Aruba Certified Switching Associate
OFFICIAL CERTIFICATION STUDY GUIDE
(EXAM HPE6-A72)

First Edition

Alvaro Tellez and Ricardo Cobos

HPE Press
660 4th Street, #802
San Francisco, CA 94107

Aruba Certified Switching Associate
Official Certification Study Guide (Exam HPE6-A72)
Alvaro Tellez and Ricardo Cobos

Published by:

Hewlett Packard Enterprise Press
660 4th Street, #802
San Francisco, CA 94107

ISBN: **978-1-7346275-5-8**

Printed in Mexico

WARNING AND DISCLAIMER

This book provides information about the topics covered in Aruba Certified Switching Associate certification exam (HPE6-A72). Every effort has been made to make this book as complete and as accurate as possible, but no warranty or fitness is implied.

The information is provided on an "as is" basis. The author, and Hewlett Packard Enterprise Press, shall have neither liability nor responsibility to any person or entity with respect to any loss or damages arising from the information contained in this book or from the use of the discs or programs that may accompany it.

The opinions expressed in this book belong to the author and are not necessarily those of Hewlett Packard Enterprise Press.

FEEDBACK INFORMATION

At HPE Press, our goal is to create in-depth reference books of the best quality and value. Each book is crafted with care and precision, undergoing rigorous development that involves the expertise of members from the professional technical community.

Readers' feedback is a continuation of the process. If you have any comments regarding how we could improve the quality of this book, or otherwise alter it to better suit your needs, you can contact us through email at hpepress@epac.com. Please make sure to include the book title and ISBN in your message.

We appreciate your feedback.

Publisher: Hewlett Packard Enterprise Press

HPE Press Program Manager: Michael Bishop

About the Authors

The material in this Study Guide was developed by Alvaro Tellez and Ricardo Cobos who created the Aruba OS-CX Switching Fundamentals, Rev. 20.21, training course. Alvaro is an Aruba Certified Instructor, ACMX, ACCP, and ACSP certified. Ricardo is an Aruba Certified Instructor, Aruba Certified Edge Expert (ACCX, ACMX, and ACDX), and ACSP certified.

About the Technical Editor

Tyler McMinn is an HPE Aruba Instructor with eleven years of experience and a background in switching, routing, data center, collaboration, design, security and wireless networks.

Introduction

This book is based on the Aruba OS-CX Switching Fundamentals, Rev. 20.21 five-day course. The material covers the fundamental skills to configure and manage modern, open standards-based wired networking solutions for small-to-midsized businesses (SMBs) and campus networks. Topics include VLANs, secure access, redundancy technologies, Aruba's Virtual Switching Framework (VSF), and more.

Certification and Learning

Hewlett Packard Enterprise Certification and Learning provides end-to-end continuous learning programs and professional certifications that can help you open doors and accelerate your career.

We provide:

- **Professional sales and technical training and certifications** to give you the critical skills needed to design, manage, and implement the most sought-after IT disciplines; and
- **Continuous learning activities and job-role-based learning plans** to help you keep pace with the demands of the dynamic, fast-paced IT industry
- **Advanced training** to help you navigate and seize opportunities within the top IT transformation areas that enable business advantage today.

As a Certification and Learning certified member, your skills, knowledge, and real-world experience are recognized and valued in the marketplace. To continue your professional and career growth, you have access to our large HPE community of world-class IT professionals, trend-makers, and decision-makers. Share ideas, best practices, business insights, and challenges as you gain professional connections globally.

To learn more about HPE Certification and Learning certifications and continuous learning programs, please visit:
http://certification-learning.hpe.com

Audience

This book is designed for network administrators tasked with implementing Aruba OS-CX switch networks. Ideal candidates for this course are networking IT professionals with an introductory level of experience in deploying small-to-medium scale network solutions.

Assumed Knowledge

This is an entry-level book and certification. Any basic knowledge of switch networking will serve to aid in your understanding of the material but is not required.

Minimum Qualifications

There are no prerequisite qualifications for the ACSA certification.

Relevant Certifications

After you pass the exam, your achievement may be applicable toward more than one certification. To determine which certifications can be credited with this achievement, log in to The Learning Center and view the certifications listed on the exam's More Details tab. You might be on your way to achieving additional certifications.

Preparing for Exam HPE6-A72

This self-study guide does not guarantee that you will have all the knowledge you need to pass the exam. It is expected that you will also draw on real-world experience and would benefit from completing the hands-on lab activities provided in the instructor-led training. To pass the certification exam, you should get as much hands-on experience as possible.

Recommended HPE Training

Recommended training to prepare for each exam is accessible from the exam's page in The Learning Center. See the exam attachment, "Supporting courses," to view and register for the courses.

Obtain Hands-on Experience

You are not required to take the recommended, supported courses, and completion of training does not guarantee that you will pass the exams. Hewlett Packard Enterprise strongly recommends a combination of training, thorough review of courseware and additional study references, and sufficient on-the-job experience prior to taking an exam.

Exam Registration

To register for an exam, go to
https://certification-learning.hpe.com/tr/learn_more_about_exams.html

CONTENTS

1 Networking Fundamentals

EXAM OBJECTIVES

- ✓ Describe computing networks
- ✓ Describe protocols and the OSI model
- ✓ Explain encapsulation and headers
- ✓ Convert numbering systems: decimal, binary, and hexadecimal
- ✓ Describe the TCP/IP protocol stack
- ✓ Compare unicast, multicast, and broadcast

Basic Network Concepts

After completing this chapter, you will be familiar with the fundamental concepts that serve as a foundation for mastering computer network technology.

What is a Computing Network?

A computing network is defined as a group of computing resources that permit digital data exchange between computer devices—regardless of the type or vendor (Figure 1-1).

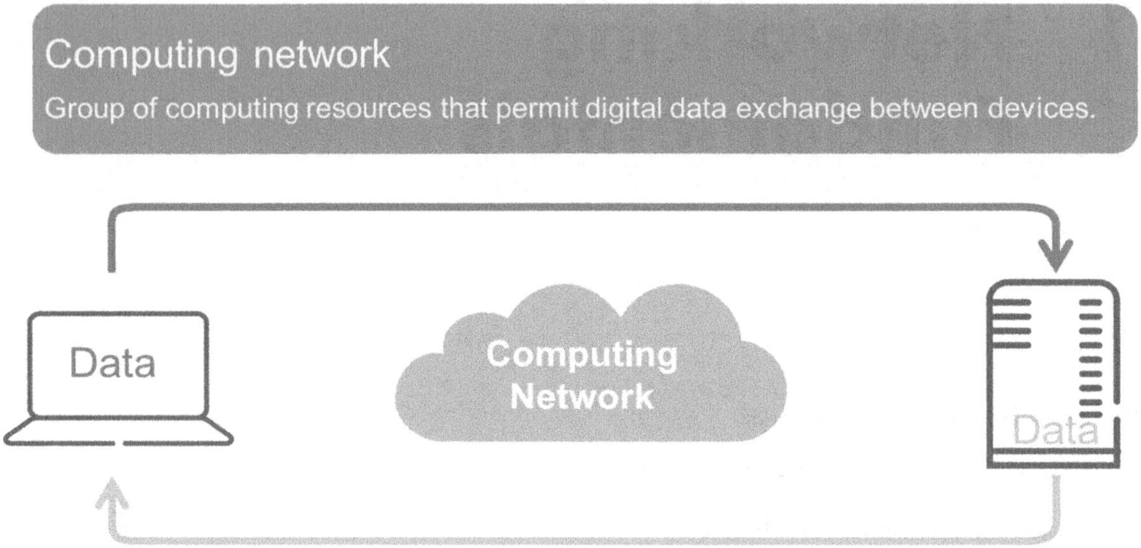

Figure 1-1 Computing Network

Network Classifications

Based on the geographical coverage a computing network can be categorized as a Local Area Network (LAN) or a Wide Area Network (WAN). A **LAN** is a group of computer devices that are geographically co-located in the same place. For example, a group of devices within a building can be considered a LAN.

LANs are used in several settings:

- Small Office/Home Office (SOHO)
- Office LANs
- Building LANs
- Campus LANs

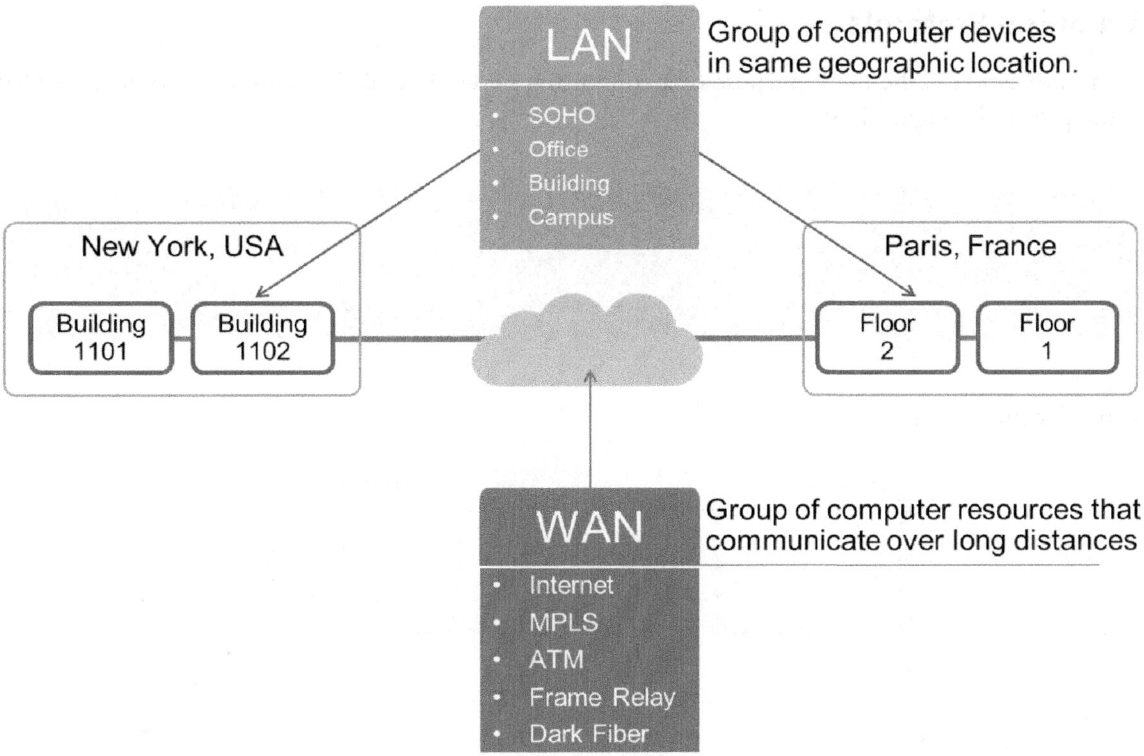

Figure 1-2 Classification

A **WAN** on the other hand is a group of computer resources that can communicate over large geographical distances—typically a few kilometers or miles, and perhaps thousands of miles, such as the Internet. The Internet is considered a WAN since it permits communication across countries and continents (Figure 1-2).

Typically, WANs are deployed by Internet Service Providers (ISP) since those companies have the economic resources to interconnect long distances. Examples of WAN technologies include the following:

- Internet
- Multi-Protocol Label Switching (MPLS)
- Asynchronous Transfer Mode (ATM)
- Frame Relay (largely obsolete)
- Dark fiber

What is a Protocol?

Communication is the main purpose of a computing network, and this communication is enabled using protocols (Figure 1-3).

> **Protocol**
> Set of rules that computer devices follow to establish and maintain communications

Consider this analogy:

Figure 1-3 Protocol

- Alice meets Bob for the first time, and starts the conversation by saying "Good morning, my name is Alice".
- Bob replies, "Good Morning Alice, my name is Bob."

This brief conversation is actually a procedure. Notice that Alice starts the communication with a greeting, and then she identifies herself. Bob's reply is also a procedure. He acknowledges Alice, and then he identifies himself by name. The implicit rules in this conversation help to establish and maintain a conversation. Likewise, computing devices exchange messages in a specific order, following specific rules.

OSI Reference Model

In the mid-1980s during the fast evolution of computing, every vendor wanted to implement their own, proprietary communication protocol. These proprietary protocols created interoperability challenges. The International Organization for Standardization (ISO) solved the problem by presenting a standard communication model for computing devices—The Open Systems Interconnection (OSI) model:

> Standard communication model for computing devices created by the ISO
> Organizes computing communication in 7 Layers

Each layer defines a phase of message processing. The OSI layers are shown in Figure 1-4, and described below:

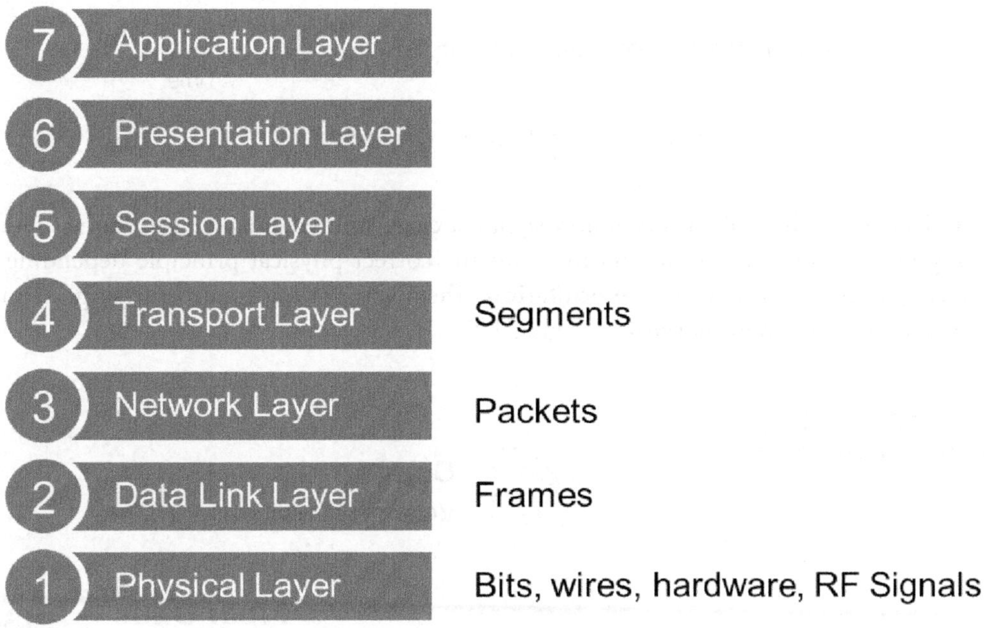

Figure 1-4 OSI Reference Model

Layer-7: Application Layer

Layer-6: Presentation Layer

Layer-5: Session Layer

Layer-4: Transport Layer, which organizes data into segments, as you will soon learn.

Layer-3: Network Layer, which organizes data into packets

Layer-2: Data Link Layer, which organizes data into frames

Layer-1: Physical Layer, which organizes the data into bits, and transmits those bits using physical hardware over wires, fiber optic cable, or RF Signals.

Layer-1: Physical Layer

Goal To dictate physical aspects of signal transmission and receipt across media

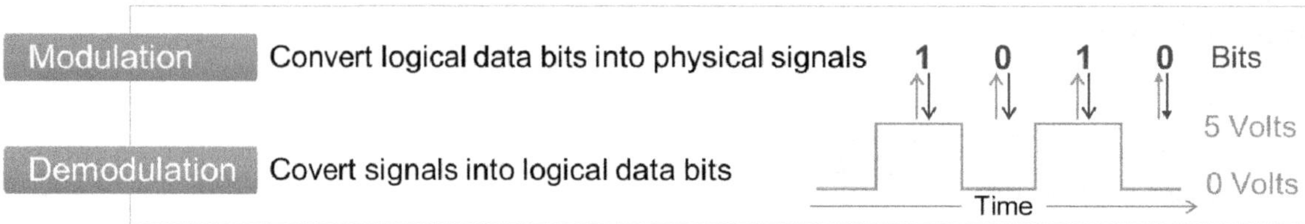

Figure 1-5 Modulation - Demodulation

This layer dictates the physical aspects of how signals are transmitted and received across some media. Computing devices convert logical data bits into the correct physical principle depending on the media in use; this process is known as **modulation**. The inverse process, converting signals into logical data bits, is known as **demodulation** (Figure 1-5).

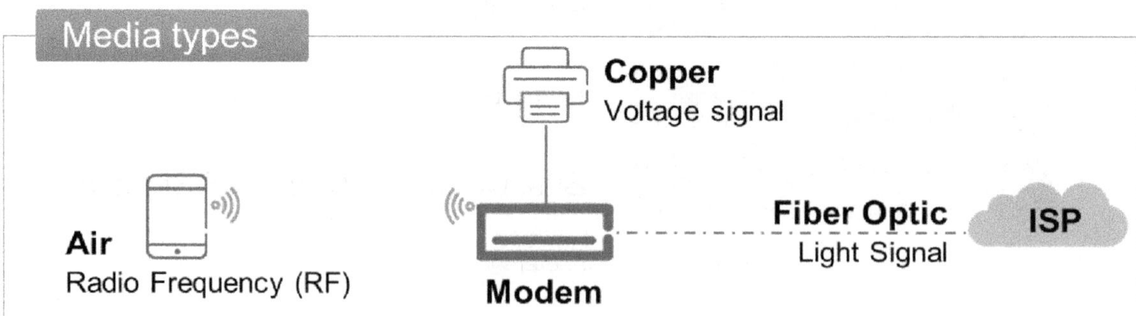

Figure 1-6 Media Types

This layer also defines the material characteristics and the components to use to achieve the correct transmission of the messages.

For example, consider the modem that is used in a home basis; your tablet connects to the modem using Radio Frequency (**RF**) signals that travel across the air. This modem connects to the Internet

Service Provider (ISP) network using Fiber Optic cables. Thus, the router converts data into optical signals. Also, the printer connects directly to the modem via a twisted pair copper patch cable. This means that print jobs are converted into electrical voltage signals before being sent to the printer (Figure 1-6).

Layer-2: Data Link Layer

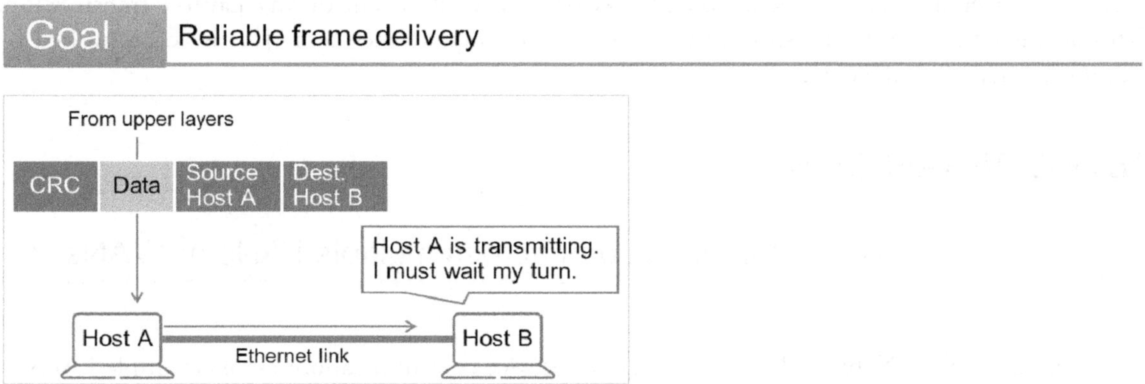

Figure 1-7 Frame Delivery

The Data Link provides 3 main functions:

Media Access Control

In polite human conversation, only one person talks at a time. While Bob talks, Alice politely listens. She detects when Bob stops talking and knows that it is her turn to speak. Similarly, only one device may transmit at a time (Figure 1-7).

Access to the media must be controlled. Many Media Access Control techniques leverage a "Carrier Sense" (CSMA/CD) mechanism. CSMA/CD says before a station may transmit, the station must sense the state of the carrier or media. If a transmission signal is detected, then the station must wait to transmit until the original signal is no longer detected.

Link Layer Addressing

Bob may call out in a crowded room, "Hey Alice, can I buy you an ice cream?" Everyone hears these sound waves as the sound travels over a shared medium. Then the air in the room provides this medium. Only Alice responds that she was identified as the intended recipient. Similarly, each station on a LAN has a unique "name". Each station is identified by a 6-byte hexadecimal number called a **MAC** address instead of an alphanumeric name like Alice or Bob.

All stations on a shared media receive the message, but only the device identified as the intended recipient processes and responds. Like humans, the other stations realize, "This message is not for me" and simply ignore the message. This information is added to the data from the upper layers as so-called "header information", about which you will soon learn.

Error Detection

For the receiver side, Layer-2 helps to detect errors that could occur during Layer-1 transmission. This avoids unnecessary processing of corrupted or incomplete messages. This is accomplished by adding a "Trailer" to the data.

Layer-3: Network Layer

Goal Establish communications across multiple LANs or WANs

The main goal of the Network Layer is to establish device communications across multiple LANs or WANs, using the best available path. This is achieved using two fundamental techniques.

- **Logical addressing**. A unique Laye-3 identifier for the source and destination is maintained across the path.
- **Path discovery and selection**. The Network Layer runs algorithms and protocols to find *all possible paths*, and then choose *the best path*. Later in this course, you will learn more about this, and things like the Routing Information Protocol (RIP) and Open Shortest Path First (OSPF).

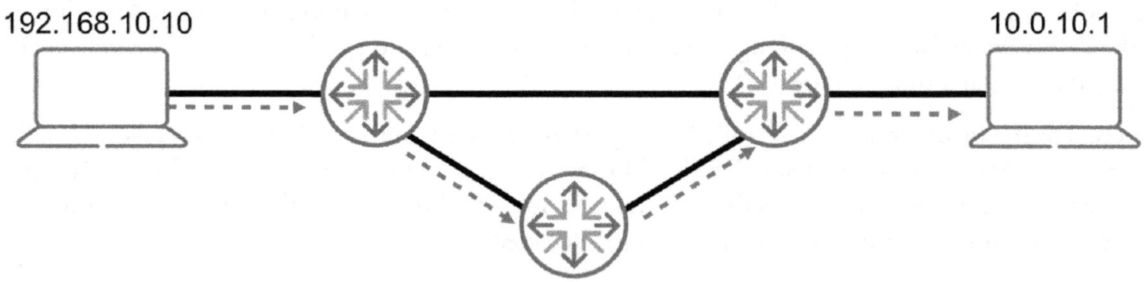

Figure 1-8 Layer-3 Delivery

The communication between two computing devices can take a specific path but not necessary the same one will be used in the future. Protocols and algorithms used in this Layer could update the path any time depending on multiple factors (Figure 1-8). You will learn more about it in this training.

Layer-4: Transport Layer

Goal Control link reliability using segmentation, and error control.

The Transport Layer controls the reliability of a given link through segmentation, de-segmentation, and error control. In this layer some protocols, like the Transmission Control Protocol (TCP), are **connection-oriented**. This means that the transport layer can keep track of the messages and retransmit those that fail. Other protocols, like the User Datagram Protocol (UDP), are **stateless** or **connectionless**. This means the transport layer does not keep track of the messages. The advantage of this is that processing these connections is relatively fast and easy to compute.

There are three main responsibilities of the transport layer, as described below:

- **Segmentation**. The sender's TCP or UDP process accepts files from the application and divides them into smaller pieces (typically 1500 bytes) called segments. Each piece is passed down to the lower layers and transmitted individually—over an Ethernet link in the example shown in Figure 1-9.
- **De-segmentation**. The receiver accepts each segment, puts them back in the correct order if need be, and reassembles the information. This then can be processed by the application.
- **Error Control**. Refers to the verification of the information received to avoid errors that could occur inthe lower Layers (1-3).

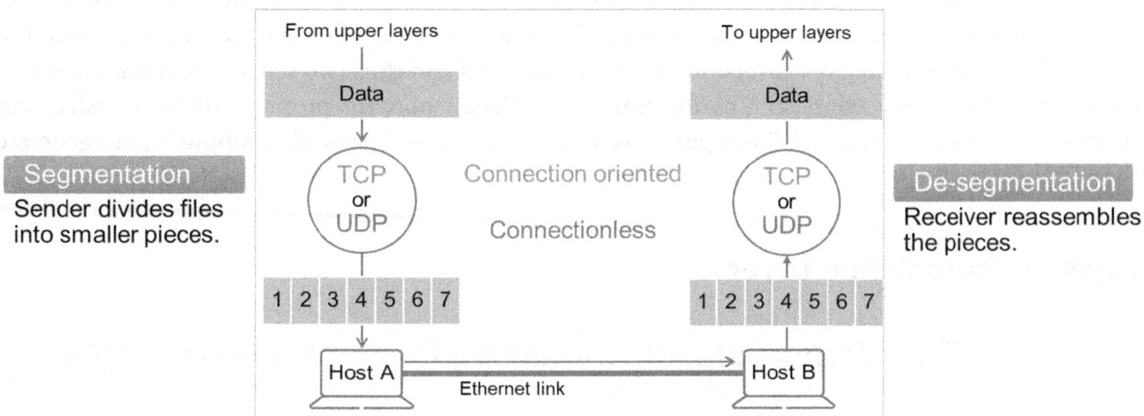

Figure 1-9 Transport Layer

Note

Error detection is a process that happens in different Layers: 2, 4, and sometimes in 7.

Layer-5: Session Layer

Goal	Setup, maintenance and teardown a session between computing devices.

Layer-5 is responsible for setup, maintenance, and tear down of sessions between two computing devices. A session is a conversation between two computer devices (Figure 1-10).

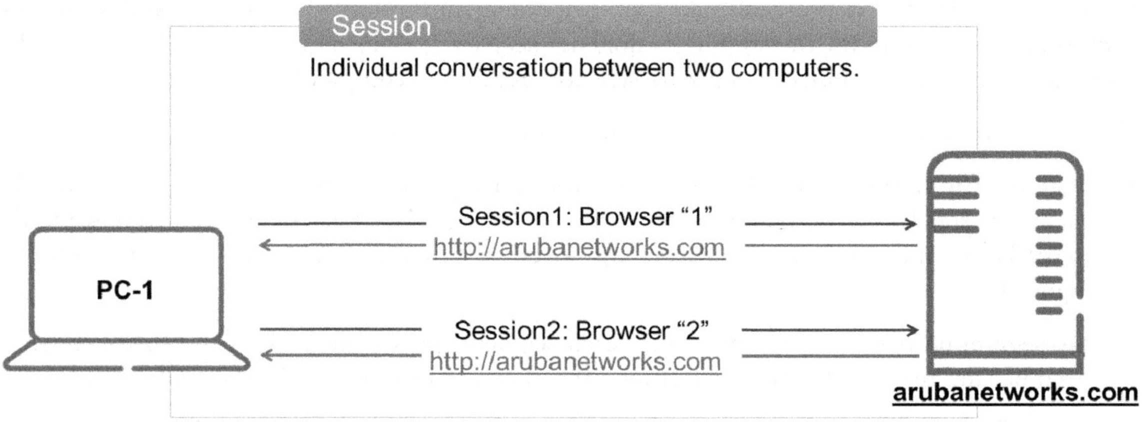

Figure 1-10 Session Layer

Suppose that some user opens a browser and connects to a web page like http://arubanetworks.com. A session is created, and the same user opens a different browser to the same destination. Since the application is different a new conversion or session is created and thus two separate sessions are maintained. The user might establish a connection to a different host for purposes of file transfer, and seven more sessions to remotely configure seven Aruba switches. A typical computer could generate thousands of sessions.

Layer-6: Presentation Layer

Goal	Transforms data into formatting the application accepts.

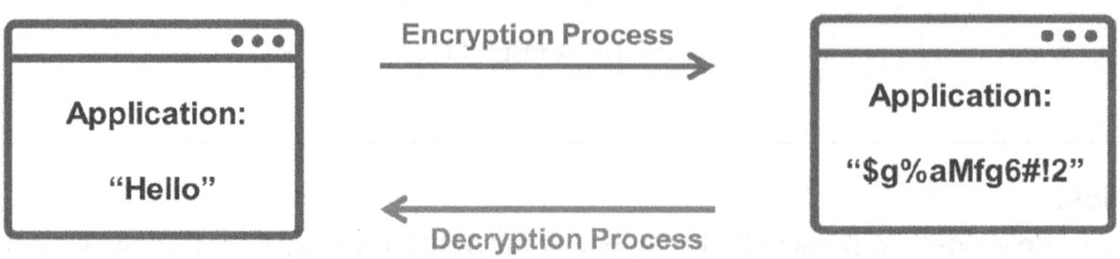

Figure 1-11 Presentation Layer

Typical processes include:

- Compression/Decompression
- Encryption/Decryption
- Code Translation (EBCDIC to ASCII)

For example, Figure 1-11shows how an application passes the clear-text message "Hello" to the Presentation Layer process, which encrypts this message before transmission. This provides confidentiality. If any bad actors or hackers intercept this data, they will not be able to read the message. Of course, upon receipt of an encrypted message, only the intended receiver has the correct digital keys to decrypt the data.

Layer-7: Application Layer

The Application Layer is the closest to the end user, which means that both the OSI Application Layer and the user interact directly with the software application.

Application Layer functions include:

- **Identifying Communication Partners**. The application layer determines the identity and availability of communication partners for an application with data to transmit.
- **Provide network resources**. This layer provides network services to user applications, such as file transfer, email, video conferencing, and many others.

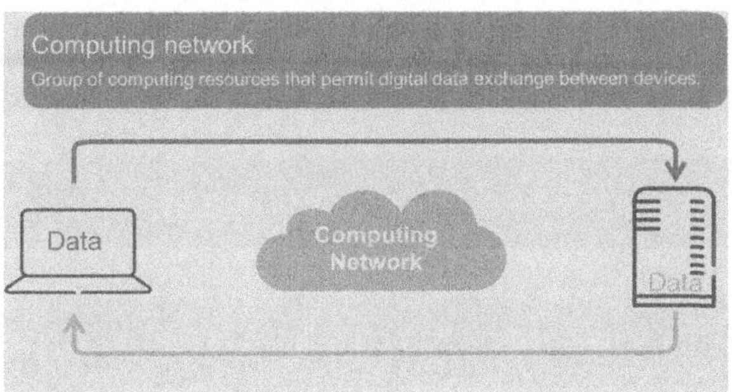

Some examples of application layer include:

- Hypertext Transfer Protocol (**HTTP**), which relies on TCP for transport
- Trivial File Transfer Protocol (**TFTP**), which uses UDP as its transport mechanism
- Domain Name System (**DNS**), which typically uses UDP, but sometimes also uses TCP
- File Transfer Protocol (**FTP**), which also relies on TCP

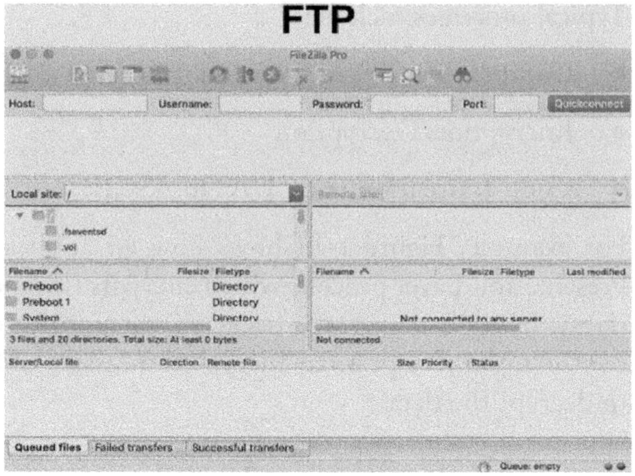

Layer Headers

On the OSI model each Layer has a specific responsibility during network communications. In the computing world, devices that establish a communication exchange control information on a particular layer (or the layers above it) using headers.

Note

A header that is generated on a specific layer by the sender can only be read at the same level on the receiver side.

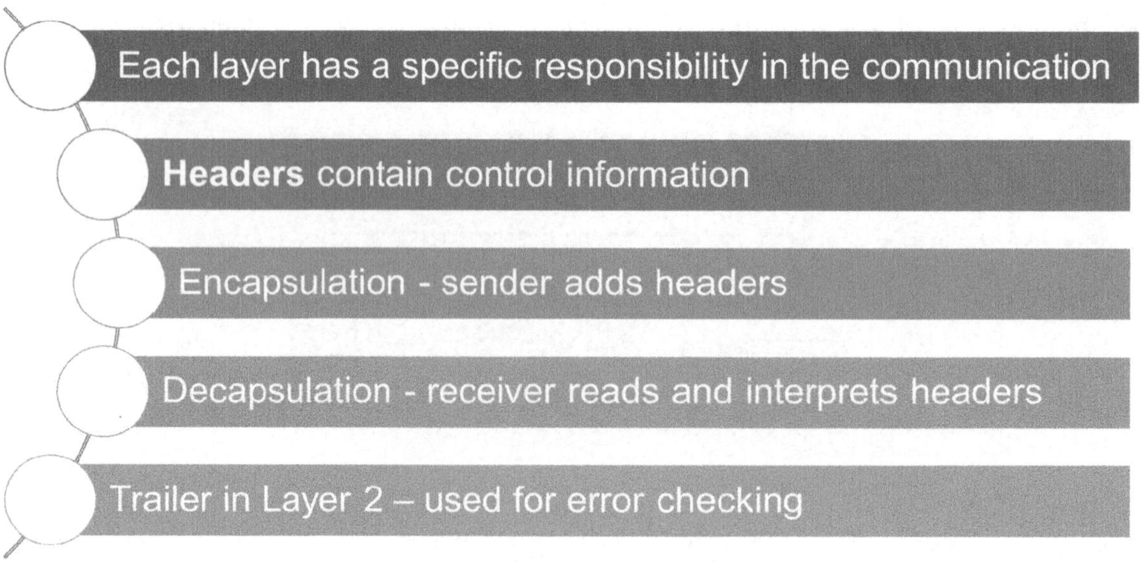

Figure 1-12 Layers

- **Encapsulation**. Is the process where each OSI Layer adds a header. This process is always done by the sender device.
- **Decapsulation**. Is the process to read and interpret the header information. This process is always done by the receiver device (Figure 1-12).

Protocol Data Units (PDUs)

The OSI model introduces the concept of a Protocol Data Unit (**PDU**). This is simply a structure that considers the header and payload or data for each layer.

The following table summarizes the PDUs from Layer-7 to Layer-2.

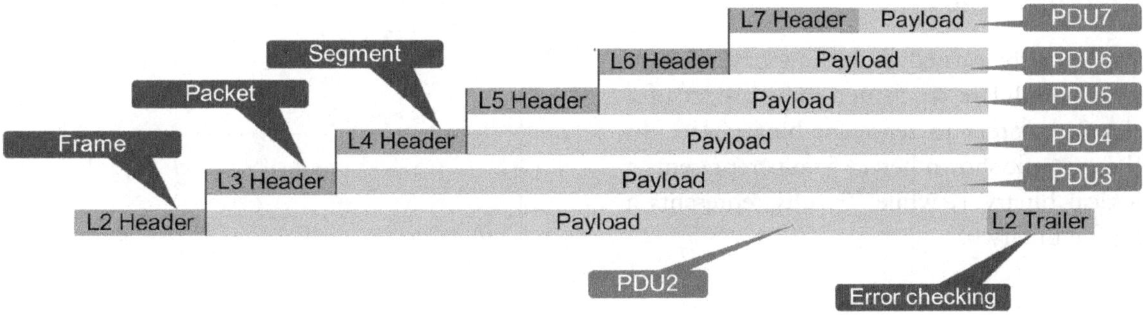

Figure 1-13 PDUs

Note
PDU1 does not exist; remember that Layer-1 refers to signals that cross the media.

There are three key terms related to PDUs that you should know:

- **Segment**. Refers to the encapsulation that is done in Layer-4. A segment is equivalent to PDU4. So, you might hear networking people speak about a TCP segment or a UDP segment.
- **Packet**. Refers to the encapsulation that is done in Layer-3. A packet is equivalent to PDU3. You might talk about Layer-3 IP packets.
- **Frame**. Refers to the encapsulation that is done in Layer-2. A frame is equivalent to PDU2. You might talk about Ethernet frames or Wi-Fi frames.

You might notice that PDU2 (a Layer-2 Frame) not only includes a Header but also a Trailer that is appended after data, labeled "L2 Trailer" in Figure 1-13.

The trailer is typically is used to detect errors during the transmission of the message. You recently learned about this during the discussion of Layer-2 of the OSI model. Layer-2 protocols like Ethernet and Wi-Fi add a Trailer, often labeled "Cyclic Redundancy Check" (CRC) or perhaps as a "Frame Check Sequence" (FCS).

Physical Media

After completing this section, you will learn how data is transmitted over some physical transmission medium—copper or fiber optic cables, or radio waves in the case of Wi-Fi.

Physical Media—Copper

Computing devices might use different media to transmit information, and each media type has different characteristics. Recall that Fiber Optic media modulates light waves, Wi-Fi modulates Radio Waves, and Copper-based media modulates electrical properties like voltage (Figure 1-14).

Copper Cables

You recently learned about how Layer-1 processes modulate or change some aspect of a signal, in order to represent binary data. In the example shown here, +5 volts represents a logical binary 1, while -5 volts represents a logical binary 0.

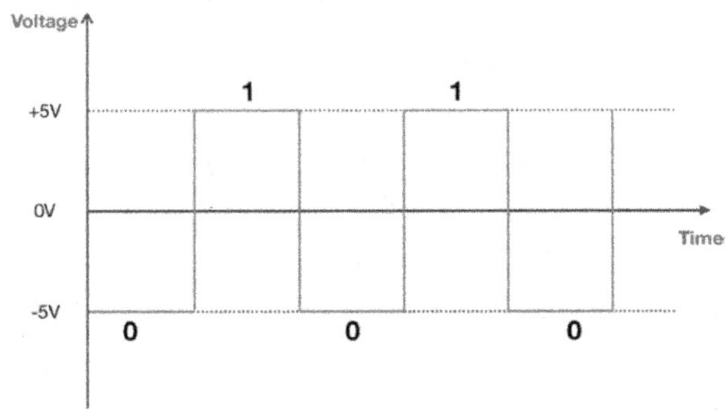

Figure 1-14 Voltage

The typical copper cable that is used to transmit digital data in a network is called Twisted Pair. With this media, wire pairs are twisted, to reduce electromagnetic radiation and interference. The most common type of Twisted pair is Unshielded Twisted Pair (UTP). Other variations also exist, such as shielded or Foiled Twisted Pair (FTP)—commonly deployed to provide superior protection from external electromagnetic interference (EMI). This is useful in highly sensitive environments, or those with high levels of EMI.

UTP cabling contains 8 color-coded wires, grouped into 4 pairs. Two wires are used for transmission (Tx) and two are used for reception (Rx). The remaining 4 lines are used to power some devices such as telephones or cameras, using a feature called Power over Ethernet (PoE). The typical connector used with UTP is an RJ-45 connector.

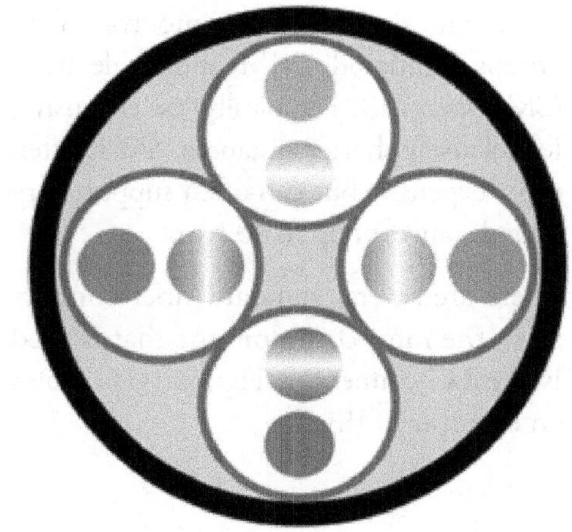

To maintain a data rate of up to 1Gbps, the maximum length of UTP cable cannot be more than 100 meters (300 feet).

Physical Media—Fiber Optic

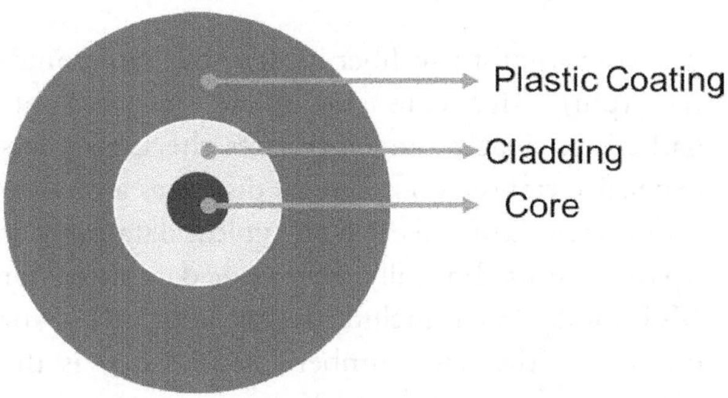

Figure 1-15 Fiber Cladding

Built from glass or plastic fiber, Fiber Optic uses light signals to transmit and receive data. Light is guided down the center of the fiber, which is called **core**. The core is surrounded by an optical material called the **cladding** that traps the light in the core using a technique called **total internal refection** (Figure 1-15).

Fiber optic cables can interconnect devices that are separated by much longer distances than Ethernet UTP's 100 meters, and with higher data rates. Distances and speeds depend on quality, type of fiber, and transceiver type. Common data rates are 1Gbps, 10Gbps, 25Gbps 40Gbps, 50Gbps, or even 100Gbps.

Note

A fiber optic transceiver is an optical module installed in the computing device. It is responsible for modulating and demodulating light signals.

Fiber optic is categorized into two main groups, Multimode (MM) and Single mode (SM) fiber. MM is typically less expensive, for relatively shorter distances. SM is often more expensive but can often support very long distances of up to 40 Km.

There are several standard fiber connectors. The most common one that is used is the **LC** connector. Figure 1-16 shows an example of this.

Figure 1-16 LC connector

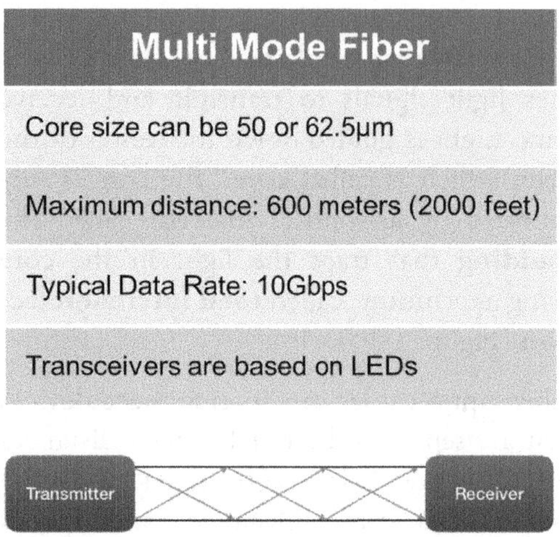

Figure 1-17 Multi-Mode Fiber

Multimode (MM)

The core size for this fiber is 50 or 62.5 micrometers (μm). This core size allows greater light-gathering capacity and facilitates the use of less expensive transceivers. Typical distances are up to 600 meters (2000 feet) with typical data rates of up to 10Gbps. Typically, fiber optic data sheets for Multimode Fiber include terms like 50/125 or 65.5/125. The first number (50 or 62.5) is the diameter of the core and 125 represents the diameter of the cladding.Multi-mode fiber with 50μm has a faster light transmission but with shorter distance (Figure 1-17).

Single Mode (SM)

The core size is only 9μm and carries light directly down the fiber. Light reflection created during light transmission decreases as a result. This lowers attenuation (loss of signal strength) and allows the signal to successfully travel over longer distances. Usuallythis fiber is more suitable to be used to interconnect devices using higher data rates such as 40Gbps or even 400Gbps. As you might imagine 9/125 refers to the fact that the core is 9μm and the cladding is still 125μm (Figure 1-18).

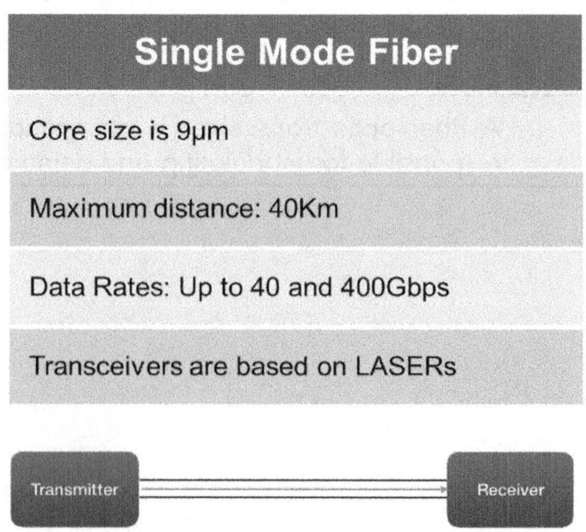

Figure 1-18 Single-Mode Fiber

Full Duplex and Half Duplex

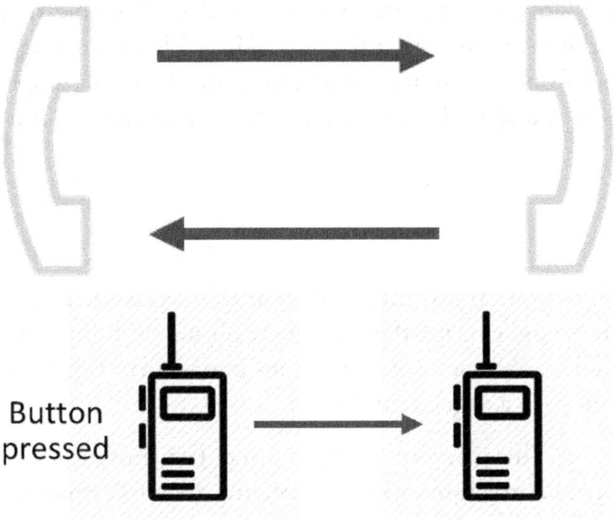

A Duplex communication system is a system composed by two or more connected parties that can communicate with one another in both directions. There are two types of duplex communication systems: Full duplex (FDX) and Half duplex (HDX).

Full Duplex: Both parties can communicate with each other simultaneously. An example of full duplex is a telephone; parties in both ends can speak and can be heard by the other party simultaneously.

Half Duplex: Both parties can communicate with each other but not simultaneously; the communication is one direction at the time. An example of half duplex is a walkie-talkie; on this communication each person must press a "push-to-talk" button when they want to talk, when the button is pressed then the user cannot hear the remote person. To listen, the button has to be released.

Types of Traffic

Unicast, Multicast, Broadcast

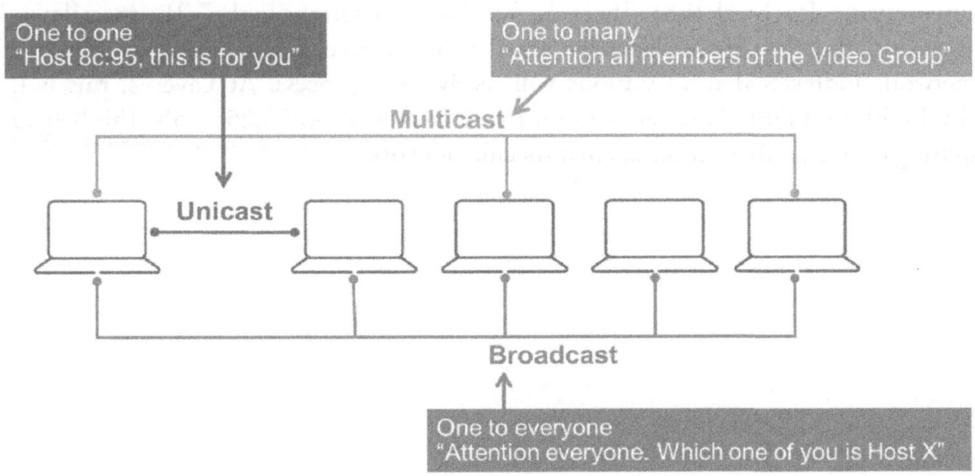

Figure 1-19 Unicast, Multicast, and Broadcast

Computing communications can be classified in three types, as shown in Figure 1-19:

Unicast

This traffic refers to one-to-one communication—one transmitter and one receiver. Imagine that there are several learners in a classroom. Bob is the instructor. He calls out, "Alice, I have a message for you from the front desk". This message came from one source—Bob and is destined to a single destination—Alice. Similarly, when a PC needs to transfer a file to a server, the two devices use unicast communications.

Multicast

This traffic refers to one-to-many communication—one transmitter and multiple receivers. In our classroom analogy, suppose that lunch has been brought in for the learners. Bob may call out, "All vegetarians can find their meals on the green table". The message came from one source: Bob. The message is destined for several people in the room with a vegetarian diet.

A common networking example is video streaming. This is where a video source (transmitter) sends a video stream to multiple devices that are capable and interested in receiving that information. Examples could include a PC, tablet, or smartphone.

Note

Multicast traffic can include many devices but not all the devices in the network.

Broadcast

This type of traffic refers to the communication one-to-all. In our classroom analogy, Bob calls out, "Attention everyone. It is break time. There are free doughnuts in the lobby." The special word "everyone" means that all people in the classroom are intended to receive this message. Similarly, there are special network addresses that all stations will receive and process. At Layer-2, this is the MAC address FF:FF:FF:FF:FF:FF. At Layer-3, this is the IP address 255.255.255.255. This helps a particular computing device to discover others in a specific network.

Numerical Systems

Binary Numerical System

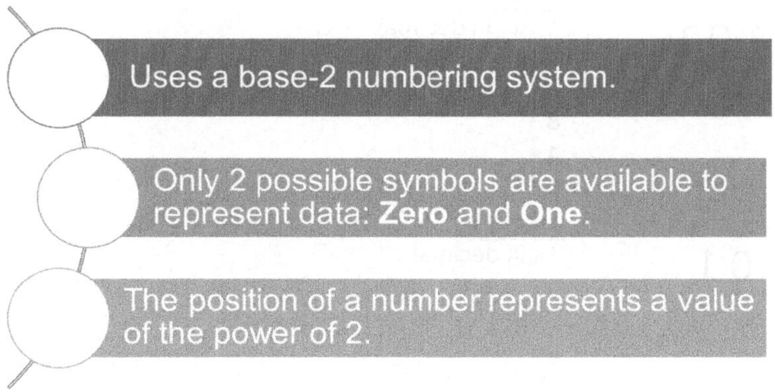

Decimal	Binary
0	0
1	1
2	10
3	11
4	100
5	101
6	110
7	111
8	1000

Power of 2	2^7	2^6	2^5	2^4	2^3	2^2	2^1	2^0
Decimal	128	64	32	16	8	4	2	1

Figure 1-20 Binary Numerical System

Familiarization with the binary numerical systems is key to understand how computing systems process and communicate information. The binary system uses a base-2 numbering system; this means that there are only two possible symbols available to represent data: zero and one (Figure 1-20). In the binary system the position of a number represents a value of the power of two. The table below shows the first eight positions and the decimal number associated to each.

Note

To avoid any confusion this text will use an index after a number to indicate the base numerical system, for example 100_{10} will represent the number 100 (one hundred) on the decimal system.

Counting in Binary

The table shows the first eight decimal numbers and their representation in binary. The first two values only require one digit (2^0), and so **zero** and **one** are the same for both numerical systems. Please note that for decimal number "2" in binary we need to add a new number to the left indicating 2^1 and the number to the right 2^0. Let us make a quick comparison of binary and decimal numbering systems.

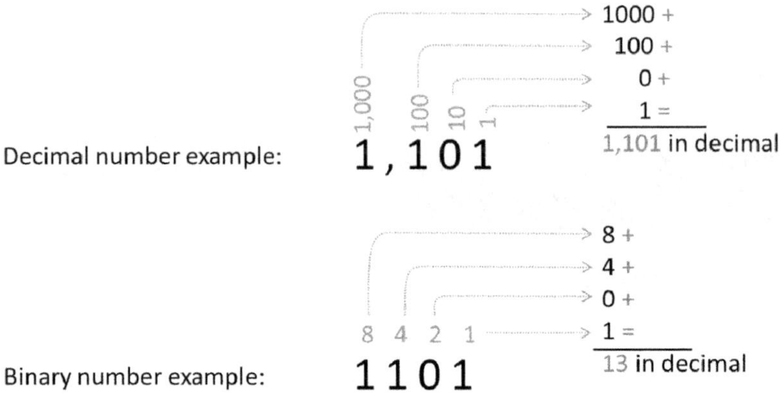

Power of 2	2^7	2^6	2^5	2^4	2^3	2^2	2^1	2^0
Decimal	128	64	32	16	8	4	2	1

Figure 1-21 Binary Powers of 2

Consider the decimal number 1,101, as shown in Figure 1-21. You know that the right-most digit "3" is in the "1's" column, then 0 is in the 10's column, the 1 is in the 100's column, and the 1 is in the 1,000 column. Therefore, the first 1 (left to right) does not merely represent a quantity of 9, it represents a quantity of one thousand—1 X 1000 = 1,000. Similarly, 1 x 100 = 100. 0 x 10 = 0, and 1 x 1=1.

You know this already, right? And 1000 + 100 + 0 + 1 = 1,101

Binary works exactly the same way. Yes, the numbering system changed from base-10 to base-2, but the fundamental rules never change. The only difference is that instead of 1000, 100, 10, and 1 the columns are 8, 4, 2, and 1.

For example, consider the binary number 1101. The left-most number is 1 and it is in the "8's" column where 1 x 8 = 8. The next number is 4 where 1 x 4 = 4. The next number is 0 where 0 x 2 = 0. The right-most number is 1 where 1 x 1 = 1. Now add them up, just like before. 8 + 4 +1 =13.

Let us take this a bit further, using a more methodical step-by-step process.

Converting Binary to Decimal

There are several methods to convert a binary number into decimal; however, the comparison method is the easiest to learn. This method simply uses the position value of each number (remember that in binary system each position is a power of 2) and simply sums all the values where the binary number is set to 1.

As an example, let us convert the binary number **10001010**$_2$ as shown in Figure 1-22:

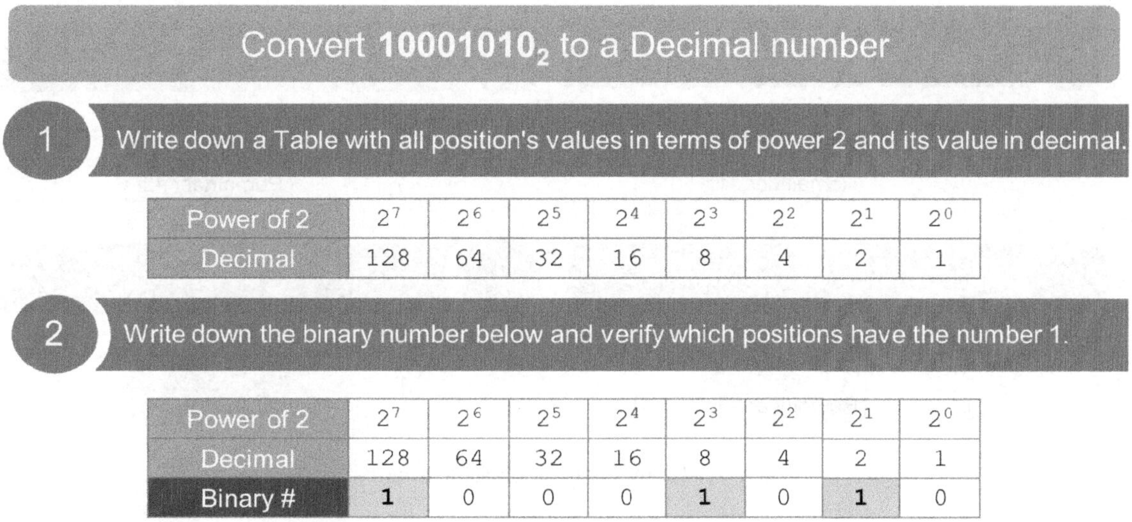

Figure 1-22 Converting Binary to Decimal

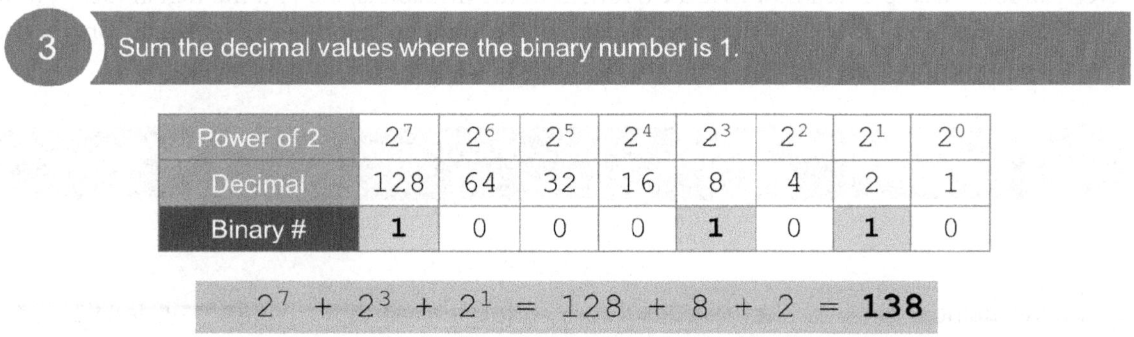

Figure 1-23 Converting Binary to Decimal Step 3

As a result, we can conclude that **10001010** in binary is equivalent to **138** in decimal (Figure 1-23).

Converting Decimal to Binary

Consider the following example, where the number **13**$_{10}$ is converted into its binary representation.

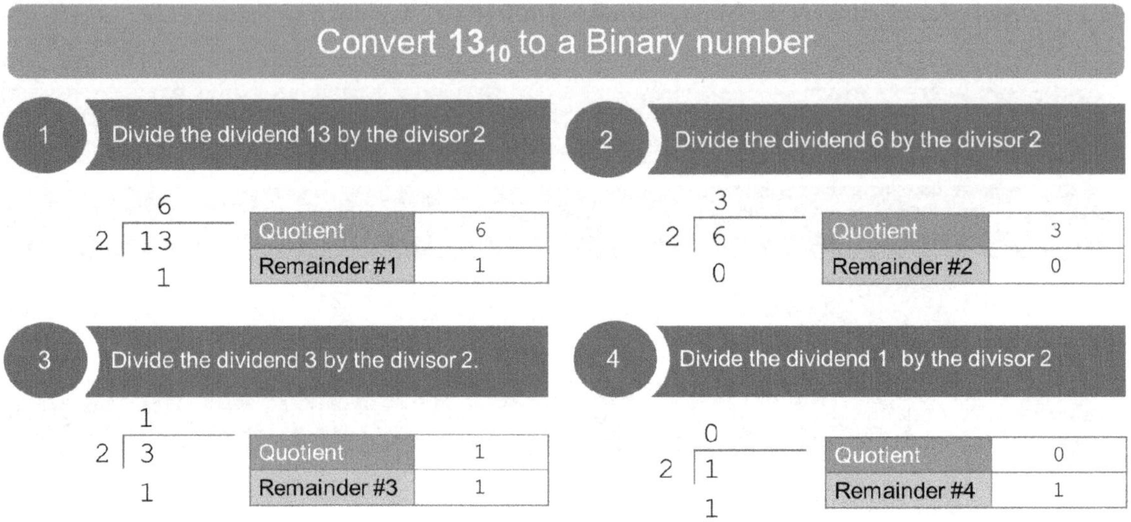

Figure 1-24 Converting Decimal to Binary Steps

The conversion from decimal to binary is not based on a sum but in a repeated divide-by-2 process. Start by dividing the decimal number by 2. Notice of the quotient and the remainder. Continue dividing the quotient by 2 until you get a quotient of zero, then just write out the remainders in the reverse order. On step 4 we know that the quotient of the division is, 0.5 and the Remainder 0; however the process only focus on the integer part of the quotient in this case is 0 and on the last Remainder before the operation is done, in this case the last Remainder is 1 (Figure 1-24).

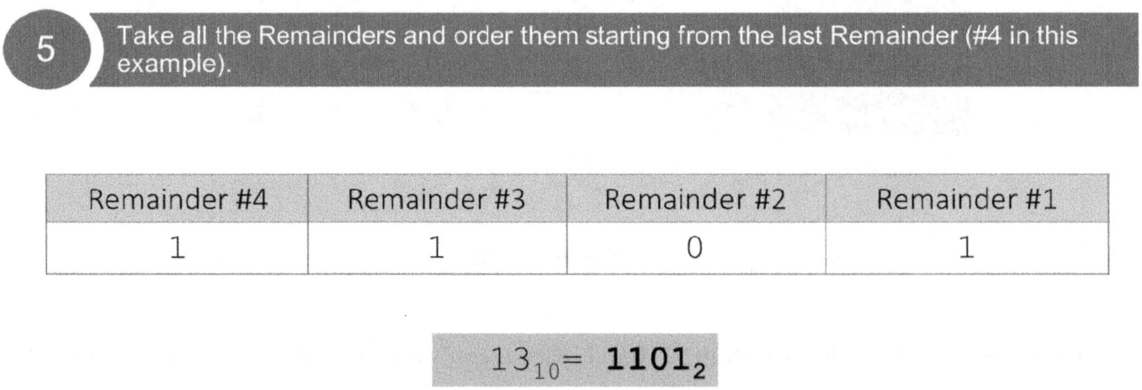

Figure 1-25 Converting Decimal to Binary Continued

The result of step 5 implies that the binary number for 13_{10} is $\mathbf{1101_2}$. Let us briefly review another approach (Figure 1-25).

Converting Decimal to Binary—Alternate Method

As before, you wish to convert decimal 15 to binary.

Power of 2	2^7	2^6	2^5	2^4	2^3	2^2	2^1	2^0
Decimal	128	64	32	16	8	4	2	1
	0	0	0	0	1	1	0	1 = 13

Figure 1-26 Decimal to Binary—Alternative Method

Look at the column values for the binary number system and compare. Is 13 greater than or less than 128? Less than, therefore you must place a 0 in the "128's" column.

13 is also less than 64, 32, and 16, so those columns must all have a 0, as shown in the figure.

Now, 13 is obviously greater than 8, so you must place a 1 in the "8's" column. We are still not to 13 yet, so keep going.

Add the next lowest column: 8+4 = 12. We have not reached 13, so keep going.

12+2 = 14 and this value is greater than 13 then place a 0 on the "2's" column.

12+1 = 13, which is equal to the number you are finding, then place a 1 on the "1's" column.

So, 13 in decimal = 00001101 in binary (Figure 1-26).

Let us try one more example.

Converting Decimal to Binary—Compare and Add

Now you wish to convert decimal 187 to binary.

Power of 2	2^7	2^6	2^5	2^4	2^3	2^2	2^1	2^0
Decimal	128	64	32	16	8	4	2	1
	1	0	1	1	1	0	1	1 = 187

Figure 1-27 Comparing and Adding

Look at the column values for the binary number system and compare. Is 187 greater than or less than 128? Greater than, so that column gets a 1.

Now add 128+64=192. That is too high, so the "64's" column gets a 0. Go to the "32's" column.

128+32 = 160. Lower than 187, so put a 1 in the "32's" column.

160+16 = 176. Lower than 187, so put a 1 in the "16's" column.

176+8 = 184. Lower than 187, so put a 1 in the "8's" column.

184+4=188. Too high, so put a 0 in the "4's" column.

184+2 = 186…a 1 in the "2's" column.

And 186+1 = 187…a 1 in the "1's" column.

So, 187 in decimal equals 10111011 in binary.

With just a small bit of practice, you will soon have the columns memorized 128, 64, 32, 16, 8, 4, 2, 1 (Figure 1-27).

With just a bit of experience, you will begin to learn certain patterns, and this will become more intuitive for you.

Let us look at some common time-saving patterns that might give you an intuitive edge and speed your conversion efforts.

Converting Decimal to Binary—Patterns for Speed

128	64	32	16	8	4	2	1	
0	0	0	0	0	0	0	0	= 0
0	0	0	0	0	0	0	1	= 1
0	0	0	0	0	0	1	1	= 3
0	0	0	0	0	1	1	1	= 7
0	0	0	0	1	1	1	1	= 15
0	0	0	1	1	1	1	1	= 31
0	0	1	1	1	1	1	1	= 63
0	1	1	1	1	1	1	1	= 127
1	1	1	1	1	1	1	1	= 255

128	64	32	16	8	4	2	1	
1	0	0	0	0	0	0	0	= 128
1	1	0	0	0	0	0	0	= 192
1	1	1	0	0	0	0	0	= 224
1	1	1	1	0	0	0	0	= 240
1	1	1	1	1	0	0	0	= 248
1	1	1	1	1	1	0	0	= 252
1	1	1	1	1	1	1	0	= 254
1	1	1	1	1	1	1	1	= 255

Figure 1-28 Patterns for Speed

Look at this left-most set of binary to decimal conversions. Notice that it goes from "all zeros" at the top example, to "all 1s" in the bottom example.

Now look at the third example from the top: 00000011 is equal to 3. Suppose you then add a 1 to the "128" column. You shouldnot need a lengthy process to convert this to decimal.

You know that the 1 in the "128's" column represents a value of 128. Then add 3 to that and you get 131. With some practice, this begins to seem intuitive and you can do it in your head.

Consider the next example where 00000111 is equal to 7. If a 1 were flagged in the "32's" column then the result would be 32 plus 7 to total 39.

Do you also notice that 3 is one number less than the next column to the right; the "4's" column? The 7 is also one less than the next column to the right; the "8's" column. Do you see the pattern? Once you understand this, you will not even have to memorize the chart shown in Figure 1-28. If you see the binary sequence 00111111, you can simple subtract the "8's" and "7's" columns to equals 63. The sequence of binary 1's ends right before the "64's" column, therefore 00111111 will equal 63.

Look at the right-hand column, which shows another set of sequential patterns. Look at the second example from the top where 11000000 is equal to 192. Suppose you saw another identical example, except that the "4's" column was also set to 1. This would add the values of 192 and 4 to equal 196.

With just 30 to 60 minutes of practice, this conversion process will continue to become ever more intuitive. You will discover other useful patterns on your own and quickly be able to convert from binary to decimal. Revisit and stay sharp with this skill. This ability to convert numbers is useful for passing Aruba exams. It will also help you as you advance in your training. Subnetting will help in your ability to apply complex subnet masking and advanced IP address assignment. There are additional subnetting applications such as advanced route filtering, and other concepts that you will learn about when you take more in-depth courses.

Now that you know about decimal and binary, let us learn about the hexadecimal numbering system.

Hexadecimal Numerical System

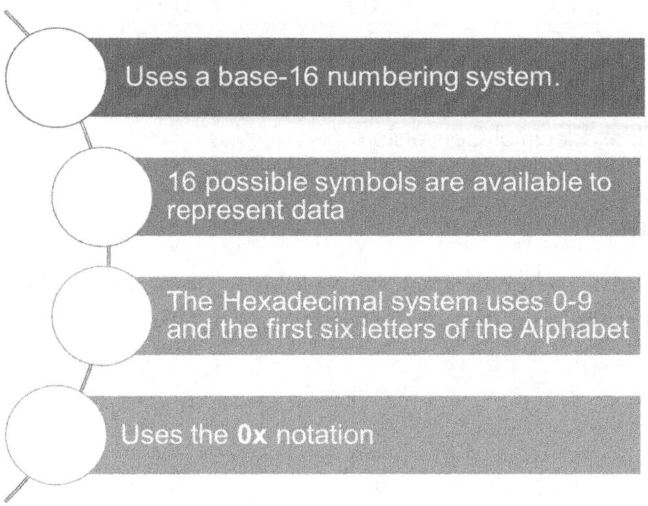

Decimal	Binary	Hexadecimal
0	0	0x0
1	1	0x1
2	10	0x2
3	11	0x3
4	100	0x4
5	101	0x5
6	110	0x6
7	111	0x7
8	1000	0x8
9	1001	0x9
10	1010	0xA
11	1011	0xB
12	1100	0xC
13	1101	0xD
14	1110	0xE
15	1111	0xF

Figure 1-29 Hexadecimal Numerical System

The Hexadecimal system uses a base-16 numbering system; this means that there are 16 possible symbols available to represent data. In this case the hexadecimal system uses numbers (0-9) and the first six letters of the alphabet (A-F). In the hexadecimal system the position of a number represents a value of the power of 16 (Figure 1-29).

Note

It is common to represent hexadecimal numbers with a preceding **0x**. This notation helps to differentiate hexadecimal numbers from decimal numbers. The hexadecimal number 0x29 is a very different value from the decimal number 29.

Converting Binary to Hexadecimal

The conversion between Binary to Hexadecimal is simple. Just know that four binary digits represent a single hexadecimal number. Based on this property, the conversion process is just a substitution, as shown in Figure 1-30. Let us look at this in another way.

Four binary digits represent a single hexadecimal number

Binary	Hexadecimal	Binary	Hexadecimal
0000	0x0	1000	0x8
0001	0x1	1001	0x9
0010	0x2	1010	0xA
0011	0x3	1011	0xB
0100	0x4	1100	0xC
0101	0x5	1101	0xD
0110	0x6	1110	0xE
0111	0x7	1111	0xF

Figure 1-30 Hexadecimal Conversion

Converting Binary to Hexadecimal

When you are going to convert a binary number to hexadecimal, group 4 binary numbers (nibble), and assign column values of 8,4,2,1 to each group, as shown in the figure.

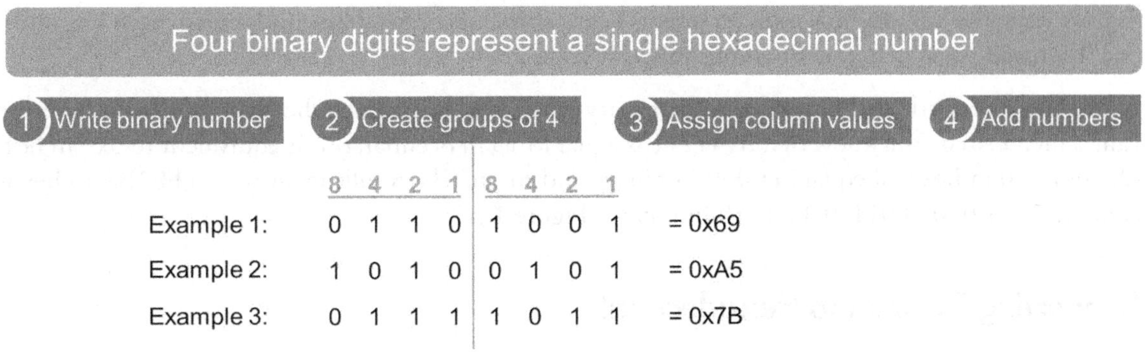

Figure 1-31 Converting Binary to Hexadecimal

Now look at Figure 1-31 example 1. In the most significant nibble, there are binary "1's" in the "4's" column and the "2's" column resulting in 4 plus 2 to equal 6. In the least significant nibble, there are binary "1's" in the "8's" column and the "1's" column making 8 plus 1 to equal 9. Therefore, 0110 1001 would equal 0x69 in hexadecimal.

Now consider the second example. The high nibble has "1's" in the "8's" and "4's" column resulting in 8 plus 4 to equal 12 in decimal, and 12 to equal 0xC in hex. The low nibble has "1's" in the "4's" and "1's" column resulting in 4 plus 1 to equal 5. Therefore, 1010 0101 in binary equals 0xC5 in hex.

In the third example, the high nibble is 4+2+1 = 7. The low nibble is 8+2+1 = 11 in decimal, which equals 0xB in hex. Thus, 0111 1011 = 0x7B in hex.

Converting Hexadecimal to Binary

Now suppose you need to convert from hexadecimal to binary.

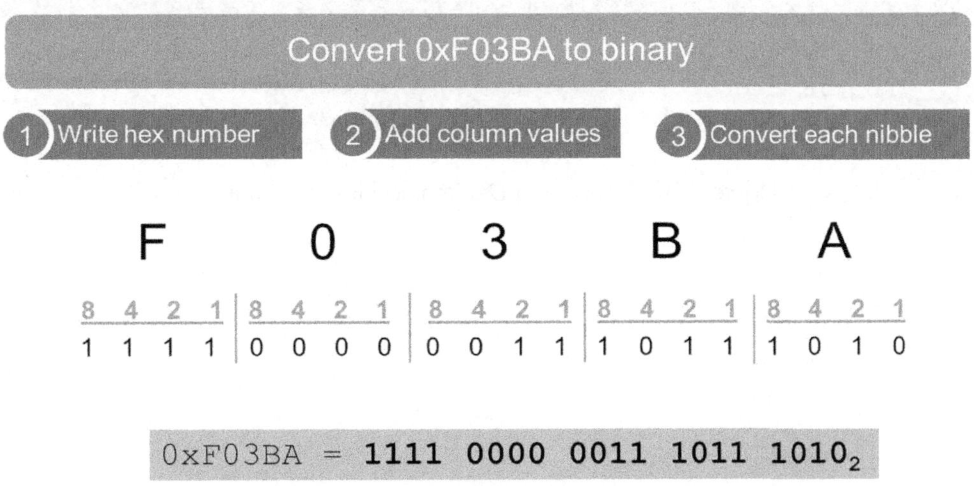

Figure 1-32 Steps to Converting Hexadecimal to Binary

Simply write the hexadecimal number down. Leave ample space for 4 bits underneath each hex number. Then add the 8,4,2, and 1 column values if you like.

Now simple convert each hex value to its binary equivalent. Reference the chart until you have the values memorized. You know that 8+4+2+1 is equal to 15 in decimal; this is equivalent to 0xF in hex. Of course, 0 in hex will equal in 0000 in binary and so on. The resulting answer 0xF03BA in hex is equal to 1111 0000 0011 1011 1010 in binary (Figure 1-32).

Converting Decimal to Hexadecimal

The process relies on a repeated division-by-16 process. Start dividing the decimal number by 16. Keep track of the quotient and the remainder. Continue dividing the quotient by 16 until you get a quotient of zero, then just write out the remainders in the reverse order.

Consider the following example, where the number 897_{10} is converted to its hexadecimal representation (Figure 1-33).

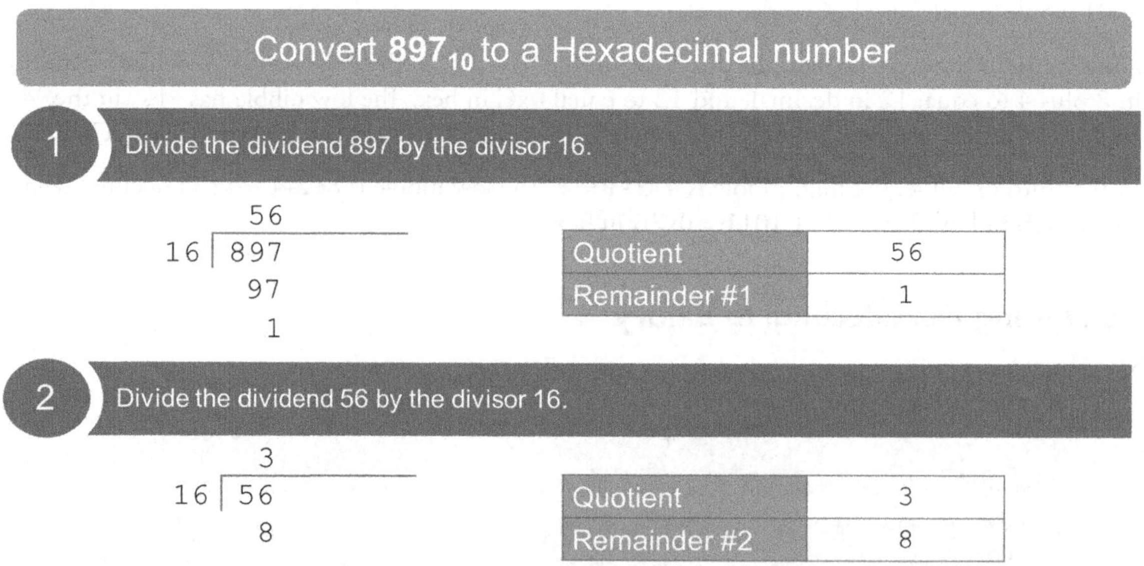

Figure 1-33 Converting Decimal to Hexadecimal

3 Divide the dividend 3 by the divisor 16.

```
     0
16 | 3
```

Quotient	0
Remainder #3	3

4 Take all the Remainders and order them starting from the last Remainder (#3 in this example).

Remainder #3	Remainder #2	Remainder #1
3	8	1

897_{10}= **0x381**

Figure 1-34 Converting Decimal to Hexadecimal Continued

Note
On step 3 we know that the quotient of the division is in reality a fraction number (0.1875). However, the process only focuses on the integer part of the quotient and the last Remainder before the operation is actually done (Figure 1-34).

Converting Hexadecimal to Decimal

There are several methods to convert a hexadecimal number into decimal; however, the comparison method is the easiest to learn. This method simply uses the position value of each number (remember that in hexadecimal system each position is a power of 16) and then sum the values (Figures 1-35, 1-36, and 1-37).

As an example, let us convert the hexadecimal number **0xC89A** to decimal.

Convert 0xC89A to a Decimal number

1 Write down a Table with all position's values in terms of power 16 and its value in decimal.

Power of 16	16^3	16^2	16^1	16^0
Decimal	4096	256	16	1

2 Write down the Hexadecimal number below

Power of 16	16^3	16^2	16^1	16^0
Decimal	4096	256	16	1
Hexadecimal #	**C**	**8**	**9**	**A**

Figure 1-35 Converting Hexadecimal to Decimal

3 Convert the letters into numbers in case that exist.

Power of 16	16^3	16^2	16^1	16^0
Decimal	4096	256	16	1
Hexadecimal #	**C**	**8**	**9**	**A**
Decimal	**12**	**8**	**9**	**10**

4 Write down the Hexadecimal number below

Power of 16	16^3	16^2	16^1	16^0
Decimal	4096	256	16	1
Hexadecimal #	**C**	**8**	**9**	**A**
Decimal	**12**	**8**	**9**	**10**
Multiplication	12x4096= **49152**	8x256= **2048**	16x9= **144**	1x10= **10**

Figure 1-36 Converting Hexadecimal to Decimal Continued

Note

Please refer to the table presented previously. You will soon have this memorized, with only a bit of practice.

5 Sum the values

Power of 16	16^3	16^2	16^1	16^0
Decimal	4096	256	16	1
Hexadecimal #	**C**	**8**	**9**	**A**
Decimal	**12**	**8**	**9**	**10**
Multiplication	12x4096= **49152**	8x256= **2048**	16x9= **144**	1x10= **10**

$$0xC89A = 49152_{10} + 2048_{10} + 144_{10} + 10_{10} = \mathbf{51354_{10}}$$

Figure 1-37 Converting Hexadecimal to Decimal Continued

Lab 1: Numerical Conversion

Although this guide assumes no previous networking knowledge and is intended to transmit solid fundamental concepts, some tasks will cover details in depth, from the ground up.

Except for Lab 1, the rest of the book will take you into a scenario where a company called BigStartup needs your professional networking services to achieve business success. The current lab is limited to practicing some binary and hexadecimal conversions.

Task 1: Binary to Decimal Conversion

In this task you will convert decimal numbers to binary, hexadecimal, and vice versa.

Steps

1. Fill out Table 1-1 with the "Power of two" information shown in chapter 1 "Numerical Systems."
2. Use Table 1-1 for completing your conversions.

Tip

In your time off, practice writing the table down. The more times you do it, the easier for you to remember it. This is a good shortcut for decimal to binary conversion whenever a calculator is not close.

Table 1-1 Binary to Decimal

Power of 2								
Decimal								

Binary a)								
Decimal a)								

Binary b)								
Decimal b)								

Binary c)								
Decimal c)								

Binary d)								
Decimal d)								

Binary e)								
Decimal e)								

Task 2: Decimal to Binary Conversion Method 1

Convert the following decimal values into binary using the division method:

a) 315

b) 116

c) 39 (optional)

d) 240 (optional)

Steps

1. Convert 315

Rem. 9	Rem. 8	Rem. 7	Rem. 6	Rem. 5	Rem. 4	Rem. 3	Rem. 2	Rem. 1

2. Convert 116

Rem. 7	Rem. 6	Rem. 5	Rem. 4	Rem. 3	Rem. 2	Rem. 1

3. Convert 39

Rem. 6	Rem. 5	Rem. 4	Rem. 3	Rem. 2	Rem. 1

4. Convert 240

Rem. 8	Rem. 7	Rem. 6	Rem. 5	Rem. 4	Rem. 3	Rem. 2	Rem. 1

Task 3: Decimal to Binary Conversion Method 2

Convert the following decimal values into binary using the powers of two method. Fill out Table 1-2 with the "Decimal to Binary" information shown in chapter 1 "Numerical Systems." Use Table 1-2 for completing your conversions:

a) 224

b) 17

c) 199 (optional)

d) 46 (optional)

Steps

1. Convert 224
2. Convert 17
3. Convert 199 (optional)
4. Convert 46 (optional)

Table 1-2 Decimal to Binary

Power of 2							
Decimal							

Binary a)							
Decimal a)							

Binary b)							
Decimal b)							

Binary c)							
Decimal c)							

Binary d)							
Decimal d)							

Binary e)							
Decimal e)							

Task 4: Decimal to Hexadecimal Conversion (Optional)

Convert the following decimal values into hexadecimal using the division method. Fill out Table 1-3 with the "Decimal to Hexadecimal" information shown in chapter 1 "Numerical Systems." Use Table 1-3 for completing your conversions.

Steps

1. 898
2. 2033
3. 1572
4. 78

Table 1-3 Decimal to Hexadecimal

Decimal	Hexadecimal

5. Convert 898

Rem. 3	Rem. 2	Rem. 1

6. Convert 2033

Rem. 3	Rem. 2	Rem. 1

7. Convert 1572

Rem. 3	Rem. 2	Rem. 1

8. Convert 78

Rem. 2	Rem. 1

Task 5: Hexadecimal to Decimal Conversion (Optional)

Convert the following decimal values into binary using the division method. Use Table 1-4 for completing your conversions.

Steps

1. F3A
2. 15B
3. 111
4. 7C

Table 1-4 Decimal to Hexadecimal

Power of 16				
Decimal				

Hexadecimal a)				
Decimal				
Multiplication				
Decimal a)				

Hexadecimal b)				
Decimal				
Multiplication				
Decimal b)				

Hexadecimal c)				
Decimal				
Multiplication				
Decimal c)				

Hexadecimal d)				
Decimal				
Multiplication				
Decimal d)				

Task 6: Binary to Hexadecimal Conversion

Convert the following binary values into hexadecimal. Use Table 1-5 for completing your conversions.

a) 01100110

b) 10100101

c) 00010010 (optional)

d) 01011010 (optional)

Table 1-5 Binary to Hexadecimal

Binary	Hexadecimal

Steps

Fill in the "Decimal to Hexadecimal" information shown in chapter 1 "Numerical Systems".

1. Convert 01100110
2. Convert 01100110
3. Convert 01100110
4. Convert 01100110

Task 7: Hexadecimal to Binary Conversion

Convert the following hexadecimal values into binary using the division method. Use Table 1-6 for completing your conversions.

a) AB

b) AB3

c) 3F4 (optional)

d) 0C (optional)

Table 1-6 Hexadecimal to Binary

Hexadecimal	Binary

Steps

1. Convert AB
2. Convert AB3
3. Convert 3F4
4. Convert 0C

You have completed Lab 1!

Learning Check

Here are some questions that will help you review the information covered in this chapter. Please refer to the Appendix to verify your answers.

Chapter 1 Questions

Computer Networks

1. Which of the following are concepts or technologies that are **specific** to a LAN? Pick two.
    a. Ethernet
    b. Wi-Fi
    c. Multi-Protocol Label Switching (MPLS)
    d. The Transmission Control Protocol (TCP)
    e. Modulation and demodulation

The OSI Model

2. Which of the following are aspects of Layer-4 of the OSI model? Pick three.
    a. TCP
    b. IP
    c. UDP
    d. Segmentation
    e. Session Management

Physical Media

3. Under which circumstances is it most appropriate to use Single Mode fiber optic mode? Pick two.
    a. When you need to connect two devices in a single equipment rack
    b. When you must connect two buildings that are 10km apart

c. When you are concerned about electromagnetic interference
d. When you want to use UDP instead of TCP

Binary to Decimal Conversion

4. What does 11010110 equal to in decimal?
   a. 212
   b. 198
   c. 214
   d. 218
5. What does 10101110 equal to in decimal?
   a. 230
   b. 89
   c. 174
   d. 43
6. What does 01000101 equal to in decimal?
   a. 223
   b. 48
   c. 85
   d. 69
7. What does 11111110 equal to in decimal?
   a. 254
   b. 49
   c. 146
   d. 265
8. What does 10000001 equal to in decimal?
   a. 149
   b. 161
   c. 230
   d. 129

2 TCP/IP

EXAM OBJECTIVES

✓ Describe network devices and common network services

✓ Explain network hierarchical models

Basic Network Concepts

After completing this module, you will be able to describe the typical devices that are used to create a network, switches, routers, Multi-Layer Switches, access points, firewalls, and servers. You will also be able to explain common networking services that are used over these networks including DHCP, DNS, HTTP, Telnet and SSH, and FTP.

TCP/IP Stack

The Internet Protocol Suite is a conceptual model and set of communication protocols used in Internet and computing networks. It is commonly known as the TCP/IP Stack because the foundational protocols in the suite are Transmission Control Protocol (TCP) and the Internet Protocol (IP). This model provides end-to-end data communication. It specifies how data should be packetized, addressed, transmitted, routed, and received. This functionality is organized into four abstraction Layers. The TCP/IP model is often compared to the OSI model, as shown in Figure 2-1.

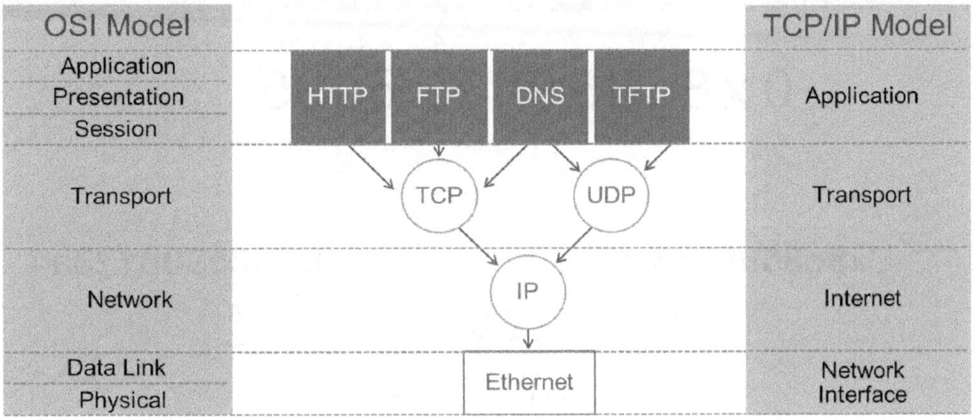

Figure 2-1 TCP/IP Stack

The OSI model has seven Layers which map to the four Layers of the TCP/IP model. The functionality of the OSI model's Application, Presentation, and Session Layers all map to a single TCP/IP Application Layer. This means that TCP/IP-based applications are responsible for interfacing with users and creating the data (Application Layer), putting it in the proper format (Presentation Layer), and managing sessions (Session Layer).

The Transport Layers of each model directly map. Recall that this Layer is responsible for flow and error control. This Layer establishes an end-to-end connection of two devices whose logical connection traverses a series of networks. The two choices used in a TCP/IP network are UDP and TCP.

The OSI Network Layer maps to the TCP/IP Internet Layer. Both perform the same function—routing data across logical network paths by defining a packet format and an addressing format. IP version 4 (IPv4) and IP version 6 (IPv6) are the protocols that work on this Layer.

The OSI models Data Link and Physical functions are all defined in a single Layer in the TCP/IP model: Network Interface Layer. These Layers contain protocols relating to the physical communication medium (copper wires, fiber optics, and radio waves). Recall that physical media access control also occurs here. Ethernet and Wi-Fi are common protocols that work at this Layer.

Ethernet

Ethernet is a family of computer networking technologies that are used at Layer-1 and Layer-2 of the OSI model. At Layer-2, this standard provides for the assignment of 6-byte (48-bit) Media Access Control (MAC) addresses to each device. Each manufacturer assigns a globally unique hexadecimal MAC address to each Network Interface Controller (NIC). This address is stored in permanent Read Only Memory (ROM) on the NIC (Figure 2-2). In other words, every Ethernet NIC in the world has a unique MAC address. How is this possible?

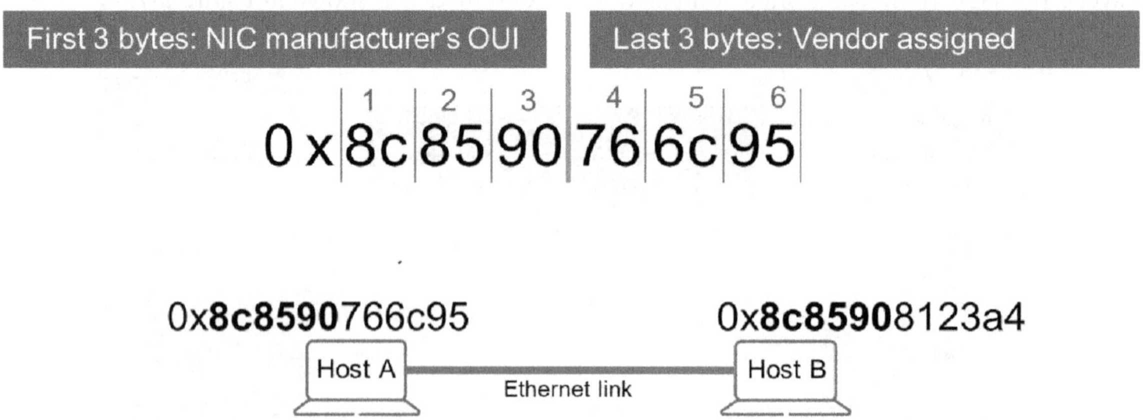

Figure 2-2 Ethernet Addressing

The most significant first three bytes of each MAC address are referred to as the manufacturer's Organizationally Unique Identifier (OUI). A standards body assigns each manufacturer in the world a unique 3-byte number. All NICs from that vendor therefore have the same number in the first 3 bytes.

The last three bytes of the MAC address comprise the NIC serial number. Recall that with hexadecimal a single byte is comprised of two characters. Thus, each MAC address is represented with 12 hexadecimal characters, each Byte or octet is typically separated by either a colon or dash. For example for the MAC address 8c:85:90:76:6c:95, the OUI is 8c:85:90, while the NIC serial number is 76:6c:95. As you progress through this course, we will often use fictitious, 2-byte MAC addresses such as 8c::95. This just makes it easier for you to focus on fundamental concepts, as opposed to always trying to read out large, 6-byte hexadecimal numbers.

To verify the vendor of an NIC by its MAC address, access a website like https://macvendors.com, which allows you to perform OUI lookups. If you were to lookup the address in this example, you would determine that the manufacture is Apple.

Ethernet Frame

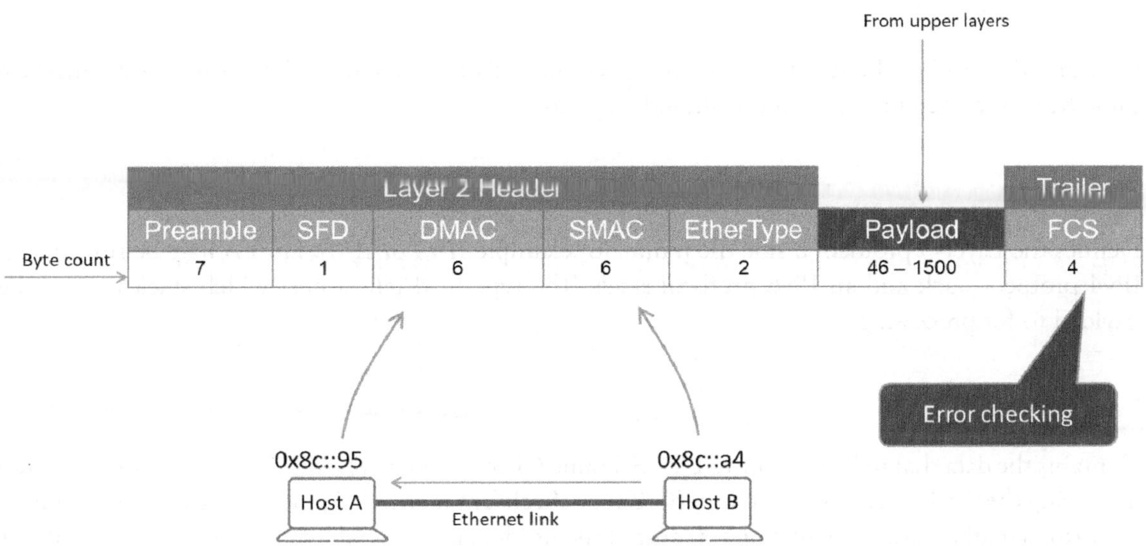

Figure 2-3 Ethernet Frame

Suppose that Host B receives data from the upper Layers of the OSI model. Think of Ethernet as an employee of the upper Layers. They have given Ethernet this payload and asked Ethernet to get this over to host A. To do this, the Ethernet process must wrap this payload with a header and trailer, as shown in Figure 2-3. Each field in the header and trailer is described below:

Preamble

Informs the receiving system that a frame is starting and enables synchronization.

SFD (Start Frame Delimiter)

Indicates that the Destination MAC address field begins with the next byte. There might be several hosts on this Ethernet segment. The preamble and SFD are seen by every host as a kind of signal, "Hey, here comes a frame and it might be for you!" How does the receiving station know whether the frame is for it, or some other host? By reading the next field, the destination MAC address.

Destination MAC(DMAC)

Identifies the NIC of the receiving computing system. In this example Host A reads the MAC address and knows, "Hey, this is my MAC address. I should accept this frame." All other stations read the MAC address, realize the message is not for them, and drop the frame. This is like someone yelling in a room, "Hey Marta, can I buy you an ice cream?" Only Marta will respond.

Source MAC(SMAC)

Identifies the NIC of the sending computing system. This is how Host A knows where the message came from and therefore to whom it should respond.

EtherType

Defines the Layer-3 protocol inside the frame, for example IPv4 or IPv6. Host A may be running an IPv4 protocol stack and an IPv6 protocol stack. The type field tells a host which stack to pass the payload to for processing.

Payload

Contains the data that to be transmitted. FCS(Frame Check Sequence). Allows detection of corrupted data using the Cyclic Redundancy check (CRC) or checksum method. As Host B creates this Frame, it performs a mathematical calculation on most of the header and payload bits. It places the result of this calculation in the FCS field. When Host A receives the frame, it performs the same calculation. If it comes up with the same result that is stored in the FCS field, the frame is not corrupted. But if you have bad wiring or strong electromagnetic interference (EMI) the data may become corrupted. In this case, Host A's calculation will not match the FCS and so the frame is discarded; no need to accept bad data.

It is important to understand that the Ethernet payload not only carries application data; it also includes the header information from the upper Layers. Remember, TCP adds a header, which IP considers part of the payload. Then IP adds a header, which Ethernet considers part of the payload. Let us look now at this IP header information.

Note

As promised, we are only showing the first and last bytes of each 6-byte MAC address, to ease the learning experience.

IPv4 Header

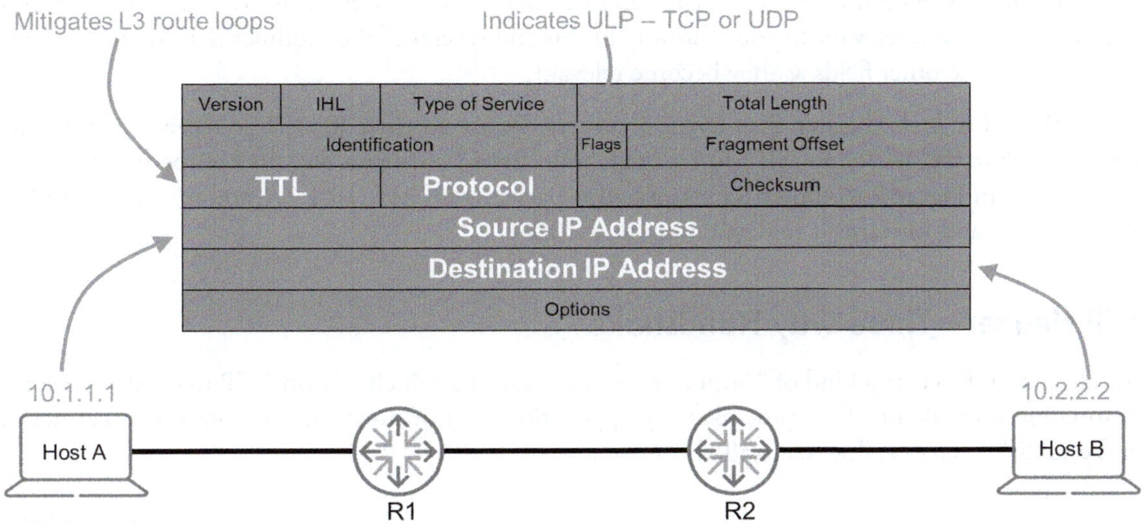

Figure 2-4 IPv4 Header

Figure 2-4 shows the IPv4 header information added to a packet at Layer-3 with a special emphasis on the most important fields in this header as described below:

Time to Live (TTL)

This field mitigates Layer-3 route loops. If routers are misconfigured, IP packets could be bounced around between two or more routers forever. To prevent this, the original places a number in this field from 0 to 255. For example, suppose that TTL=15. Each router that routes this packet decrements this field by 1. So, after this packet "hops" through the first router, TTL=14. After the next router, TTL=13 and so on. The router that decrements the TTL field to zero discards the packet.

Protocol

This field indicates whether this IP packet carries TCP traffic or UDP traffic. Recall that application data is passed down to TCP or UDP, which adds a header and passes this on down to IP. From IP perspective, TCP, UDP, and other protocols are at higher Layers in the model and so can be collectively referred to as Upper Layer Protocols (ULP).

Source IP Address

This originator of this IP packet adds its IP address to the source address field. In Figure 2-4, host 10.1.1.1 sends a packet to host 10.2.2.2. Thus, the Source IP Address fields = 10.1.1.1 and the Destination IP address field = 10.2.2.2.

Destination IP Address

The ultimate destination of the packet is described above. The other fields are shown here in gray because they are not relevant to your learning in this and several of the modules that follow. You will learn about these other fields as they become relevant.

Remember, this is the header that Layer-3 routers use to do their job. They receive an inbound packet, analyze the destination IP address field, and forward packets along the best path toward that destination. In Figure 2-4, router R1 receives this packet from host 10.1.1.1 and forwards it to R2. R2 receives it and forwards it to destination host 10.2.2.2.

TCP Header—Three-way Handshake

Recall that TCP acts as a kind of "employee" for applications, which rely on TCP to get data to some destination host. Before TCP processes any application data, it must first contact the target device and establish a reliable, flow-controlled connection.

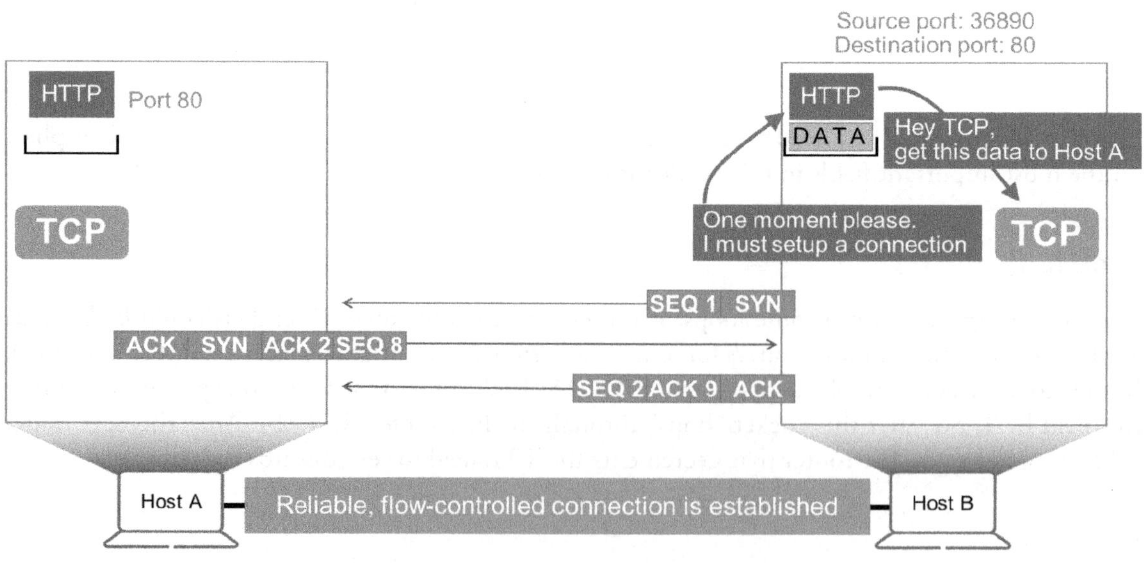

Figure 2-5 TCP Three-Way Handshake

In Figure 2-5, the Host B's HTTP application has data; sitting in a kind of "out box", waiting to be transmitted to Host A. It is as if HTTP says, "Hey TCP, I need you to get this data to Host A." TCP says, "OK boss, but first I must establish a connection with Host A to ensure that your data is sent in a controlled reliable manner."

There are four primary fields in the TCP header that are used to establish this connection: the sequence (SEQ) number, the acknowledgement (ACK) number, the Synchronize (SYN) flag, and the Acknowledgement (ACK) flag.

Host B starts by creating a TCP packet. This packet carries no data; it only signals Host A, "We should establish a connection."

In this example, Host B sets SEQ=1 and raises its SYN flag (sets it to a binary 1).

Host A receives this and knows, "This packet came from Host B with the SYN flag raised; Host B wants to connect."

Host A must inform Host B that it received SEQ=1 and so expects SEQ=2 next. To do this, Host A sends a packet with ACK=2, and both the SYN and ACK flags are raised. Understand that Host A is independent of Host B. Host B tagged its packet with SEQ=1. Host A chooses to tag its packet with SEQ=8.

Host A is saying, "I'm using my packet number 8 to acknowledge receipt of your packet number 1."

Host B receives and responds to this packet, "You expected SEQ=2 next, so here it is. I am using my packet number 2 to acknowledge receipt of your packet number 8. I expect packet number 9 next."

As you can see, both the SYN and ACK flags are raised in this packet. At this point, a reliable, flow-controlled connection is established. Each host has successfully received and acknowledged a sequence of packets from the other. Now TCP is ready to start transferring that data for the application.

HTTP uses a specific port to transmit the information; in this case the destination port number is 80 the source port in this case is randomly selected on Host B. In this case Host B selects the port 36890 as the source port.

TCP Header—Sequence Numbers

TCP may be asked to transfer large files, too big to transfer all at once. Therefore, Host B's TCP process breaks up the large file into smaller pieces called segments and assigns a unique sequence (SEQ) number to each segment. In this example we want to transmit the word "DATA". Host B then creates 2 pieces—one for the letters "DA" and the other for the letters "TA."

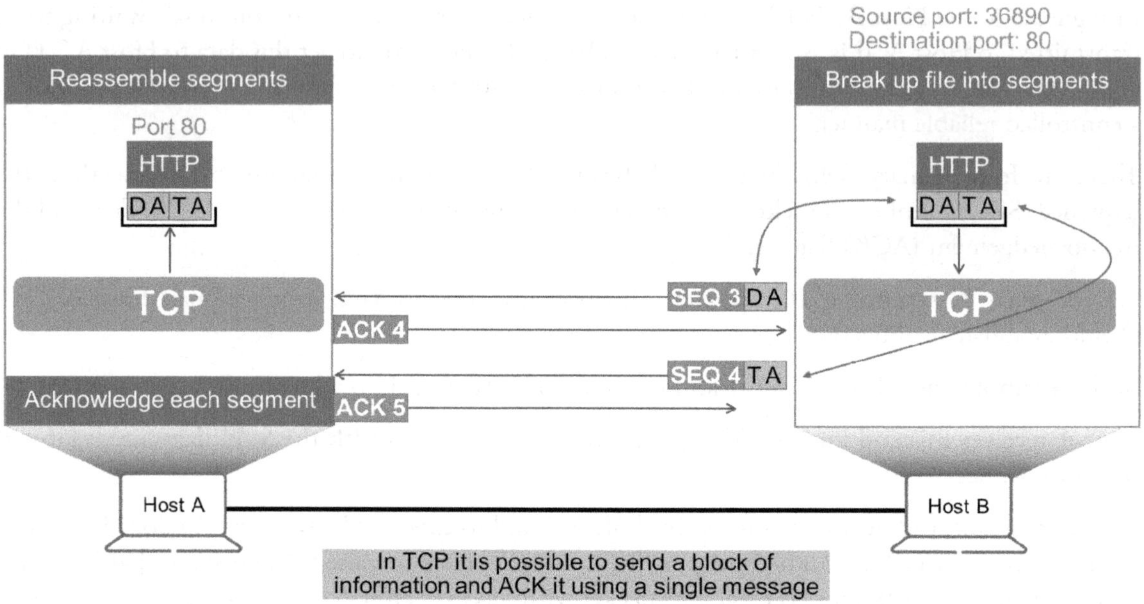

Figure 2-6 TCP Sequencing

In Figure 2-6, TCP assigns Sequence = 3 to the first piece (DA) and transmits it to Host B. Host A acknowledges this by sending a packet with Acknowledgement (ACK) number = 4. Essentially, Host A is saying, "I received segment 3 and so I expect segment 4 next." Host B then takes the next piece (TA) adds Sequence = 4 and sends it to Host A. Host A acknowledges this by sending ACK = 5. As Host A receives this data, it reassembles the pieces back into a complete file and passes it up to the application. The host knows of course that SEQ.

Note

In TCP it is possible to send a block of information and acknowledge all the blocks of data using a single ACK message.

TCP Header—Port Numbers

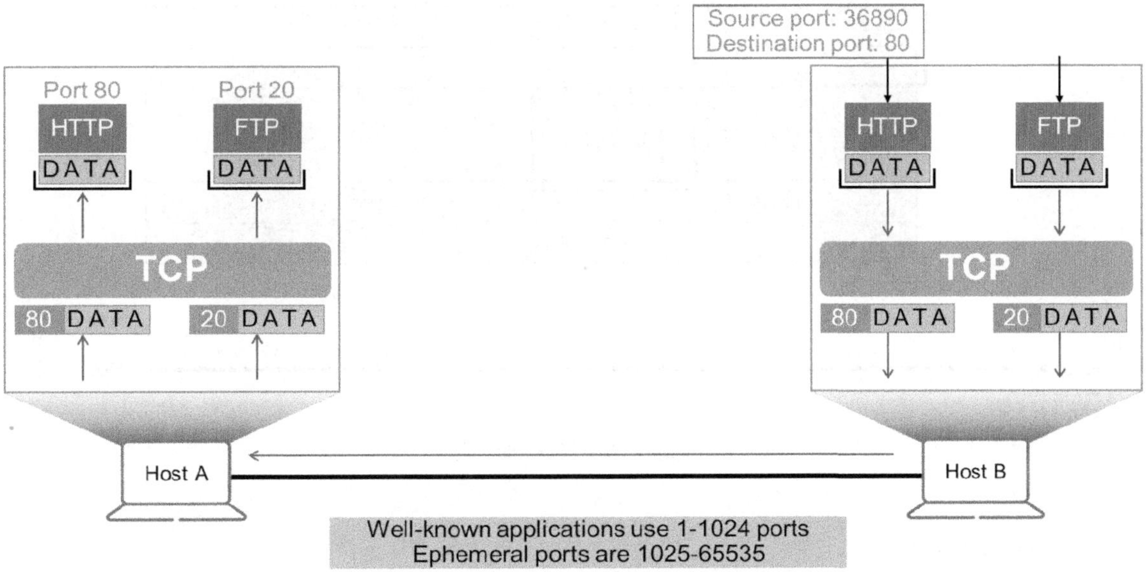

Figure 2-7 TCP Port Numbers

Recall that TCP acts as a kind of "employee" for applications. TCP receives requests from HTTP, FTP, and many other applications. It is as if the application says, "Hey TCP, establish a connection with the target host and make sure my data gets there reliably." TCP uses the destination port number to keep track of each application it serves. To accommodate this, each application is assigned a standard port number. FTP uses port 20 for data transfer, HTTP uses port 80, and so on. When Host B's TCP process accepts data from HTTP it sets Destination Port = 80. Thus, when Host A receives this data, it knows to pass this data up to its HTTP application as opposed to DNS or FTP. In TCP you can use up to 65535 ports; however the well-known applications use the first 1024 ports. From 1025 to 65525 ports are known as Ephemeral Port numbers (Figure 2-7).

TCP Header

As described below, Figure 2-8 shows the entire TCP header information added to a Layer-4 segment, with a special emphasis on the most important fields in this header:

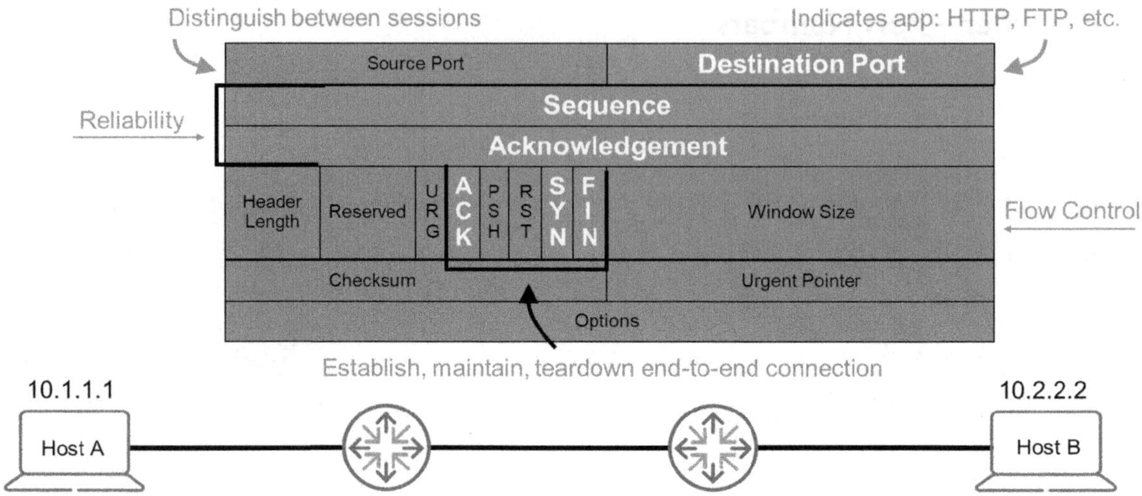

Figure 2-8 TCP Header

Destination Port

The first fields added are the source and destination port numbers. You just learned hosts use the destination port to distinguish the various applications that it serves. But what if you form two or more HTTP connections? You point your browser to your favorite search engine. Then open another tab in the browser and point it to www.arubanetworks.com. Both sessions have Destination Port = 80. How does TCP know which data is for the search engine and which data is for arubanetworks.com?

TCP sets the source port to a random number. The session to the search engine has Source Port = 58936, Destination Port = 80. The session to Aruba has Source Port = 57576, Destination Port = 80. Thus, TCP can distinguish multiple simultaneous sessions for the same application.

Sequence and Acknowledgement Numbers

You also learned about the sequence and acknowledgement numbers. They are used along with the ACK and SYN flags to ensure reliability and flow control. Host B sends SEQ=5, Host A responds with ACK=6, and so on. But what if Host A responded with ACK = 5? Host B says, “Hmm. I guess host A did not receive segment 5, so I will resend it.” In this way, TCP ensures reliability, resending any packets that are lost in transmission.

Flags

You learned how the SYN and ACK flags are used to formally synchronize TCP packet (sequence) numbers and acknowledge receipt of packets. There is also a Final (FIN) flag, which tells the receiver, “Hey Host A, this is the last piece of the file.” There are the Urgent (URG) and Push (PSH) flags to indicate that certain data is urgent and should be quickly pushed up to the receiving application. The URG flag is used in conjunction with the Urgent Pointer field, which indicates where the urgent data is located. There is also a Reset (RST) flag used to reset the connection.

Window Size

There is a checksum for reliability and a Window size field used for flow control. If Host B is sending too much data at a time, Host A may not be able to handle the load. Host A may lower the window size, telling Host B, "Slow down, please do not send so much data at a time." The remaining fields are not either rarely used or not relevant to this initial discussion. You will learn about these fields as you continue your training, as appropriate.

UDP Header

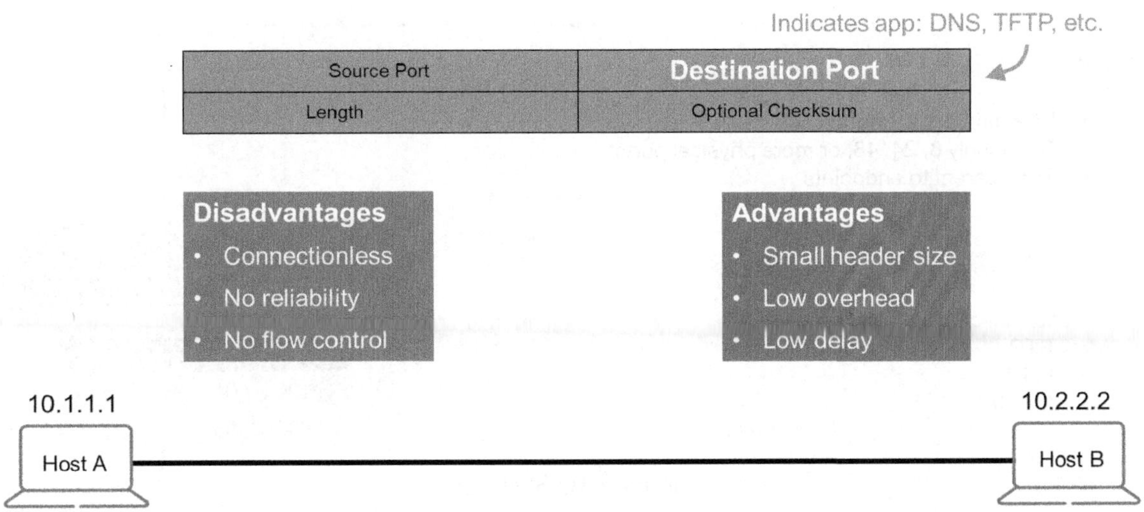

Figure 2-9 UDP Header

Figure 2-9 shows the entire UDP header information added to a Layer-4 segment. Look how simple this is. There are only source and destination ports, used in the same way as for TCP. Then there is a Length field and an optional checksum. For applications, TCP acts as a very dedicated employee. TCP established a connection with the other side and retransmits any lost packets. This makes sure the receiver does not become overwhelmed with data. In contrast, UDP is like a lazy employee, no connection, no reliability, and no flow control. Did the packets get to the destination? UDP says, "I don't care." Is the network or destination host overwhelmed with the data that I transmit? "I don't care." UDP might be lazy, but it is inexpensive. The small header size means that there is low overhead. The lack of services means that UDP can transfer data with lower delay. It is not reliable, but it is quick. This is perfect for applications like Voice over IP (VoIP) or video streaming. These applications do not need all of TCP's reliability and they do not want to pay for it. Programmers who build applications can simply build the needed reliability into the application itself. In UDP you can use up to 65535 ports; however the well-known applications use the first 1024 ports. From 1025 to 65525 ports are known as Ephemeral Port numbers, same concept as TCP.

Networking Devices

Switches

Switches have multiple ports that are used to connect computing devices into one or more Local Area Networks (LAN). This can include PCs, printers, video cameras, Voice-over-IP (VoIP) phones, and more. You may encounter switches that have 8, 24, 48, or more ports. Understand that switches are "transparent" to endpoints. Connected devices are not aware of the existence of the switch; they perceive themselves as being directly connected to each other.

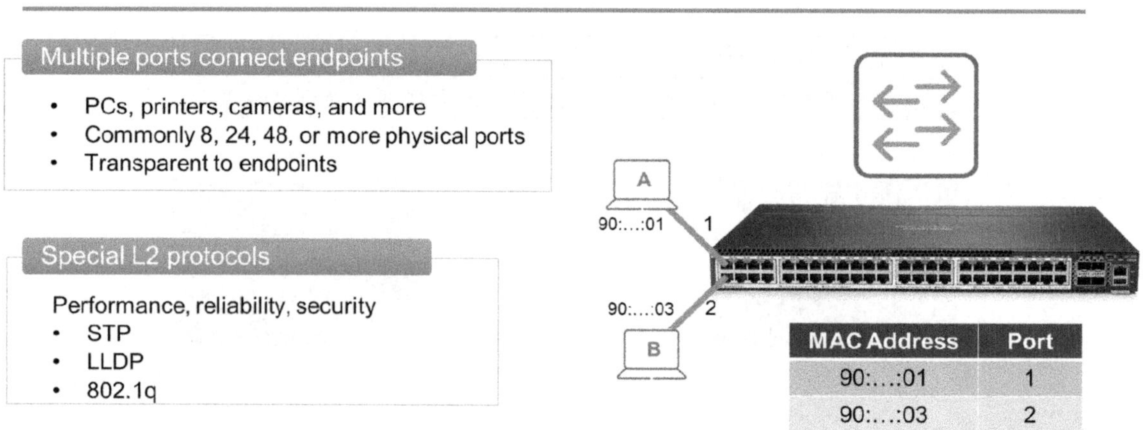

Figure 2-10 Switches

A switch is a Layer-2 network device that forwards Ethernet frames, based on destination MAC addresses. Recall that MAC addresses are part of the Data Link Layer and so switches are considered Layer-2 network devices. Figure 2-10 shows the Aruba icon used for a switch and below that a physical switch example. You also see a simplified MAC address table that is maintained in switch memory. The switch has learned that a device with MAC address 90::01 is connected to port 1 of the switch and a device with MAC address 90::03 is connected to port 2.

Switches also have special languages or protocols that they use to increase network performance, reliability, and security. Examples of these protocols include the following:

- Spanning Tree Protocol (STP)
- Link Layer Discovery Protocol (LLDP)
- 802.1q

Note
You will learn more about these protocols later in this course.

Routers

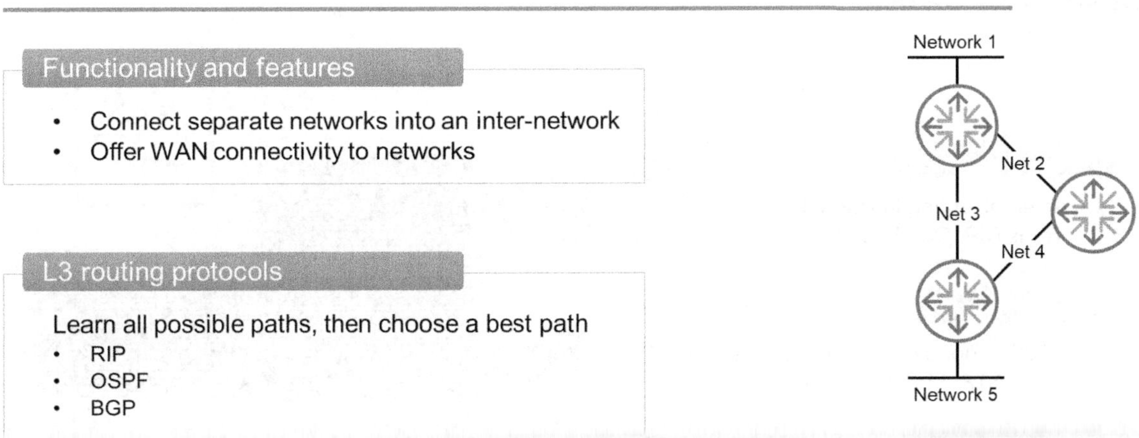

Figure 2-11 Routers

A router is a Layer-3 network device that forwards packets based on the destination IP address. Since IP addresses are part of the Network Layer, routers are considered Layer-3 devices. You know that switches connect computing devices into one or more networks. It is a router's job to connect those separate networks together to create an inter-network. The Internet is the largest most common example of an inter-network. Figure 2-11 shows three routers used to interconnect five networks. While switches might have a few dozen or a couple hundred ports, routers have a relatively small port count, often between 2 and 6, which are used to connect to WAN networks.

When you take a long trip in your car, there are often several paths you could take to arrive at your destination. You consider all possible paths and then choose the best path. You judge the best path based on some criteria that is important to you, such as whether, the route is the fastest, the shortest, or whether the route is particularly scenic. Then you drive along that path. Similarly, routers run protocols between them to learn all possible paths between all available networks. They then choose a best path for each destination and forward packets along those best paths.

Examples of these routing protocols are:

- Routing Information Protocol (RIP)
- Open Shortest Path First (OSPF)
- Border Gateway Protocol (BGP)

Note
You will learn more about these protocols later in this course.

Multi-Layer Switch

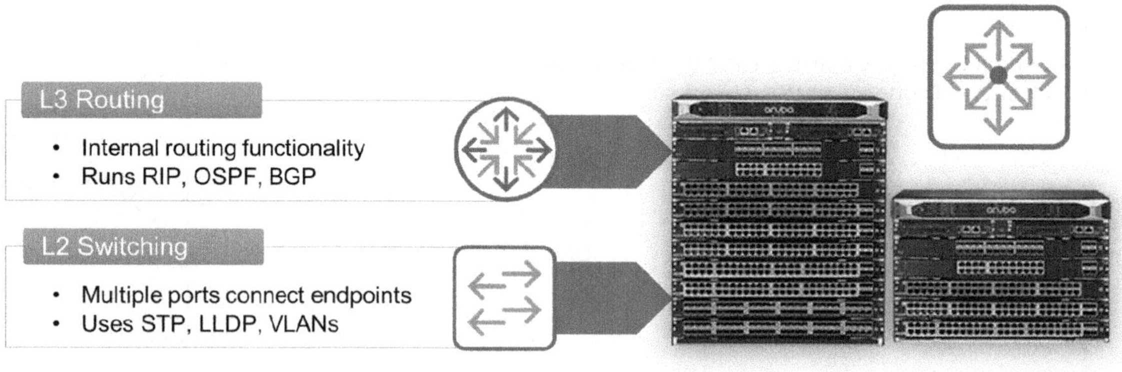

Figure 2-12 Multi-Layer Switch

The OSI model sets clear distinctions between a Layer-2 switch and a Layer-3 router. However, networking professionals know that it is often good to have a single device that can perform both functions, a hybrid between a router and a switch.

A Multi-Layer Switch has all the functionality of a Layer-2 Switch. They support typical Layer-2 functionality such as STP, LLDP, and VLANs. Multiple ports connect various endpoint devices together into one or more networks. A Multi-Layer Switch also has all or most of the functionality of a Layer-3 router, so it can route between those separate LANs internally: an internetwork in a box! Like most standard routers, a Multi-Layer switch supports routing protocols like RIP, OSPF, and BGP. Of course, Multi-Layer switches support Layer-1 to transmit and receive data and it can even perform some Layer-4 functions, especially as relates to certain security features. These devices help to build a secure and flexible network (Figure 2-12).

Wireless Access Points

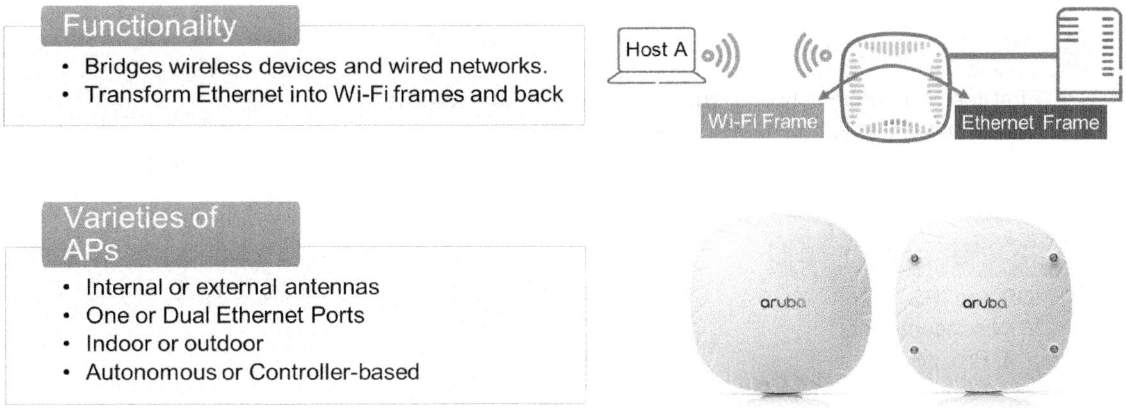

Figure 2-13 Wireless Aps

Access Points (AP) enable wireless users to access wired resources. Without being tethered to an Ethernet cable, users are free to roam about. APs are translational bridges; they accept Wi-Fi frames from endpoints, translate them into Ethernet frames, and forward them on to some wired resource. This could be an internal corporate server, storage, application, or an Internet resource. Responses from wired devices route back to the AP. The AP accepts those Ethernet frames and translates them into a Wi-Fi frame. This wireless frame is then transmitted over the air to a wireless host, as shown in Figure 2-13.

There are many varieties of APs to meet your technical and budgetary needs. They may be built with internal or external antennas, with one or dual Ethernet ports. Some may be for indoor use only, while others may be mounted outside. Wi-Fi systems may be designed to use Autonomous APs or Controller-based AP. Autonomous APs can perform all necessary functions to create a functional system. They process wireless and Ethernet frames and provide a certain amount of manageability and control. As the name implies, they work autonomously, without control from some external device. This type of deployment is relatively simple and easy, but it is not very scalable. It is suitable for smaller environments. With Controller-based AP solutions, the APs send and receive Wireless and Ethernet frames, much like Autonomous APs. However, much of the processing and management functions are off-loaded to one or more centralized controllers. These centralized configuration and control features might increase the initial complexity of the deployment, but once in place they provide far superior visibility into network health, enable more proactive network management, and can scale from medium to large deployments.

Firewalls

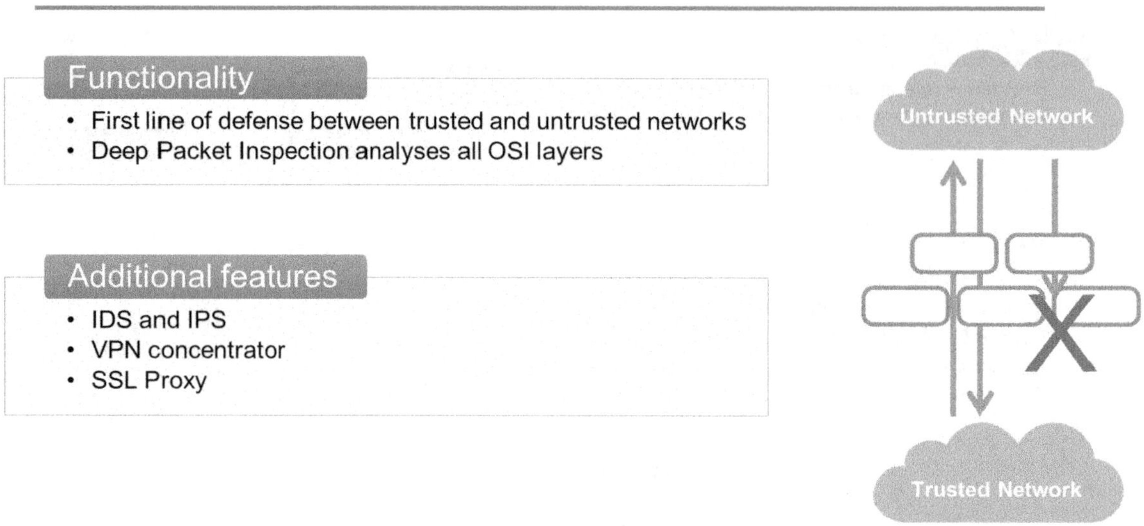

Figure 2-14 Firewalls

Firewalls are security devices that monitor and control network traffic, based on security rules. Appropriate traffic is permitted, while suspicious traffic is denied and determine whether each packet should be permitted or denied, based on security rules. Firewalls are commonly deployed as the first line of defense between trusted networks (managed by a corporation) and untrusted networks such as Internet, permitting only the valid connections. Many firewalls can inspect all OSI Layers, permitting engineers to create elaborate rules based on applications. Compared with older firewalls that only understand up to OSI model Layer-4, these newer firewalls can get deeper into the packet headers; all the way to Layer-7. This is known as Deep Packet Inspection (Figure 2-14).

Some firewalls can integrate other functions such as:

- Intrusion Detection Systems (IDS)
- Intrusion Prevention Systems (IPS)
- VPN Concentrators
- SSL proxy

Servers

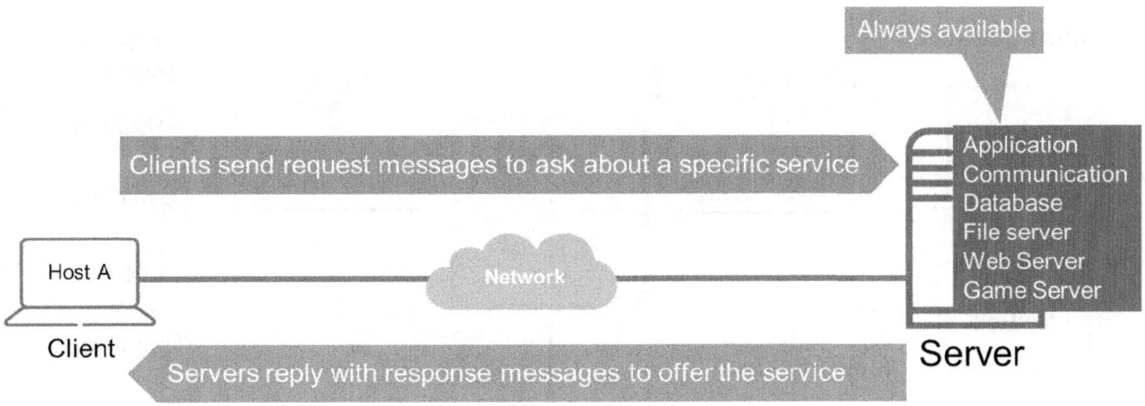

Figure 2-15 Servers

A server is a computing device that provides services for other programs or devices called clients.

The underlying switches, routers, APs and firewalls facilitate this client-server communication. Clients often send request messages to servers to ask about a specific service. Servers reply with response messages to offer the service. Clients can contact a server anytime, and servers use hardware and software that is designed to be available all time. Servers are often classified based on the services that they provide (Figure 2-15).

Some examples include the following:

- Application Servers
- Communication Servers
- Database Servers
- File Servers
- Web Servers
- Game Servers

Operational Planes: Control, Management, and Data

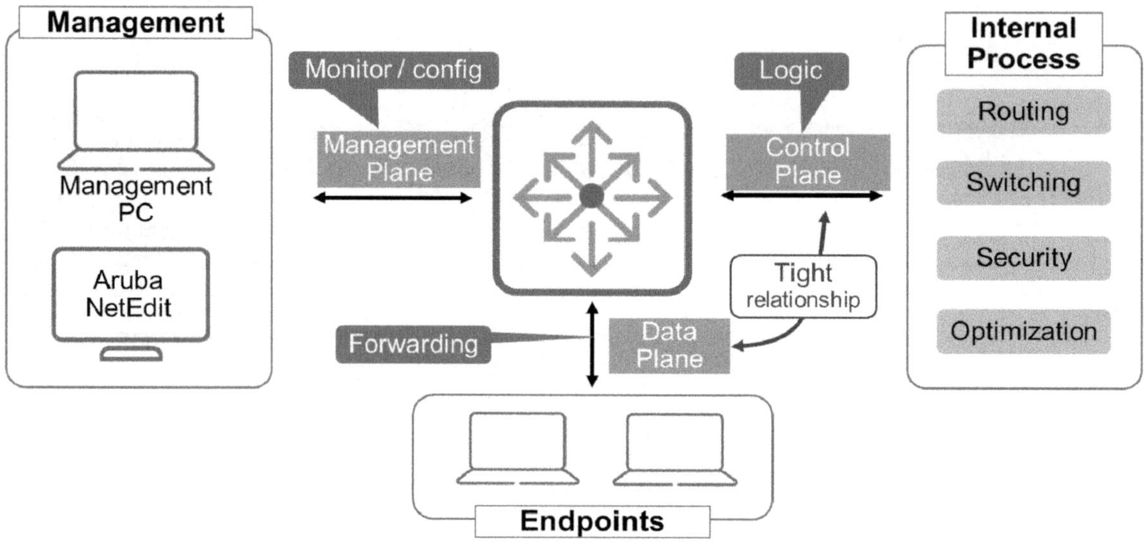

Figure 2-16 Operational Planes: Control, Management, and Data

A network device is logically composed of three operational planes, and each plane performs specific tasks (Figure 2-16).

Data Plane

The data plane receives and sends frames using specialized hardware called Application-Specific Integrated Circuits (ASIC), which is much faster than using software. ASICs modulate and demodulate data and handle other functions related to frame transmission and receipt.

Control Plane

The control plane logic determines what to do with the data that has been received. These decisions are made with internal processes, routing, switching, security, and flow optimization. Data plane and Control planes have a tight relationship to process any data as fast as possible.

Management Plane

You use the management plane to monitor and configure the device. This plane must be separate from the data plane, for security and accessibility reasons. You do not want your access to the device to be completely reliant on things like VLANs or VRFs. You must be able to access the device even if the control and data planes fail. Also, you do not want end users to gain access to the management plane; this could be an egregious security issue.

Note

Aruba OS-CX devices have a specific Interface and VRF that is used for Out-of-Band Management which maintains separation from the data plane.

Common Networking Services

DHCP

Challenge

Every device on a TCP/IP network requires an IP address, which can be manually configured. But imagine the overhead of manually assigning IP addresses to hundreds or thousands of hosts. Even worse, if your laptop has a statically assigned address appropriate for work, it will unlikely be the correct information when you then connect at home or at your favorite café.

Solution

DHCP dynamically assigns network information to clients. Thus, when a host boots up, it automatically acquires its IP address, subnet mask, default gateway, and other configurable parameters.

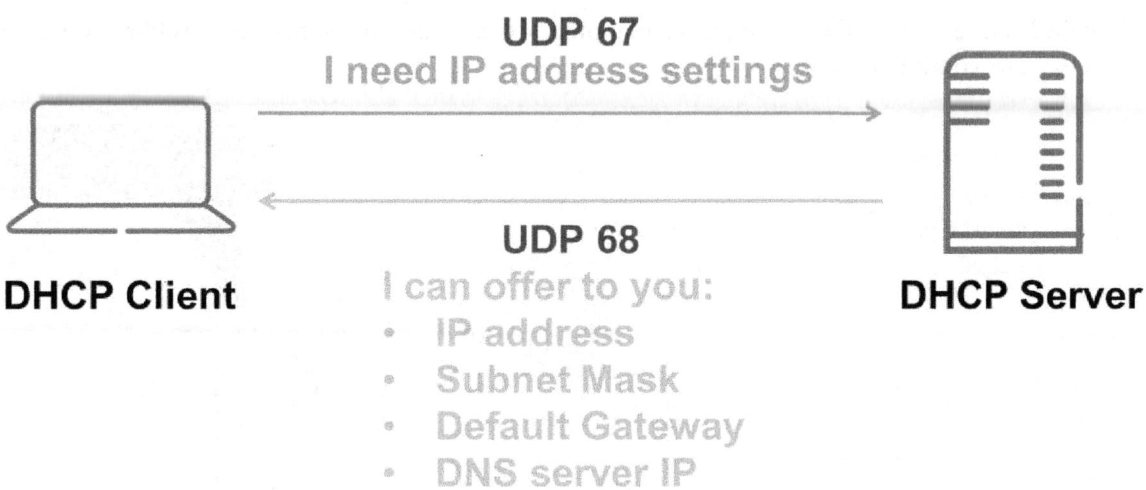

Figure 2-17 DHCP

Clients typically initiate the communication by broadcasting a DHCP query on the network, "Attention everyone! I need an IP address." The DHCP server receives this query and replies with an offer. If the offer is valid, the client uses the provided information. Recall that both UDP and TCP headers include a destination port number, which indicates the type of application data that is received. Clients use UDP port 67 for the DHCP query and servers reply with an offer on UDP port 68. For larger enterprise-class deployments, this DHCP service is often implemented on a server. For smaller deployments, DHCP can be implemented on routers and Multi-Layer Switches (Figure 2-17).

DNS

Challenge

To send or receive data all devices in a computing network must have a valid IP address. Two problems arise in a typical internal network with hundreds or thousands of devices. First, how can users identify the target computing device to which they must connect? And secondly, how can users know the IP address of that target destination device? To solve the first problem, endpoints can be assigned an intuitive name, like "fileserver1" or "PC-of-John."

Groups of devices can exist in a common domain, like www.arubanetworks.com or www.hpe.com. This naming makes computer systems more user friendly for humans, but the underlying network devices still require Layer-3 IP addresses to communicate. This brings us to the second problem—how can users identify a device by its name and have that name translated to the correct IP address?

Solution

Domain Name Service (DNS) maintains a mapping between the names that humans like and the IP addresses that computers need.

Figure 2-18 DNS

The client device sends a unicast request to the DNS server on UDP port 53, "What IP address is associated with www.hpe.com?" The server performs a name lookup in its database, finds a matching record and responds to the client with the associated IP address. DNS uses UDP for smaller more common operations like name queries. However, for larger operations like "Zone Transfer" DNS occasionally uses TCP port 53. Unlike DHCP service, DNS cannot run in most network devices like routers or Multi-Layer Switches. It is recommended to use a dedicated name server for this purpose (Figure 2-18).

HTTP

The HTTP protocol is used to transfer hypertext pages from web servers to web clients. Hypertext pages are documents with tags or links. When users click on these tags they gain access to new pages. Typically, tags are defined by a language such as the Hyper-Text Markup Language (HTML) or the extensible Markup Language (XML). HTTP access methods provide a flexible communication mechanism (Figure 2-19).

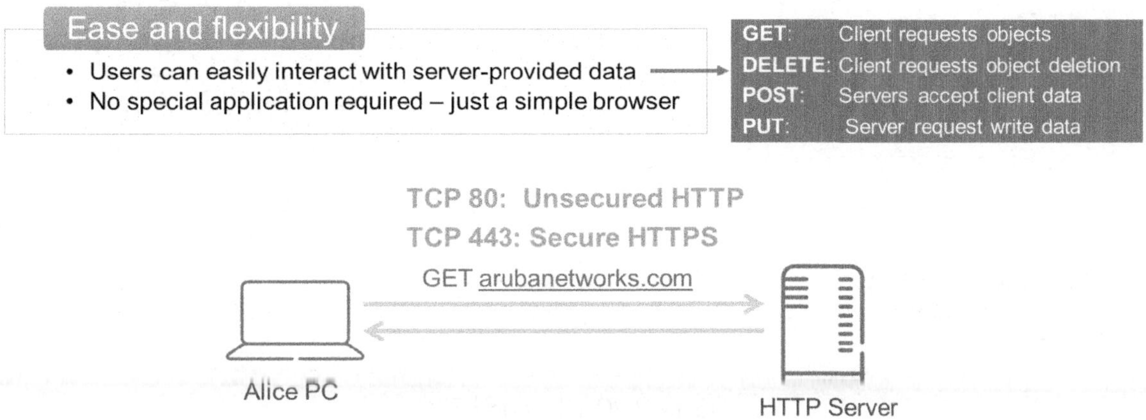

Figure 2-19 HTTP/HTTPS

Clients do not require specialized applications; only a simple web browser is used to establish HTTP sessions. Although HTTP is a well-known protocol, it can be dangerous to use it when browsing public internet sites. This is because HTTP provides no security mechanisms; your activity can be monitored and manipulated by hackers. Are you really accessing your bank's website, or a fake site stood up by hackers? Is someone viewing or copying the data that I transmit or receive? These issues are addressed by using HTTPS, the secure version of HTTP. HTTP sessions are established on TCP port 80 while HTTPS uses TCP port 443.

Telnet and SSH

Challenge

Network administrators may need to configure and troubleshoot dozens, hundreds, or even thousands of network devices. To directly, physically connect to them might require a hike across campus or flying to another city. Perhaps you are in your office and you need to configure or view the status of a router or switch. Instead of walking across the campus, going up to the 12th floor and sitting in a small network closet, you can simply Telnet to the device.

Solution

The Telnet protocol enables you to remotely connect to and control other devices, using that device's Command Line Interface (CLI). This protocol does not provide for the use of a graphic interface.

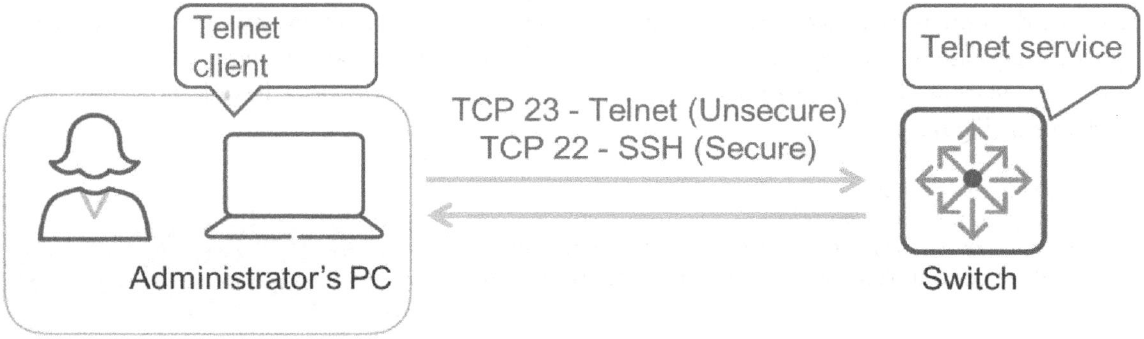


```
6300 login: admin
Password: admin
6300#
```

Figure 2-20 Telnet and SSH

First you establish a telnet session using a telnet client such as the common PuTTY application. Then you send commands that are executed on the remote device. The remote device must be running a telnet service. In the example shown, the administrator has remotely attached to the switch and issued the command **show mac-address-table**. This reveals the Layer-2 MAC addresses of all devices connected to the switch, and to which ports they are connected. You will learn more about show commands later in this module.

Like HTTP, Telnet has no security mechanisms. Hackers can intercept your sessions and harvest your data including usernames and passwords. For this reason, many people avoid using Telnet and use the Secure Shell (SSH) instead. Other than SSH's security and encryption mechanisms, the functionality is about the same as telnet (Figure 2-20).

FTP

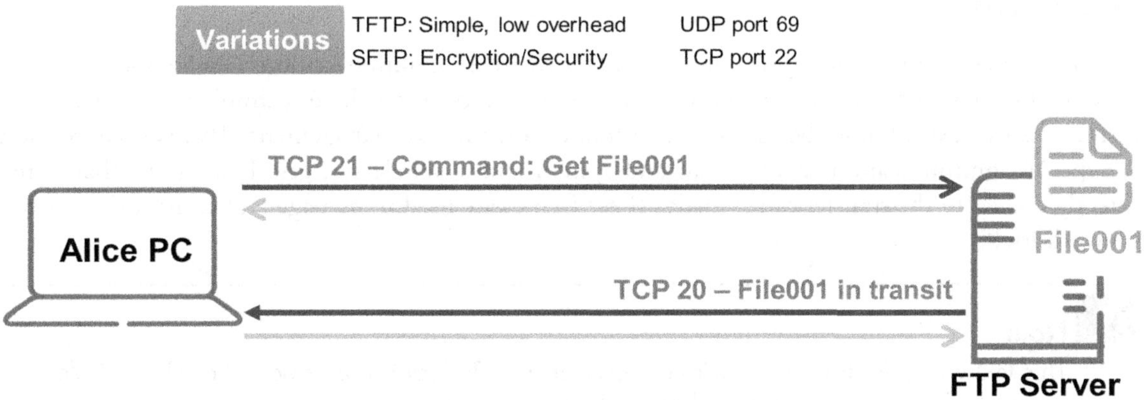

Figure 2-21 FTP

FTP enables you to upload and download files from a server, regardless of the operating system they are using. FTP uses TCP as the control protocol a reliable, flow-controlled mechanism that ensures complete file transmission. FTP uses TCP port 20 for Data and TCP port 21 for Control. FTP provides for user authentication, where you enter valid credentials to access the FTP server.

Clients could use dedicated applications to establish FTP connections; however a simple web browser also works. If you want to use a web browser, make sure you use the correct URL. When you browse to a website, the URL always starts with http://. When you connect via FTP, the URL always starts with ftp://.

In Figure 2-21, Alice connects to and authenticates the FTP server. Her username is alice@arubalab.com. She sees a list of directories and files. She selects the file named File001 and chooses to download it. This results in an FTP GET action. Alice's PC connects on the FTP control port 21 and makes a file request, "I need File001." The actual file is transferred from server to PC using the FTP data session, TCP port 20.

There are two common FTP variations: TFTP which uses UDP port 69 and Secure File Transfer Protocol (SFTP) that runs over an SSH session, usually on TCP port 22. SFTP offers enhanced security and encryption not available with FTP. The Trivial File Transfer Protocol (TFTP) works like FTP, except it relies on UDP instead of TCP.

UDP has few headers and lower overhead making transfer faster. However, UDP has no reliability mechanisms. Protocols like TFTP may have required reliability built into the application itself.

Wi-Fi Frames

802.11 Frame

Wi-Fi technology is used at Layer-1 and Layer-2 for wireless communications. Remember, Ethernet only works for wired connections. One major difference between these technologies is that Wi-Fi introduces two extra frames besides the data frame: control and management. This is because there are special communications between an end system and a Wireless Access Point (AP) that is not directly related to the transfer of payloads. These frames are used to manage and control the wireless network itself.

Note

This text will only discuss the wireless data frame. To learn more about the other wireless frames, refer to the Aruba Mobility Fundamentals training.

Wi-Fi Header								Wi-Fi Trailer
Frame Control	Duration ID	Address 1	Address 2	Address 3	Sequence Control	Address 4	Payload	FCS
2 Bytes	2 Byte	6 Bytes	6 Bytes	6 Bytes	2 Bytes	6 Bytes	46 – 1500 Bytes	4 Bytes

Figure 2-22 802.11 Frame

The fields shown in Figure 2-22 are described below:

- **Frame Control**. Indicates the type of frame (Control, management, or data) also includes fragmentation and privacy information.
- **Duration/Connection ID**. If used, indicates the time in microseconds the channel will be allocated for successful transmission of a control frame.
- **Addresses**. MAC addresses for the devices that are participating in the communication. The number of addresses depends on frame type and on context. Typically, only the first three address fields are used.
- **Sequence Control**. This field includes information about the fragmentation and reassembly.

- **Payload**. Contains the data that we want to transmit.
- **FCS (Frame Check Sequence)**. Allows detection of corrupted data using the CRC or checksum method.

Understanding the Wi-Fi Header

To understand how the address fields are used, consider the following example:

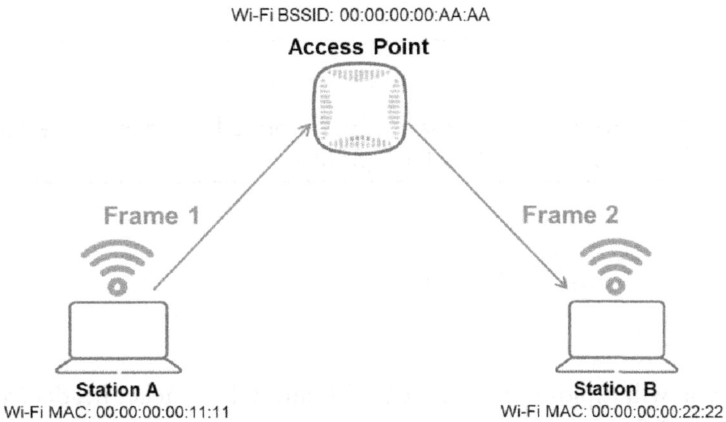

	Address 1 (receiver)	Address 2 (transmitter)	Address 3	Address 4
Frame 1	BSSID (AP) 00:00:00:00:AA:AA	MAC of Station A 00:00:00:00:11:11	MAC of Station B 00:00:00:00:22:22	Not Used
Frame 2	MAC of Station B 00:00:00:00:22:22	BSSID (AP) 00:00:00:00:AA:AA	MAC of Station A 00:00:00:00:11:11	Not Used

Figure 2-23 802.11 Example

Stations A and B want to communicate each other. Each station has a specific MAC address assigned to their Wireless NIC. Station A has 00:00:00:00:11:11 while Station B has 00:00:00:00:22:22. This is a typical scenario, where an Access Point (AP) acts as a central device. Stations do not communicate directly with each other; they only communicate via the AP. Therefore, 2 frames are generated, one from station A to the Access Point and the other from the Access Point to Station B. The table summarizes how the MAC addresses are used in this scenario. You see that Station A is the wireless transmitter of this frame, so its MAC address is placed in the frame's Address 2 field. The AP is the wireless receiver of the frame, so its address is placed in the frame's Address 1 field. Station B is the ultimate destination, so its address is in the Address 3 field. The Address 4 field is not used. This is typical. This field is typically only used in special "repeater" scenarios, where frames must pass between multiple APs before arriving at their destination. The AP receives this frame, creates a new frame, and transmits it to Station B. In this case the AP is the transmitter, so its address is in the Address 2 field. Station B is the wireless receiver of the frame, and so its MAC address is in the Address 1 field. Station A is the original sender of the frame, and so its address is in the Address 3 field (Figure 2-23).

Note

In Wi-Fi, the MAC address associated to a Wireless LAN and a specific radio band is known as the Basic Service Set Identifier (BSSID).

Lab 2.1: Packet Exploration

Overview

In the current lab you will explore Ethernet, IP, TCP, and UDP packet headers and be familiar with their contents (Figure 2-24).

Note: References to equipment and commands are taken from Aruba's hosted remote lab. These are shown for demonstration purposes in case you wish to replicate the environment and tasks on your own equipment.

Objectives

After completing this lab, you will be able to:

- Capture packets using Wireshark
- Explore Layer-2, 3, and 4 headers
- Identify most significant fields in headers

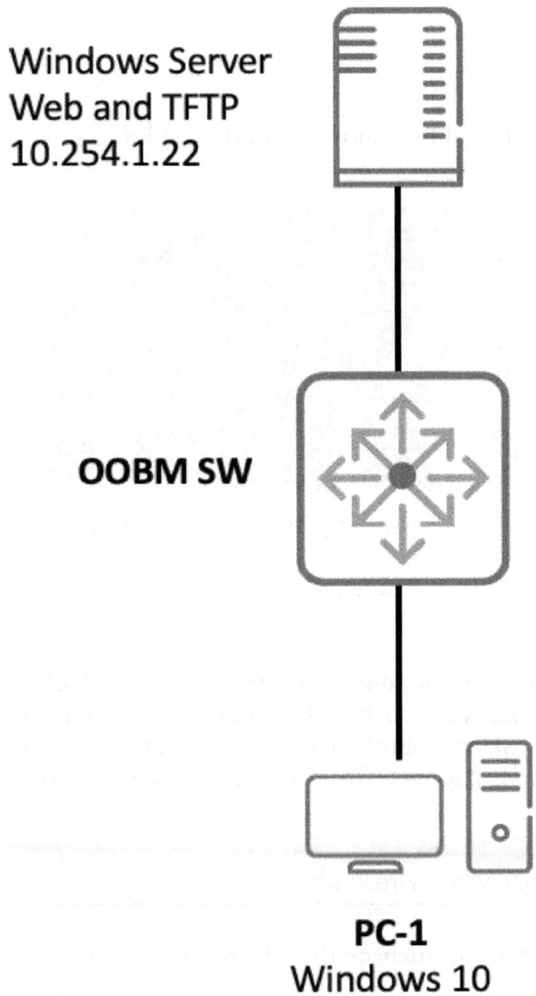

Figure 2-24 Lab2.1 Topology Example

Task 1: Discover Headers and Encapsulation

Objectives

A key step for better learning data forwarding and networking protocols is being able to look at packets and identify their OSI model headers, and the headers contents. In this task you will explore Ethernet, IP, UDP, and TCP headers.

Steps

1. Open a console session to PC-1.
2. Open Wireshark; there should be a shortcut on the Desktop.

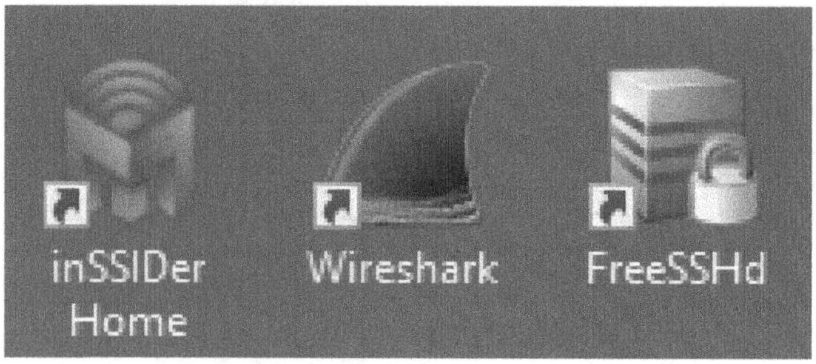

Figure 2-25 Wireshark Shortcut

Note

Wireshark is a well-known, open-source packet analyzer tool. It is capable of capturing traffic in different media types such as Ethernet, 802.11, Bluetooth, USB, and more. It is supported on main desktop operating systems such as Microsoft Windows, MacOS, and many Linux distributions (Figure 2-25). For more information please go to:

www.wireshark.org

https://wikipedia.org/wiki/Wireshark

---

3. Expand the "View" menu and uncheck the "Packet Bytes" option (Figure 2-26).

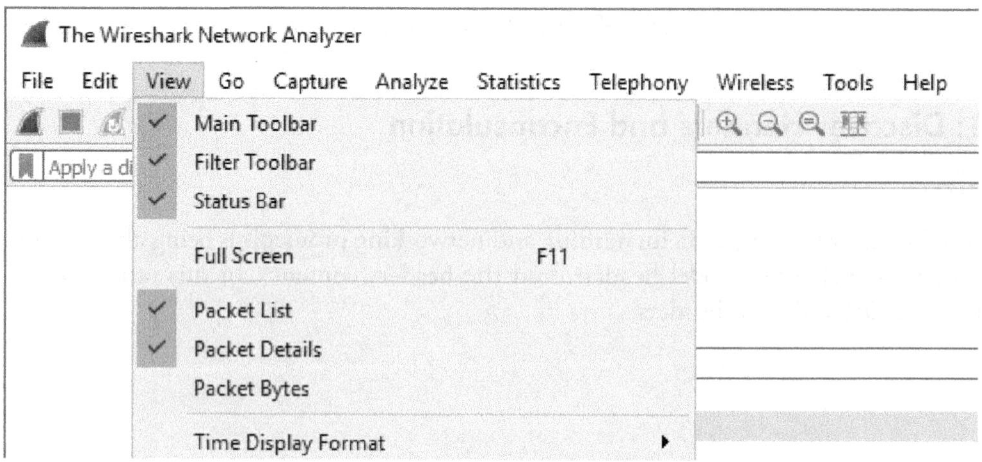

Figure 2-26 Wireshark View > Packet Bytes

4. Double click the OOBM entry. That will begin the packet capture in that interface (Figure 2-27).

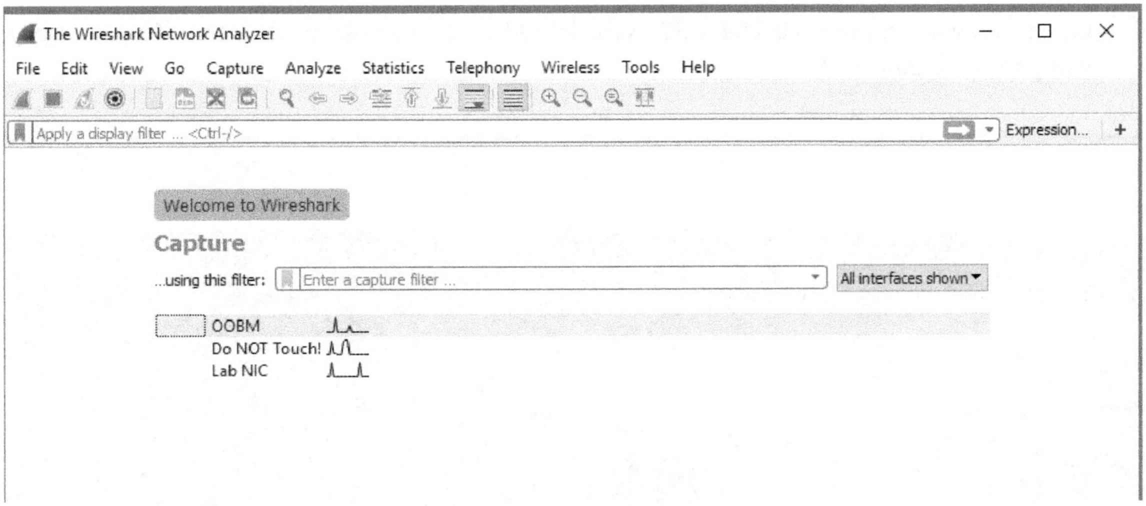

Figure 2-27 Wireshark NICs

5. Identify the components shown (Figure 2-28).

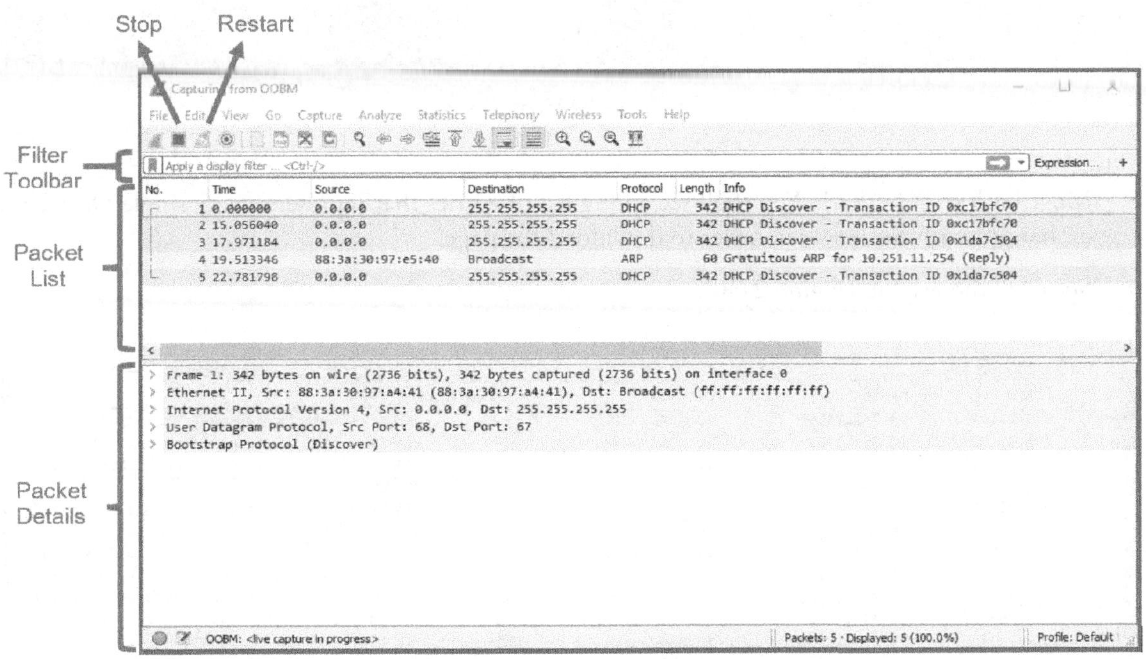

Figure 2-28 Wireshark Sections

6. On filter toolbar type **"ip.addr == 10.254.1.22"** with no quotes and hit [**Enter**]. That will instruct Wireshark to only display packets to and from that server.
7. Open a browser and type **10.254.1.22** as the IP address in the URL field and hit [**Enter**]. A page will pop up (Figure 2-29).

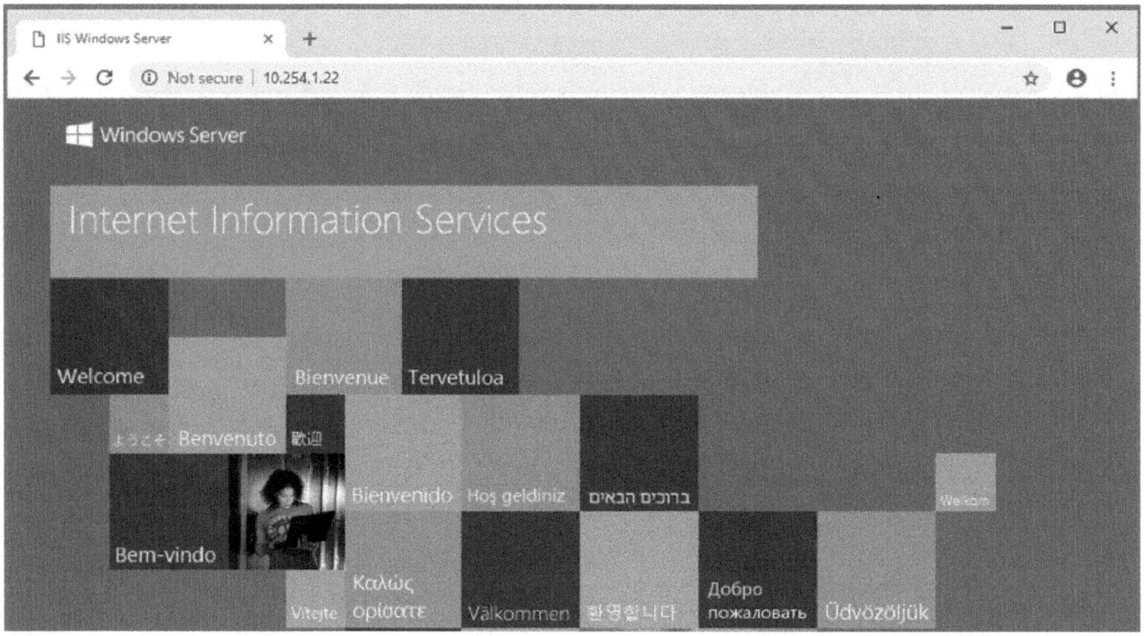

Figure 2-29 Web Page

8. Move back to Wireshark. You shall see a long list of entries that represent every single Data Unit exchanged with the server in order to download the page.
9. Scroll all the way up (Figure 2-30).

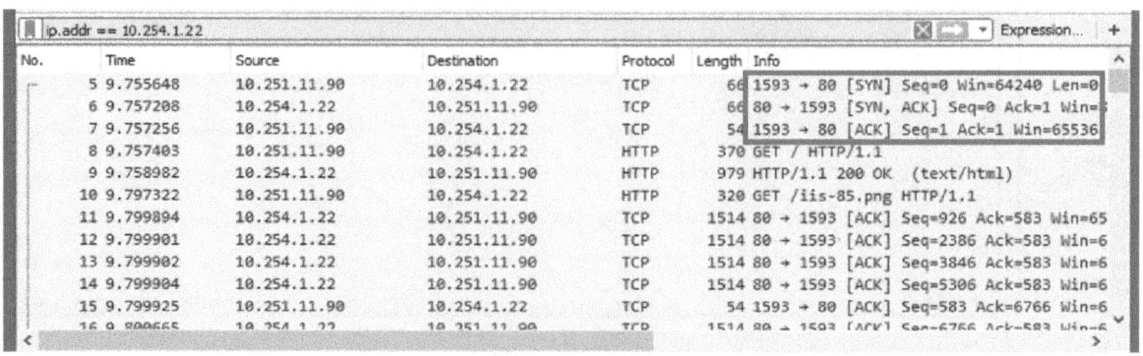

Figure 2-30 Capture of Data Packets

You will first see three packets listed as "SYN", "SYN, ACK", and "ACK" under the Info column.

What do they mean? ______________________________

What are these three packets for? ______________________________

10. Select the entry that lists "GET/HTTP/1.1" in the Info column (Figure 2-31). Five entries will appear in the "Packet Details" section including Frame details and Data Link, Network, Transport, and Application headers.

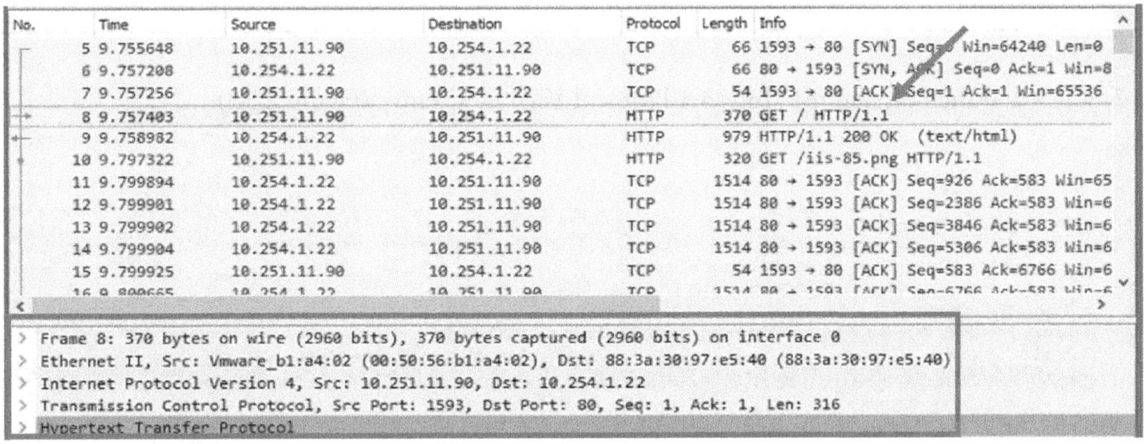

Figure 2-31 Capture of Data Headers

What protocols are listed in the "Frame details" section and what OSI model Layers do they belong to?

Data Link header: ______________________________

Network header: ______________________________

Transport header: ______________________________

Application header: ______________________________

11. Click and then expand the "Ethernet II" entry (Figure 2-32).

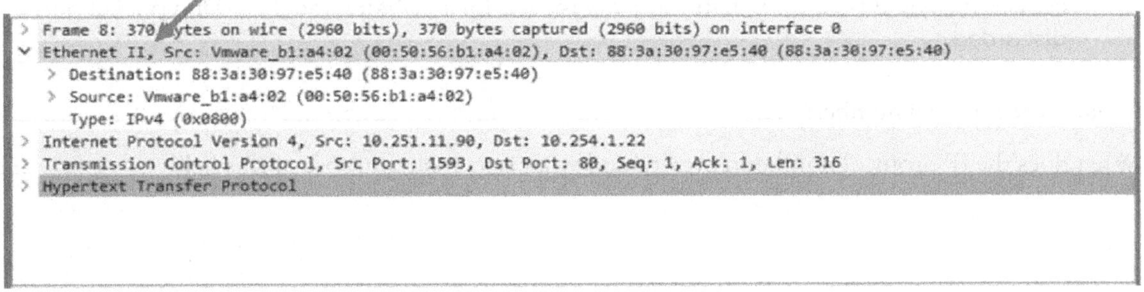

Figure 2-32 Capture of Data Link Layer Header

What is the length of the header? ______

What are the values of Destination and Source fields? ______

What is the Type value (also known as Ethertype)? ______

Tip

You can see the header length at the very bottom of the window.

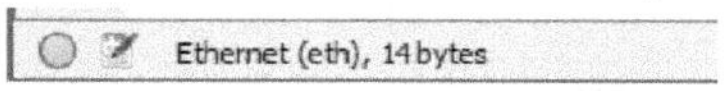

12. Click and then expand the "Internet Protocol Version 4" entry (Figure 2-33).

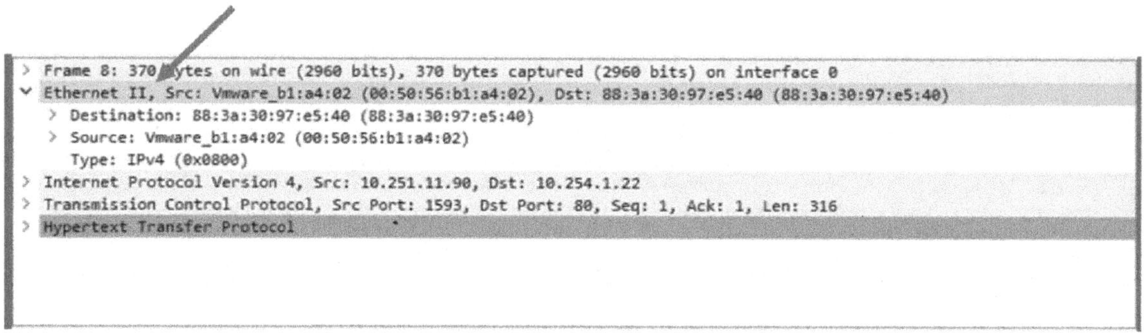

Figure 2-33 Capture of the Network Layer Header

What is the length of the header? ______

What is the protocol version? ______

What is the Time to live value? ______

Answer

TTL is an 8-bit field with an initial value when the packet is created, every time the packet crosses a Layer-3 boundary then TTL is decreased by 1, when it reaches 0 the packet gets discarded.

What is the Protocol number? ______

What does the IP protocol number represent and what is its main purpose of this field? ______

Answer

IP protocol number or Protocol for short is a numeric identification of the upper Layer protocol contained in the packet's payload. The IANA has assigned unique values to each IP protocol, for example, ICMP is IP protocol 1, TCP is 6, UDP is 17, and GRE is 47.

What are the values of the Destination and Source fields? ______________________

13. Click and then expand the "Transport Control Protocol" entry (Figure 2-34).

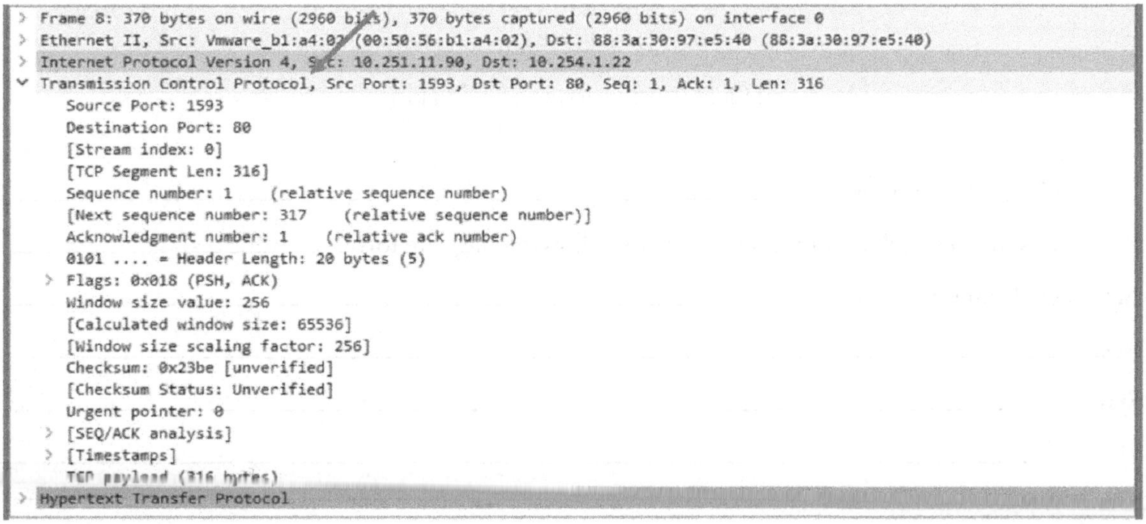

Figure 2-34 Capture of Transport Layer Header

What is the length of the header? ______________________

What are the first two fields? ______________________

What are they for? ______________________

What is the sequence number for? ______________________

14. Expand "Flags" (Figure 2-35).

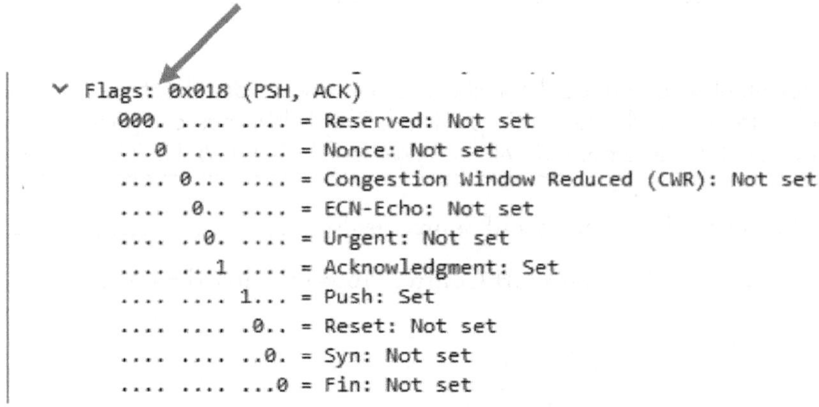

Figure 2-35 Capture of TCP Flags

Do you know any of them? ______________________________

Please do some research and find out what the following flags are for? ______________

Acknowledgement: ______________________________

Reset: ______________________________

Syn: ______________________________

Fin: ______________________________

Answer

Flag types are:

- Acknowledgement: Indicates that the acknowledgement field is significant. All packets after the initial SYN packet sent by the client should have this flag set.
- Reset: Reset the connection. Seen on rejected connections.
- Syn: Synchronize the sequence numbers. Seen on new connections.
- Fin: No more data from sender. Seen after a connection is closed.

What is the Window size? ______________________________

What is the Window size for? ______________________________

Answer

The window size field is the number of bytes the sender will buffer for the response. During 3-way handshake both sender and receiver will say how large their receive window is.

15. Expand the "Hypertext Transfer Protocol" entry (Figure 2-36).

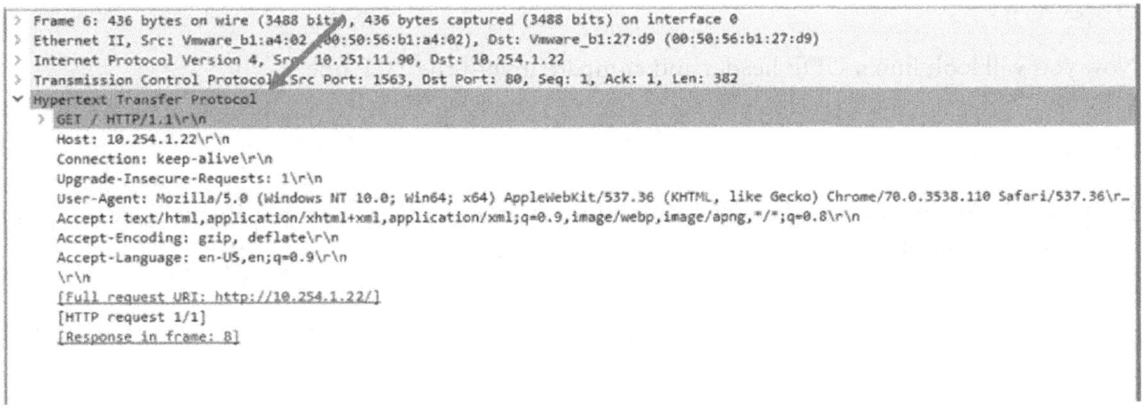

Figure 2-36 Capture of the Application Header

Important

In Hyper Transfer Protocol or HTTP's header there are four main commands: GET, PUSH, PUT, and DELETE. Usually after the 3-way handshake, the first HTTP payload has a GET instruction in order to download the web page.

After requesting the web page, there will be a lot of packets coming from the server. These are acknowledged by the client and displayed as the black with red entries (image below in Figure 2-37), they contain the web page itself. Once the page is fully loaded in the browser there is a FIN segment coming from the client signaling the end of the session. It is followed by a similar one from the server, and finally a last ACK is sent by the client.

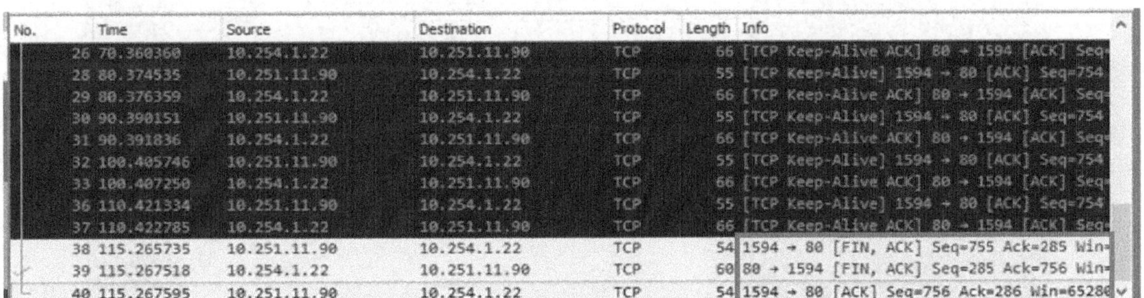

Figure 2-37 Capture of FIN and ACK

Task 2: UDP Header

Objectives

Now you will look into a UDP header and compare it with the TCP one.

Steps

16. Click the restart button; then click "Continue without Saving" button. This will clean up the packet capture (Figure 2-38).

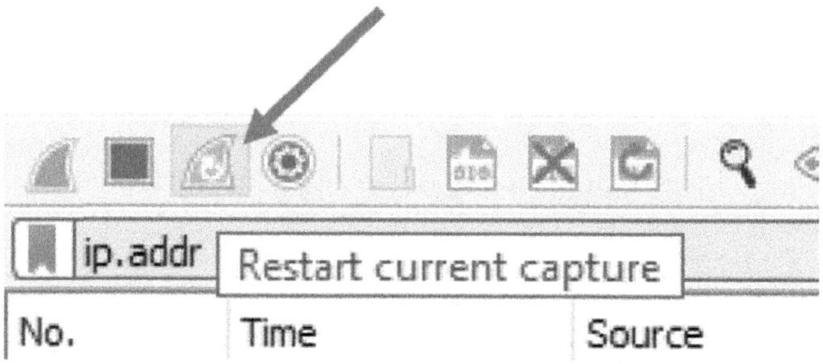

Figure 2-38 Wireshark Restart Button

17. Open Tftpd64; there should be a shortcut on the Desktop (Figure 2-39).

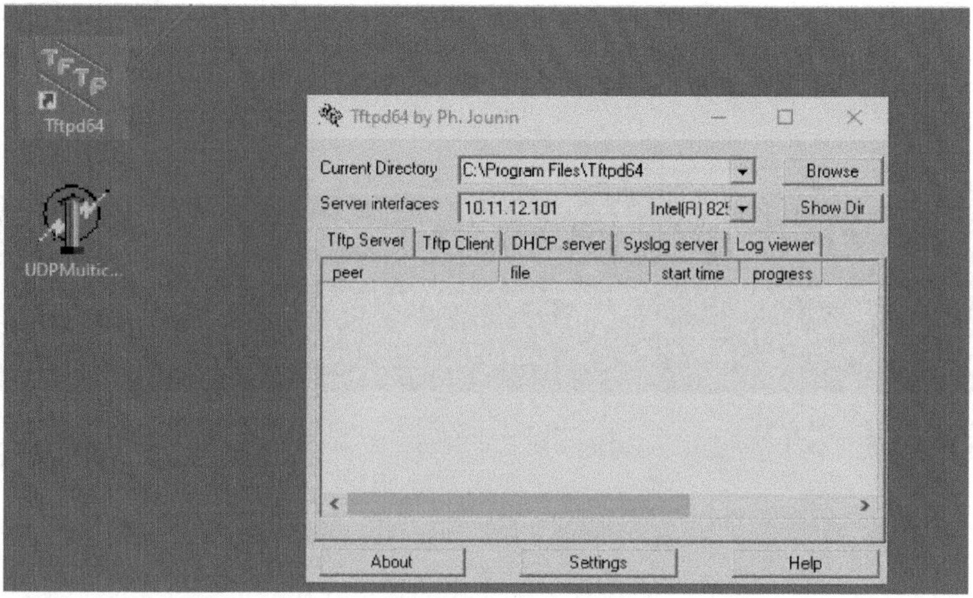

Figure 2-39 Tftpd64

18. Click on the "Tftp Client" tab.

19. Click the "**...**" button next to "Local File" field, then select Desktop as destination directory, and type CXF.txt as file name (Figure 2-40).

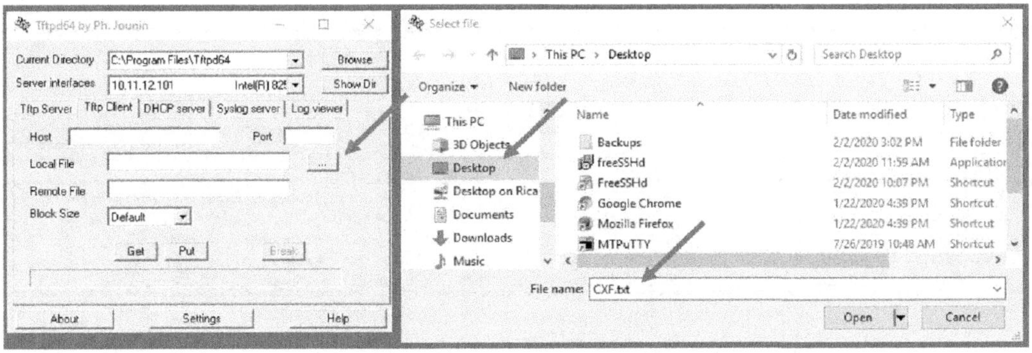

Figure 2-40 TFTP Client to Opening Local File

20. Click Open button.

21. Back in "Tftp Client" tab, fill out the fields with the following information (Figure 2-41):

- Host: 10.254.1.22
- Port: 69
- Remote File: CXF.txt

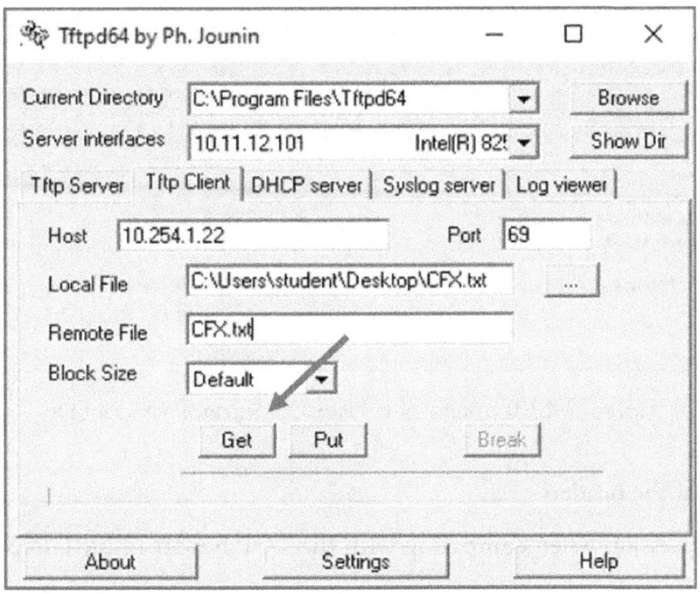

Figure 2-41 TFTP Client Settings

22. Click the get button. The software will begin a TFTP connection and download the file.
23. Click OK to the transfer confirmation message; then move to Wireshark. You will see a new capture with all packets involved in the transfer (Figure 2-42).

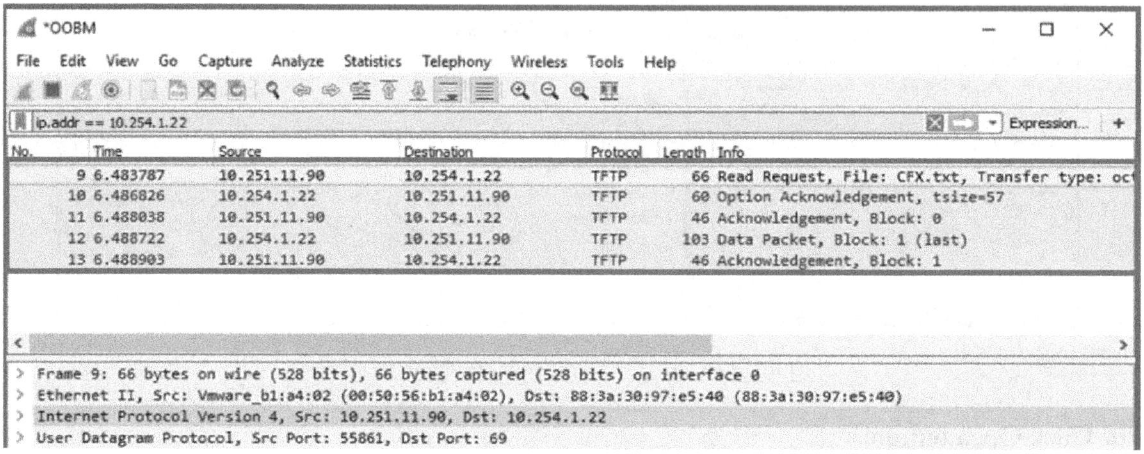

Figure 2-42 TFTP Traffic Capture

Is there any Three-way handshake session establishment? ____________________

24. Click the first packet (Read Request).
25. Select and expand the "User Datagram Protocol" entry in the Packet Details section (Figure 2-43).

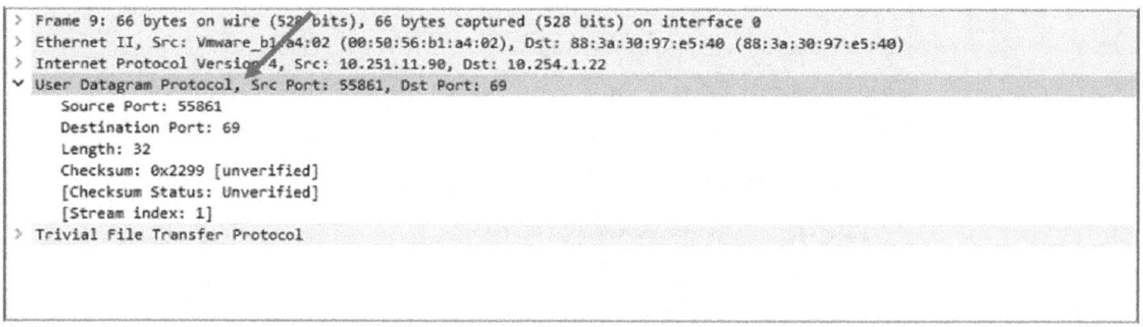

Figure 2-43 Capture of a User Datagram Protocol Entry

What is the length of the header? ____________________

What is the first impression when comparing with the TCP header (Task 1 step 13)?

____

What fields do they have in common? ______________________________

Can you see any Acknowledgment flag embedded in the header? ______________________________

26. Click and expand the "Trivial File Transfer Protocol" entry (Figure 2-44).

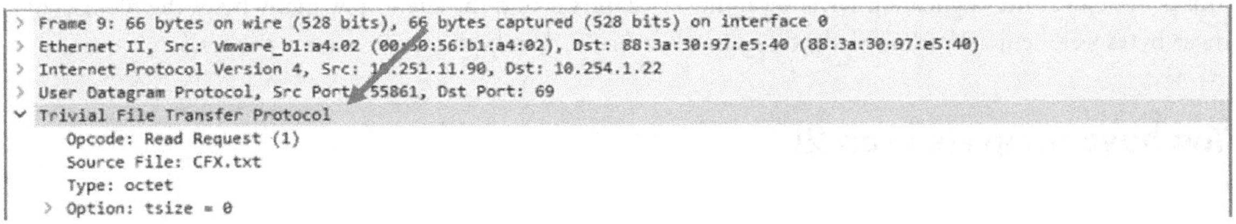

Figure 2-44 TFTP Traffic Capture

Note

This is the TFTP application header, just by looking in its contents you can tell this is the CXF.txt file request sent by the client.

---

27. Click the last packet (Acknowledgement). It will automatically show the TFTP header contents (Figure 2-45).

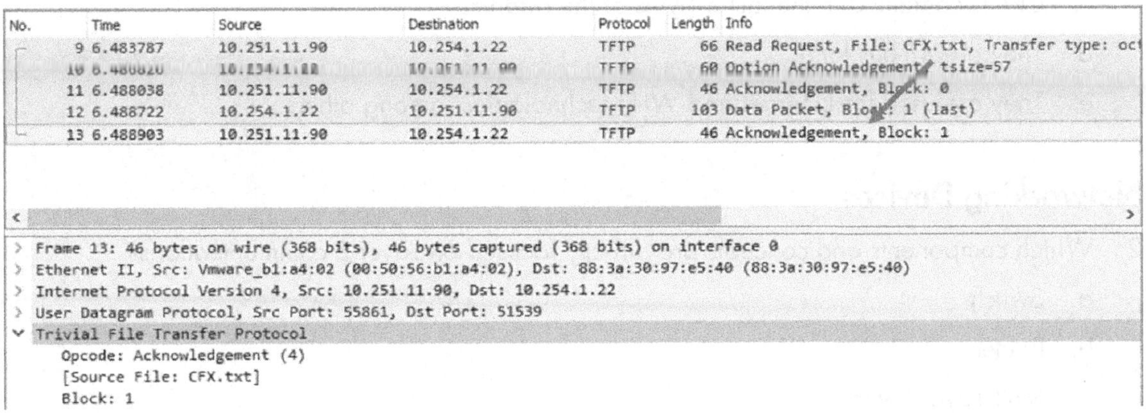

Figure 2-45 TFTP Traffic Capture

What is the "Opcode" field value? ______________________________

____

> **Important**
> Due to the lack of acknowledgement at the transport level, some UDP-based applications do support the feature at Layer-7 level; this is the case of TFTP.

Also notice how, unlike TCP, the transmission suddenly stops without any FIN signaling at the transport Layer. This is because at the application Layer level the TFTP server told the client how many bytes the file has, once those bytes were sent and acknowledged (again at Layer-7), then both parties assume the session is over.

You have completed Lab 2!

Learning Check

Chapter 2 Questions

The OSI Model

1. Which of the options below accurately describe MAC addresses?
   a. They are used at Layer-2 of the OSI model.
   b. They are used at Layer-3 of the OSI model.
   c. OUI is contained in the last 3 bytes of the address.
   d. They are 48-bits long.
   e. They are used for Ethernet and Wi-Fi technologies, among others.

Networking Devices

2. Which components and concepts are directly focused on Layer-2 communications?
   a. Switch
   b. Router
   c. Multi-Layer Switch
   d. MAC addresses
   e. IP addresses
   f. Access Points

3. Which components and concepts are directly focused on Layer-3 communications?
    a. Switch
    b. Router
    c. Multi-Layer Switch
    d. MAC addresses
    e. IP addresses
    f. Access Points
4. Which of the following statements accurately describe common networking services?
    a. Use DNS to dynamically provide network addressing information to clients.
    b. Use DHCP to map names to IP addresses.
    c. All common network services use either TCP or UDP.
    d. The advantage of HTTPS over HTTP is that HTTPS is more secure.
    e. You can use SSH to gain remote access to a switch CLI interface.

3 Basic Networking with Aruba Solutions

EXAM OBJECTIVES

- ✓ Explain network hierarchical models
- ✓ Compare the Aruba switch portfolio
- ✓ Describe AOS-CX Operating system
- ✓ Discover switch information with CLI show commands
- ✓ Perform basic configuration tasks
- ✓ Discover network status and connectivity

Overview

You begin this module by understanding of two-tier and three-tier network design models; you have a good network design and troubleshooting foundation on which to build. Next you will review Aruba's portfolio of switches. This will help you to select the proper device for a given scenario. You will learn how to use Aruba switches, how to connect to them, and how to use the CLI to glean basic network health. This allows you to gather status information, perform basic configuration, and to discover how an unknown network is connected. This ability to document a network will serve you well when you must diagnose network outages.

Network Design

Hierarchical Model

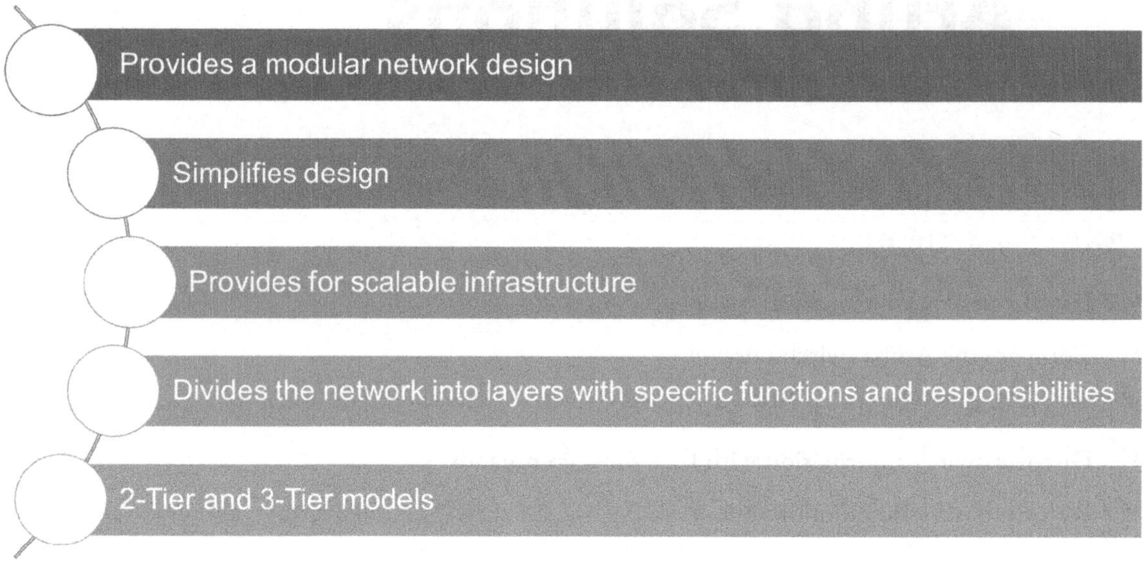

Figure 3-1 Hierarchical Model

A hierarchical model provides a modular view of the network, simplifies the design, and provides a scalable infrastructure (Figure 3-1).The hierarchical model divides the network into layers, and each layer has specific functions and responsibilities. This helps to ensure that you have an available, fault tolerant, flexible, and secure network. Some engineers may choose a two-tier hierarchy, while others might choose a three-tier hierarchy. This decision is based on various factors:

- Number of wired and wireless users
- Mobility requirements
- Number of wireless Access Points deployed
- Cabling
- Number of buildings in the campus
- Desired security level
- Features and protocols needed

Two-Tier Hierarchy

A two-tier design divides the network in two layers: Access and Core. This means that Layer-2 and Layer-3 protocols run close to the endpoints. This design can secure the network by deploying Access

Control Lists (ACLs). Quality of Service (QoS) can analyze and prioritize traffic. This ensures the best performance for the most business-critical and delay-sensitive applications (Figure 3-2).

Wireless Networks can also benefit from this two-tier design. Multilayer access switches receive and process critical wireless traffic from APs. Appropriate security and QoS policies are applied, and the traffic is routed toward its destination.

You want three key things at the Core Layer: speed, speed, and speed! This core must switch and route packets as fast as possible. Therefore, most of the more processing-intensive end-user services are off-loaded to the Access layer. You also need reliability at the core, so High Availability (HA) is also critical, as is the ability to quickly respond to changes in the network.

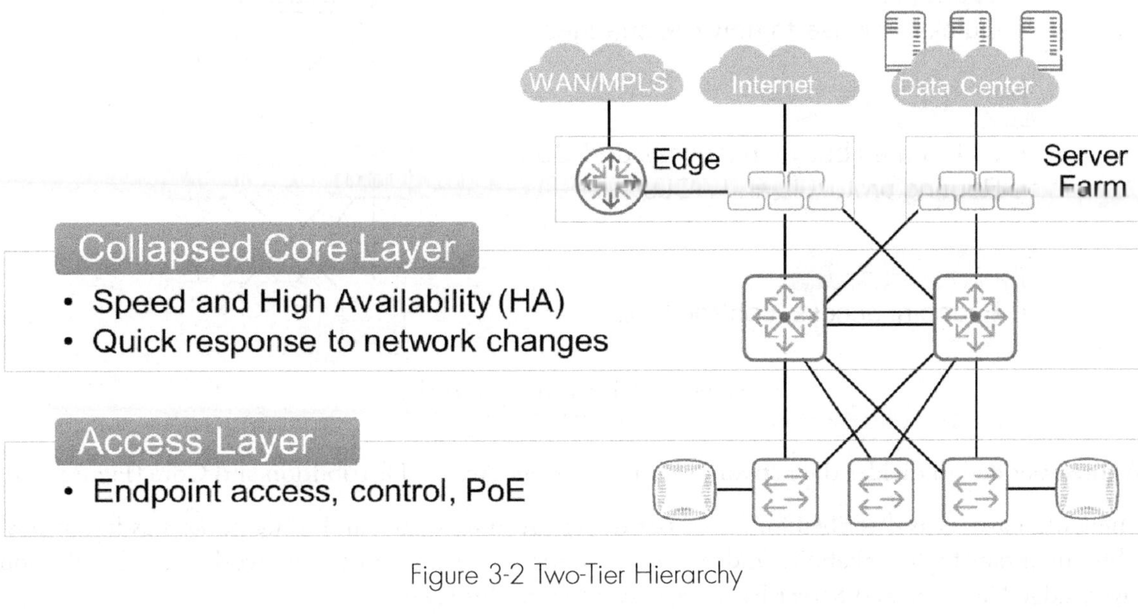

Figure 3-2 Two-Tier Hierarchy

Access Layer switches have redundant connections to the core to improve resiliency and mitigate outages. The Access Layer provides endpoint device connectivity, with Power over Ethernet (PoE), and several Layer-2 and Layer-3 features.

Other sections of the network may also connect to the core. For example, the Edge Network contains network devices that provide secure connectivity to WAN links and the Internet. The Server Farm contains racks of physical and/or virtual servers and their associated switches and hypervisors.

Note
ACLs and QoS are out of the scope for this training.

Three-Tier Hierarchy

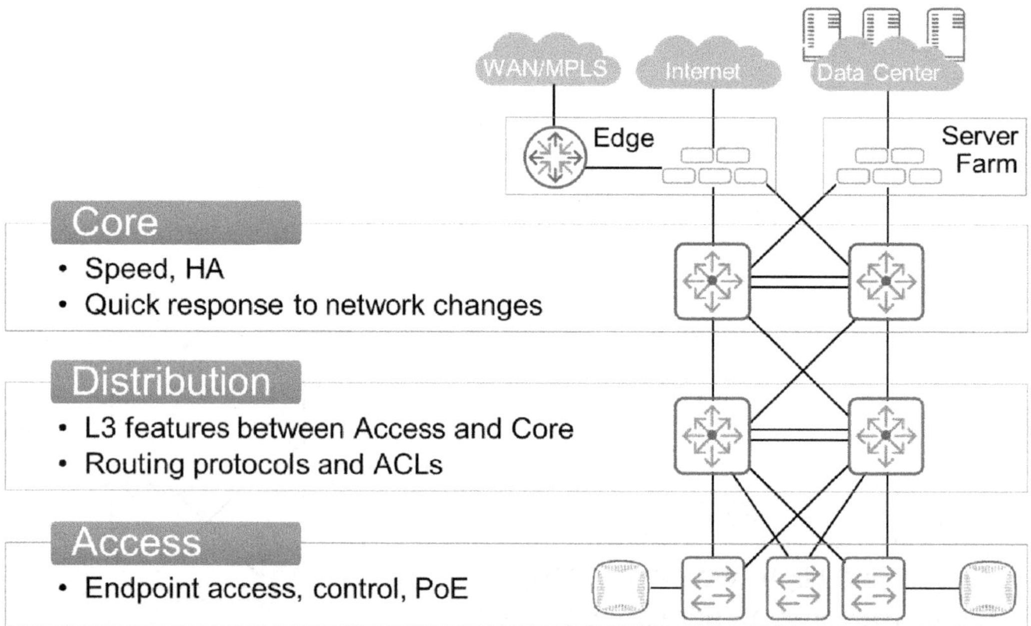

Figure 3-3 Three-Tier Hierarchy

A three-tier design divides the network into three layers, Access, Distribution and Core (Figure 3-3).

The Core Layer is as described for a two-tier design. It must switch and route packets as fast as possible, maintain high availability and quickly respond to changes in the network. The distribution layer, Edge Network, and Server Farms may connect to this layer.

The Access Layer provides for endpoint access with PoE and Layer-2 features, as with a two-tier design.

The Distribution Layer provides Layer-3 features for traffic to and from the access layer. Routing protocols and ACLs ensure that the correct traffic is routed along the best path. Essentially, you have expanded the core into two separate layers. This can increase cost and perhaps complexity. However, it may make the network more scalable in certain larger deployments.

Aruba Switching Portfolio

Modern Switching Requirements

Traditionally the network switch had one job: to provide wired access to computing devices. These legacy switches had low port bandwidth utilization and minimal power requirements. Each wired user connected to a separate switch port, and each port handled traffic from a single user.

Today, the role of the switch has dramatically changed. Many users prefer a wireless connection.They connect to APs, which in turn connect to switches. Thus, the switch has become an aggregation device, each port handles traffic from multiple endpoints. For many organizations, good wireless communication is mission critical. Resilient, reliable, and high-performance aggregation must ensure the best mobile user experience.

Also, there is an increasing number of Internet-of-Things (IoT) devices, often deployed throughout the organization. To support these devices, switches must offer security, authentication, and services such as Power over Ethernet (PoE) to devices that request it. The Power over Ethernet (PoE) feature enables a switch to provide device power, in addition to data connectivity. This eliminates the need to run separate power cables to every device, and drastically reduces cost. However, this means that the switch must have big enough power supplies to not only power itself, but all connected PoE devices.

Aruba Networks has created a switching portfolio that meets today's requirements in terms of performance, security, manageability, automation, and wireless optimization. The portfolio accommodates any organization, regardless of their size and complexity. To meet the objectives of modern network deployments, Aruba Networks has developed two Network Operating Systems (NOS): Aruba OS-S and AOS-CX.

Switching Portfolio: AOS-S

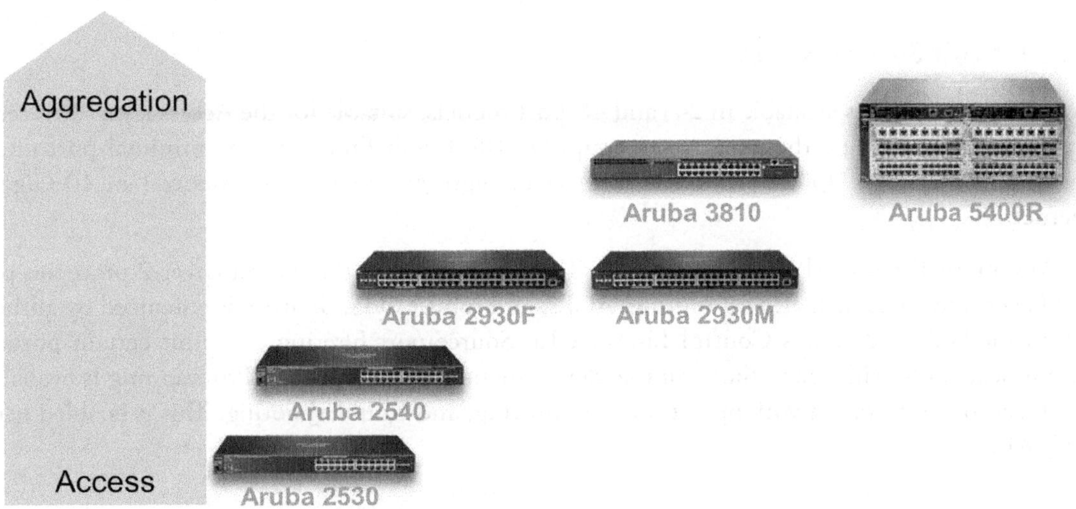

Figure 3-4 AOS-S

This family of switches offer excellent performance in Campus LANs, offering Layer-2 and Layer-3 features (Figure 3-4).

Aruba 2530 Switches Series

These are fixed switches available in 8-, 24-, and 48-port models, suitable for the Access layer. They have typical Layer-2 features, along with simplified Quality of Service (QoS) and security features. This series supports 10/100 Mbps only ports and Gigabit Ethernet ports, with up to 4 Small Form-factor Pluggable (SFP) uplinks. Full PoE support provides up to 370 Watts of power pooled to be shared to Access Points, IP Cameras, IoT devices, and more.

Multiple authentication methods are available in this series. This includes the very robust 802.1X authentication and the simpler, but less secure MAC authentication. Web-based authentication is available for clients that do not support 802.1X. This enhances security by controlling access to the network.

This series can be integrated into the Aruba Central cloud-based management platform. This offers a simple, secure, and cost-effective way to manage switches anywhere and anytime.

ZeroTouchProvisioning (ZTP) simplifies installation of the switch infrastructure in remote locations.

Note

Small Form-Factor Pluggable (SFP) is a compact, hot-pluggable network interface module which gives the switch the interface port to be equipped with any suitable type of transceiver as needed. For example, some SFP interfaces support copper media, while others may support Multi-Mode (MM) or Single Mode (SM) fiber optic connections.

Aruba 2540 Switches Series

These are fixed switches available in 24- and 48-port models, suitable for the Access layer. This series differ from 2530 because the ports do not support 10/100mb Ethernet. The minimal port rate is Gigabit Ethernet. The Uplink ports that connect to aggregation switches support 1 or 10 Gigabit Ethernet.

Full Power over Ethernet (PoE+) is supported. This series supports the typical Layer-2 protocols plus basic Layer-3 features such as: RIP routing, ACLs, and robust QoS. Security is enhanced by authentication methods and Access Control Lists (ACL). Source-port filtering can limit certain ports to communicate only with each other. Simple deployment with Zero Touch Provisioning is available, as is the automation of network operations, monitoring, and troubleshooting. This is enabled using REST APIs.

Aruba 2930F Switches Series

These fixed switches are available in 8-, 24-, and 48-port models, suitable to be deployed in the Access Layer. This series uses Gigabit Ethernet ports with 1 and 10 Gbps uplinks. Full PoE+ support provides up to 740 watts of power.

The 2930F series offers Layer-3 capabilities including OSPF, Dynamic segmentation, ACLs, IPv6, and robust QoS: all without requiring an additional software license.

This series also supports Virtualized switching or stacking. When switches are stacked, they appear as a single chassis, to simplify management. Up to 8 members can be stacked in a ring topology. Zero Touch Provisioning (ZTP) simplifies installation of the switching infrastructure using Aruba Activate or a DHCP-based process. Aruba Central management is also available. Security is enhanced by running user authentication methods, ACLs, STP protection, and Private Virtual LANs (VLAN).

Aruba 2930M Switches Series

This series is available in 24- and 48-port models and has similar software capabilities to the Aruba 2930F switches series. The key difference is modularity. A modular switch allows you to choose the right module for the uplink ports, add a secondary power supply, use modular 10 or 40 Gigabit Ethernet uplinks, and select models with Smart Rate ports.

HPE Smart Rate multi-gigabit Ethernet delivers faster connectivity than a regular Gigabit Ethernet port, along with PoE, using existing campus cabling. Full PoE+ is supported with the newer 802.3bt Class 6 cabling standard. This means that you can power devices that require up to 60W. A redundant power supply is available, to provide up to 1440 total watts of power.

Aruba 3810M Switches Series

These fixed switches are available in 16-, 24-, and 48-port models, with or without full PoE+ and Smart Rate ports. These Smart Rate ports can deliver high-speed rates and power for 802.11ax and 802.11ac devices using existing CAT5e and CAT6 twisted pair wiring.

The 3810 series supports typical Layer-2 features and Layer-3 features such as OSPF, BGP. They also support the Virtual Router Redundancy Protocol (VRRP), as well of QoS and security features.

The switch series supports Virtualized switching or stacking, and an available slot accepts both 10 and 40 Gigabit Ethernet modules. Stacking has been designed for high performance and provides up to 336Gbps of stacking throughput. Using a ring topology, you can stack up to 10 switches. In a mesh topology, the maximum is 5.

Aruba 5400R ZL2 Switches Series

These modular switches are available in 6-slot or 12-slot chassis and can be deployed at the Access or Core of a campus network, depending on the size of the network. The 5400R ZL2 switches support the most demanding network features, including QoS and security. Redundant management modules and redundant power supplies provide high availability for environments that cannot tolerate down time.

The switch supports any combination of 10/100Mbps Ethernet and 1/10/40 Gigabit Ethernet with full PoE+ on all ports. Smart Rate ports are also supported, based on the 802.3bz standard.

5400 ZL2 switches can run Layer-3 features such as: OSPF, BGP, VRRP, and Protocol Independent Multicasting (PIM). They also support the Virtual Switching Framework (VSF), which enables you to combine two switches into one virtual switch, called a fabric.

Switching Portfolio: AOS-CX

AOS-CX is a modern software system for the enterprise core and aggregation that automates and simplifies many critical and complex network tasks. It delivers enhanced fault tolerance and facilitates zero-service disruption during planned or unplanned control-plane events. The key innovations in AOS-CX are its micro-services style modular architecture, REST APIs, Python scripting capabilities, and the Aruba Network Analytics Engine (NAE). AOS-CX is based on modular architecture that allows individual processes to re-start and be upgraded. Its REST APIs and Python scripting enables fine-grained programmability of the switch functions and its unique Aruba Network Analytics Engine (NAE) provides for easy network monitoring and troubleshooting (Figure 3-5).

A data center is a facility that centralizes an organization's IT operations and equipment, as well as where it stores, manages, and disseminates its data. Data centers house a network's most critical systems and are vital to the continuity of daily operations. The security and reliability of data centers and their information is top priority for organizations.

A Data Center architecture could include a three-tier layer approach. Access, Aggregation and Core Layers help to create a resilient network. AOS-CX switches were designedto work in the Campus LAN network and as well as in the data center, offering a rich set of features and high performance.

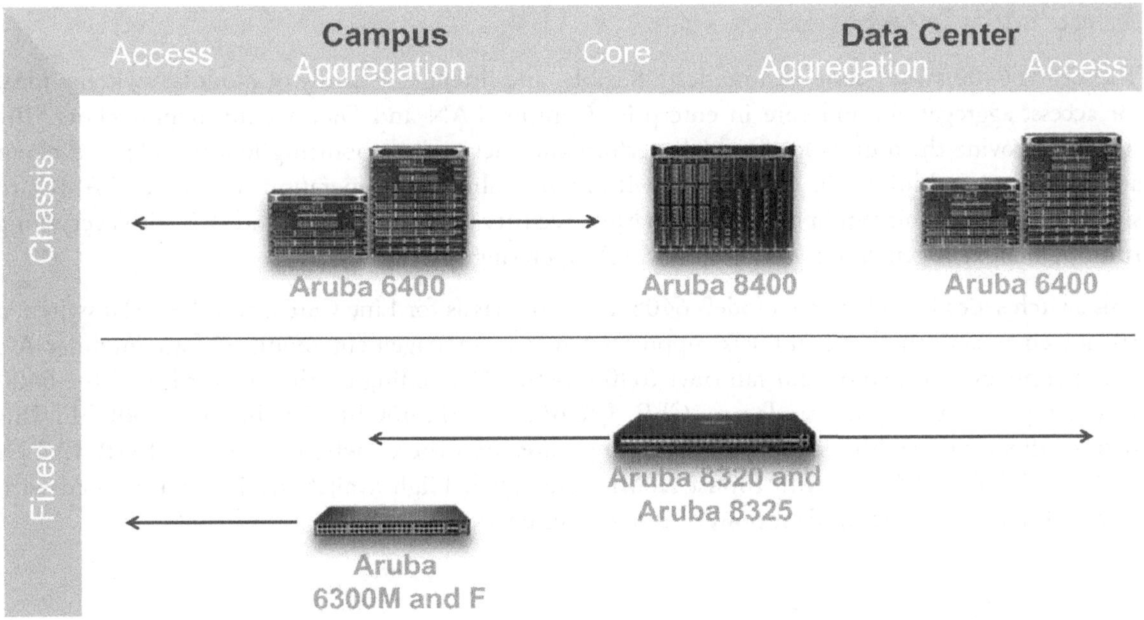

Figure 3-5 AOS-CX

Aruba 8400 Switches Series

The Aruba 8400 switch is suitable for deployments as a Campus Core switch or as a Core/Aggregation switch in the Data Center. This series switch has been designed to provide high availability and resiliency in every part of the hardware, supporting 99.999% availability.

These modular switches are available in 8-slot chassis for interface modules or Line Cards (LC). Options for Line Cards include 32-port 10GbE modules, 8-port 40GbE, and 6-port 100GbE modules. Fabric modules provide the ability for traffic to flow between the line cards. The 8400 switch supports up tothree fabric modules which provide redundancy and keep line rate speeds in case of a failure. The switch offers up to 19.2 Terabit per second switching capacity.

The 8400 series switch supports redundant Management Modules (MM), fan assemblies, and power supplies. All modules are hot-swappable, permitting upgrade or replacement without powering off the chassis. These switches also include the Aruba Network Analytics Engine (NAE) a framework for monitoring, troubleshooting, and capacity planning.

AOS-CX advanced Layer-2 and Layer-3 features include BGP, OSPF, VRF, Multicasting, and IPv6. Also, this switch supports VSX and Multi-chassis Link Aggregation (MLAG) which enables you to create one virtualized switch composed of two individual physical switches.

Aruba 6400 Switches Series

The Aruba 6400 switch series is a modern, flexible, and intelligent family of modular switches ideal for access, aggregation, and core in enterprise Campus LAN and Data Center deployments. The switches provide the foundation for high-performance networks supporting IoT, mobile, and cloud applications. In addition, the 6400 comes with high-quality next-generation Aruba Gen7 ASICs to support multi-Gigabit requirements, automation, security, high availability, and PoE with everything running on a next generation modular AOS-CX operating system.

This switch series introduce the models 6405, a 5-slot chassis for Line Cards, and the 6410 switch, a 10-slot chassis. Both chassis models support up to two management modules, four modular AC power supplies, and two or four fan trays (6405/6410). Depending on the line card used the 6400 series supports a variety of interfaces: 1GbE, 10GbE, 25GbE, 40GbE, 50GbE, and 100GbE. This switch offers 24 Terabit per second switching capacity. These switches support BGP, EVPN, VXLAN, VRF, and OSFP with robust security and QoS. High availability is accomplished with VSX redundancy and redundant power supplies and fans.

Aruba 8325 Switches Series

The Aruba 8325 switch series offers a flexible and innovative approach to addressing the application, security and scalability demands of the mobile, cloud and IoT era. These switches serve the needs of the core and aggregation layers, as well as Top of Racks (ToR) and End of Row (EoR) Data Center requirements. This switch series provide over 6.4 Terabit per second switching capacity with line-rate Gigabit Ethernet interfaces including 1Gbps, 10Gbps, 25Gbps, 40Gbps, and 100Gbps.

This 1 Rack Unit switch supports advanced Layer-2 and 3 features that includes BGP, OSPF, VRF-Lite, and IPv6. Dynamic VXLAN with BGP-EVPN for deep segmentation in Data Center and Campus networks. This switch series offer two models with 48 and 32 ports; both models include 6 fans and 2 power supplies. Also, each switch model offers the choice to select the airflow front-to-back and back-to-front.

Aruba 8320 Switches Series

The Aruba 8320 switches are powerful with 1 Rack Unit (RU) devices designed to provide core and aggregation services in mid-sized Campus networks. These switches offer three fixed-port models with 10GbE and 40GbE interfaces offering up to 2.5 Terabits per second switching capacity. This model offers similar features as the 8325 switches series including BGP, OSPF, VRF, IPv6, VSX, and Multi-chassis link aggregation. The 8320 switches are also built for resiliency. They offer redundant power supplies and fans.

Aruba 6300 Switches Series

The Aruba CX 6300 switch series is a modern, flexible, and intelligent family of stackable switches ideal for enterprise access and aggregation layers. This switch series is built around the new Aruba Gen7 ASIC, a highly capable CPU and the next-generation modular AOS-CX switch software platform. The Aruba Virtual Stacking Framework (VSF) allows for stacking of up to 10 switches, providing scale and simplified management. This flexible series has built-in 1GbE, 10GbE, 25GbE, and 50GbE uplinks and supportshigh-density High-Power PoE interfaces, offering up to 880 Gbps system switching capacity.

This series support one touch deployment with the Aruba CX Mobile App. Aruba Dynamic Segmentation extends Aruba's foundational wireless role-based policy capability to Aruba wired switches. What this means is that the same security, user experience, and simplified IT management can be enjoyed throughout the network. Regardless of how users and IoT devices connect, consistent policies are enforced across wired and wireless networks, keeping traffic secure and separate.

AOS-CX Software Architecture

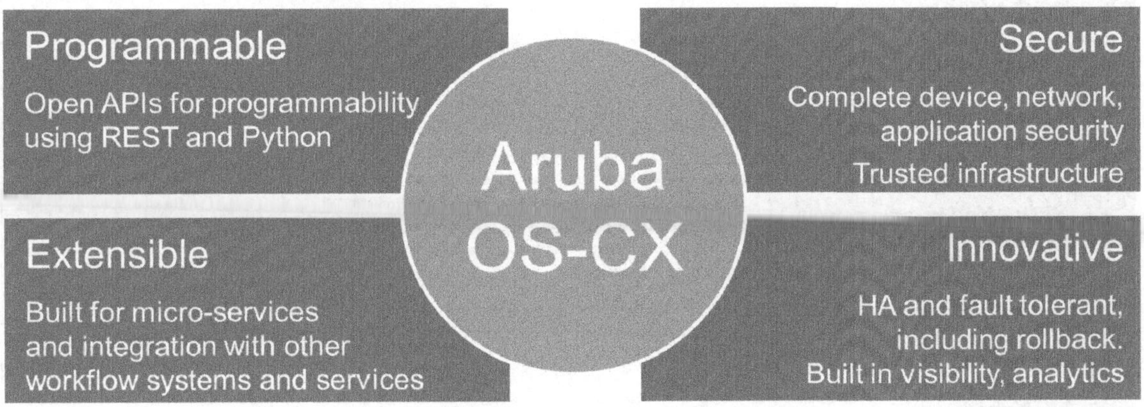

Figure 3-6 AOS-CX Software Architecture

The AOS-CX software is a modern, database-driven operating system that automates and simplifies many critical and complex network tasks (Figure 3-6). A built-in time series database enables customers and developers to use software scripts for historical troubleshooting and to analyze past trends. This helps to predict and avoid future problems due to scale, security, and performance.

This network operating system is built on a modular Linux architecture with a stateful database which helps to offer the following unique capabilities:

- Easy access to all network state information allowing unique visibility and analytics.
- REST APIs and Python scripting for fine-grained programmability of network tasks.

- A micro-services architecture that enables full integration with other workflow systems and services.
- Continual state synchronization that provides superior fault tolerance and high availability.
- Security best practices were applied to completely create a trusted platform.

Aruba Network Analytics Engine (NAE) Overview

The Aruba Network Analytics Engine (NAE) is a built-in framework for network assurance and remediation. Combining the full automation and deep visibility capabilities of the AOS-CX, this framework allows monitoring, troubleshooting, and easy network data collection using simple scripting agents (Figure 3-7).

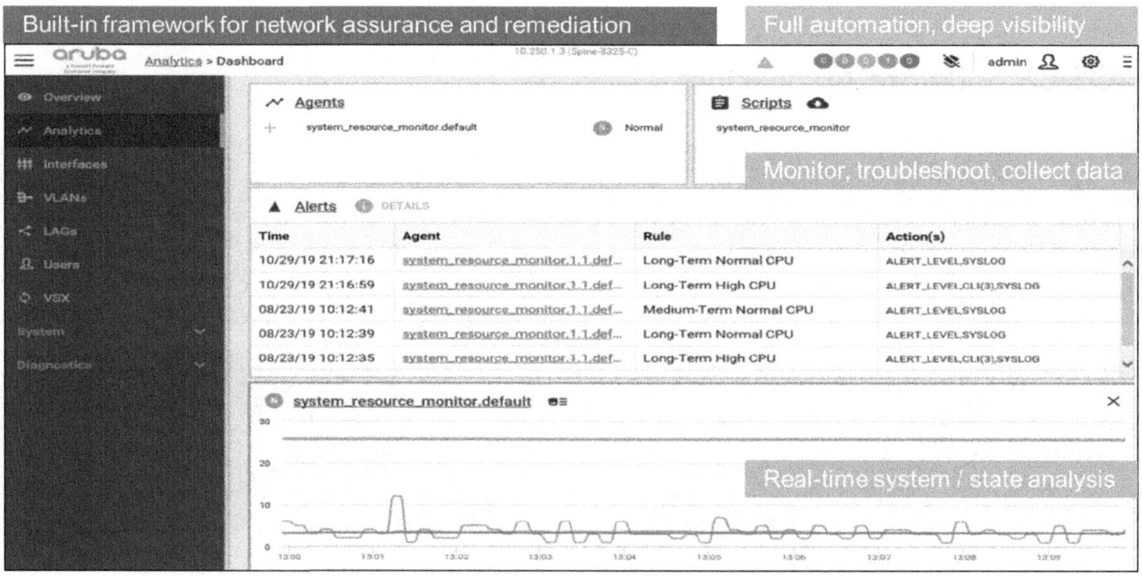

Figure 3-7 Network Analytics Engine (NAE)

This framework analyzes a problem in real time giving you the insight you need to resolve the issue or take corrective action based on established policies. When an anomaly is detected, it can proactively collect additional statistics and data.

AOS-CX Feature Set

The AOS-CX has the following feature set. Bold protocols are covered on this training:

Layer-2 Switching

- VLAN support and tagging for 802.1Q
- Jumbo packet support
- VXLAN encapsulation protocol
- Rapid Spanning Tree Protocol (RSTP)
- Rapid Per-VLAN Spanning Tree (RPVST+)
- Multiple Spanning Tree Protocol (MSTP)
- Internet Group Management Protocol (IGMP)
- Port mirroring

Layer-3 Routing

- Bidirectional Forwarding Detection (BFD)
- Border Gateway Protocol (BGP)
- Equal-Cost Multipath (ECMP)
- Multi-protocol BGP
- Open shortest path first (OSPF)
- Static routing
- Policy-based routing
- IP performance optimization
- IPv6 capabilities
- Protocol Independent Multicast (PIM)

Security

- Access Control Lists (ACL) for both IPv4 and IPv6
- RADIUS
- TACACS+
- Control plane policing
- Authentication based on 802.1X, MAC, and web based

- DHCP Protection
- Secure encryption for all access methods including: SSH, SSL, and SVMPv3
- Switch CPU protection
- Identity-driven ACL

High Availability (HA) and Resiliency

- Virtual Router Redundancy Protocol (VRRP)
- Uni-direction Link Detection (UDLD)
- Link Aggregation Control Protocol (LACP)
- Aruba Virtual Switching Extension (VSX)
- Aruba Virtual Switching Framework (VSF)

Quality of Service (QoS)

- Strict Priority queuing
- Deficit Weighted Round Robin (DWRR)
- Traffic prioritization (802.1p)
- Layer-4 prioritization based on TCP/UDP port numbers
- Class of Service (CoS)
- Rate limiting
- Unknown Unicast Rate
- Large buffers for graceful congestion management

Note

The features listed do not apply to all switch models; please refer to the specific data sheet for each model to verify if the feature is supported. This text considers the feature set for AOS-CX 10.4 release.

AOS-CX CLI Access

Accessing AOS-CX CLIConsole Port

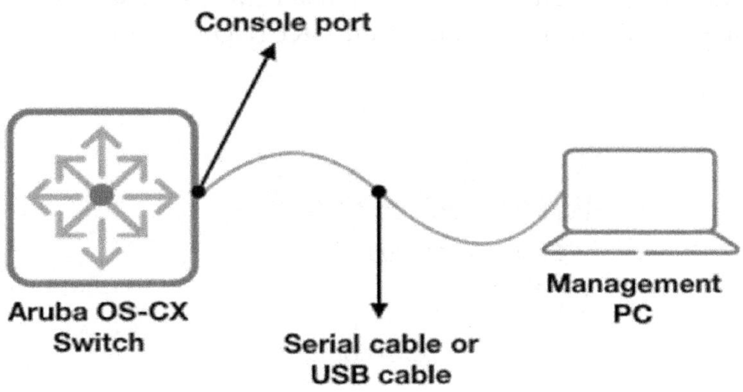

Figure 3-8 Console Port

When you initially configure a switch, you will typically use out-of-band Management (OOBM) on a console port (Figure 3-8). This special console port is integrated on all switch models and types, to facilitate configuration, troubleshooting, and management. Depending on the switch model, the console can be a USB-C port or an RJ-45 port; however for both port types you must establish a serial connection between the management station, perhaps your laptop, and the switch. To do this you need the following items:

If the Switch has an RJ-45 Port:

- Serial cable (shipped with the switch) (Figure 3-9).
- A USB-to-Serial converter—modern laptops no longer include a serial port.
- Software on your laptop or management station that emulates the serial session. Some common examples include PuTTY, TeraTerm, and Secure CRT.

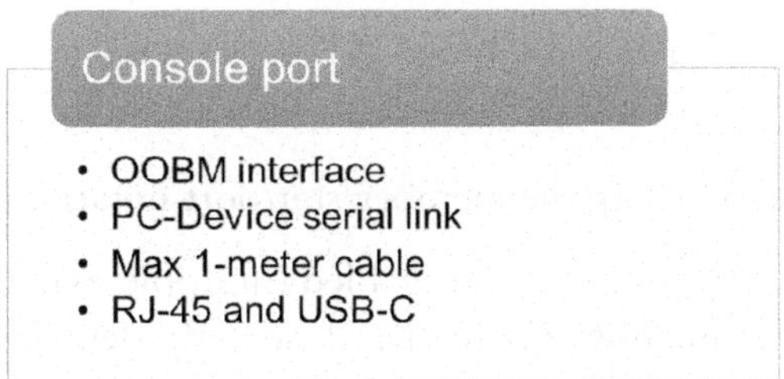

Figure 3-9 Console Port

If the switch has a USB-C Port:

- USB-C cable.
- Software on your laptop or management station that emulates the serial session. Some common examples include PuTTY, TeraTerm, and Secure CRT (Figure 3-10).

Figure 3-10 Serial Connection

AOS-CX: Port Numbering

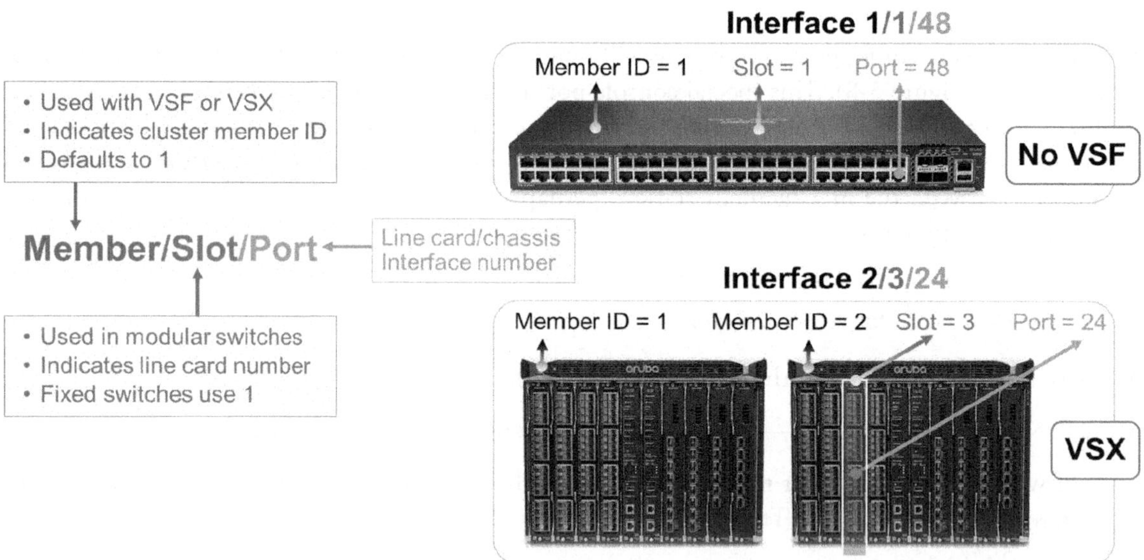

Figure 3-11 AOS-CX Port Numbering

AOS-CX reference interfaces following the member/slot/port notation (Figure 3-11).

- Member: When VSF or VSX protocols are enabled (multiple switches can be seen as one virtual) this number indicates the member ID in the cluster. By default, an AOS-CX switch will be member 1.
- Slot: In modular switches like 8400 and 6400, this number represents the slot being used by a particular line card. For fixed switches (8320,8325 and 6300) this number will always be1.

- Port: This number refers to the individual interface in the line card (modular switches) or in the chassis (fixed switches).

The image in Figure 3-11 shows an example with a fixed switch and with a Modular switch with VSX enabled.

Note
VSF is available for 6300 switch series; VSX is supported on the other platforms. You will know more about this technology later in this course.

AOS-CX: Prompt Modes

AOS-CX is organized into different configuration contexts or levels. Each context determines which parts of the switch can be managed and which commands are available to users with the appropriate authority (Figure 3-12).

Prompt	Context	Description
`Switch>`	Operator	View commands, no configuration commands
`Switch#`	Manager	Use commands that need not be saved
`Switch(config)#`	Global config	Change switch configuration
`Switch(config-if)#`	Interface config	Descendants of global config. Use commands that apply to a specific configuration or protocol
`Switch(config-router)#`	Router config	
`Switch(config-vlan-100)#`	VLAN 100 config	

Figure 3-12 AOS-CX Prompt Modes

The operating system defines the following contexts:

Operator Context (>)

This operator context enables you to execute commands to view but not change configuration. This context requires the least user privilege to execute commands. When in operator context, the CLI prompt is the switch name, followed by a greater than sign (>).

```
Switch>
```

Manager Context (#)

This context will show the name of the switch followed by a hashtag. To navigateto the manager context, start at the operator context (>). Then enter the **enable** command, as shown. You must have manager access to the switch to enter the enable command.

```
Switch> enable

Switch#
```

Global Configuration (config)

In the global configuration context (**config**) is where you can execute commands that change the switch configuration, as shown. To access this mode, start in Manager mode, then enterthe command **configure terminal**, or shorten it to just **config**, as shown in the figure. To move back up one level from this or any other context, issue the **exit** command.

All other configuration command contexts are descendants of the global configuration command context (config). From these command contexts you can execute commands that apply to specific configuration or protocol such as an interface or a VLAN.

Examples:

```
Switch(config-if)#

Switch(config-router)#

Switch(config-vlan-100)#
```

To return to Manager context from any child or descendent context, enter the **end** command.

For example:

```
Switch(config-vlan-100)# end

Switch#
```

AOS-CX: Context-Sensitive Help

Show the available commands in the current context

```
Switch# ?
boot                    Reboot all or part of the system
checkpoint              Checkpoint information
<<<Omitted Output>>>
Switch#
```

Figure 3-13 AOS-CX Context-Sensitive Help

The AOS-CX CLI provides you with built-in help features. For example, to show the available commands that you can execute in the current command context enter the question mark (?) symbol. This is shown in the top example in Figure 3-13. The question mark (?) does not display on the screen when you enter it.

Show the available parameters for a command

```
Switch# show access-list ?
  all          All access-lists
  ip           Internet Protocol v4 (IPv4)
  ipv6         Internet Protocol v6 (IPv6)
  log-timer    Set ACL log timer length (frequency)
  mac          Ethernet MAC Protocol
Switch(config)# access-list
```

Figure 3-14 Show Access-List

To show the available parameters for a command, enter the command followed by a space and then enter the question mark symbol (?). This is shown in the bottom example in Figure 3-14. Please notice that after the CLI displays the information, it automatically displays the text you entered before without including the help symbol (?).

AOS-CX: Command Abbreviation andCompletion

The AOS-CX supports both command abbreviation and command completion. To save time by only typing in abbreviated version of the full syntax, enter enough letters to uniquely specify a valid command, and the CLI accepts the command. For example, you can enter **conf** instead of **configure** to navigate from the manager context to the global configuration context.

```
Switch# conf
Switch(config)#
```

Command completion means that if you enter part of command word and then press the **Tab** key, one of the following occurs:

- If you enter enough letters to match a valid command, the CLI displays the reminder of the word.
- If you have not entered enough letters to match a valid command, the CLI does not complete the command.

For example:

```
Switch(config)# int <Tab>
Switch(config)# interface
```

If you press the Tab key twice after a completed word, the CLI displays the command options. For example:

```
Switch(config)#interface<Tab><Tab>
lag
loopback
mgmt
tunnel
```

Getting Switch Information Using Show Commands

In this section you will learn about basic commands that will help you to verify your networking equipment, along with its general capabilities. This is some of the most valuable information you can learn during an entry-level networking course. Good network engineers and administrators must be adept at discovering the ACTUAL connectivity of the network. This will help you to verify the accuracy of existing documentation, or to create new network documentation from scratch.

AOS-CX—The Value of Show Commands

Show commands are valuable for baselining and troubleshooting. Using these commands, you can view many switch performance and health parameters, including CPU and memory utilization. Suppose that your network is healthy, everyone is happy, and all your switches are generally at about 5% CPU utilization. You have been paying attention to this for months now; you know your network.

During an outage or slowdown, you find a switch that is running at 85% utilization. You might focus your diagnostic efforts on that switch and its directly attached devices. Because you paid attention while the network is healthy, you are more efficient when the network is not healthy. If you had not paid attention, you would have no idea whether 85% utilization is normal or abnormal. Of course, Aruba has amazingly effective management platforms that ease and automate these baseline processes, but it can still be valuable to use the CLI to check network device health and status.

Mastering the commands that you are about to learn, creating good documentation, and having good baseline information is kind of like getting the answers to a test before you take the test. Only this is the real world, and the "test" relates to how effective you are when the network is down.

AOS-CX Show Version

Show version displays version information about the network operating system software, service operating system software, and BIOS. In the figure, you see that this system is running the AOS-CX, version GL.10.04.0003. Near the bottom you see the Service OS and BIOS versions. This is useful for your general knowledge, and to help to determine if upgrades are needed.

```
Switch# show version
-----------------------------------------------------------------
ArubaOS-CX
(c)Copyright 2017-2019 Hewlett Packard Enterprise Development LP
-----------------------------------------------------------------
Version                  : GL.10.04.0003
<output deleted for clarity>
Service OS Version       : GL.01.05.0002
BIOS Version             : GL-01-0013
```

Command context: Operator (>) or Manager (#)

Authority: Operators or administrators.

AOS-CX Show System

Show system displays general status information about the system. During remote access, the device platform and version information may not be obvious. In the example shown, you are attached to device named "Switch": An Aruba model 8325-48YC. It has 48 25gbps ports, and 8 100Gbps ports. You see the serial number, base MAC address, and uptime, as well as CPU and memory utilization. This can give you some idea of the general health of the system. By baselining these parameters, you can begin to establish what "normal" is for your network.

```
Switch# show system
Hostname                 : Switch
SystemDescription        : GL.10.04.0003
SystemContact            :
SystemLocation           :
Vendor                   : Aruba
ProductName              : JL635A Aruba 8325-48Y8C 48p 25G 8p 100G swch
Chassis Serial Nbr       : TW98KM003P
Base MAC Address         : 9020c2-bced00
ArubaOS-CX Version       : GL.10.04.0003
Time Zone                : UTC
```

```
Up Time                      : 1 week, 1 day, 11 hours, 20 minutes
CPU Util (%)                 : 4
MemoryUsage (%)              :19
```

Command context: Operator (>) or Manager (#)

Authority: Operators or Administrators

AOS-CX Top CPU

The **top cpu** command shows detailed CPU utilization information. You learned how to see high-level CPU utilization with the command **show system**. The **top cpu** command provides more detailed information (Figure 3-15).

```
Switch# top cpu

top - 20:40:46 up 17 days, 23:45, 1 user, load average: 0.32, 0.26, 0.24

Tasks: 238 total, 1 running, 194 sleeping, 0 stopped, 0 zonbie

%Cpu(s): 2.5 us, 1.6 sy, 0.0 ni, 95.9 id, 0.0 wa, 0.0 hi, 0.0 si, 0.0 st

KiB Mem : 7868164 total, 3013360 free, 13999328 used, 3455476 buff/cache

KiB Swap: 2097148 total, 2095868 free,     1280 used. 6079420 avail Mem
```

```
  PID USER     PR  NI    VIRT    RES    SHR S  %CPU %MEM     TIME+ COMMAND
26308 admin    20   0    3344   2064   1612 R  11.8  0.0   0:00.03 top -b -n 1 -s -c -o %CPU
  629 root     20   0   33928  17084   6124 S   5.9  0.2 777:57.14 /usr/sbin/ovsdb-server
 3047 root     20   0  791184  84416  32232 S   5.9  1.1 189:43.13 /usr/bin/prometheus
    1 root     20   0    7600   6312   2960 S   0.0  0.1   0:28.14 /sbin/init
```

Figure 3-15 Example Output: **Top Cpu**

Command Context: Operator (>) or Manager (#)

Authority: Operators or administrators

Note

Top memory is a related command that shows memory utilization information.

AOS-CX Show Events

The **Show events** command displays the event logs generated by the switch modules since the last reboot. Log analysis is a powerful tool to investigate and troubleshoot system and protocol-related problems. You can use the **-r** parameter to list the most recent log events first. The **show event** command also has other parameters that you can use like -e, -s, -a, -n, -c, and -d. You can learn more about how to use these parameters in the *Command-Line Interface Guide for ArubaOS-CX* document.

```
Switch# show events -r
---------------------------------------------------
Event logs from current boot
---------------------------------------------------
2019-12-06T10:24:18.679695+00:00  Spine-8325-C  hpe-sysmond[3212]:
Event|6303|LOG_INFO|AMM|1/1|Current system memory usage is 27%
2019-12-06T09:09:19.067316+00:00     Spine-8325-C     lldpd[2165]:
Event|106|LOG_INFO|AMM|1/1|LLDP neighbor 90:20:c2:bc:7c:00 deleted
on 1/1/35
```

Command Context: Manager (#)

Authority: Administrators or auditors

AOS-CX Interface Brief

The **show interface brief** command helps the administrator to see what the available interfaces and the current status are. This command also briefly shows Layer-2 and Layer-3 configuration applied to the interface. This is a frequently used command for many network engineers. At a glance, you can tell the status of every interface on the entire device, with a specific focus on the Enabled and Status columns.

Enabled "yes" means that the interface is not disabled in the switch configuration: no administrator has disabled the interface. "Up" in the status column means that something is attached to that interface, and there is at least a good Layer-1/Layer-2 connection between them.

```
Switch# show interface brief
-----------------------------------------------------------------------
Port       Native  Mode   Type             Enabled Status  Reason
Speed
(Mb/s)     VLAN
-----------------------------------------------------------------------
```

```
1/1/1        1            routed  SFP28DAC3        yes      up
25000
1/1/2        1            trunk   SFP28DAC3        yes      up
25000
1/1/3        1            trunk   SFP28DAC3        yes      up
25000


<<<Omitted Output>>>
```

Command Context: Operator (>) or Manager (#)

Authority: Operators or Administrators

Basic Configuration

Configuring Hostname

You should name each network device. This ensures that you can easily identify them, especially in large networks. In a real environment this is one of the first configuration steps that you will do. Many corporations have documented, standardized naming conventions. For example, one standard might be Building-Floor-Rack_Name. The switches in Rack 2 on the 2nd floor of building 9 might be named 9-2-2_SWA, 9-2-2_SWB, 9-2-2_SWC, and so on.

Command Context: **Config**

Syntax: **Hostname**<*Hostname*>

For example:

```
Switch(config)# hostname Access-1
Access-1(config)#
```

Enabling an Interface

In AOS-CX, all ports are disabled by default. However, you can modify this state using the **no shutdown** command.

Command context: config-if (interface level)

Syntax: shutdown/no shutdown

For example, to enable an interface:

```
Switch(config)# interface 1/1/1
Switch(config-if)# no shutdown
```

Or to disable interface:

```
Switch(config)# interface 1/1/1
Switch(config-if)# shutdown
```

A description can be configured for each interface; this facilitates management.

Command context: config-if (interface level)

Syntax: **description** <*Description*>

For example:

```
Switch(config)# interface 1/1/1
Switch(config-if)# description To-Core-switch
```

Verifying an Interface Status

The **show interface** command shows status and configuration for all interfaces on the switch.

For example "Administratively down" means that a **shutdown** command was configured on that interface. You can also see that an interface description was configured on that interface with the **description** command.

```
Interface 1/1/1 is down (Administratively down)
 Admin state is down
 State information: Group speed mismatch
 Link transitions: 0
 Description: To-Core-switch
 Hardware: Ethernet, MAC Address: 90:20:c2:bc:3f:00
 MTU 1500
 Type SFP-BT
```

Notice if the interface shows as"up", somebody would have entered the **no shutdown** command.

```
Switch# show interface 1/1/1

Interface 1/1/1 is up
 Admin state is up
 State information: Group speed mismatch
```

```
Link transitions: 0
Description: To-Core-switch
Hardware: Ethernet, MAC Address: 90:20:c2:bc:3f:00
MTU 1500
Type SFP-BT
```

Command context: Manager (#)

Syntax: **show interface** *<Interface-ID>*

Discovering the Network

Link Layer Discovery Protocol

Imagine that you are remotely configuring an AOS-CX switch in a production environment. This switch is connected to multiple network devices.You must configure only the interface that is facing an Aruba Controller. The onsite IT team is not available and somehow you must identify the correct interface so you can apply the configuration. This problem is easily addressed using LLDP.

LLDP is a vendor-neutral, IEEE standard, link layer (Layer-2) protocol. It is used by network devices to advertise their identity and capabilities over a wired Ethernet connection. This protocol enables you to discover and document network device interconnections.Media Endpoint Discovery is an enhancement of LLDP known as LLDP-MED. This provides for Auto-discovery of LAN policies such as VLAN-ID, Layer-2 priority, and Differentiated services for QoS. This helps to enable **plug and play** networking.

Devices send LLDP information on a regular interval, encapsulated in Ethernet frames. In AOS-CX LLDP is enabled by default. Directly connected devices receive these frames and store the information in a table in local memory. You can view this information with commands like **show lldp neighbor-info**.

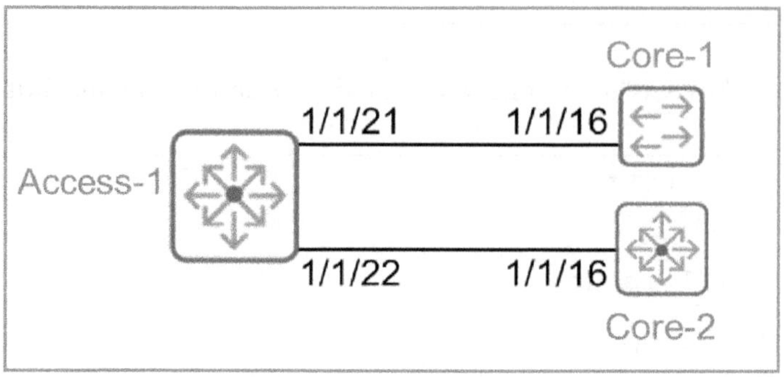

Figure 3-16 LLDP Scenario

In the scenario (Figure 3-16), Access-1's port 1/1/21 connects to port 1/1/16 of Core-1. Access-1's port 1/1/22 connects to port1/1/16 of Core-2. If someone has already taken the time to create a diagram like the one shown in the figure, you do not need to use LLDP for discovery, it has already been done for you. However, network documentation is often incorrect, out of date, or was simply never created. You can verify existing documentation and create new documentation using LLDP information.

Many folks do not believe that it is worth the time and money to create and maintain good, accurate network documentation, "The network is fine, why waste time making documents". However, when the network fails, instead of having to discover the network or rely on that one person who has the network memorized, everyone can look at the document and be far more effective troubleshooters. Documentation is an insurance policy against slow, ineffective, troubleshooting. It can be the difference between a four-hour network outage and a 15-minute outage.

Using the **Show LLDP neighbor-info** command displays information about neighboring devices for all interfaces or for a specific interface.

```
Switch-A# show LLDP neighbor-info

LLDP Neighbor Information
=========================

 <output omitted>

LOCAL-PORT   CHASSIS ID          PORT-ID PORT-DESC  TTL    SYS-NAME
--------------------------------------------------------------------------

1/1/21       90:20:c2:bc:a8:00 1/1/16  1/1/16     120    Core-1

1/1/22       90:20:c2:bb:8b:00 1/1/16  1/1/16     120    Core-2
```

To get more information about a specific entry you can append the interface at the end of the previous command. **Show LLDP neighbor-info 1/1/21**, as shown below.

```
Access-1# show LLDP neighbor-info 1/1/21


Port                              : 1/1/21

Neighbor Entries                  : 1

Neighbor Entries Deleted          : 0

Neighbor Entries Dropped          : 0
```

```
Neighbor Entries Aged-Out             : 0
Neighbor Chassis-Name                 : Core-1
Neighbor Chassis-Description          : Aruba JL635A  GL.10.04.0001
Neighbor Chassis-ID                   : 90:20:c2:bc:a8:00
Neighbor Management-Address           : 10.250.1.3
Chassis Capabilities Available        : Bridge, Router
Chassis Capabilities Enabled          : Bridge, Router
Neighbor Port-ID                      : 1/1/16
Neighbor Port-Desc                    : 1/1/16
Neighbor Port VLAN ID                 : 1107
TTL                                   : 120
```

Command context: Manager (#)

Authority: Operators or Administrators

ICMP

Suppose that a new printer is added into the network and a laptop wants to use this device. The first troubleshooting step is to verify connectivity between these two devices, to ensure that the network is properly configured. ICMP helps you to address this problem.

The Internet Control Message Protocol (ICMP) is a supporting protocol in the Internet protocol suite. ICMP messages do not include any TCP or UDP headers. ICMP messages are placed directly into an IP packet. Thus, ICMP is often considered to be an extension of the Network Layer. Network devices use ICMP to send error messages and operational information, to indicate success or failure when communicating with another IP address. For example, an error is indicated when a requested service is not available or that a host or router could not be reached.

Table 3-1 shows the common messages that are used in ICMP, starting with Destination unreachable. Other messages include:

Table 3-1 ICMP Messages

Message	Description
Destination unreachable	Inform source of delivery issue
Time exceeded	TTL expired, packet discarded
Redirect	Inform others of a better L3 path
Echo request/reply	Ping: validate connectivity

Ping

The ping command sends ICMP Echo request messages to the destination device. The remote device responds to each received Echo request with an Echo reply message. When the source device receives the messages back, it is sure that the network was properly configured, communication succeeded between the two devices.

In AOS-CX the ping command must specify the IPv4 or hostname. The ping command is supported in most of the Client Operating Systems. The example ping session shown in the figure is from the command prompt of a Windows Client (Figure 3-17).

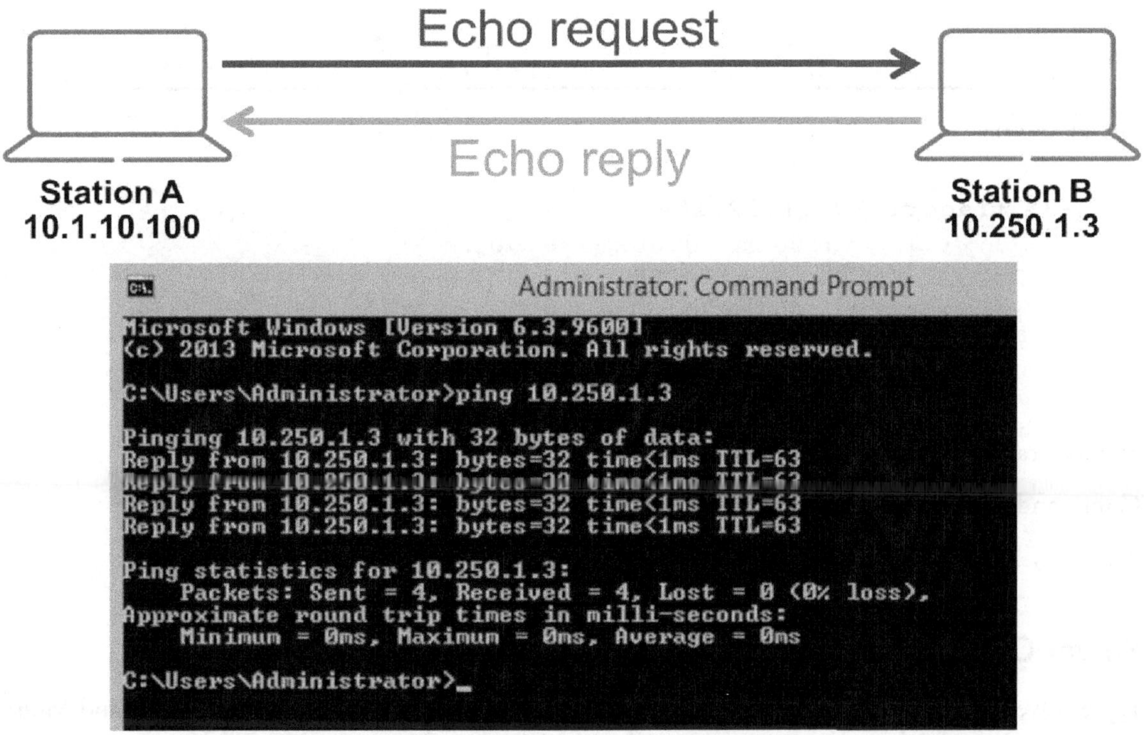

Figure 3-17 Echo Request and Reply

Syntax: **ping** <IPv4-address or hostname>

Command context: Operator (>) Manager (#)

Authority: Operators or Administrators

Traceroute

Traceroute is a variant of the ICMP protocol and it is a useful troubleshooting tool when you deploy a Layer-3 technology, such as a routing protocol. This command tracks the path that a packet takes to reach its destination listing the Layer-3 devices that are in the path. In AOS-CX the traceroute command must specify an IPv4 address or hostname (Figure 3-18).

Many firewalls block ping and trace commands. If you are attempting to use ping and trace commands to test connectivity through a firewall, the tests may fail. This does not necessarily mean that anything is wrong; it just means that the firewall is dropping your ping and trace commands as a security measure.

In this example, the switch tries to establish connectivity to the destination 10.11.12.104, via two intermediate routers (10.11.11.1 and 10.11.0.2). You will learn more about routing and Layer-3 in the next chapters.

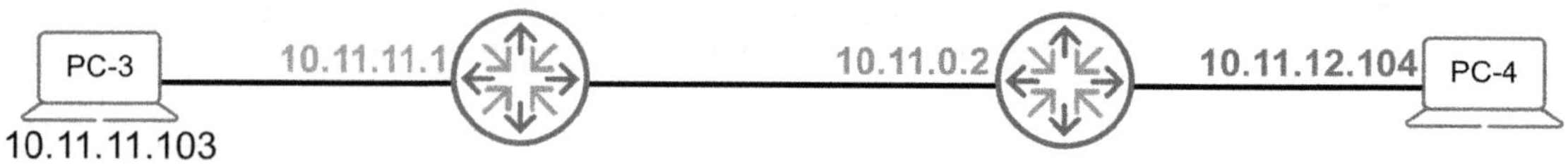


```
PC-3> tracert 10.11.12.104
1 10.11.11.1     0.002ms 0.002ms 0.001ms
2 10.11.0.2      0.002ms 0.001ms 0.001ms
3 10.11.12.104   0.001ms 0.002ms 0.002ms
```

Figure 3-18 Traceroute

Syntax: **traceroute** <IPv4-address or hostname>

Command context: Operator (>) Manager (#)

Authority: Operators or Administrators

Power Over Ethernet

Power Over Ethernet or PoE is a feature implemented on network devices such as Layer-2 and Multi-Layer switches, which provides power to endpoints using an Ethernet cable. This feature eliminates the need of external power sources saving expenses on materials and installation time.

PoE uses the twisted pairs of aUTP cable (described in module 1) to send power to PoE-enabled devices. The first PoE standard uses two twisted pairs to transmit data while the other two are used for power transmission. With the new PoE standards power and data are sent over the four twisted pairs. If you are thinking how is that possible, the answer is that power and data use different frequencies, electricity uses low frequency (60 Hz or less) and data uses high frequencies (10-100MHz).

The standard considers two types of devices—Powered devices (PDs) are devices that receive PoE power, while power sourcing equipment (PSE) provides the power. Typical PDs are Access Points, IP Phones, cameras, and some IoT devices. On the other hand, network switches are considered PSEs.

AOS-CX switches support all standards. PSEs and PDs can negotiate the power that PDs require more precisely using LLDP messages. Table 3-2 displays the 4 different standards that are available in the industry.

Name	IEEE Standard	Power to PD	Maximum power per port	Energized Pairs
PoE	802.3af	12.95 W	15.4 W	2-pairs
PoE+	802.3at	25.5 W	30 W	2-pairs
PoE++	802.3bt (Type 3)	51 W	60 W	4-pairs
PoE++	802.3bt (Type 4)	71.3 W	100 W	4-pairs

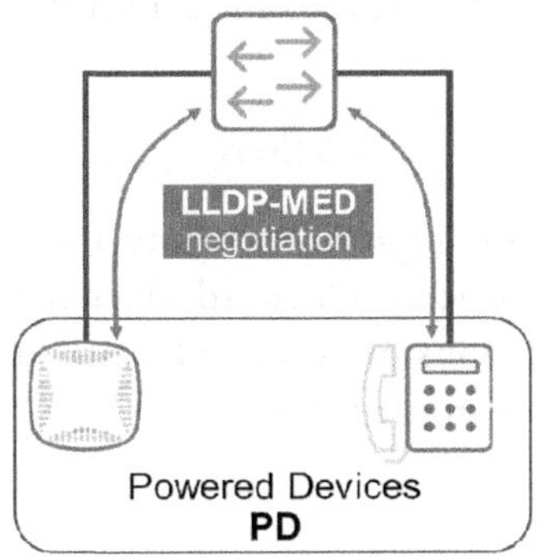

Table 3-2 Power Over Ethernet

AOS-CX Switch Architecture

AOS-CX Hardware Architecture

The AOS-CX modular switch series (Aruba 6400 and 8400) hardware architecture includes three major components: Management Modules, Fabric Modules, and Line Cards. The diagram in Figure 3-19 simplifies the components and the communication paths between them.

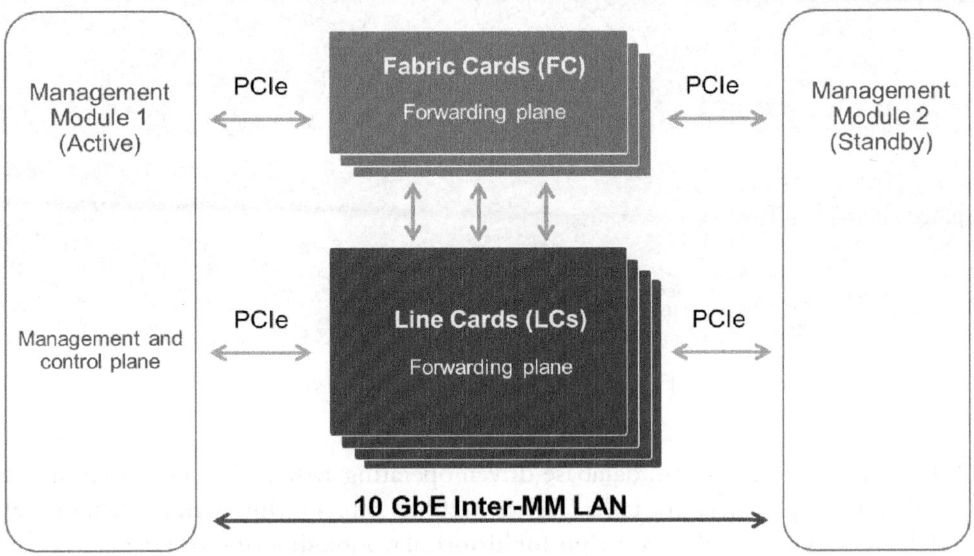

Figure 3-19 Hardware Architecture

Management Modules

This component has two main purposes. First, it runs the management plane, for monitoring and configuration services. The management module also runs the control plane, which defines what to do with the incoming information by running protocols and algorithms.

Fabric Modules

This component helps to interconnect the multiple Line Cards that can be installed in the switch. A fabric card forwards data between the ingress Line card and the egress line card. This device makes decisions based on information derived from data packets,and so is considered part of the data or Forwarding plane.

Line Cards

This component works on the Forwarding plane. It decides where traffic should be sent. Data that must be forwarded to another port on the same line card uses an internal process within that line card. Traffic that must be sent to a different line card is sent via the Fabric Module, which selects the proper destination line card.

AOS-CX Software Architecture

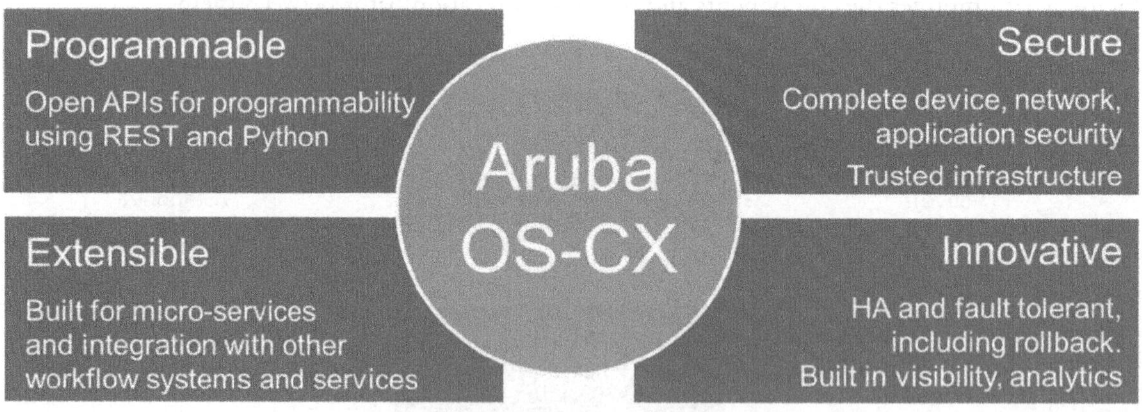

Figure 3-20 Software Architecture

The AOS-CX software is a modern, database-driven operating system that automates and simplifies many critical and complex network tasks (Figure 3-20). A built-in time series database enables customers and developers to use software scripts for historical troubleshooting and to analyze past trends. This helps to predict and avoid future problems due to scale, security, and performance.

This network operating system is built on a modular Linux architecture with a stateful database which helps to offer the following unique capabilities:

- Easy access to all network state information allowing unique visibility and analytics.
- REST APIs and Python scripting for fine-grained programmability of network tasks.
- A micro-services architecture that enables full integration with other workflow systems and services.
- Continual state synchronization that provides superior fault tolerance and high availability.
- Security best practices were applied to completely create a trusted platform.

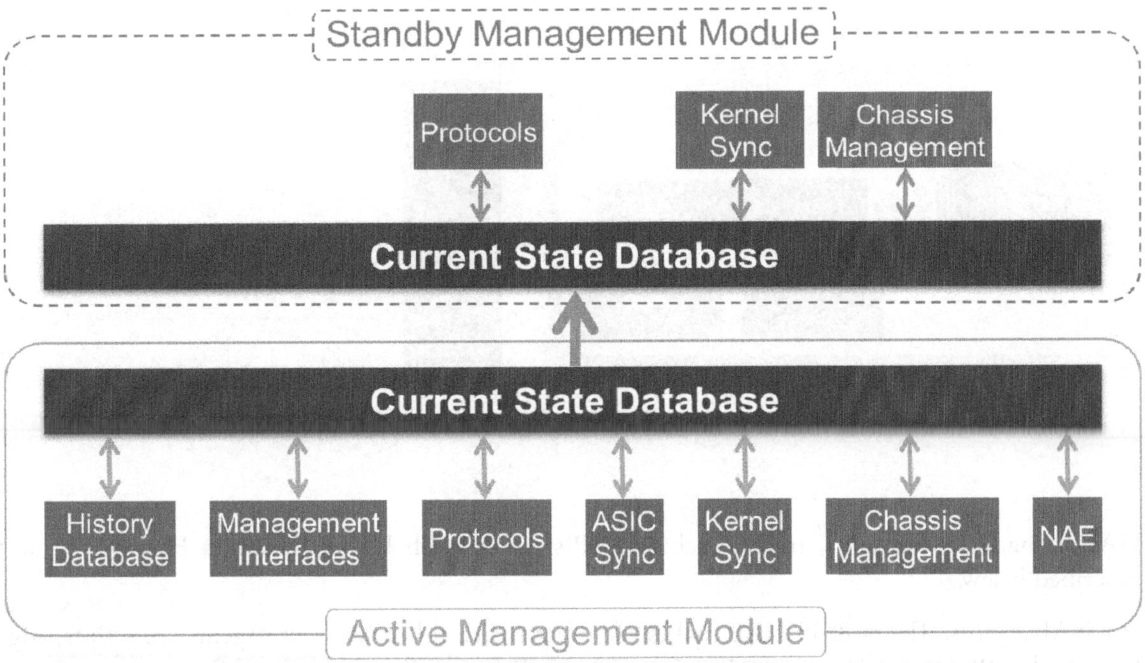

Figure 3-21 Management Module

Figure 3-21 shows how the Active Management Module (MM) can synchronize information on the standby MM. This ensures a fault tolerant system that reduces downtime. Network Protocols do not have to wait and re-converge.

The Current State Database is the most important aspect of the AOS-CX software architecture. All software processes communicate with the data base rather than each other. This model ensures near real-time state and resiliency. Using the Current State Database, you can upgrade software modules independently.

The figure shows how processes like the History Database or Protocols interact directly with the database and not between each other. This streamlined approach allows all processes to only use one language to talk to the database. Without this model, direct inter-process communication would be less efficient, wasting CPU resources.

The database also maintains the current configuration, status of all features, and statistics. The unified database ensures that all information is visible in a single place. Thus, interaction is accomplished through a single, open API.

Aruba Network Analytics Engine (NAE) Components

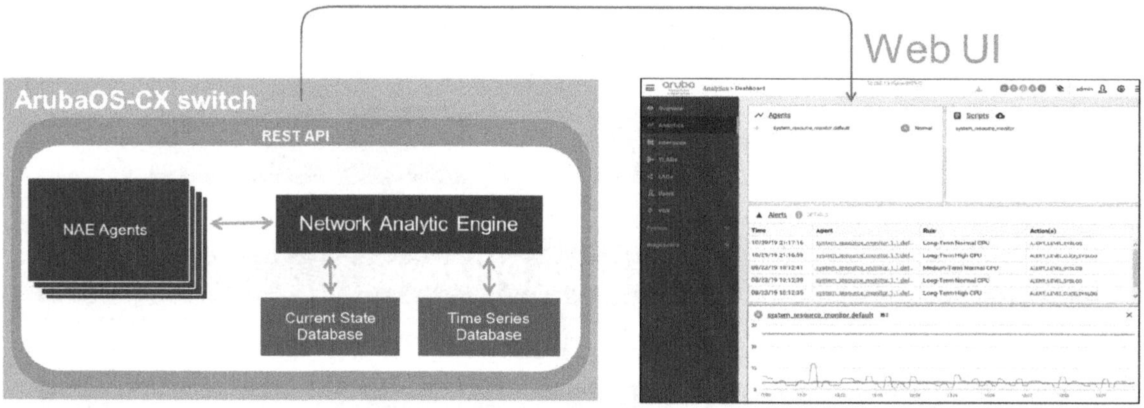

Figure 3-22 Network Analytics Engine (NAE)

NAE is made up of agents, rules, databases, APIs, and a Web UI, as shown in Figure 3-22 and described below.

- NAE Agents: The built-in NAE makes use of agents to collect context. Agents are scripts, triggered in the device when a specific event occurs. Then it collects additional interesting and relevant network information.
- NAE Rules: Agents are triggered by user-defined rules. For example, you can create a rule to collect information when CPU utilization exceeds a certain threshold for a specified period.
- Configuration and State Database: This database enables NAE's direct access to the current configuration and switch operational states. Data retrieved from this database can be used to analyze trends and predict future capacity requirements.
- Time Series Database: This database gives the users the ability to rewind and playback the network context surrounding a network event. Under normal use, storage is estimated at 400 days.

- REST APIs: This communication method enables integration with external systems, such as SIEM tools and log analytic engines. Also, operators can use the APIs to request information from other devices in the network. This helps to create a complete picture of the network state when a specific event occurs.
- Web UI: Allows you to access, view, and configure NAE agents, scripts, and alerts. Automatically generated graphs provide additional context, useful for troubleshooting networks.

AOS-CX Top Memory

The **top memory** command shows memory utilization information.

```
Switch# top memory

top - 20:41:22 up 17 days, 23:46, 1 user, load average: 0.31, 0.26,
0.24

Tasks: 238 total, 2 running, 193 sleeping, 0 stopped, 0 zonbie

%Cpu(s): 2.5 us, 1.6 sy, 0.0 ni, 95.9 id, 0.0 wa, 0.0 hi, 0.0 si,
0.0 st

KiB Mem : 7868164 total, 3013768 free, 1398760 used, 3455636 buff/
cache

KiB Swap: 2097148 total, 2095868 free,    1280 used. 6080024 avail
Mem
```

PID	USER	PR	NI	VIRT	RES	SHR	S	%CPU	%MEM	TIME+	COMMAND
2366	root	20	0	2013036	129684	45568	S	0.0	1.6	739:59.05	/usr/bin/switchd_agent -i 1 -s
3047	root	20	0	791184	84416	32232	S	0.0	1.1	189:43.37	/usr/bin/prometheus --
701	root	20	0	1212616	75652	19316	S	0.0	1.0	18:02.19	/usr/bin/hpe-restd

Table 3-3 Results of Top Memory

Command context: Operator (>) or Manager (#)

Authority: Operators or administrators

AOS-CX Show Interfaces Transceiver Detail

The **show interfaces transceiver detail** command lists the transceivers installed in the switch.

```
Switch# show interface transceiver detail
Transceiver in 1/1/1
Interface Name        : 1/1/1
Type                  : SFP28DAC3
Connector Type        : No separable connector
Transfer Distance     : 0.00km (SMF), 0m (OM1), 0m (OM2), 0m (OM3)
Diagnostic Support    : None
Product Number        : JL488A
Serial Number         : CN97KBG0BJ
Part Number           : 8121-1743
```

Command context: Operator (>) or Manager (#)

Authority: Operators or administrators

Lab 3: Initial Setup

Overview

BigStartup is a small business that just started operations a few months ago. The owners have determined the need to rent a small portion of a nearby building's floor (The East Wing) from Cheap4Rent Properties in order to house a new group of employees they just hired. These employees will be using Windows PCs and will have a few networking connectivity requirements in their daily operations, such as printing and file sharing.Because of this, you have been contacted toprovide network consulting services,as well astake care of configuring and managing the switching equipment thatBigStartuprecently purchased.

Note: References to equipment and commands are taken from Aruba's hosted remote lab. These are shown for demonstration purposes in case you wish to replicate the environment and tasks on your own equipment.

Objectives

After completing this lab, you will be able to:

- Set your gear in factory values
- Navigate through the AOS-CX command line interface (CLI)
- Define a hostname on 6300-A switch
- Disable unused interfaces
- Save device's configuration and create checkpoints

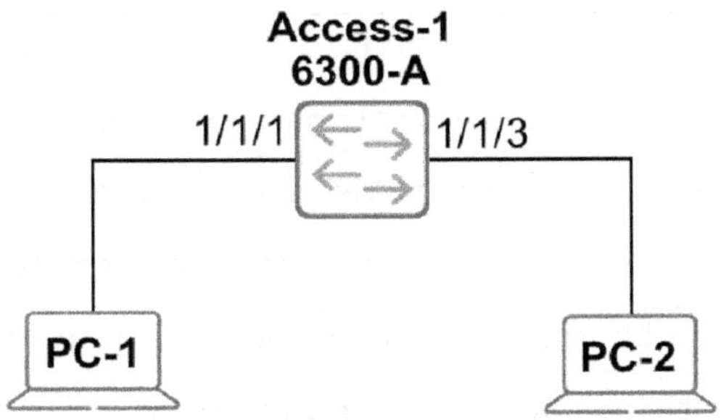

Figure 3-23 Lab Topology

Task 1: Explore the AOS-CX Switch CLI

Objectives

In this task, you will explore and become more familiar with the AOS-CX switch CLI. Do not be afraid to try out different commands on the CLI: you will learn by experimenting!

Steps

6300-A

1. Open a console connection to the **6300-A**. Log in using **admin** and **no password**.
2. Hit the [?] key to show the available commands that you can execute in the current command context.

```
6300# ?
  auto-confirm   Disables user confirmation, and executes the opera-
tion without
                 prompting
  boot           Reboot all or part of the system; configure default
                 boot
  parameters
  checkpoint     Checkpoint information
  clear          Reset functions
  configure      Configuration from vty interface
  copy           Copy data or files to/from the switch
  debug          Configure debug logging
```

```
  diagnostics   Change diagnostic commands availability
  disable       Turn off privileged mode command
  end           End current mode and change to enable mode
  erase         Erase device information or files
  exit          Exit current mode and change to previous mode
  https-server  HTTPS Server management
  list          Print command list
  member        VSF member selection
  no            Negate a command or set its defaults
  page          Enable page break
  ping          Send IPv4 ping requests to a device on the network
  ping6         Send IPv6 ping requests to a device on the network
  port-access   Port based network access.
  repeat        Repeat a list of commands from history
  show          Show running system information
ssh             Configure SSH.
  start-shell   Start Bash shell
  top           Top command
  traceroute    Trace the IPv4 route to a device on the network
  traceroute6   Trace the IPv6 route to a device on the network
usb             Commands to control the USB Port
vsf             Virtual Switching Framework (VSF) commands
  write         Write running configuration to memory, network, or
terminal
```

Page through the commands available at this level. Some important commands available at this level include:

- **show**, which enables you to examine current configuration parameters
- **copy**, which enables you to back up the switch configuration
- **ping** and **traceroute**, which are connectivity test tools

3. List the parameters available for the **show** command. By typing "**show**" followed by[**?**].

```
6300# show ?
aaa                    Authentication, Authorization and Accounting.
access-list            Access control list (ACL)
  accounting               Show local accounting information
active-gateway         Show active gateway settings
  alias                    Short names configured for a set of commands
  allow-unsafe-updates  Show allowed non-failsafe updates
arp                    Show IPv4 addresses from neighbor table
aruba-central          Configure Aruba-Central
  banner                   Show one of the configured system banners
  bfd                      BFD information
bgp                    BGP specific commands
bluetooth                  Display information about Bluetooth wire-
less management
  boot-history             Display boot history details
  capacities               Show system capacities and its values.
  capacities-status  Show system capacities status and its values.
cdp                        Show various CDP settings
  checkpoint               Checkpoint information
                    ←---- output omitted ---→
```

4. Scroll through
5. Type "disable"

```
6300# disable
6300>
```

How has the prompt changed? ______________________________

Answer

This turns privileged mode off, which means only basic commands with no control upon the device will be available.

6. Hit the **[?]** key to show the available commands that you can execute in this non-Privileged command context.

```
6300>?
  clear    Reset functions
  enable   Turn on privileged mode command
  exit     Exit current mode and change to previous mode
  list     Print command list
  no       Negate a command or set its defaults
  page     Enable page break
  repeat   Repeat a list of commands from history
  show     Show running system information
  top      Top command
  user     User account
                  ←---- output omitted ---→
```

Important

Available commands in both privileged and non-privileged modes are different. Protecting privileged mode is used as a basic role-based access control for defining what operators can do when logged into the device.

7. Type **"enable"** and hit enter; this will turn privileged mode back again.

```
6300>enable
6300#
```

8. Type "**co**" and then hit the [**tab**] key twice to list commands that start with "co":

```
6300# co[tab][tab]
```

What does the CLI display? ____________________

9. Type "**con**" followed by a single **[tab]** hit.

```
6300# configure
```

What has just happened to the command? ______________________________

Tip
You can execute any command as soon as you have entered an unambiguous character string. For instance, **conf** will have the same effect as **configure**.

10. Hit **[Enter]** key. This takes you to global configuration mode, where you can start making changes that take immediate effect upon the device's configuration.

```
6300# configure
6300(config)#
```

11. Hit **[?]** key to show the available commands that you can execute in the global config mode.

```
6300(config)# ?
aaa                      Configure Authentication, Authorization and
Accounting
                         feature.
access-list              Access control list (ACL)
  alias                  Create a short name for the specified command(s)
  allow-unsafe-updates   Allow non-failsafe updates of programmable
                         devices
  apply                  Apply a configuration record
aruba-central            Configure Aruba-Central
  banner                 Customize login banner
  bfd                    Enable Bidirectional Forwarding Detection
                         (BFD)
bluetooth                Configure Bluetooth wireless management
cdp                      Configure CDP operating mode
  checkpoint             Configure checkpoint related feature
  class                  Configure classifier class
  cli-session            Configure CLI session management
                         ←---- output omitted ---→
```

> **Note**
> You can notice how commands available here are different than in previous CLI modes due to the configuration nature of them.

12. Type **interface 1/1/1** and then hit **[enter]**. You will be moved to the interface sub configuration mode.

```
6300(config)# interface 1/1/1
6300(config-if)#
```

13. Hit **[?]** key. Again, you will see a different list of available commands for this sub context.

```
6300(config-if)# ?
aaa                         Configure Authentication, Authorization and
Accounting feature.
  apply                  Apply a configuration record
arp                    Configure ARP commands
  bfd                    Set BFD configuration
cdp                    Configure CDP operating mode
  description            Add an interface description
  dhcpv4-snooping        Configure DHCPv4-Snooping
  dhcpv6-snooping        Configure DHCPv6-Snooping
  end                    End current mode and change to enable mode
  exit                   Exit current mode and change to previous mode
  flow-control           Configure flow control
```

14. Type "**end**" and hit **[Enter]**.

```
6300(config-if)# end
6300#
```

What has just happened to the command prompt? ______________________________

Next, you will enter a command that is invalid, and then fix issues with it by using the command-recall feature.

15. Enter this command exactly as shown: "**show hitory**".

```
6300# show hitory
Invalid input: hitory
```

16. Recall the command by pressing the **[Up]** arrow key.
17. Go to the beginning of the command with the **[CTRL][a]** shortcut.
18. Go to the end of the command line with the **[CTRL][e]** shortcut.
19. With the **[Left]** and **[Right]** arrow keys, move your cursor to the correct position in "**hitory**" and place the letter "s".
20. Press the **[Enter]** key at any time (no matter where your cursor is) to execute the command.

Tip
Repeating commands can be a useful way to enter similar commands more quickly, as well as to correct mistakes in commands.

```
6300# show history
6      disable
5      enable
4      configure
3      interface 1/1/1
2      end
1      show hitory
6300#
```

21. Recall the wrong command by pressing the **[Up]** arrow key two times.
22. Delete the last word with the **[CTRL][w]** shortcut.

```
6300# show hitory[CTRL][w]
6300# show
```

Important

Using the **[CTRL]+[w]** shortcut for removing the word that is preceding the cursor is useful in cases you want to either quickly correct a typo or you intend to use another form of the root command.

23. Add "**system**" to the show command followed by "**?**".

```
6300# show system ?

   resource-utilization   Utilization metrics of various system
resources

serviceos               Display serviceOS information

<cr>

6300# show system
```

What options are available for the "show system" command? ____________________

Note

Notice the **<cr>** at the end; this means that you can execute the command without supplying any further parameters.

24. View the system resource utilization on the switch.

```
6300# show system resource-utilization

                    ←---- output omitted ---→

dhcp-server-ada          0          1          8

systemd-udevd            0          0         14

hpe-restd                0          1         14

hpe-entityd              0          0         10

ata_sff                  0          0          0

mmcqd/0                  0          0          0

bled                     0          0         12

mmcqd/0rpmb              0          0          0

vlanremapd               0          0          9

powerd                   0          0         12
```

```
rpciod                  0                0                0
nfsd                    0                0                0
rcu_sched               0                0                0
```

Tip

You will notice that a long output automatically populates overrunning on the screen, not giving you the chance to read the first lines. You can use the "page" command for displaying subsequent command outputs in portions and giving you the ability to control when to display the next page by hitting the space bar.

25. Use the "**page**" command followed by "**system resource-utilization**".

```
6300# page
6300# show system resource-utilization
System Resources:
Processes: 202
CPU usage(%): 1
Memory usage(%): 16
Open FD's: 6048
mmc-type-a: Endurance = 0-10%, Health = normal
mmc-type-b: Endurance = 0-10%, Health = normal
ProcessCPU Usage(%)Memory Usage(%)  Open FD's
----------------------------------------------------------------
kworker/u8:2            0                0                0
tacacs-srv-trkd         0                0                9
acctsyslogd             0                0                6
watchdogd               0                0                0
prometheus 0             1               11
nginx                   0                0              ' 13
kblockd                 0                0                0
ovsdb-server          14              0              125
```

```
migration/3             0            0            0
fpsLink1                0            0            0
kauditd                 0            0            0
mmcqd/0gp1          0            0            0
-- MORE --, next page: Space, next line: Enter, quit: q
```

What has changed in this new output? ______________________

____

Answer

The command shows the current CPU and memory utilization of the system and the per process utilization.

What is current CPU and Memory utilization of the switch? ______________________

____

Tip

Alternately you can use the "top cpu" and "top memory" commands for displaying these numbers. A key difference between "show system resource-utilization" and "top" commands is that "top"commands list higher resource usingcommands first. Also, the output displays the processes' ID, status, and the user that is running the command (the system or a real user logged into the device).

Notice

High CPU utilization is a symptom of an unstable process or situation happening in the system, such as layer-2, layer-3, or layer-7 loop.

26. Hit **[space]** a few times to scroll all the way down or **[q]** key.
27. Try "**show system**"command. This version of the command will also show current hostname, description SNMP contact and location, serial number, base MAC address, up time, etc.

```
6300# show system
Hostname             : 6300
System Description : FL.10.04.0030
System Contact       :
System Location      :
Vendor               : Aruba
Product Name         : JL668A 6300F 24G 4SFP56 Sw
```

```
Chassis Serial Nbr : SG90KN70HX
Base MAC Address   : 883a30-983000
AOS-CX Version : FL.10.04.0030

Time Zone          : UTC

Up Time            : 2 hours under a minute
CPU Util (%)       : 5
Memory Usage (%)   : 16
```

What is current Hostname? ____________________

What is Chassis serial number? ____________________

What is system base MAC address? ____________________

What is system Up Time? ____________________

28. Execute the "**list**" command.

```
6300# list
  show hostname
  show domain-name
  list
  configure { terminal }
  disable
  exit
  end
  page
  page <2-1000>
  no page
  show running-config
  show session-timeout
  start-shell
  auto-confirm
  no auto-confirm
```

```
  diagnostics
  no diagnostics
  show history {timestamp}
  repeat { id <A:1-500>|count <1-1000>|delay <1-1000> }
  show vrf
  show vrf VRF
  show dhcp client vendor-class-identifier
  show ztp information
 -- MORE --, next page: Space, next line: Enter, quit: q
```

What does the output display? ____

Important

"List" command shows the right syntax for all commands available at the current context along with their variants and extensions. This can be helpful for discovering new commands and previewing their different forms.

29. Execute the "**show version**" command.

```
6300# show version
-----------------------------------------------------------------------------
AOS-CX
(c) Copyright 2017-2019 Hewlett Packard Enterprise Development LP
-----------------------------------------------------------------------------
Version      : FL.10.04.0030
Build Date   : 2019-11-15 10:37:55 PST
Build ID     : AOS-CX:FL.10.04.0030:ff84f1ebd5b2:201911151752
Build SHA    : ff84f1ebd5b2765e65cc6de982b8ce8d16228050
Active Image : primary

Service OS Version : FL.01.05.0003
BIOS Version       : FL.01.0002
6300#
```

What main AOS-CX code version is running in the system?

30. Execute the "**show images**" command. ____________________

```
6300# show images
---------------------------------------------------------------------------
AOS-CX Primary Image
---------------------------------------------------------------------------
Version : FL.10.04.0030
Size    : 722 MB
Date    : 2019-11-15 10:37:55 PST
SHA-256 : abe5ec454be522ce6e3947db1c09fbdb2bfe72ae0447f5055ad592d
          adc422deb

---------------------------------------------------------------------------
AOS-CX Secondary Image
---------------------------------------------------------------------------
Version : FL.10.04.0030
Size    : 722 MB
Date    : 2019-11-15 10:37:55 PST
SHA-256 : abe5ec454be522ce6e3947db1c09fbdb2bfe72ae0447f5055ad592d
          adc422deb

Default Image : Primary

------------------------------------------------------
Management Module 1/1 (Active)
------------------------------------------------------
Active Image       : primary
Service OS Version : FL.01.05.0003
BIOS Version       : FL.01.0002

6300#
```

How many images does the system support? ____________________

What is the default image? ____________________

31. Execute the "**show capacities**" command (be prepared for a long output).

```
6300# show capacities
System Capacities:
Capacities                                                    Name
Value
------------------------------------------------------------------
                   ←---- output omitted ---→
Maximum number of entries in an Access Control List           8000
Maximum number of entries in a class                          1000
Maximum number of entries in an Object Group                    64
Maximum number of entries in a policy                          128
                   ←---- output omitted ---→
Maximum number of IP neighbors (IPv4+IPv6) that can be configured
on the system                                                49152
Maximum number of IP source lockdown bindings allowed on the system
16384
Maximum number of GRE IPv4, "IPv6 in IPv4" and "IPv6 in IPv6" tun-
nels in a system                                               127
Maximum number of IPv4 neighbors to hold in ARP cache before per-
forming garbage collection                                  262144
Maximum number of IPv4 neighbors that can be configured on the
system                                                       49152
Maximum number of IPv6 neighbors in hold in ARP cache before per-
forming garbage collection                                  131072
Maximum number of IPv6 neighbors that can be configured on the
system                                                       49152
Maximum number of L2 MAC addresses supported in the system
                                                             32768
Maximum number of L3 Groups for IP Tunnels and ECMP Groups
                                                              2047
```

```
Maximum number of L3 Destinations for Routes, Nexthops in Tunnels
and ECMP groups                                                 2045

Maximum number of configurable LAG ports                         256

Maximum number of members supported by a LAG port                  8

                  ←---- output omitted ---→

Maximum number of unique tunnel TTLs in a system                   4

Maximum number of routes (IPv4+IPv6) on the system             65536

Maximum number of IPv4 routes on the system                    65536

Maximum number of IPv6 routes on the system                    61440

Maximum number of VLANs supported in the system                 4094

Maximum number of VLAN Translation rules supported              4000

                  ←---- output omitted ---→
```

What is the maximum amount of access control entries per Access-list supported in the system?

____

What is the maximum amount of MAC addresses supported in the system? ______________

What is the maximum amount of IP routes (IPv4 and IPv6 combined) supported in the system?

____

What is the maximum amount of VLANs supported in the system? ______________

Tip

A similar command "**show capacities-status**" displays similar information plus the amount of resources/entries already consumed by the current device state.

32. Execute the "**show interface 1/1/1**" command.

Important

Output displays among many things, the interface state, interface type, current speed and duplex settings, MTU configured, port VLAN mode: access or trunk, and interface counters.

```
6300# show interface 1/1/1
Interface 1/1/1 is up
 Admin state is up
 Link transitions: 1
 Description:
 Hardware: Ethernet, MAC Address: 88:3a:30:98:30:27
 MTU 1500
Type 1GbT
 Full-duplex
qos trust none
 Speed 1000 Mb/s
 Auto-negotiation is on
 Flow-control: off
 Error-control: off
 MDI mode: MDIX
 VLAN Mode: access
 Access VLAN: 1
 Rx
           22 input packets            4695 bytes
            0 input error                22 dropped
            0 CRC/FCS
 Tx
           352 output packets          46087 bytes
             7 input error                 7 dropped
             0 collision
6300#
```

What is the interface type? ______________________________

33. Now try “show interface 1/1/28” command.

```
6300# show interface 1/1/28

Interface 1/1/28 is up

 Admin state is up

 Link transitions: 3

 Description:

 Hardware: Ethernet, MAC Address: 88:3a:30:98:30:0d

 MTU 1500

Type SFP+DAC1

 Full-duplex

qos trust none

 Speed 10000 Mb/s

 Auto-negotiation is off

 Flow-control: off

 Error-control: off

 VLAN Mode: access

 Access VLAN: 1

 Rx

        37775 input packets        5124978 bytes

            0 input error            40317 dropped

            0 CRC/FCS

 Tx

         2216 output packets        279307 bytes

           10 input error               10 dropped

            0 collision

6300#
```

What is the interface type? ____________________

Answer

Interfaces 1/1/25 to 1/1/28 in a 24 ports switch model and 1/1/49 to 1/1/52 in a 48 ports switch model are SPF+ 25Gig capable interfaces that support either transceivers or Direct Attached Cables (DACs). In this case port 28 has a 10Gig DAC attached.

34. Execute the "show interface transceiver" command.

```
6300# show interface transceiver
-----------------------------------------------------------------
Port      Type          Product   Serial            Part
                        Number    NumberNumber
-----------------------------------------------------------------
1/1/25    SFP+DAC1      J9281D    CN97KBZ55Y        8121-1300
1/1/26    SFP+DAC1      J9281D    CN97KBZ46K        8121-1300
1/1/27    SFP+DAC1      J9281D    CN94KBZ97T        8121-1300
1/1/28    SFP+DAC1      J9281D    CN94KBZ9RZ        8121-1300
```

Task 2: Configure Initial Settings

Objectives

In this task, you will explore the AOS-CX configuration script and make minor customization changes like setting a hostname, setting interface descriptions, and disabling unused ports. Also, you will ask the system to display the event log contents.

Steps

6300-A

1. Open a console connection to the 6300-A. Log in using **admin** and **no password**.
2. Issue the "**show running-config**" command to display the current configuration of the system.

Note

You will notice that most portions of the configuration are shown by listing the switch ports and their settings. The code version and actual admin account are listed first.

```
6300# show running-config
Current configuration:
!
!Version AOS-CX FL.10.04.0030
!export-password: default
user admin group administrators password ciphertext
AQBapRp8LdLe6JVQcygkkgkv/oylHnTJxLb0P2kWEByJaxIhYgAAAMYWl-
wysPrGTTG/dRu2WG5zqNV4OiNx7ZRZiyhYyJ1T0T4dW3yFaOcCbxCb4qVq1gdlHi
4qdcjN2ILQQyQi39b5rVsZSv1LjaoluZnvyvyZTC2+kN7fTKxxl16Nf8Fq6T+8I
!
!
ssh server vrf default
ssh server vrfmgmt
!
!
vlan 1
no spanning-tree
interface mgmt
   no shutdown
ipdhcp
interface 1/1/1
   no shutdown
   no routing
   vlan access 1
interface 1/1/2
   no shutdown
   no routing
   vlan access 1
                  ←---- output omitted ---→
interface 1/1/27
```

```
   no shutdown
   no routing
   vlan access 1
interface 1/1/28
   no shutdown
   no routing
   vlan access 1
interface vlan1
ipdhcp
https-server vrf default
https-server vrfmgmt
vsf member 1
   type jl668a
6300#
```

3. Move to configuration mode and change the switch's hostname to **T11- Access-1**.

```
6300#configure terminal
6300(config)# hostname T11-Access-1
```

4. Apply the console session timeout to 1 day (1440 minutes) to prevent a logout during the lab activities.

```
T11-Access-1(config)# session-timeout 1440
T11-Access-1(config)#
```

Tip
An alternative method you can use is the next configuration script:
T11-Access1(config)# **cli-session**
T11-Access1(config-cli-session)# **timeout1440**

5. T11-Access1(config-cli-session)# **exit.** Use "**show interface brief**" for displaying a table of ports and their more relevant settings.

What are the ports "Mode" values? ______________________________

What ports are enabled? ______________________________

```
T11-Access-1# show interface brief
------------------------------------------------------------------
Port       Native  Mode    Type            Enabled Status  Reason
Speed
(Mb/s)      VLAN
------------------------------------------------------------------
1/1/1     1      access 1GbT         yes    up      1000
1/1/2     1      access 1GbT         yes    down    1000
1/1/3     1      access 1GbT         yes    up      Waiting for link
1/1/4     1      access 1GbT         yes    down    Waiting for link
                   ←---- output omitted ---→
1/1/24    1      access 1GbT         yes    down    Waiting for link
1/1/25    1      access SFP+DAC1     yes    up      10000
1/1/26    1      access SFP+DAC1     yes    up      10000
1/1/27    1      access SFP+DAC1     yes    up      10000
1/1/28    1      access SFP+DAC1     yes    up      10000
vlan1     --     --                  yes    up
```

Note

6300 and 6400 AOS-CX switches have all their ports configured as layer-2 interfaces (VLAN and Spanning Tree capable) and are enabled by default vs 8300 switches that have administratively disabled routed ports.

6. Disable ports **1/1/2 to 1/1/28**.

```
T11-Access-1(config)# interface 1/1/2-1/1/28
T11-Access-1(config-if-<1/1/2-1/1/28>)# shutdown
T11-Access-1(config-if-<1/1/2-1/1/28>)# exit
```

7. Enable port **1/1/3**.

```
T11-Access-1(config)# interface 1/1/3
T11-Access-1(config-if)# no shutdown
T11-Access-1(config-if)# exit
```

8. Issue the "**show interface brief**" command again.

```
T11-Access-1(config)# show interface brief
------------------------------------------------------------------
Port   Native   Mode            Type   Enabled     Status    Reason
Speed VLAN
(Mb/s)
------------------------------------------------------------------
1/1/1     1     access   1GbT   yes    up     1000
1/1/2     1     access   1GbT   no     down   Administratively  down
1/1/3     1     access   1GbT   yes    up     1000
1/1/4     1     access   1GbT   no     down   Administratively  down
                    ←---- output omitted ---→
1/1/24    1     access   1GbT          no     down   Administratively
down
1/1/25    1     access   SFP+DAC1no    down     Administratively down
1/1/26    1     access   SFP+DAC1 no down     Administratively down
1/1/27    1     access   SFP+DAC1 no down     Administratively down
1/1/28    1     access   SFP+DAC1 no down     Administratively down
vlan1                yes        up
```

What is the Enabled and Status values of ports 1/1/27 and 1/1/28 now? ____________________

9. Display the "**event log**" in reverse mode.

```
T11-Access-1(config)# show events -r -n 10
---------------------------------------------------
Event logs from current boot
---------------------------------------------------
2020-01-08T20:23:22.656240+00:00 T11-Access-1 lldpd[2773]:
Event|106|LOG_INFO|MSTR|1|LLDP neighbor 88:3a:30:97:a4:40 deleted
on 1/1/28
2020-01-08T20:23:22.656240+00:00 T11-Access-1 lldpd[2773]:
Event|106|LOG_INFO|MSTR|1|LLDP neighbor 88:3a:30:97:a4:40 deleted
on 1/1/27
2020-01-08T20:23:11.652815+00:00 T11-Access-1 lldpd[2773]:
Event|106|LOG_INFO|MSTR|1|LLDP neighbor 90:20:c2:bc:26:00 deleted
on 1/1/26
2020-01-08T20:23:32.660046+00:00    T11-Access-1    lldpd[2773]:
Event|106|LOG_INFO|MSTR|1|LLDP neighbor 90:20:c2:bc:ee:00 deleted
on 1/1/27
2020-01-08T20:21:27.949674+00:00    T11-Access-1    intfd[715]:
Event|404|LOG_INFO|||Link status for interface 1/1/28 is down
2020-01-08T20:21:27.949674+00:00    T11-Access-1    intfd[715]:
Event|404|LOG_INFO|||Link status for interface 1/1/27 is down
2020-01-08T20:21:27.938854+00:00    T11-Access-1    intfd[715]:
Event|404|LOG_INFO|||Link status for interface 1/1/26 is down
2020-01-08T20:21:27.921704+00:00    T11-Access-1    intfd[715]:
Event|404|LOG_INFO|||Link status for interface 1/1/25 is down
2020-01-08T20:21:06.717715+00:00   T11-Access-1   hpe-restd[702]:
Event|4646|LOG_ERR|AMM|-|Aruba  Activate  server  https://devices-
v2.arubanetworks.com is not reachable through any supported VRF.
2020-01-08T20:16:06.716627+00:00      6300      hpe-restd[702]:
Event|4646|LOG_ERR|AMM|-|Aruba  Activate  server  https://devices-
v2.arubanetworks.com is not reachable through any supported VRF.
```

What link stats messages can you see at top related to 1/1/27 and 1/1/28 ports? ______________

What other messages in the event log do you get? ______________

Answer

You should see notifications informing you that LLDP neighbors have been deleted, because the ports have been disabled. Also,since AOS-CX switches periodically attempt to contact the Aruba Activate Cloud service and the switch has no internet connectivity the device complains that the service is unreachable.

10. Define interface descriptions for port **1/1/1** and **1/1/3**. Do not leave interface 1/1/3 yet.

```
T11-Access-1# configure terminal
T11-Access-1(config)# interface 1/1/1
T11-Access-1(config-if)# description TO_PC-1
T11-Access-1(config-if)# interface 1/1/3
T11-Access-1(config-if)# description TO_PC-3
T11-Access-1(config-if)#
```

11. Inside of interface 1/1/3 type the "**show running-config current-context**" command.

```
T11-Access-1(config-if)# show running-config current-context
interface 1/1/3
no shutdown
    description TO_PC-3
    no routing
    vlan access 1
    exit
```

Important

This command is a shortcut for displaying only the commands available at the context/subcontext level. Get used to it, since it is of great use when configuring and editing ports, protocols, access control lists, etcetera.

12. Run the "show interface 1/1/3" command followed by "include Description".

Note

The information will be filtered out, listingthe lines that include the "Description" string only, hence it is removing any other line part of that command's regular out.

```
T11-Access-1(config-if)# end
T11-Access-1# show interface 1/1/3 | include Description
Description: TO_PC-3
```

Notice

The pipe (|) command filters the output of show commands according to the criteria specified by the parameter include, exclude, count, begin, or redirect. Strings of characters that follow the filtering tool (for example, "Description" in command above) are case sensitive. Typing the wrong capitalization may lead to the absence of output.

13. Try the same command but use "**| begin 3 Interface**" instead.

Note

The information will be filtered out, listing only the lines that include the "Interface" string along with the 3 subsequent lines.

```
T11-Access-1#show interface 1/1/3 | begin 3 Interface
Interface 1/1/3 is up
 Admin state is up
 Link transitions: 1
 Description: TO_PC-3
T11-Access-1(config-if)# end
```

How was the output modified now? ______________________________

Task 3: Create and Explore Checkpoints.

Objectives

You have made some configuration changes in 6300-A. Now is a good time tokeep those changes stored in the system and protect them from any power cycle events. Next you will explore checkpoints, see how they are created, and make your own to save your progress.

Steps
Access-1

1. Open a console connection to **Access-1**.
2. Show the current system's checkpoints.

```
T11-Access-1# show checkpoint list
CPC20200108211347
CPC20200108212625
T11-Access-1#
```

How many entries did you get? ____________________

Important
AOS-CX systems are 100% database driven. This means that configuration scripts you save are stored in a local database instead of a regular configuration file. The database is periodically tracked and whenever the changes are made, they will be automatically stored after a 5-minute idle period. Any new configuration change, followed by a 5-minute idle period, will create a new checkpoint that can later be used to back up or restore the running configuration state of the system. On demand checkpoints can be generated by saving the runningconfiguration or creating custom checkpoints.

3. Issue the "**write memory**" command.

```
T11-Access-1# write memory
Configuration changes will take time to process, please be patient.
T11-Access-1#
```

4. List the checkpoints again.

```
T11-Access-1# show checkpoint list
CPC20200108211347
CPC20200108212625
startup-config
T11-Access-1#
```

Is there any new checkpoint? ____________________
What is its name? ____________________

5. Create a checkpoint called **Lab3** using the **running-configuration** as the source.

```
T11-Access-1# copy running-config checkpoint Lab3
Configuration changes will take time to process, please be patient.
T11-Access-1#
```

6. Display the checkpoints one more time.

```
T11-Access-1# show checkpoint list
CPC20200108211347
CPC20200108212625
startup-config
Lab3
```

7. Now make a checkpoint called **Lab3_final** using the **running-config** as the source.

```
T11-Access-1# copy running-config checkpoint Lab3_final
Configuration changes will take time to process, please be patient.
cannot create duplicate checkpoint, configuration already exists in
checkpoint Lab3
T11-Access-1#
```

What error message did you get? ____________________

Note
AOS-CX cannot have two different configuration snapshots with identical contents in its database (that would not be resource efficient). If you want to rename a checkpoint, then you will have to delete it first, and then create a new one.

8. Erase checkpoint Lab3.

```
T11-Access-1# erase checkpoint Lab3
```

9. Try creating the checkpoint again.

```
T11-Access-1# copy running-config checkpoint Lab3_final
Configuration changes will take time to process, please be patient.
T11-Access-1#
```

10. Last, issue the "**show checkpoint list all**" command.

```
T11-Access-1# show checkpoint list all
|NAME              |TYPE        |WRITER  |DATE(UTC)              |IMAGE
VERSION|
|CPC20200108211347  |checkpoint    |System    |2020-01-08T21:13:47Z
|FL.10.04.0030|
|CPC20200108212625|checkpoint     |System     |2020-01-08T21:26:25Z
|FL.10.04.0030|
|startup-config     |startup        |User        |2020-01-08T22:18:31Z
|FL.10.04.0030|
|Lab3_final   |latest   |User   |2020-01-08T22:28:33Z |FL.10.04.0030|
```

Important

You will see the same list of checkpoints along with more detailed data about them, like checkpoint type, user who created it, date and time it was created, and OS release that was running when they were created. Keeping track of when checkpoints are created is important during regular maintenance tasks. This is the reason configuring all switches with Network Time Protocol server is important. Since IP connectivity is not enabled yet, you will continue working without setting up an NTP server and trust the system clock for now. NTP configuration will be covered in a later Module.

```
T11-Access-1# copy checkpoint Lab3_final running-config
Configuration changes will take time to process, please be patient.
T11-Access-1#
```

Important

Checkpoints can be restored by using the copy command and applying the checkpoint's contents into the running-configuration (or startup configuration and invoking the "boot system" command), like in the example below.

```
T11-Access-1# copy checkpoint Lab3_final running-config
Configuration changes will take time to process, please be patient.
T11-Access-1#
```

You have completed Lab 3!

Learning Check

Chapter 3 Questions

Network Design

1. Which options below describe differences between 3-tier and 2-tier network designs?
   a. In a 3-tier design, the core must quickly respond to network changes.
   b. The 2-tier Access Layer must often provide PoE for end systems.
   c. The 2-tier distribution layer is less robust than a 3-tier design.
   d. A 3-tier design might be more scalable than a 2-tier design.

Switch Platforms

2. What are some advantages of a modular, chassis-based switch?
   a. They are more scalable.
   b. They tend to cost less.
   c. They use less power.
   d. They include optional PoE capabilities.
   e. They are more flexible.

Console Port

3. What kind of cables might you use to connect to an Aruba OS-CX Switch console port?
   a. Ethernet cable
   b. Fiber optic cable
   c. USB cable
   d. Serial cable

Getting Switch Information

4. Which command could you use to validate network connectivity for an AOS-CX switch?
   a. show running-config
   b. show system
   c. show interfaces brief
   d. show events
   e. show interface transceiver detail

Network Discovery

5. Which of the options below accurately describe network discovery commands or techniques?
   a. LLDP is a Layer-2 discovery protocol.
   b. You typically use the ping command to help document your network.
   c. If the ping or traceroute command fails, you know that you have a connectivity issue.
   d. The ping command leverages ICMP echo requests and echo replies.
   e. It is best to use LLDP after your network documentation is complete.

4 VLANs

EXAM OBJECTIVES

- ✓ Compare and describe collision and broadcast domains
- ✓ Describe and configure VLANs
- ✓ Explain 802.1Q tagging and
- ✓ Configure trunk ports
- ✓ Describe MAC address and ARP forwarding tables
- ✓ Describe the frame delivery process

Overview

This chapter is intended to improve your understanding of vital Layer-2 switch concepts, which will speed your journey toward mastery of Layer-2 network design, deployment, configuration, and troubleshooting.

First you will learn about Layer-2 collision domains and broadcast domains, which is important for both your theoretical knowledge and your practical ability to improve network performance. Then you will learn about VLANs and how vital they are to create scalable, flexible, and secure networks. Related concepts include switch ports, Switch Virtual Interfaces (SVI), and physical routed ports. You will turn this theoretical knowledge to practical use by learning how to configure all these entities.

You will learn about some potential limitations of VLANs and how they are eliminated with the 802.1Q trunking protocol. With this knowledge and configuration ability, you will be able to extend the VLAN concept across multiple physical switches.

With such an ability to create larger, more scalable networks comes a need to understand forwarding tables, including the MAC address table that is built by Layer-2 switches and the ARP cache, which is maintained by both end systems, Layer-2 switches, and Layer-3 routers.

Armed with this prerequisite knowledge, you will be ready to explore a typical scenario of two devices communicating over a network. This will unite the earlier information from this module into a real-world scenario. You will see the interaction of Layer-2 frame addressing, VLANs, 802.1Q, the MAC address table, and the ARP cache. In the Lab activity you will create a couple of VLANs and you will configure a trunk port to expand the VLAN concept across different switches. Finally, you will explore the MAC address table.

Domains

Collision Domains

Suppose that Alice and Bob are having a conversion. Alice has something to say, but her ears detect that Bob is speaking, so she politely waits her turn.

If Alice and Bob happen to speak at the same time (Figure 4-1), the sound of their voices collide, making it difficult to understand. Alice and Bob realize what is happening and stop. Bob says, "I'm sorry, please go ahead and speak." Alice says, "No, please you go ahead." They both back off, and then try again.

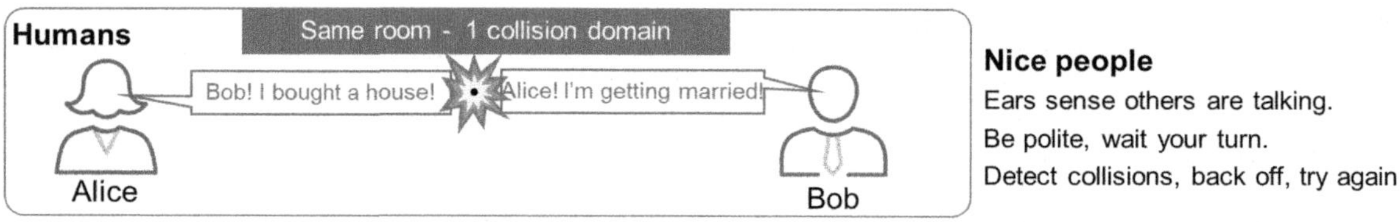

Figure 4-1 Collision Domain Scenario 1

Ethernet is similar in that only one Ethernet host on a particular segment may transmit at a time. This is all controlled by an algorithm running on all Ethernet NICs called Carrier Sense Multiple Access/Collision Detection (CSMA/CD). This works very much like humans, as described above.

Multiple humans can be in the same small room and all of them can access the airwaves and speak any time they want; it is a Multi-access system, like Ethernet. Before speaking however, a polite human first listens to sense if others are currently speaking, this is like Ethernet's Carrier Sense mechanism. Ethernet cards sense the state of a "carrier signal" that indicates a currently transmitting NIC.

If two devices transmit at the same time (Figure 4-2), the electrical signals collide and become corrupted. This is called a collision. This condition is detected, and each station backs off and tries again. This is like when Alice and Bob both start talking at the same time, realize what is happening, and stop. Bob says, "I'm sorry, please go ahead and speak." Alice says, "No, please you go ahead." They both back off, and then try again.

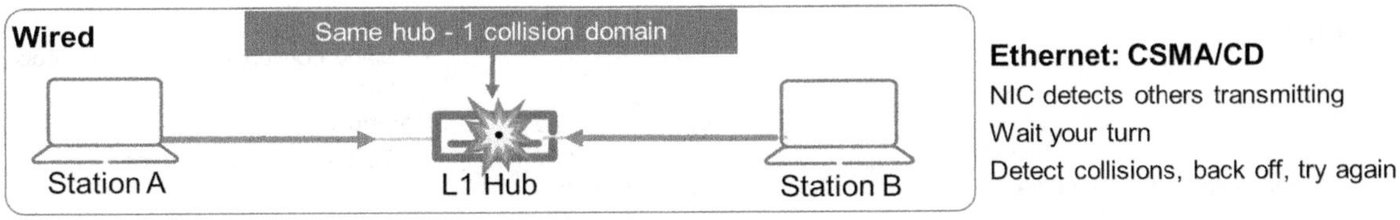

Figure 4-2 Collision Domain Scenario 2

Ethernet collisions occur when a **hub** is deployed in networks. A hub is a Layer-1 device that receives digital 1s and 0s, and repeats them, near instantaneously, out all other ports. Therefore, a hub is also known as a multi-port repeater. All 16 devices connected to a 16-port hub are in the same collision domain, if one device transmits, 15 other devices must wait. If two hosts transmit at the same time, a collision occurs, everyone backs off, waits a few milliseconds, and tries again.

Thankfully, hubs are outdated devices that are no longer used. These unintelligent, Layer-1 repeaters have been replaced by intelligent Layer-2 switches. For a properly deployed and configured switch under normal circumstances, collisions do not occur on Layer-2 switches.

Similarly, Wi-Fi uses an algorithm called Carrier Sense Multiple Access/Collision Avoidance (CSMA/CA). This works very much like Ethernet's CSMA/CD, only it adds additional mechanisms to pre-emptively avoid collisions (Figure 4-3).

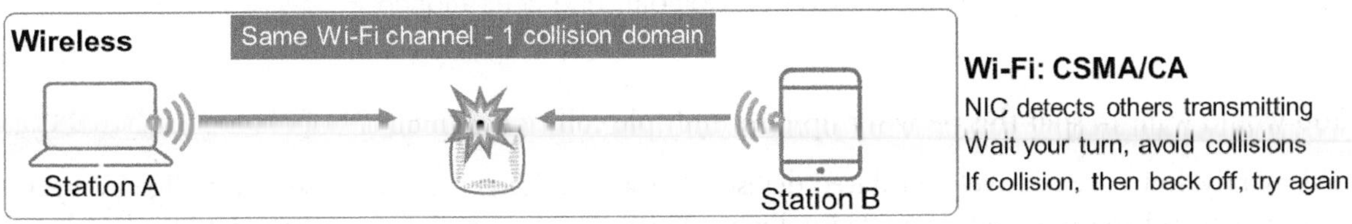

Figure 4-3 Collision Domain Scenario 3

Everyone attached to the same wireless Access Point (AP) channel is in the same collision domain. Therefore, only one of them may transmit at a time.

Collision Domains and Performance

Your understanding of collision domains enables you to optimize network performance.

Consider the humans. With only two people in the room, conversation is quick, easy, and efficient. Then there are 8…10…50 people in the room.

Multiple conversations occur, causing distractions and "collisions" (people talking at the same time).

Figure 4-4 Collision Domains and Performance 1

You may want to split people off into different rooms to improve communications and prevent people from having to wait too long (Figure 4-4).

Suppose that you have an Ethernet hub with 8 connected devices (Figure 4-5). While one host transmits, seven hosts must wait their turn. If you had a 48-port hub, then 47 hosts must wait. Imagine the performance impact!

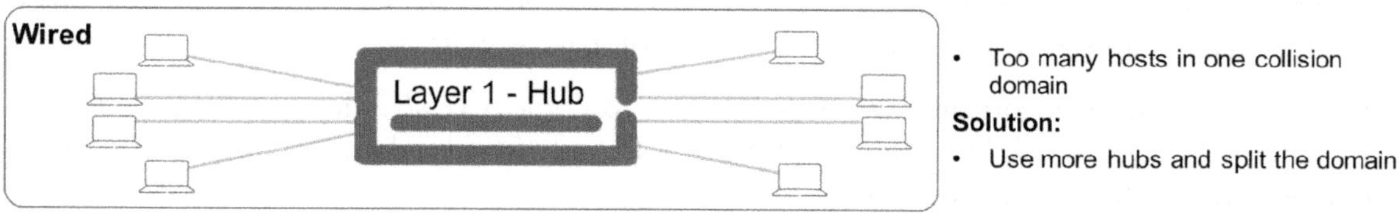

Figure 4-5 Collision Domains and Performance 2

You would want to split this network up into multiple collision domains.

Thankfully, hubs are relatively outdated devises that are no longer used. These unintelligent, layer-1 repeaters have been replaced by more intelligent Layer-2 switches. For a properly deployed and configured switch under normal circumstances, collisions do not occur on Layer-2 switches.

Similarly, consider 1 AP, with transmit power set to maximum. This increases its coverage area, such that it can service all 75 people in the room. This is nice, because you save money, you provided coverage for everyone with a single AP. However, while 1 host transmits, 74 people must wait. People complain that wireless is slow. Nobody is happy (Figure 4-6).

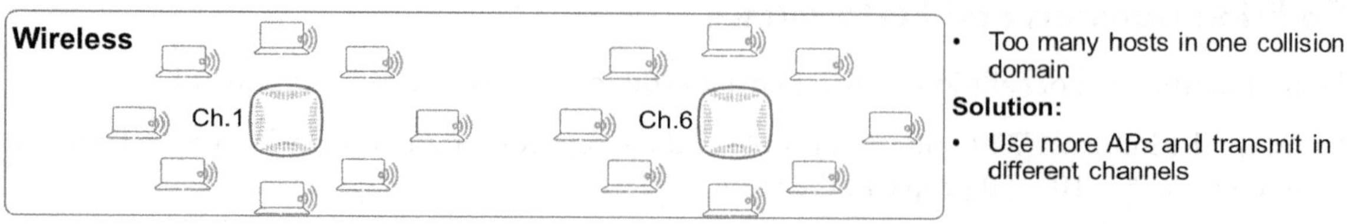

Figure 4-6 Collision Domains and Performance 3

To resolve the issue, you purchase more APs, set their transmit power much lower, and set each to a unique channel. Now about 25 people are connected to each AP, and each is a different collision domain. Now three people can transmit at a time, and performance is greatly improved. Most good wireless engineers add more APs and reduce their power, such that only 10-25 people connect. This can drastically increase performance.

Broadcast Domains

A broadcast domain is simply a group of devices that are on the same network, capable of receiving and responding to a broadcast frame from any device.

Recall that Module 1 introduced a **broadcast** as a type of communication where a single device contacts all other devices. A broadcast message uses a special Layer-2 MAC address: **FF:FF:FF:FF:FF:FF** and a special Layer-3 IPv4 address: **255.255.255.255**.

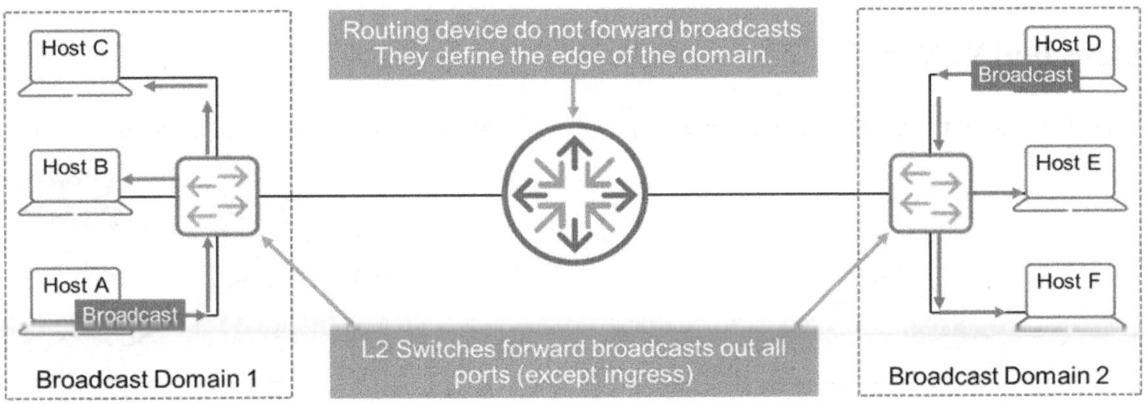

Figure 4-7 Broadcast Domains

In Figure 4-7, Host A transmits a broadcast address. Perhaps it is saying, "Hey everyone! Who has IP address 10.1.1.1?" Because switch SW1 forwards this out all other ports, hosts B and C receive the message. Of course, nobody in broadcast domain 2 receives the message – they are not even connected!

Similarly, when Host D sends a broadcast, all hosts in domain 2 receive it, and nobody in domain 1 receives it.

But now suppose that you want to connect these two networks into an internetwork. Do you recall what type of device does this? The answer is a Layer-3 device such a router. Now the two networks are connected. However, unlike Layer-2 switches, Layer-3 routers do not forward broadcasts. In other words, they define the edge of the broadcast domain. Thus, broadcast traffic travels exactly as before; all domain 1 hosts receive broadcasts from domain 1, but not from domain 2, and vice versa. Of course, now that they are connected, all devices can communicate with unicast or multicast traffic.

But why not simplify this network? Eliminate the router, and simply connect all hosts together on a single network and in a single broadcast domain. You save money because there is no need to purchase a router.

As with collision domains, large broadcast domains cause performance issues. For unicast traffic, from Host A to Host F, only those two stations must fully process packets. However, with broadcast frames, all stations must process the traffic. Switches must forward, or flood broadcast frames out all ports (except the ingress port). This can increase utilization on switches and increase bandwidth utilization. The result is every switch link must carry every broadcast. Hackers might even write programs to generate millions of broadcast packets and flood the network, leaving no resources for valid traffic. This is called a Denial of Service (DoS) attack. Smaller broadcast domains mean better performance.

Virtual LAN

LANs and VLANs

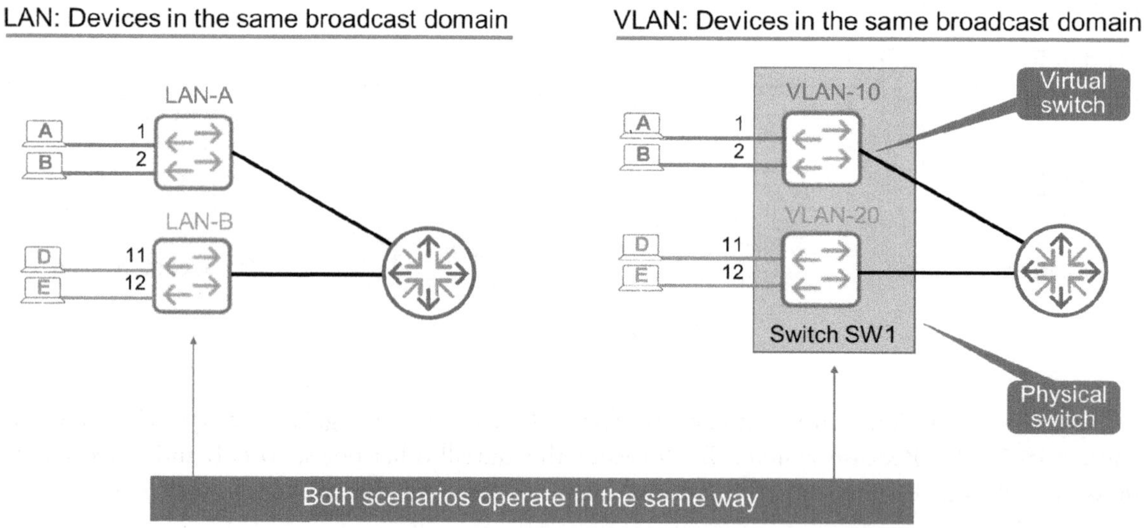

Figure 4-8 LANs and VLANs

Recall that if a switch receives a broadcast on any port, it floods it out all other ports, except the ingress port. Therefore, if Host A in Figure 4-8 sends a broadcast, the LAN-A switch forwards it out all other ports and so host B receives the frame. Of course, hosts D and E do not receive this frame, there is no connection between LAN-A and LAN-B. They are physically separate LANs, connected to physically separate switches.

What if you wanted to connect these three Local Area Networks into an Internetwork?

Simply add a router, which can route unicast and multicast traffic between the LANs.

Now consider a Virtual LAN (VLAN), which is, just like a physical LAN, a group of devices in the same broadcast domain. Suppose that you have a single, physical Aruba switch named SW1.

In Figure 4-8, hosts A to E connect to ports 1, 2, 11, and 12 on this switch. By default, all these devices are in the same broadcast domain. If Host A sends a broadcast, all other hosts receive the frame. Now suppose that you learned some new switch syntax, and created a Virtual LAN named "VLAN10."

It is as if you have created a small virtual switch, inside the physical switch. This virtual switch exists, but it is not connected to any of the physical switch ports.

Therefore, you can define or "map" physical ports 1 and 2 as being members of the red VLAN 10.

Similarly, you create VLAN20, and assign ports 11 and 12 as members of the blue VLAN 20.

You have now created two separate broadcast domains on a single physical switch. When host A sends a broadcast, the switch knows to only forward that frame out all ports that are in the same VLAN, except the ingress port. Only host B receives the broadcast. If host D broadcasts, only E receives it.

You have effectively recreated the scenario on the left, using a single physical switch. Just like the physical scenario on the left, there is NO connectivity between the separate VLANs. No unicast, multicast, nor broadcast traffic shall pass between the VLANs.

Of course, you could always connect a router to create an internetwork, just like you did with the physical switches.

But if the scenarios operate in the same way, why bother with VLANs? Let us talk about the advantages of VLANs and learn some new syntax.

VLAN Creation

AOS-CX refers to VLANs by their VLAN-ID, a number between 1 and 4094. In AOS-CX VLAN 1 is created by default and cannot be removed. By default, all ports are members of this VLAN. This is a common default for many switches. The VLAN command creates a VLAN, which is enabled by default.

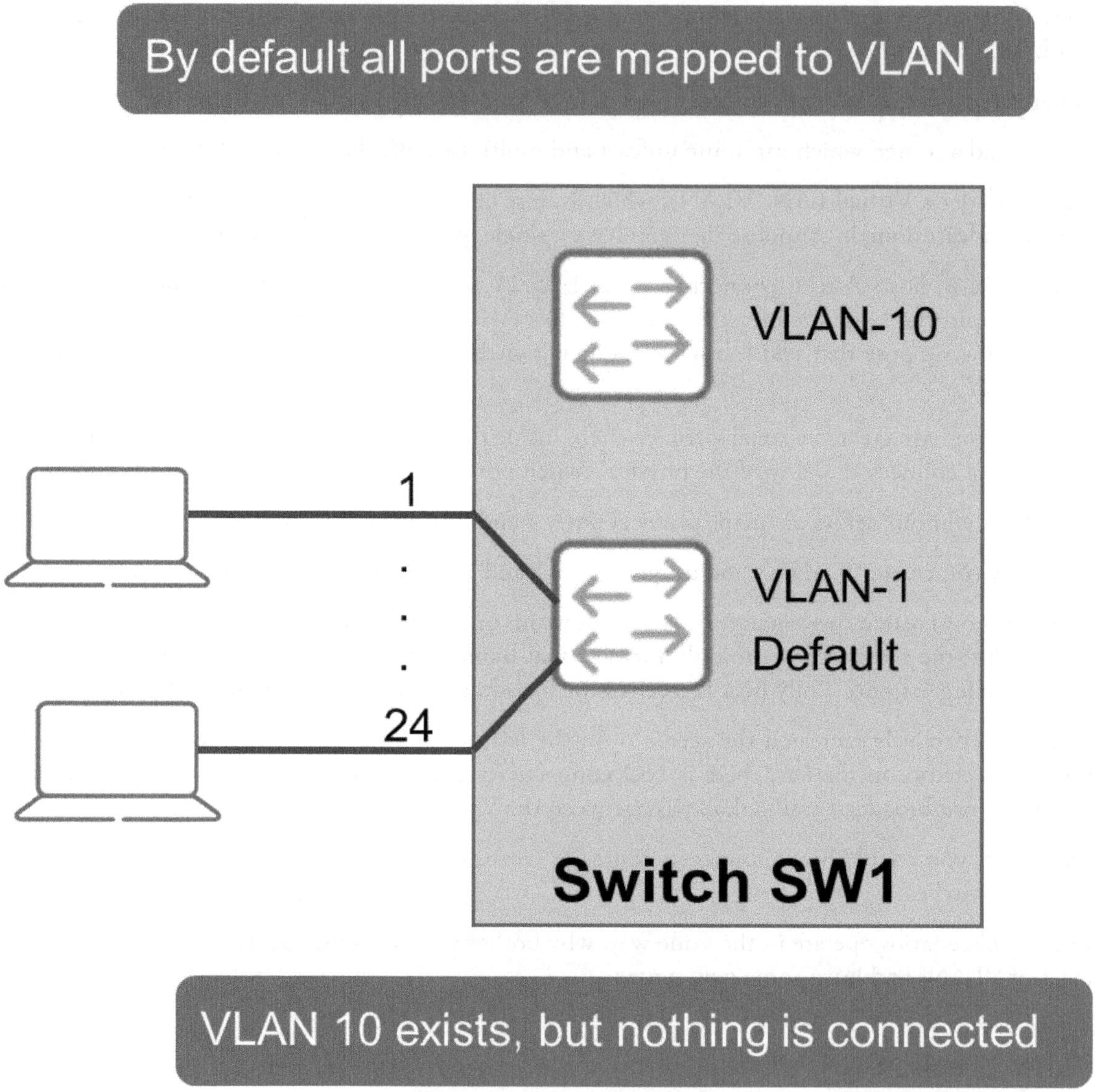

Figure 4-9 VLAN Creation

In the Figure 4-9 example above, you can create VLAN 10:

```
SW1(config)# VLAN 10
SW1(config-VLAN-10)#
```

You can also create a series of VLANs with a single command:

```
SW1(config)# VLAN 2-5,10
```

To remove the VLAN, use the command no VLAN 10:

```
SW1(config)# no VLAN 10
```

Or, instead of deleting it, you could use the shutdown command to disable the VLAN:

```
SW1(config)# VLAN 10
SW1(config-VLAN-10)# shutdown
```

It is also a good idea to name the VLAN, as shown in the figure, with the name command:

```
SW1(config)# VLAN 10
SW1(config-VLAN-10)# name Sales
```

Remember, when you use the command VLAN 10 to create a VLAN, it is as if you have created a virtual switch inside of the actual, physical switch. Although it exists, no ports have yet been defined as members of this VLAN. No devices are yet attached to this virtual switch, as shown in the figure. The next thing you probably want to do is associate or "map" physical interfaces as members of the VLAN.

Access Ports

Figure 4-10 shows SW1, with four connected devices, all in VLAN 1 by default.

- You define VLAN 10, name Sales.
- You define VLAN 20, name Service.

```
SW1(config)# vlan 10
SW1(config-vlan-10)# name Sales
SW1(config-vlan-10)# exit
SW1(config)# vlan 20
SW1(config-vlan-20)# name Service
SW1(config-vlan-20)# exit
```

```
SW1(config)# interface 1/1/1-1/1/2
SW1(config-if-<1/1/1-1/1/2)# vlan access 10
SW1(config-if-<1/1/1-1/1/2)# exit
SW1(config)# interface 1/1/11-1/1/12
SW1(config-if-<1/1/4-1/1/5)# vlan access 20
SW1(config-if-<1/1/4-1/1/5)# exit
```

```
SW1# show vlan
-----------------------------------------------------------------------
VLAN   Name             Status   Reason   Type      Interfaces
-----------------------------------------------------------------------
1      DEFAULT_VLAN_1   up       ok       default   <output omitted>
10     Sales            up       ok       static    1/1/1-1/1/2
20     Service          up       ok       static    1/1/11-1/1/12
```

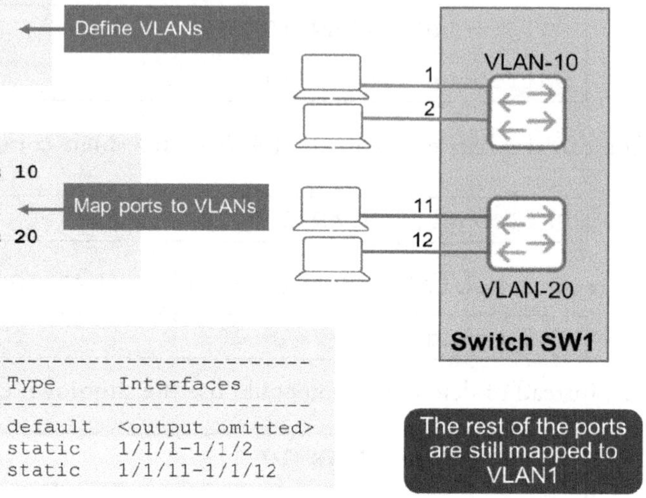

Figure 4-10 Access Ports

Now you need to assign or "map" ports to these VLANs.

From the global configuration context, you choose to configure a range of interfaces at the same time: ports 1/1/1 through 1/1/2. Then you assign these ports to VLAN 10 as shown.

You repeat these steps for ports 1/1/11–12, as shown.

Understand that only one VLAN ID can be assigned to an interface. Therefore interface 1/1/1 cannot be a member of both VLAN 10 and VLAN 20 at the same time. This would be like you trying to be in the sales room for a meeting and in the engineering room for another meeting at the same time.

Use the **show VLAN** command to verify VLAN creation and mapping.

AOS-CX 6300 series interfaces are Layer-2 by default; those other AOS-CX switches areLayer-3. To convert these interfaces to Layer-2 mode, use the command "no routing."

802.1Q

Extending VLAN Across Multiple Switches

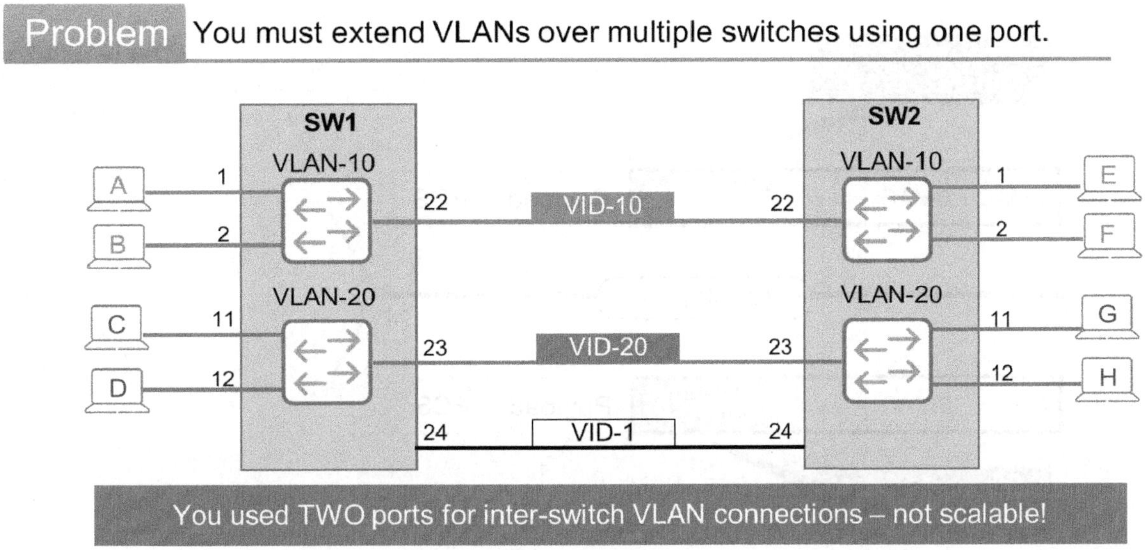

Figure 4-11 Extend VLANs

Figure 4-11 shows two switches, each with ports in VLANs 10 and 20.

Now you want to connect these two switches, so you connect port 24 of SW1 to port 24 of SW2. What happens? Will all devices be able to communicate?

Recall that by default ports are members of VLAN1, including port 24 on both switches. This means that port 24 is not connected to VLANs 10 and 20, and so cannot carry that traffic. Effectively, you still do not have connectivity between the switches for VLANs 10 and 20. How can we fix this?

One way is to connect two more pairs of ports.

Map port 22 on both switches to VLAN 10, and port 23 as to VLAN 20. Now all VLANs can communicate. A broadcast from host A is flooded out all ports in VLAN 10 (except ingress port), and so all members of VLAN 10 receive the broadcast. This is good, but there is a problem.

You used up two physical ports on each switch. What if we had 100 VLANs? We would need 100 physical switch ports just for interconnects, that is not feasible.

We need a way to use one single physical port to connect multiple VLANs.

Solution: 802.1Q Tagging

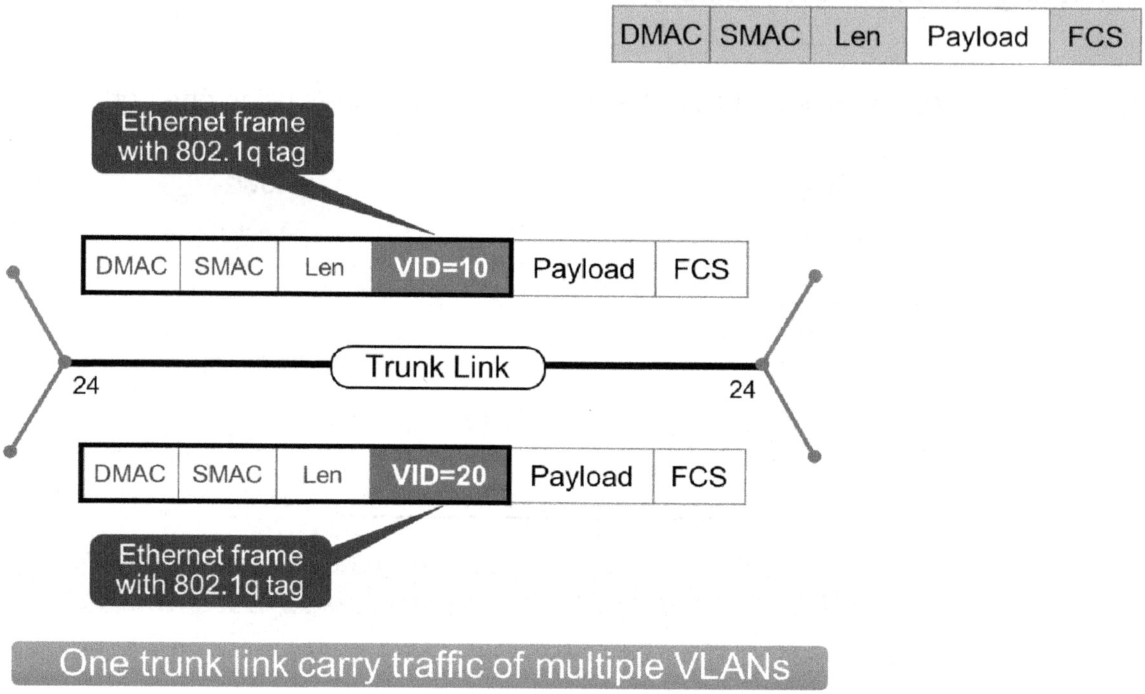

Figure 4-12 802.1Q Tagging

Look at the standard Ethernet frame shown in the diagram (Figure 4-12). Suppose that this was a broadcast frame from host A, that flooded out all ports in VLAN 10, including port 24. There is no field in this frame to inform receiving switches about the intended destination VLAN. If SW2 could talk, it might ask, "What do I do with this? Is this for VLAN 10? VLAN 20? VLAN1?"

We need a tagging mechanism, as defined in the IEEE 802.1Q standard. This standard adds an additional field between the length and payload fields, the 802.1Q Tag field. The most important part of this field is the VLAN tag or VLAN-ID or simply VID. Before SW1 floods this broadcast frame across this specially defined "trunk port", it adds this tag to the frame.

Thus, SW2 receives the frame, looks at the tag, and knows, "Ahhh! This frame is for VLAN 10." It strips off the special tag, and forwards a standard Ethernet frame out all ports in VLAN 10, to hosts E and F.

Next host G sends a broadcast. SW2 floods a standard Ethernet frame out its local ports. Before flooding the frame out port 24, it is a tag, "This frame is for VLAN 20." SW1 receives this frame, sees that it is for VLAN 20, strips off the tag, and forwards a standard Ethernet frame out all ports in VLAN 20 (11 and 12).

Thus, you can now extend the VLAN concept across multiple switches, using a single physical port.

802.1Q Tagging

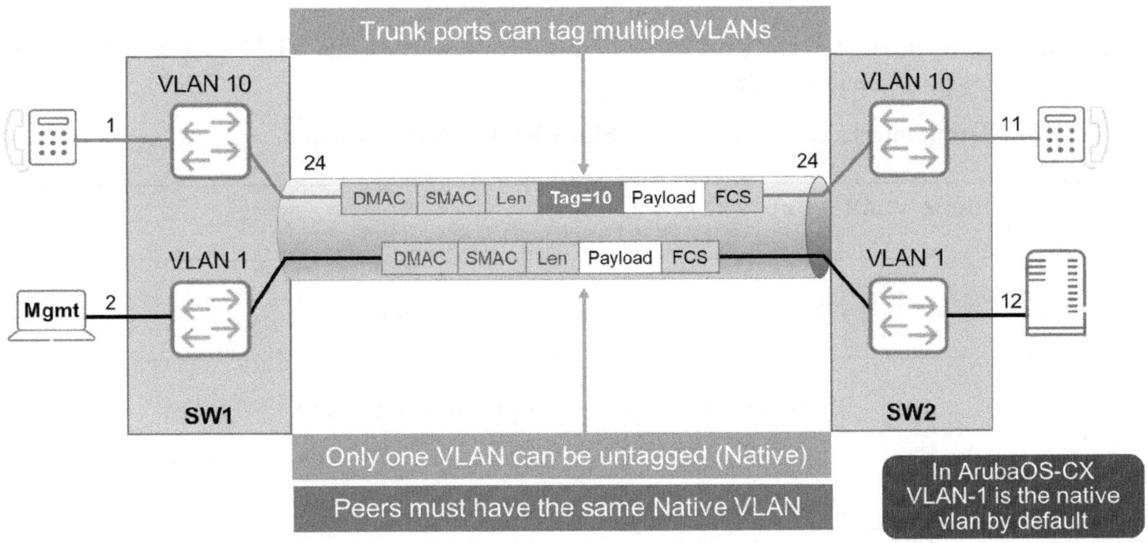

Figure 4-13 802.1Q Tagging

The 802.1q standard allows administrators to select a single VLAN on which no tag or VID is included in the Layer-2 header. This means that a standard, untagged Ethernet frame is sent out of the port. This VLAN is known as the Native VLAN or Untagged VLAN. By default, in AOS-CX VLAN 1 is considered the native VLAN. You can modify this by using **VLANTrunkNative <VLAN-ID>** command. To avoid inconsistencies, it is recommended that the same Native VLAN is used in both peers (Figure 4-13).

Note

The VLAN-ID field is 12-bits long; this length allows a switch to carry traffic up to 4094 VLANs.

Configure VLAN Trunks: Allowed VLANs

In AOS-CX, use the command **VLAN Trunk Allow** to allow a VLAN-ID to traverse a trunk interface. Multiple VLAN-IDs can be assigned to a trunk interface. In this example, interface 1/1/25 is configured as a trunk link, and only allows VLANs 1, 10, and 20. Other VLANs shall not traverse this link:

```
SW1(config)# interface 1/1/24
SW1(config-if)#VLAN trunk allow 1,10,20
```

This example is focused on Trunk port configuration. It is assumed that VLANs are already configured, and access ports are mapped to them.

To verify the Trunk interface, you can use the **Show VLAN Port** command:

```
SW1# Show VLAN Port 1/1/24
--------------------------------------------------------------------
VLAN          Name                        Mode                 Mapping
--------------------------------------------------------------------
1               DEFAULT_VLAN_1       native-untagged     port
10              Sales                trunk               port
20              Service              trunk               port
```

Configure VLAN Trunks—Native VLAN

Recall that by default, all VLAN traffic is tagged to traverse a trunk link except the native VLAN, which defaults to VLAN 1. However, you can change the native VLAN as desired. Note that peers must have the same Native VLAN. As in the example, use the **VLAN Trunk native** command to change the untagged VLAN, to 10 in this case:

```
SW1(config)# interface 1/1/24
SW1(config-if)# VLAN Trunk native 10
```

This configuration must match on both switches, so be sure to apply this command to the appropriate port of the attached switch.

This is a good opportunity to remember earlier lessons. You can use the "show LLDP neighbor-info" command to see which switch is connected to port 1/1/24 of the switch you are currently configuring.

Verify your efforts with the command **Show VLAN Port**:

```
SW1# Show VLAN Port 1/1/24
--------------------------------------------------------------------
VLAN          Name                  Mode                   Mapping
```

```
-------------------------------------------------------------------
1                   DEFAULT_VLAN_1     trunk               port
10                  Sales              native-untagged     port
20                  Service            trunk               port
```

Forwarding Tables

MAC Address Table

Layer-2 switches use the MAC address table to make forwarding decisions. The switch builds this table automatically, based on the source MAC addresses of the frames that it receives from connected devices. How?

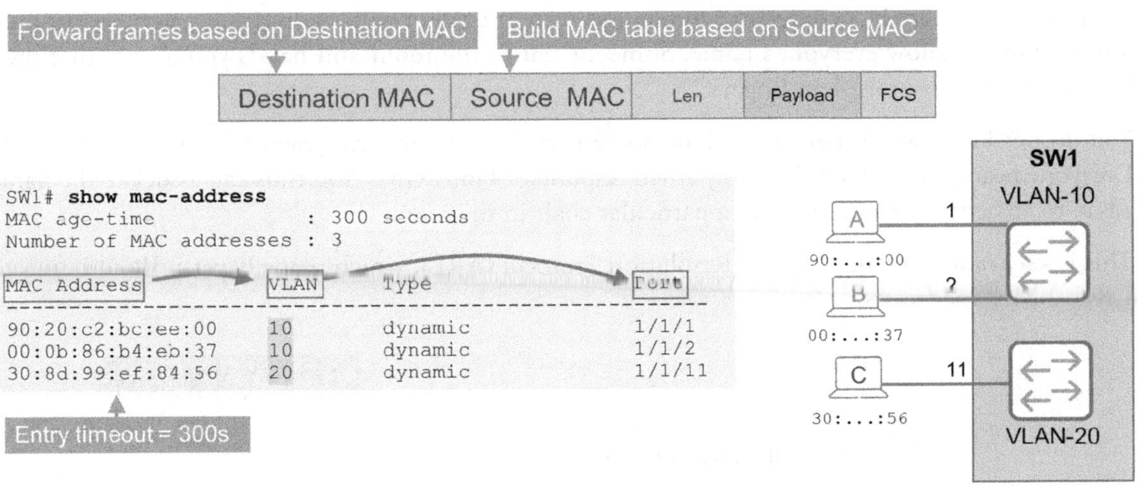

Figure 4-14 MAC Address Table

Suppose that you power up switch SW1. Its MAC address table is blank. You see this here in the **show mac-address** output in Figure 4-14.

Then Host A transmits a frame to Host B. Switch 1 receives this frame with source MAC address = 90:...:00 on Port 1, defined as being a member of VLAN 10.

Thus, it adds the top entry to the MAC address table, as shown in the figure.

It maps the MAC address to its VLAN and port.

Suppose that at this point there are no other entries in the table. The switch does not yet know where to forward frames to destination 00:...:37, so it floods this frame out all ports in VLAN 10. All

VLAN 10 hosts receive this frame and see the destination MAC address, "This is not for me", and they discard the frame. Except for Host B, "This is my MAC address, I will respond."

And so Host B responds to Host A with source MAC = 00:...:37, and destination MAC = 90:...:00.

Now the switch adds the second entry you see in the table MAC 00:0b:86:b4:eb:37 is in VLAN 10, connected to port 2.

A similar process will happen with host C on port 11.

So, switches automatically build the MAC table based on source MAC addresses, and forward frames based on destination MAC addresses.

By default, table entries are maintained for 300 seconds (5 minutes). You can verify the MAC address table in ArubaOS-CX using the **show mac-address** command.

Address Resolution Protocol (ARP)

Imagine that you are in a conference room, leading a discussion with people that you have just met. You do not yet know everyone's name. Someone enters the room and hands you a note that says, "Important message for Alvin Rogers."

You do not know which person is Alvin, so you say, "Excuse me everyone. Who is Alvin Rogers?" Everyone hears your request, but only Alvin responds, "I'm Alvin." You thus can associate the name Alvin to an actual person, seated at a particular chair in the room.

This is very much like the Address Resolution Protocol (ARP), which maps Layer-3 IP addresses to Layer-2 MAC addresses.

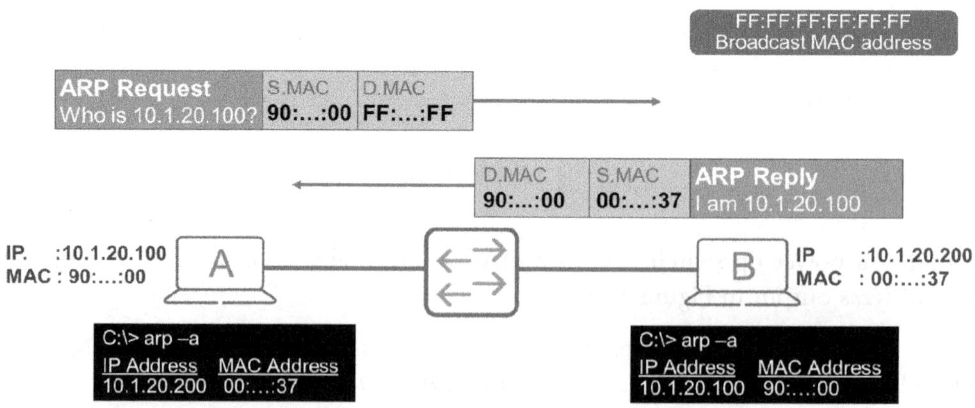

Figure 4-15 Address Resolution Protocol (ARP)

In Figure 4-15, Host A knows that it must communicate with the host at IP address 10.1.20.200. To do this it must build an Ethernet frame, which requires its own source MAC address (90::00), and Host B's destination MAC address, which it does not yet know.

To learn it, Host A broadcasts an ARP request, destination MAC address ff:ff:ff:ff:ff:ff. (In the IP header, the destination IP address is 255.255.255.255). You know that switches forward broadcasts out all ports in the same VLAN (except for ingress port). Thus, all hosts in the VLAN receive this frame and ignore it, "I'm not 10.1.20.200."

Except for Host B, which responds with an ARP reply, unicast to Host A's MAC address, "I am 10.1.20.200 and my MAC address is 00::37."

Host A receives this reply and creates an entry in its ARP table, sometimes called an ARP cache. It maps 10.1.20.200 to 00:0b:86:b4:eb:37. Thus, the next time Host A must communicate with Host B, it need not use ARP.

Also know that when Host B received the ARP request from host A, it learned about Host A's MAC address and IP address. Thus, Host B creates an entry in its ARP table, mapping 10.1.20.100 to MAC address 90:20:c2:bc:ee:00.

On a Windows PC's command prompt, use the command **arp –a** to see which IP addresses have been resolved to a MAC address.

Frame Delivery

Frame Delivery Overview

In this section you will learn how two devices in the same VLAN communicate across multiple switches. In this scenario, the user on PC-1 wants to establish an FTP session to download a file from PC-2 (Figure 4-16).

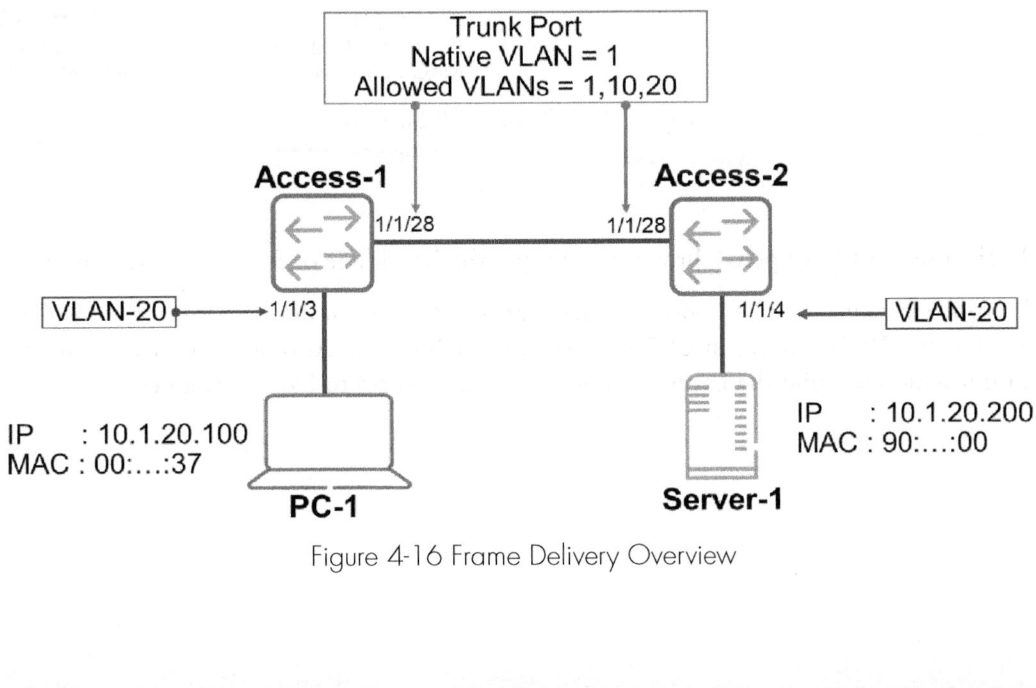

Figure 4-16 Frame Delivery Overview

The scenario is as follows:

- PC-1 and Server1 are correctly configured with an IP address.
- Both switches are configured with 3 VLANs: 1, 10, and 20.
- The switch-to-switch links are configured as trunk ports allowing VLANs 1, 10, and 20, and the Native VLAN = 1.
- Port 1/1/3 on Access-1 switch and Port 1/1/4 on Access-2 switch are mapped to VLAN=20.
- PC-1 has not initiated any previous communication to Server-1.

Initiate FTP Session

Layer 2 Header		Layer 3 Header		Layer 4 Header		Layer 5-7 Header	L2T
S-MAC	D-MAC	S-IP	D-IP	S-Port	D-Port	FTP GET	CRC
00:...:37	?	10.1.20.100	10.1.20.200	23561	21	Get **file.txt** from 10.1.20.200	

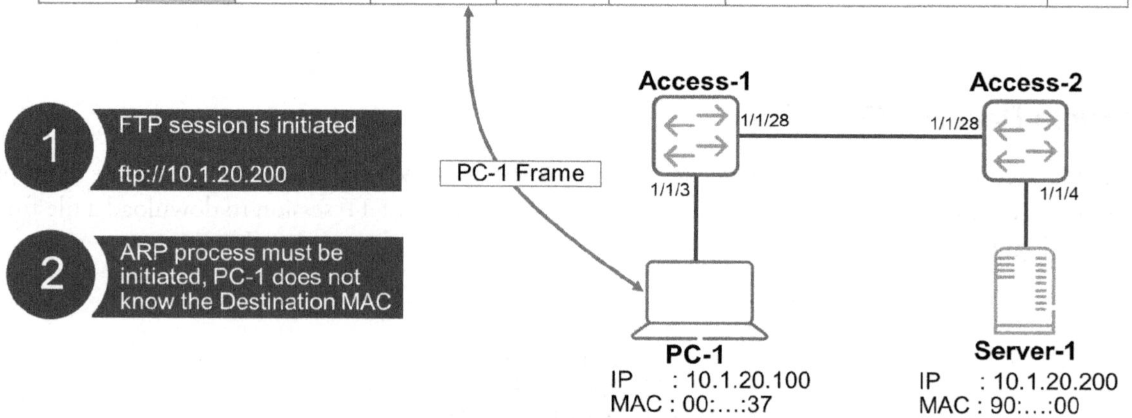

Figure 4-17 Initiate FTP Session

Step 1: The user on PC-1 opens a browser and types the IP address of Server-1 as ftp://10.1.20.200.

Step 2: Notice that even if PC-1 knows the Destination IP address it does not know the MAC address associated to this IP. Therefore, an ARP process must be initiated. Also notice that PC-1 has the rest of the information to build the Layer-2 frame including Layer-3 to Layer-7 (Figure 4-17).

ARP Request

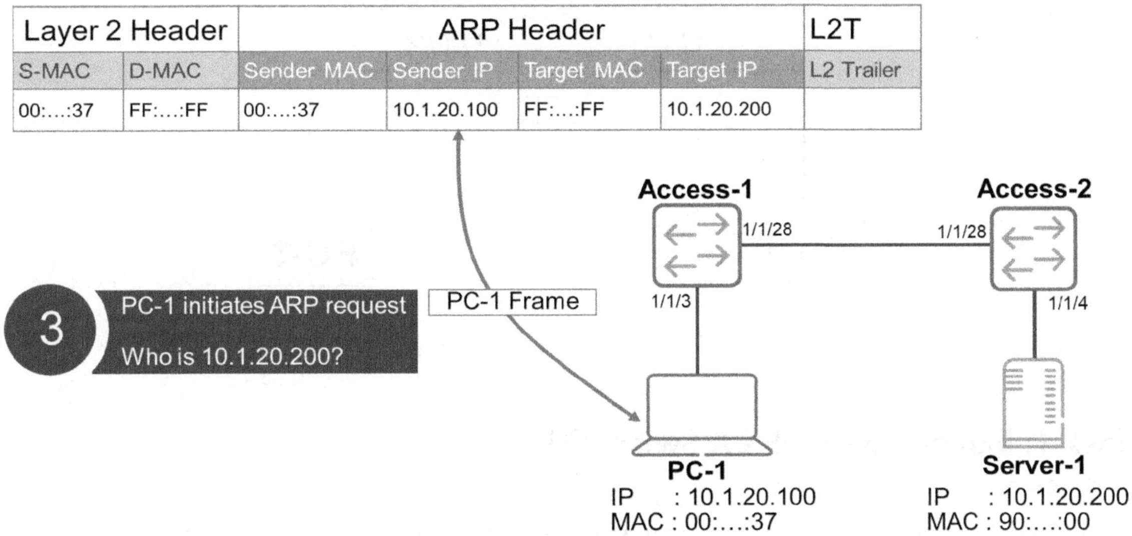

Figure 4-18 ARP Request

Step 3: PC-1 generates an **ARP request**. Notice that the ARP request has a Layer-2 broadcast destination MAC address (FF:FF:FF:FF:FF:FF) (Figure 4-18).

Lab 4.1: Configure a VLAN

Overview

At this point the Access-1 switch is up and running and ready for configuration. The next task in your initial network deployment will be to place wired EMPLOYEES in a custom VLAN to enable inter-user communication (Figure 4-19).

Note: References to equipment and commands are taken from Aruba's hosted remote lab. These are shown for demonstration purposes in case you wish to replicate the environment and tasks on your own equipment.

Objectives

After completing this lab, you will be able to:

- Create a custom VLAN and assign it to access ports
- Configure clients with static IP addresses
- Explore the Switch MAC address table

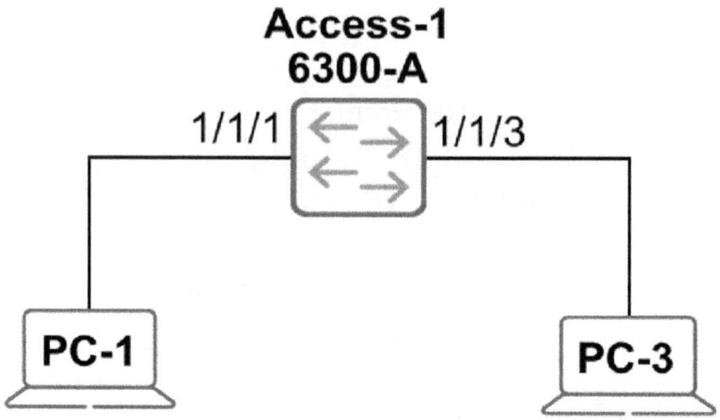

Figure 4-19 Lab Topology

Task 1: Explore the AOS-CX Switch CLI

Objectives

In this task you will create the employee VLAN and configure Windows PCs with IP addresses of the corresponding IP segment according to the network design. Then you will verify IP connectivity between clients and explore the MAC address table.

Steps

Access-1

1. Open a console connection to Access-1. Log in with **admin** and no password.
2. Use the **Show VLAN** command to display current Virtual Local Area Networks configured in the switch. You should only see VLAN 1 assigned to all ports. This is the default setting for the switch.

```
T11-Access-1# show VLAN

---------------------------------------------------------------------------

--------------

VLAN   Name                        Status   Reason                     Type
Interfaces

---------------------------------------------------------------------------

1      DEFAULT_VLAN_1             up       ok                      default
1/1/1-1/1/28

T11-Access-1#
```

3. Create **VLAN 1111** and name its**EMPLOYEES**.

```
T11-Access-1# configure terminal
T11-Access-1(config)# VLAN1111
T11-Access-1(config-VLAN-1111)# name EMPLOYEES
T11-Access-1(config-VLAN-1111)# exit
```

4. Repeat the show VLAN command.

```
T11-Access-1(config)# Show VLAN
--------------------------------------------------------------------------------
--------------
VLAN  Name                          Status  Reason                    Type
Interfaces
--------------------------------------------------------------------------------
--------------
1     DEFAULT_VLAN_1                up      ok                        default
1/1/1-1/1/28
1111  EMPLOYEES                     down    no_member port  static
T11-Access-1(config)#
```

Is the output reflecting your previous configuration change? ____________

What is the newly created VLAN status? ____________

What caused the new VLAN to have this status? ____________

Answer

Since the VLAN has not been assigned to any enabled physical port, the status is down. No MAC address learning process is happening in the switch for that VLAN.

5. Assign **VLAN 1111** to interfaces **1/1/1** and **1/1/3** as an access VLAN.

```
T11-Access-1(config)# interface 1/1/1
T11-Access-1(config-if)# VLAN access 1111
T11-Access-1(config-if)# interface 1/1/3
T11-Access-1(config-if)# VLAN access 1111
T11-Access-1(config-if)# exit
```

6. Try the "**Show VLAN**" command again.

```
T11-Access-1(config)# Show VLAN
--------------------------------------------------------------------------------

--------------
VLAN   Name                          Status   Reason                     Type
Interfaces
--------------------------------------------------------------------------------

--------------
1      DEFAULT_VLAN_1              down     no_member_forwarding  default
1/1/2,1/1/4-1/1/28
1111   EMPLOYEES                     up       ok                       static
1/1/1,1/1/3
T11-Access-1(config)#
```

What is the VLAN1111 status now? ______________________________

Note

Currently, only ports 1/1/1 and 1/1/2 are UP. When you replaced VLAN 1 with VLAN 1111 on the ports, both VLANs will still appear, but VLAN 1 is no longer associated with any port in the UP state. Therefore, VLAN 1's status was changed to down.

7. Issue the "**Show VLAN Port 1/1/1**" command.

```
T11-Access-1(config)# Show VLAN Port 1/1/1
--------------------------------------------------------------------------------
VLAN   Name                                   Mode          Mapping
--------------------------------------------------------------------------------
1111   EMPLOYEES                              access        port
T11-Access-1(config)#
```

What VLAN is present on the interface and what is its mode? ______________________________

8. Use the "**Show VLAN Summary**" command. This command shows the VLAN count in the system.

```
T11-Access-1(config)# Show VLAN Summary
Number of existing VLANs: 2
Number of static VLANs:   2
Number of dynamic VLANs:  0
```

9. Issue the "**show interface 1/1/1**" command. You will be able to see VLAN ID and VLAN Mode at the bottom of the command.

```
T11-Access-1(config)# show interface 1/1/1
Interface 1/1/1 is up
  Admin state is up
  Link transitions: 1t
  Description: TO_PC-1
  Hardware: Ethernet, MAC Address: 88:3a:30:98:30:27
  MTU 1500
  Type 1GbT
Full-duplex
  qos trust none
  Speed 1000 Mb/s
  Auto-negotiation is on
  Flow-control: off
  Error-control: off
  MDI mode: MDIX
VLAN Mode: access
  Access VLAN: 1111
```

10. Finally, try the "**show interface brief**" command followed by a filtering option "**begin 5 Port**."

Note
The information will be filtered out, listing only the lines that include the "Port" string along with the 5 subsequent lines.

```
T11-Access-1(config)# show interface brief | begin 5 Port
Port   Native      Mode  Type  Enabled     Status    Reason    Speed
          VLAN                                                   (Mb/s)
----------------------------------------------------------------------
1/1/1 1111   access      1GbT  yes         up                   1000
1/1/2 1      access      1GbT  no     down Administratively down --
1/1/3 1111   access      1GbT  yes         up                   1000
T11-Access-1(config)#
```

Note
The pipe (|) command filters the output of show commands according to the criteria specified by the parameter include, exclude, count, begin, or redirect.

What is the value under Native VLAN for ports 1/1/1 and 1/1/3 vs 1/1/2? ____________________

Task 2: Explore MAC Address Table

Objectives

In this second task, you will statically define IP addresses to PC-1 and PC-2, so they can achieve intra VLAN layer-3 connectivity, and users on those machines can start collaborating to run their company's daily operations.

Steps

PC-1

1. Access PC-1's console.
2. Under search field in the task bar, type **control panel**. Windows will automatically display all items matching the string.
3. Click the top result (**Control Panel**). A new window will pop up (Figure 4-20).

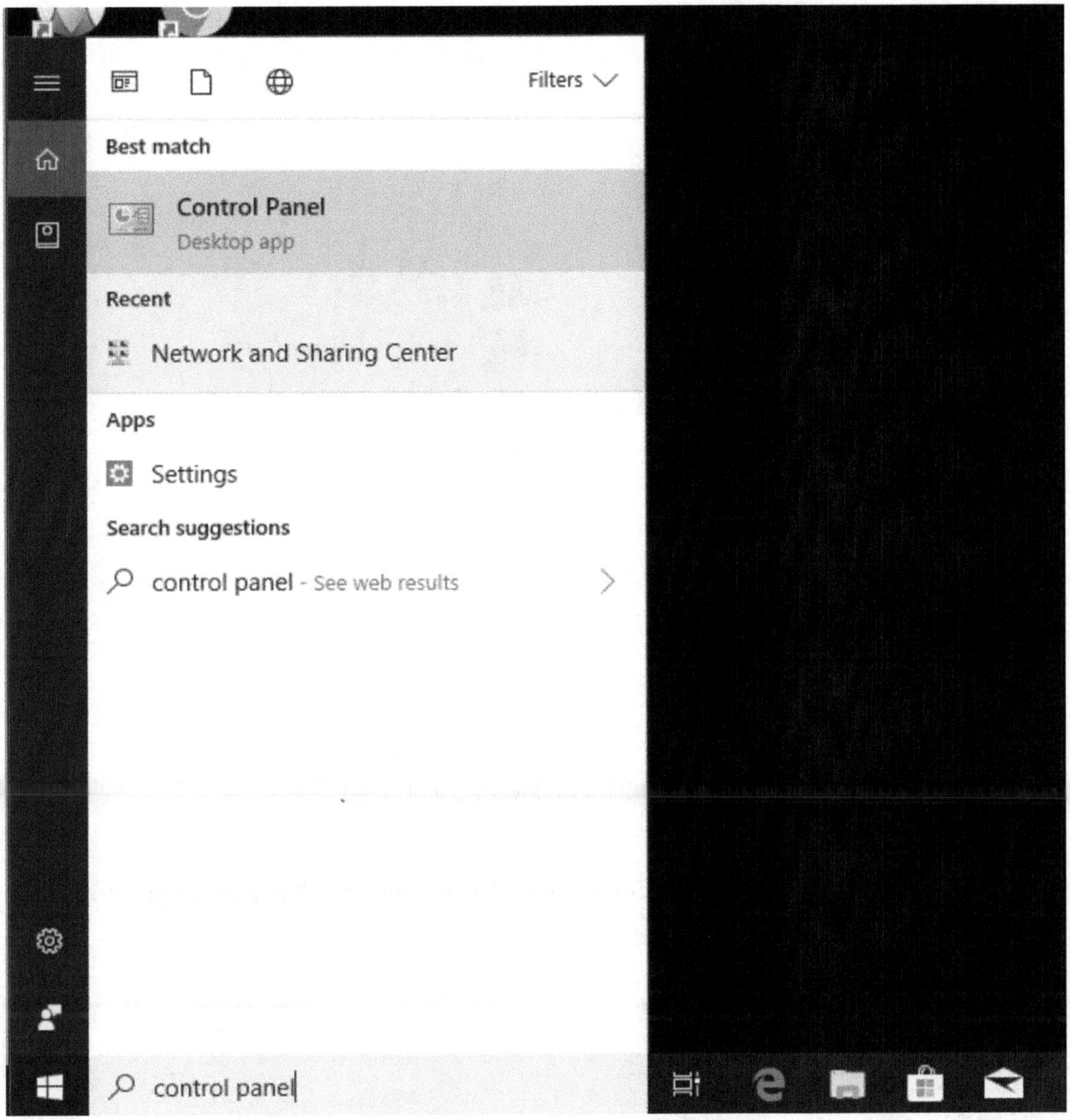

Figure 4-20 Windows Search

4. In Control Panel, click "**View network status and tasks**" under Network and Internet (Figure 4-21).

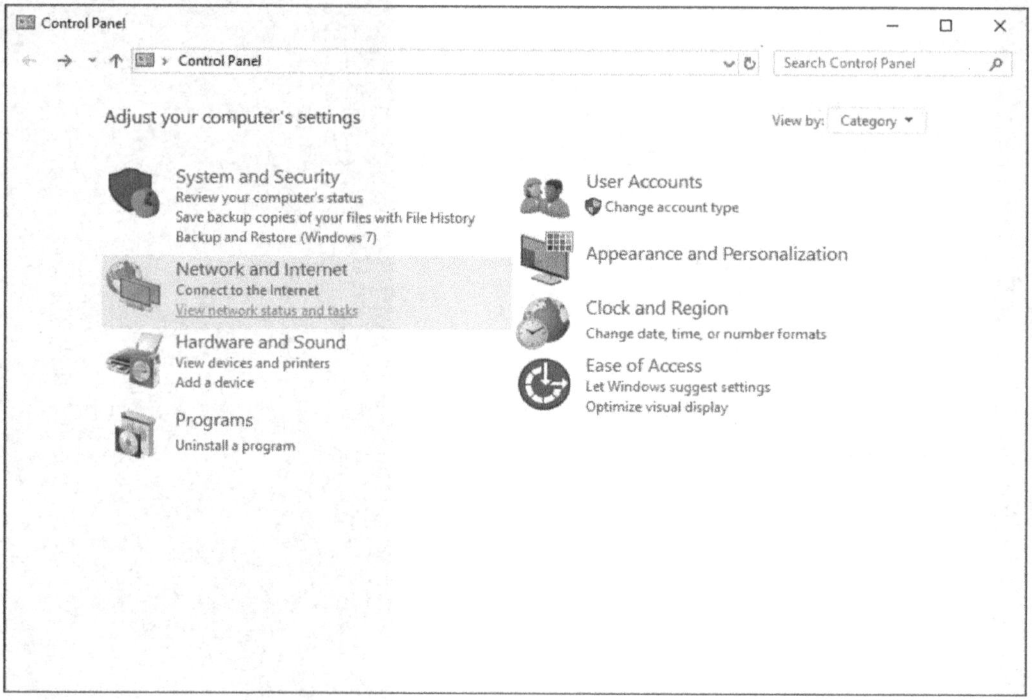

Figure 4-21 Windows Control Panel

5. Click **Lab NIC** under Access type Connections. A new window will pop up (Figure 4-22).

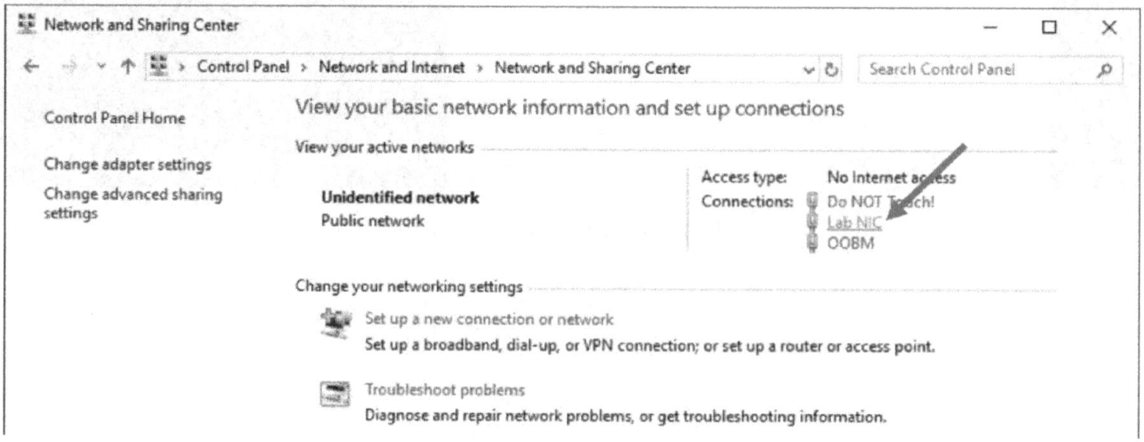

Figure 4-22 Network and Sharing Center

6. In Lab NIC status window, click **Properties** button (Figure 4-23).

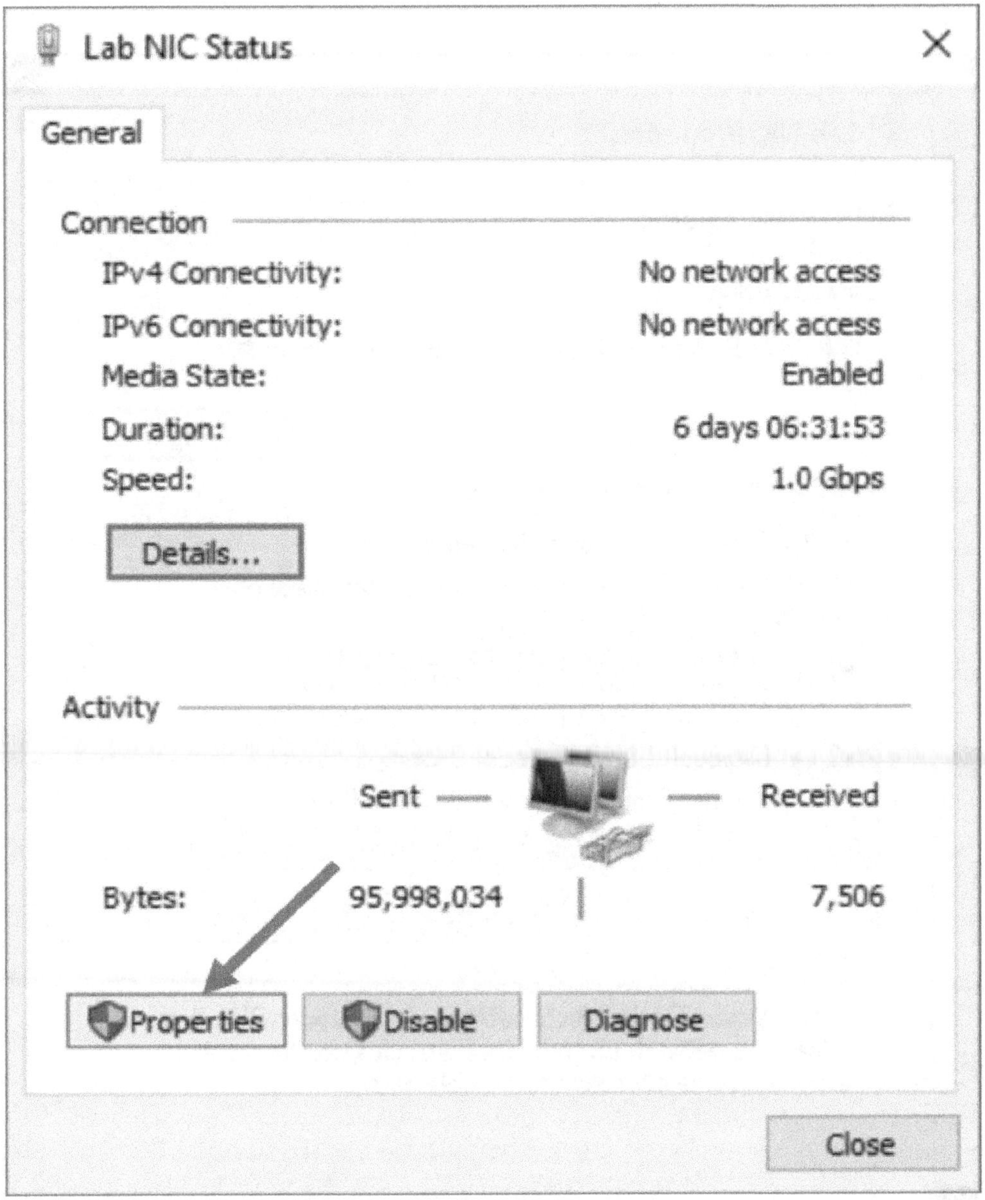

Figure 4-23 Lab NIC Status

7. In Lab NIC Properties section, select **Internet Protocol Version 4 (TCP/IPv4)**, then click **Properties** button (Figure 4-24).

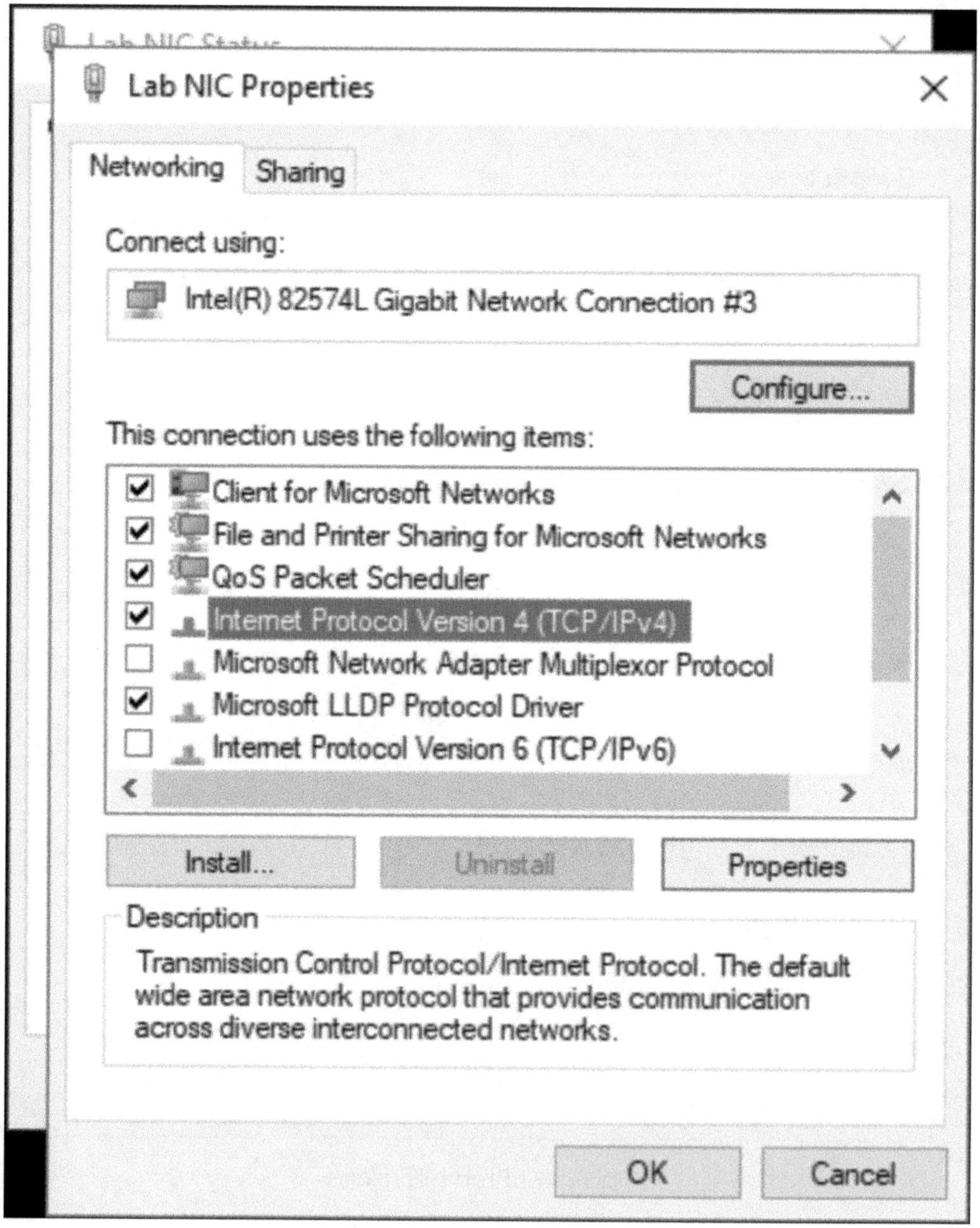

Figure 4-24 Lab NIC Properties

8. In Internet Protocol Version 4 (TCP/IPv4) Properties, choose "**Use the following IP address:**" under General tab.
9. Type **10.11.11.101** and **255.255.255.0** under IP address and Subnet mask, respectively (Figure 4-25).

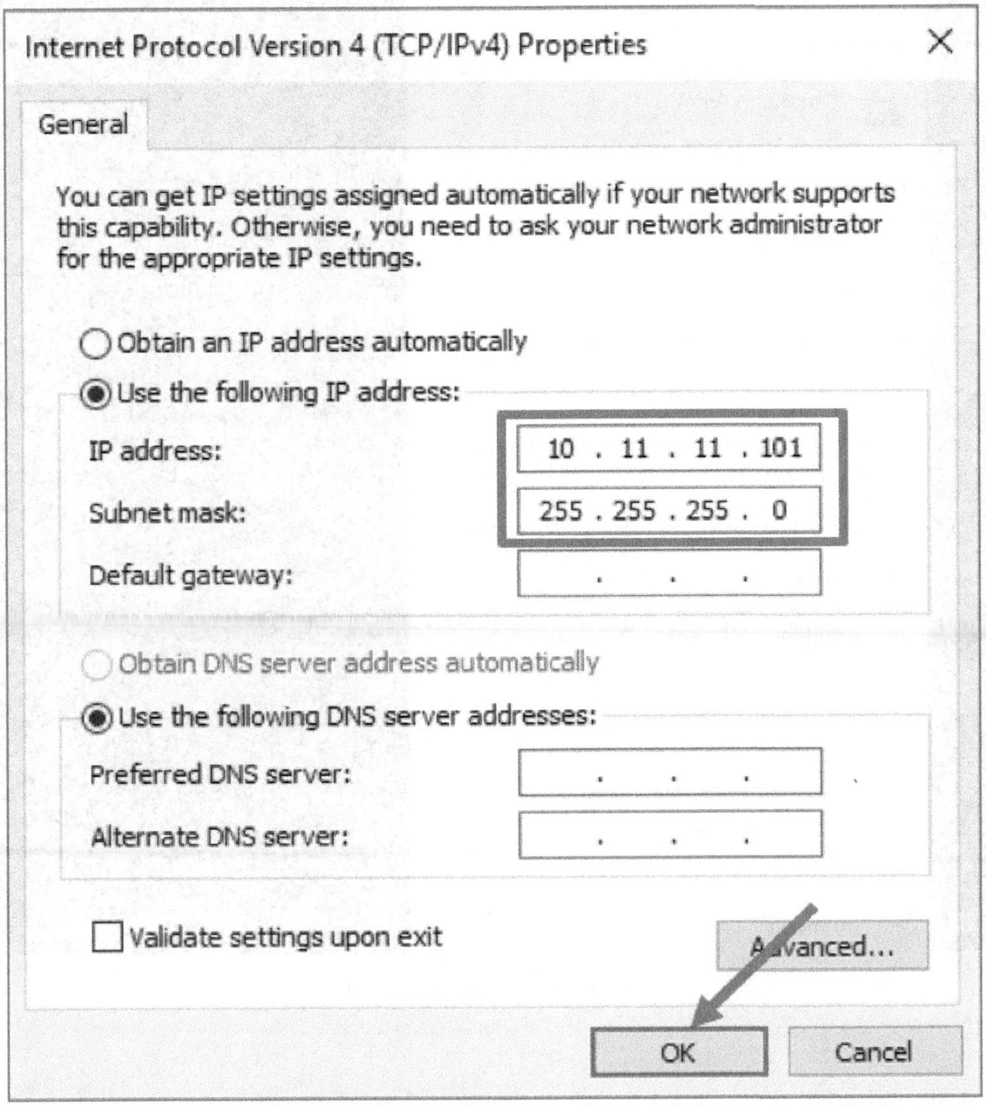

Figure 4-25 Internet Protocol Version 4 Properties

10. Click **OK** button, then **Close** button twice.
11. Under search field in the task bar, type **command**. Windows will automatically display all items matching the string (Figure 4-26).

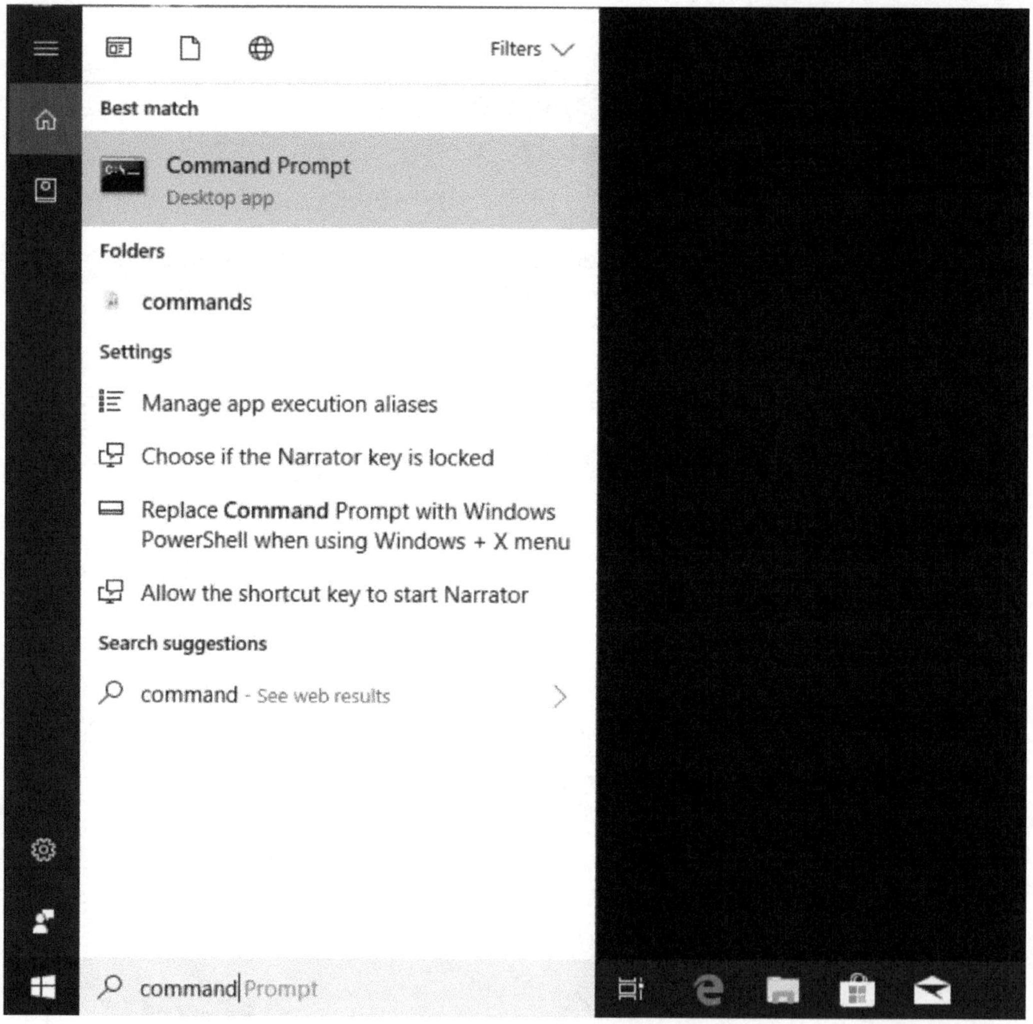

Figure 4-26 Windows Search 2

12. Click the top result (**Command Prompt**). A new window will pop up.
13. Type **ipconfig** and hit **[Enter].** This command will display IPv4 settings of all NICs in the system.
14. Confirm the Ethernet adapter called Lab NIC has the IPv4 address you just configured (Figure 4-27).

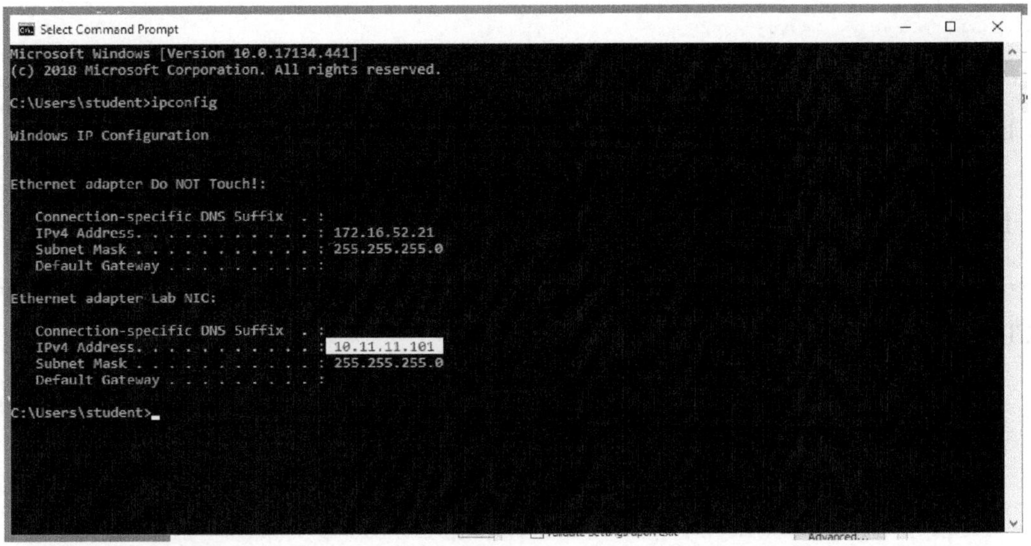

Figure 4-27 Ipconfig

15. Type **ipconfig -all** version of the command and hit **[Enter].** This command displays additional information like DNS servers, IP addresses (if configured), and the NICs physical address (MAC) (Figure 4-28).

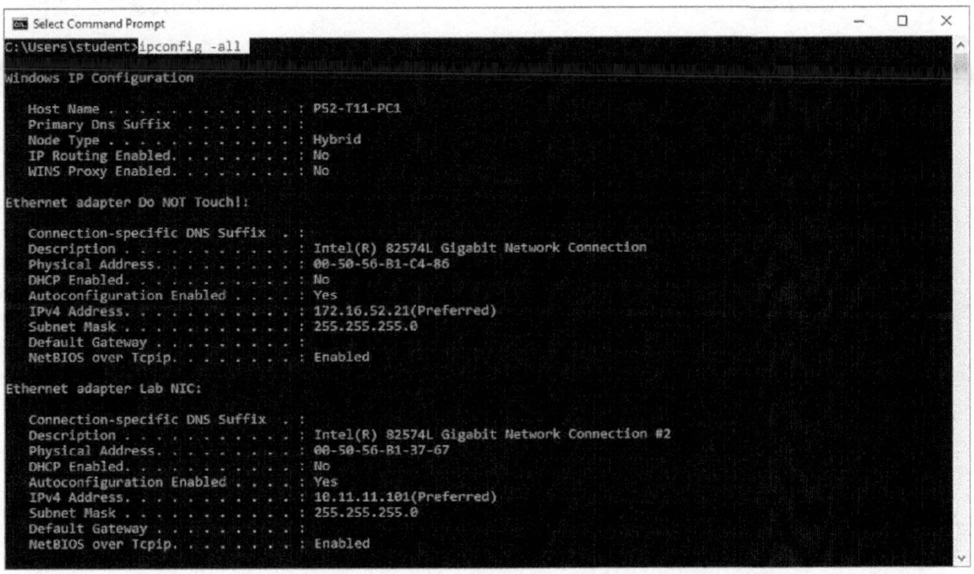

Figure 4-28 Command: ipconfigall

What is PC-1's Lab NIC MAC address? ______________________________

This is the typical IP address configuration process in a Windows system. You will now repeat it on PC-3.

PC-3

16. Access PC-3's consoleand repeat steps 2 to 10 using **10.11.11.103** IP address instead.
17. Click **OOBM** under Access type Connections. A new window will pop up.

Notice
If in your lab environment, PC-3 does not have this NIC; then move to step 19.

---

18. Click "**Disable**" button (Figure 4-29).

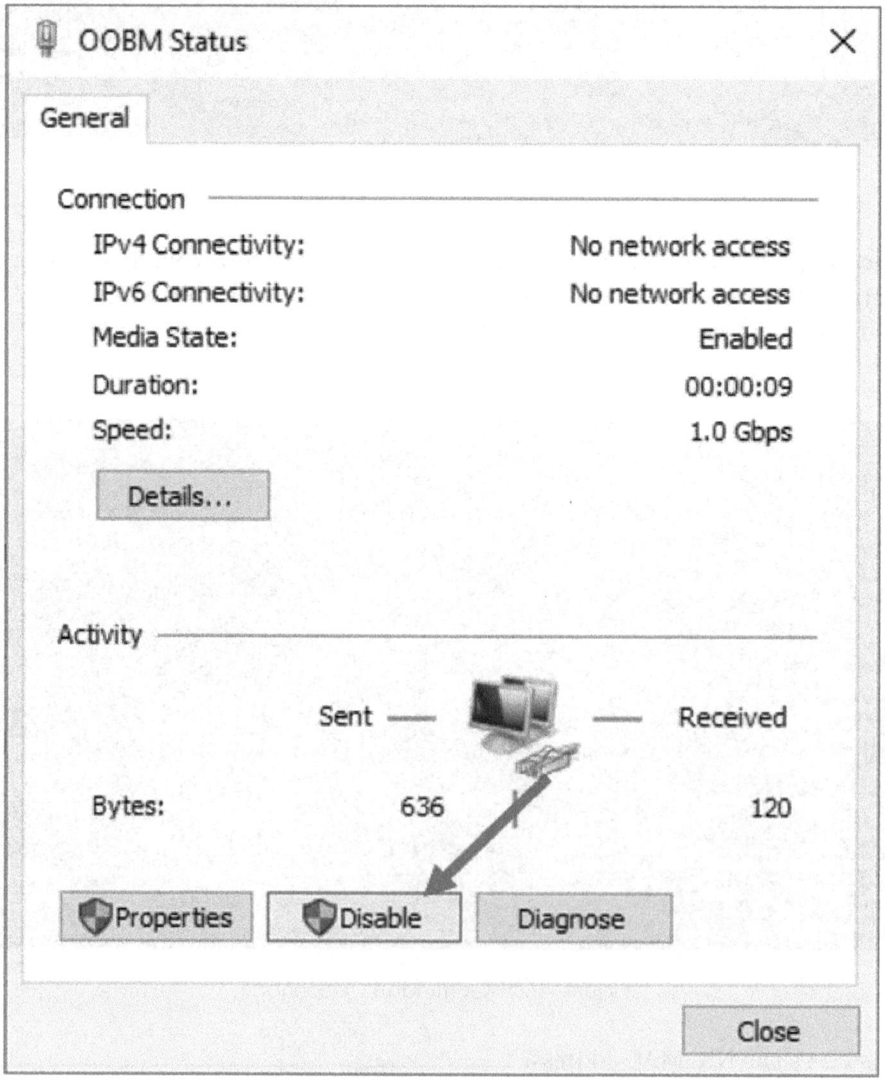

Figure 4-29 NIC Disabled

19. Repeat steps 11 to 15.

    What is PC-3's Lab NIC MAC address? ____________________

20. Confirm OOBM NIC is not listed.

21. From PC-3, ping PC-1's IP address (at **10.11.11.101**). Ping should be successful (Figure 4-30).

```
Command Prompt
Microsoft Windows [Version 10.0.17134.441]
(c) 2018 Microsoft Corporation. All rights reserved.

C:\Users\TEMP>ping 10.11.11.103

Pinging 10.11.11.103 with 32 bytes of data:
Reply from 10.11.11.103: bytes=32 time<1ms TTL=128
Reply from 10.11.11.103: bytes=32 time<1ms TTL=128
Reply from 10.11.11.103: bytes=32 time<1ms TTL=128
Reply from 10.11.11.103: bytes=32 time<1ms TTL=128

Ping statistics for 10.11.11.103:
    Packets: Sent = 4, Received = 4, Lost = 0 (0% loss),
Approximate round trip times in milli-seconds:
    Minimum = 0ms, Maximum = 0ms, Average = 0ms

C:\Users\TEMP>
```

Figure 4-30 Ping to PC-3

22. In Access-1, display the mac-address-table (Figure 4-31).

```
T11-Access-1# show mac-address-table
MAC age-time              : 300 seconds
Number of MAC addresses : 2
MAC Address          VLAN     Type                  Port
--------------------------------------------------------------
00:50:56:b1:37:67    1111     dynamic               1/1/1
00:50:56:b1:ae:e8    1111     dynamic               1/1/3
T11-Access-1#
```

What entries are listed in the output? ____________________

23. Using the output information, write down the client's MAC addresses in Figure 4-30, along with ports and VLAN IDs.

Mac Address	Port	VLAN
PC-1's MAC		
PC-3's MAC		

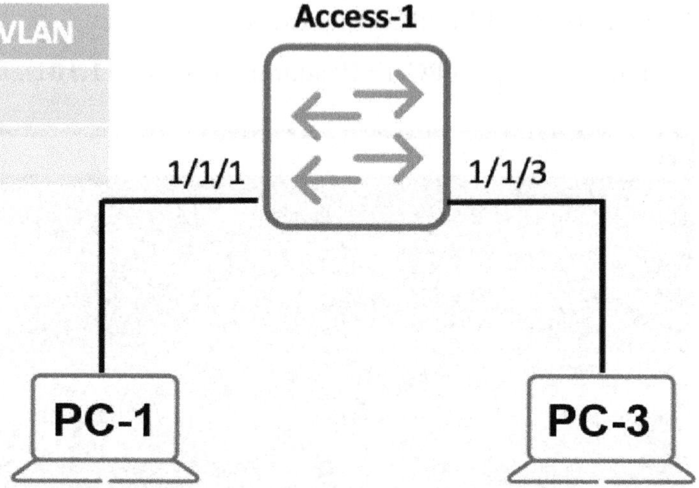

Figure 4-31 Access-1's MAC Address Table

Were these MAC addresses discovered on the ports you expected them?

Tip

There are multiple forms of the "show mac-address-table" command that can be used for displaying only entries that match a certain criteria,such as an address learned in a particular VLAN or port, or learned dynamically versus configured statically in the MAC table, use the [?] key at the end of the command for displaying the options.

```
T11-Access-1# show mac-address-table ?
  address   Show a specific MAC address
  count     Number of MAC addresses
  detail
  dynamic   Show learnt MAC addresses
  lockout   Show MAC lockout address information
  port      Show MAC addresses learnt on port
  static    Show static MAC address information
VLAN        Show MAC addresses learnt on VLANs
<cr>
```

Task 3: Save Your Configurations

Objectives

You will now proceed to save your configurations and create checkpoints. Please note that final lab checkpoints may be used in later activities.

Steps

Access-1

24. Save the current Access-1's configuration in the startup checkpoint.

```
T11-Access-1# write memory
Configuration changes will take time to process, please be patient.
```

25. Backup the current Access-1's configuration as a custom checkpoint called **Lab4-1_final**.

```
T11-Access-1# copy running-config checkpoint Lab4-1_final
Configuration changes will take time to process, please be patient.
```

You have completed Lab 4.1!

Lab 4.2: Add a Second Switch to the Topology

Overview

Good news! BigStartup seems to be a successful business and management has decided to hire more personnel. More ports are required, and it is time to add a second switch. You have been asked to make an onsite visit to integrate the second switch and span the employee VLAN.

Objectives

After completing this lab, you will be able to:

- Enable an Interswitch link
- Configure trunk ports by enabling 802.1Q tagging on them
- Extend the broadcast domain
- Enable Inter-switch client communication (Figure 4-32).

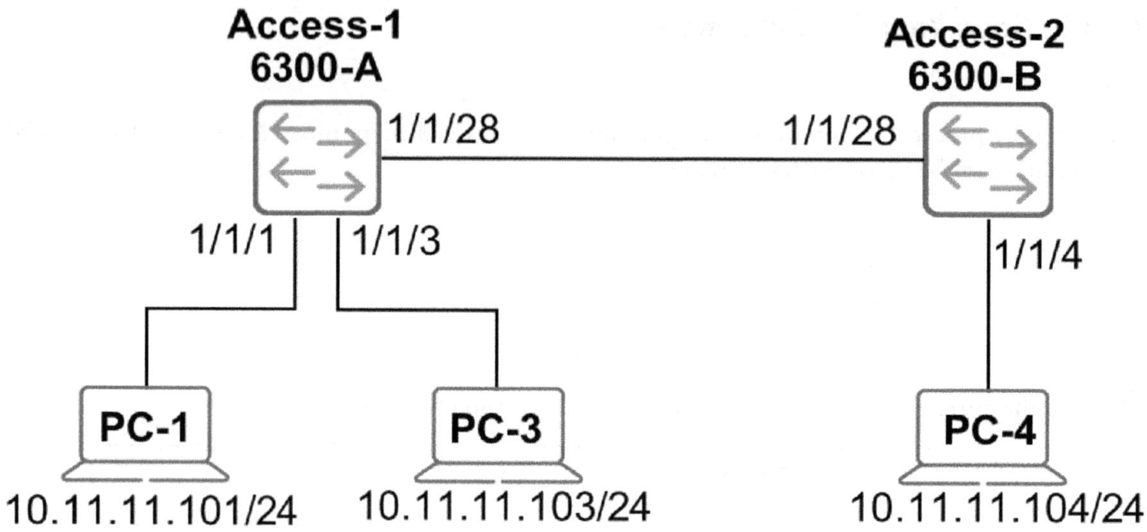

Figure 4-32 Lab Topology

Task 1: Configure Initial Settings on T11-Access-2

Objectives

Task 1 of lab 4.2 defines the initial settings for Access-2 and disables all ports but the one for the Windows client. Then you will move to PC-4 and assign an IP address to its NIC.

Steps

6300-B

26. Open a console connection to the **6300-B**. Log in using **admin** and **no password**.
27. Move to configuration mode and change the switch's hostname to **T11-Access-2** and set session timeout to 1440 minutes.

```
6300# configure terminal
6300(config)# hostname T11-Access-2
T11-Access-2(config)# session-timeout 1440
T11-Access-2(config)#
```

28. Disable all ports.

```
T11-Access-2(config)# interface 1/1/1-1/1/28
T11-Access-2(config-if-<1/1/2-1/1/28>)# shutdown
T11-Access-2(config-if-<1/1/2-1/1/28>)# exit
```

29. Access interface **1/1/4** and set a description (this interface connects to PC-4).

```
T11-Access-2(config)# interface 1/1/4
T11-Access-2(config-if)# description TO_PC-4
```

30. Enable the port.

```
T11-Access-2(config-if)# no shutdown
T11-Access-2(config-if)# exit
```

You will now give PC4 an IP address.

PC-4

31. Open a console to **PC-4.**
32. Click the top result (**Control Panel**). A new window will pop up (Figure 4-33).

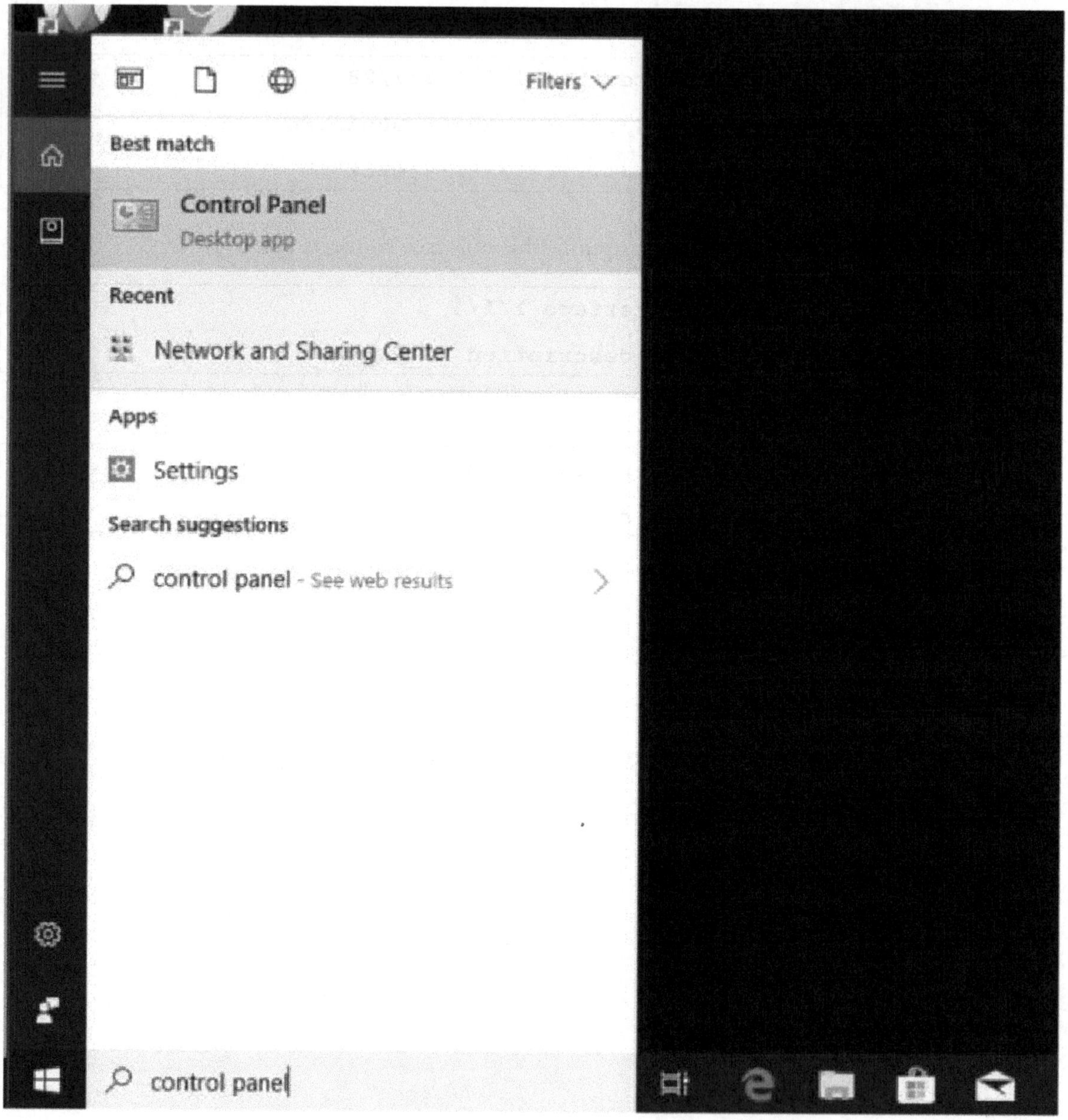

Figure 4-33 Windows Search

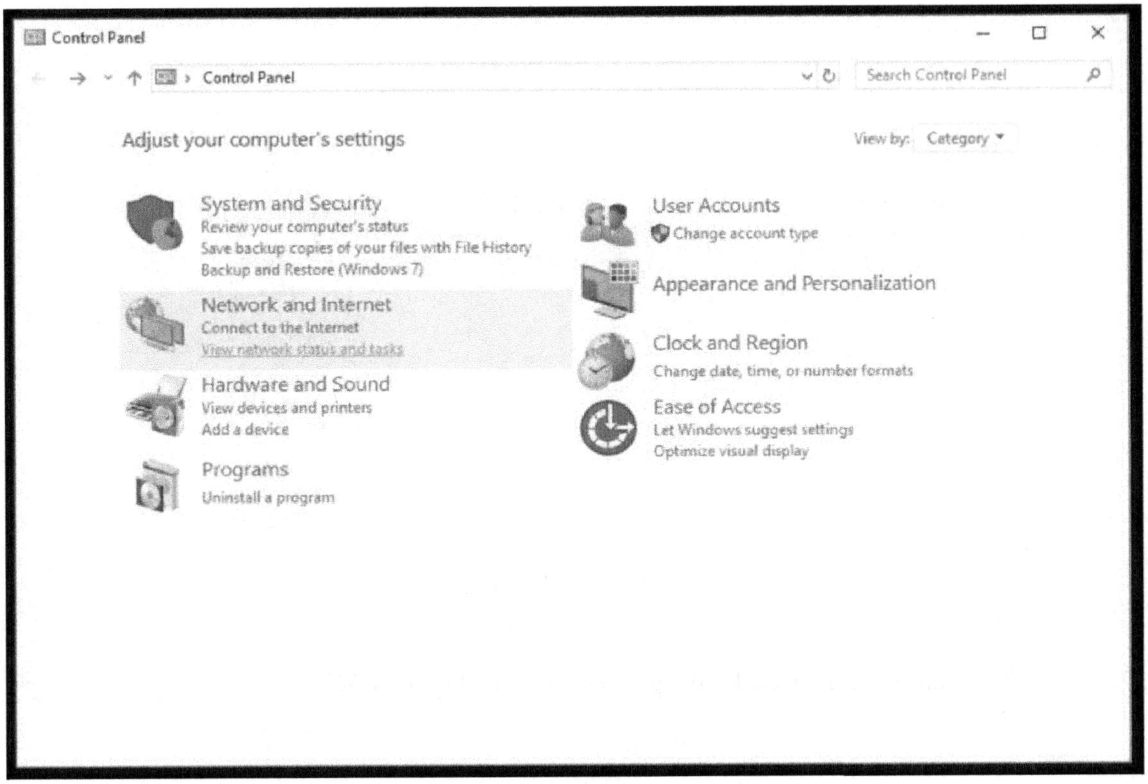

Figure 4-34 Control Panel

33. Under Control Panel (Figure 4-34), click "**View network status and tasks**" under Network and Internet.
34. In Control Panel, click "**View network status and tasks**" under Network and Internet.
35. Click in "**Change adapter settings**" in the left pane.
36. Right click the "**Lab NIC**" adapter icon and select "**Properties**" from the menu that appears (Figure 4-35).

Figure 4-35 NIC Properties

37. In Lab NIC status window, click "**Properties**" button (Figure 4-36).

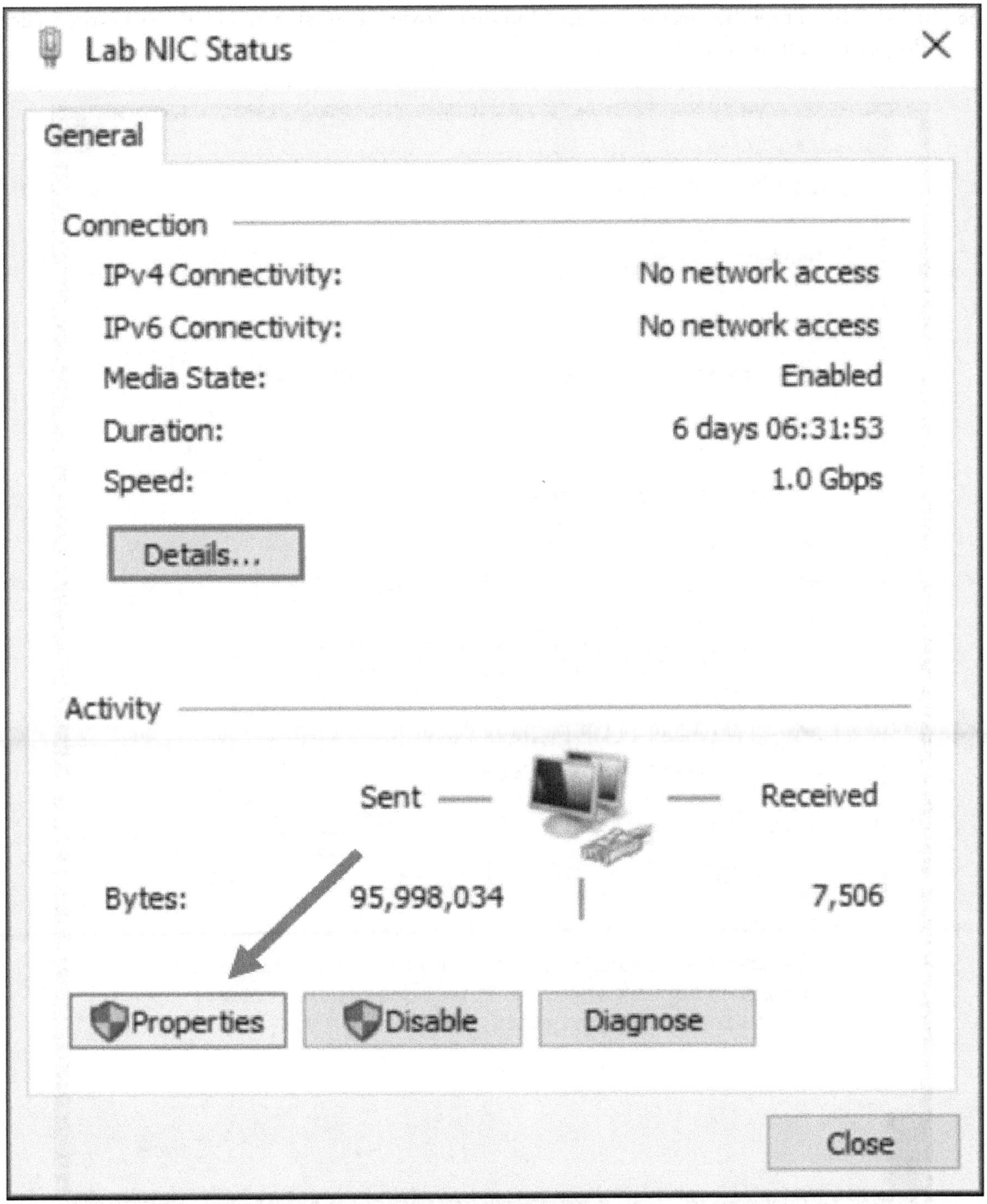

Figure 4-36 NIC Status

38. In Lab NIC Properties section, select "Internet **Protocol Version 4 (TCP/IPv4)**, then click "**Properties**" button (Figure 4-37).

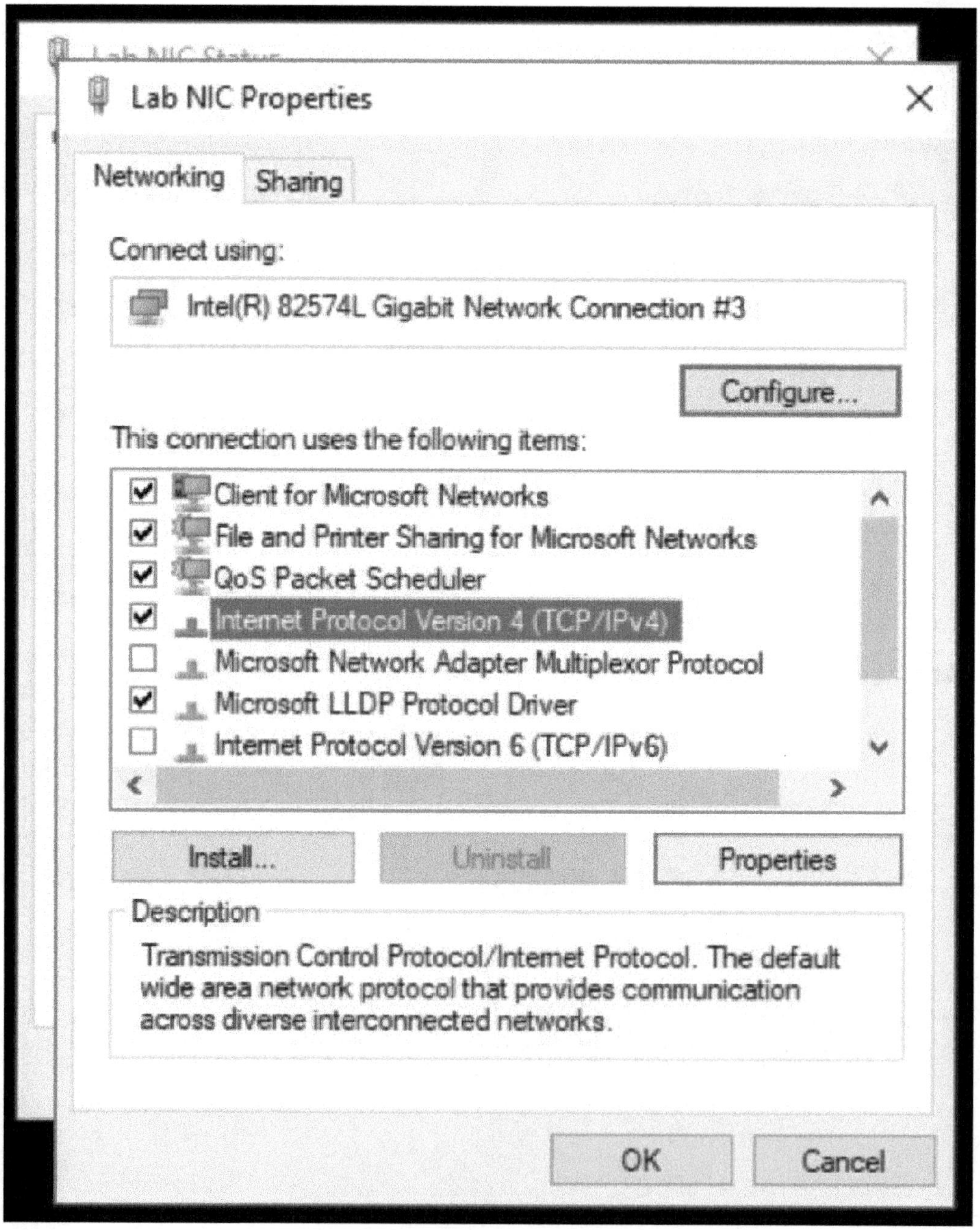

Figure 4-37 Lab NIC Properties

39. In Internet Protocol Version 4 (TCP/IPv4) Properties, choose "**Use the following IP address:**" under General tab.

40. Type **10.11.11.104** and **255.255.255.0** under IP address and Subnet mask respectively (Figure 4-38).

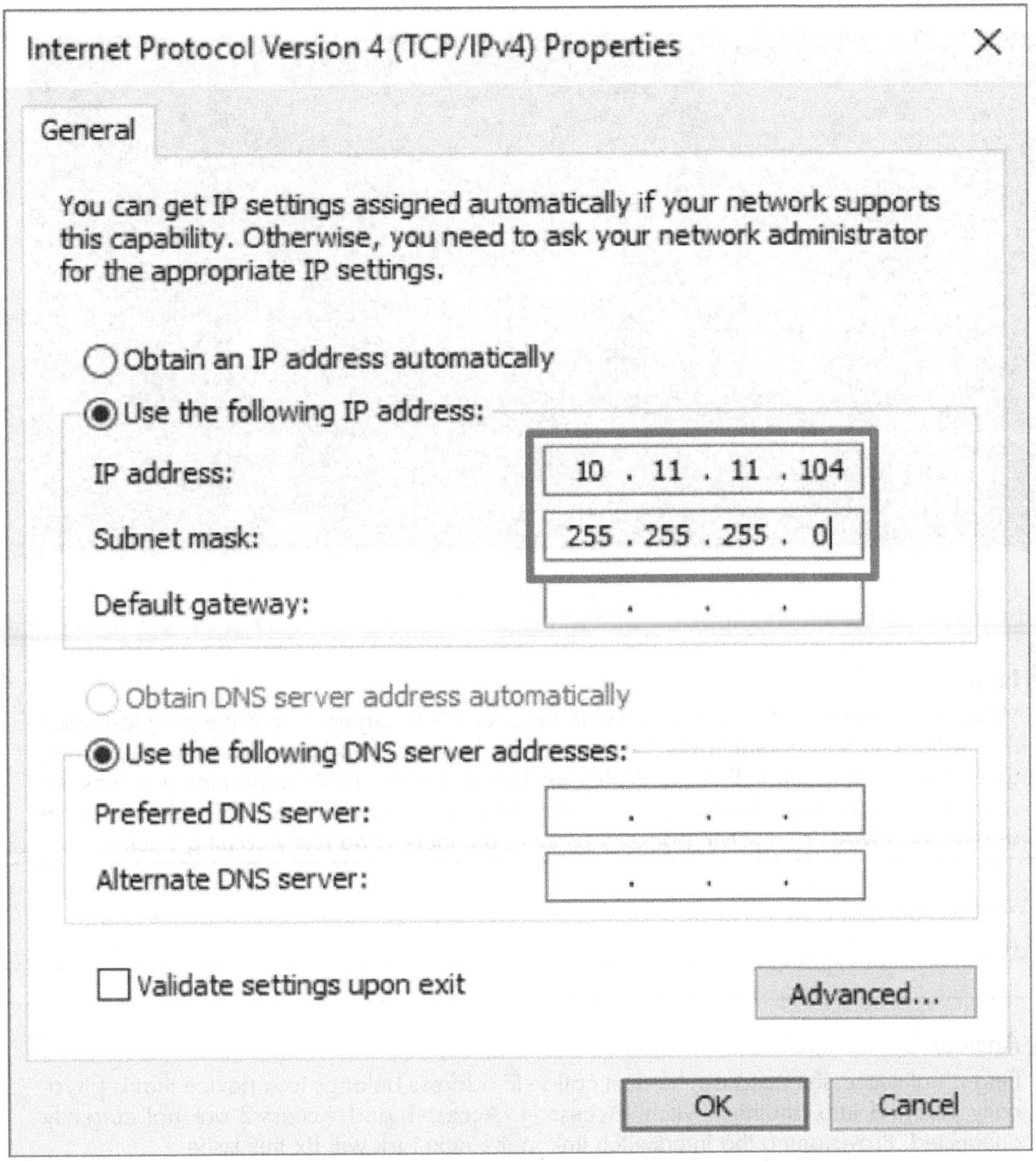

Figure 4-38 Internet Protocol Version 4

41. Click "**OK**" button, then "**Close**" button twice.
42. Open the **Command Prompt**.
43. Ping **PC-3**'s IP address (**10.11.11.103**) (Figure 4-39).

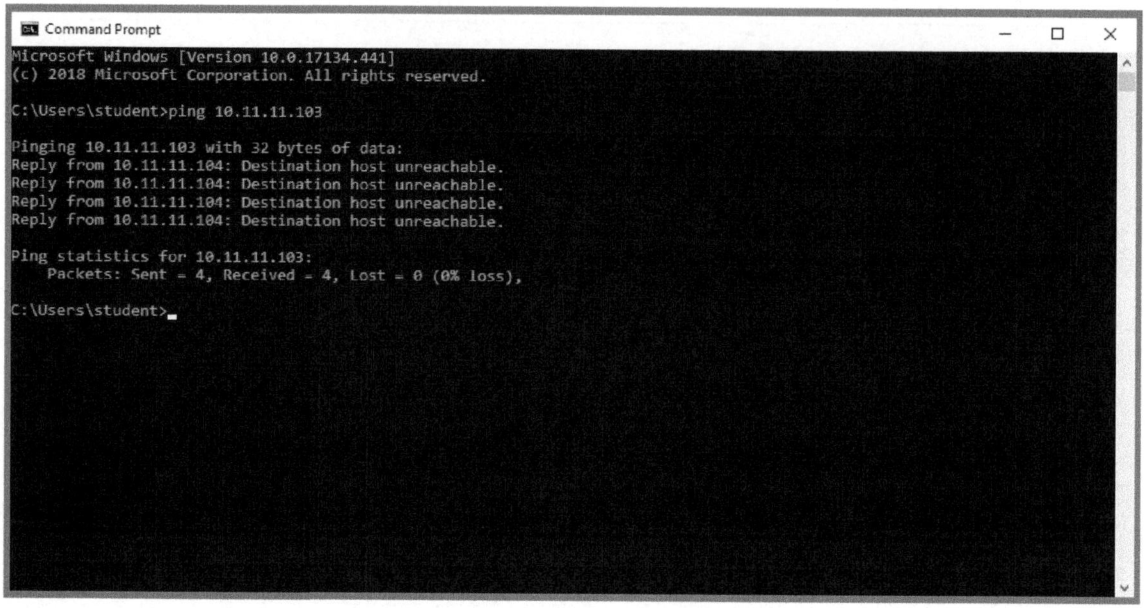

Figure 4-39 Ping Failure

Note

When the destination IP address is within the source's IP segment, and the ping test result is "Destination host unreachable." It means that the Layer-3 to Layer-2 address resolution using Address Resolution Protocol (ARP) has failed, and the ICMP echo message was not sent at all. However, if the result is "timeout" then it means that host was able to resolve destination's MAC and ICMP packet was sent, but there is no reply coming back.

Was ping successful? ____________________

Why? ____________________

Answer

Ping is not successful because the destination IP address belongs to a device that is physically plugged into another switch (Access-1). Access-1 and Access-2 are not currently connected. Provisioning the Interswitch link in the next task will fix this issue.

Task 2: Enable Link Between Access Switches

In this task you will enable an ethernet connection between Access switches using a DAC in order to increase the number of portson the network. Next, you will explore the information that Link Layer Discovery Protocol (LLDP) can provide.

Objectives

- Factory reset
- Remove all checkpoints

Steps

Access-1

44. Open a console connection to the **Access-1.**
45. Enable interface 1/1/28.

```
T11-Access-1# configure terminal
T11-Access-1(config)# interface 1/1/28
T11-Access-1(config-if)#no shutdown
T11-Access-1(config-if)#end
```

Access-2

46. Move toAccess-2.
47. Enable interface 1/1/28.

```
T11-Access-2# configure terminal
T11-Access-2(config)# interface 1/1/28
T11-Access-2(config-if)#no shutdown
T11-Access-2(config-if)#end
```

48. Confirm interface 1/1/28 came up using the "**show interface brief**" command followed by the filter "**exclude down**."

Note

The information will be filtered out, listing all the lines except the ones that contain the "down" string.

```
T11-Access-2# show interface brief | exclude down
--------------------------------------------------------------------------------
Port     Native  Mode    Type        Enabled   Status    Reason      Speed
         VLAN                                                        (Mb/s)
--------------------------------------------------------------------------------
1/1/1     1112    access 1GbT          yes      up                    1000
1/1/28    1      access  SFP+DAC1      yes      up                    10000
VLAN1     --               --          yes      up                    --
```

Note

The pipe (|) command filters the output of show commands according to the criteria specified by the parameter include, exclude, count, begin, or redirect.
Strings of characters that follow the filtering tool (for example, "down" in command above) are case sensitive. Typing the wrong capitalization may lead to the absence of output.

Is port 1/1/28 up? ____

What is port 1/1/1 and port 1/1/28 speeds? ________________________________

Important

In wired networking it is common practice to use faster speed links for connections between switches than those to the clients.Best practice for switch-to-switch connections is to limit oversubscription ratios to 24:1 or less (depending on the traffic generated by the endpoints). This guarantees that regardless of the traffic pattern, the link between switches does not get congested.Next, you will use LLDP to analyze the information the protocol can provide regarding what device is connected tospecific interfaces.

Note

LLDP is on by default on AOS-CX switches.

49. Issue the "**show LLDP configuration**" command.

```
T11-Access-2# show LLDP configuration

LLDP Global Configuration
=========================

LLDP Enabled                 : Yes
LLDP Transmit Interval       : 30
LLDP Hold Time Multiplier    : 4
LLDP Transmit Delay Interval : 2
LLDP Reinit Time Interval    : 2

TLVs Advertised
===============

Management Address
Port Description
Port VLAN-ID
System Capabilities
System Description
System Name
OUI

LLDP Port Configuration
=======================

PORT           TX-ENABLED          RX-ENABLED
-----------------------------------------------
1/1/1          Yes                 Yes
1/1/2          Yes                 Yes
                ←---- output omitted ---→
1/1/27         Yes                 Yes
1/1/28         Yes                 Yes
```

What is the current LLDP state? ____________________

What are the transmit interval and hold time multiplier values? ____________________

What are the LLDP transmit and receive modes on all the ports? ____________________

Note

LLDP is enabled by default both globally and per port (on all ports). It can be disabled/enabled globally and/or per port using the commands shown below:
T11-Access-1(config)# **no LLDP**
T11-Access-1(config)# **LLDP**
T11-Access-1(config-if)# **no LLDP receive**
T11-Access-1(config-if)# **no LLDP transmit**
T11-Access-1(config-if)# **LLDP receive**
T11-Access-1(config-if)# **LLDP transmit**

---

50. Issue the "**show LLDP local device**" command. This will show the information the local device shares/advertises with LLDP messages.

```
T11-Access-2# show LLDP local-device
Global Data
===========
Chassis-ID                : 88:3a:40:97:a4:40
System Name               : T11-Access-2
System Description        : Aruba JL668A  FL.10.04.0030
Management Address        : 88:3a:30:97:a4:40
Capabilities Available    : Bridge, Router
Capabilities Enabled      : Bridge, Router
TTL                       : 120
Port Based Data
===============
Port-ID             : 1/1/4
Port-Desc           : "1/1/4"
Port Mgmt-Address   :
Port VLAN ID        : 1
```

```
Port-ID              : 1/1/28
Port-Desc            : "1/1/28"
Port Mgmt-Address    :
Port VLAN ID         : 1
```

What is the "System Description"? ____________________

What are the available capabilities supported by the system? ____________________

Important
AOS-CX systems have IP routing service enabled by default and cannot be disabled. This means they will automatically populate entries in the Routing Table for whatever IP segment they are configured with in Layer-3 ports (ether physical or logical), and start moving packets at Layer-3 between those segments. IP routing cannot be disabled in these systems.

51. Write down System Name and Chassis ID to Figure 4-40.

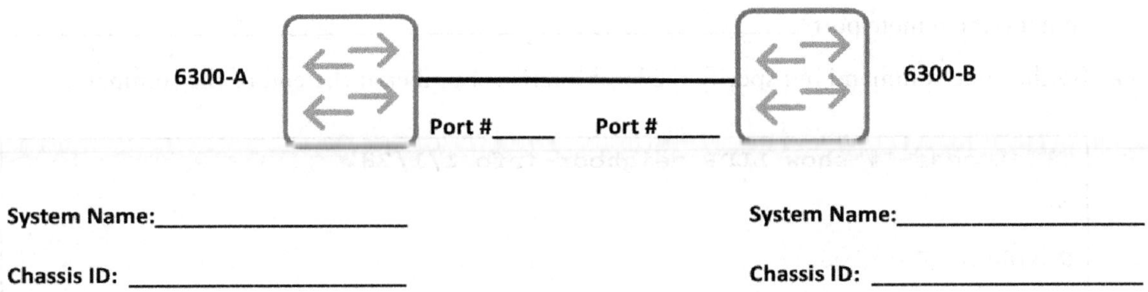

Figure 4-40 System Name and Chassis ID

What interfaces are currently running the protocol? ____________________

Steps
Access-1

52. Move to **Access-1**.
53. Issue the "**show LLDP neighbor-info**" command. You should see only one entry in the output.

```
T11-Access-1# show LLDP neighbor-info

LLDP Neighbor Information
=========================

Total Neighbor Entries          : 1
Total Neighbor Entries Deleted  : 0
Total Neighbor Entries Dropped  : 0
Total Neighbor Entries Aged-Out : 0

LOCAL-PORT  CHASSIS-ID          PORT-ID         PORT-DESC       TTL
SYS-NAME
---------------------------------------------------------------------------
1/1/28      88:3a:30:97:a4:40   1/1/28          1/1/28          120
T11-Access-2
```

Does the entry match the Chassis-ID and System Name seen in step 8? ____________________

What is the local port? ____________________

What is the remote port? ____________________

54. Try the same command but specify the local interface number at the end of the command.

```
T11-Access-1# show LLDP neighbor-info 1/1/28

Port                           : 1/1/28
Neighbor Entries               : 1
Neighbor Entries Deleted       : 0
Neighbor Entries Dropped       : 0
Neighbor Entries Aged-Out      : 0
Neighbor Chassis-Name          : T11-Access-2
Neighbor Chassis-Description   : Aruba JL668A  FL.10.04.0030
Neighbor Chassis-ID            : 88:3a:30:97:a4:40
Neighbor Management-Address    : 88:3a:30:97:a4:40
Chassis Capabilities Available : Bridge, Router
Chassis Capabilities Enabled   : Bridge, Router
```

```
Neighbor Port-ID                  : 1/1/28
Neighbor Port-Desc                : 1/1/28
Neighbor Port VLAN ID             : 1
TTL                               : 120
Neighbor Mac-Phy details
Neighbor Auto-neg Supported       : true
Neighbor Auto-Neg Enabled         : false
Neighbor Auto-Neg Advertised      : Other
Neighbor MAU type                 : 10 GIGBASEER
```

Note

This version of the command displays the detailed data of the neighbor just like the command, "show LLDP local-device" used earlier on Access-2.

55. Finally, run "**show LLDP local-device**" on Access-1. Then use the output of this step and the previous step to complete the remaining fields of Figure 4-9.

```
T11-Access-1# show LLDP local-device
Global Data
===========
Chassis-ID               : 88:3a:30:98:30:00
System Name              : T11-Access-1
System Description       : Aruba JL668A  FL.10.04.0030
Management Address       : 88:3a:30:98:30:00
Capabilities Available : Bridge, Router
Capabilities Enabled     : Bridge, Router
TTL                      : 120
Port Based Data
===============
Port-ID            : 1/1/1
Port-Desc          : "1/1/1"
Port Mgmt-Address  :
Port VLAN ID       : 1111
```

```
Port-ID              : 1/1/3
Port-Desc            : "1/1/3"
Port Mgmt-Address :
Port VLAN ID         : 1111

Port-ID              : 1/1/28
Port-Desc            : "1/1/28"
Port Mgmt-Address :
Port VLAN ID         : 1
```

Note

Understanding LLDP and the information it providescan help you verify and troubleshoot Layer-1 communication between devices.

Now that you are sure about which ports are used, you are ready to set the interface descriptions.

56. Set descriptions on both switches' interface 1/1/28.

```
T11-Access-1# configure terminal
T11-Access-1(config)# interface 1/1/28
T11-Access-1(config-if)# description TO_T8-ACCESS-2_PORT-28
T11-Access-1(config-if)# end
T11-Access-2# configure terminal
T11-Access-2(config)# interface 1/1/28
T11-Access-2(config-if)# description TO_T11-ACCESS-1_PORT-28
T11-Access-2(config-if)# end
```

PC-4

57. Move back to PC-4 and **ping PC-3**'s IP address (**10.11.11.103**) (Figure 4-41).

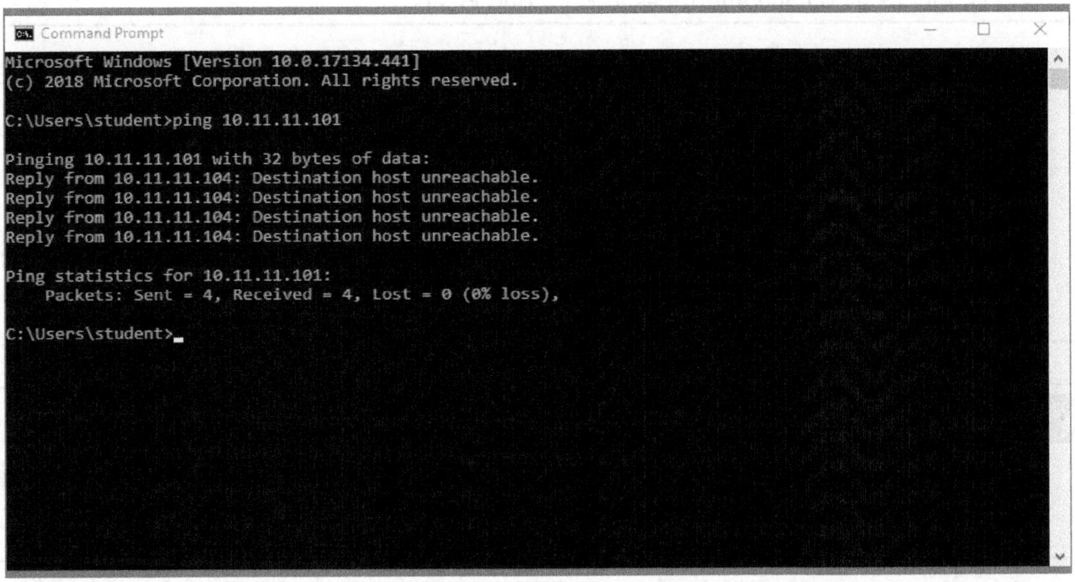

Figure 4-41 Destination Host Unreachable

Was ping successful? ______________________

Why? ______________________

Answer

Even though a link between both switches has been enabled, ping still fails. In order to better understand why, you should explore the mac-address-table of either switch. Let us do it on Access-1.

---

58. Open console session to Access-1 and use the "**show mac-address-table**" command.

```
T11-Access-1# show mac-address-table
MAC age-time                : 300 seconds
Number of MAC addresses : 2
MAC Address          VLAN     Type                          Port
--------------------------------------------------------------
88:3a:30:97:a9:86    1        dynamic                       1/1/28
00:50:56:b1:ae:e8    1111     dynamic                       1/1/3
```

Tip

This output may give you more entries than the ones in the example above (for example, PC-1), ignore all but the interfaces to PC-3 and PC-4s.

What Port and VLAN is PC-3 seen on? ______________________

What Port and VLAN is PC-4 seen on? ______________________

Answer

As you can see both PCs are on different ports (which is expected) and on different VLANs. PC-4 is seen on VLAN 1 because that is the only VLAN that exists on Access-2, and the only VLAN it forwards in its 1/1/28 interface.

Note

As seen in this step, understanding the fundamentals of layer-2 forwarding and exploring the MAC Address table of switches are key tools for troubleshooting the lack of connectivity between two endpoints

Task 3: Extend Connectivity for VLAN 1111

Objectives

After finding the root cause that prevents communication between two endpoints it is time to apply a configuration that solves the issue. You will proceed now to extend VLAN 1111 to Access-2 switch.

Steps

Access-1

1. Configure Access-1's interface 1/1/28 as trunk link that permits VLANs 1 and 1111.

```
T11-Access-1# configure terminal
T11-Access-1(config)#interface1/1/28
T11-Access-1(config-if)# VLAN Trunk allowed 1,1111
T11-Access-1(config-if)# end
```

2. Display trunk interfaces.

```
T11-Access-1# show interface trunk
------------------------------------------------------------------
Port    Native VLAN Trunk VLANs
------------------------------------------------------------------
1/1/28  1           1,1111
```

Access-2

3. Move to **Access-2.**
4. Create **VLAN 1111** and name its **EMPLOYEES**.

```
T11-Access-2# configure terminal
T11-Access-2(config)# VLAN 1111
T11-Access-2(config-VLAN-1111)# name EMPLOYEES
T11-Access-2(config-VLAN-1111)# exit
```

5. Configure **Access-2's** interface 1/1/28 as trunk link that permits **VLANs 1 and 1111**.

```
T11-Access-2(config)# interface 1/1/28
T11-Access-2(config-if)# VLAN trunk allowed 1,1111
T11-Access-2(config-if)# exit
```

6. Last configure interface **1/1/4** as access port in **VLAN 1111**.

```
T11-Access-2(config)# interface 1/1/4
T11-Access-2(config-if)# VLAN access 1111
T11-Access-2(config-if)# end
```

7. Confirm **VLAN 1111** is now member of ports **1/1/1 and 1/1/28**.

```
T11-Access-2# show VLAN 11111
------------------------------------------------------------------
VLAN     Name        Status        Reason      Type      Interfaces
```

```
--------------------------------------------------------------------------
--------1111   employees                                      up         ok
static     1/1/4,1/1/28
```

8. Display trunk interfaces. You should have only one trunk port.

```
T11-Access-2# show interface trunk
--------------------------------------------------------------------------
Port     Native VLAN Trunk VLANs
--------------------------------------------------------------------------
1/1/28   1               1,1111
```

9. Move back to PC-4 and ping **PC-3**'s IP address (**10.11.11.11**) (Figure 4-42).

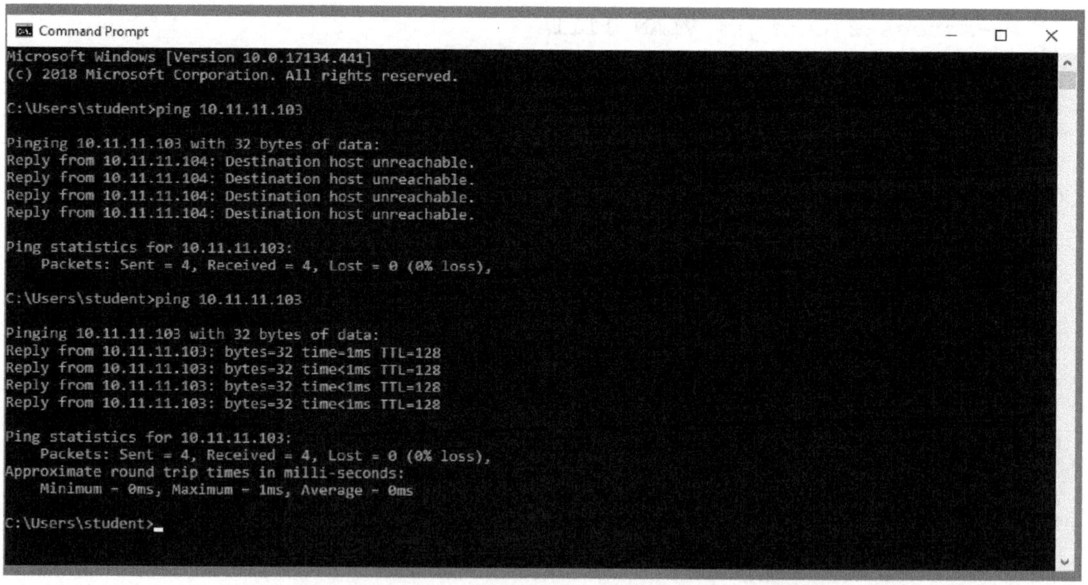

Figure 4-42 Ping Successful

Was ping successful? ______________________________

Let us now explore the MAC address tables of both switches and trace the MAC addresses of each station in order to confirm they are learned in the expected ports and VLANs.

Access-1 and Access-2

10. Display the mac address table of both Access-1 and Access-2.

```
T11-Access-2# show mac-address-table
MAC age-time                : 300 seconds
Number of MAC addresses : 4
MAC Address             VLAN      Type                          Port
--------------------------------------------------------------
00:50:56:b1:a9:86       1111      dynamic                       1/1/4
00:50:56:b1:ae:e8       1111      dynamic                       1/1/28
T11-Access-1# show mac-address-table
MAC age-time                : 300 seconds
Number of MAC addresses : 3
MAC Address             VLAN      Type                          Port
--------------------------------------------------------------
00:50:56:b1:a9:86       1111      dynamic                       1/1/28
00:50:56:b1:ae:e8       1111      dynamic                       1/1/3
```

11. With the information shown please fill out the fields on Figure 4-43.

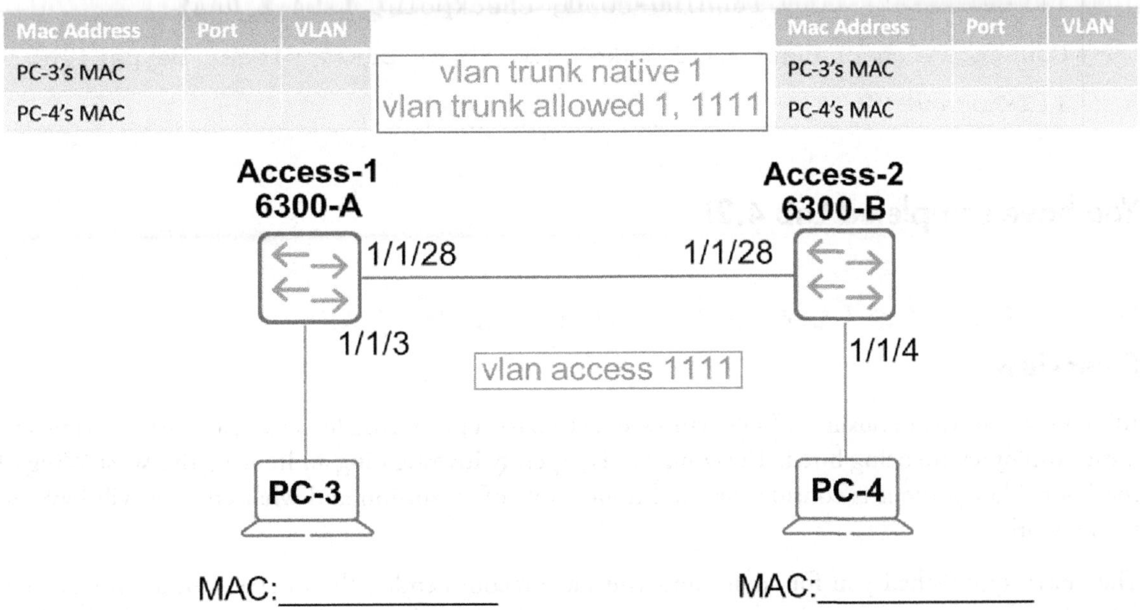

Figure 4-43 MAC Address Tables

Task 4: Save Your Configurations

Objectives

You will now save your configurations and create checkpoints. Remember, final lab checkpoints may be used in later activities.

Steps

Access-1 and Access-2

12. Save the current Access switches' configuration in the startup checkpoint.

```
T11-Access-1# write memory
Configuration changes will take time to process, please be patient.
T11-Access-2# write memory
Configuration changes will take time to process, please be patient.
```

13. Backup the current Access switches' configuration as a custom checkpoint called **Lab4-2_final**.

```
T11-Access-1# copy running-config checkpoint Lab4-2_final
Configuration changes will take time to process, please be patient.
T11-Access-1#
T11-Access-2# copy running-config checkpoint Lab4-2_final
Configuration changes will take time to process, please be patient.
T11-Access-2#
```

You have completed Lab 4.2!

Lab 4.3: Add a Core Switch to the Topology

Overview

After a few months in business, BigStartup seems to have a promising forecast. Sales are growing and more employees are being hired. The company is urgently investigating andrenting the West Wing of the floor. Management is considering the implications of expansion and what effect it will have on the network.

They have approached you for advice and you have recommended the insertion of a Core switch, following a two-tier design that can assure future growth with no complexity (instead of a daisy chain-based topology). You suggest an 8325 AOS-CX switch, which assures a consistent OS across the board, high port density, unprecedented throughput, and no blocking switching. While management agrees with your recommendation and can budget for the new gear, it turns out that the building owner, Cheap4Rent, also offers some degree of network services for all their tenants.

Cheap4Rent offers to include the same 8325 AOS-CX switch in the lease. This permits the company to save capital and invest in other assets such as servers, IP telephony, video surveillance, etc.

BigStartup is the first tenant to be offered the Core Switching service and to facilitate the integration, they are giving you limited network operations access over SSH and will allow you to use the default VRF for now.

Objectives

After completing this lab, you will be able to:

- Deploy a Core Switch to the topology
- Configure uplinks as trunk ports by enabling 802.1Q
- Add a new VLAN for another users' type
- Enable DHCP server on Access-1 (Figure 4-44).

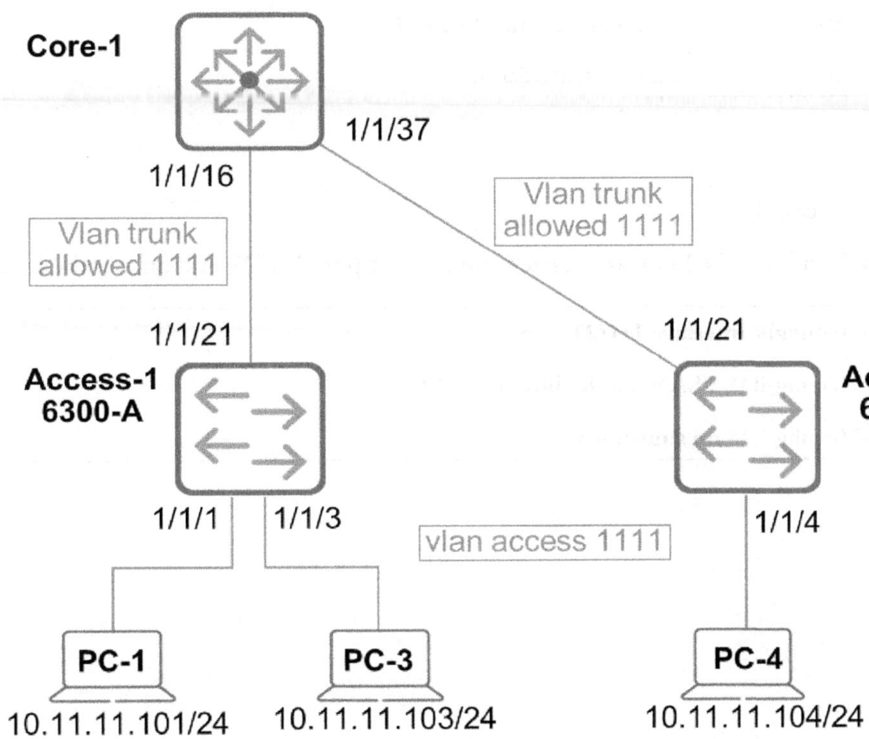

Figure 4-44 Lab Topology

Task 1: Add Core-1 to the Topology

Objectives

In this task, you will change the switching topology and enable ports on the Access switches that have been connected to the 8325 AOS-CX Core Switch that resides in the Building's MDF. You will also configure the core switch side of the links and validate the topology.

Even though 8300 platforms come with disabled routed ports by default, Cheap4Rent has turned the Core ports on and made them switch interfaces. They have provided ethernet wire drops for establishing Layer-1 connectivity between the Core and Access switches.

Steps

Access-1 and Access-2

14. Disable the link between **Access-1** and **Access-2**.

```
T11-Access-1# configure terminal
T11-Access-1(config)# interface 1/1/28
T11-Access-1(config-if)# shutdown
T11-Access-2# configure terminal
T11-Access-2(config)# interface 1/1/28
T11-Access-2(config-if)# shutdown
```

Access-1

15. Move back to Access-1.
16. Allow VLAN 1 and VLAN 1111 as a tagged member of port 1/1/21 and enable the interface.

```
T11-Access-1(config)# interface 1/1/21
T11-Access-1(config-if)# VLAN trunk allowed 1,1111
T11-Access-1(config-if)# no shutdown
```

Tip

You were told by the Cheap4Rent team that your switches were connected on ports 1/1/3 and 1/1/6 on the Core side, nonetheless you know from experience that it is always better to verify third-party technical information using LLDP.

17. Use the "**show LLDP neighbor-info**" command, to validate the port Access-1 is connected to.

```
T11-Access-1(config-if)# show LLDP neighbor-info

LLDP Neighbor Information
=========================

Total Neighbor Entries          : 2

Total Neighbor Entries Deleted  : 1

Total Neighbor Entries Dropped  : 0

Total Neighbor Entries Aged-Out : 1

LOCAL-PORT  CHASSIS-ID          PORT-ID        PORT-DESC       TTL
SYS-NAME

-----------------------------------------------------------------

1/1/21      90:20:c2:bc:ed:00   1/1/16         1/1/16          120
Core-1
```

Tip

This output may still show Access-2 on port 1/1/28. That would be an old entry that is about to age out.

Was the information given by Rent4Cheap accurate? ____________________

18. On Access-1, set the proper description on port 1/1/21.

```
T11-Access-1(config-if)# description TO_CORE-1_PORT-16
```

19. Move back to **Access-2** and **repeat steps 3 to 5**. Do not forget to draw the connections in Figure 4-44.

Access-2

```
T11-Access-2(config)# interface 1/1/21
T11-Access-2(config-if)# VLAN trunk allowed 1111
T11-Access-2(config-if)# no shutdown
```

```
T11-Access-2(config-if)# show LLDP neighbor-info
LLDP Neighbor Information
=========================
Total Neighbor Entries          : 2
Total Neighbor Entries Deleted  : 1
Total Neighbor Entries Dropped  : 0
Total Neighbor Entries Aged-Out : 1
LOCAL-PORT  CHASSIS-ID          PORT-ID        PORT-DESC      TTL
SYS-NAME
--------------------------------------------------------------------------
1/1/21      90:20:c2:bc:ed:00   1/1/37         1/1/37         120
Core-1
T11-Access-2(config-if)#
T11-Access-2(config-if)# description TO_CORE-1_PORT-37
T11-Access-2(config-if)#end
```

Just as a sanity check you will connect to Core-1 and confirm the connection status on that device. To access it you will connect to PC-1 and use it as a "jump host" running an SSH session to Core-1's IP address.

Tip

PC-1 has two Lab-related ethernet connections, "LAB NIC" and "OOBM" (Out of Band Management). You will access Core-1 using the second one as shown in Figure 4-45.

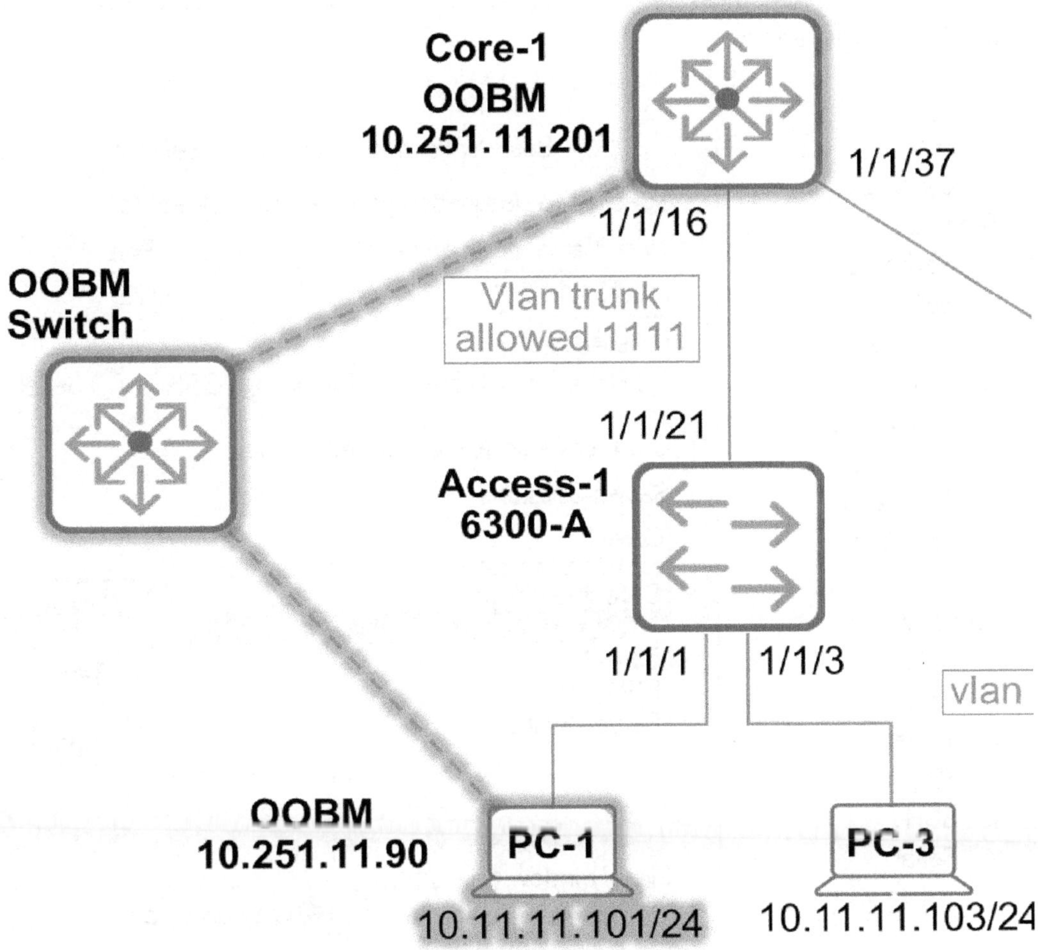

Figure 4-45 Using OOBM Network

PC-1

20. Access the PC-1.
21. Open Putty. You can create saved sessions to Core-1 and the other three devices (Figure 4-46).

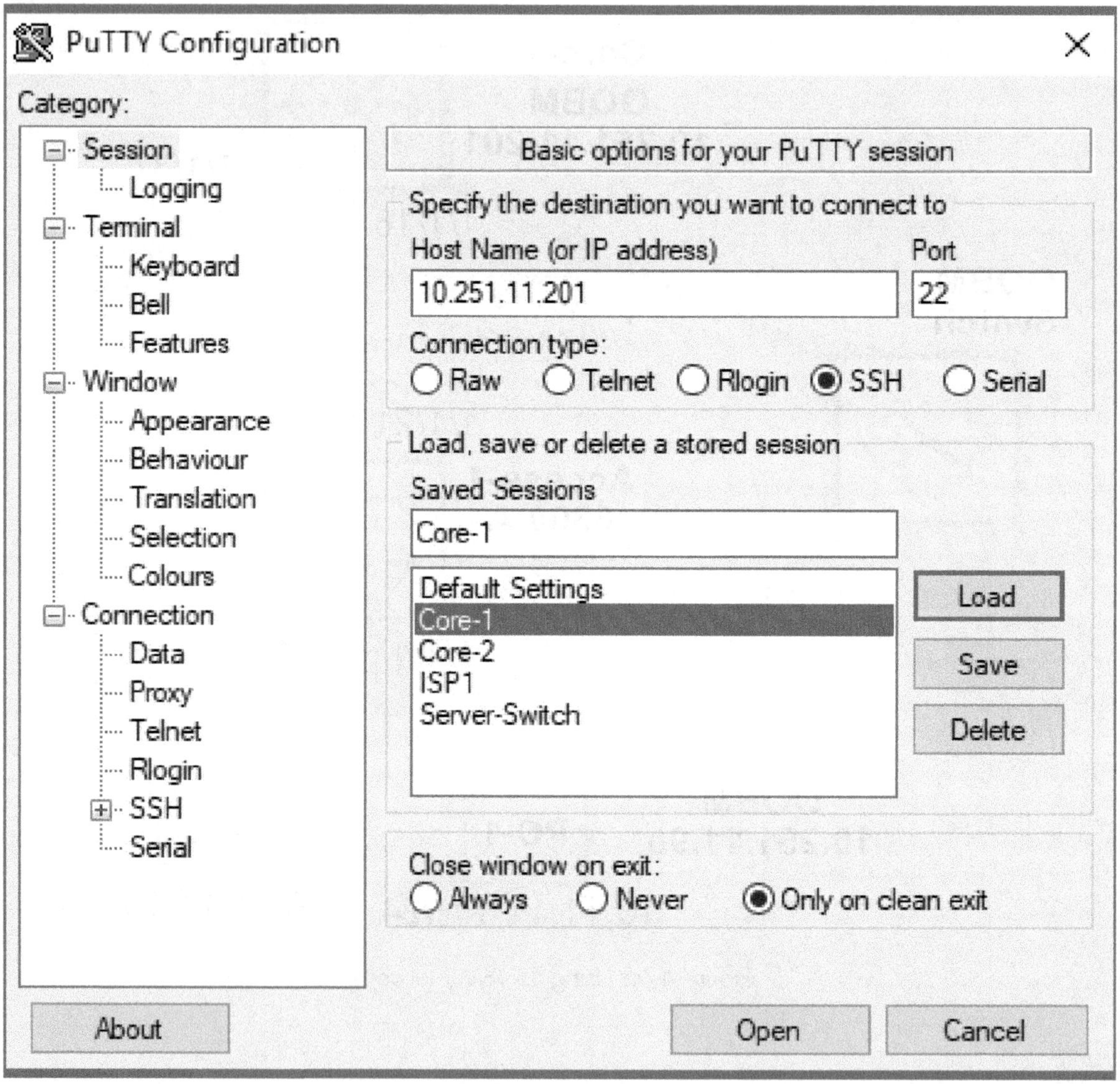

Figure 4-46 Putty

22. Double-click **Core-1** saved session.

Core-1 (via PC-1)

23. Log in using **cxf11/aruba123.**
24. Define the height of the page as 40 lines.

```
Core-1# page 40
```

25. Type **show LLDP neighbor-info | include T11.**

Note

The information will be filtered out, listing only the lines that include the "T11" string.

```
Core-1# show LLDP neighbor-info | include T11

1/1/16        88:3a:30:98:30:00   1/1/21        1/1/21        120
T11-Access-1

1/1/37        88:3a:30:97:a4:40   1/1/22        1/1/22        120
T11-Access-2
```

Notice

The pipe (|) command filters the output of show commands according to the criteria specified by the parameter include, exclude, count, begin, or redirect.

Strings of characters that follow the filtering tool (for example, "T4" or "T11" in example above) are case sensitive. Typing the wrong capitalization may lead to the absence of output.

Does the output match what you recorded on Figure 4-46? ______________________

26. Create **VLAN 1111** and name it **T11_EMPLOYEES.**

```
Core-1# configure terminal

Core-1(config)# VLAN 1111

Core-1(config-VLAN-1111)# name T11_EMPLOYEES

Core-1(config-VLAN-1111)# exit
```

Notice

Command-based authorization is enabled on all SSH sessions you will run in this training lab. This means that every command you type on SSH sessions will be validated with a list of permitted commands. If the command you type is not in the list, you will get an error message like the following:

```
Core-2(config)# VLAN 1999
Cannot execute command. Command not allowed.
```

27. Access port **1/1/16**, then set the **TO_T11-ACCESS-1_PORT-21** description, and make the interface switch port and a trunk interface member of **VLAN 1111**.

```
Core-1(config)# interface 1/1/16
Core-1(config-if)# description TO_T11-ACCESS-1_PORT-21
Core-1(config-if)#VLAN trunk allowed 1111
```

28. Move to port **1/1/37**;then repeat **step 11** using **TO_T11-ACCESS-2_PORT-21** as description.

```
Core-1(config)# interface 1/1/37
Core-1(config-if)# description TO_T11-ACCESS-2_PORT-21
Core-1(config-if)#VLAN trunk allowed 1111
```

PC-1

29. From PC-1 **ping PC-4**(10.11.11.104). Ping should be successful (Figure 4-47).

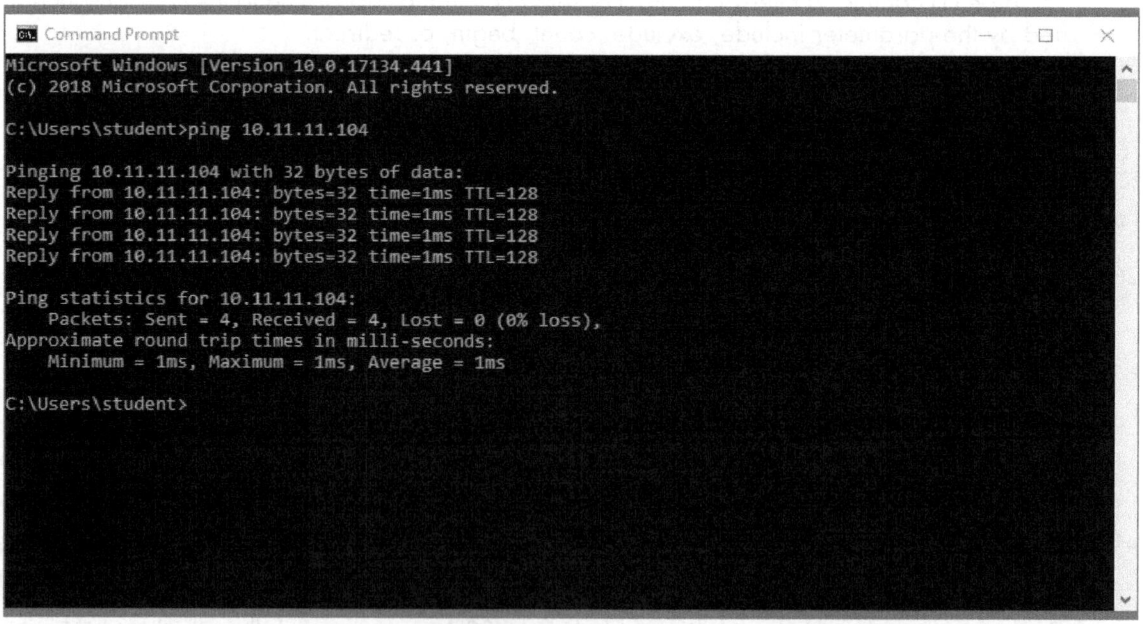

Figure 4-47 Ping Successful

Core-1 (via PC-1)

30. **OPTIONAL**—You can display the MAC address table to see what ports Core-1 learned the clients' MAC addresses from, which are the ports it uses for forwarding traffic to them at Layer-2.

```
Core-1# show mac-address-table VLAN 1111

MAC age-time                : 300 seconds

Number of MAC addresses : 3

MAC Address          VLAN     Type                       Port

--------------------------------------------------------------

00:50:56:b1:ae:e8    1111     dynamic                    1/1/16

00:50:56:b1:37:67    1111     dynamic                    1/1/16

00:50:56:b1:a9:86    1111     dynamic                    1/1/37

Core-1#
```

Task 2: Adding a Second VLAN.

Objectives

After more hiring, BigStartup is now interested in improving privacy and traffic separation between regular employees and managers. They are asking you if there is any way you can achieve that with networking devices they already have. You can improve privacy and traffic separation by adding another VLAN.

The next steps will be focused on creating VLAN 1112 for managers across all switches and moving PC-1 and PC-4 into that broadcast domain (Figure 4-48).

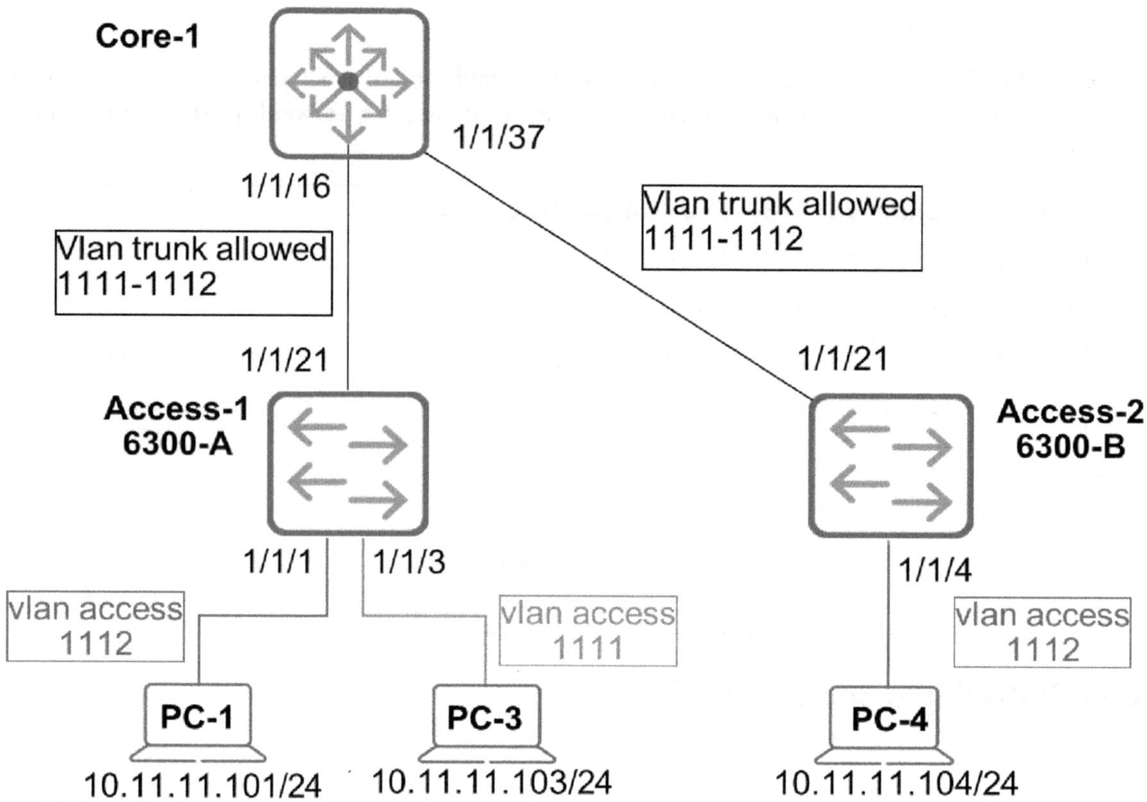

Figure 4-48 Task 2: Logical Topology

Steps

Access-1

31. Open a console connection to Access-1. Log in using **admin** and **no password**.
32. Create **VLAN 1112** and name its**MANAGERS**; then apply it on port **1/1/21**.

```
T11-Access-1# configure terminal
T11-Access-1(config)# VLAN 1112
T11-Access-1(config-VLAN-1112)# name MANAGERS
T11-Access-1(config-VLAN-1112)# exit
T11-Access-1(config)# interface 1/1/21
T11-Access-1(config-if)# VLAN trunk allowed 1112
T11-Access-1(config-if)# exit
```

33. Use the "**show VLAN**" command to see the new added VLAN and the port members.

```
T11-Access-1(config)# show VLAN
--------------------------------------------------------------------------------
VLAN  Name                        Status  Reason                   Type
Interfaces
--------------------------------------------------------------------------------
1     DEFAULT_VLAN_1.            down    no_member_forwarding  default
1/1/2,1/1/4-1/1/20,1/1/22-1/1/28
1111  EMPLOYEES                   up      ok                      static
1/1/1,1/1/3,1/1/21,1/1/28
1112  MANAGERS                    up      ok                      static
1/1/21
```

Access-2

34. Open a console connection to Access-2. Log in using **admin** and **no password**.

35. Repeat step 2.

```
T11-Access-2# configure terminal
T11-Access-2(config)# VLAN1112
T11-Access-2(config-VLAN-1112)# name MANAGERS
T11-Access-2(config-VLAN-1112)# exit
T11-Access-2(config)#
T11-Access-2(config)# interface 1/1/21
T11-Access-2(config-if)# VLAN trunk allowed 1112
T11-Access-2(config-if)# exit
T11-Access-2(config)#
```

Core-1 (via PC-1)

36. Move back to Core-1 SSH session.

37. Create VLAN 1112, name it **T11_MANAGERS**.

```
Core-1# configure terminal
Core-1(config)# VLAN 1112
Core-1(config-VLAN-1112)# name T11_MANAGERS
Core-1(config-VLAN-1112)# exit
```

38. Apply VLAN 1112 on port 1/1/16.

```
Core-1(config)# interface 1/1/16
Core-1(config-if)# VLAN trunk allowed 1112
```

39. Repeat **step 8** on interface **1/1/37**.

Note
All switches have VLANs 1111 and 1112 now, and they have been assigned in all switch-to-switch links. Now you will move PC1 and PC4 into VLAN 1112 and test connectivity.

Access-1

40. Move to Access-1.
41. Make interface 1/1/1 an access port on VLAN 1112.

```
T11-Access-1(config)# interface 1/1/1
T11-Access-1(config-if)# VLAN access 1112
```

Access-2

42. Move to Access-2.
43. Make interface 1/1/4 an access port on VLAN 1112.

```
T11-Access-2(config)# interface 1/1/4
T11-Access-2(config-if)# VLAN access 1112
T11-Access-2(config-if)#
```

You will now change the IP segment where PC-1 and PC-4 belong.

PC-1

44. Access PC-1 and change the "**Lab NIC**" IP address to **10.11.12.101/24** (Figure 4-49).

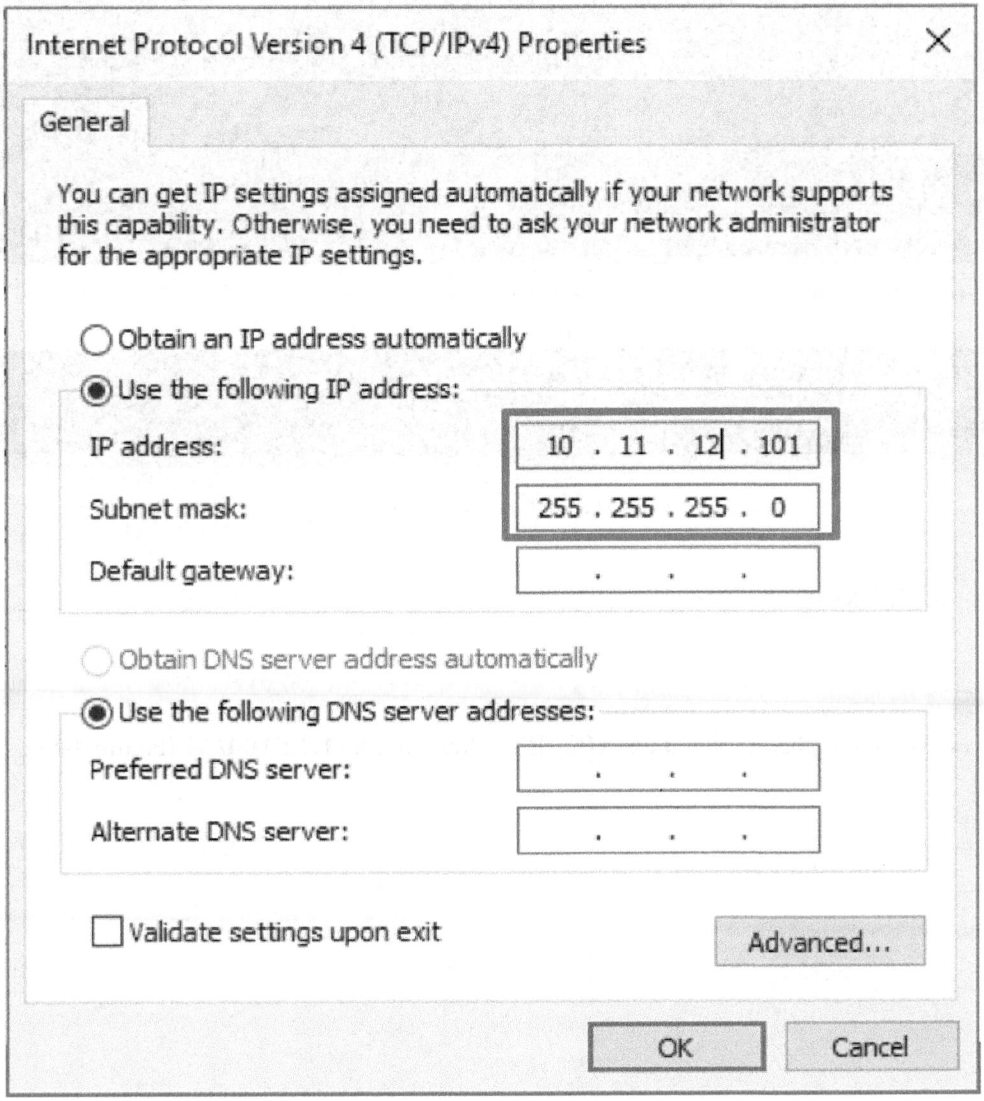

Figure 4-49 PC-1's IP Address Setting

45. Use the "**ipconfig -all**" command and confirm the client is using the new IP address (Figure 4-50).

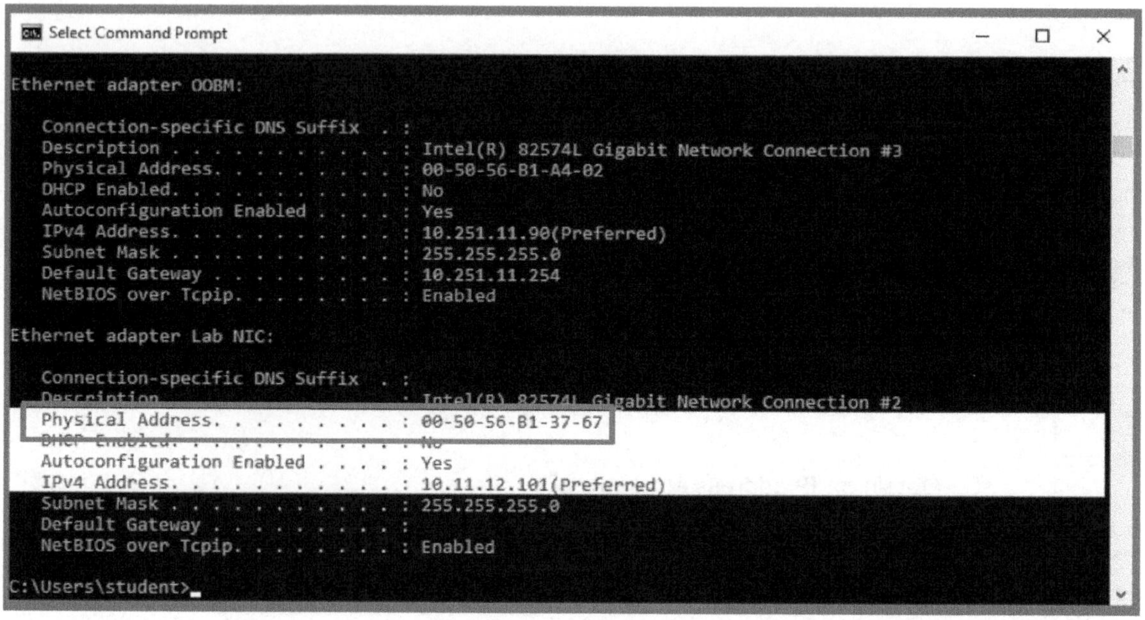

Figure 4-50 PC-1 Network Settings

What is the NIC MAC address? ____

PC-4

46. Access PC-4 and change the "**Lab NIC**" IP address to **10.11.12.104/24** (Figure 4-51).

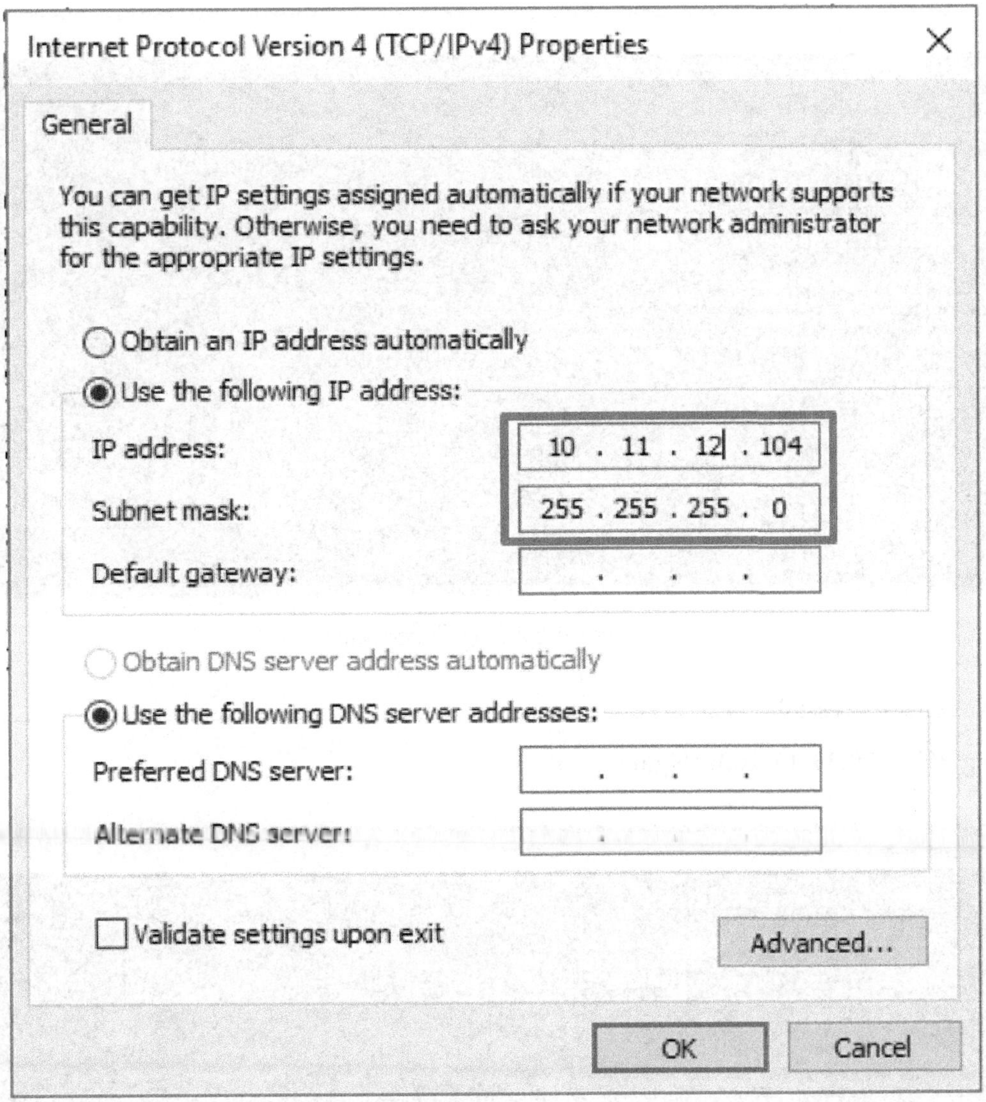

Figure 4-51 IPv4 Address

47. Ping PC-1 (**10.11.12.101**) (Figure 4-52).

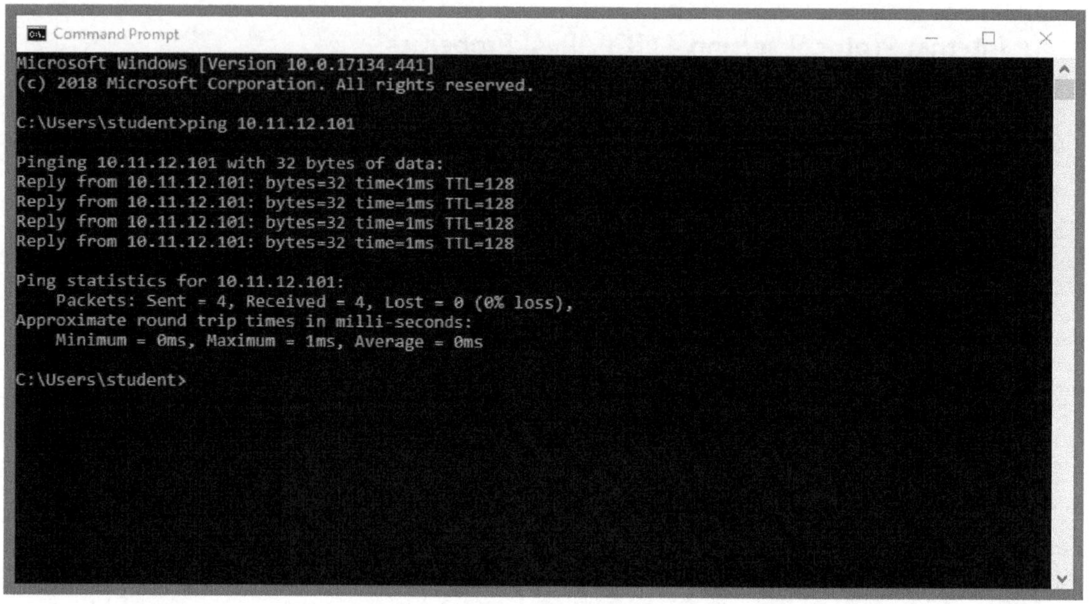

Figure 4-52 Ping Successful

Was ping successful? ______________________________

48. Ping PC-3 (**10.11.11.103**) (Figure 4-53).

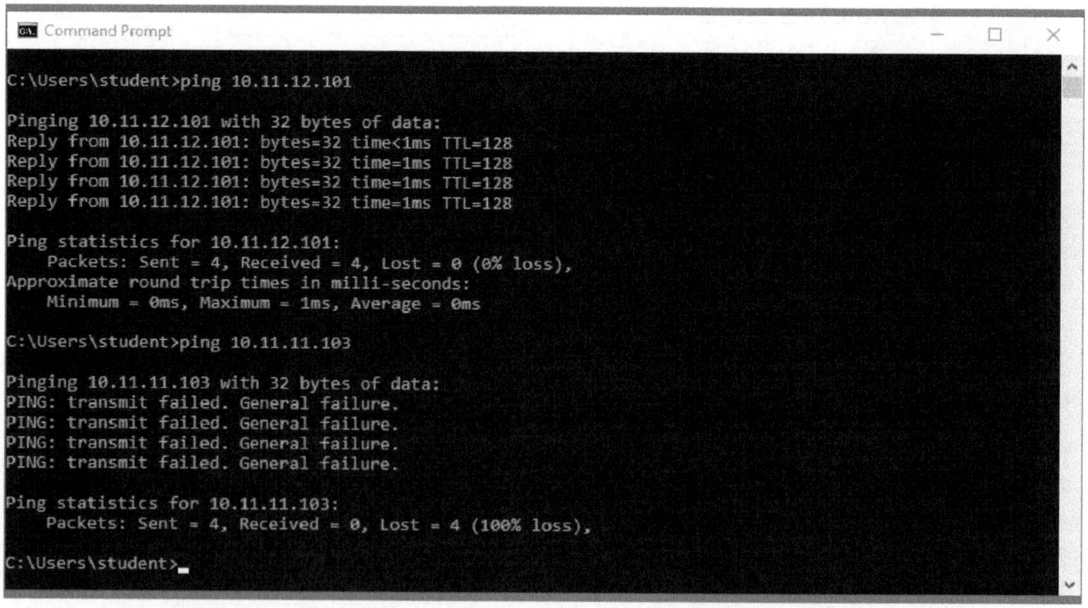

Figure 4-53 Ping Unsuccessful

Was ping successful? ______________________________

Answer

Pinging PC-3 will fail because it is now in a different network.

49. Display the ARP Table using the "**arp -a**" command and look for the **10.11.12.101** entry (Figure 4-54).

Tip

You can use the filtered version of this command "arp -a -N 10.11.12.101" for only displaying entries associated with "Lab NIC" interface.

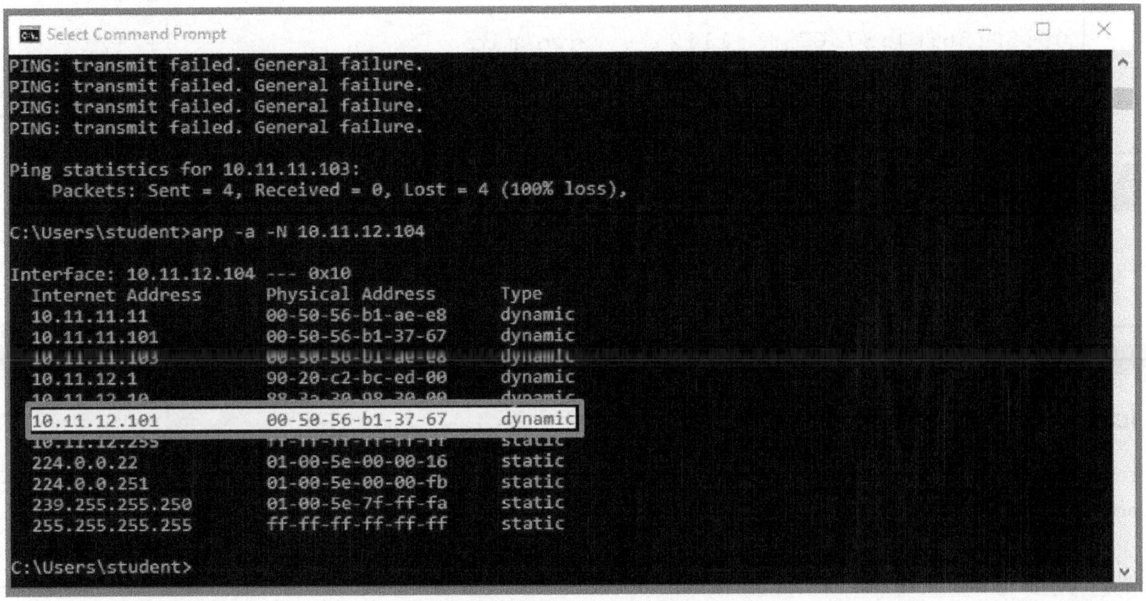

Figure 4-54 PC-4's ARP Table

Is the MAC address in the entry the same you recorded in step 15?

Note

You might also see a 10.11.11.101 entry associated with the same MAC. That is an old record from the time PC-1 and PC-4 were both in VLAN 1111, this entry will eventually expire.

Access-1

50. Move to Access-1.
51. Display the MAC address table. You will see one entry associated with VLAN 1111 and another with VLAN 1112.

```
T11-Access-1# show mac-address-table
MAC age-time                : 300 seconds
Number of MAC addresses : 3
MAC Address           VLAN     Type                      Port
---------------------------------------------------------------
00:50:56:b1:ae:e8     1111     dynamic                   1/1/3
00:50:56:b1:37:67     1112     dynamic                   1/1/1
00:50:56:b1:a9:86     1112     dynamic                   1/1/21
```

Note

If you do not get an entry mapped to port 1/1/3, artificially generate some traffic on PC-3 to let Access-1 re-learn its MAC address again. A single ping to 10.11.11.101 is enough. It will work even if the ping is unsuccessful.

Task 3: Save Your Configurations

You will now proceed to save your configurations and create checkpoints. Notice that final lab checkpoints might be used by later activities.

Steps

Access-1, Access-2, and Core-1 (via PC-1)

52. Save the current Access switches and Core-1 configuration in the startup checkpoint.

```
T11-Access-1# write memory
Configuration changes will take time to process, please be patient.
T11-Access-2# write memory
Configuration changes will take time to process, please be patient.
```

```
Core-1# write memory
Configuration changes will take time to process, please be patient.
```

Access-1 and Access-2

53. Backup the current Access switches' configuration as a custom checkpoint called Lab4-3_final.

```
T11-Access-1# copy running-config checkpoint Lab4-3_final
Configuration changes will take time to process, please be patient.
T11-Access-2# copy running-config checkpoint Lab4-3_final
Configuration changes will take time to process, please be patient.
```

You have completed Lab 4.3!

Learning Check

Chapter 4 Questions

Domains

1. Which of the options below accurately describe collision domains and broadcast domains?
   a. Collision domains relate to Layer-2 processes, while broadcast domains are a Layer-3 concept.
   b. Collisions are quite common in modern network switches.
   c. Multi-Layer Switches eliminate the need for collision domains.
   d. A routing device defines the edge of a broadcast domain.
   e. A router defines the edge of a collision domain.
   f. Broadcast domains are mainly a problem when you use a hub device.

VLANs

2. What are the benefits of creating VLANs?
   a. Simplify the network deployment.
   b. Minimize the need for routing.

c. Smaller broadcast domains can improve performance.

d. MAC address tables are smaller.

e. Separate VLANs mitigate risk.

802.1Q

3. What is true from the following lines of configuration?

```
SW1(config)# interface 1/1/24
SW1(config-if)# vlan trunk allow 1,20
```

a. VLAN-20 is the Native VLAN.

b. VLAN-10 is permitted in the trunk port.

c. There is no Native VLAN.

d. Native VLAN is VLAN-1.

MAC Address and ARP Tables

4. Which options below accurately describe MAC address and ARP tables?

a. Switches automatically build the MAC table based on destination MAC addresses.

b. MAC address tables are build based on source IP addresses.

c. The ARP reply packet uses a broadcasting mechanism.

d. The ARP table maps IP addresses to MAC addresses.

e. Switches use the MAC address table to properly forward frames.

Frame Delivery

5. When does a switch add a VLAN tag to a frame?

a. When it forwards the frame to a server.

b. When it forwards the frame to a PC or client.

c. When it forwards the frame to another switch.

d. When it accepts a frame from another switch.

e. When it accepts a frame from a server.

5 Spanning-Tree Protocol

EXAM OBJECTIVES

- ✓ Describe redundant network links.
- ✓ Describe Spanning-Tree Protocols.
- ✓ Explain and Configure Rapid STP.
- ✓ Elements and operation.
- ✓ Ports and links.
- ✓ Proposals and Agreements.
- ✓ Describe and Configure MST.

Overview

You are about to explore the most vital aspect of designing Layer-2 switched networks, especially as relates to resiliency, path optimization, and network efficiency: The Spanning-Tree protocols.

You will begin by learning how single points of failures can be mitigated by connecting redundant switches and redundant links. However, this causes the network breaking problem of Layer-2 loops, broadcast storms, and MAC table instability.

You will learn to solve these problems with the 802.1d Spanning-Tree Protocol (STP). You learn about RSTP elements, and how they work together to create a functional system that provides Layer-2 resiliency, while avoiding loops. You will dive deeper into RSTP operation. You will explore how edge ports and link types, as well as the RSTP proposal and agreement process can be leveraged to further increase the efficiency and uptime of your systems. In addition, you will learn how to resolve this issue by deploying the IEEE 802.1s standard Multiple Spanning-Tree (MST) solution. All these topics will allow you to engage in hands-on lab activities to solidify your knowledge.

Redundancy

Redundant Network

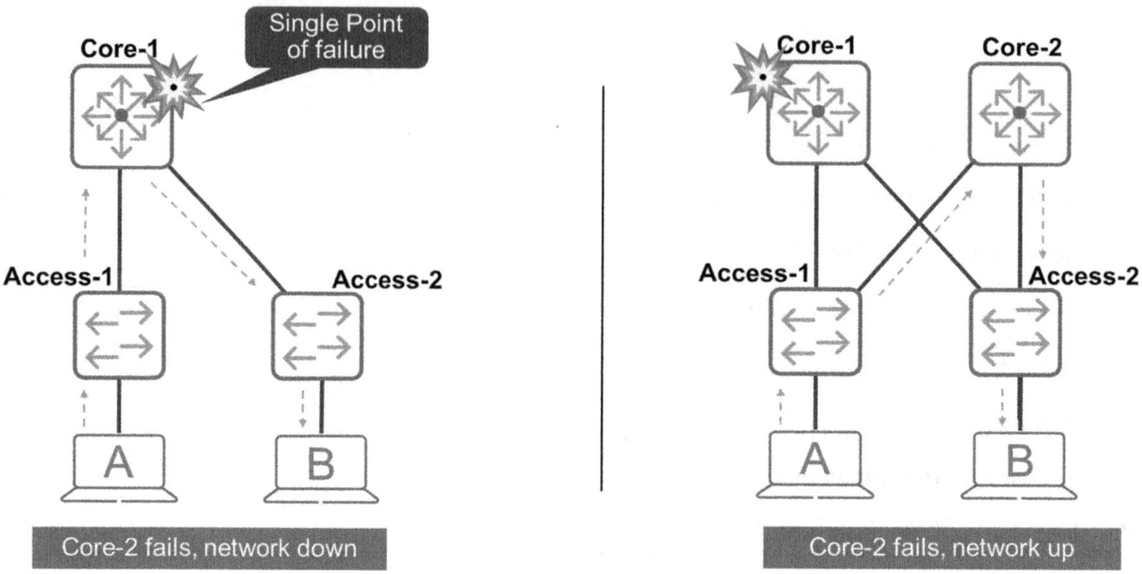

Figure 5-1 Redundant Network

Network communications is often mission-critical. Layer switch or link failures cannot be tolerated. For example, the left-hand example shows a single path to connect two Access switches using Core-1. This design has single points of failure. If Core-1 fails, the network is down. Host A and B cannot communicate.

One common way to mitigate this is by adding a redundant Core switch, as in the figure's right-hand example (Figure 5-1). In this scenario, if the Core-1 fails, the network will remain viable. Hosts A and B can still communicate over the redundant link using Core-2.

While this redundant link mitigates a single point of failure issue, it creates a new challenge.

Layer-2 Loops

Connecting Layer-2 switches with redundant links creates Layer-2 loops. A loop is even created if you connect an Ethernet cable from one port on a switch to another port on that same switch. The slide shows three different ways to create Layer-2 loops (Figure 5-2).

If not properly handled, these loops cause serious problems that can effectively disable a network.

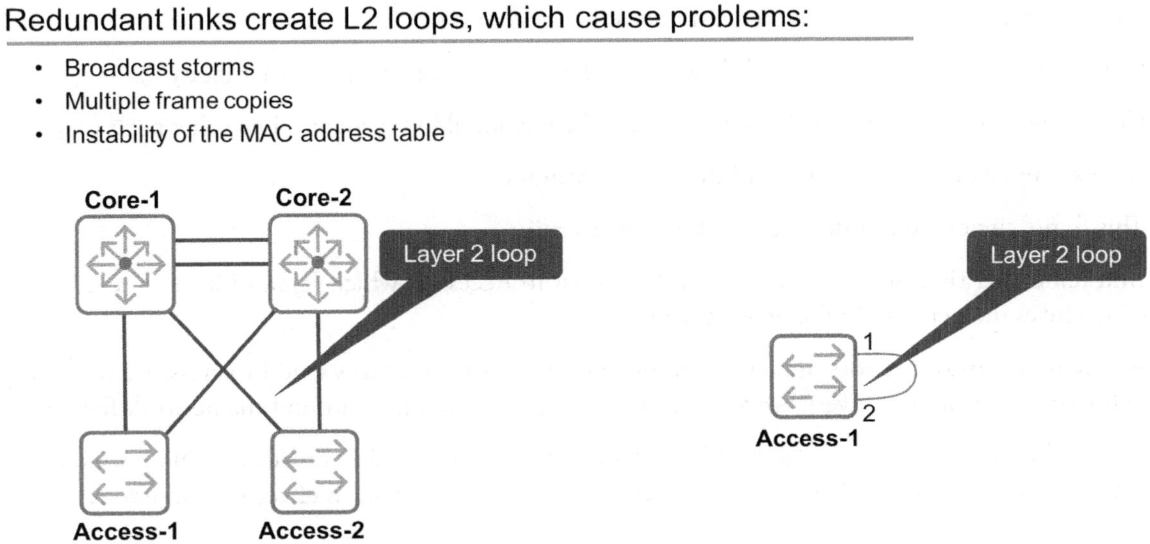

Figure 5-2 Layer-2 Loops

Broadcast Storms

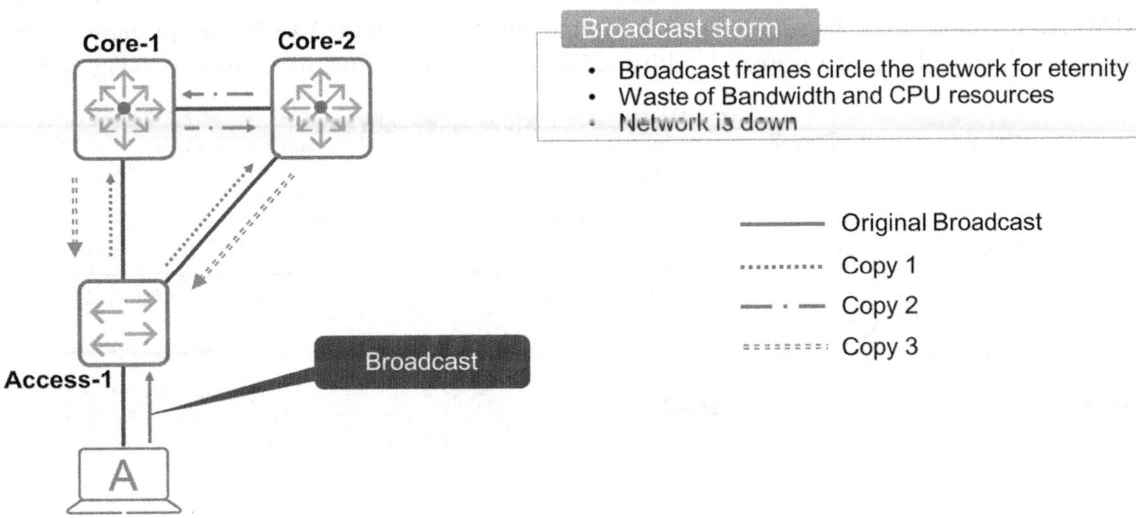

Figure 5-3 Broadcast Storms

You learned in module 3 that switches flood broadcasts out all interfaces in the same VLAN, except the ingress port. This can cause problems on a redundant, looped network like the one in Figure 5-3.

Suppose that Host A sends a broadcast frame.

Switch Access-1 receives this frame, and floods it out (copy 1).

Core-1 and Core-2 receive this and flood it out their connections to each other (copy 2).

Core-1 and Core-2 and Access-2 receive the second copy, and flood them out their other ports (copy 3).

Access-1 receives the third copy, and the cycle continues.

This frame circles around the network for all of eternity.

And remember that Access-1 flooded this broadcast to Access-2, which forward it to Core-2, etc. A copy circles the network in the other direction.

As a natural part of network and endpoint operation, nearly all devices send broadcast frames, often many times per minute. Every broadcast from every device circulates around the network forever.

Soon, all available bandwidth and CPU cycles are used up processing broadcasts. No resources are available to process normal data communication frames. The network is effectively unusable.

Multiple Frame Copies

You may recall that switches not only flood broadcasts out all ports in the VLAN (except the ingress port), but they do the same thing with unicasts to an unknown destination. If a switch receives a unicast packet to some destination MAC address, and that address has not yet been learned in the MAC address table, then the switch floods the frame out all ports in the VLAN (except ingress port). These can also circulate and waste bandwidth and CPU cycles. They also cause other issues (Figure 5-4).

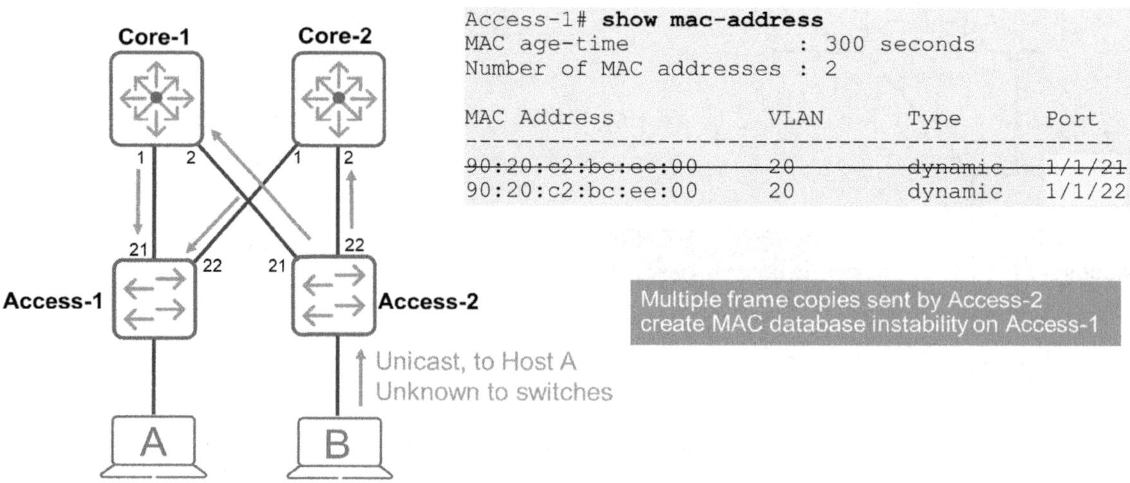

Figure 5-4 Multiple Frame Copies

Suppose that Host B sends a frame to Host A.

Access-2 has not yet learned Host A's MAC address, and so it floods this frame out ports 21 and 22. Thus, Core-1 and Core-2 both switches receive a frame with source MAC 90:...:00, inbound on port 21.

Both cores send a copy to Access-1 switch.

Access-1 now believes that it can reach Host B via ports 21 and 22.

Access-1 is thus confused, Host B can only exist in one place, but it appears to exist in two places.

The multiple frame copies generated by Access-2 create MAC database instability on Access-1.

As you can see, these are serious problems. You need redundant links for reliability, but this redundancy can bring your network to its knees. It is time to learn about the solution to these challenges, the Spanning-Tree Protocol invented in 1984 by the brilliant Miss Radio Perlman. Legend has it that she created the algorithm for this protocol in a few hours. She was so pleased with her creation that she then wrote a poem about it, and then went home for the day.

Spanning-Tree Protocol

Operation Overview

The IEEE 802.1d standard version of the Spanning-Tree Protocol (STP) was developed to build and maintain redundant, yet loop-free networks. With STP, you eliminate single points of failure, while avoiding loops and MAC table instability. STP creates a loop-free topology by automatically disabling redundant links.

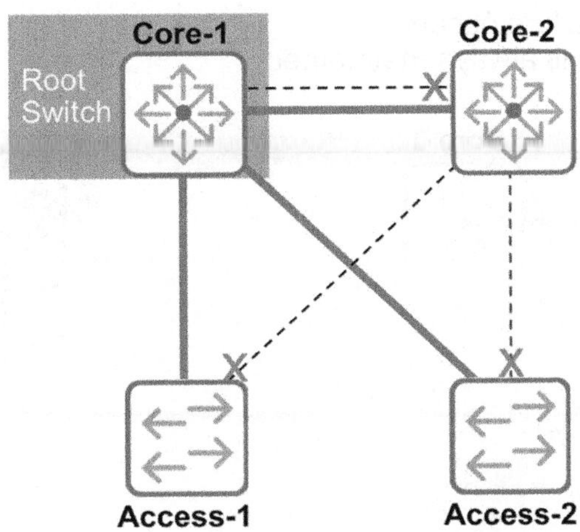

Figure 5-5 Operation Overview

Figure 5-5 shows a highly redundant network for resiliency and fault-tolerance. These redundant links could cause loops and their associated issues.

However, once STP is engaged, certain redundant links are automatically disabled. If there are no loops, there should not be problems with broadcast storms or MAC address table instability. However, these disabled links remain available to provide redundancy as needed.

To accomplish its goal, one switch in the Spanning-Tree domain is elected as a bridge or root switch. Many trees grow out of the ground, from its roots, as a single trunk, and then branch out from there. Likewise, the root bridge is the reference from which the spanning tree grows. All other switches are non-root bridges (switches), sometimes knows as designated switches. A loop-free path "grows" from this root switch out to all non-designated (non-root) switches.

Note

What we now call a "switch" is a very fast, multiple-port version of what used to be called a "bridge" (many years ago). When discussing STP, you will often see the term bridge. In this context, "bridge" and "switch" can be thought of as the same thing. When you see "bridge", know that we are talking about a switch.

Spanning-Tree Protocol (STP)

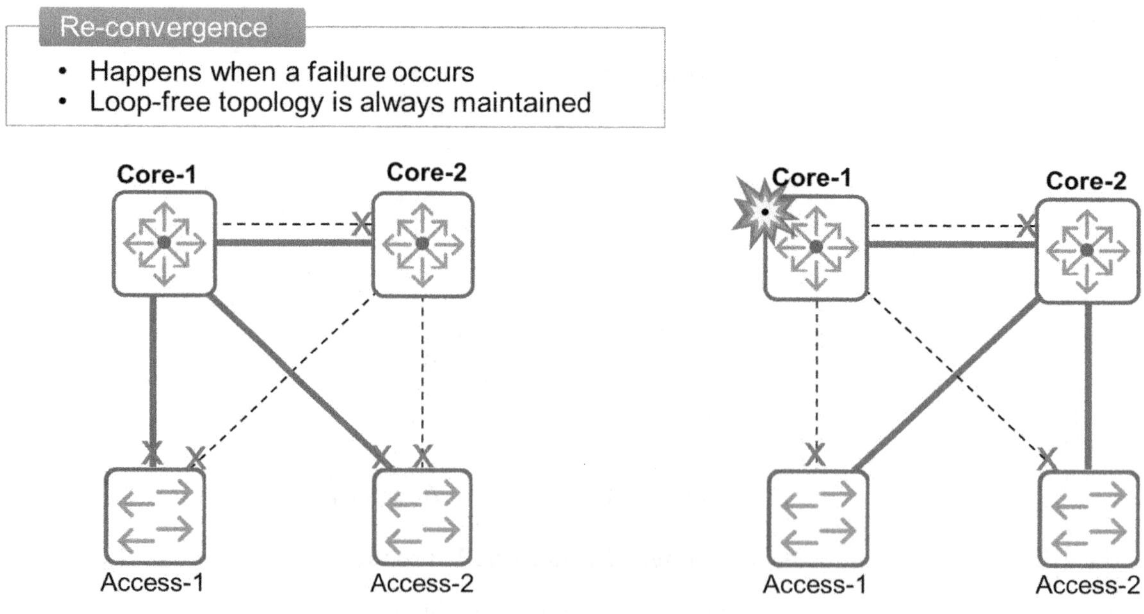

Figure 5-6 Spanning-Tree Protocol

The STP algorithm runs on all switches, and redundant links have been disabled to avoid loops.

However, if a failure occurs, STP converges on a new topology of active links, which are used to forward frames. A loop-free topology is always maintained (Figure 5-6).

Note

The word "converge" can mean something like "to meet at some point". Convergence, in the context of networking, means that the devices all come to an agreement about a new network topology. All devices converge on a new set of active paths to be used for frame forwarding.

Overview of Spanning-Tree Protocol

STP	RSTP	MSTP
802.1D (pre-2004)	**802.1w** merged into **802.1D 2004**	**802.1s** merged into **802.1Q 2005**
• Original protocol • Slow convergence	• Faster convergence • Costs that fit with modern port speeds	RSTP behavior in multiple instances
• Obsolete • Not recommended	Default *operation* between ArubaOS-CX switches (when no MSTP region is set up)	Default *mode* for **ArubaOS-CX** switches (but no MSTP region settings)

Figure 5-7 Spanning-Tree Overview

In the original standard the failure detection is based on timers. With the IEEE 802.1d default, the root switch (and only the root switch) originates a "hello" packet every 2 seconds. These hello packets are forwarded on out to the rest of the switches in the domain. If some switch downstream (farther away from the root switch) ceases to receive hello packets for 20 seconds (the default Max Age timer), an outage is assumed, and all switches begin to converge on a new topology. The duration of this process is defined by the Forward Delay timer, which is 15 seconds by default. This protocol is considered obsolete and its use is no longer recommended in modern networks (Figure 5-7).

Rapid Spanning-Tree Protocol (RSTP) was developed in 1998 to speed convergence. Instead of only the root switch originating hello packets, ALL switches originate them. This means that RSTP now has a true keepalive mechanism that can respond in seconds (or less). The need for old and slow Max Age and Forward Delay timers is eliminated. You will soon learn the details of this new convergence process.

Note

RSTP is backward compatible with the original standard 802.1d. However, to maintain this capability, some benefits of RSTP are lost.

802.1s or Multiple Spanning Tree was developed to improve the performance of the protocol for implementing multiple Loop-free Topologies or Instances to load balance the traffic across all links. This protocol helps to create optimal paths.

MSTP runs on AOS-CX switches by default. However, if no setting is configured then this protocol behaves like RSTP. You will understand why this happens later in this training.

Note

- AOS-CX 6300 Spanning Tree is globally enabled by default.
- AOS-CX 8325 Spanning Tree is globally disabled by default.

Rapid Spanning-Tree Protocol Elements

Overview

In this section we introduce the key elements that the Rapid Spanning-Tree Algorithm uses to decide on which ports will be enabled and capable of forward traffic and which ones will not.

- Bridge Identifier
- Bridge Protocol Data Unit
- Rapid Spanning-Tree Port States
- Rapid Spanning-Tree Port Cost
- Rapid Spanning-Tree Port Roles

Bridge Identifier

Spanning Tree assigns each switch a unique identifier called Bridge ID. This identifier is composed of a 2-byte priority and 6-byte MAC address. The priority defaults to 32768. By default, all switches have the same priority. However, each switch has a unique MAC address, and so each Bridge ID (BID) will be unique (Figure 5-8).

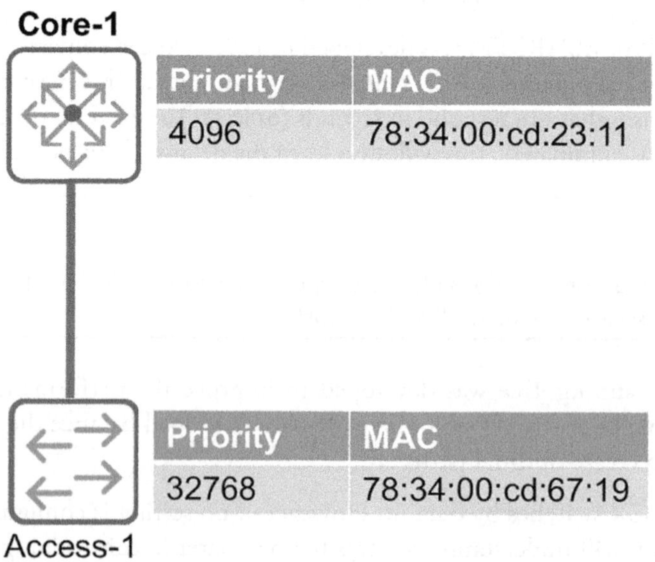

Figure 5-8 Bridge Identifier

Bridge Protocol Data Unit

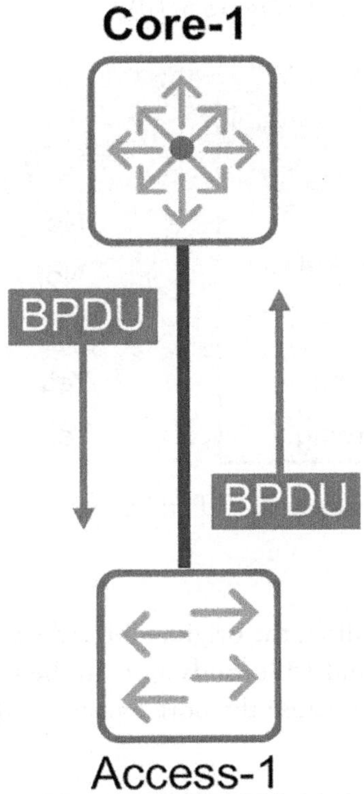

Figure 5-9 BPDUs

All switches that participate in the Spanning-Tree Algorithm exchange control messages called Bridge Protocol Data Units (BPDU). In the original 802.1d standard, BPDUs were generated only by the root switch, and then had to "trickle down" to other switches. This led to the need for the slow MAX AGE and Forward Delay timers.

With RSTP, all switches originate BPDUs with its current information, every 2 seconds, the default hello-time period. Thus, if a port stops receiving BPDUs for three consecutive hello timers, the switch quickly knows that it has lost connectivity to its neighbor. It ages out the protocol information and begins to converge. Because each switch originates BPDUs, this becomes a true keepalive mechanism. Failure detection will take no longer than 6 seconds (Figure 5-9).

Port States

During original tree establishment and any ensuing convergence, switches must decide which ports will forward data and which ports must be disabled to prevent Layer-2 Loops. Spanning Tree uses port states to transit from a Blocking port to a Forwarding port. The table in the slide summarizes the port states and their specific task. This table lists the states that were used on 802.1d and compares them against the new port states in 802.1w (Figure 5-10).

STP (802.1d) Port State	RSTP (802.1w) Port state	Port Included in Active Topology	Port learning MAC addresses?
Disabled	Discarding	No	No
Blocking		No	No
Listening		No	No
Learning	Learning	Yes	Yes
Forwarding	Forwarding	Yes	Yes

Figure 5-10 Port States

To transition from Blocking to Forwarding, the original 802.1d standard takes 30 seconds where 15 seconds are spent in a Listening state, and 15 seconds more in the Learning state. One of the reasons RSTP is more efficient than 802.1d is because the port transitions quickly from discarding to learning to forwarding.

Note

Blocking and Listening state are also deprecated in MSTP.

Note

In RSTP the Learning state is a transitory state and is only used during a re-convergence of the protocol when a change happens in the topology. Stable states will be Discarding or Forwarding states.

Path Cost

RSTP may have several possible paths to get from the root switch to some non-root switch. It chooses the best path based on cost, which is based on link speed. Figure 5-11 shows the AOS-CX default port costs.

Link Speed	RSTP Port Cost in ArubaOS-CX
100 Mbps	200,000
1Gbps	20,000
10 Gbps	2,000
100 Gbps	200
1 Tbps	20

BPDUs advertise the path cost

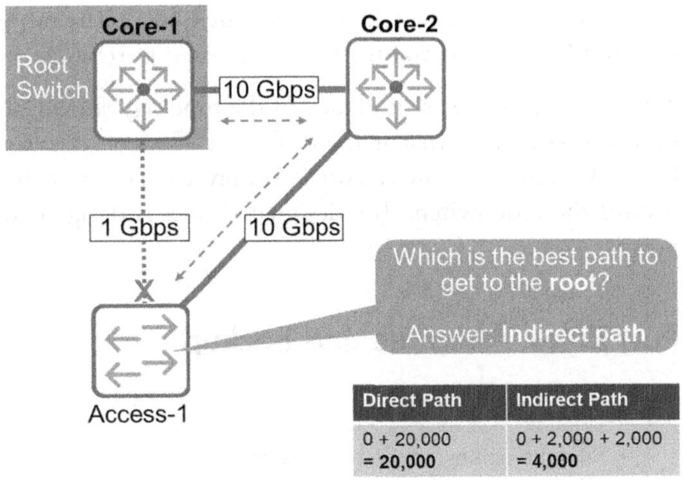

Figure 5-11 Path Cost

Consider the example shown in Figure 5-11. Intuitively, you might think the root switch's best path to Access-1 is the direct path. However, this is a 1Gbps link, which has a cost of 20,000.

The indirect path to Access-1 via Core-2 requires two 10Gbps links, which only have a cost of 2,000 each. 2,000 + 2,000 = 4,000 (far less than 20,000). Strictly speaking the root switch will add its cost to itself in this case the cost is equal to 0. Thus, this is the preferred best path. The redundant path is disabled to avoid loops.

Port Roles: Designated and Root

Switches that use 802.1w RSTP do not have a complete view of the topology. They build and maintain the loop-free topology by exchanging BPDUs, which indicate how close they are to the root switch. BPDUs help switches to calculate the correct port role for each of their ports (Figure 5-12).

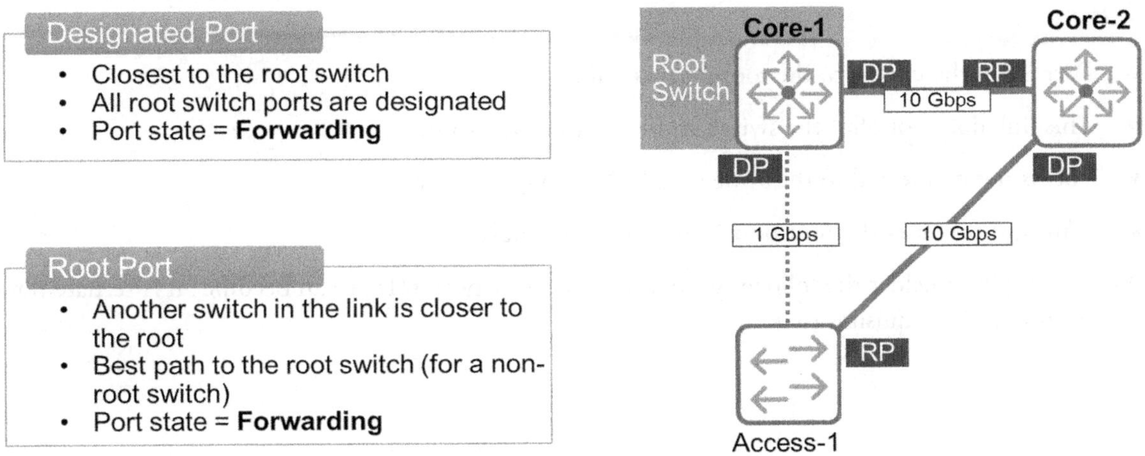

Figure 5-12 Port Roles

All ports on the root switch are Designated ports. The root switch is like the "boss" of the domain. It does not block its ports; only non-designated ports must worry about that.

Note also that there are no loops in the topology shown, so all ports are forwarding. Looking at the non-root switches, what is the difference between the Root Port and Designated port? They both forward frames. The Root Port is simply the port that is closest to the root switch, the best path toward the root switch. The designated port is designated to accept traffic from downstream root ports.

Port Roles: Alternate and Backup

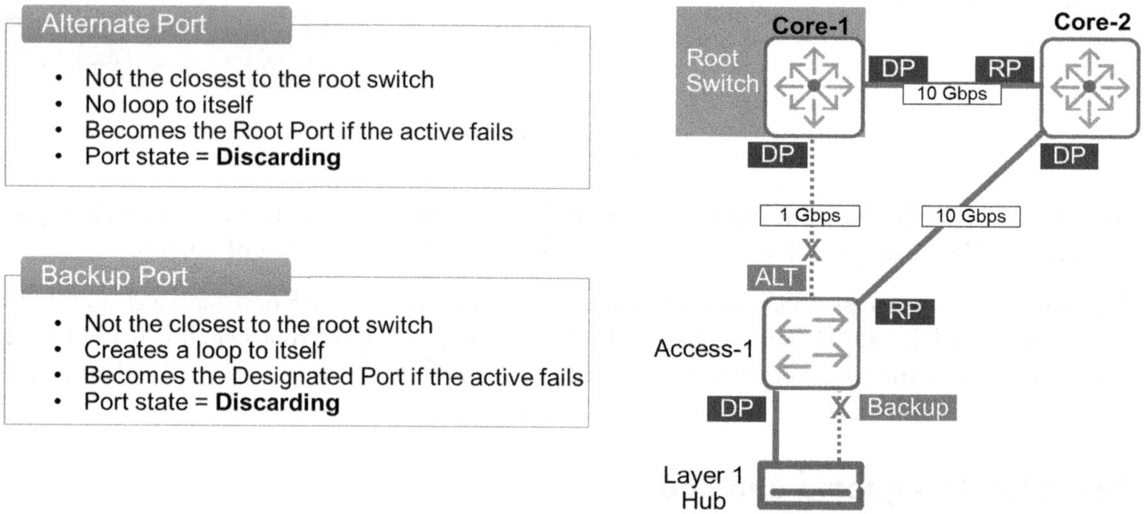

Figure 5-13 Port States: Alternate and Backup

Alternate

- Port is not the closest to the root on this link.
- This link does not offer the switch its best path to the root.
- Port is not connected to the same switch. No Loop to itself.
- This port becomes the root port if the active port fails.

As an example, consider the following situation. Access-1 port 1/1/21 can become an Alternate port since it fulfills the requisites to it.

Backup

- Port is not the closest to the root in this link.
- This link does not offer the switch its best path to the root.
- Port is connected to the same switch. The switch has a looped connection to itself or it has a loop created by a Layer-1 hub.
- The backup port becomes designated port if the existing designated port fails.

A loop could be caused when a Layer-1 hub is placed on the topology. As an example, take in consideration the following image, in this situation ports 1/1/26 and 1/1/27 on Access-1 are in a loop situation because a Hub was introduced to the topology. If RTSP was running on Access-1 neither of these ports (1/1/25 and 1/1/26) will become an Alternate Port.

A backup port is considered when a Hub is connected to the network. In this case Port 1/1/26 becomes the backup port (Figure 5-13).

Note

Introducing Layer-1 Hubs into the topology must be avoided.

RSTP Operation

Operational Overview

The Rapid STP algorithm converges on a loop-free topology by performing the following steps:

- Elects Root switch.
- Select the root port on all non-root switches or Non-designated bridges.
- Select the designated port on each switch-to-switch links.

Other ports move to a blocking state to prevent loops.

Root Switch Election

For both the 802.1d and 802.1w standards, root switch election is based on the Bridge ID (BID) the lowest value wins. Recall that the two-part BID is composed of a priority, which defaults to 32,768 for all switches, and a globally unique MAC address.

You can rely on this default, rather random behavior, but it is not recommended. Some small, low-powered switch on the edge of your network might win the election. This makes for a less stable tree, with sub-optimal paths and poor resiliency.

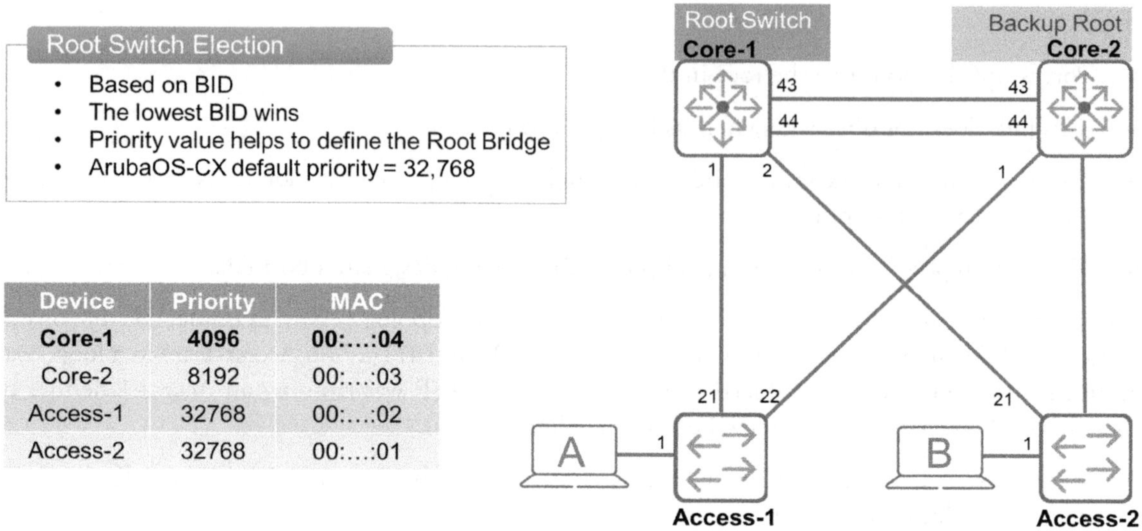

Figure 5-14 Root Switch Election

Consider the topology shown in Figure 5-14. If the priority is set to the default, then Access-2 will become the Root Switch; it has the Lowest MAC address.

You want to ensure that one of the high-powered, more centrally located core switches wins the election. You have a more robust, resilient, and optimally pathed tree structure. To do this, you simply lower the priority value of the preferred switches, lower than the 32,768 default. In this example, Core-1 becomes the Root Switch simply by setting its priority to 4096. However, if Core-1 fails, then Access-2 will become the Root Switch, which would not be optimal. Therefore, it is important that Core-2 becomes the second-best option. In this case Core-2 is setup with a priority of 8192.

Recall that the priority value must be configured in increments of 4096. You might lower the value of Core-1 to 4096, and the value of Core-2 to 8192.

Select Root Ports in Non-Root Switches

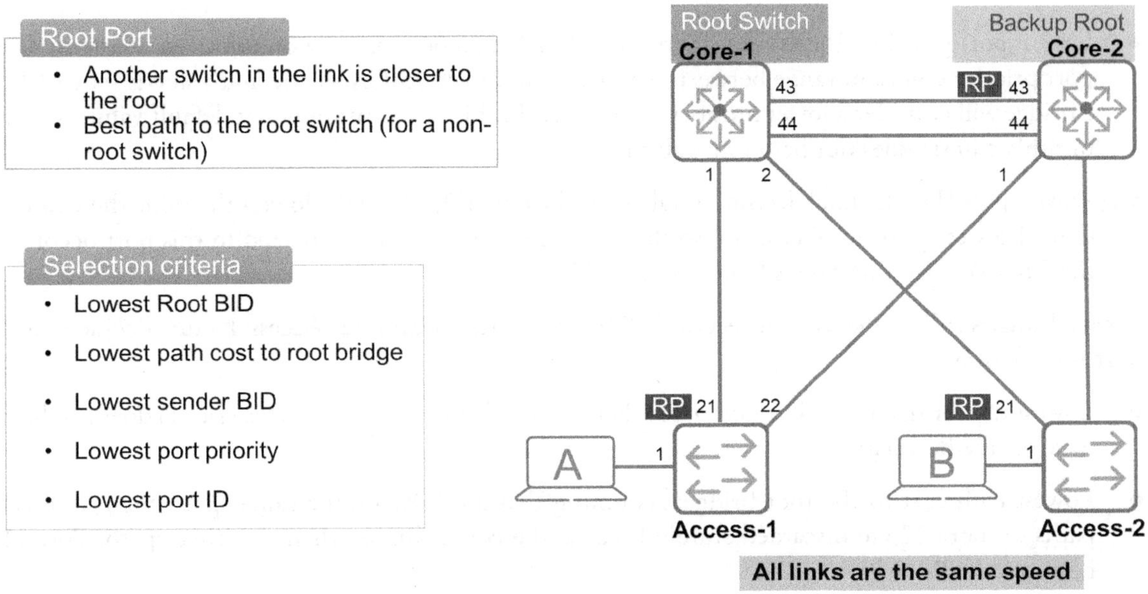

Figure 5-15 Root Ports in Non-Root Switches

Non-root switches or Non-Designated bridges must select the best path to the root switch, by selecting its root port, the port connected to this best path (Figure 5-15). Root port selection criteria are as follows:

1. Lowest root bridge ID
2. Lowest path cost to the root bridge
3. Lowest sender bridge ID
4. Lowest port priority
5. Lowest port ID

Core-2 analysis: This device will receive BPDUs on ports 1, 2, 43, and 44. Core-2 must decide which port is the best one.

- Lowest Root Bridge ID: All devices agree that the root bridge is Core-1. This does not help to select the best path.
- Lowest path cost to the root bridge: Assuming that all links are the same speed then, indirect paths on port 1 and 2 are discarded simply because the cost is higher than direct paths. Ports 43 and 44 have the same cost; the next criteria must be used.

- Lowest sender Bridge ID: BDPUs received on ports 43 and 44 are generated by the same device (Core-1), this criteria does not help to break the tie.
- Lowest port priority: The sender (Core-1) will include a port priority on the advertisement. The port priority comes in range between 0 and 240 and in AOS-CX the default value is set to 128, a bridge will consider a lower number the winner. In this case assuming that default values are set but this criteria does not help to break the tie.
- Lowest port ID: The final decision is taken on the port ID, where the lowest the value the winner. Core-1 lowest port number is 43, so the port on Core-2 that is connected to this port becomes the Root Port (in this case is Core-2's port 43).

Access-1 analysis: This device will receive BPDUs on ports 21 and 22. Access-1 must decide which port is the best one.

- Lowest root bridge ID: All devices agree that the root bridge is Core-1. This criteria does not help to select the best path.
- Lowest path cost to the root bridge: Assuming that all links are the same speed then, indirect paths on port 22 are discarded simply because the cost is higher than the direct path. Port 21 becomes the Root Port.

Access-2 analysis: This device will receive BPDUs on ports 21 and 22. Access-2 must decide which port is the best one.

- Lowest root bridge ID: All devices agree that the root bridge is Core-1. This criteria does not help to select the best path.
- Lowest path cost to the root bridge: Assuming that all links are the same speed then, indirect paths on port 22 are discarded simply because the cost is higher than the direct path. Port 21 becomes the Root Port.

Selecting Designated Ports and Alternate Ports

The criteria to select a Designated port is the same as root port.

1. Lowest root bridge ID
2. Lowest path cost to the root bridge
3. Lowest sender bridge ID
4. Lowest port priority
5. Lowest port ID

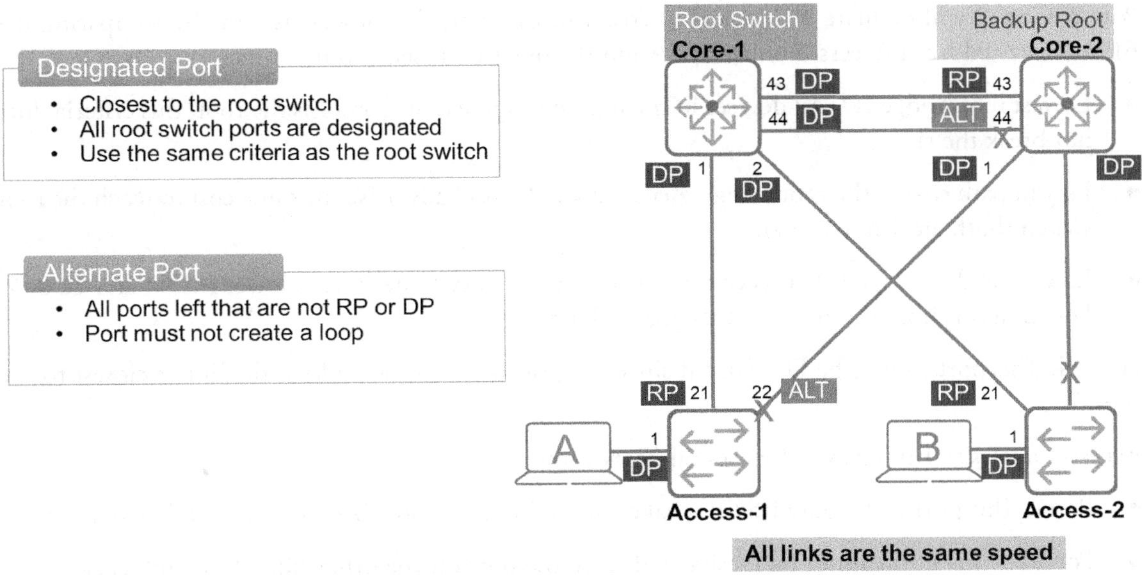

Figure 5-16 Designated Ports and Alternate Ports

The following statements are a shortcut to determine a designated port on a link.

All ports in the root switch are always designated ports.

- In a switch-to-switch link where previously a root port was elected on one side, the other side must always be a designated port.

Core-1 analysis: This is the Root switch and its ports will always be the closest to the root bridge; therefore ports 1, 2, 43, and 44 on Core-1 become Designated Ports.

Core-2 analysis: The analysis focuses on ports 1, 2, and 44.

Port 1. Core-2 will evaluate if this port is closest to the root; this process is done by comparing the BPDU received from Access-1 on this port and the one that it sends out. This process follows the same rules as the root port, so let's start the analysis:

- Lowest root bridge ID. All devices in the topology agree that Core-1 is the root; this criteria does not break the tie.
- Lowest path cost to the root bridge. Access-1 and Core-2 advertise the same cost to reach the root switch (both are 1 hop away).
- Lowest sender bridge ID. This criteria breaks the tie since Core-2 has a lower BID than Access-1. Port 1 in this link becomes the Designated Port.

Port 2. Core-2 will evaluate if this port is closest to the root; this process is done by comparing the BPDU received from Access-2 on this port and the one that it sends out.

- Lowest root bridge ID. All devices in the topology agree that Core-1 is the root; this criteria does not break the tie.
- Lowest path cost to the root bridge. Access-2 and Core-2 advertise the same cost to reach the root switch (both are 1 hop away).
- Lowest sender bridge ID. This criteria breaks the tie since Core-2 has a lower BID than Access-2. Port 2 in this link becomes the Designated Port.

Port 44. This port cannot be Designated since the port on the other side of the link is closest to the root.

Access-1 analysis: This analysis focuses on ports 1 and 22.

- Port1. This port is the only RSTP speaker in the link; this port becomes the Designated Port.
- Port22 . This port cannot be Designated since the port on the other side of the link is closest to the root.

Access-2 analysis: This analysis focuses on ports 1 and 22.

- Port1. This port is the only RSTP speaker in the link; this port becomes the Designated Port.
- Port22 . This port cannot be Designated since the port on the other side of the link is closest to the root.

In this example, the topology does not include any Layer-1 hub which implies that there will not exist a Backup port only Alternate Ports. Simply all ports that were not elected as Designated or Root ports will become Alternate and their state will be discarding. In the slide you can notice that Access-1's port 22, Access-2's port 22, and Core-2's port 44 become Alternate ports (Figure 5-16).

Edge Ports

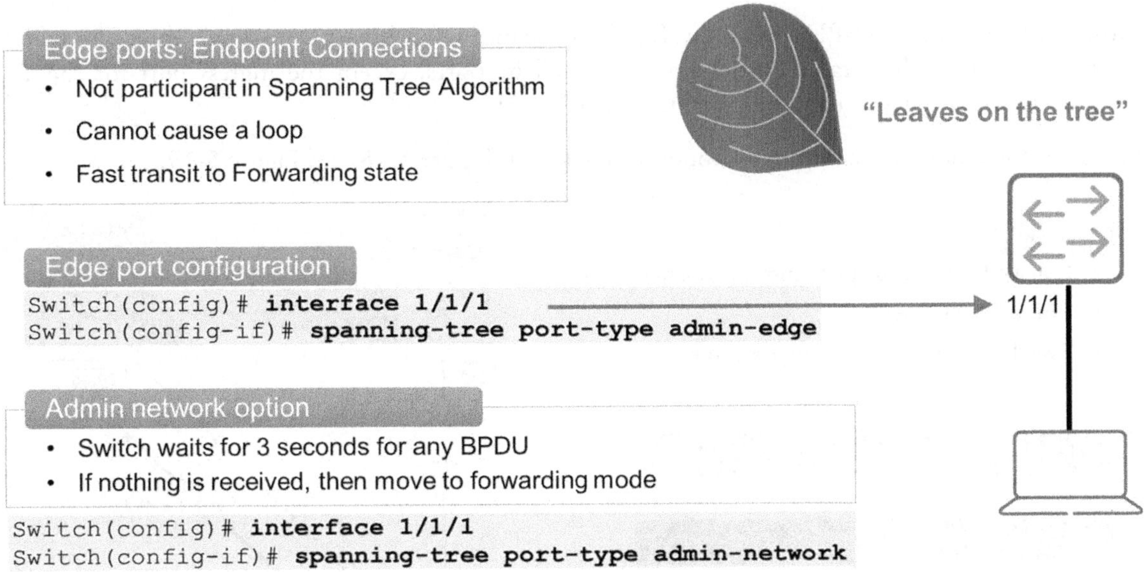

Figure 5-17 Edge Ports

Edge ports connect to endpoint, and therefore should not be receiving BPDUs. Because edge ports do not need to participate in the spanning-tree algorithm they are referred to as the "leaf on the spanning tree". Since they cannot cause loops, they can quickly transition to a forwarding state with no intermediate steps (Figure 5-17).

If BPDUs are received on an edge port, then the port will act as a normal Spanning-Tree port and participate in the Spanning-Tree algorithm to prevent Layer-2 Loops. You must manually configure edge ports, as shown here.

```
Switch(config)# interface 1/1/1
Switch(config-if)# spanning-tree port-type admin-edge
```

An alternative to the admin-edge option is the AOS-CX administrative-network option. With this option, the port looks for BPDUs for the first 3 seconds after the link is up. If no BPDUs are received, the port becomes an edge port and immediately forwards frames. If BPDUs are detected, the port becomes as a non-edge port. It participates in normal STP operation.

```
Switch(config)# interface 1/1/1
Switch(config-if)# spanning-tree port-type admin-network
```

Topology Change Mechanism

In RSTP, a topology change occurs when non-edge ports move to a different state, or when BPDUs are no longer received. A switch detects this topology change. The switch actively informs the rest of the switches in the network of the Topology Change. It sets the TC bit in BPDUs and transmits these BPDUs. It flushes the MAC address table entries associated with all non-edge ports.

Other switches receive a BPDU with the Topology Change (TC) bit set from a neighbor. The switch clears the MAC address table entries learned on all its ports, except the ingress port for the TC BPDU. These switches in turn send BPDUs with TC set.

Consider the following example of a topology change in Figure 5-18 and Figure 5-19.

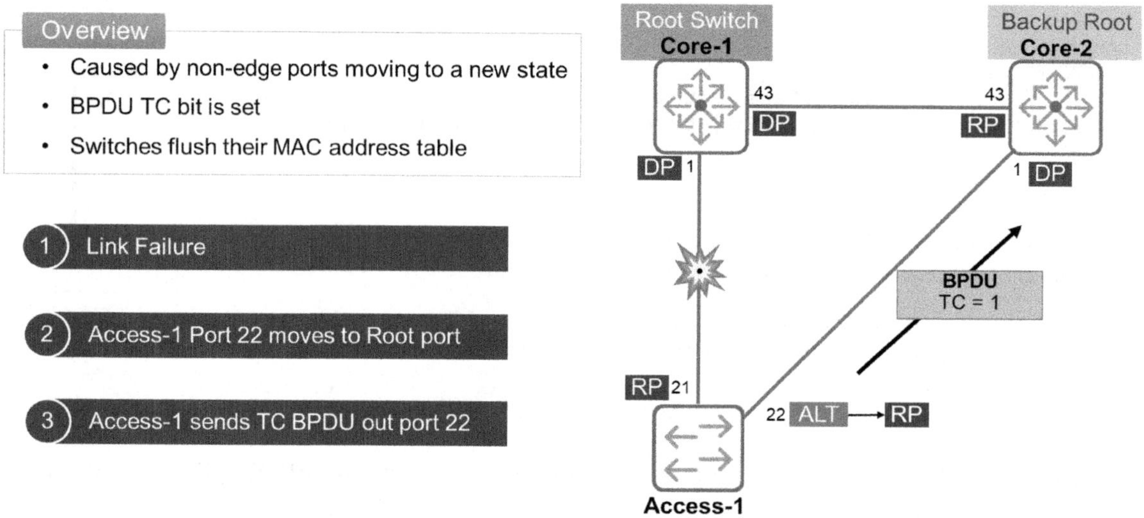

Figure 5-18 Topology Change Mechanism

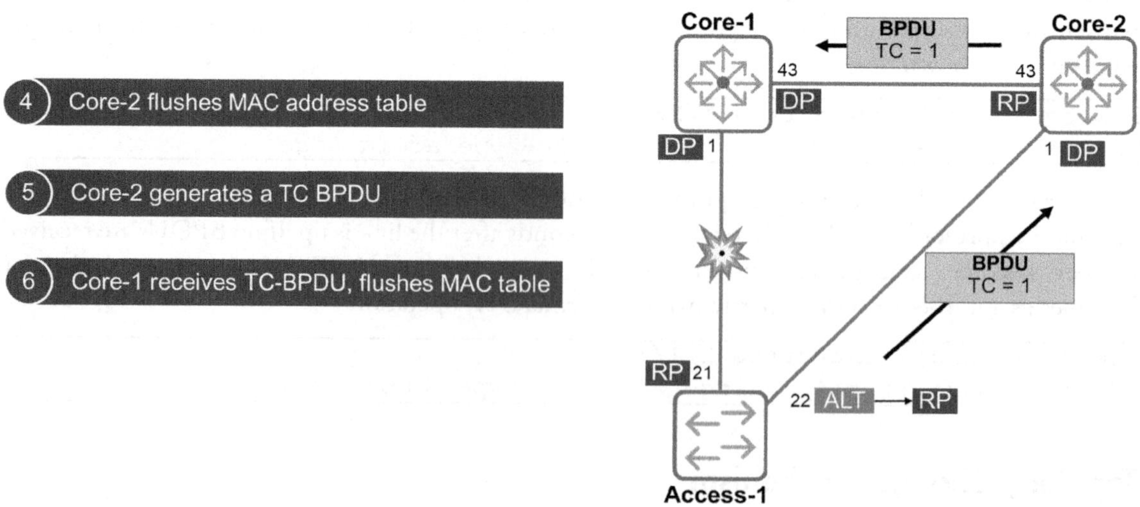

Figure 5-19 Topology Change Continued

Note

In the original 802.1d standard, any switch could send TC BPDUs to notify others, but the instruction to clear the MAC address table must always come from the Root switch. This two-step process takes more time to be completed.

Lab 5.1: Configuring Rapid Spanning-Tree Protocol

Overview

Your Core switch integration has proven successful and the network is more scalable; however, experience tells you that a single Core switch is a single point of failure. If an uplink or the Core itself goes down all business operations will be disrupted. During a conversation you share this concern with BigStartup management. A formal request for a second 8325 switch was sent to Rent4Cheap Properties who agreed to supply the second unit and modify the lease. A few weeks later the switch arrived and was connected to Core-1.

BigStartup has notified you the additional Core switch is operational and has asked you to complete the integration.

Note that references to equipment and commands are taken from Aruba's hosted remote lab. These are shown for demonstration purposes in case you wish to replicate the environment and tasks on your own equipment.

Objectives

After completing this lab, you will be able to:

- Add a redundant core switch.
- Enable redundant links.
- Verify the spanning-tree functionality.
- Find the Root bridge.
- Discover the CST topology.

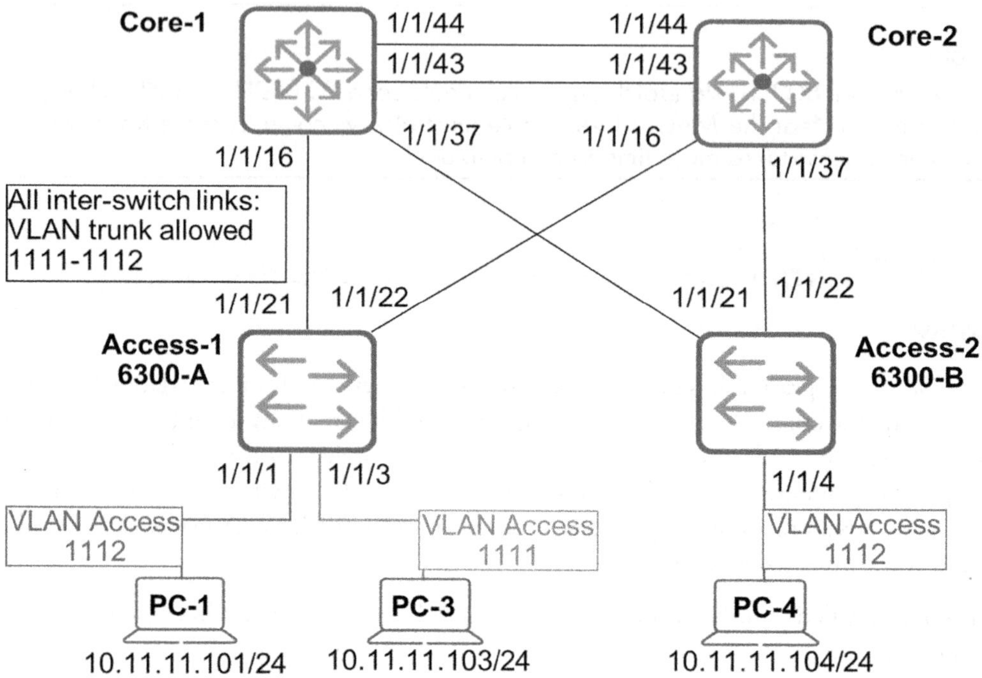

Figure 5-20 Lab Topology

Task 1: Add the Redundant Core Switch and Redundant Links

Objectives

In this task you will add a fourth component to the topology: Core-2. First you will make sure that the Core and Access switches are running Spanning Tree. Next, you will prepare port 1/1/22 on both Access switches to act as uplinks to Core-2 and enable them. Finally, you will confirm that connectivity between hosts is still in place (Figure 5-20).

Steps

PC-1

1. Access PC-1.
2. Open Putty and open an SSH session to Core-1 (**10.251.0.1**), and login with **cxf11/aruba123**.

Tip
Putty should have Saved Sessions to Core-1 and Core-2; you can use these as shortcuts.

Core-1 (via PC-1)

3. Define the height of the page to 40 lines.

```
Core-1# page 40
```

4. Confirm STP is active.

```
Core-1(config)# show spanning-tree
Spanning-tree status        : Enabled Protocol: MSTP

MST0
  Root ID     Priority     : 0
              MAC-Address : 90:20:c2:bc:ed:00
              This bridge is the root
              Hello time(in seconds):2  Max Age(in seconds):20
              Forward Delay(in seconds):15

  Bridge ID  Priority   : 0
              MAC-Address: 90:20:c2:bc:ed:00
              Hello time(in seconds):2  Max Age(in seconds):20
              Forward Delay(in seconds):15

Port          Role          State         Cost          Priority   Type
----------------------------------------------------------------------
1/1/1           Disabled         Blocking       20000             128
point_to_point
1/1/2           Disabled         Blocking       20000             128
point_to_point
←---- output omitted ---
```

PC-1

5. Open Putty and open an SSH session to Core-2 (10.251.0.2), and login with: **cxf11/aruba123**.

Core-2 (via PC-1)

6. Confirm STP is active.

```
Core-2(config)# show spanning-tree | include Spanning
Spanning-tree status      : Enabled Protocol: MSTP
Core-2(config)#
```

Access-1 and Access-2

7. Repeat step 6 on Access-1 and Access-2.

```
T11-Access-1# show spanning-tree | include Spanning
Spanning-tree status        : Enabled Protocol: MSTP
```

Notice

The pipe (|) command filters the output of show commands according to the criteria specified by the parameter include, exclude, count, begin, or redirect. Strings of characters that follow the filtering tool (for example, "T4" or "T11" in example above) are case sensitive. Typing the wrong capitalization may lead to the absence of output.

```
T11-Access-2# show spanning-tree | include Spanning
Spanning-tree status       : Enabled Protocol: MSTP
```

Important

Spanning-Tree Protocol is enabled by default on 6300s; however in the case of the **8325s** its initial configuration state is **disabled**. Once enabled, default STP mode is Multiple-Instance Spanning Tree (MST).

Important

MST0 relates to instance 0 of MST; this instance is used for interoperating with RSTP switches and MST switches in other regions and to create the Common Spanning Tree (CST): a single Spanning-Tree topology for all VLANs.

As a sanity check you will connect to Core-1 and confirm the connections from that device.

Access-1

8. Move back to Access-1.
9. Allow VLANs 1111 and 1112 on interface 1/1/22 and enable the port.

```
T11-Access-1(config)# interface 1/1/22
T11-Access-1(config-if)# vlan trunk allowed 1111-1112
T11-Access-1(config-if)# no shutdown
```

10. On the Access switch use LLDP to discover which Core-2 remote port is connected to interface 1/1/22. This will be port 1/1/37.

```
T11-Access-1(config-if)# show LLDP neighbor-info

LLDP Neighbor Information
=========================

←---- output omitted ---→
```

```
LOCAL-PORT  CHASSIS-ID          PORT-ID         PORT-DESC       TTL       SYS-
NAME
------------------------------------------------------------------------------
-------
1/1/21      90:20:c2:bc:ed:00  1/1/16          1/1/16          120       Core-
1
1/1/22      90:20:c2:bc:3f:00  1/1/16          1/1/16          120       Core-
2
```

11. Apply a description to the port.

```
T11-Access-1(config-if)# description TO_CORE-2_PORT-16
```

Access-2

12. Move to Access-2 and repeat steps 9 to 11. The remote port that interface 1/1/22 is connected to on the Core-2 side will be 1/1/37.

```
T11-Access-2(config)# interface 1/1/22
T11-Access-2(config-if)# VLAN trunk allowed 1111-1112
T11-Access-2(config-if)# no shutdown
T11-Access-2(config-if)# show LLDP neighbor-info

LLDP Neighbor Information
=========================

←---- output omitted ---→


LOCAL-PORT  CHASSIS-ID          PORT-ID         PORT-DESC       TTL       SYS-
NAME
------------------------------------------------------------------------------
-------
1/1/21      90:20:c2:bc:ed:00  1/1/37          1/1/37          120       Core-
1
1/1/22      90:20:c2:bc:3f:00  1/1/37          1/1/37          120       Core-
2
T11-Access-2(config-if)# description TO_CORE-2_PORT-37
```

You have prepared the Access switches uplinks; now you will prepare the connections between the cores and their downlinks.

Core-1

13. Use LLDP to discover the ports used for the connection to Core-2. Use a filtered version of this command to display relevant output only.

```
Core-1# show LLDP neighbor-info | exclude 1/21


←---- output omitted ---→

LOCAL-PORT  CHASSIS-ID          PORT-ID        PORT-DESC     TTL      SYS-
NAME
-----------------------------------------------------------------------
-------
1/1/43      90:20:c2:bc:3f:00  1/1/43         1/1/43         120      Core-
2
1/1/44      90:20:c2:bc:3f:00  1/1/44         1/1/44         120      Core-
2
```

What are the Core-2 local ports? ____________________

What are Core-2 remote ports? ____________________

14. Move to ports 1/1/43 and 1/1/44 and make each port a trunk interface that allows VLANs1111 and 1112.

```
Core-1(config)# interface 1/1/43-1/1/44
Core-1(config-if-<1/1/43-1/1/44>)# VLAN trunk allowed 1111-1112
```

Notice

If when applying configuration above you get the following error message:

Core-1(config-if-<1/1/43-1/1/44>)# **VLAN trunk allowed 1111-1112**

Operation not allowed on an interface part of a LAG (LAG10).

This implies that your instructor has already run Lab - 6.1 - Link demonstration. This means that interface LAG 10 is replacing ports 43 and 44. Please configure the LAG interface instead using this script:

Core-1(config)# **interface LAG 10**

Core-1(config-LAG-if)# VLAN trunk allowed 1111-1112

Core-2

15. Open the SSH session of Core-2.

16. Define the height of the page to 40 lines.

```
Core-2# page 40
```

17. Create VLAN 1111 and name it T11-EMPLOYEE.

```
Core-2(config)# VLAN 1111
Core-2(config-VLAN-1111)# name T11_EMPLOYEES
```

18. Create VLAN 1112 and name it T11_MANAGERS.

```
Core-2(config)# VLAN 1112
Core-2(config-VLAN-1112)# name T11_MANAGERS
```

19. Access port 1/1/16. Make the description TO_T11-ACCESS-1_PORT-22 and make the interface a trunk interface that allows VLANs 1111 and 1112.

```
Core-2(config)# interface 1/1/16
Core-2(config-if)# description TO_T11-ACCESS-1_PORT-22
Core-2(config-if)# VLAN trunk allowed 1111-1112
```

20. Move to port 1/1/37, then set the TO_T11-ACCESS-2_PORT-22 description, and make the interface a trunk interface that allows VLANs 1111 and 1112.

```
Core-2(config)# interface 1/1/37
Core-2(config-if)# description TO_T11-ACCESS-2_PORT-22
Core-2(config-if)# VLAN trunk allowed 1111-1112
```

21. Access ports 1/1/43 and 1/1/44; make the port a trunk interface that allows VLANs 1111 and 1112.

```
Core-2(config)# interface 1/1/43-1/1/44
Core-2(config-if-<1/1/43-1/1/44>)# VLAN trunk allowed 1111-1112
```

Notice

If you get the following error message:

Core-2(config-if-<1/1/43-1/1/44>)# **VLAN trunk allowed 1111-1112**

Operation not allowed on an interface part of a LAG (LAG10).

This implies that your instructor has already run Lab - 6.1 - Link demonstration. This means that interface LAG 10 is replacing ports 43 and 44. Please configure the LAG interface instead using this script:

Core-2(config)# **interface LAG 10**

Core-2(config-LAG-if)# VLAN trunk allowed 1111-1112

Core-2(config-LAG-if)# **exit**

Task 2: Verify the Topology

Objectives

Obtain and record the Bridge ID of the switches then, identify designated bridges for each link, and locate the Root Bridge as well as link costs. This information will allow you to draw the current logical Common Spanning-Tree (CST) topology.

Steps

Access-1

1. Access the terminal session to Access-1.

2. Show a filtered version of the "show spanning-tree" to get the switch MAC address and switch priority only.

```
T11-Access-1# show spanning-tree | begin 1 Bridge
  Bridge ID  Priority  : 32768
             MAC-Address: 88:3a:30:98:30:00
```

Important

Some of the command output depends on your switch hardware. For example, the system MAC address is unique to your equipment.

Tip

Since the output of the show spanning-tree command is quite long, we have decided to use a shorter version of it by displaying only the information that is relevant to us at this moment. You will use a regular version of this command later in this lab.

Was the switch MAC address? ______________________________

Was the switch Priority? ______________________________

3. Use this information to determine the Bridge ID of Access 1 and write down the value in Figure 5-21 down below.

Tip

You can obtain the Bridge ID by concatenating the value of Switch Priority with the Switch MAC address, for example, 32768:**88:3a:30:98:30:00** for output above.

Core-1, Core-2, and Access-2

4. Repeat steps 1 and 2 with Core-1, Core-2, and Access-2.

```
T11-Access-2# show spanning-tree | begin 1 Bridge
  Bridge ID  Priority   : 32768
             MAC-Address: 88:3a:30:97:a4:40
Core-1# show spanning-tree | begin 1 Bridge
  Bridge ID  Priority   : 4096
             MAC-Address: 90:20:c2:bc:ed:00
Core-2# show spanning-tree | begin 1 Bridge
  Bridge ID  Priority   : 8192
             MAC-Address: 90:20:c2:bc:3f:00
```

5. On Figure 5-21, put a start by the switch that you have identified as Root Bridge. Other fields you will fill out in later steps.

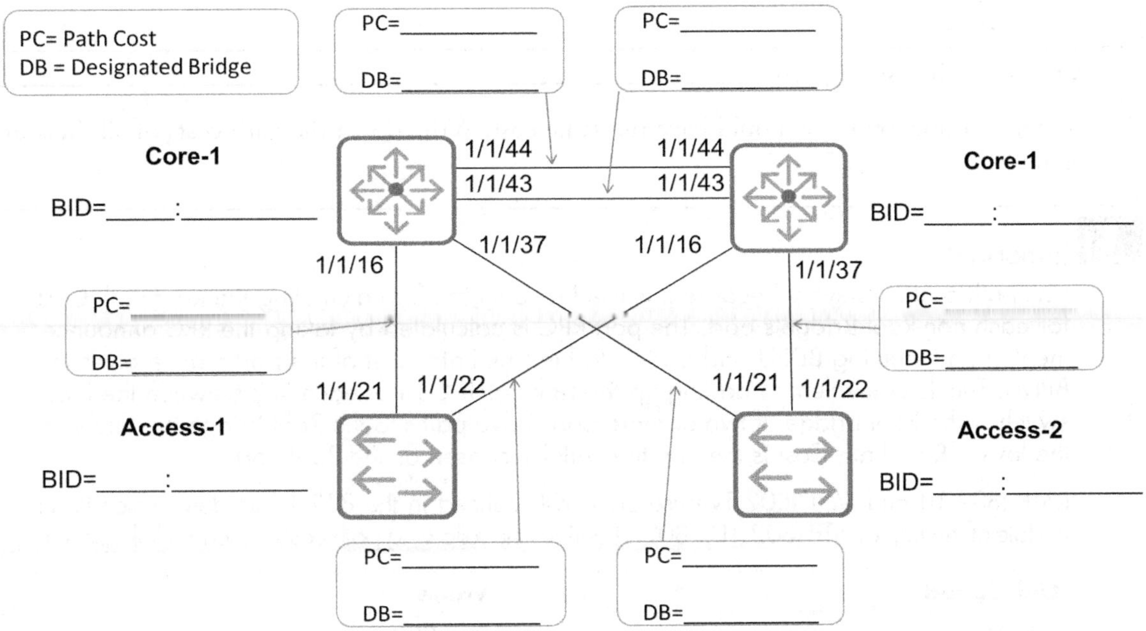

Figure 5-21 Bridge ID, Designated Bridge, and Costs

Access-1

6. Move back to **Access-1** and run the "**show spanning-tree**" command. What are the path costs of the ports?

```
T11-Access-1# show spanning-tree | begin 30 Port
Port            Role            State          Cost          Priority   Type
------------------------------------------------------------------------
----
1/1/1            Designated       Forwarding     20000                    128
point_to_point
1/1/2           Disabled         Blocking        20000                    128
point_to_point
1/1/3            Designated       Forwarding     20000                    128
point_to_point
1/1/4           Disabled         Blocking        20000                    128
point_to_point
1/1/5           Disabled         Blocking        20000                    128
point_to_point
1/1/6           Disabled         Blocking        20000                    128
point_to_point
←---- output omitted ---→
```

What are path costs of ports? ________________________________

7. All ports in this topology should have the same cost. Write down the path costs of all links on Figure 5-21.

Important

Link path cost is relevant because it is used as a metric for calculating the Root Path Cost for each non-Root Bridge's port. The port RPC is calculated by taking the RPC announcement in an incoming BDPU and adds it to the Link Path Cost of the port that receives the BPDU. This is equivalent to adding up the Link Patch Cost of each link between the local switch to the Root Bridge. If two or more ports have paths to the Root Bridge the one with the lowest Root Path Cost is the one that will be chosen as the Root Port.

RSTP (802.1r) and MST (802.1w) use path costs defined in the 802.1t standard which is an update of the legacy STP (802.1D). 802.1t defines the following path costs based on link speeds:

Link Speed	Value
100 Mbps	200,000
1 Gbps	20,000
10 Gbps	2,000
100 Gbps	200

8. Issue the "**show spanning-tree detail**" command. The output will be very long.

Note

"**show spanning-tree detail**" displays the role and state of the ports, similar to the "show spanning-tree" command, with the addition of which switch is the Designated Bridge for each link, the number of transitions to forwarding state, and the number of BPDUs being exchanged.

9. Now try a filtered version of the "**show spanning-tree detail**" command in order to find the Designated bridge on each uplink.

```
T11-Access-1(config)# show spanning-tree  detail | begin 12 "Port 1/1/21"
Port 1/1/21 id 21
Designated  root  has  priority                          :4096  Address:
90:20:c2:bc:ed:00
Designated  bridge  has  priority                        :4096  Address:
90:20:c2:bc:ed:00
Designated port id                          :16
Number of transitions to forwarding state   :11
Bpdus sent 1015, received 23535

Port 1/1/22 id 22
Designated  root  has  priority                          :4096  Address:
90:20:c2:bc:ed:00
Designated  bridge  has  priority                        :8192  Address:
90:20:c2:bc:3f:00
Designated port id                          :37
Number of transitions to forwarding state   : 6
Bpdus sent 23, received 24183
T11-Access-1(config)#
```

What is the Switch's BID of the Designated Bridge on port 1/1/21 (port connected to Core-1)? ______________________________

What is the designated port ID and who owns it? ______________________________

What is the Switch's BID of the Designated Bridge on port 1/1/22 (port connected to Core-2)? ______________________________

What is the designated port ID and who owns it? ______________________________

10. Write down the Designated Bridge of these links on Figure 5-21.

Access-2

11. Move to Access-2 and repeat step 9.

```
T11-Access-2# show spanning-tree detail | begin 12 "Port 1/1/21"
Port 1/1/21 id 21
Designated root has priority                              :4096 Address:
90:20:c2:bc:ed:00
Designated bridge has priority                            :4096 Address:
90:20:c2:bc:ed:00
Designated port id                              :37
Number of transitions to forwarding state       : 1
Bpdus sent 5, received 21209

Port 1/1/22 id 22
Designated root has priority                              :4096 Address:
90:20:c2:bc:ed:00
Designated bridge has priority                            :8192 Address:
90:20:c2:bc:3f:00
Designated port id                              :16
Number of transitions to forwarding state       : 1
Bpdus sent 7, received 21209
```

What is the Switch's BID of the Designated Bridge on port 1/1/21 (port connected to Core-1)? ______

What is the designated port ID and who owns it? ______

What is the Switch's BID of the Designated Bridge on port 1/1/22 (port connected to Core-2)? ______

What is the designated port ID and who owns it? ______

12. Write down the Designated Bridge of these links on Figure 5-21.

Core-2

13. Move to Core-2 and repeat step 9 for ports 1/1/43 and 1/1/44.

```
Core-2# show spanning-tree  detail | begin 12 "Port 1/1/43"
Port 1/1/43 id 43
Designated root has priority                              :4096 Address:
90:20:c2:bc:ed:00
Designated bridge has priority                            :4096 Address:
90:20:c2:bc:ed:00
Designated port id                              :43
Number of transitions to forwarding state       : 1
Bpdus sent 23556, received 23418
```

```
Port 1/1/44 id 44
Designated  root  has  priority                                    :4096  Address:
90:20:c2:bc:ed:00
Designated  bridge  has  priority                                  :4096  Address:
90:20:c2:bc:ed:00
Designated port id                                  :44
Number of transitions to forwarding state   : 2
Bpdus sent 23558, received 23416
```

What is the Switch's BID of the Designated Bridge on port 1/1/43 (port connected to Core-1)? ____________________

What is the designated port ID and who owns it? ____________________

What is the Switch's BID of the Designated Bridge on port 1/1/43 (port connected to Core-2)? ____________________

What is the designated port ID and who owns it? ____________________

At this point you have obtained enough information to accurately determine the Root Bridge, the roles of ports from the Root Bridge to all the other switches, and to draw the CST topology. Start with the Root Bridge and ports' roles identification first.

Read the following notes to refresh how these elections take place.

! Important

Bridge role assignments are aligned with the following rules:

Rule 1: In a topology with redundant switch ports the Switch with lowest Bridge ID (Bridge Priority + MAC address) is elected Root Bridge.

Rule 2: A switch is closer to the Root Bridge if it has the lowest Root Path Cost from the root port and lowest BID combination. On a switch-to-switch link a designated bridge is the switch that is closest to the Root Bridge while the other switch will be non-designated bridge.

Rule 3: The Root Bridge is always the Designated bridge for all its links.

Rule 4: On a link connected to a collision domain where there is only one switch running STP, that switch will be the Designated Bridge for that link.

! Important

Port role assignment follows the following rules:

Rule 5: On a switch-to-switch link the port in the designated bridge side will be chosen as a designated port, unless there is a local loop on the same switch in which case the interface with the lowest Port ID will be designated port and the other will be the blocked port.

Rule 6: If a non-root bridge has only one switch-to-switch link, then the port used for that link is the Root Port.

Rule 7: If a non-root bridge has two or more switch-to-switch links to different remote devices, then:

The one with the lowest Root Path Cost is the root port. In case of a tie of two or more links with the same RPC then the one whose upstream switch is considered closest to the Root Bridge will be the Root port.

For any other links on which this switch was elected designated bridge, the interface will be chosen as designated port.

Rule 8: If a non-designated bridge has two or more links with equal RPC to the same Designated Bridge, then the local interface that connects neighbor's with lowest Port ID will be selected Root Port.

Rule 9: Any other interface on links where the local switch was not elected a designated bridge will be considered an alternate port.

As a side note the final state of designated and root ports is Forwarding, unless there is a security feature triggering an action like root-guard, bpdu-protection, or loop-guard, in which case it will be either blocking or inconsistent.

Alternate ports' final state will always be discarding.

Based on recorded information on Figure 5-21, who is the Root Bridge? Remember that Root bridge is the switch with the lowest Bridge ID. ________________________

What was the Bridge ID component that made this switch the Root Bridge, the MAC address of the priority value? ________________________

Which switch will become Root if the current one fails? ________________________

14. Label the Root bridge on Figure 5-22.
15. All Root Bridge's ports are Designated Ports; tag them as DP on Figure 5-21. (→ Rule 3).
16. Each Access Switch has two ports with different Root Path Costs (RPC), the one with the lowest value (20,000) is the root port (either port 21 or 22), tag them as RP (→ Rule 7a).
17. The non-Root Core switch has two connections to the Root, since both have the same RPC value (20,000) the local port connected to the neighbor's interface with lowest Port ID will be the RP (interface 1/1/43) (→ Rule 8).
18. On the other link between the non-Root Core Switch and Access-1, one of them is closest to the Root, that is the designated bridge; tag its port as DP. (→ Rule 2, Rule 7b).
19. Repeat step 17 for the connection between the non-Root Bridge Core Switch and Access-2.
20. Last, both port Access Switches have one or two ports that are the only STP speaker (1/1/1 and 1/1/3 in Access-1 and 1/1/4 in Access-2). Therefore, Access Switches will be Designated Bridges for those ports, and the interfaces considered designated ports; tag them as DP (→ Rule 4).
21. Any other interface will be considered an Alternate port. Draw an X on them to indicate the blocked link (→ Rule 9).

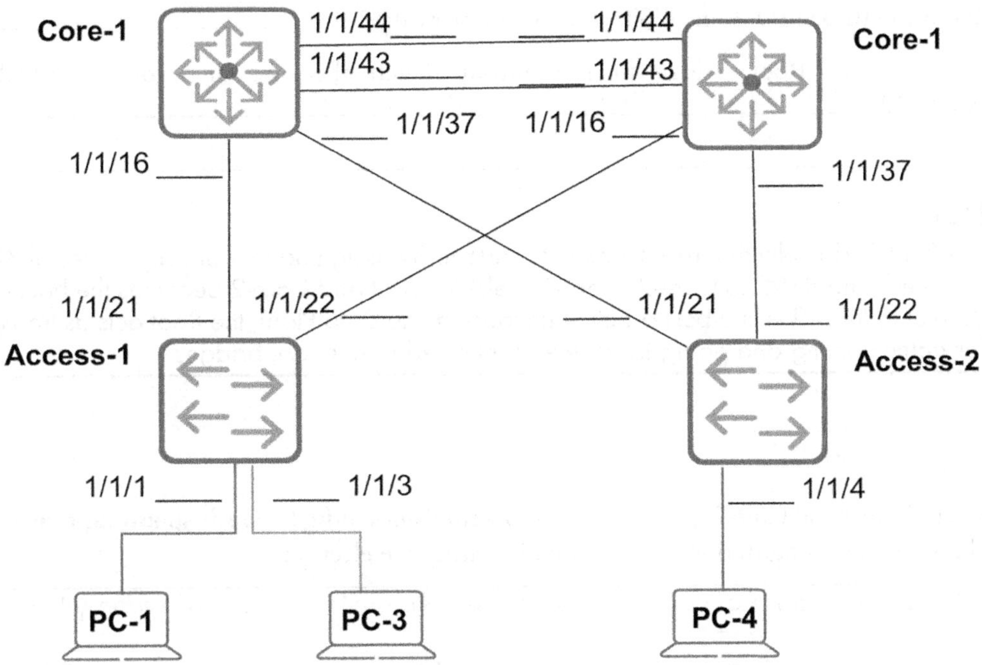

Figure 5-22 Devices and Ports Roles

Tip

You can find a larger copy of this diagram in Appendix 3.

At this point you have a good idea of how the topology should look; in next steps this analysis will be validated.

22. On any switch run the filtered version of the "**show spanning-tree**" command (you should be currently on Core-2).

```
Core-2# show spanning-tree | begin 12 Spanning
Spanning-tree status      : Enabled Protocol: MSTP

MST0
  Root ID     Priority   : 4096
              MAC-Address: 90:20:c2:bc:ed:00
              Hello time(in seconds):2  Max Age(in seconds):20
              Forward Delay(in seconds):15

  Bridge ID   Priority  : 8192
              MAC-Address: 90:20:c2:bc:3f:00
              Hello time(in seconds):2  Max Age(in seconds):20
              Forward Delay(in seconds):15
```

What is the Bridge ID of the CST (MST0) Root Bridge? ______________________

Does the CST Root Bridge in the output match the one that you identified as in Figure 5-22? ______________________

Note

The Root Bridge election result was not random. By assigning low priority values of 4096 to Core-1 and 8192 to Core-2, Core-1 is elected root and Core-2 becomes the backup in case of failure. This is a best practice because at the Data Plane the Root acts as transport for traffic coming and going to devices connected to non-root bridges.

Core-1 and Core-2 (via PC-1)

23. Move to Core-1 and Core-2, then run the "**show running-config | include spanning-tree priority**", and review the configuration used for manipulating the election.

```
Core-1# show running-config | include "spanning-tree priority"
spanning-tree priority 1
Core-2# show running-config | include "spanning-tree priority"
spanning-tree priority 2
```

Important

802.1D standard says that switch priority can be set in increments of 4096. AOS-CX reflects that rule by allowing the administrator to define a multiplying factor (called step) of these 4096 increments in a range between 0 and 15 where the default value is 8. See help output below:

Core-2(config)# spanning-tree priority?

<0-15> Enter an integer number (Default: 8)

Access-1 and Access-2

24. On Access Switches, use filtered versions of the "**show spanning-tree**" command for validating the roles of the ports.

```
T11-Access-1# show spanning-tree | exclude Disabled

<---- output omitted --->

Port            Role            State        Cost            Priority   Type
------------ -------------- ------------ -------------- ---------- ---
-------
1/1/1               Designated       Forwarding    20000               128
point_to_point
1/1/3               Designated       Forwarding    20000               128
point_to_point
1/1/21          Root                Forwarding    20000                128
point_to_point
1/1/22          Alternate        Blocking        20000                 128
point_to_point
T11-Access-1#
T11-Access-2# show spanning-tree | exclude Disabled

<---- output omitted --->

Port            Role            State        Cost            Priority   Type
------------ -------------- ------------ -------------- ---------- -----
-----
1/1/1           Designated       Forwarding    20000                  128
point_to_point
1/1/21          Root               Forwarding    20000                128
point_to_point
1/1/22          Alternate        Blocking       20000                 128
point_to_point
```

Do the outputs match your Figure 5-22 results? ______________________________

Note

If they do not, it may be because some of the ports are either down or the Access switches priorities are not 32768. Please fix that portion of the configuration before moving forward.

Core-1 and Core-2 (via PC-1)

25. On Core-1 and Core-2 use filtered versions of the "**show spanning-tree**" command for validating the roles of the ports. Look specifically for ports 1/1/16, 1/1/37, 1/1/43, and 1/1/44.

```
Core-1# show spanning-tree | begin 40 Port
Port           Role              State          Cost           Priority   Type
--------------------------------------------------------------------------------
----
1/1/1             Designated        Forwarding     20000                  128
point_to_point
*****omitted*****
1/1/16            Designated        Forwarding     20000                  128
point_to_point
*****omitted*****
1/1/37            Designated        Forwarding     20000                  128
point_to_point
*****omitted*****
1/1/43            Designated        Forwarding     20000                  128
point_to_point
1/1/44            Designated        Forwarding     20000                  128
point_to_point
*****omitted*****
Core-2# show spanning-tree | begin 40 Port
Port           Role              State          Cost           Priority   Type
--------------------------------------------------------------------------------
----
1/1/1             Designated        Forwarding     20000                  128
point_to_point
*****omitted*****
1/1/16            Designated        Forwarding     20000                  128
point_to_point
*****omitted*****
1/1/37            Designated        Forwarding     20000                  128
point_to_point
*****omitted*****
1/1/43           Root                Forwarding     20000                 128
point_to_point
1/1/44           Alternate          Blocking        20000                 128
point_to_point
*****omitted*****
```

Do the outputs match your Figure 5-22 results? ______________________________

After validating your results, you are now ready to draw the CST which is the logical topology that will be used by switches for learning MAC addresses on each VLAN and determine how traffic is forwarded from all VLANs at Layer-2.

26. Based on your results and the current state of the diagram in Figure 5-22, use Figure 5-23 to draw the CST. Use solid lines for active links and dotted lines for inactive ones.

Note

Active links are those with ports in forwarding mode at both sides of the cable while inactive links have an Alternate port on either side of the connection.

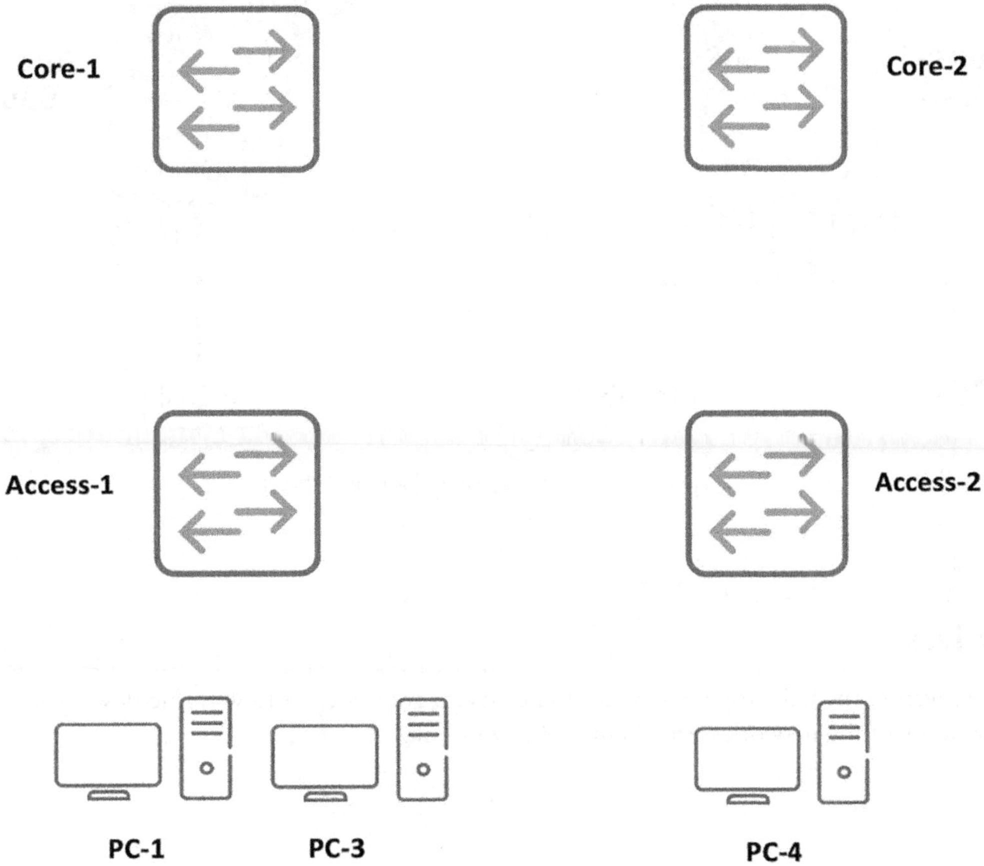

Figure 5-23 Drawing CST

Resultant topology should be like Figure 5-24:

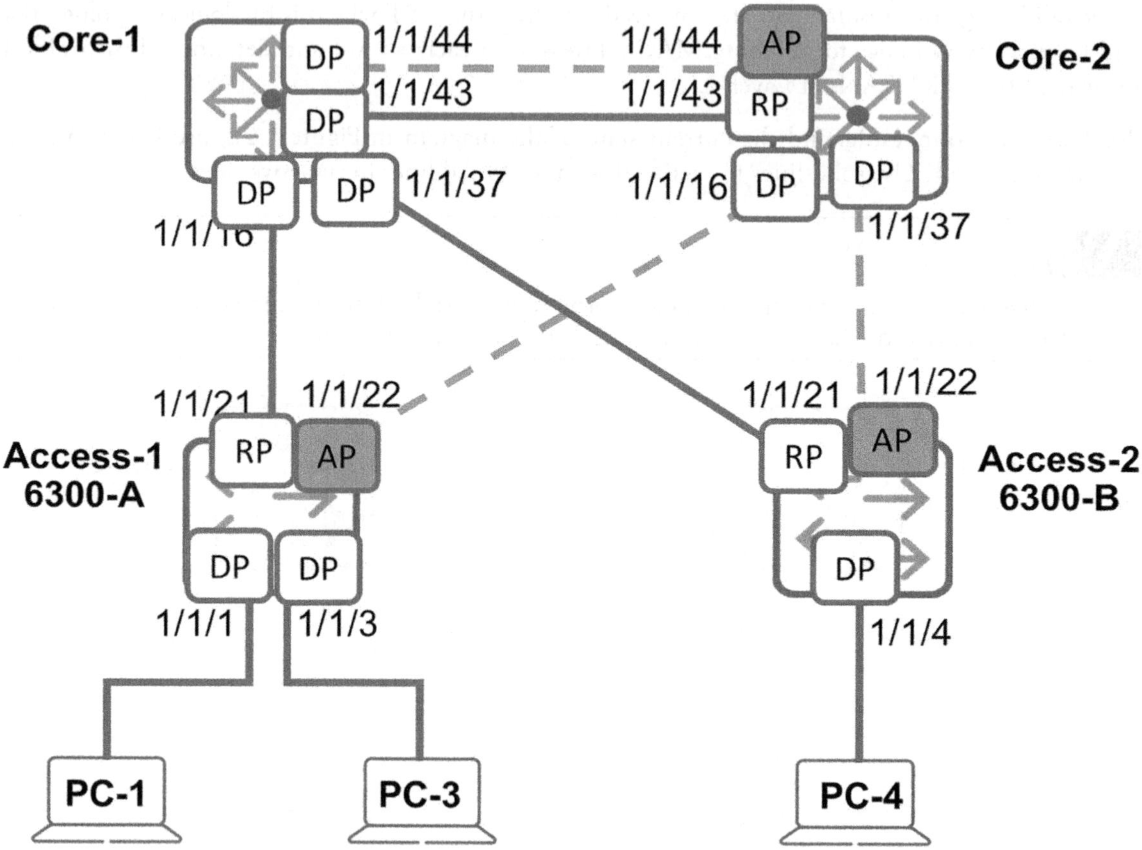

Figure 5-24 CST Topology Detailed Result

Task 3: Test Link Failure

Objectives

After discovering the CST topology, you should have a good idea of how traffic flows; you will now test how resilient the network is to a failure of any uplink.

Steps

PC-1

1. Access PC-1 and run a continuous ping to PC-4 (**10.11.12.104**). Ping should be successful (Figure 5-25).

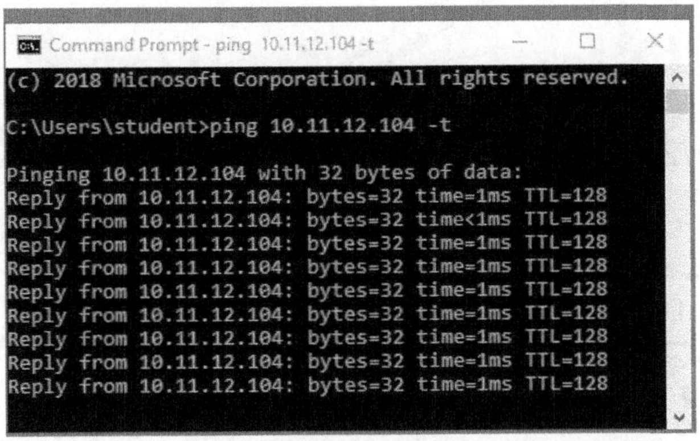

Figure 5-25 Ping to PC-4

Important

At this point and based on Figure 5-26 traffic is flowing from PC-1 to Access-1 → Access-1 to Core-1 (using port 1/1/21 to 1/1/16 link) → Core-1 to Access-2 (using 1/1/37 to 1/1/21 link) → Access-2 to PC-4. You will now modify the topology and analyze the traffic path.

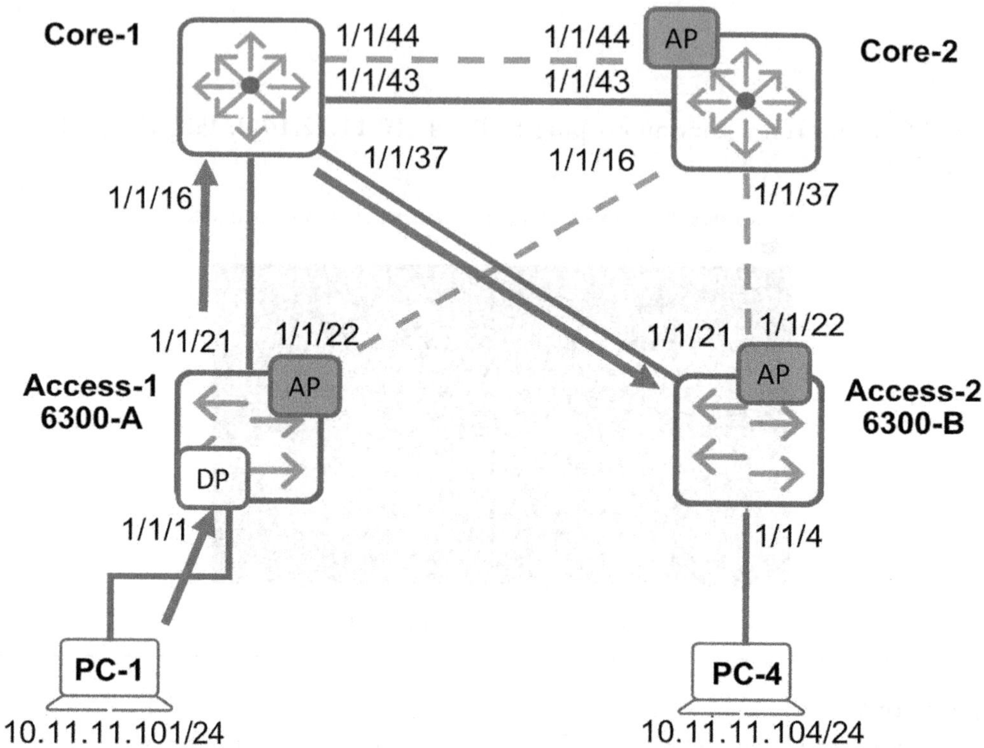

Figure 5-26 CST Topology

Access-1

2. Move to Access-1 and use the "**show spanning-tree**" command to verify the current Root port. It should be 1/1/21.

```
T11-Access-1# show spanning-tree | include Root
   Root ID.  Priority   : 4096
1/1/21           Root                   Forwarding    20000               128
point_to_point
```

3. Disable port 1/1/21.

```
T11-Access-1# configure terminal
T11-Access-1(config)# interface 1/1/21
T11-Access-1(config-if)# shutdown
```

4. Repeat step 2.

```
T11-Access-1(config-if)# show spanning-tree | include Root
   Root ID.  Priority  : 4096
1/1/22         Root                     Forwarding     20000              128
point_to_point
```

PC-3

5. Move back to PC-1 and verify the ping.

   Is ping still running? ______________________________

   How many packets did you lose? ______________________________

   What is the traffic flow now? ______________________________

> **Important**
> Traffic is now flowing from PC-1 to Access-1 → Access-1 to Core-2 (using port 1/1/22 to 1/1/Y link) → Core-2 to Core-1 using port 1/1/43 link → Core-1 to Access-2 (using port 1/1/Z to 1/1/21 link) → Access-2 to PC-4, as seen in Figure 5-27.

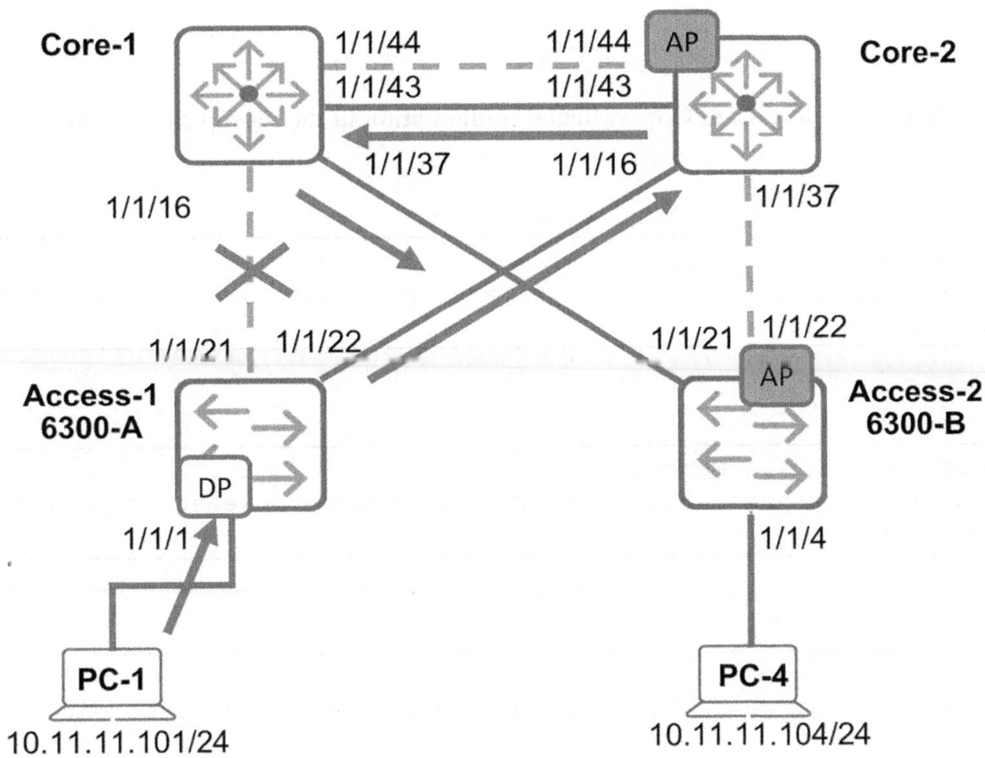

Figure 5-27 CST Topology After Failure

Access-1

6. Move to Access-1 and re-enable port 1/1/21. The topology should return to normal.

```
T11-Access-1(config-if)# no shutdown
T11-Access-1(config-if)# show spanning-tree | include Root
   Root ID.  Priority  : 4096
1/1/21          Root                   Forwarding    20000          128
point_to_point
```

Task 4: Save Your Configurations

Objectives

You will now proceed to save your configurations and create checkpoints. Notice that final lab checkpoints might be used by later activities.

Steps

Access-1, Access-2, Core-1, and Core-2 (via PC-1)

1. Save the current Access and Core switches' configuration in the startup checkpoint.

Access-1

```
T11-Access-1# write memory
Configuration changes will take time to process, please be patient.
T11-Access-1#
```

Access-2

```
T11-Access-2# write memory
Configuration changes will take time to process, please be patient.
T11-Access-2#
```

Core-1

```
Core-1# write memory
Configuration changes will take time to process, please be patient.
Core-1#
```

Core-2

```
Core-2# write memory
Configuration changes will take time to process, please be patient.
Core-2#
```

Access-1

2. Backup the current Access switches' configuration as a custom checkpoint called Lab5-1_final.

```
T11-Access-1# copy running-config checkpoint Lab5-1_final
Configuration changes will take time to process, please be patient.
T11-Access-1#
```

Access-2

```
T11-Access-2# copy running-config checkpoint Lab5-1_final
Configuration changes will take time to process, please be patient.
T11-Access-2#
```

You have completed Lab 5.1!

Lab 5.2: Deploying MSTP

Overview

Surprisingly enough, two days after the second Core was deployed a fiber connection was broken in the MDF. This affected the Access-1 main uplink; however your previous STP configuration avoided any network disruption. BigStartup (your customer) only realized there was a failure in the link when they received notification from Rent4Cheap Properties. Your customer is very satisfied with your advice. Your business relationship and their trust in you are growing (Figure 5-28).

Nonetheless, the failover event made BigStartup management wonder: Are the uplinks in an idle state when there is no failure? Are there connections that normally do not forward any traffic? Is it possible to share the load across those uplinks?

When you were asked those questions, the answer was "yes" to all of them. You went on to explain there is a new version of the STP protocol that not only provides loop avoidance and fast failover, but also provides load sharing and that it could be easily deployed. It is called Multiple Instance Spanning Tree. The next morning you received a request to deploy the solution.

Objectives

After completing this lab, you will be able to:

- Deploy an MST Region Configuration.
- Draw per instance topologies.
- Validate the load sharing effect.

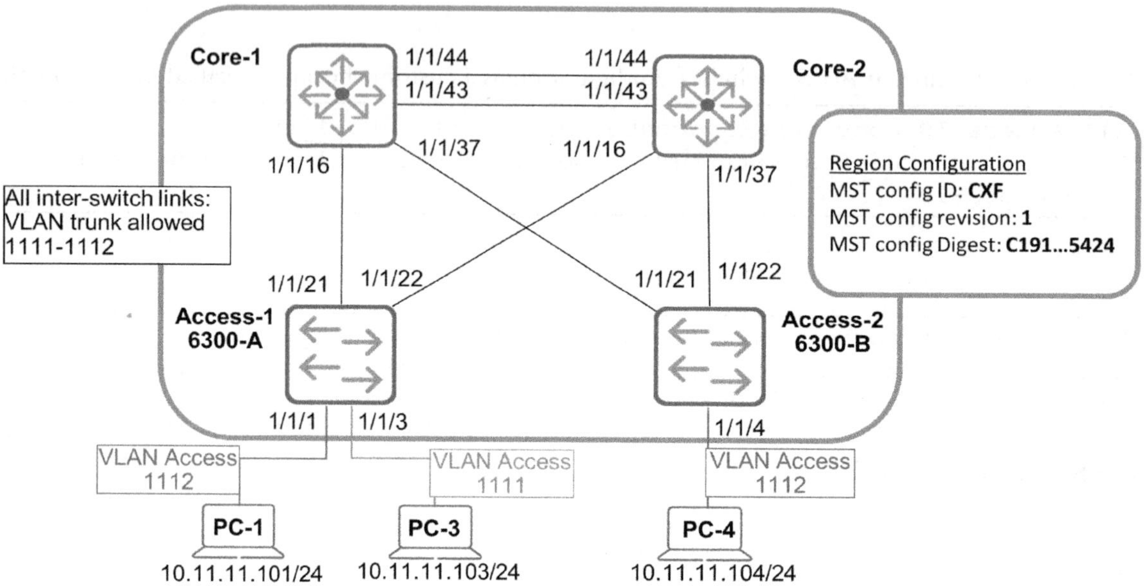

Figure 5-28 MST Topology

Task 1: Inspect MST Region Configuration

Objectives

Core switches have been pre-provisioned with an MST region configuration that cannot be modified. Therefore, in this lab you will deploy the same MST region script on your Access Switches. Then you will explore the current Core's priority values and confirm that all switches agree on the Root Bridge in each Instance (Figure 5-29).

Core-1 (via PC-1)

3. Access Core-1.
4. Display the current MST region configuration.

```
Core-1(config)# show spanning-tree mst-config
MST configuration information
   MST config ID          : CXF
   MST config revision    : 1
   MST config digest      : C1918786A14CE2765D013B62CCCD5424
   Number of instances : 2
```

```
Instance ID      Member VLANs
--------------- -----------------------------------
0
1-110,113-210,213-310,313-410,413-510,513-610,613-710,713-810,813-910,913-
1010,
                 1013-1110,1113-1210,1213-1310,1313-1410,1413-4094
1
111,211,311,411,511,611,711,811,911,1011,1111,1211,1311,1411
2
112,212,312,412,512,612,712,812,912,1012,1112,1212,1312,1412
```

What are the MST config ID and revision number values? ____________________

What is the config digest value? ____________________

What is the Instance to VLAN mapping configuration? ____________________

Instance 1: ____________________

Instance 2: ____________________

Note

Since the Core switches are a shared resource in a multitenancy environment, several VLANs terminate on them. Although many of these VLANs are not applicable to your environment, they must be part of the MST Region configuration in order to distribute these VLANs' traffic across multiple uplinks based on the Root Bridge of each instance.

Important

The MST config digest is the result of hashing the instance to VLAN mapping configuration. The digest along with the region ID (region name) and revision number are contained within the MST BDPUs sent by the switches. Switches transmit their region to one another. If the region announced in an incoming BPDU matches the local MST configuration, then the local switch forms part of its neighbor's region. Switches belonging to the same region converge toward each instance's root bridge and form part of each instance's topology.

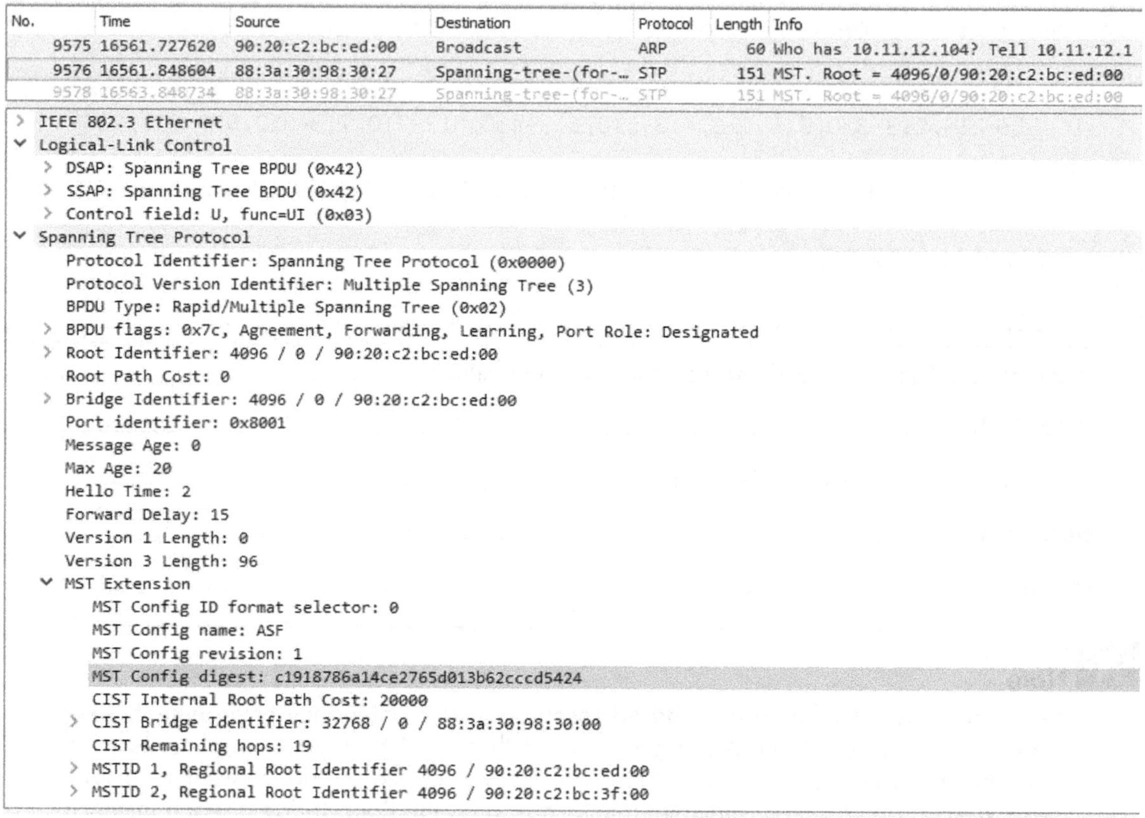

Figure 5-29 STP BPDU with MST Extensions

Core-2 (via PC-1)

5. Move to Core-2 and repeat step 2.

```
Core-2(config)# show spanning-tree mst-config
MST configuration information
   MST config ID        : CXF
   MST config revision  : 1
   MST config digest    : C1918786A14CE2765D013B62CCCD5424
   Number of instances : 2

Instance ID     Member VLANs
--------------- ----------------------------------
0
1-110,113-210,213-310,313-410,413-510,513-610,613-710,713-810,813-
910,913-1010,
                1013-1110,1113-1210,1213-1310,1313-1410,1413-4094
```

```
1
111,211,311,411,511,611,711,811,911,1011,1111,1211,1311,1411
2
112,212,312,412,512,612,712,812,912,1012,1112,1212,1312,1412
```

Do region parameters match the ones of Core-1? ______________________

Answer

It does; this confirms that both Core switches are part of the same region; however your Access switches are not since they do not have any custom region configuration.

Access-1

6. Move to Access-1 and use the "**show spanning-tree**" command. Then move to Access-2 and use it again.

```
T11-Access-1# show spanning-tree mst-config
MST configuration information
   MST config ID          : 88:3a:30:98:30:00
   MST config revision    : 0
   MST config digest      : AC36177F50283CD4B83821D8AB26DE62
   Number of instances : 0

Instance ID     Member VLANs
--------------- ------------------------------------
0               1-4094
```

What is the default Config ID and revision number? ______________________

What is the default VLAN to Instance mapping? ______________________

Access-2

7. Move to Access-2 and use a filtered version of the same command.

```
T11-Access-2# show spanning-tree mst-config | include MST
MST configuration information
   MST config ID          : 88:3a:30:97:a4:40
   MST config revision    : 0
   MST config digest      : AC36177F50283CD4B83821D8AB26DE62
```

Are Access switches in the same region as the Core switches? ______________________

Are the two Access switches part of the same region? ______________________

Answer

As you can see, the Access switches' configuration is different from the Core switches and although Access-1 and Access-2 share the same Digest (result of having all VLANs mapped to Instance 0) they do not share the region ID or revision number and therefore they belong to different regions. See Figure 5-30.

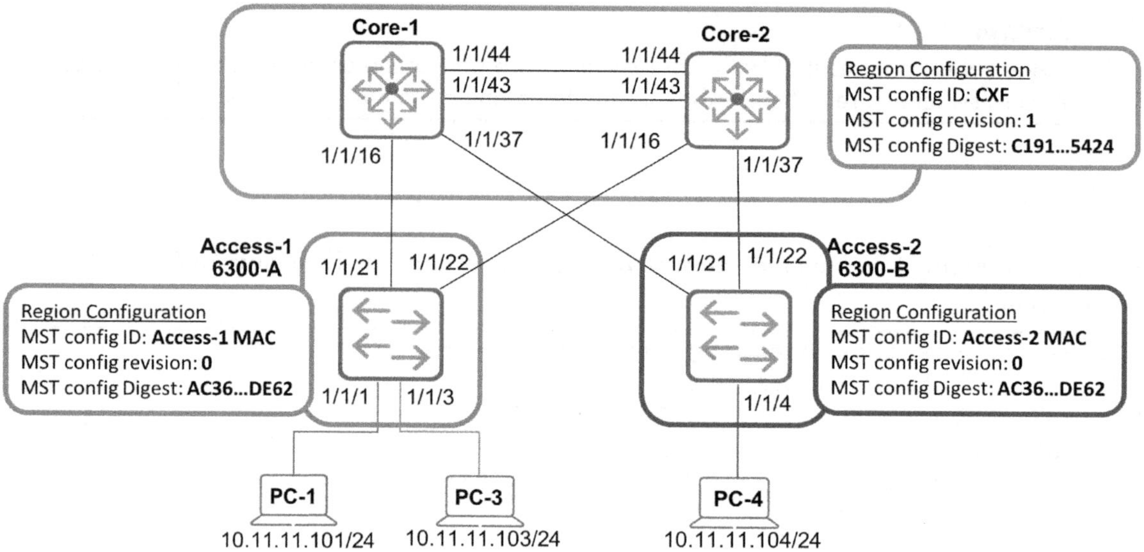

Figure 5-30 Multi-Region Topology

Important

Switches that do not share a common region configuration will belong to different regions; if this is the case then they will run RSTP, negotiate roles within the CST, and form part of the CST topology only. They will lack any MST-based load sharing support. In this type of design, root and designated ports will forward traffic for all VLANs and similarly alternate ports will discard traffic from all VLANs.

Task 2: Inspect Load Balancing

Objectives

Confirm what link Access-1 is using for each VLAN by inspecting its MAC Address table, then apply the same Core switch configuration to the Access switches and inspect the MAC table.

This test is easy for VLAN X12 because PC-1 and PC-4 (members of that VLAN) are connected to different access switches and their traffic has to cross the Core. However, testing VLAN X11 is more difficult because there is a single client (PC-3) on Access-1. In order to generate IP traffic on VLAN X11, you will simulate a host on Access-2 by adding an IP address on that switch using Switched Virtual Interfaces (SVI).

Steps

Access-2

8. Move to Access-2's console.
9. Create interface VLAN 1111; then assign it IP address **10.11.11.4/24.**

```
T11-Access-2(config)# interface VLAN 1111
T11-Access-2(config-if-VLAN)# IP address 10.11.11.4/24
```

10. See the newly created SVI details using "**show IP interface VLAN1111**".

```
T11-Access-2# show IP interface VLAN1111

Interface VLAN1111 is up
 Admin state is up
 Hardware: Ethernet, MAC Address: 88:3a:30:97:a4:40
 IP MTU 1500
 IP Directed Broadcast is Disabled
 IPv4 address 10.11.11.3/24
 L3 Counters: Rx Disabled, Tx Disabled
```

Important

This command is case sensitive; make sure to type lowercase "VLAN" immediately followed by the VLAN number, for example, "**show IP interface VLAN1111**".

What is the SVI state? ________________

Record the MAC address of Interface VLAN 1111 of Access-2.

Access-2's MAC address ________________

PC-4

11. Access **PC-4**.
12. Record the MAC address of PC-4.

PC-4's MAC address ________________

PC-3

13. Access **PC-3**.
14. Run a continuous ping to Access-2 IP address on VLAN 1111 (**10.11.11.4**). Ping should be successful.

PC-1

15. Access PC-1.
16. Run a continuous ping to PC-4's IP address on VLAN 1112 (**10.11.12.104**). Ping should be successful.

Access-1

17. Move back to Access-1.
18. Display the MAC address table.

```
T11-Access-1(config)# show mac-address-table
MAC age-time            : 300 seconds
Number of MAC addresses : 3

MAC Address          VLAN     Type                        Port
--------------------------------------------------------------
88:3a:30:97:a4:40    1111     dynamic                     1/1/21
00:50:56:b1:ae:e8    1111     dynamic                     1/1/1
00:50:56:b1:a9:86    1112     dynamic                     1/1/21
```

What port is used to reach Access-2's MAC address? ______________________

What port is used to reach PC-4's MAC address? ______________________

19. Apply the STP region configuration:

- Config-name: **CXF**.
- Config-revision: **1**.
- Instance 1 VLANs: **111, 211, 311, 411, 511, 611, 711, 811, 911, 1011, 1111, 1211, 1311, and 1411**.
- Instance 2 VLANs: **112, 212, 312, 412, 512, 612, 712, 812, 912, 1012, 1112, 1212, 1312, and 1412**.

```
T11-Access-1# configure terminal
T11-Access-1(config)# spanning-tree config-name CXF
T11-Access-1(config)# spanning-tree config-revision 1
T11-Access-1(config)# spanning-tree instance 1 VLAN 111, 211, 311, 411,
511, 611, 711, 811, 911, 1011, 1111, 1211, 1311, 1411
T11-Access-1(config)#spanning-tree instance 2 VLAN 112, 212, 312, 412,
512, 612, 712, 812, 912, 1012, 1112, 1212, 1312, 1412
T11-Access-1(config)# end
```

Notice

You should be careful when applying the region configuration. The smallest difference will make the integration into the region fail. Config-name is case sensitive, revision level must be "1" in this case, and every single VLAN listed in the script must be included regardless of whether they apply to your table or not.

20. Confirm config ID; revision number and digest match the ones seen on Task 1 step 3.

```
T11-Access-1# show spanning-tree mst-config | include MST
MST configuration information
   MST config ID         : CXF
   MST config revision   : 1
   MST config digest     : C1918786A14CE2765D013B62CCCD5424
T11-Access-1#
```

21. Move to Access-2 and repeat steps 12 and 13.

```
T11-Access-2# configure terminal
T11-Access-2(config)# spanning-tree config-name CXF
T11-Access-2(config)# spanning-tree config-revision 1
T11-Access-2(config)# spanning-tree instance 1 VLAN 111, 211, 311, 411,
511, 611, 711, 811, 911, 1011, 1111, 1211, 1311, 1411
T11-Access-2(config)# spanning-tree instance 2 VLAN 112, 212, 312, 412,
512, 612, 712, 812, 912, 1012, 1112, 1212, 1312, 1412
T11-Access-1(config)# end
T11-Access-2# show spanning-tree mst-config | include MST
MST configuration information
   MST config ID         : CXF
   MST config revision   : 1
   MST config digest     : C1918786A14CE2765D013B62CCCD5424
```

Note

At this point Spanning Tree is running 3 processes simultaneously, one per instance. The topology that is used is 100% dependent on who the Root is for each instance, which in turn depends on the BID of the switches. Currently Access switches have no custom priority whatsoever, but the Cores are already provisioned with certain values; please proceed and validate those values.

Core-1 (via PC-1)

22. Move to Core-1 and explore its STP priorities configuration.

```
Core-1(config)# show running-config | include priority
spanning-tree priority 1
spanning-tree instance 1 priority 1
spanning-tree instance 2 priority 2
```

Core-2 (via PC-1)

23. Move to Core-2 and repeat the previous step.

```
Core-2(config)# show running-config | include priority
spanning-tree priority 2
spanning-tree instance 1 priority 2
spanning-tree instance 2 priority 1
```

Based on the outputs, who is the Root for each instance? ______

Root for Instance 0: ______

Root for Instance 1: ______

Root for Instance 2: ______

Important

Instance 0 or Internal Spanning Tree (IST) is used as both: a regular instance in MST and the creation of the CST in a multi-region deployment for backward compatibility with RSTP speakers, for this reason Instance 0 is known as CIST (Common Internal Spanning Tree).

Validate your conclusions.

Access-1

24. Move to Access-1.

25. Use the "**show spanning-tree mst 0**" command to look at information about instance 0.

Tip

Since this command's output is long, a filtered version of it is used below.

```
T11-Access-1# show spanning-tree mst 0 | begin 25 Root | exclude Disabled
Root            Address:90:20:c2:bc:ed:00   Priority:4096
                Port:1/1/21                 Path cost:0
Regional Root   Address:90:20:c2:bc:ed:00   Priority:4096
                Internal cost:20000         Rem Hops:19

Port            Role            State       Cost        Priority    Type
-------------------------------------------------------------------------
1/1/1                Designated          Forwarding       20000            128
point_to_point
1/1/3                Designated          Forwarding       20000            128
point_to_point
1/1/21              Root                  Forwarding       20000            128
point_to_point
1/1/22              Alternate            Blocking         20000            128
point_to_point

Topology change flag             : True
Number of topology changes       : 9
Last topology change occurred : 1422 seconds ago
```

Who is the Root bridge for this instance? ____________________

What are the Root and Alternate ports? ____________________

26. Repeat step 19 for instance 1 and 2.

```
T11-Access-1# show spanning-tree mst 1 | begin 25 Root | exclude Disabled
Root            Address:90:20:c2:bc:ed:00    Priority:4096
                Port:1/1/21, Cost:20000, Rem Hops:19

Port            Role             State       Cost      Priority   Type
-------------- -------------- ------------ ------- ---------- ----------
1/1/1                    Designated        Forwarding      20000       128
point_to_point
1/1/3                    Designated        Forwarding      20000       128
point_to_point
1/1/21                 Root                 Forwarding      20000       128
point_to_point
1/1/22                  Alternate         Blocking           20000       128
point_to_point

Topology change flag            : True
Number of topology changes      : 4
Last topology change occurred : 1449 seconds ago
```

Who is the regional root for this instance? ______________________

What are the Root and Alternate ports? ______________________

```
T11-Access-1# show spanning-tree mst 2 | begin 25 Root | exclude Disabled
Root            Address:90:20:c2:bc:3f:00    Priority:4096
                Port:1/1/22,   Cost:20000, Rem Hops:19

Port            Role             State        Cost      Priority   Type
-------------- -------------- ------------ ------- ---------- ----------
1/1/1                    Designated        Forwarding      20000       128
point_to_point
1/1/3                    Designated        Forwarding      20000       128
point_to_point
1/1/21                  Alternate         Blocking           20000       128
point_to_point
1/1/22                 Root                 Forwarding      20000       128
point_to_point

Topology change flag            : True
Number of topology changes      : 5
Last topology change occurred : 1488 seconds ago
```

Who is the regional root for this instance? ______________________

What are the Root and Alternate ports? ______________________

Tip

There is no need to validate the same information on Access-2. Since it has the same region configuration, the results will be the same.

Note

As you can see Instance 0 and 1 share the same Root and same roles on uplinks; however Instance 2 does not. This is because Core-2 is root for this instance. Instance topologies are like the ones in in Figures 5-31 and 5-32 below.

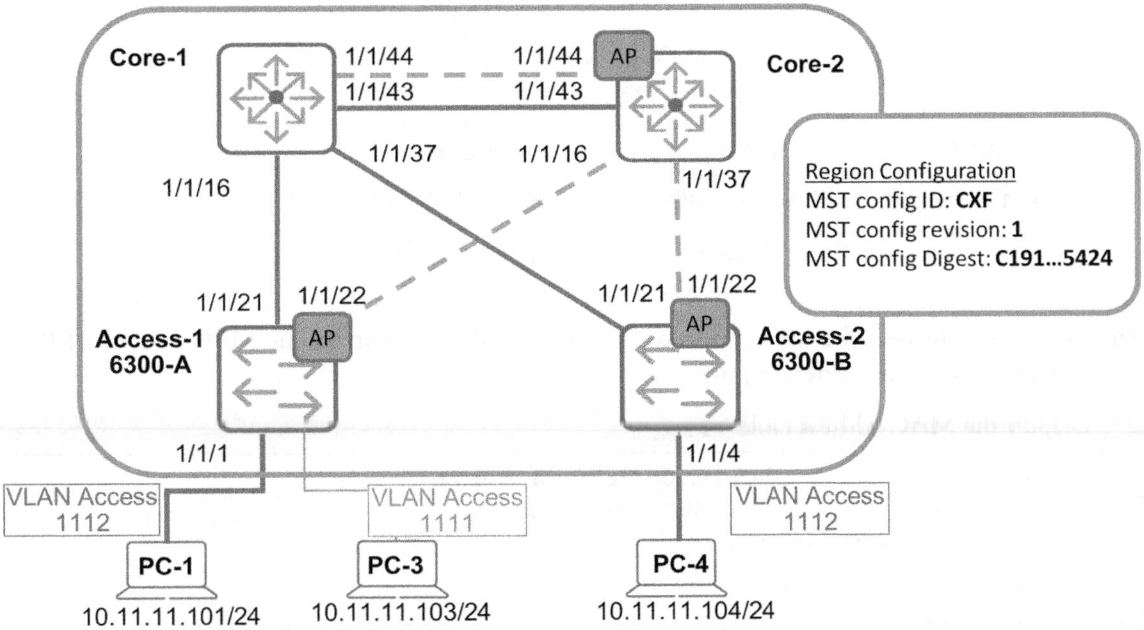

Figure 5-31 Topology of Instances 0 and 1

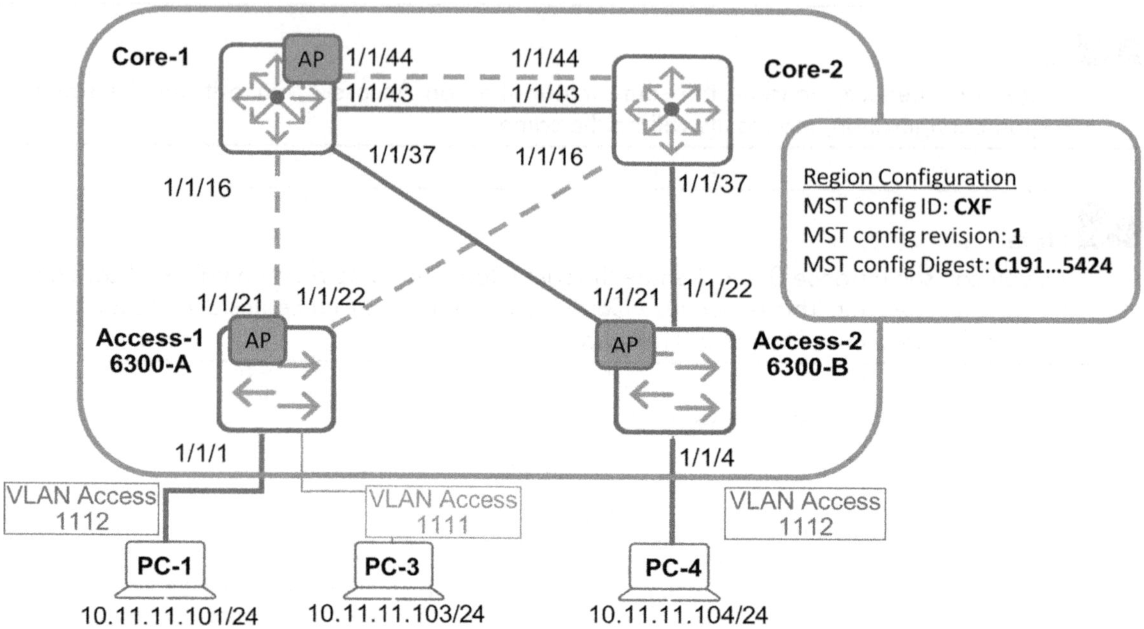

Figure 5-32 Topology of Instance 2

Finally, you will inspect the MAC address table; if everything is correct the MAC address of PC-4 should be seen now on a different port.

27. Display the MAC address table.

```
T11-Access-1(config)# show mac-address-table
MAC age-time                : 300 seconds
Number of MAC addresses : 3

MAC Address          VLAN      Type                        Port
---------------------------------------------------------------
88:3a:30:97:a4:40    1111      dynamic                     1/1/21
00:50:56:b1:ae:e8    1111      dynamic                     1/1/1
00:50:56:b1:a9:86    1112      dynamic                     1/1/22
```

What port is used to reach Access-2's MAC address? ____________________

What port is used to reach PC-4's MAC address? ____________________

What has changed from what you saw in step 7? ____________________

PC-1 and PC-3

28. Stop the pings.

Task 3: Save Your Configurations

Objectives

Save your configurations and create checkpoints. Note that lab checkpoints might be used by later activities.

Steps

Access-1, Access-2, Core-1, and Core-2 (via PC-1).

1. Save the current Access and Core switches' configuration in the startup checkpoint.

Access-1

```
T11-Access-1# write memory
Configuration changes will take time to process, please be patient.
```

Access-2

```
T11-Access-2# write memory
Configuration changes will take time to process, please be patient.
```

Core-1

```
Core-1# write memory
Configuration changes will take time to process, please be patient.
```

Core-2

```
Core-2# write memory
Configuration changes will take time to process, please be patient.
```

2. Backup the current Access switches' configuration as a custom checkpoint called Lab5-2_final.

Access-1

```
T11-Access-1# copy running-config checkpoint Lab5-2_final
Configuration changes will take time to process, please be patient.
```

Access-2

```
T11-Access-2# copy running-config checkpoint Lab5-2_final
Configuration changes will take time to process, please be patient.
```

You have completed Lab 5.2!

Learning Check

Chapter 5 Questions

Redundancy

1. Which of the following are issues created from redundant Layer-Two loops?
    a. Routing loops
    b. Broadcast storms
    c. Multiple frame copies
    d. Voltage drops to Power-Over-Ethernet ports
    e. Instability of the MAC address sable

Spanning-Tree Protocol

2. Which Spanning-Tree protocols are considered open standards?
    a. PVRSTP+
    b. GLBP
    c. 802.1D
    d. 802.1W
    e. 802.11AX
    f. 802.1S

RSTP Operation

3. What is the command to enable an **edge** port in Aruba OS-CX?
    a. **Spanning-tree port-type admin-edge**
    b. **Spanning-tree port-type edge**
    c. **Port-type admin-edge**
    d. **Spanning-tree port-type access**

6 Link Aggregation

EXAM OBJECTIVES

- ✓ Describe Link Aggregation Group (LAG) and its interface requirements
- ✓ Explain, configure, and verify LAG
- ✓ Describe, configure, and verify load balancing

Overview

Switch-to-switch links are busy links! Without knowledge of LAG, you could easily oversubscribe these links, poor performance with no resiliency.

You will explore Link Aggregation Group advantages and requirements, before learning about the difference between static and dynamic LAG, which relies on the Link Aggregation Control Protocol (LACP). You learn about LACP operation modes and then apply that knowledge to configure and verify it.

You will learn about load balancing algorithms and inputs, and then learn how to configure and verify LAG load balancing.

Link Aggregation Overview

You know that switches provide connectivity for many devices, on many different VLANs. All that traffic must share the switch-to-switch links. So, you add multiple switch interconnects, as shown in the left side example in Figure 6-1.

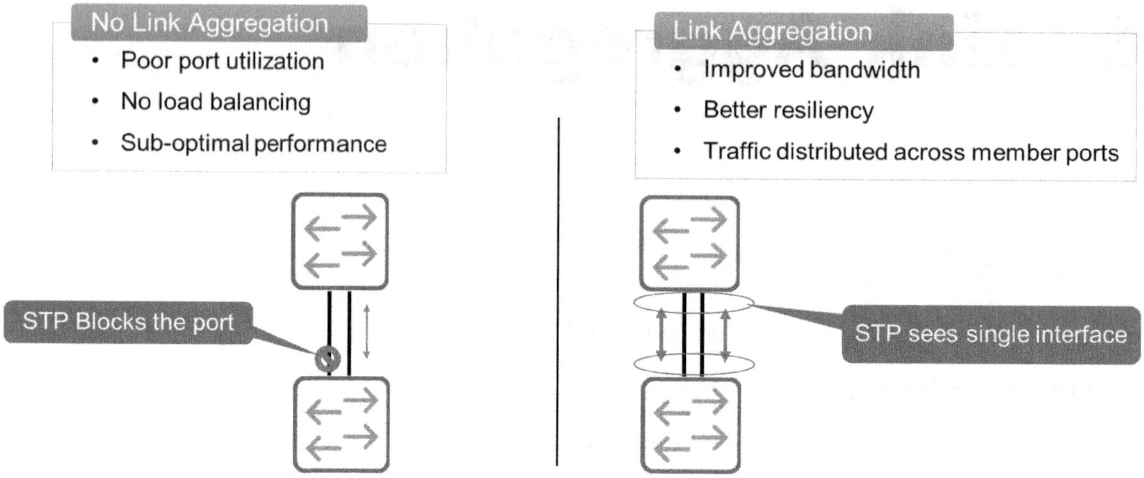

Figure 6-1 Link Aggregation Overview

While this does add some resiliency, it does not add additional bandwidth. The two links would create a loop, and so STP will automatically block one of the ports. You have two links, but only one of them isused, poor link utilization, no load balancing, and sub-optimal performance.

The solution is Link aggregation, which bundles multiple physical interfaces into a single logical interface, as shown in Figure 6-1's right-hand example. Since protocols like STP perceive this bundle as a single interface, there is no blocking. All switch interconnects carry traffic. You might go from one 10GBPS link to two, four, or more bundled links. You get far more bandwidth because traffic is distributed across member ports. You get better resiliency because if one member fails, remaining links carry the load. Convergence is faster than spanning tree, because there is no need for an STP Topology Change notification.

Note

Link aggregation can be used not only for switch-to-switch links, but it can be used on other links to servers and routers. This text however finds an easy way to introduce this topic by talking about switch-to-switch links that were discussed on previous modules.

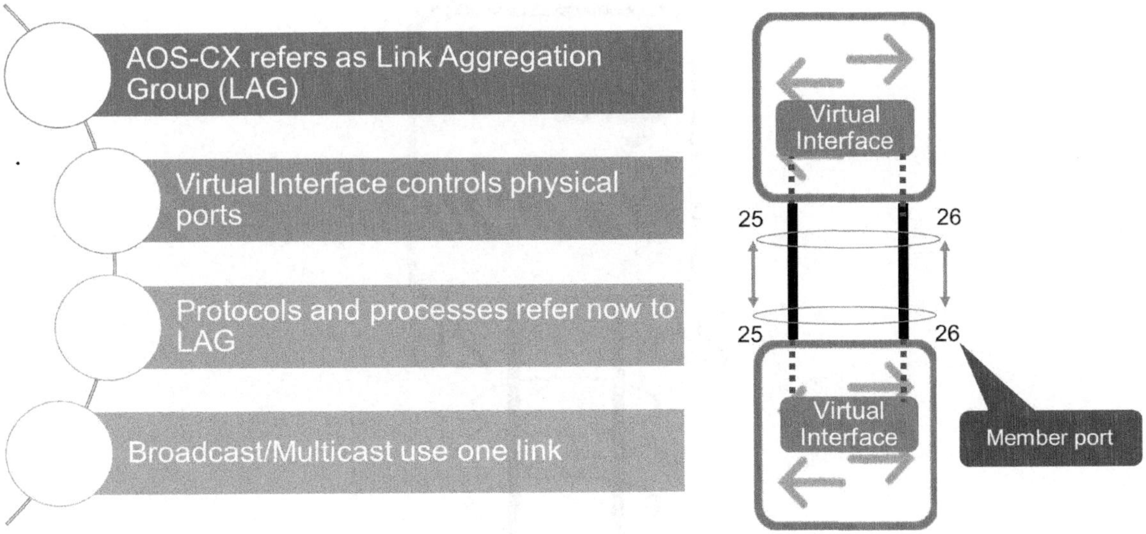

Figure 6-2 Link Aggregation Overview Continued

When you enable Link aggregation on a switch the protocol creates a virtual interface. You then configure physical ports to be members of that virtual interface. The switch's various protocols and processes will only perceive and refer to the virtual interface. They no longer perceive the individual physical interface members (Figure 6-2).

In AOS-CX the virtual interface is referred as LAG (Link Aggregation Group) and the interfaces are called member ports.

It is important to mention that broadcast and multicast traffic is sent across only one physical link in the bundle. This behavior ensures that Link Aggregation does not create a Layer-2 loop.

Link Aggregation—Interface Requirements

Interfaces that are mapped to the same Link Aggregation Group must be configured in a consistent manner (Figure 6-3).

The following items must match:

- Duplex mode (Full-duplex or Half-duplex)
- Link speed
- Media

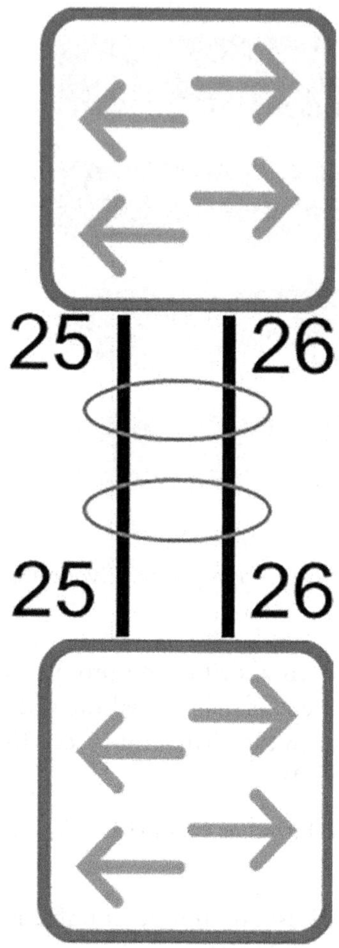

Figure 6-3 LAG

AOS-CX displays a warning if you attempt to map mismatched interfaces to a LAG. For example, Interface 5 with speed of 10 Gb/s cannot be added to LAG10 with base speed of 1 Gb/s. Each Link Aggregation Group can have up to eight individual ports. Use the command show capacities to verify your switch capacity.

Static and Dynamic LAG

Now that you understand LAG, you should learn about two operating modes:Static LAG and Dynamic LAG, which uses the Link Aggregation Control Protocol (LACP).

Static LAG

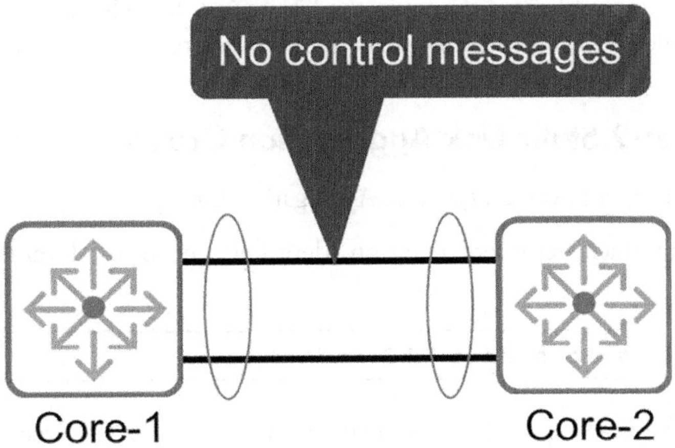

Figure 6-4 Static LAG

In Static Link Aggregation mode devices do not exchange any control information. There is no signaling between switch peers about LAG. You simply configure LAG independently on each peer. If your configuration is good, LAG works. However, the switch peers have no knowledge of who they are connected to, or whether they are connected to the same peer.

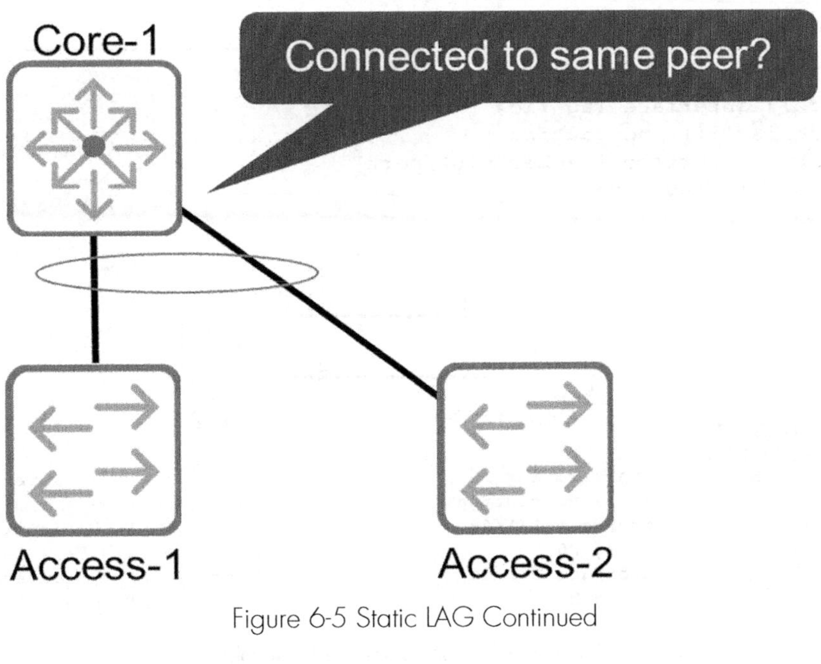

Figure 6-5 Static LAG Continued

This mode is not recommended because a misconfiguration on one side is not detected by the peer. This can lead to unexpected behavior, which can be challenging to detect and troubleshoot. Another scenario that could cause problems is shown in the Figure 6-4. Switch Access-1 is not aware that you have erroneously connected LAG member ports to two separate physical switches (Figure 6-5).

Configuring Layer-2 Static Link Aggregation Group

The following steps create a Layer-2 Dynamic Aggregation Group:

1. Create a LAG interface, represented by an identifier: any unused value between 1 and 256 (Figure 6-6).

```
Switch(config)# interface LAG <id>
```

2. Disable routing (Layer-3 capabilities) in the new LAG interface. This step limits the LAG to only process Layer-2 frame headers.

```
Switch(config-LAG-if)# no routing
```

3. Map a port member to the LAG.
4. In the interface context level:

```
Switch(config)# interface 1/1/1
Switch(config-if)# LAG <id>
```

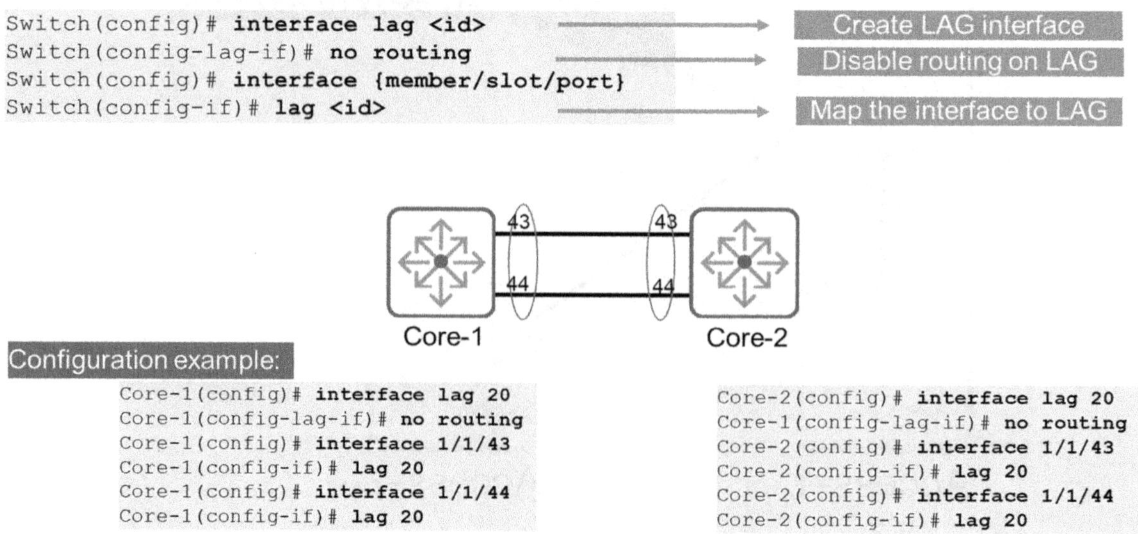

Figure 6-6 Configuration Example

Dynamic LAG or LACP

Peer devices that use Dynamic Link Aggregation exchange control messages to establish and maintain the LAG. This mechanism will also detect link failures and ensure that LAG port members terminate on the same device.

The standard used to implement this exchange is Link Aggregation Control Protocol (LACP). LACP exchanges periodic messages called LACP Data Units**.** These messages include:

- **System ID**which uniquely identifies the switch.
- **Operational key** which uniquely identifies the Link aggregation group.

Dynamic LAG or LACP is the recommended method to implement Link Aggregation, to avoid unexpected network problems.There are some flags that are included in the LACP-DU. The extra content section shows the meaning of these flags.

LACP Data Unit Flags

Flag	Meaning
LACP_Activity	Indicates a participant's intent to detect or maintain the LAG • Set = Active LACP • Not Set = Passive LACP
LACP_Timeout	The participant wishes to receive periodic transmissions. • Set = Short timeout • Not Set = Long Timeout
Aggregate	The participant allow the link to be used as part of LAG
Synchronization	The participant multiplexor component is in sync with the system ID and key information
Collecting	The reception component of the multiplexor is on
Distributing	Participant distributor is not off

Figure 6-7 LACP-Data Units Defined

LACP Operational Modes

LACP can be configured in one of two modes, which controls how peer negation proceeds.

With Passive mode, the device passively waits to receive an LACP Data Unit message from the peer, to dynamically create the Link Aggregation Group. This mode places the LAG in a listening state. It is as if the switch is thinking, "I'll just sit here and wait until I hear from my peer." If you configure the peer switch to also be in passive mode, then it is thinking the same thing. Both switches wait to hear from the other, and so a functional LAG connection is never formed. At least one peer must be in Active mode.

With Active mode, the device actively transmits LACP Data Unit messages over its member ports, "Hey! Let us form a LAG." Whether the peer is Passive or Active, it responds, negotiation continues, and the LAG successfully forms. This is shown in Figure 6-7.

Device A port mode	Device B port mode	LAG formed?
Passive	**Passive**	**No**
Passive	Active	Yes
Active	Passive	
Active	Active	

Figure 6-8 LACP Operational Modes

Let us talk about configuration.

Configuring Layer-2: Dynamic Aggregation Group

The configuration for Dynamic LAG is the same as static except for an extra line where you need to specify the LACP mode (Figures 6-8 and 6-9).

```
Switch(config)# interface lag <id>                       → Create LAG interface
Switch(config-lag-if)# no routing                        → Disable routing on LAG
Switch(config-lag-if)# lacp mode {active | passive}      → LACP Mode
Switch(config)# interface {member/slot/port}
Switch(config-if)# lag <id>                              → Map the interface to LAG
```

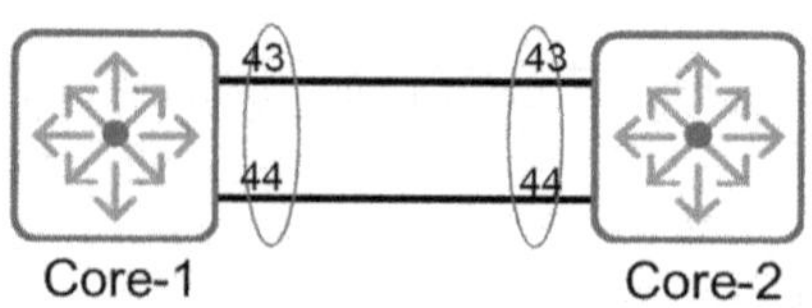

Configuration example

```
Core-1(config)# interface lag 20
Core-1(config-lag-if)# no routing
Core-1(config-lag-if)# lacp mode active
Core-1(config)# interface 1/1/43
Core-1(config-if)# lag 20
Core-1(config)# interface 1/1/44
Core-1(config-if)# lag 20
```

```
Core-2(config)# interface lag 20
Core-2(config-lag-if)# no routing
Core-2(config-lag-if)# lacp mode active
Core-2(config)# interface 1/1/43
Core-2(config-if)# lag 20
Core-2(config)# interface 1/1/44
Core-2(config-if)# lag 20
```

Figure 6-9 Configuring Layer-2: Dynamic Aggregation Group

Verifying the LAG Interface

Use **show interface LAG** to verify your efforts. You can also use **show interface LAG brief** to see the LAG's total available bandwidth (Figure 6-10).

```
Switch# show interface lag

 Aggregate lag1 is up
 Admin state is up
 Description :
 MAC Address                  : 88:3a:30:97:59:c0
 Aggregated-interfaces        : 1/1/25 1/1/26 2/1/25 2/1/26
 Aggregation-key              : 1
 Aggregate mode               : active
 Speed                        : 40000 Mb/s
 L3 Counters: Rx Disabled, Tx Disabled
 <<<<Omitted output>>>>
```

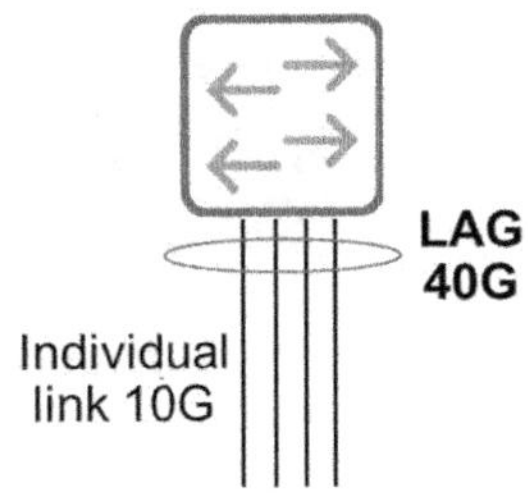


```
Switch# show interface lag brief
--------------------------------------------------------------------------------
Port        Native  Mode    Type          Enabled Status  Reason            Speed
            VLAN                                                            (Mb/s)
--------------------------------------------------------------------------------
lag1        1       trunk   --            yes     up      --                40000
```

Figure 6-10 Verifying the LAG Interface

Load Sharing

Load Balancing Algorithm

Peer LAG devices must balance the traffic load across multiple physical interfaces. How does the switch decide which member port should be used for a given packet? It uses a **Hash** algorithm.

A hash algorithm is a mathematical function that is applied to an input (x). Interestingly, if you see the output (y) of this function, you cannot derive or infer input (x). Therefore, it is referred to as a one-way function. Another characteristic of a hash is that if the same input (x) has been entered, the result will be always the same. So, what does the switch use as inputs to this function?

The switch uses packet header information as hash function inputs, and the result is the port member to be used for that particular packet. Depending on switch algorithm used, inputs for the hash could be:

- Layer-4 TCP/UDP ports
- Layer-3 Source and Destination IP addresses
- Layer-2 Source and Destination MAC addresses

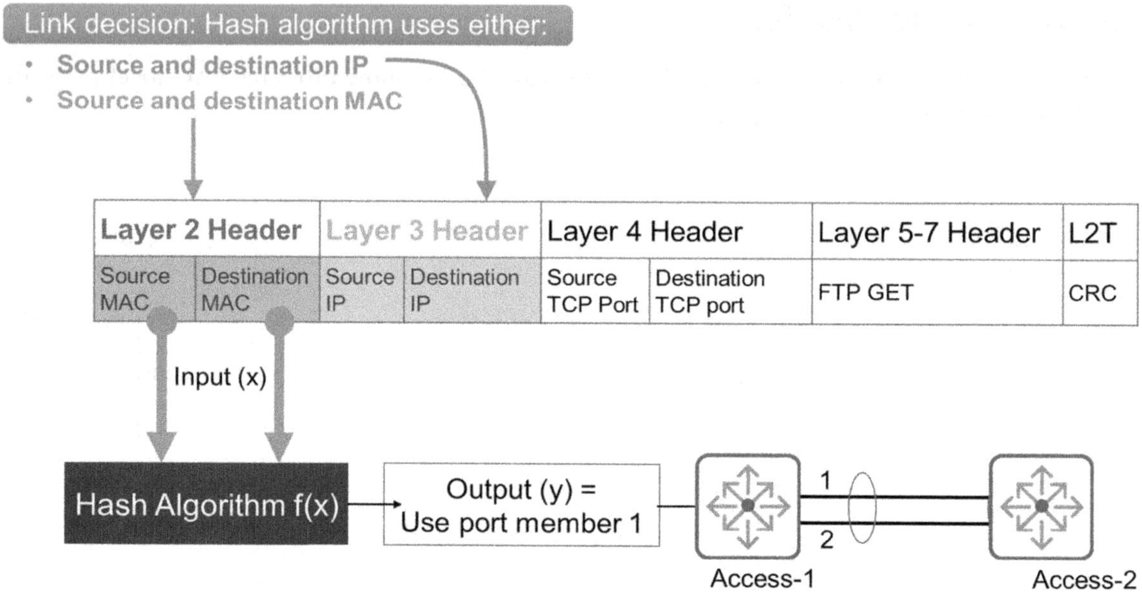

Figure 6-11 Load Balancing Algorithm

Figure 6-11 shows how the Layer-2 source and destination MAC addresses are taken as inputs for the algorithm. The output is to use physical port 1 for all packets with this source and destination MAC address combination. Only a link failure will cause port 2 to be used for these packets.

Link Aggregation Load Balancing

In AOS-CX the default input information for the hash algorithm are the Source and Destination IP addresses. You can verify with the **show LACP aggregates** command. Notice that the highlighted hash information is "l3-src-dst." You know "L3" means Layer-3, which is IP addresses.

In some cases, the hash algorithm's use of source/destination IP addresses may not properly distribute the load equally among port members.This could lead to traffic congestion and poor performance.

In that case, you can modify the hash input data. As shown in Figure 6-11, you have decided to use Layer-2 source and destination MAC addresses as inputs to the hash function. This might help to avoid port member oversubscription (Figure 6-12).

Verifying Hash algorithm

```
Switch# show lacp aggregates

Aggregate name    : lag1
Interfaces        : 2/1/26 1/1/25 2/1/25 1/1/26
Heartbeat rate    : Fast
Hash              : l3-src-dst              Default
Aggregate mode    : Active
```

Changing algorithm to L2

```
Switch(config)# interface lag <ID>
Switch(config-lag-if)# hash l2-src-dst
```

Figure 6-12 Link Aggregation Load Balancing

Lab 6.1: Link Aggregation between Core Switches

Overview

After successfully deploying MST-based load sharing on links between Core switches, the network administrator of Rent4Cheap Properties has been monitoring the bandwidth utilization of links of ports 43 and 44. They have calculated an average of 10% utilization of one link versus 55% in the other. Although neither link is congested yet, the network administrator would like to look for a better way to share the load among links.

Although moving VLANs from one instance to the other looks like a good solution in the short term, this may not be a scalable option. Nothing guarantees that traffic patterns will not change.

The network administrator has approached you and asked for advice. You propose deploying link aggregation, since load sharing is not VLAN based but hash based (based on Layer-2 or Layer-3 source and destination addresses) which commonly leads to more even resource utilization.

Note that references to equipment and commands are taken from Aruba's hosted remote lab. These are shown for demonstration purposes in case you wish to replicate the environment and tasks on your own equipment.

Objectives

After completing this lab, you will be able to:

- Deploy static Link Aggregation
- Understand the nature of transient loops when creating static aggregations
- Monitor LAG interfaces in AOS-CX (Figure 6-13).

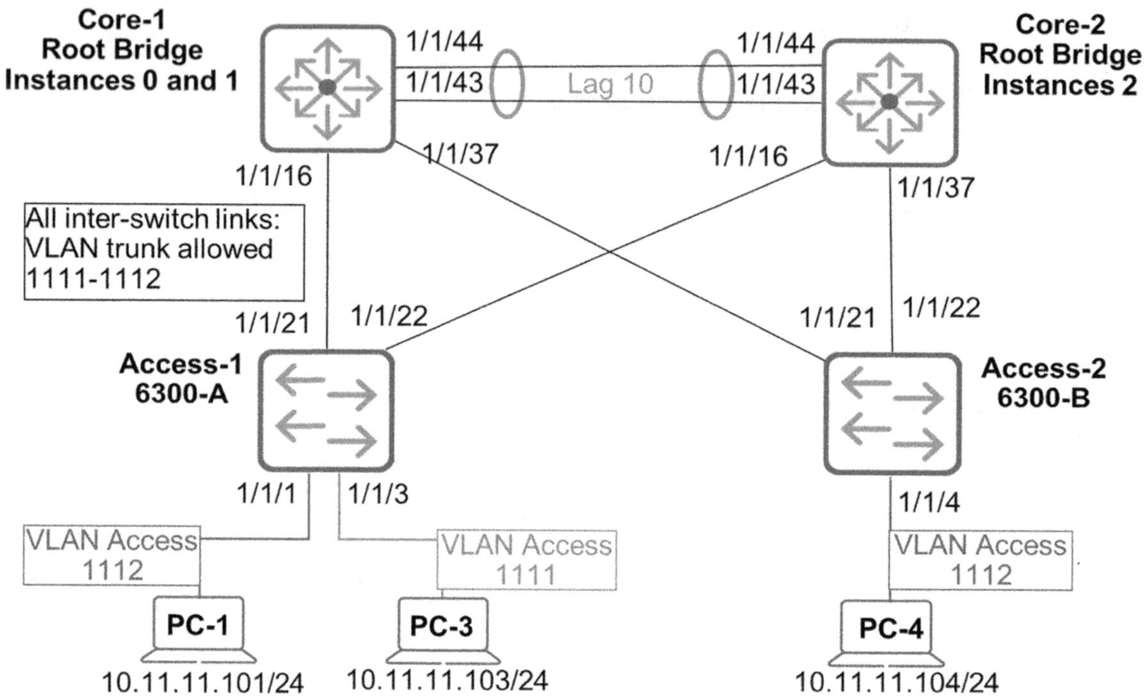

Figure 6-13 Lab Topology

Task 1: Pre-Lab Setup

Objectives

In this activity you will load **Lab5-2_final** checkpoint in Access-1 and Access-2, where those two switches were interconnected to the Core switches using ports 1/1/21 and 1/1/22.

> **Note**
>
> This activity is dependent on Lab 5.2 configuration, so make sure you have completed that lab before starting the current one. Do not proceed if this is not the case.

Steps

Access-1 and Access-2

1. Display the checkpoint list and confirm the **Lab5-2** checkpoint is there.

```
T11-Access-1# show checkpoint list | include Lab5
Lab5-1_final
Lab5-2_final
Lab5-3_final
Lab5-3_task1_done
```

```
T11-Access-2# show checkpoint list | include Lab5
Lab5-1_final
Lab5-2_final
Lab5-3_final
Lab5-3_task1_done
```

2. Load the checkpoint using the "**checkpoint rollback**" command.

```
T11-Access-1# checkpoint rollback Lab5-2_final
Configuration changes will take time to process, please be patient.
```

```
T11-Access-2# checkpoint rollback Lab5-2_final
Configuration changes will take time to process, please be patient.
```

Task 2: Configure Manual Link Aggregation

Objectives

The network administrator of Rent4Cheap Properties (your instructor) will demonstrate and test out static aggregation on the links between the Core switches. He researched the configuration commands and is ready to add them during a maintenance window.

Steps
PC-3

1. Access PC-3.
2. Run a continuous ping to the IP address of Access-2 on VLAN 1111 (10.11.11.4). Ping should be successful.

Core-1(via PC-1)

3. Open the SSH session to Core-1.
4. Create LAG 10 interface and apply a description. This will be used as a logical Layer-2 connection between Cores.

```
Core-1# configure terminal
Core-1(config)# interface LAG 10
Core-1(config-LAG-if)# description TO_CORE-2_PORTS-43_&_44
```

5. Disable routing and enable the interface.

```
Core-1(config-LAG-if)# no routing
Core-1(config-LAG-if)# no shutdown
```

6. Allow VLANs 1111 and 1112.

```
Core-1(config-LAG-if)# VLAN trunk allowed 1111-1112
```

7. Create a port range with interfaces 1/1/43 and 1/1/44 and make these two ports members of LAG 10.

```
Core-1(config-if)# interface 1/1/43-1/1/44
Core-1(config-if-<1/1/43-1/1/44>)# LAG 10
Core-1(config-if-<1/1/43-1/1/44>)# end
```

8. Display detailed information about LAG 10.

```
Core-1# show interface LAG 10


Aggregate LAG10 is up
 Admin state is up
 Description : TO_CORE-2_PORTS-43_&_44
 MAC Address                  : 90:20:c2:bc:ed:00
Aggregated-interfaces        : 1/1/43 1/1/44
 Aggregation-key              : 10
```

```
 Speed                           : 2000 Mb/s
 L3 Counters: Rx Disabled, Tx Disabled
 qos trust none
VLAN Mode: native-untagged
 Native VLAN: 1
Allowed VLAN List: 1111-1112
 Rx
164524 input packets       24564243 bytes
           0 input error             2766 dropped
           0 CRC/FCS
 Tx
276626 output packets      46476581 bytes
           0 input error             2774 dropped
           0 collision
```

What is the state of LAG 10? __________

What are the member ports? __________

What is the speed of the link? __________

How is that speed determined? __________

What VLANs are forwarding traffic on this LAG? __________

How many packets are being sent and received? __________

Are all these packets generated by the continuous ping you are running?

____

Note

Right now, interface LAG 10 is up because the previous configuration has created a local static aggregation that does not depend on any control plane protocol-based negotiation with the remote end (Core-2). However, this has data plane implications, the number of sent and received packets are not the result of a continuous ping. The question is: what else can be creating that amount of traffic? After all, you are in the middle of a maintenance window and nobody else is working in the network (Figure 6-14).

PC-3

9. Move back to PC-3.

   Is the ping still running? ____________________

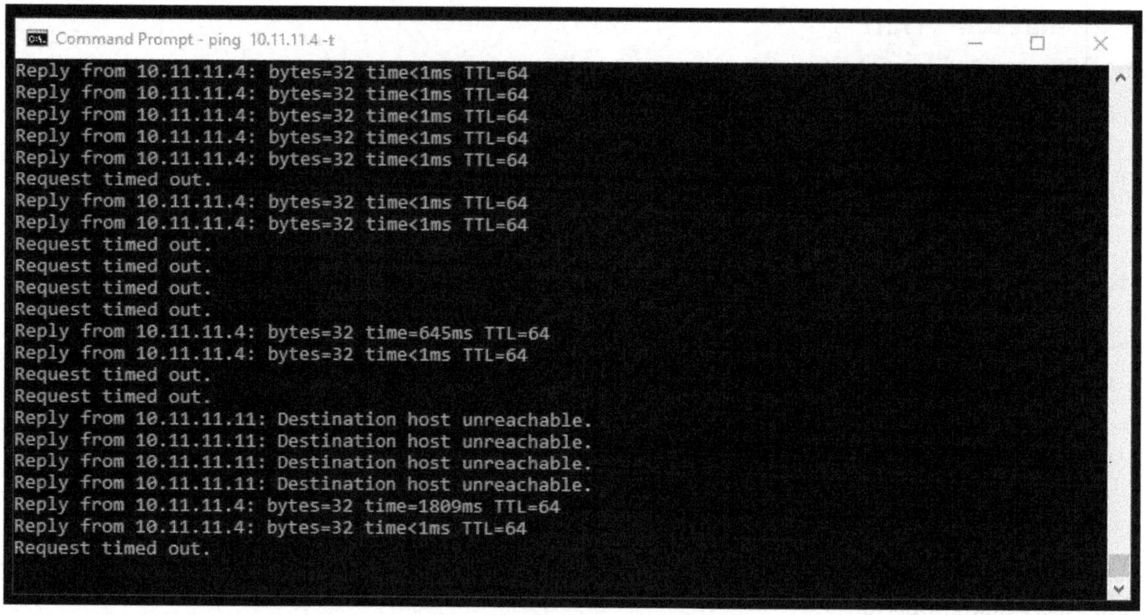

Figure 6-14 Failed Ping

You are experiencing a transient Layer-2 loop. When you configured static link aggregation, on Core-1 it started sending every single frame to Core-2 on either port 43 or 44 based on a load sharing mechanism that uses Source and Destination IPs (or Source and Destination MACs in the absence of IP headers) as input and gives a hash result as output: either 0 or 1 that representsport 43 and 44 respectively. This includes the BPDUs, since at the STP level,LAG 10 is a single logical port.

Core-2 is not running static aggregation yet, and its STP processes see two physical ports instead of one, and Core-2 only receives BPDUs on one of these ports. After a few seconds, the lack of BPDUs in one port forces it to transition its role to Designated (as if it was an interface connected to an end-point) while the other interface becomes Root, these events happen on Instances 0 and 1, because on Instance 2 both ports on Core-2 are already Designated.

Another potential loop situation can take place when configuring Static Aggregation in Access switches uplinks that terminate on different non-related/non-stacked physical devices.

Therefore, before configuring static aggregation, you must verify the following:

- All LAG member ports except one are disabled on one side.
- Confirm cabling is correct and involves two switching entities only.

Since you are already facing the issue, you will begin by removing the transient loop, then you will complete Core-2's portion of the setup.

Core-2(via PC-1)

10. Move to Core-2.
11. Disable port 1/1/43.

```
Core-2# configure terminal
Core-2(config)# interface 1/1/43
Core-2(config-if)# shutdown
```

PC-3

12. Move back to PC-3 (Figure 6-15).

    Is the ping still failing?____

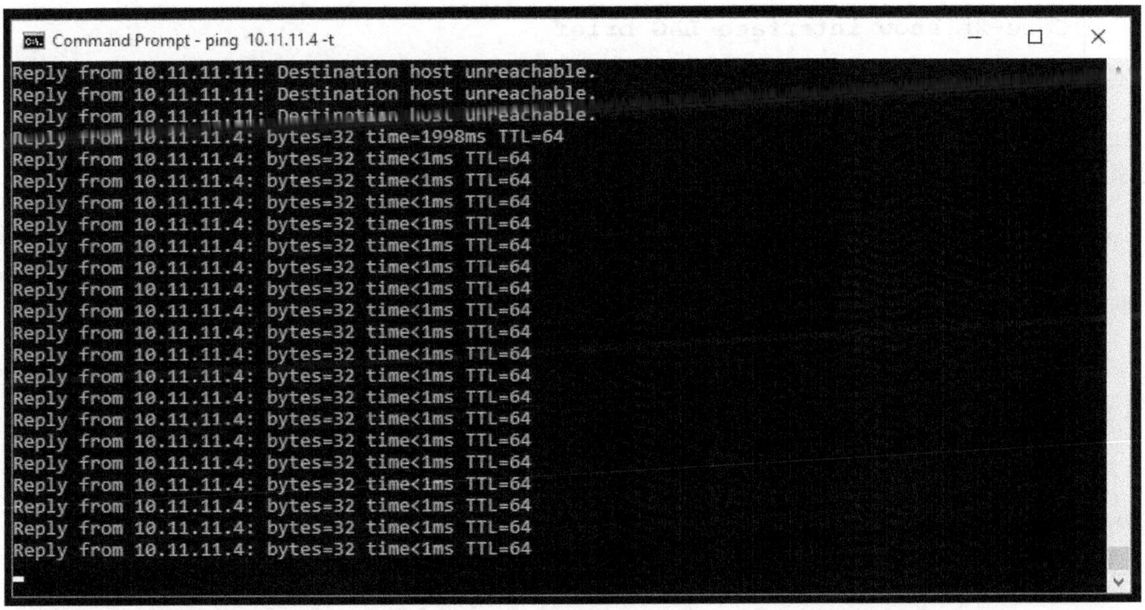

Figure 6-15 Pings Running

Core-2

13. Move back to Core-2.
14. Repeat steps 4 to 8.

```
Core-2(config)# interface LAG 10
Core-2(config-LAG-if)# description TO_CORE-1_PORTS-43_&_44
Core-2(config-LAG-if)# no routing
Core-2(config-LAG-if)# no shutdown
Core-2(config-LAG-if)# VLAN trunk allowed 1111-1112
Core-2(config-if)# interface 1/1/43-1/1/44
Core-2(config-if-<1/1/43-1/1/44>)# LAG 10
```

15. Enable interface 1/1/43 back.

```
Core-2(config)# interface 1/1/43
Core-2(config-if)# no shutdown
```

16. Show interface **LAG 10** status.

```
Core-2# show interface LAG brief
-----------------------------------------------------------------------------
Port        Native  Mode   Type              Enabled Status  Reason
Speed
VLAN
(Mb/s)
-----------------------------------------------------------------------------
LAG10    1         trunk  --        yes      up       --          2000
```

Is LAG 10 working normally?____

PC-3

17. Move back to PC-3.

Is the ping still working? ____

Task 3: Normalize Configuration for All Kits

Objectives

You will now proceed to save your configurations and create checkpoints. Notice that final lab checkpoints might be used by later activities.

Steps

Core-1 and Core-2

18. Add the following VLANs to Core-1 and Core-2s:

```
Core-1# configure terminal
Core-1(config)#                                                                    VLAN
111-112, 211-212, 311-312, 411-412, 511-512, 611-612, 711-712, 811-812, 911-912, 1
011-1012, 1111-1112, 1211-1212, 1311-1312, 1411-1412
Core-1(config-VLAN-<111-112,211-212,311-312,411-412,511-512,611-612,7>)#
interface LAG 10
Core-1(config-LAG-if)#              VLAN              trunk              allowed
111-112, 211-212, 311-312, 411-412, 511-512, 611-612, 711-712, 811-812, 911-912, 1
011-1012, 1111-1112, 1211-1212, 1311-1312, 1411-1412
Core-1(config-LAG-if)# end
Core-1# write memory
Configuration changes will take time to process, please be patient.
Core-1#copy running-config checkpoint Lab6-1_final
```

```
Core-2# end
Core-2# configure terminal
Core-2(config)#                                                                    VLAN
111-112, 211-212, 311-312, 411-412, 511-512, 611-612, 711-712, 811-812, 911-912, 1
011-1012, 1111-1112, 1211-1212, 1311-1312, 1411-1412
Core-2(config-VLAN-<111-112,211-212,311-312,411-412,511-512,611-612,7>)#
interface LAG 10
Core-2(config-LAG-if)#              VLAN              trunk              allowed
111-112, 211-212, 311-312, 411-412, 511-512, 611-612, 711-712, 811-812, 911-912, 1
011-1012, 1111-1112, 1211-1212, 1311-1312, 1411-1412
Core-2(config-LAG-if)# end
Core-2# write memory
Configuration changes will take time to process, please be patient.
Core-2#copy running-config checkpoint Lab6-1_final
```

You have completed Lab 6.1!

Lab 6.2 Deploying LACP-based Link Aggregation

Overview

When LAG 10 was created between both Core switches, BigStartup saw the value of the technology and asked about other potential use cases. When you mentioned link aggregations can be used between switches, routers, firewalls, and servers,the customer became more interested.They asked if it is possible to deploy aggregated links without any chance of loops and can you demonstrate the technology?

Objectives

After completing this lab (Figure 6-16), you will be able to:

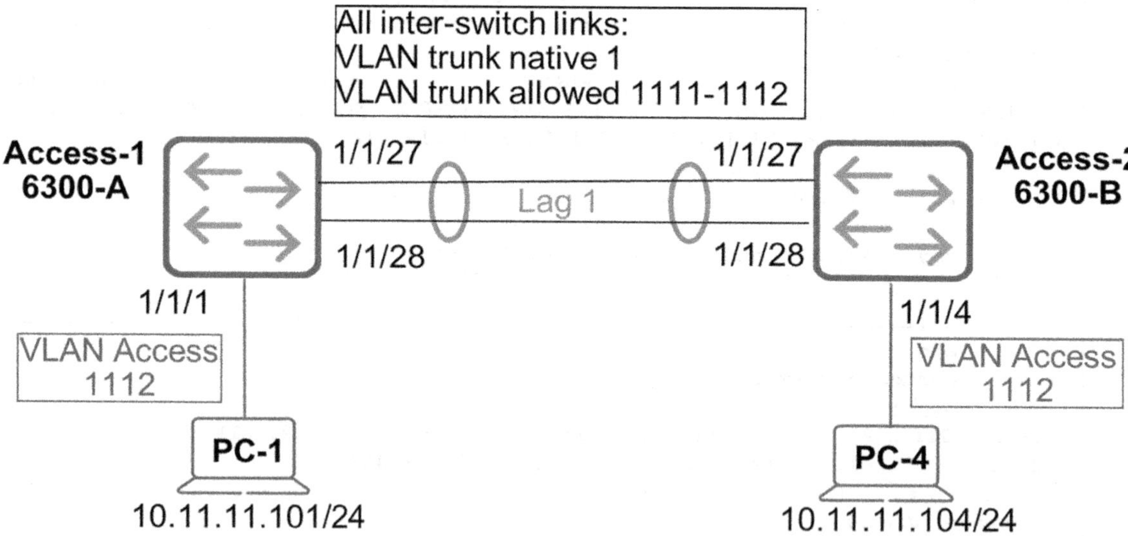

Figure 6-16 Lab Topology

- Deploy LACP-based Link Aggregation
- Demonstrate the benefits of LACP vs Static aggregation

Task 1: Pre-lab Setup:

Objectives

In this activity, you will isolate Access-1 and Access-2 from the rest of the network and then enable a dual-homed topology using ports 27 and 28.

Access-1

19. Open a console connection to Access-1. Log in using **admin** and **no password**.
20. Disable ports 1/1/21 and 1/1/22.

```
T11-Access-1# configure terminal
T11-Access-1(config)# interface 1/1/21-1/1/22
T11-Access-1(config-if-<1/1/21-1/1/22>)# shutdown
T11-Access-1(config-if-<1/1/21-1/1/22>)# exit
```

21. Access port **1/1/27** and set a description.

```
T11-Access-1(config)# interface 1/1/27
T11-Access-1(config-if)# description TO_T11-ACCESS-2_PORT-27
```

22. Create a port range including 1/1/27 and 1/1/28, allow VLANs 1, 1111, and 1112, then enable them

```
T11-Access-1(config)# interface 1/1/27-1/1/28
T11-Access-1(config-if-<1/1/27-1/1/28>)#    VLAN    trunk    allow
1,1111-1112
T11-Access-1(config-if-<1/1/27-1/1/28>)# no shutdown
T11-Access-1(config-if-<1/1/27-1/1/28>)#exit
```

23. Confirm port 1/1/21 to 1/1/22 are down.

```
T11-Access-1(config) # show interface 1/1/21-1/1/22 link-status
--------------------------------------------------
Port      Type          Physical    Link
                        Link State  Transitions
--------------------------------------------------
1/1/21    1GbT          down        4
1/1/22    1GbT          down        2
```

Notice

Remember that you are about to create a Layer-2 loop, which has the potential of affecting other students. In order to limit the effects, you have to make sure that both uplinks 1/1/21 and 1/1/22 are down. If this is not the case, go to those ports and shut them down.

Access-2

24. Move to Access-2; then repeat steps 2 through 4.

```
T11-Access-2# configure terminal
T11-Access-2(config-if-<1/1/21-1/1/22>)# interface 1/1/21-1/1/22
T11-Access-2(config-if-<1/1/21-1/1/22>)#shutdown
T11-Access-2(config-if-<1/1/21-1/1/22>)#exit
T11-Access-2(config)# interface 1/1/27
T11-Access-2(config-if)# description TO_T11-ACCESS-1_PORT-27
T11-Access-2(config-if)#exit
T11-Access-2(config)# interface 1/1/27-1/1/28
T11-Access-2(config-if-<1/1/27-1/1/28>)#    VLAN    trunk    allow
1,1111-1112
T11-Access-2(config-if-<1/1/27-1/1/28>)# no shutdown
T11-Access-2(config-if-<1/1/27-1/1/28>)#exit
```

25. Confirm ports 1/1/21 to 1/1/22 are down and 1/1/27 to 1/1/28 are up.

```
T11-Access-2(config)#  show  interface  1/1/21-1/1/22,1/1/27-1/1/28
link-status
--------------------------------------------------
Port       Type             Physical    Link
                            Link State  Transitions
--------------------------------------------------
```

```
1/1/21     1GbT          down        0
1/1/22     1GbT          down        4
1/1/27     SFP+DAC1      up          11
1/1/28     SFP+DAC1      up          17
```

Notice

Remember that you are about to create a Layer-2 loop. It has the potential of affecting the entire network; in order tolimit the effects, you have to make sure that both uplinks 1/1/21 and 1/1/22 are down. Do not proceed if this is not the case.

---

26. Increase Access-2 spanning-tree priority to 15 (61440). This will make Access-1 the root bridge and force Access-2 to choose a root and alternate port.

```
T11-Access-2(config)# spanning-tree priority 15
```

27. Use the show spanning-tree command and look at **1/1/27 and 1/1/28** ports.

```
T11-Access-2# show spanning-tree | exclude Disabled
Spanning tree status       : Enabled Protocol: MSTP
MST0
  Root ID     Priority    : 28672
              MAC-Address: 88:3a:30:98:30:00
              Hello time(in seconds):2  Max Age(in seconds):20
              Forward Delay(in seconds):15
  Bridge ID  Priority   : 61440
              MAC-Address: 88:3a:30:97:a4:40
              Hello time(in seconds):2  Max Age(in seconds):20
              Forward Delay(in seconds):15
Port           Role            State      Cost          Priority  Type
------------- -------------- ------------- ---------------- ---------
1/1/4          Designated      Forwarding    20000            128
point_to_point
```

```
1/1/27          Root            Forwarding    2000           128
point_to_point
1/1/28          Alternate       Blocking      2000           128
point_to_point
```

What interface is the root port? ____________________

Whatinterface is the alternate port? ____________________

Since the current Access-1 and Access-2 configurations will be used later, create checkpoints now.

Access-1 and Access-2

28. Backup the current Access switches' configuration as a custom checkpoint called **Lab5-3_task1_done**.

```
T11-Access-1# copy running-config checkpoint Lab5-3_task1_done
Configuration changes will take time to process, please be patient.
```

```
T11-Access-2# copy running-config checkpoint Lab5-3_task1_done
Configuration changes will take time to process, please be patient.
```

Task 2: Configure LACP Link Aggregation

Objectives

In the current task you will deploy an aggregated link between both Access Switches using LACP for negotiating the physical ports' states.

Steps

Access-1

1. Open a console connection to Access-1.
2. Create LAG 1 and add a description.

```
T11-Access-1(config)# interface LAG 1
T11-Access-1(config-LAG-if)# description LAG_TO_Access-2
```

3. Run Active LACP and fast rate heartbeats on the link aggregation.

```
T11-Access-1(config-LAG-if)# LACP mode active
T11-Access-1(config-LAG-if)# LACP rate fast
```

4. Allow VLANs 1, 1111, and 1112; then enable the interface.

```
T11-Access-1(config-LAG-if)# VLAN trunk allowed 1,1111,1112
T11-Access-1(config-LAG-if)# no shutdown
T11-Access-1(config-LAG-if)# exit
```

5. Make ports 1/1/27 and 1/1/28 part of the LAG.

```
T11-Access-1(config)# interface 1/1/27-1/1/28
T11-Access-1(config-if-<1/1/27-1/1/28>)# LAG 1
T11-Access-1(config-if-<1/1/27-1/1/28>)# exit
```

6. Use the **show LACP configuration** for displaying the local System-ID and Priority.

```
T11-Access-1(config)# show LACP configuration
System-ID       : 88:3a:30:98:30:00
System-priority : 65534
```

7. Display the LACP-based LAG status information.

```
T11-Access-1(config)# show LACP interfaces
State abbreviations :
A - Active          P - Passive        F - Aggregable I - Individual
S - Short-timeout L - Long-timeout N - InSync       O - OutofSync
C - Collecting     D - Distributing
X - State m/c expired                  E - Default neighbor state
Actor details of all interfaces:
-----------------------------------------------------------------------------
IntfAggr         Port   Port   State    System-ID          System Aggr
Forwarding
       Name        Id     PriPri     Key  State
-----------------------------------------------------------------------------
1/1/27   LAG1       28     1      ASFOE    88:3a:30:98:30:00 65534   1
LACP-block
1/1/28   LAG1       29     1      ASFOE    88:3a:30:98:30:00 65534   1
LACP-block
```

```
Partner details of all interfaces:
----------------------------------------------------------------------------
IntfAggr        Port  Port  State    System-ID           System Aggr
       Name        Id     PriPri     Key
----------------------------------------------------------------------------
1/1/27  LAG1       0      65534 PLFOEX  00:00:00:00:00:00 65534  0
1/1/28  LAG1       0      65534 PLFOEX  00:00:00:00:00:00 65534  0
```

What is the local system ID? ______________________________

What is the remote system ID? ______________________________

What is the forwarding state? ______________________________

Answer

Forwarding state is LACP-block; this prevents data packets from being transmitted on such physical ports until the local switch receives inbound LACP Data Units from a peer, preventing any transient loops.

Access-2

8. Open a console connection to Access-2.
9. Repeat steps 2 to 5 using VLANs 1111 and 1112.

```
T11-Access-2(config)# interface LAG 1
T11-Access-2(config-LAG-if)# description LAG_TO_Access-1
```

```
T11-Access-2(config-LAG-if)# LACP mode active
T11-Access-2(config-LAG-if)# LACP rate fast
T11-Access-2(config-LAG-if)# VLAN trunk allowed 1,1111,1112
T11-Access-2(config-LAG-if)# no shutdown
T11-Access-2(config-LAG-if)# exit
T11-Access-2(config)# interface 1/1/27-1/1/28
T11-Access-2(config-if-<1/1/27-1/1/28>)# LAG 1
T11-Access-2(config-if-<1/1/27-1/1/28>)# exit
```

10. Display the LACP-based LAGs' status information.

```
T11-Access-2(config)# show LACP interfaces

State abbreviations :

A - Active          P - Passive       F - Aggregable I - Individual

S - Short-timeout L - Long-timeout N - InSync     O - OutofSync

C - Collecting     D - Distributing

X - State m/c expired                E - Default neighbor state

Actor details of all interfaces:

-----------------------------------------------------------------

IntfAggr         Port  Port  State   System-ID          System Aggr
Forwarding

       Name        Id     PriPri     Key  State

-----------------------------------------------------------------

1/1/27  LAG1     28    1    ASFNCD  88:3a:30:97:a4:40 65534  1    up

1/1/28  LAG1     29    1    ASFNCD  88:3a:30:97:a4:40 65534  1    up


Partner details of all interfaces:

-----------------------------------------------------------------

IntfAggr      Port  Port       State   System-ID          System Aggr

Name           Id     PriPri     Key

-----------------------------------------------------------------

1/1/27  LAG1        28    1      ASFNCD  88:3a:30:98:30:00 65534  1

1/1/28  LAG1        29    1      ASFNCD  88:3a:30:98:30:00 65534  1
```

What physical ports are a member of the LAG? ____________________

What are the state flags on the local and remote ports? ____________________

What is their meaning? ____________________

11. Issue the **show spanning-tree** command.

What is the spanning-tree state of ports 1/1/27, 1/1/28, and LAG 1? ______________________

```
T11-Access-2(config)# show spanning-tree | exclude Disabled
                        ←---- output omitted ---→
Port        Role          State         Cost            Priority   Type
------------------------------------------------------------------------
1/1/4    Designated   Forwarding     20000    128         point_to_point
LAG1     Root         Forwarding     2000     64          point_to_point
```

Answer

Ports 1/1/27 and 1/1/28 are not listed, while LAG1 is Root. When LAG1 was created and ports 1/1/27 and 1/1/28 became part of it, then Spanning Tree stopped considering the physical interfaces in its calculations and started using LAG1 instead.

12. Run the**show LACP aggregates** command.

```
T11-Access-2(config)# show LACP aggregates
Aggregate name     : LAG1
Interfaces         : 1/1/28 1/1/27
Heartbeat rate     : Fast
hash               : l3-src-dst
Aggregate mode     : Active
```

What is the current (default) hashing algorithm? ______________________

PC-1

13. Open a console session to PC-1.

14. Ping PC-4 (10.11.12.104). Ping should be successful.

Note

Since this traffic will always have the same source and destination IP addresses, only one link is being used for sending the traffic in either direction. If multiple clients were connected on both switches, then the traffic between them would be shared across both links in an Active/Active way.

Task 3: Save Your Configurations

Objectives

You will now proceed to create checkpoints.

Steps

Access-1 and Access-2

15. Save the current Access switches' configuration in the startup checkpoint.

```
T11-Access-1# write memory
Configuration changes will take time to process, please be patient.
```

```
T11-Access-2# write memory
Configuration changes will take time to process, please be patient.
```

16. Backup the current Access switches' configuration as a custom checkpoint called **Lab6-2_final**.

```
T11-Access-1# copy running-config checkpoint Lab6-2_final
Configuration changes will take time to process, please be patient.
```

```
T11-Access-2# copy running-config checkpoint Lab6-2_final
Configuration changes will take time to process, please be patient.
```

You have completed Lab 6.2!

Learning Check

Chapter 6 Questions

Static and Dynamic LAG

1. What is correct when referring to Static versus Dynamic LAG?
   a. Static Link Aggregation mode devices do not exchange any control information.
   b. Switches can establish a LAG between each other as long as one side is Dynamic.

c. Dynamic LAG uses the Aruba proprietary LACP protocol.

d. LACP is not available on Layer-Three routed ports.

e. Dynamic LAG can detect link failures and ensure that LAG port members terminate on the same device.

Load Sharing

2. What can be used to determine the hashing algorithm used for load balancing traffic across a LAG in Aruba OS-CX switches?

   a. Layer-4 TCP/UDP ports

   b. Layer-3 Source and Destination IP addresses

   c. Layer-2 Source and Destination MAC addresses

   d. Layer-1 Port numbers

   e. Layer-7 application type if Deep-Packet inspection is enabled.

Deploying LACP

3. What is the command to enable a Link Aggregation interface 99 in Aruba OS-CX?

   a. SW1(config)# **interface LAG 99**

   b. SW1(config)# **Dynamic LAG 99**

   c. SW1(config)# **Static LAG 99**

   d. SW1(config)# **LAG 99**

   e. SW1(config-if)# **LAG 99**

7 IPv4 Routing Part 1

EXAM OBJECTIVES

- ✓ Describe routing, IP addressing, and masking
- ✓ Explain IP routes and the default gateway
- ✓ Describe inter-VLAN routing
- ✓ Describe the packet delivery process
- ✓ Explain Virtual Routing and Forwarding

Overview

You have learned quite a bit about Layer-2 processes and Layer-2 frames, communications within a single VLAN. Now you learn how to connect those VLANs together and route between them. Routing devices use Layer-3 packet analysis to forward Layer-3 IP packets, explore IP addressing, and masking. These are vital skills to design, deploy, and diagnose scalable routed networks.

You will see how IP routes and Default Gateways (DG) benefit end systems, before exploring Inter-VLAN routing and DHCP helper addresses. Armed with this information, you will explore a Layer-3 packet delivery scenario.

You will learn how a single physical router can be divided into multiple virtual routers using Virtual Routing and Forwarding (VRF). Then you will apply this knowledge in a lab activity.

Routing Introduction

Routing

You have learned how devices communicate within the same network (broadcast domain), using Layer-2 switching. Layer-2 switches forward frames among devices in the same LAN by processing Layer-2 frame headers. Recall that switches build a MAC address table based on source MAC addresses, and forward frames based on destination MAC addresses. Now you will learn how Layer-3 routers move packets between different LANs or broadcast domains, based on Layer-3 IP addresses (Figure 7-1).

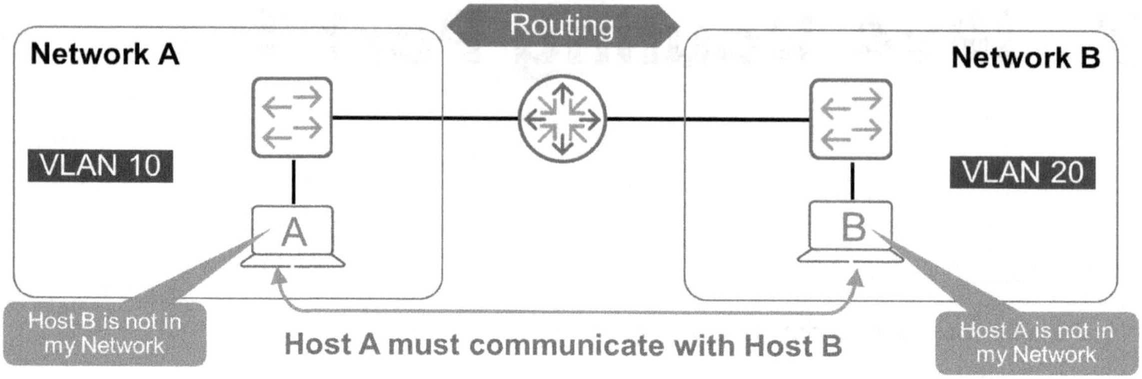

Figure 7-1 Host A to B Routing

Routing Layer-3 Analysis

The ability to analyze the Layer-3 header is known as **routing**.

Layer-3 devices perform routing. They analyze Layer-3 IP addresses, select the best path to get from original source to ultimate destination, and the forward packets along that path (Figure 7-1).

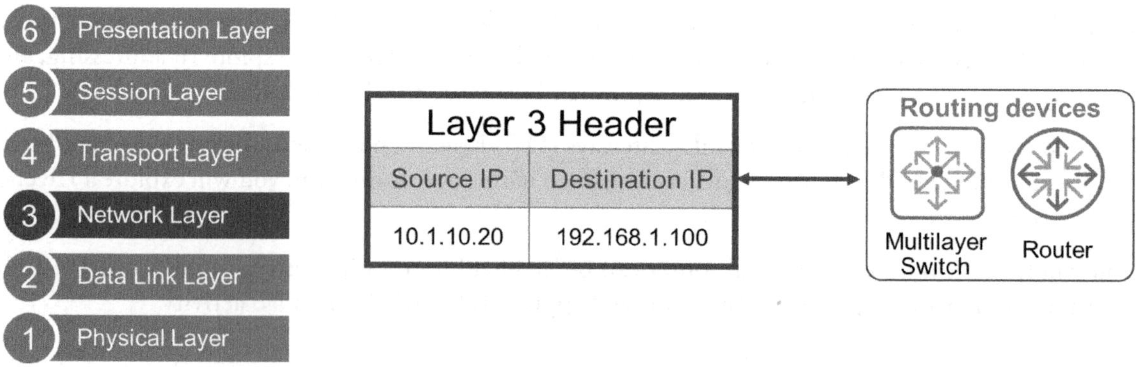

Figure 7-2 Layer-3 Analysis

IP Addressing

Basic routing decisions are based on the analysis of the Layer-3 addressing (Figure 7-2). The Internet Protocol (IP) provides an identification or address for each device in a network.

Currently there are two versions of IP that are widely used: IP version 4 (IPv4) and version 6 (IPv6). The main difference between these two protocols is the addressing space. Version 4 can allocate approximately 4.29 billion addresses, while version 6 can allocate 3.4×10^{38} addresses. This module is focused on IPv4 addressing and routing.

An IPv4 address consists of 32bits expressed in a dotted decimal notation. This notation divides the address intofour sections called octets. As the name implies, each octet is composed by 8bits, a byte. This dotted decimal notation makes it easy for humans to work with IPv4 addresses. Figure 7-3 shows three hosts in the same LAN, each with a unique IP address.

Feature	IPv4	IPv6
Size of address	32 bits – 4 octets	128 bits – 16 octets
Example of address	192.168.10.250	fe80:0000:0000:0000:844d:a9ff:febb:62c3
Number of possible addresses	4.29 Billion	340 Undecillion (3.4×10^{38})

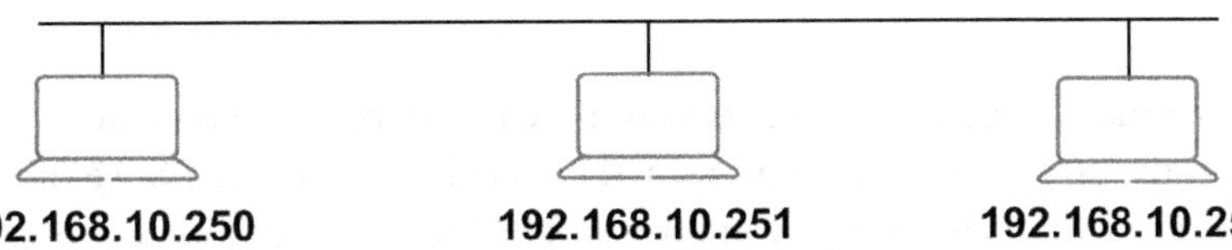

Figure 7-3 IPv4 Versus IPv6

Note
Since an octet is composed by 8 bits, this implies that valid decimal values in an octet are from 0 to 255.

IPv4 address

An IP address consists of two parts: network ID and the host ID. The network ID is the most significant part of the address (left side) that identifies the network. The host ID on the other hand is the less significant part of the address (right side) that identifies an individual host (Figure 7-4).

IPv4 binary notation	11000000101010000000101000000011			
Octet	11000000	10101000	00001010	00000011
Decimal	192	168	10	3
IPv4 dot-decimal notation	192.168.10.3			

Figure 7-4 IPv4 Address Format

To help you understand the relationship between these two concepts, you can think that the network ID is analogous to the street name and the host ID is analogous to the house number in that street. IPv4 addresses are always 32 bites long. Sometimes, 16 bits represent the network, and 16 bits represent the host. Sometimes there are 24 bits to specify the network, and 8 bits for hosts. There can be nearly any combination of network and host bits. This is all controlled by the subnet mask.

Network Mask

The network mask is an IP parameter that indicates how many bits represent the network portion of an address, and how many bits represent the host portion of an address. The 32-bit network mask is a mandatory IP parameter for all IP network devices.

The network mask determines if two endpoints are on the same network or on different networks. This process is done by a simple comparison.

- If the network ID for the source and destination is the same, then both devices are in the same broadcast domain. Layer-2 switching is enough to complete the communication.
- If the network ID for the source and destination is different, then the devices are in different networks. Layer-3 routing is required for this communication.

A network mask is 32-bits long, just like an IPv4 address. The mask is simply a contiguous string or block of binary ones, followed by a block of zeros. The ones indicate the portion of the IPv4 address that is assigned to the network ID and the zeros will represent the portion of the IPv4 address assigned to the Host ID.

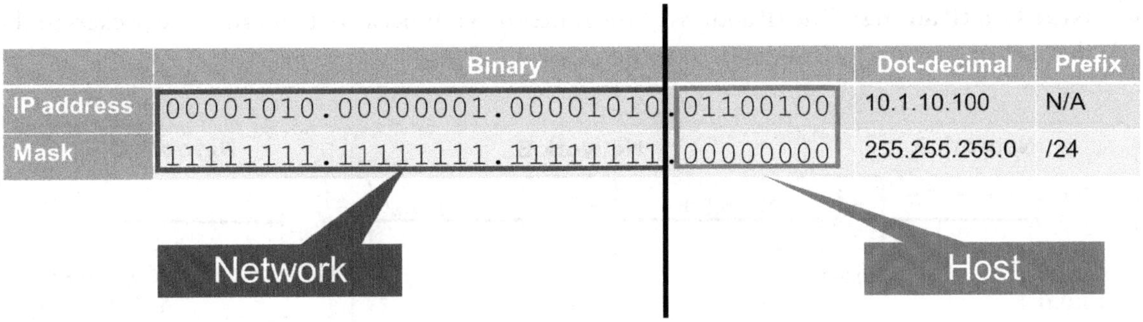

Figure 7-5 IPv4 Dotted Decimal to Binary

Figure 7-5 shows the relationship between an IP address and the network mask. Where the binary 1s in the mask end and the 0s begin defines the line between the network and host portions of an IP address.

The network mask usually is represented in two different ways:

- Dotted Decimal notation: Same as an IPv4 address, the mask uses four different octets and each one is separated by a dot, for example, 255.255.255.0.
- Prefix notation: This notation in decimal indicates the number of bits that are set to one. This notation uses a *slash + number* and is commonly placed next to an IP address, for example, 10.1.10.100/24. This notation indicates that the first 24 bits are set to one.

IP Routes and Default Gateway

IP Route

When a device must communicatewith others in a different network, it must know which local network device on its broadcast domain can route the traffic toward the destination network. This information is provided to computers using IP Routes.

For endpoints, this information must be manually added, in the form of a so-called "static route." However, routers and multilayer switches can use manually added static routes or they can dynamically and automatically determine the best routes to each destination, using a routing protocol. You will soon learn about dynamic routing protocols in a later module.

A static route must specify the following information, as shown in the figure for Router 1 and Router 2:

- **Destination IP address**: Where you want to go
- **Subnet mask**: How that destination IP address is split into a network portion and a host portion

- **Next-hop IP address**: The IP address of the router on your network that can route packets to the destination.

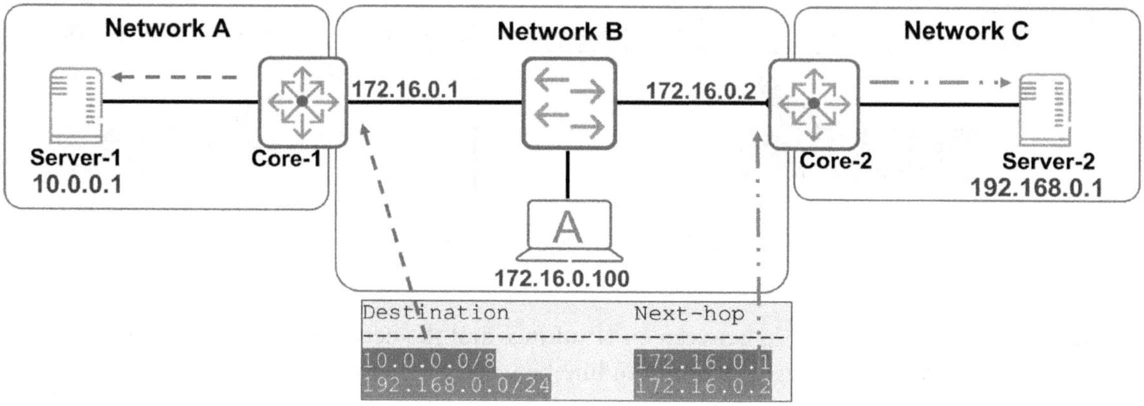

Figure 7-6 Static Route Scenario

Look at the scenario shown in Figure 7-6, which shows three networks connected by two routers. Core-1 connects Networks A and B, while Core-2 can route between networks B and C.

If Host A (in network B) must communicate with Server-1 in Network A, it must use Route 1. Route 1 says, "To get to destination 10.0.0.1, which has a mask of 255.0.0.0 (/8), you must use next-hop router at IP address 172.16.0.1.

What if Host A must use Server-2? To arrive at 192.168.0.1 with the 255.255.255.0 (/24) mask, you must send the packets to next-hop router at IP address 172.16.0.2 according to Route 2.

Default Gateway

A default gateway (DG) is the device that routes all network destinations for the endpoint devices in a broadcast domain or network. It is like telling a host, "To get to everywhere in the known universe, go to this next-hop address." The default gateway optimizes and simplifies endpoint routing decisions, since only a single route is required.

Figure 7-7 shows how router Core-1 acts as the DG for all devices in Network B. These devices must only install a single route.

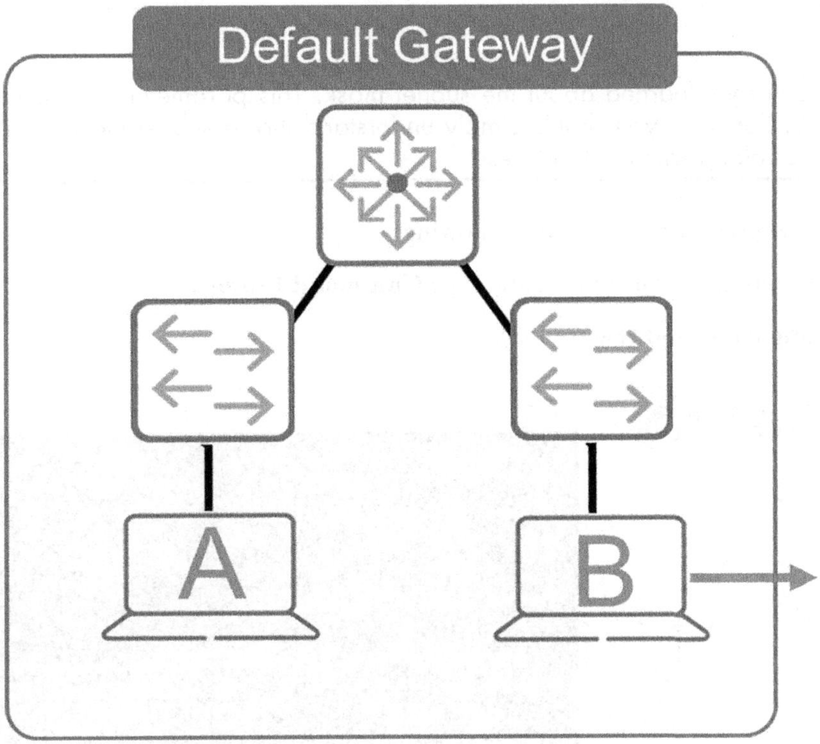

Figure 7-7 Default Gateway Scenario

Note
Different endpoints in the same subnet could have different default gateways if there is more than one router on the network.

In a windows device a static IP address and Default Gateway can be set up in the same place. For windows 10 devices you can follow the next instructions:

1. Click on the windows start button and type Control Panel.
2. Navigate to Network and Internet → Network and Sharing Center → Change adapter settings.
3. Right click on the Network Interface Card (NIC) that you want to set up and select Properties.
4. Double click on Internet Protocol Version 4 (TCP/IPv4).
5. Enter the proper information for the IP address, subnet mask, Default Gateway. Optionally you can enter DNS server information.
6. Click OK twice.

Note

You have not yet learned about the subnet mask. This parameter will be discussed on Module 8. For now, you should simply understand that a subnet mask must always be configured, along with an IP address.

To verify the previous set up you, do the following:

1. Click on the windows start button and type **Command Prompt**.
2. Type **ipconfig** command (Figure 7-8).

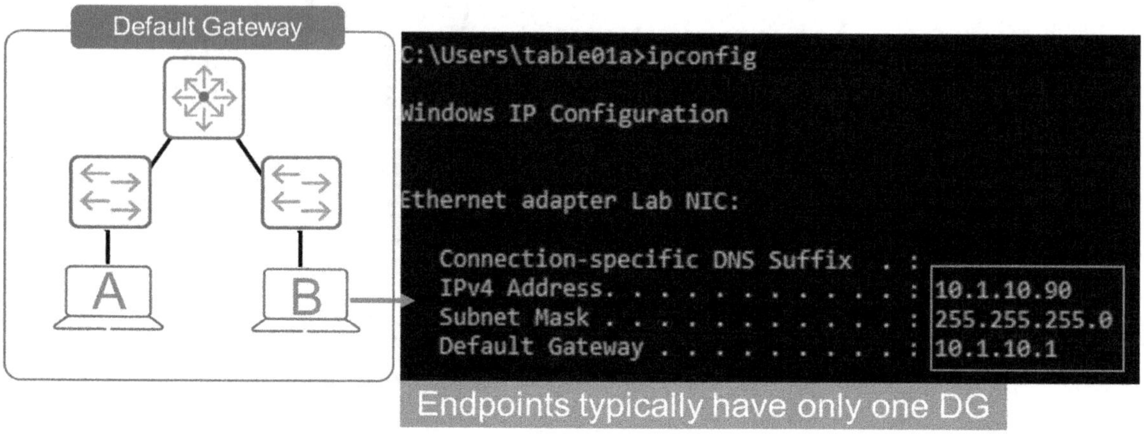

Figure 7-8 IPCONFIG

Inter-VLAN Routing

Multi-Layer Interface Types

A switch port can only run Layer-2 features and protocols—like being a member of a VLAN, for example.

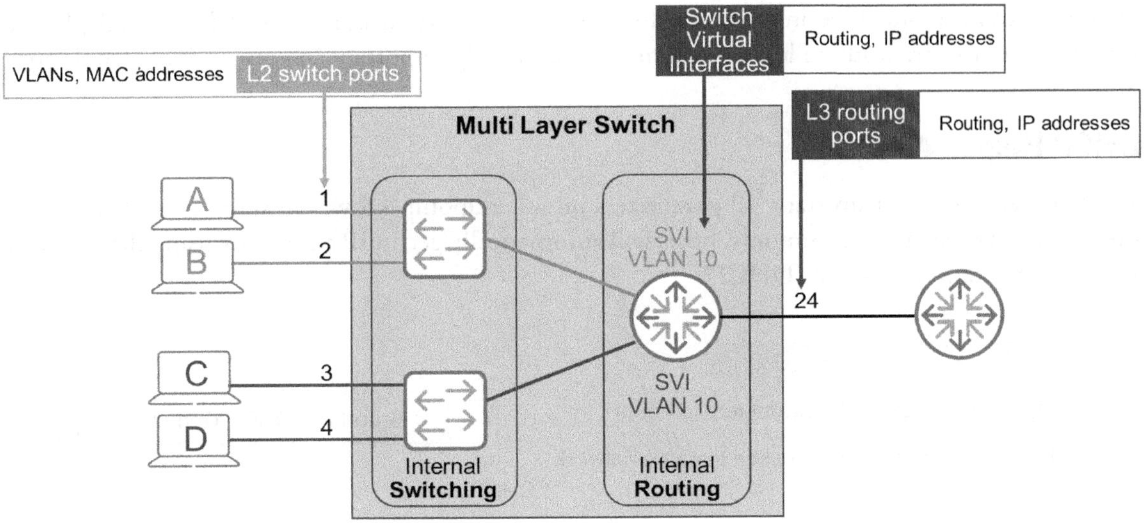

Figure 7-9 Multi-Layer Interfaces

Figure 7-9 shows ports 1–4 being used as Layer-2 interfaces. They attach to end systems, accept L2 frames as being a member of some Layer-2 VLAN, and forward them—based on their destination Layer-2 MAC address. You learned that Aruba OS-CX ports are Layer-3 interfaces by default, and so you must configure ports 1–4 with the command no routing.

But what if you want to route between these VLANs. The Aruba OS-CX switches are multi-layer switches;they have both internal Layer-2 switching functions and internal Layer-3 routing capabilities. You need a way to connect each Layer-2 VLAN to the internal routing functions. To do this, you must create Switch Virtual Interfaces (SVI). This is a virtual Layer-3, routed interface that exists only inside the device, as a virtual construct.

Suppose that you define SVI 10. Because it is an SVI, by definition, it connects to the internal routing construct. Because it is SVI "10", by definition, it connects to VLAN 10, and so services routable traffic from VLAN 10 to other destination networks.

Similarly, you might define SVI 20. With some routing configuration, which you will soon learn, your switch can now route traffic between your VLANs.

Now suppose that you need to connect your multi-Layer switch to an external router, perhaps using port 24, as shown in Figure 7-9. Since all ports are Layer-3 interfaces by default, Port 24 connects to the internal routing functions by default. You merely need to configure it with typical Layer-3 parameters, such as an IP address. You will soon learn about these concepts and syntax.

The SVIs are virtual Layer-3 interfaces, for internal routing, and port 24 is a physical Layer-3 interface, for external routing. Both are Layer-3 interfaces, and so perform routing functions. They accept routable Layer-3 packets and forward them based on their destination IP address.

Now you know about three important interface types, L2 switch ports, L3 SVIs, and L3 physical routed ports. You are ready to learn about another especially important interface type: a trunk port.

DHCP Helper Address

You have learned to set up static IP parameters on an endpoint. However, static IP address assignment is not typical. More commonly, hosts will automatically get an IP address by using the Dynamic Host Configuration Protocol (DHCP).

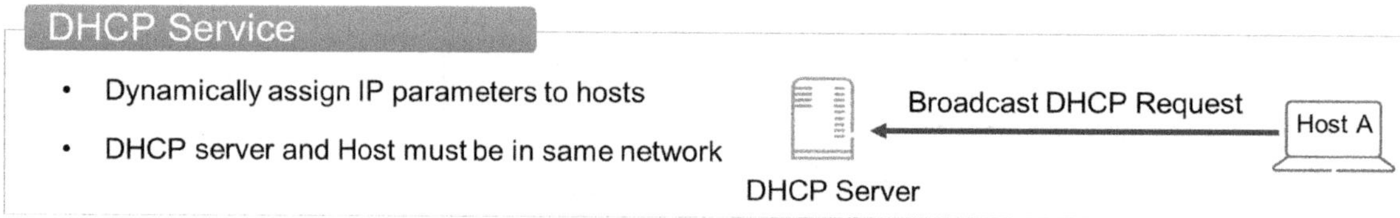

Figure 7-10 DHCP Service

Endpoints broadcast a DHCP request, "Hey everyone, I need an IP address, a mask, and a DG." Because it is a broadcast, the host and server must be on the same subnet. Remember, a router defines the edge of a broadcast domain, and does not forward broadcast. Routers on different broadcast domains (VLAN) do not hear the request, and so no address is assigned.

Now wait a minute. If an organization deploys thousands of broadcast domains (VLANs), then you would need thousands of DHCP servers; one per VLAN (Figure 7-10)! This is not realistic. You need a central DHCP service for all VLANs.

The solution is to configure a DHCP Helper address on each router interface that serves as the Default Gateway for endpoints (Figure 7-11).

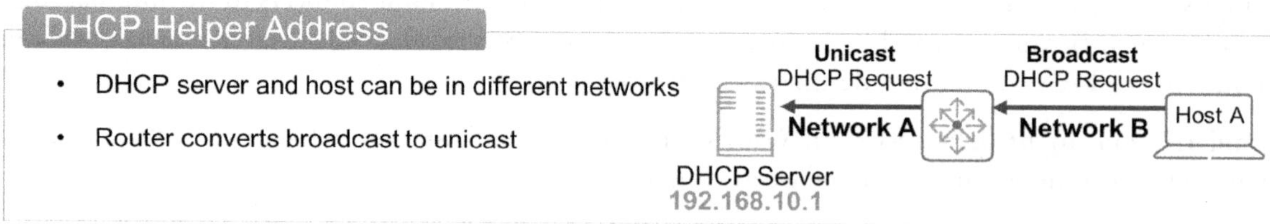

Figure 7-11 DHCP Helper Address

The following process describes how the solution works, when a router is properly configured with a helper address:

1. The client broadcasts a normal DHCP query.
2. The router that is on the client's network (the client's DG) receives this broadcasted DHCP query.
3. Instead of discarding the broadcast, as is normal, the router "helps" this broadcast by forwarding it on to the DHCP server. It converts this broadcast into a unicast, with the destination address specified in the **IP helper-address** command (192.168.10.1 in this example). Now that the message is a unicast, the router forwards it as it would any other unicast packet, toward its destination, the DHCP Server.
4. Thus, the DHCP Server receives the DHCP request and replies with a DHCP offer, a unicast message sent to the requesting host, via the router.

In AOS-CX the command **IP helper-address** defines the address of a remote DHCP server. Up to eight addresses can be defined. When more than one DHCP server has been defined the switch will send the client request to all defined servers.

This command must be used under a Layer-3 interface as show:

```
Switch(config)# interface vlan 1
Switch(config-if)# ip helper-address <IP-Address>
```

Inter-VLAN Routing

You learned about VLANs in Module 3. A VLAN is a broadcast domain, with a unique IP network number. In other words, all devices in the same VLAN have the same network address. All devices in the Sales VLAN are 10.1.10.x, where x is some unique host value. So, IP addresses might be 10.1.10.100, 10.1.10.101, 10.1.10.102, and so on. Everyone in the HR VLAN might be 192.168.20.100, 192.168.20.101, and so on.

Recall that devices in different VLANs cannot communicateunless you connect them with a router. Inter-VLAN routing connects separate VLANs into a routed internetwork of communicating devices.

In years past, multi-layer switches did not exist. Older environments used Layer-2 switches for host connectivity, and then routed between them with an external router. You see this in the left-hand example of Figure 7-12.

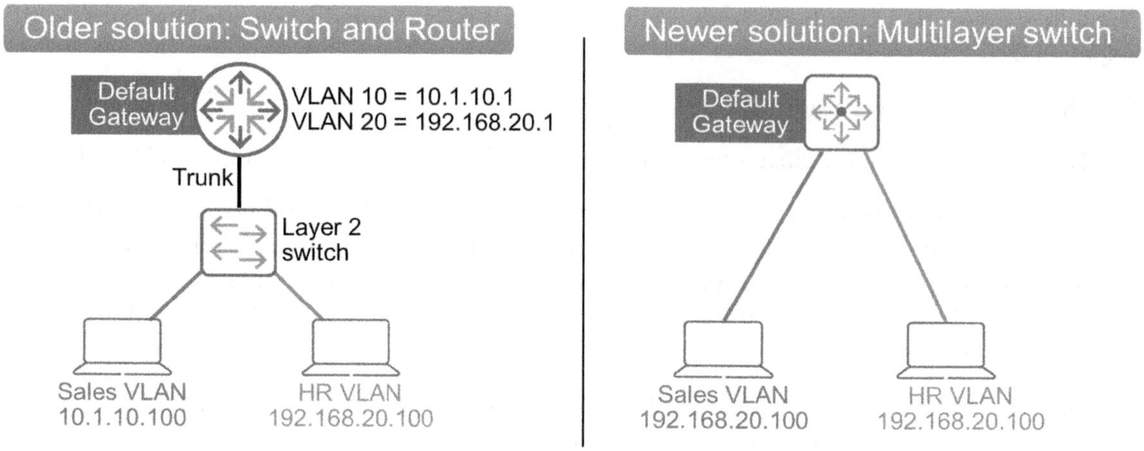

Figure 7-12 Inter-VLAN Routing

A potential problem with this deployment is that the Switch-to-router link can become oversubscribe, although LAG can alleviate this problem to some extent. Performance can also be suboptimal, because sending frames to the router requires an additional routing decision.

Multilayer switches are more efficient devices. The switching and routing functions of the device are connected via a high-speed internal backplane. Initial routing decisions and other processes all happen "in the box." This can reduce latency and increase performance.

All AOS-CX switches are multilayer switches which have routing enabled by default.

IP Routing Table

Routing devices (Routers and Multilayer switches) build and maintain a routing table that informs them of the best path to any given destination.

You can manually add entries to the route table, in the form of static routes. Alternatively, you can configure a routing protocol, which automatically builds and maintains this table. Typically, entries in the routing table do not expire unless a change in the topology causes an update. This differs from the MAC address table in Layer-2 switches where an entry expires after five minutes if the switch stops receiving traffic from the endpoint.

You will learn about all the entries that can exist in an actual route table soon. Meanwhile, Figure 7-13 shows a slightly simplified view of the route table on the Core-1 and Core-2 routers.

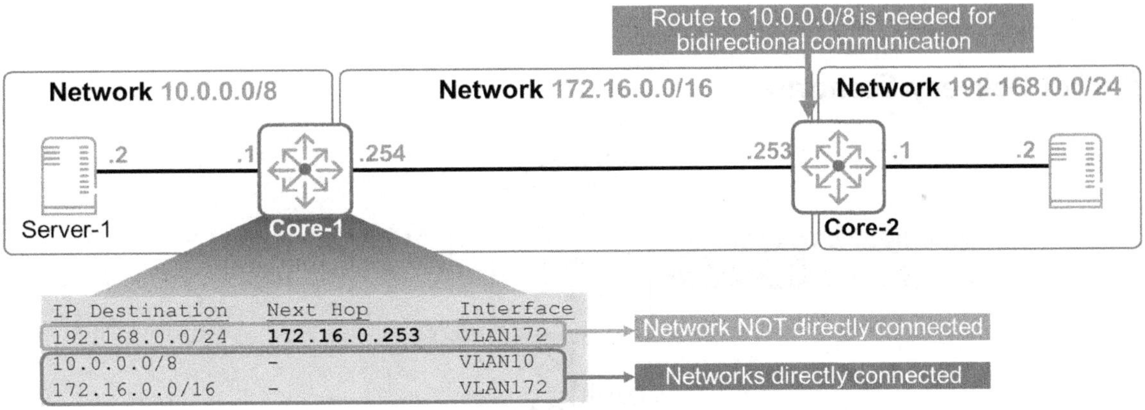

Figure 7-13 IP Routing Table

There are three networks, 10.0.0.0/8, 172.16.0.0/16, and 192.168.0.0/24. Recall that the subnet mask determines the network portion of an IP address.

OK, now let us analyze Core-1's route table. The first entry says, "To get to any host on network 192.168.0.0/24, send packets to next-hop router 172.16.0.253 (Core-2). To get to that next-hop address, forward the packet out local VLAN172."

The next entry says, "To get to any host on network 10.0.0.0/8, there is no next-hop. I am directly connected to that network. Simply forward the packet out my local VLAN interface 10." Finally, to connect to the network 172.16.0.0/16, Core-1 is directly connected to this network. There is no need to assign a next hop; simple forward the packet out of VLAN interface 172.

Consider at this moment that you configure only Core-1 when Server-1 connects to Server-2 Core-1 will properly route the packet and send it to Core-2. This device will have no problem to send the packet to Sever-2; this network is locally connected to Core-2. So, communication in oneway is successful. However, the response from Server-2 is sent to Core-2; this device receives the packet but since the destination (10.0.0.2) is not its table route the packet will be dropped. Simply bidirectional communication cannot be done.

To solve the problem, remember that Core-2 will need to be configured with a route to reach the non-directed network (10.0.0.0/8). Try to think about how this route will look like.

Answer:
Destination = 10.0.0.0/8
Next hop = 172.16.0.254
Interface = VLAN that is connected to network 172.16.0.0—for this example VLAN172.

Packet Delivery

Packet Delivery Scenario

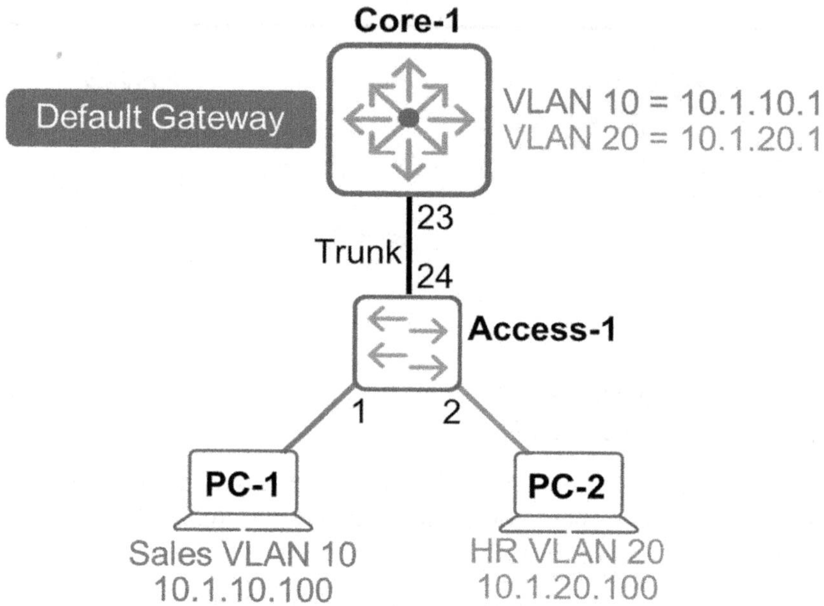

Figure 7-14 Packet Delivery Scenario

In this scenario, PC-1 must communicate with PC-2. Both endpoints connect to the same Layer-2 switch, but they are mapped to different VLANs. The Core-1 multilayer switch is there to do inter-VLAN routing (Figure 7-14).

PC-1 has IP address 10.1.10.100 on VLAN 10, and its DG is 10.1.10.1. It connects to port 1 of Access-1.

PC-2 has IP address 10.1.20.100 on VLAN 20, with DG = 10.1.20.1. It connects to port 2 of Access-1

Access-1 port 24 connects to Core-1 port 23.

Note

You learned that collapsing Layer-2 access services and Layer-3 routing services into a single multilayer switch can improve efficiency. However, for larger networks, there is typically a separate layer of pure Layer-2 switches for endpoint access, connected to a smaller set of L2/L3 multilayer switches. This design improves scalability.

Endpoint to Access Switch

1. PC-1 generates a message that contains the following information:
    - Layer-3 header: Source IP address is PC-1's 10.1.10.100 and the destination IP isPC-2's 10.1.20.100.
    - Layer-2 header: Source MAC address is PC-1's MAC address and the destination MAC address is the default gateway (the MAC address associated with 10.1.10.1) (Figure 7-15).

Layer 2 Header		Layer 3 Header		Payload	L2T
Source MAC	Destination MAC	Source IP	Destination IP	Payload data	CRC
PC-1 MAC	Gateway MAC	10.1.10.100 **(PC-1)**	10.1.20.100 **(PC-2)**		

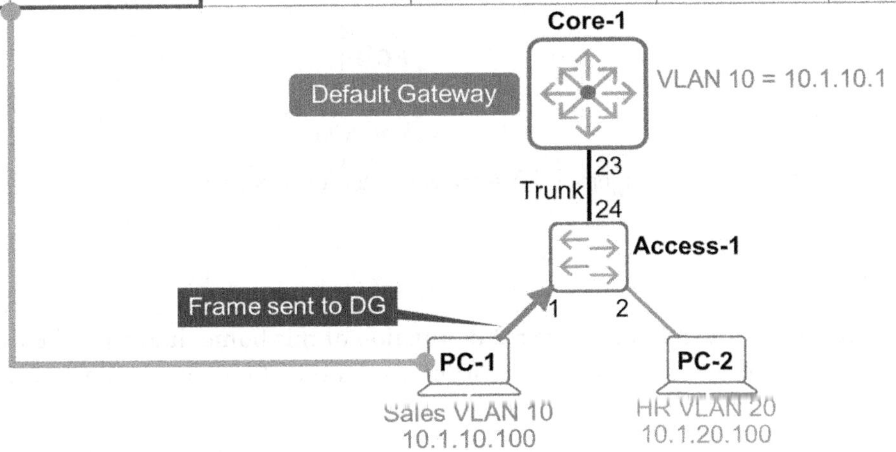

Figure 7-15 Packet Delivery: Endpoint to Access Switch

Remember, if PC-1 does not know the MAC address for 10.1.10.1, it performs an ARP process to get this information.

Access to Multilayer Switch

2. Access-1 receives the frame and analyzes the Layer-2 destination MAC address. It finds a match in its MAC address table and knows that it must forward this frame out its trunk link, port 24, to Core-1. It adds an802.1q tag, VLAN = 10, and forwards the frame (Figure 7-16).

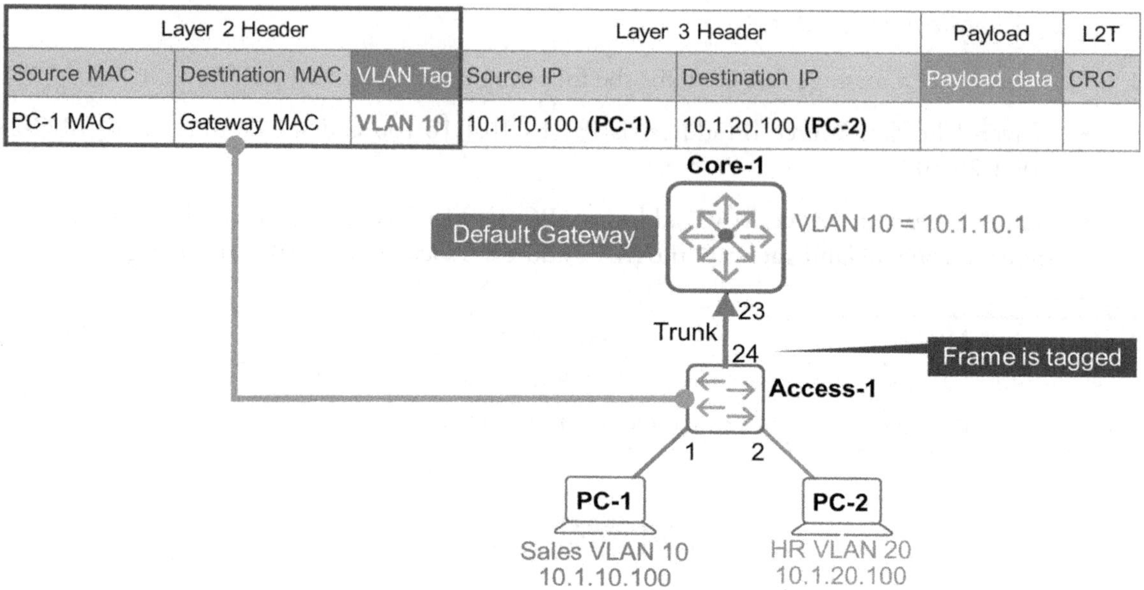

Figure 7-16 Access to Multilayer Switch

Routing Process

3. Multilayer switch Core-1 is the Layer-2 destination of this frame. It accepts the frame, strips off the Layer-2 header, and begins to perform its routing function, to analyze layer-3 header information.

4. It compares the Layer-3 destination IP address to its routing table entries. The figure shows Core-1's route table, the output of **show IP route**. Core-1 knows that destination network 10.1.20.0/24 is directly connected on its Switch Virtual Interface (SVI) VLAN20. Thus, Core-1 knows that it must forward the packet out its VLAN20 interface (Figure 7-17).

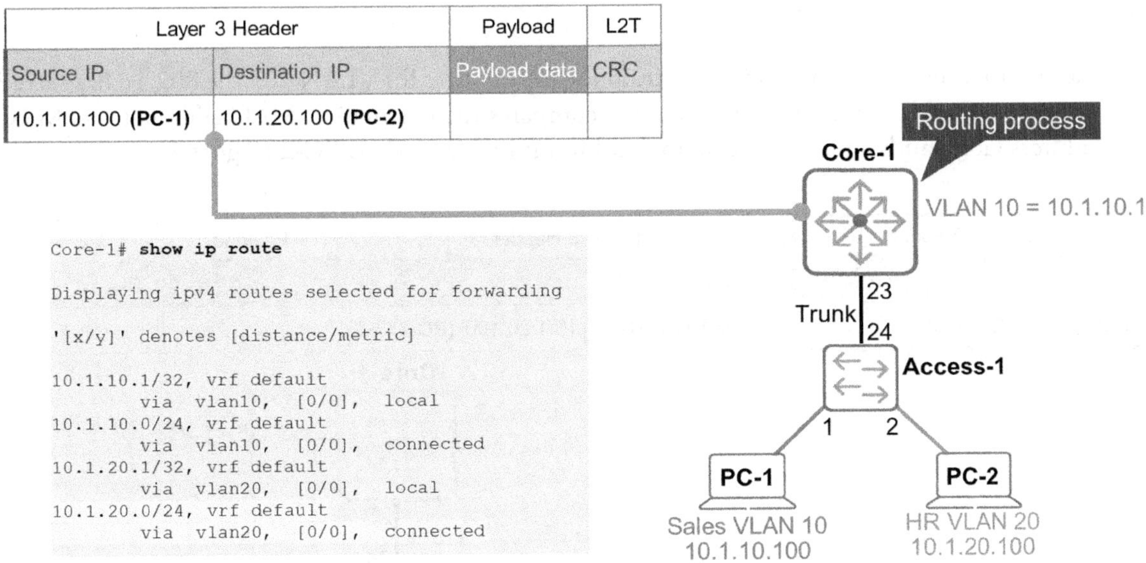

Figure 7-17 Routing Process

Multilayer to Access Switch

5. Core-1 builds a new frame to wrap around the IP packet. This frame includes an 802.1q Tag—VLAN = 20. This frame is sent to L2 switch Access-1 (Figure 7-18).

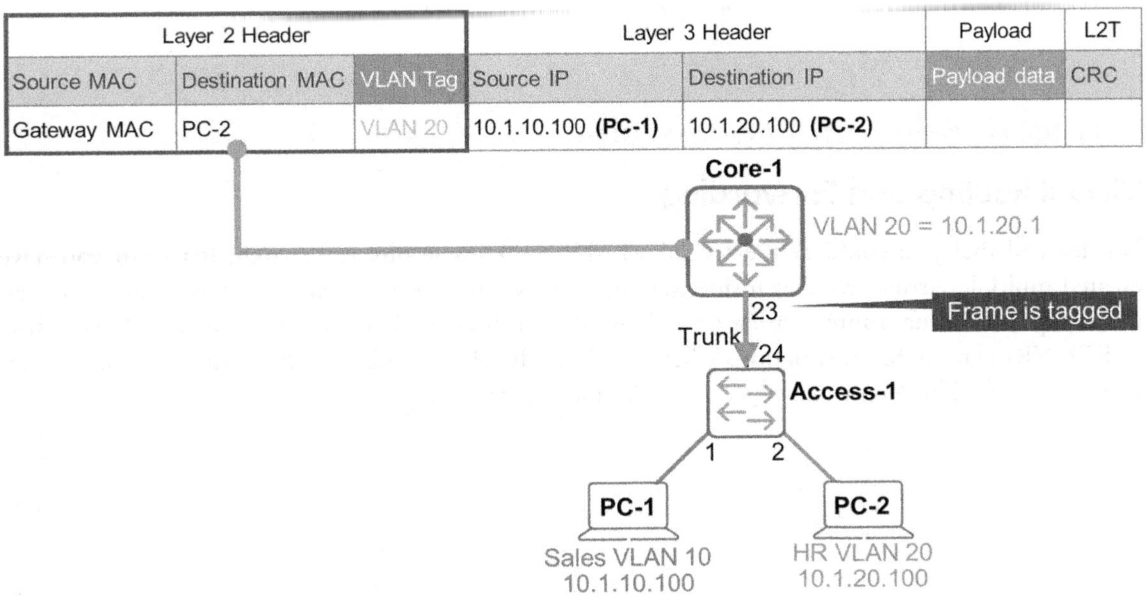

Figure 7-18 Multilayer to Access Switch

Access Switch to Endpoint

6. Access-1 receives the frame and learns from the tag that it is for VLAN 20. The 802.1q has served its purpose, and so it is removed. Access-1 compares the destination MAC address to its MAC address table, finds a match, and so forward it out port 2, toward PC-2 (Figure 7-19).

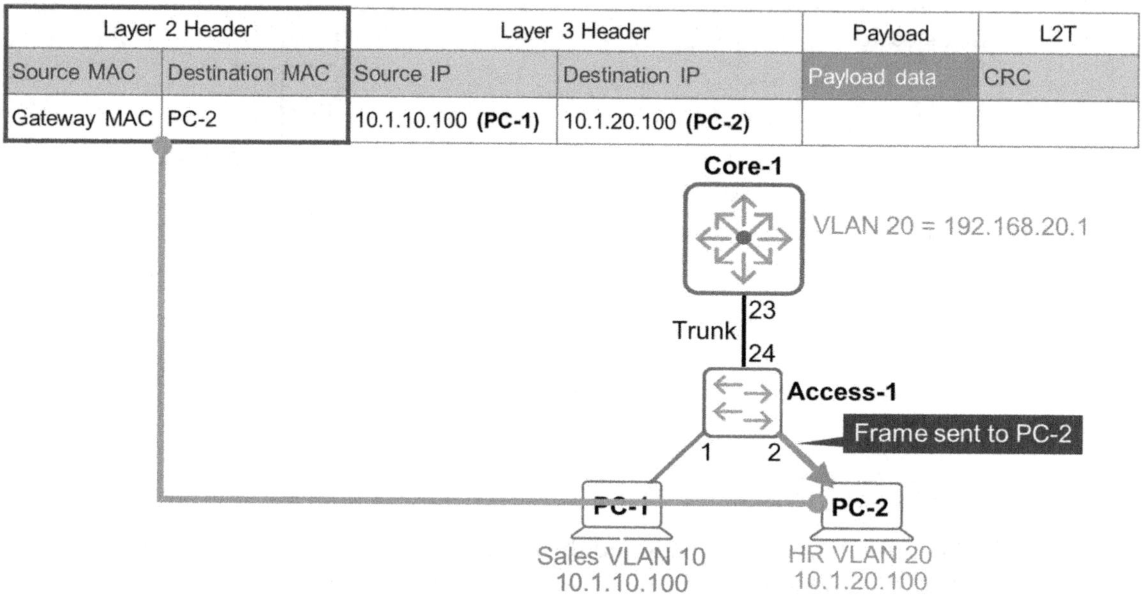

Figure 7-19 Access Switch to Endpoint

Virtual Routing and Forwarding

Virtual Routing and Forwarding

You learned that you could define several VLANs on a single physical switch. It is as if you have created multiple virtual switches inside the physical switch, one for each VLAN. Similarly, you can create separate virtual routers inside a single physical router, with Virtual Routing and Forwarding (VRF). VRFs are useful in situations where the IP addressing overlaps in different places of the network. This could happen when two companies merge, for example.

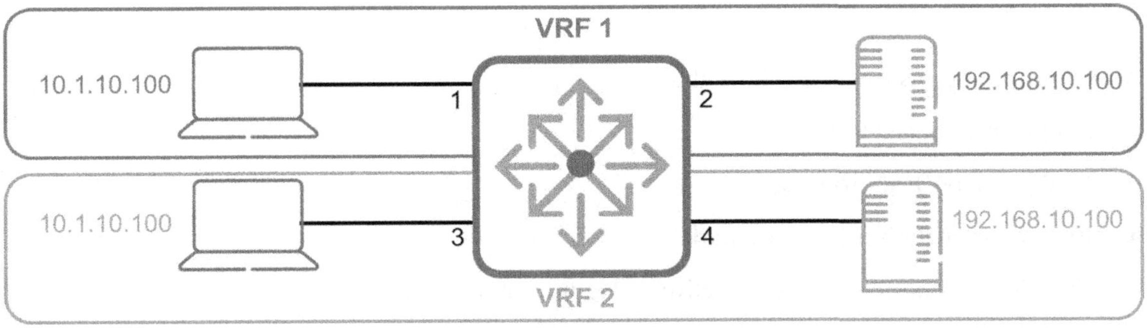

Figure 7-20 VRF Example

Figure 7-20 shows a single multilayer switch split into two separate VRFs. Interfaces 1 and 2 participate in VRF 1, and only interfaces 3 and 4 participate in VRF 2. These two VRFs do not interact. It is as if they are separate physical routers, with no connectivity between them. Therefore, the addressing can be the same in both VRFs without conflict.

In AOS-CX all interfaces (enabled with routing) by default are mapped to the Global VRF called "default." In other words, all interfaces are part of the same VRF, the physical router and the global VRF are essentially the same thing. Then you decide to create VRFs 1 and 2, to split it up as shown in the figure. You know the two VRFs do not interact by default. However, you can configure the solution to route between the two VRFs if needed.

AOS-CX also includes a specific VRF for management purposes and that can only be used in the Out-of-Band Management (OOBM) port, to separate the data and control plane from the management plane.

Lab 7.1: IPv4 Inter-VLAN Routing

Overview

As the network grows, BigStartup has realized the need for communicationsbetween departments. Services such as Zoom conferencing, Remote Printing, Remote Assistance, and Internet access move traffic across VLANs. To provide for this new requirement, you have suggested enabling inter-VLAN routing rather than reverting to a single VLAN design. This enables the connectivity level your customer is looking for and allows for blocking forbidden connection attempts using traffic filters (Routed Access Control Lists).

You will enable Layer-3 functions on one of your Core switches.Then the TCP IP stack on each client and host will require a default gateway IP address to enable using Layer-3 functions to deliver the packets destined to non-local segments.

Note that references to equipment and commands are taken from Aruba's hosted remote lab. These are shown for demonstration purposes in case you wish to replicate the environment and tasks on your own equipment.

Objectives

After completing this lab, you will be able to:

- Assign IP addresses to SVIs
- Enable Inter-VLAN routing
- Run traffic analysis using Wireshark
- Describe the end-to-end packet delivery (Figure 7-21).

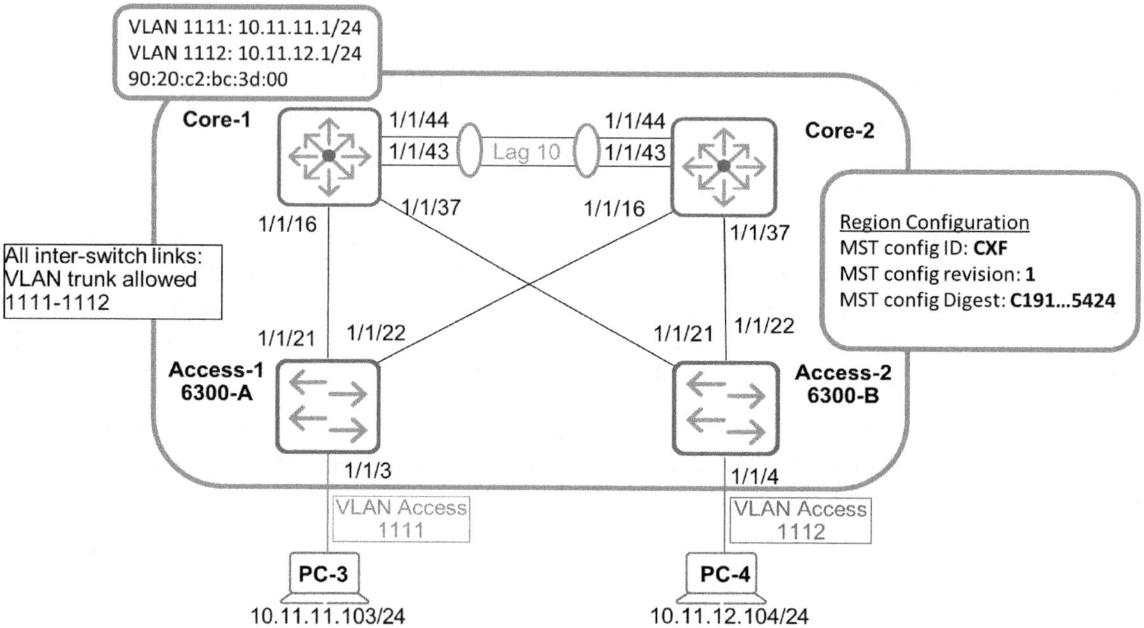

Figure 7-21 Lab Topology

Task 1: Pre-Lab Setup:

Objectives

In this activity you will load **Lab5-2_final** checkpoint in Access-1 and Access-2, where those two switches were interconnected to the Core switches using ports 1/1/21 and 1/1/22.

> **Note**
>
> This activity has a dependency on the Lab 5.2 configuration; make sure you have completed that lab before starting the current one. Do not proceed if this is not the case.

Steps

Access-1 and Access-2

1. Display the checkpoint list and confirm **Lab5-2_final** is there.

```
T11-Access-1# show checkpoint list | include Lab5
Lab5-1_final
Lab5-2_final
Lab5-3_final
Lab5-3_task1_done
```

```
T11-Access-2# show checkpoint list | include Lab5
Lab5-1_final
Lab5-2_final
Lab5-3_final
Lab5-3_task1_done
```

2. Load the checkpoint using the checkpoint rollback command.

```
T11-Access-1# checkpoint rollback Lab5-2_final
Configuration changes will take time to process, please be patient.
```

```
T11-Access-2# checkpoint rollback Lab5-2_final
Configuration changes will take time to process, please be patient.
```

Task 2: Set IP DefaultGateway

Objectives

In this first task you will configure IP addresses of both interface VLAN X11 and X12 in Core-1; then you will assign those addresses as default Gateways on PC-3 and PC-4.

Steps

Core-1 (via PC-1)

1. Open an SSH session to Core-1. Log in using **cxf11/aruba123**.
2. Create **interface vlan 1111;** then assign it IP address **10.11.11.1/24.**

```
Core-1# configure terminal
Core-1(config)# interface vlan 1111
Core-1(config-if-vlan)# ip address 10.11.11.1/24
Core-1(config-if-vlan)# exit
```

Important

This makes Core-1 a multilayer switch capable of routing traffic into the 10.X.11.0/24 segment.

3. See the newly created SVI details using **show ip interface vlan111.**

```
Core-1(config)# show ip interface vlan1111

Interface vlan1111 is up
 Admin state is up
Hardware: Ethernet, MAC Address: 90:20:c2:bc:ed:00
 IP MTU 1500
 IP Directed Broadcast is Disabled
 IP Neighbor flood is Disabled
 IPv4 address 10.11.11.1/24
 L3 Counters: Rx Disabled, Tx Disabled
```

What are the SVI state and MAC address? ________________________________

4. Repeat steps 2 and 3 for interface vlan 1112, with IP address **10.11.12.1/24.**

```
Core-1(config)# interface vlan 1112
Core-1(config-if-vlan)# ip address 10.11.12.1/24
Core-1(config-if-vlan)# end
```

```
Core-1# show ip interface vlan1112

Interface vlan1112 is up
 Admin state is up
Hardware: Ethernet, MAC Address: 90:20:c2:bc:ed:00
 IP MTU 1500
```

```
IP Directed Broadcast is Disabled
IP Neighbor flood is Disabled
IPv4 address 10.11.12.1/24
L3 Counters: Rx Disabled, Tx Disabled
```

Important

This command is case sensitive, so make sure to type lowercase "vlan" (lowercase) immediately followed by the VLAN number, for example, "**show IP interface VLAN1111**".

What is the SVI MAC address? ____________________

Note

Both SVIs use the same MAC address (the system one); this does not create any conflict because they are in two different broadcast domains.

5. Display the IPv4 routing table and look for your newly added prefixes.

```
Core-1# show ip route
Displaying ipv4 routes selected for forwarding
'[x/y]' denotes [distance/metric]
                    <---- output omitted --->
10.9.11.0/24, vrf default
        via  vlan911,  [0/0],  connected
10.9.11.1/32, vrf default
        via  vlan911,  [0/0],  local
10.9.12.0/24, vrf default
        via  vlan912,  [0/0],  connected
10.9.12.1/32, vrf default
        via  vlan912,  [0/0],  local
10.10.11.0/24, vrf default
        via  vlan1011,  [0/0],  connected
```

```
10.10.11.1/32, vrf default
        via  vlan1011,  [0/0],  local
10.10.12.0/24, vrf default
        via  vlan1012,  [0/0],  connected
10.10.12.1/32, vrf default
        via  vlan1012,  [0/0],  local
10.11.11.0/24, vrf default
        via  vlan1111,  [0/0],  connected
10.11.11.1/32, vrf default
        via  vlan1111,  [0/0],  local
10.11.12.0/24, vrf default
        via  vlan1112,  [0/0],  connected
10.11.12.1/32, vrf default
        via  vlan1112,  [0/0],  local
                    ←---- output omitted ---→
```

There are 4 prefixes published in the routing table after assigning the IP addresses. The ones with prefix length 32 are considered local and reference the IP addresses just configured in the SVIs. The /24 prefixes are the connected subnets discovered from having an interface with an IP in those segments.

IP prefixes are expressed using the following format:

PREFIX/PREFIX_LENGHT, vrf VRF_NAME

via OUTBOUND_INTERFACE, [DISTANCE/METRIC], ROUTING_PROCESS

Notice that they all contain vrf "default." VRF stands for Virtual Routing and Forwarding, which is the control plane virtual routing table the system is using for moving traffic at Layer-3 in the data plane. AOS-CX has two built-in VRFs: mgmt for management traffic and default for data traffic. Since this device is a shared resource, the output that you get out of this command may contain either entries.

When the routing table is that long, you can either use filtered versions of the command (for example, **show IP route | begin 7 10.11.11.0**) or you can use a prefix specific command:

```
Core-1# show ip route 10.11.11.0/24
Displaying ipv4 routes selected for forwarding
'[x/y]' denotes [distance/metric]
10.11.11.0/24, vrf default
        via  vlan1111,  [0/0],  connected
```

AOS-CX switches can support several virtual routing table instances that are used for keeping IP Prefixes separated into different Layer-3 logical routing domains. Under normal circumstances, control plane prefixes from one VRF cannot be shared with other VRFs and data plane traffic contained in one VRF cannot be forwarded to interfaces belonging to another VRF (unless explicit prefix leaking is intentionally enabled).

This feature is ideal in multitenancy environments like Data Centers, Service Provider networks, and Network as a Service environments such as Rent4Cheap Properties.

6. Currently Core-1 can move traffic from either IP segment. You will add the client gateways. Non-local traffic will be delivered to the local gateway using Layer-2 and then forwarded to the non-local destinations using Layer-3.

PC-3

7. Access PC-3.
8. Assign 10.11.11.1 as the default gateway in Lab NIC (Figure 7-22).

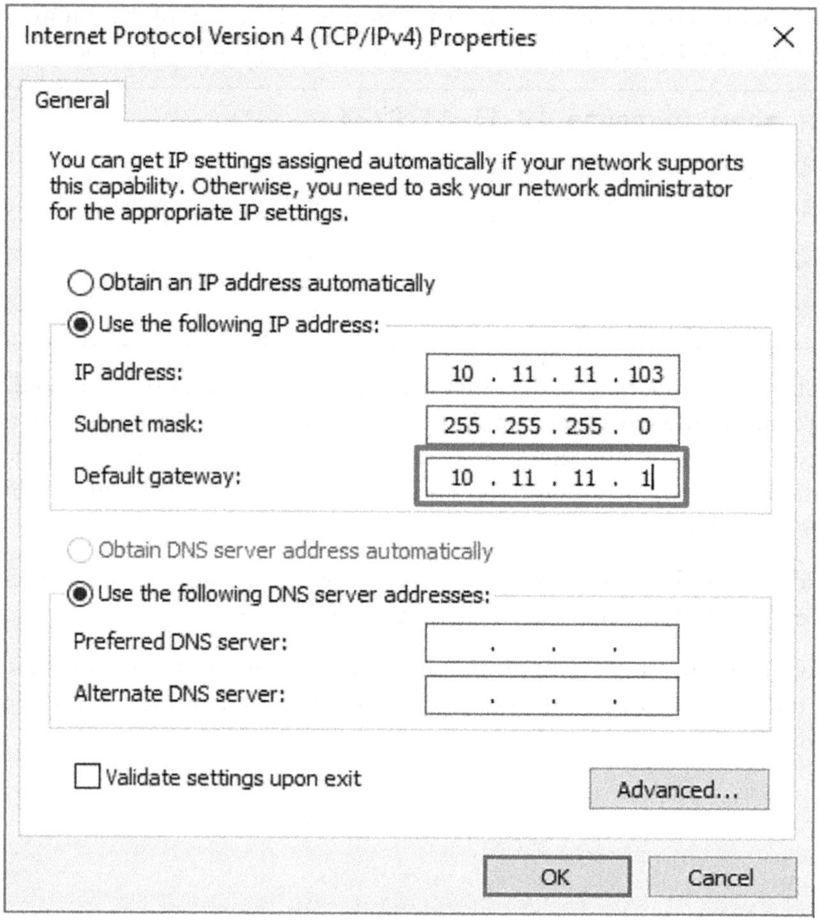

Figure 7-22 IPv4 Properties For PC-3

9. Ping the default gateway IP address. Ping should be successful (Figure 7-23).

```
Command Prompt
Microsoft Windows [Version 10.0.17134.441]
(c) 2018 Microsoft Corporation. All rights reserved.

C:\Users\TEMP>ping 10.11.11.1

Pinging 10.11.11.1 with 32 bytes of data:
Reply from 10.11.11.1: bytes=32 time<1ms TTL=64
Reply from 10.11.11.1: bytes=32 time<1ms TTL=64
Reply from 10.11.11.1: bytes=32 time<1ms TTL=64
Reply from 10.11.11.1: bytes=32 time<1ms TTL=64

Ping statistics for 10.11.11.1:
    Packets: Sent = 4, Received = 4, Lost = 0 (0% loss),
Approximate round trip times in milli-seconds:
    Minimum = 0ms, Maximum = 0ms, Average = 0ms

C:\Users\TEMP>
```

Figure 7-23 Ping to PC-3's Default Gateway

PC-4

10. Access PC-4.

11. Repeat steps 7 and 8 using 10.11.12.1 instead (Figure 7-24).

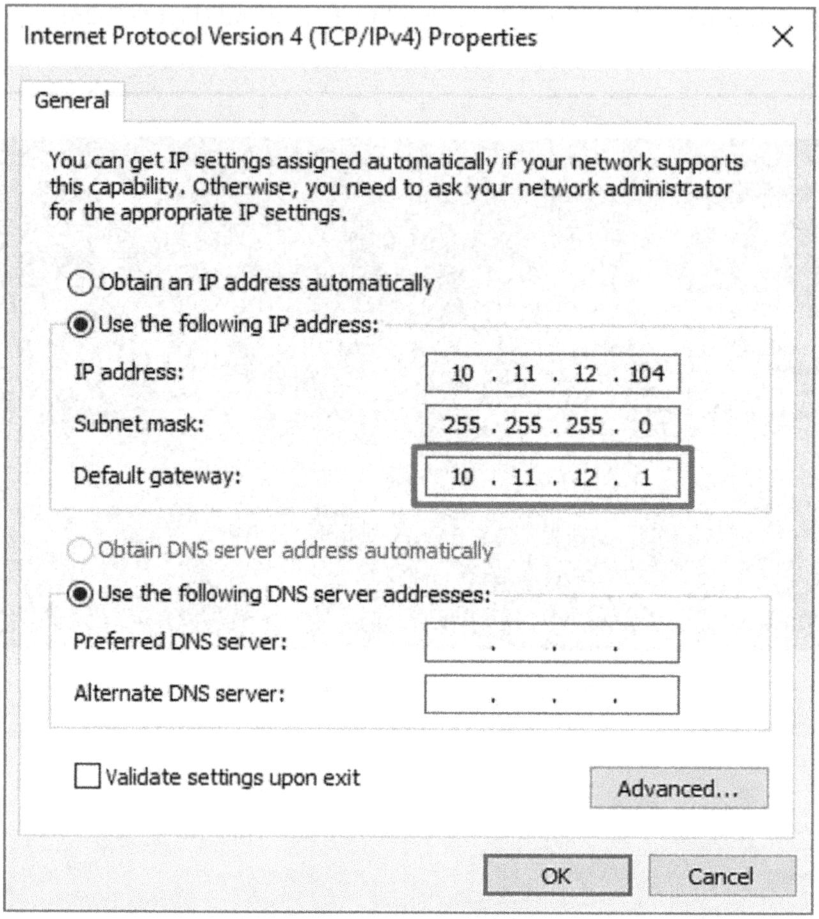

Figure 7-24 IPv4 Properties for PC-3

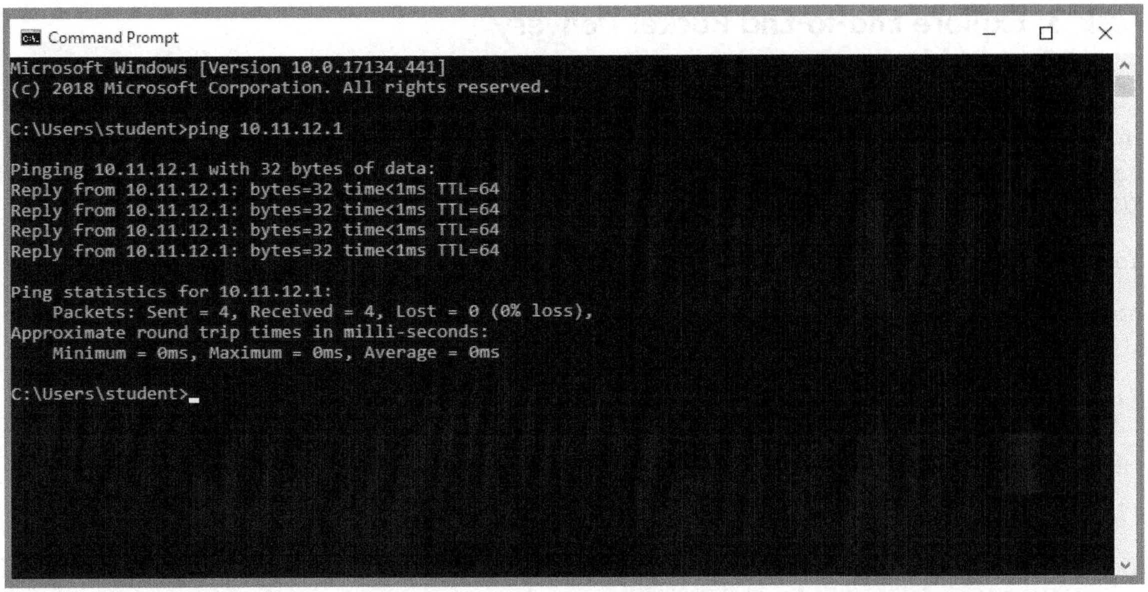

Figure 7-25 Ping to PC-4's Default Gateway

12. From PC-4, as shown in Figure 7-25, ping PC-3 (10.11.11.103). Ping should be successful now (Figure 7-26).

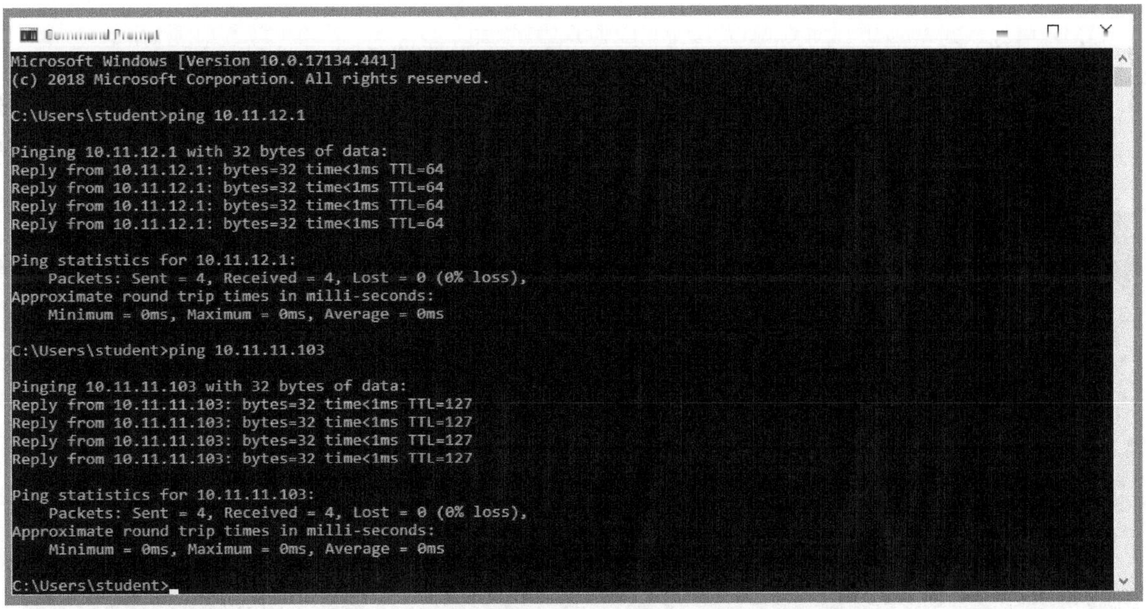

Figure 7-26 Ping PC3 and PC4

Task 3: Explore End-to-End Packet Delivery

Objectives

In this part of the lab you will explore end-to-end packet delivery. You will examine Ethernet and IP headers, their addressing, and some of their fields using anopen-source traffic analysis tool called Wireshark. Wireshark will become an essential component of your networking troubleshooting tool kit.

You can download Wireshark for free at the following URL:

https://www.wireshark.org/download.html

Steps

Core-1 (via PC-1)

1. Open an SSH session to Core-1. Log in using cxf11/aruba123.
2. Clear ARP entries associated to PC-3 and PC-4 IP addresses (10.11.11.103 and 10.11.12.104 respectively).

```
Core-1# clear arp vrf default ipv4 10.11.11.103
Core-1# clear arp vrf default ipv4 10.11.12.104
```

PC-4

3. Access PC-4.
4. Right click the Command Prompt icon in the "Start Bar"; then right click the "Command Prompt" option that shows up or type in "Cmd" and select "Run as Administrator" in the menu that appears (Figure 7-27).

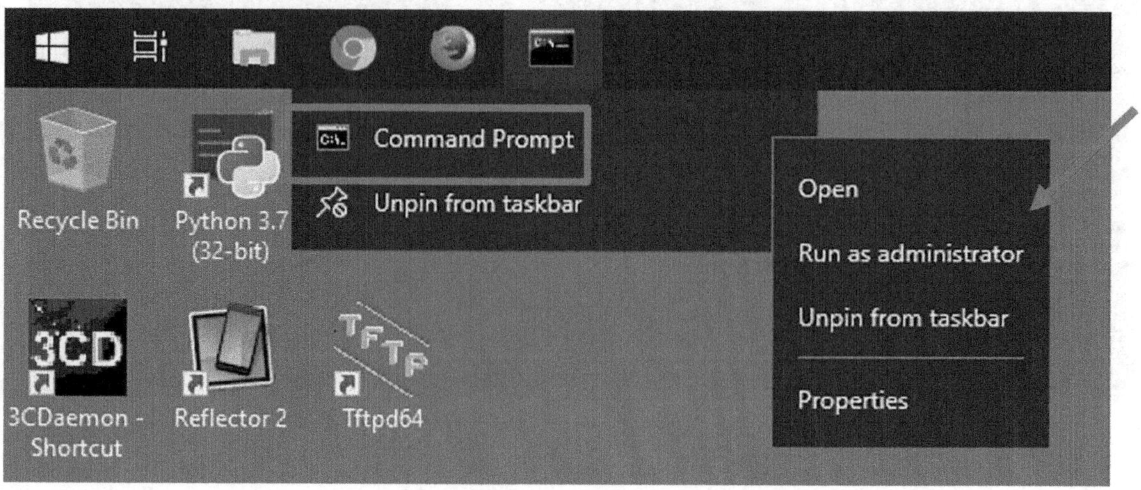

Figure 7-27 Run CMD as Administrator

5. To accept the Windows warning below click on **yes** (Figure 7-28).

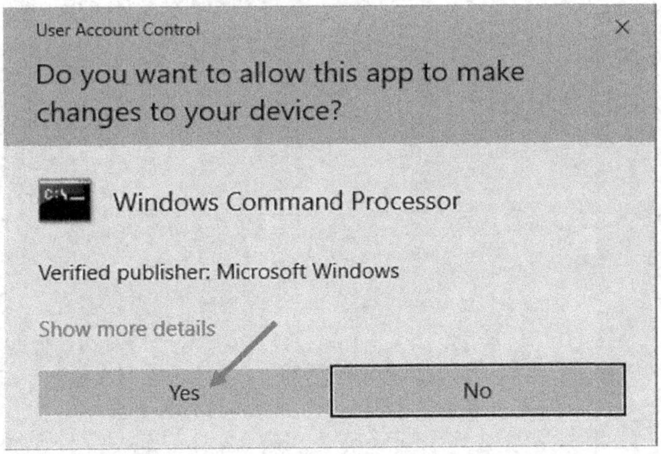

Figure 7-28 Windows User Account Control

6. Run the **arp -d** command to flush the ARP table of the host (Figure 7-29).

Figure 7-29 Flush ARP Table PC-4

7. Run the **arp -a** command to display the ARP table in the host (Figure 7-30).

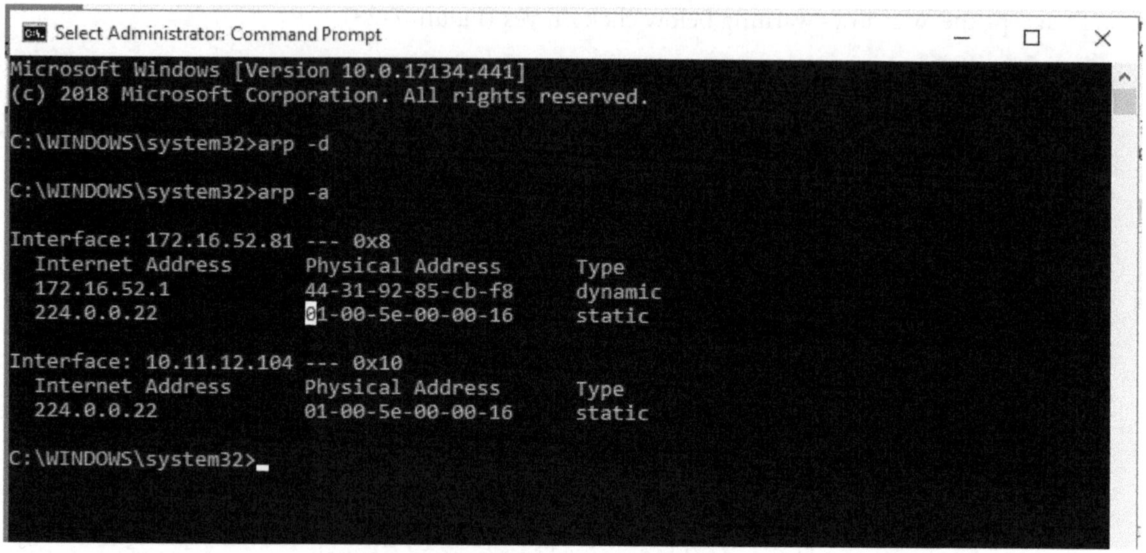

Figure 7-30 Display ARP Table

8. Open Wireshark from a shortcut on the Desktop.
9. Double click the NIC card used in your environment to connect to the lab equipment. In this example, we will use the **Lab NIC** entry. That will begin the packet capture on that interface.You will see gratuitous ARP messages coming from 10.11.12.1 (Core-1) (Figure 7-31).

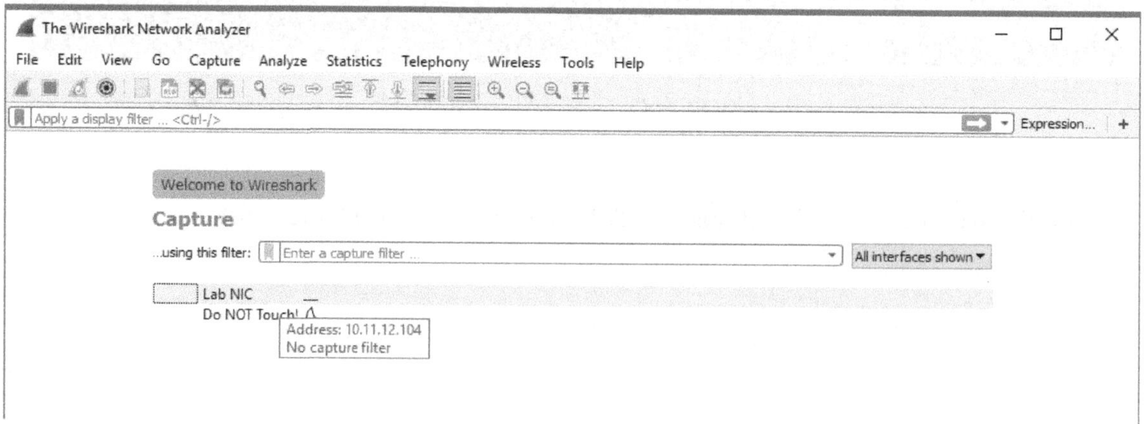

Figure 7-31 Wireshark NIC Selection

Address Resolution Protocol (ARP) is a protocol that assists in IP Layer-3 to Ethernet/802.11 Layer-2 address resolution. When devices create an IP packet, they always have to find out the MAC address of the next-hop (either the IP gateway when the Layer-3 destination is in a remote segment, or the destination host if it happens to be in the local segment of the sender). An IP packet cannot be sent out to the physical medium (copper, radio frequency, or fiber) without a Data Link layer header. A Data Link layer header requires an address to be forwarded at Layer-2 (for example, Ethernet MAC, Frame Relay DCI, 802.11 BSSID, etc.) (Figure 7-32).

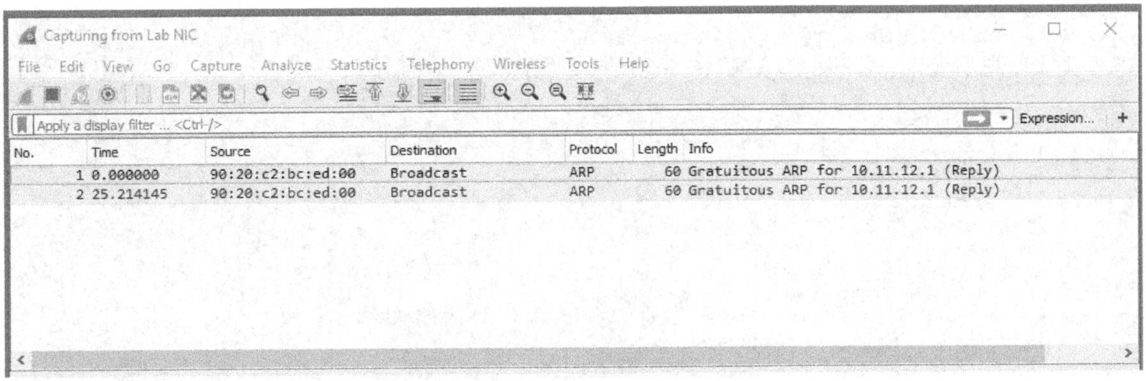

Figure 7-32 Gratuitous ARP Example

AOS-CX advertises GARP packets every 25 seconds on the interfaces that have IP addresses. This updates any IP neighbor's ARP table and provides the resolution information in advance. However, operating systems like Microsoft Windows ignore these packets for security reasons.

10. In the filter, type **(arp && not arp.isgratuitous) || ip.addr == 10.11.11.103** and hit **[Enter]**. That will instruct Wireshark to only display ARP non-gratuitous messages and IP packets that include PC-4's IP address (Figure 7-33).

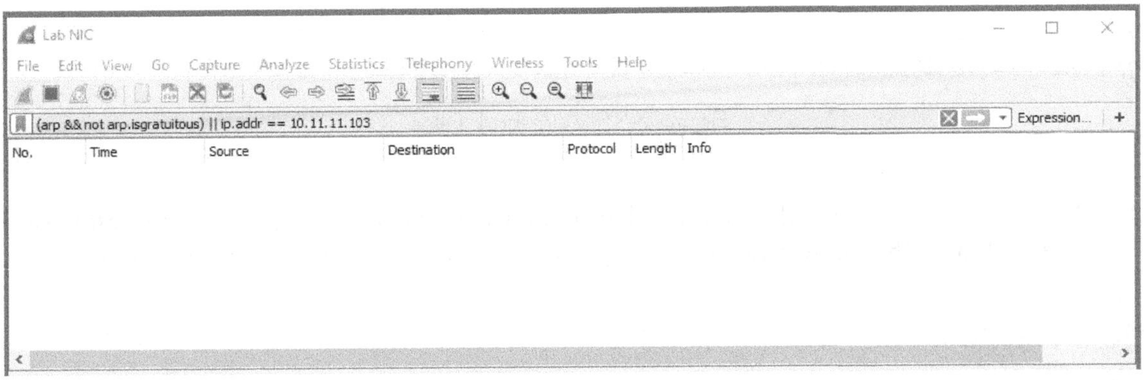

Figure 7-33 Wireshark Filter

PC-3

11. Move to PC-3.
12. Repeat steps 4 to 10 on PC-3 using **10.11.12.104** in the Wireshark filter (7-35).

Figure 7-34 Flush and Display the ARP Table

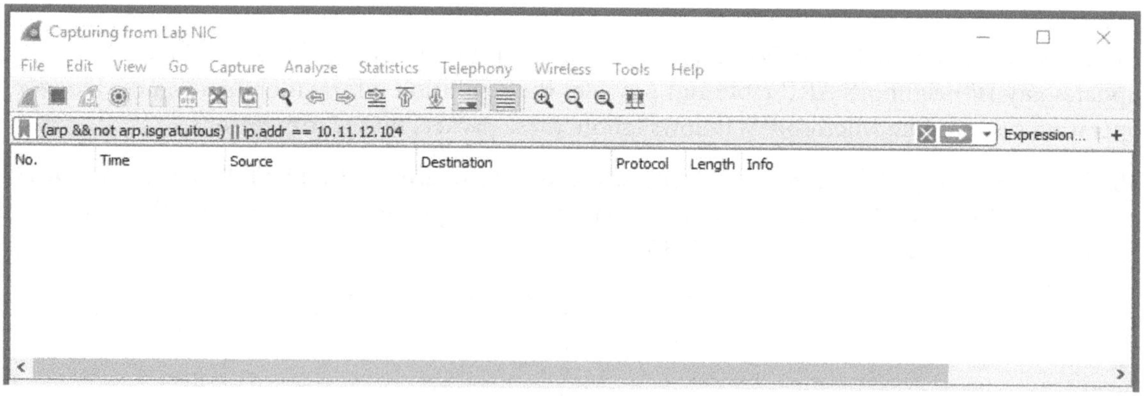

Figure 7-35 Wireshark Filter

13. Run a custom ping on the command prompt using the following command: **ping -n 1 10.11.12.104**. This command will trigger a single ICMP echotoward PC-4's IP address.

PC-3 and PC-4

14. Stop the Wireshark capture in both stations.
15. To begin the analysis, keep in mind what devices are involved in the packet forwarding. Use Figure 7-36 as a reference.

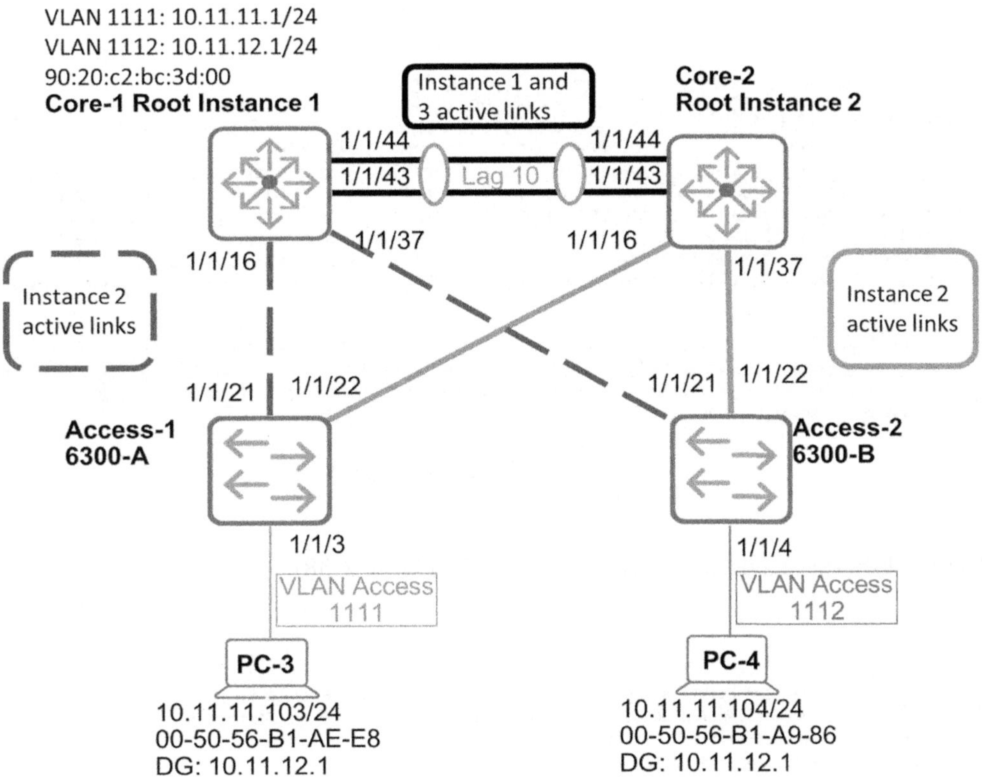

Figure 7-36 Topology for Traffic Analysis

PC-3

In Wireshark you will see 6 frames in the capture, two of them are ICMP (pink packets) and the four in yellow are ARP.

Tip

Packets might be in a different order becausethere are limited resources assigned to client VMs. Nonetheless, the explanation below should help you know the order packets are sent.

---

16. Select the packet where its Destination equals “Broadcast”, that is an ARP request. Then look at the packet details section. You will see three gray rows; the first is the summary of the packet, the second is the Layer-2 header, and the third is the actual ARP payload (Figure 7-37).

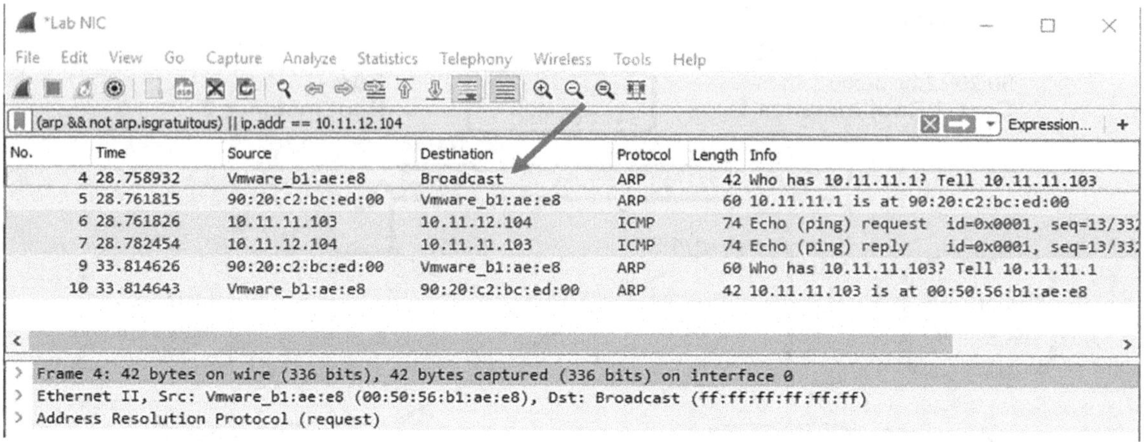

Figure 7-37 Traffic Analysis 1

17. Select the Ethernet Layer-2 header and expand it (Figure 7-38).

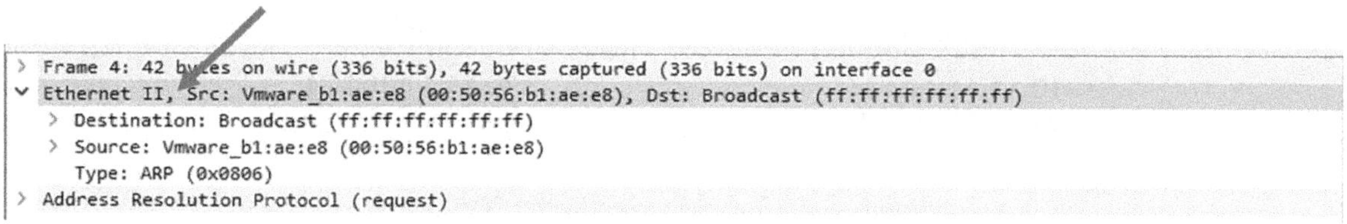

Figure 7-38 Traffic Analysis 2

What is the Destination MAC address? ______________________________

What is the Source MAC address? ______________________________

What is the Ethertype value? ______________________________

Answer

The Destination MAC is all Fs, which is the Broadcast MAC address, while the source is PC-3's MAC address. The Ethertype value is 0x0806 or ARP. This alerts the Layer-2 process what kind protocol or header comes next.

Important

In Ethernet encapsulation, the destination MAC address is one of the first values in the packet. This helps the Layer-2 switch start the forwarding decision and processing of the frame as soon as its ingresses on the inbound port. This drastically enhances the throughput of the device.

18. Expand and select the third row (ARP Payload). This is an ARP request (Figure 7-39).

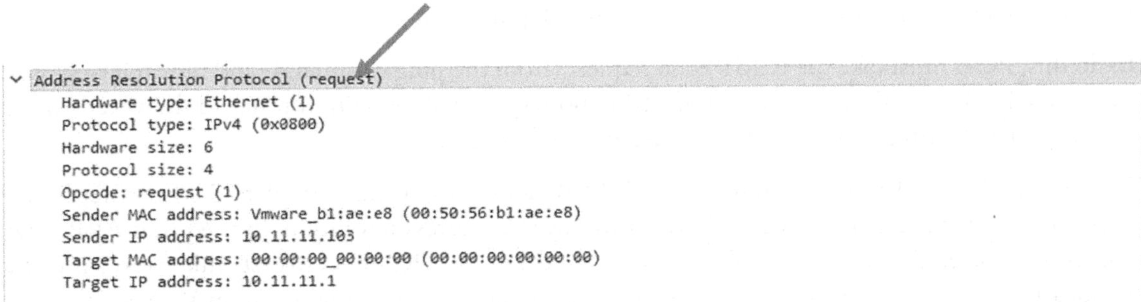

```
Address Resolution Protocol (request)
    Hardware type: Ethernet (1)
    Protocol type: IPv4 (0x0800)
    Hardware size: 6
    Protocol size: 4
    Opcode: request (1)
    Sender MAC address: Vmware_b1:ae:e8 (00:50:56:b1:ae:e8)
    Sender IP address: 10.11.11.103
    Target MAC address: 00:00:00_00:00:00 (00:00:00:00:00:00)
    Target IP address: 10.11.11.1
```

Figure 7-39 Traffic Analysis 3

What are the Sender MAC and IP addresses? ______________________________

Who do they belong to? ______________________________

What are the target MAC and IP addresses? ______________________________

Why does the MAC address all 0s? ______________________________

What is the main purpose of this packet? ______________________________

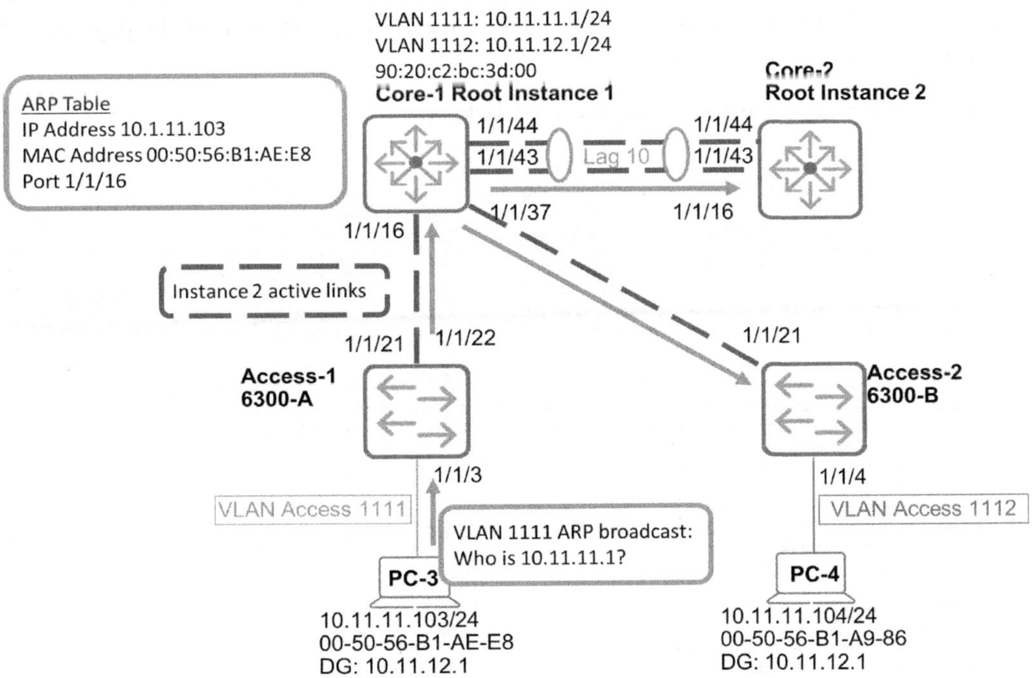

Figure 7-40 Topology for Traffic Analysis 2

The destination of the packet is not a local segment (10.11.12.103); therefore PC-3 cannot reach it directly using Layer-2 but needs to send it to the default gateway (10.11.11.1). The default gateway will take the packet and route it out using Layer-3 (Figure 7-40).

To do this, PC-3 must take the ICMP echo request (from the ping command) and return it to Core-1 on VLAN 1111. The IP header of the ICMP Echo request will remain untouched; however it must be encapsulated with an Ethernet Layer-2 header to forward it.

To achieve this, PC-3 needs to know Core-1's MAC address so it can complete the Ethernet header generation. This process is known as Layer-3 to Layer-2 address resolution and requires ARP. Since you initially deleted PC-3's ARP table, it must send out an ARP request first; this packet uses the broadcast destination MAC address to assure it reaches all devices in the common VLAN.

When the broadcast is received by Access-1, it floods it across all ports in STP Forwarding mode for VLAN X11 except the sending port (port 3). Even though this is a broadcast packet, Access-2 does not decapsulate and process it beyond Layer-2 because the Ethertype 0x0806 tells the switch that an ARP packet will follow. Since ARP is an IP protocol (Layer-3) and Access-1 is not currently running Layer-3, there is no reason to keep inspecting the packet.

Core-1 receives thepacket on port 1/1/16. Core-1 broadcasts the packet on all ports in Forwarding mode on VLAN 1111 (port 1/1/37 and LAG 10). When the packet is received by Core-2 and Access-2 they just drop it.

When Core-1 looks at the Ethertype (ARP), it inspects the header at Layer-3 because IP is running on interface VLAN 1111. After inspecting the ARP request, Core-1 recognizes the payload is asking for its own IP and prepares the reply.

19. Select the ARP reply (frame #5 in Figure 7-41 below).

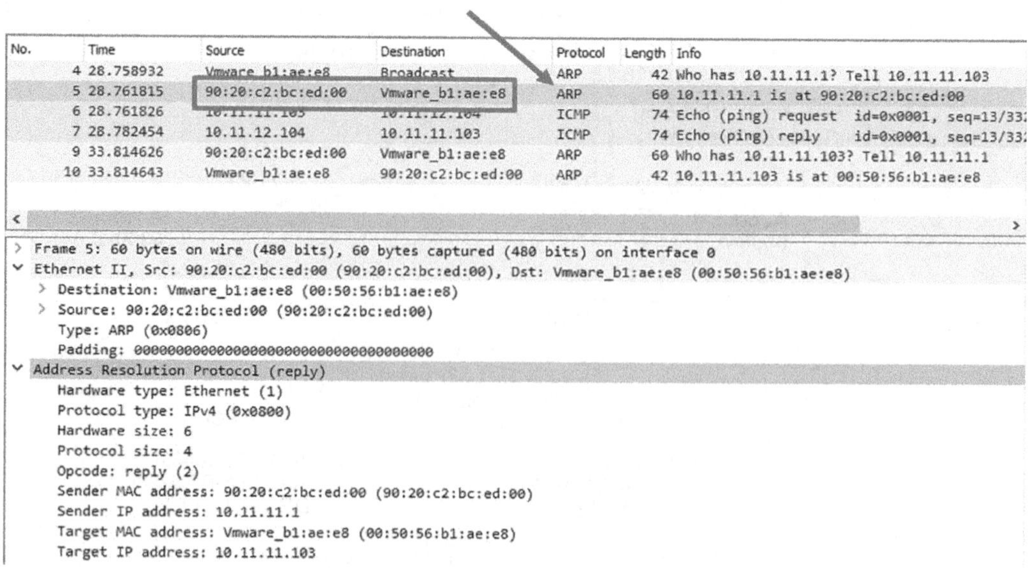

Figure 7-41 Traffic Analysis 4

In the Ethernet header, what are the Destination and Source MAC addresses? ________

What kind of packet is this: Unicast, Broadcast, or Multicast? ________

In the ARP header, what are the Sender MAC and IP addresses? ________

What are the Target MAC and IP addresses? ________

What is the main purpose of this packet? ________

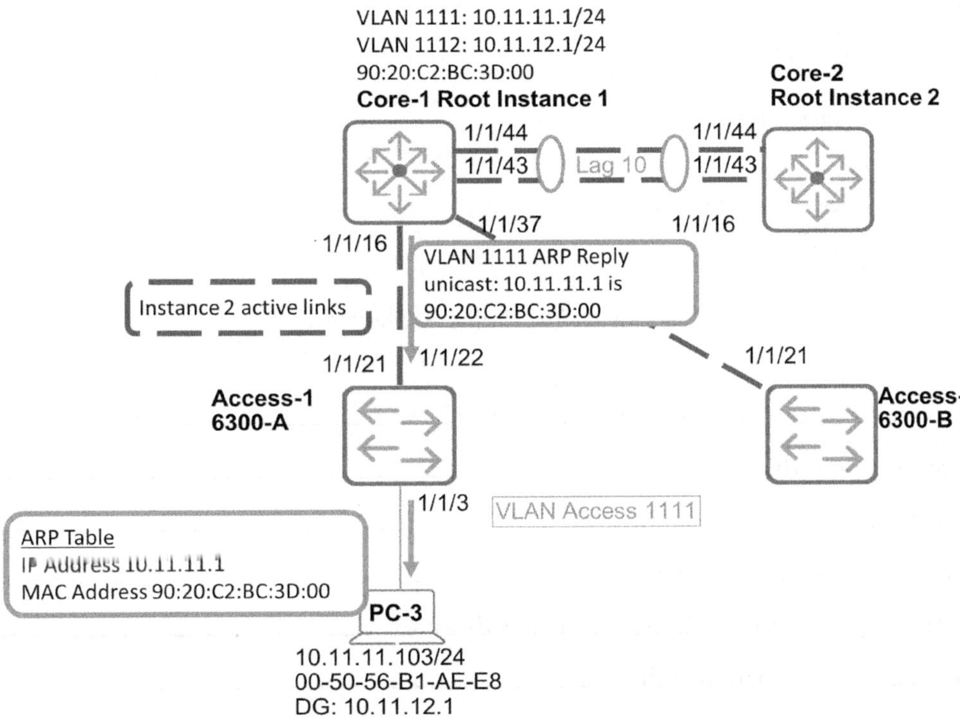

Figure 7-42 Topology for Traffic Analysis 3

The Core-1 ARP reply is a regular unicast packet with the Layer-2 destination address of PC-3's MAC. The packet is received by Access-1. Access-1uses its MAC Address table to forward the packet to port 3 and deliver it to PC-3. When examining the Layer-3 payload, PC-3 recognizes this is the expected reply and uses the contents (Sender IP and MAC address) to generate an entry in its ARP table. At this point PC-3 has completed the required Layer-2 to Layer-3 address resolution, now it can generate the Layer-2 header of the ICMP echo packet that it sends out (Figure 7-42).

20. Select the Echo (ping) request entry (frame #6 in Figure 7-43); then expand the IP and ICMP headers.

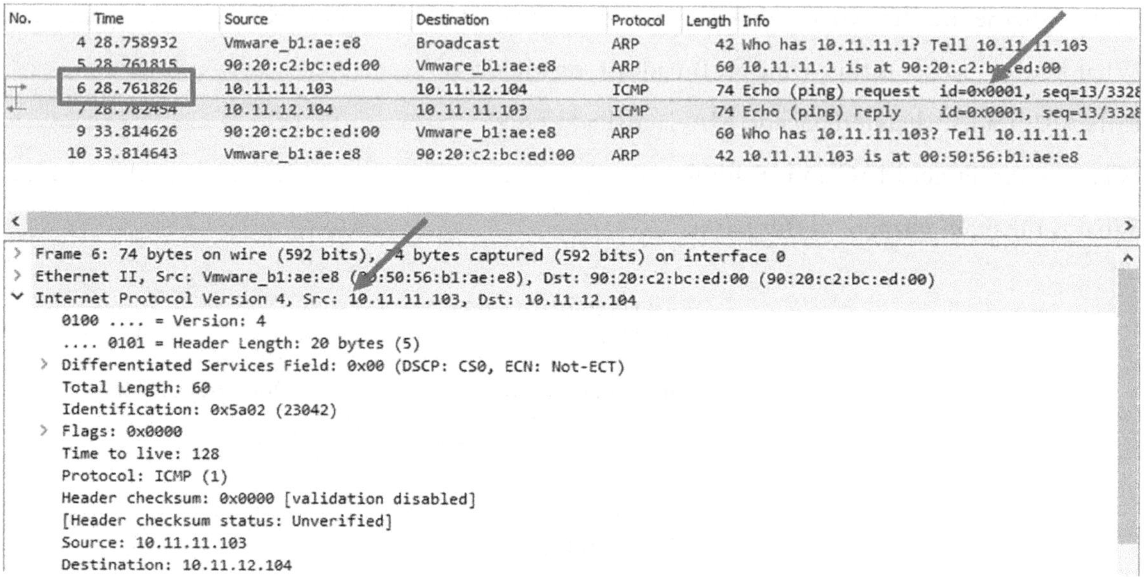

Figure 7-43 Traffic Analysis 4

On the Ethernet header, what is the Ethertype value? ____________________

What encapsulation is that? ____________________

What is the Layer-2 destination address? ____________________

What is the Layer-2 source address? ____________________

From the IP header, what is the Layer-3 source address? ____________________

What is the Layer-3 destination address? ____________________

Why are the Layer-2 and Layer-3 source addresses the same device, while the Layer-2 and Layer-3 destination addresses are different devices? ____________________

____

Answer

At the time, the ICMP Echo request packet is generated, the Layer-3 destination address is the host you want to ping (PC-4).However, PC-4 is not present in VLAN X11, so the packet must be handed over to Core-1 (the default gateway of PC-3). This makes Core-1 the layer-2 destination of the frame (Figure 7-44).

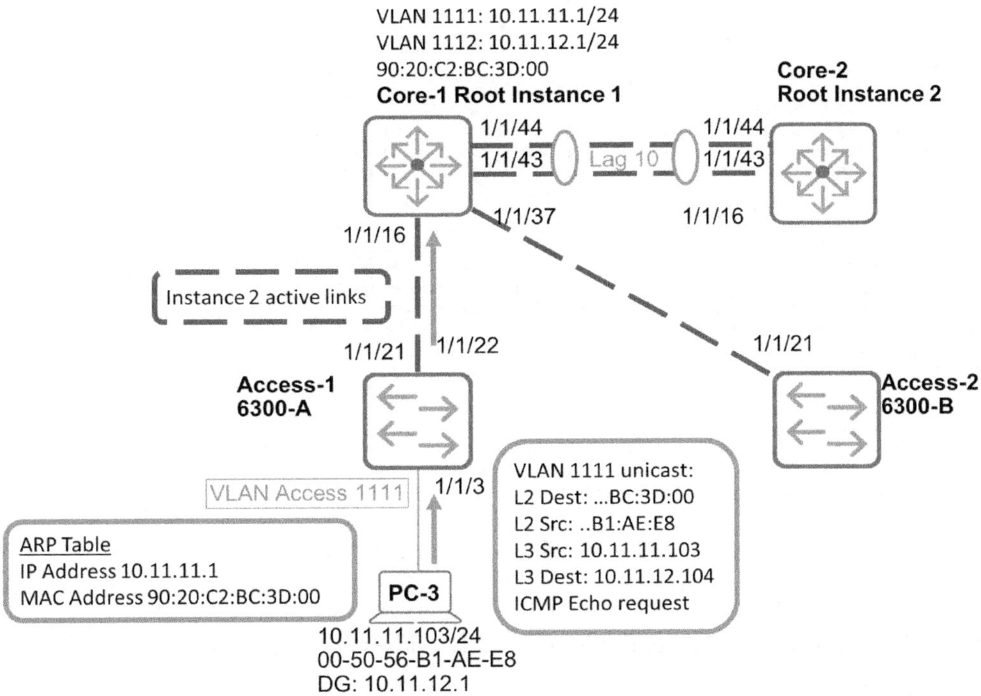

Figure 7-44 Topology for Traffic Analysis 4

What is the Time to Live value? ______________________________

What is the Protocol value? ______________________________

Answer

Time to Live is the maximum number of Layer-3 boundaries the packet will be able to cross before getting dropped. As mentioned in Module 1, IP protocol is used to signal the next layer protocol.

The following part of the process takes place on VLAN 1112. Since PC-3 is not part of that broadcast domain, move to PC-4 and continue the packet analysis from there.

PC-4

21. Move to PC-4.

22. In Wireshark, Select the packet where its Destination equals "Broadcast" and expand the Address Resolution Protocol row in the packet details section (Figure 7-45).

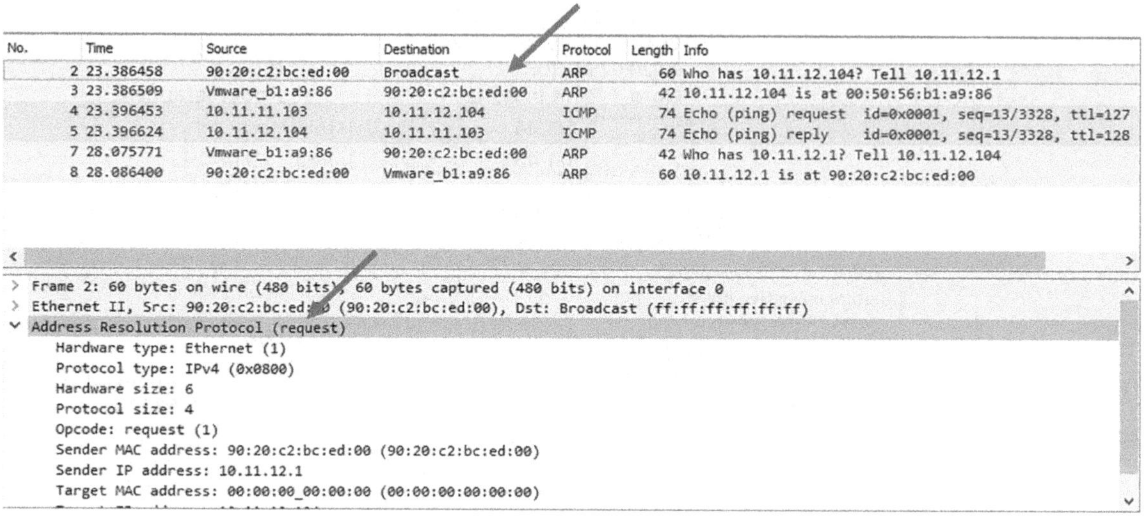

Figure 7-45 Traffic Analysis 5

On the ARP header, what are the Sender MAC and IP addresses? ______________________

What do they belong to? ______________________

What arethe target MAC and IP addresses? ______________________

What is the main purpose of this packet? ______________________

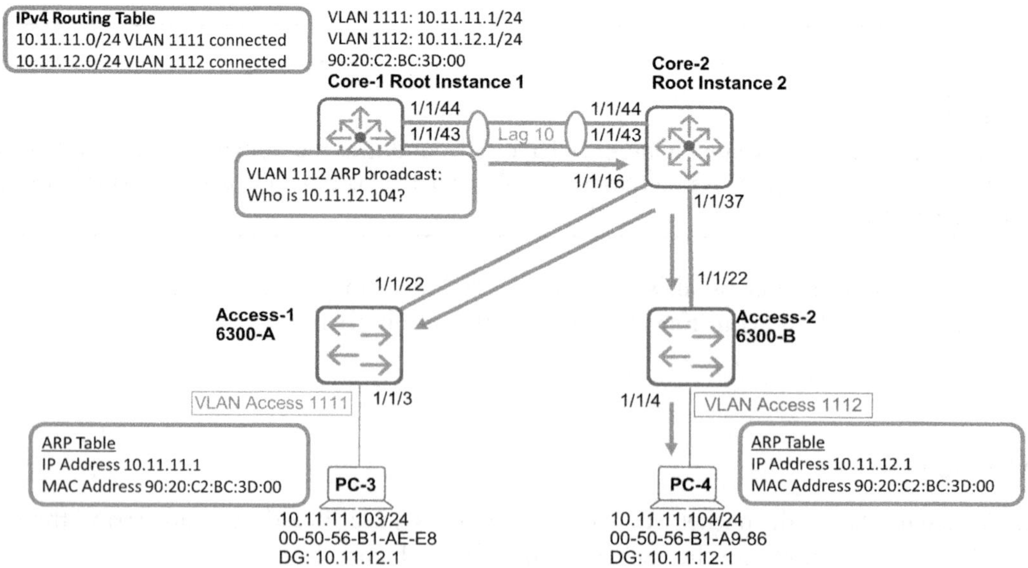

Figure 7-46 Topology for Traffic Analysis 5

When Core-1 received the ICMP packet and decapsulated it up to Layer-3, it investigated the destination IPv4 address. Core-1 determines it is not the IP destination of the packet and must move the packet between VLANs (Inter-VLAN routing).

To route between VLANs, Core-1 examines its routing table. It looks for an entry with an IP prefix or network that includes the destination IP address. If several entries are found, then the longest match (the more specific route) is used. In the current routing table, there is a valid entry: 10.X.12.0/24 out of VLAN X12 that Core-1 can use. It is a connected route (Figure 7-46).

Core-1 is now like PC-3 at the beginning of the process. It knows which outbound Layer-3 interface to use but it must create the Layer-2 header; therefore it needs to perform another Layer-2/Layer-3 address resolution requesting PC-4's MAC address.

23. Select the ARP reply from PC-4 to Core-2 (frame #3 in Figure 7-47).

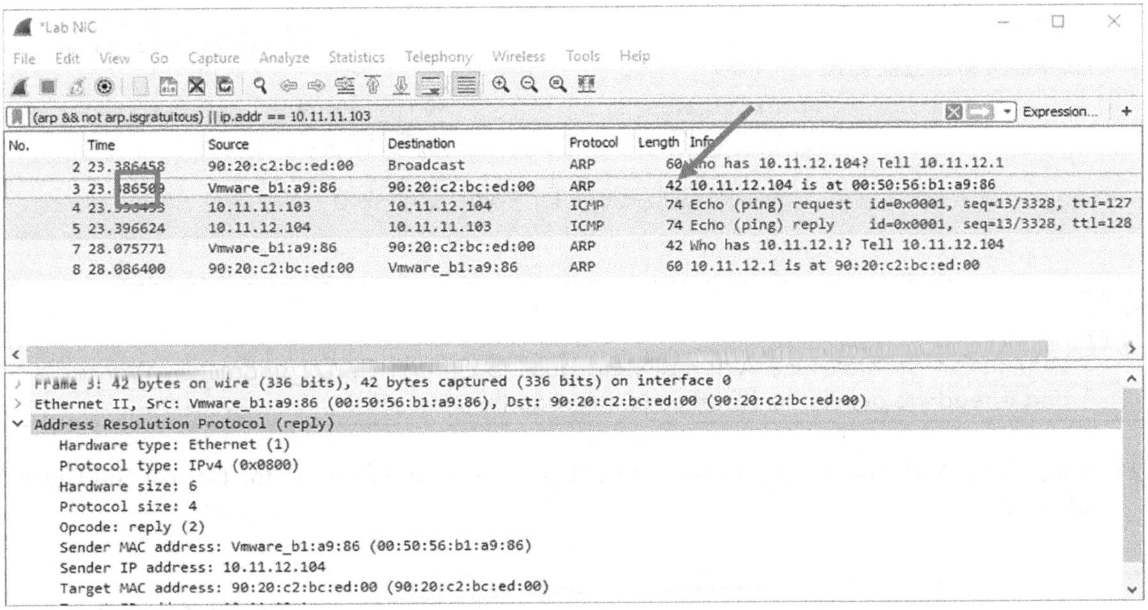

Figure 7-47 Traffic Analysis 6

What is the source MAC address? ____________________

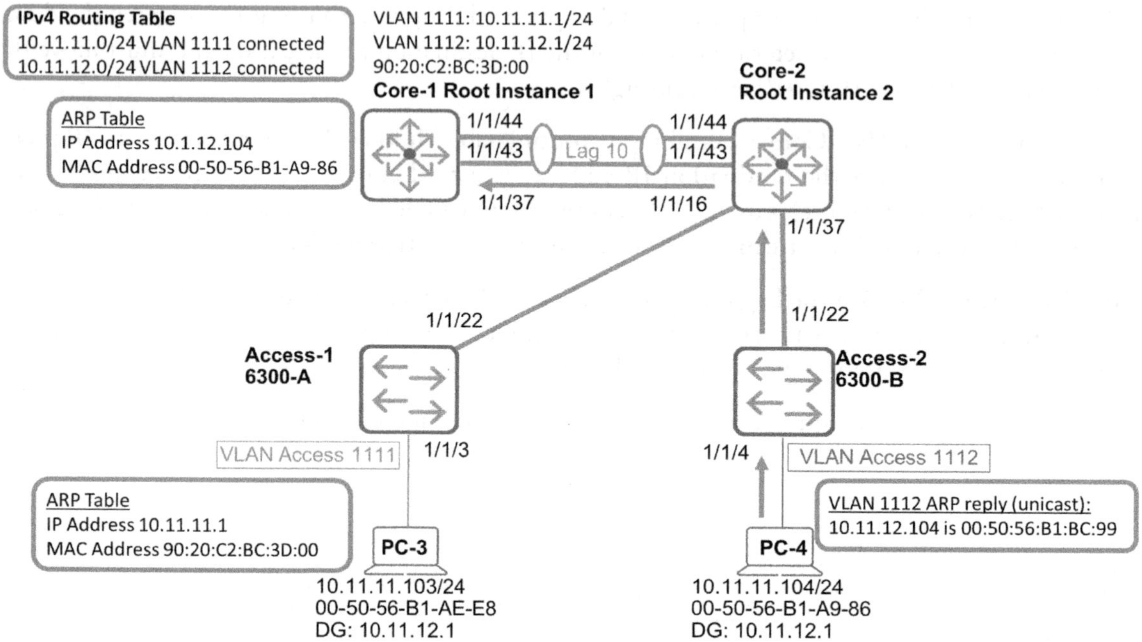

Figure 7-48 Topology for Traffic Analysis 6

Note

When PC-4 generates the ARP reply, this goes to Core-1. Core-1 updates its ARP table and is ready to deliver the ICMP echo message (Figure 7-48).

24. Select the ICMP echo message (frame #4 in Figure 7-49). And focus on the Layer-2 and Layer-3 addresses.

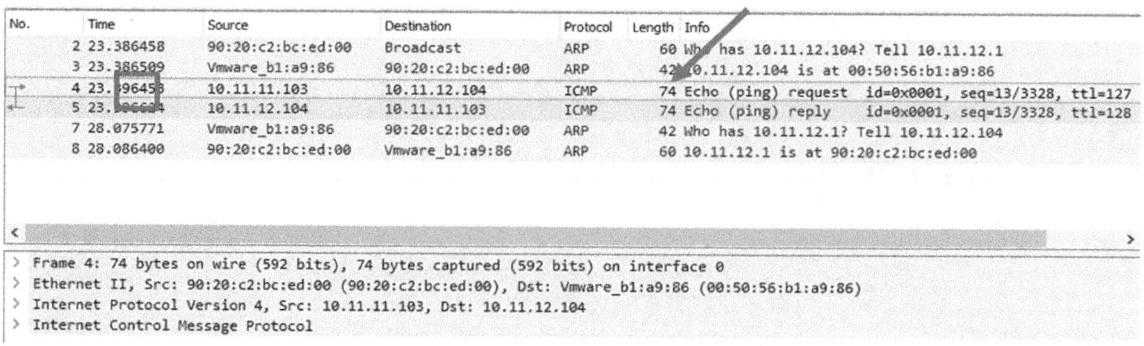

Figure 7-49 Traffic Analysis 7

What are the Layer-2 destination and source addresses? ______________________

How did they change from step 18? ______________________

What are the Layer-3 destination and source addresses? ______________________

Did they change from step 18? ______________________

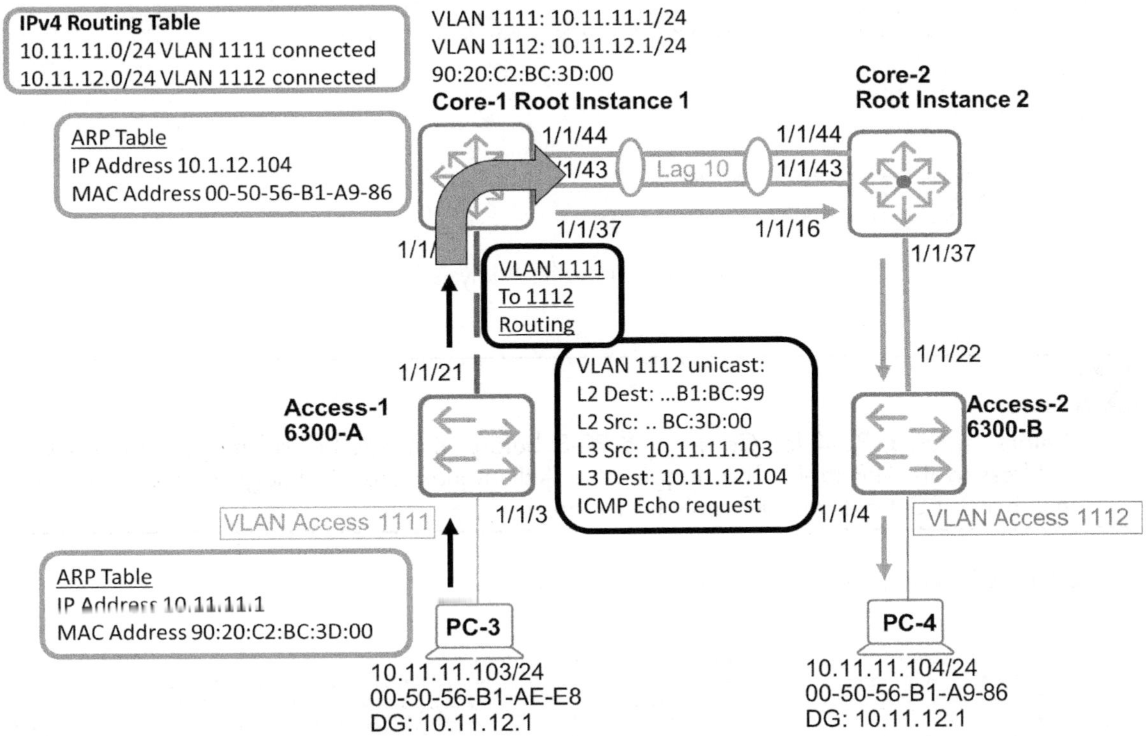

Figure 7-50 Topology for Traffic Analysis 7

After creating the Layer-2 header with PC-4's MAC address and looking into its MAC address table, Core-1 is ready to forward the packet using LAG 10 as the outbound interface for the unicast packet. When leaving Core-1 the packet crosses Core-2, Access-2 and finally gets to PC-4 (Figure 7-50).

This new version of the packet has the Core-1 MAC address as its Layer-2 source address rather than its destination address (as it was in step 18) and PC-4 is now the new destination address. Layer-2 addresses change at each routing hop.

25. Select the second ARP request (frame #7 in Figure 7-51) and inspect its contents.

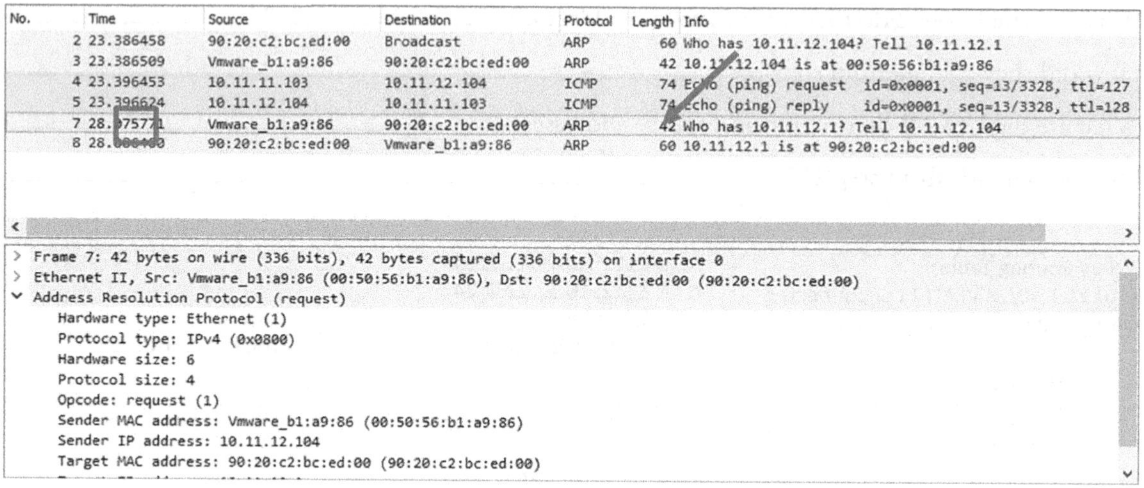

Figure 7-51 Traffic Analysis 8

Note

Before replying, PC-4 (as Core-1 and PC-3 before it) needs to add its gateway MAC address to its ARP table. That triggers the ARP request seen in image above. In entry number 8, PC-4 gets an ARP reply from Core-1.

7. Select the ICMP (ping) reply (frame #5 in Figure 7-52).

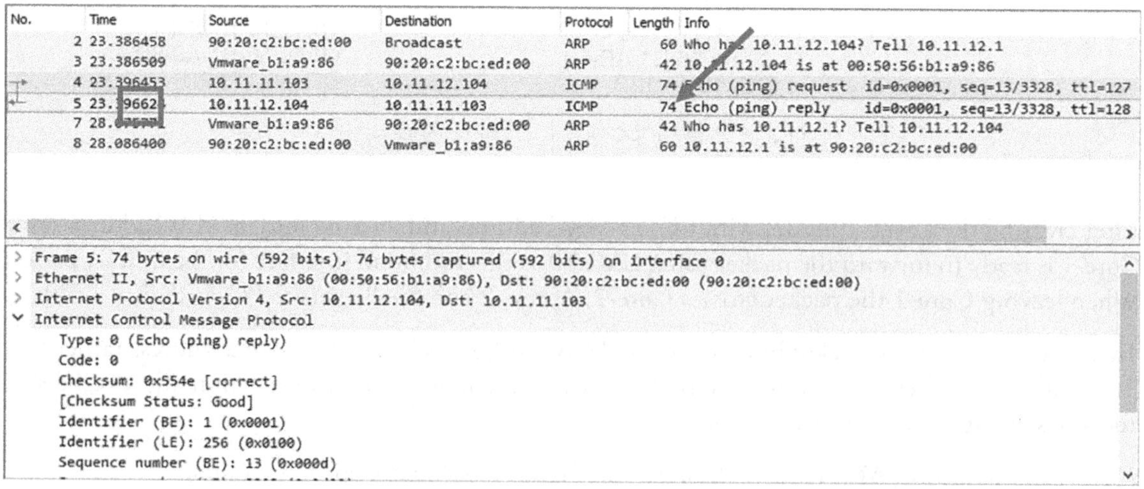

Figure 7-52 Traffic Analysis 9

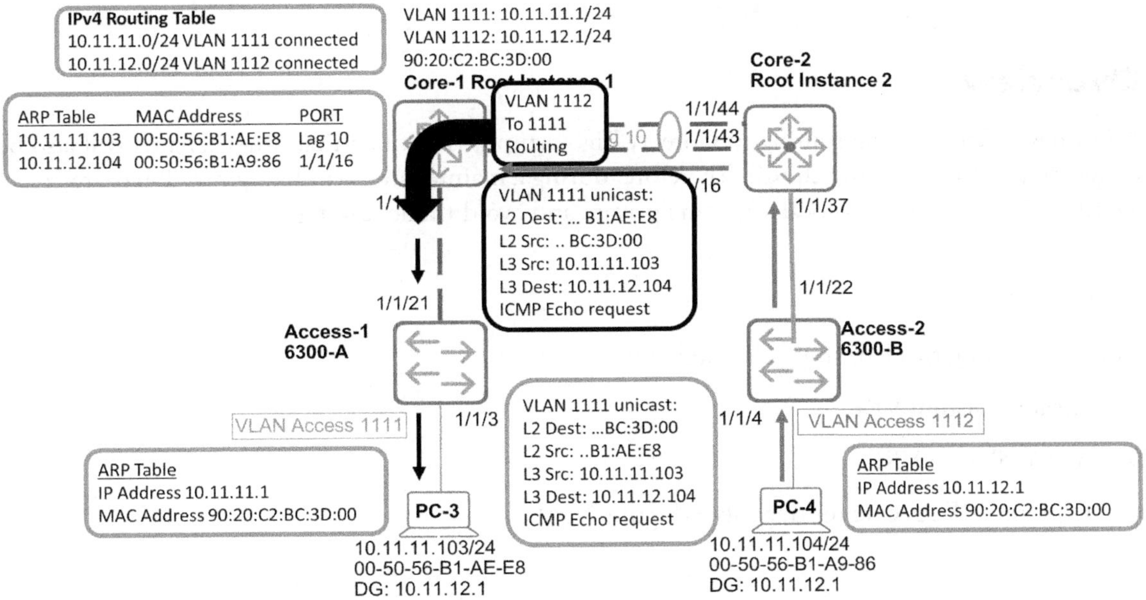

Figure 7-53 Topology for Traffic Analysis 8

When PC-4 completes the encapsulation step, it sends the packet to Core-1. Again Core-1 must perform an ARP lookup to add the PC-3 MAC address. After encapsulating the packet, Core-1 forwards the ICMP echo reply to PC-3 and the process ends (Figure 7-53).

26. Close Wireshark in both PCs.

Task 3: Save Your Configurations

Objectives

You will now proceed to save your configuration.

Steps

Core-1 (via PC-1)

1. Save the current Core-1's configuration in the startup checkpoint.

```
Core-1# write memory
Configuration changes will take time to process, please be patient.
```

You have completed Lab 7.1!

Lab 7.2: Creating a VRF

Overview

A few days after enabling routing in Core-1, BigStartup was notified that other tenants will also be connecting to the 8325-switch pair. Therefore, during a maintenance window, you will have to create a custom VRF for keeping local segments private and avoid traffic leaking.

Objectives

After completing this lab, you will be able to:

- Create a custom VRF
- Assign SVIs to VRF
- Explore VRF-specific routing table (Figure 7-54).

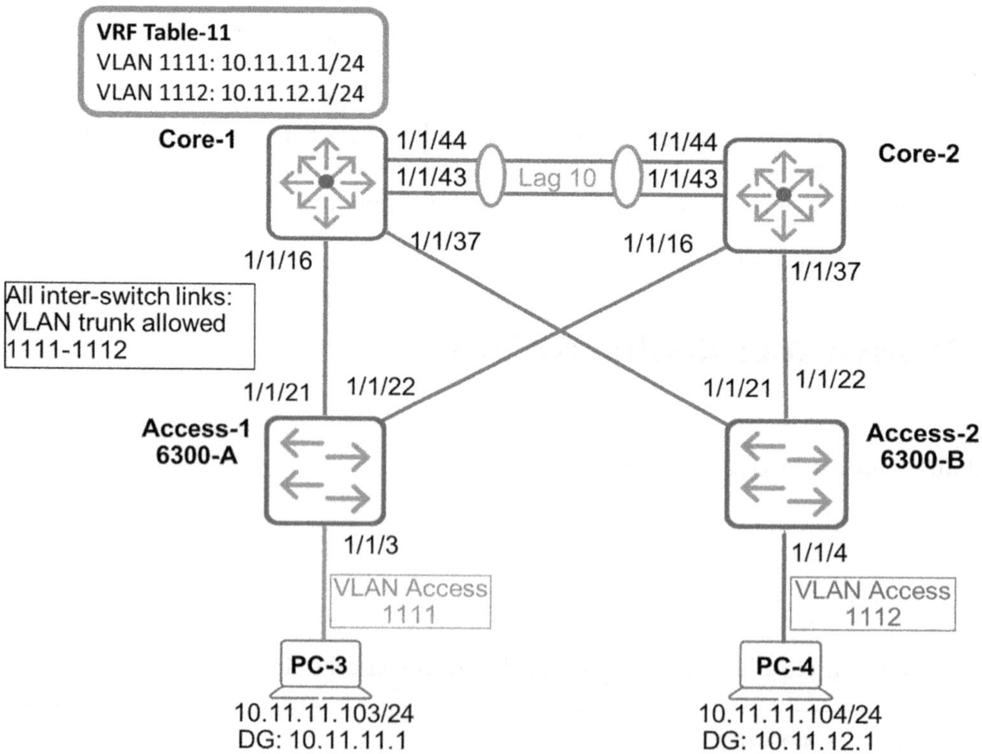

Figure 7-54 Lab Topology

Task 1: Create Table VRF

Objectives

In this step you will migrate your customer's network into an exclusive VRF. This requires creating it, assigning Layer-3 interfaces, and re-configuring the IP settings. Since the process might suspend IP services, a one-hour maintenance window has been scheduled for this task. You must act promptly!

Steps

Core-1 (via PC-1)

1. Open the SSH session to **Core-1**.
2. Ping PC-3 (10.11.11.103) and PC-4 (10.11.12.104). Pings should be successful.

```
Core-1# ping 10.11.11.103
PING 10.11.11.103 (10.11.11.103) 100(128) bytes of data.
108 bytes from 10.11.11.103: icmp_seq=1 ttl=128 time=19.0 ms
108 bytes from 10.11.11.103: icmp_seq=2 ttl=128 time=0.802 ms
108 bytes from 10.11.11.103: icmp_seq=3 ttl=128 time=0.642 ms
108 bytes from 10.11.11.103: icmp_seq=4 ttl=128 time=0.715 ms
108 bytes from 10.11.11.103: icmp_seq=5 ttl=128 time=0.706 ms

--- 10.11.11.103 ping statistics ---
5 packets transmitted, 5 received, 0% packet loss, time 4051ms
rtt min/avg/max/mdev = 0.642/4.374/19.007/7.316 ms
Core-1# ping 10.11.12.104
PING 10.11.12.104 (10.11.12.104) 100(128) bytes of data.
108 bytes from 10.11.12.104: icmp_seq=1 ttl=128 time=20.2 ms
108 bytes from 10.11.12.104: icmp_seq=2 ttl=128 time=0.817 ms
108 bytes from 10.11.12.104: icmp_seq=3 ttl=128 time=0.831 ms
108 bytes from 10.11.12.104: icmp_seq=4 ttl=128 time=0.762 ms
108 bytes from 10.11.12.104: icmp_seq=5 ttl=128 time=0.682 ms

--- 10.11.12.104 ping statistics ---
5 packets transmitted, 5 received, 0% packet loss, time 4053ms
rtt min/avg/max/mdev = 0.682/4.661/20.217/7.778 ms
```

3. Move to configuration mode and create a VRF named TABLE-11.

```
Core-1# configure terminal
Core-1(config)# vrf TABLE-11
Core-1(config-vrf)# exit
```

Notice

VRF names are case sensitive in both cases: when you create them and apply them to layer-3 interfaces, make sure you are using the right capitalization.

4. Move to interface VLAN 1111 and move it to the VRF.

```
Core-1(config)# interface vlan 1111
Core-1(config-if-vlan)# vrf attach TABLE-11
```

5. Move to interface VLAN 1112 and move it to the VRF.

```
Core-1(config)# interface vlan 1112
Core-1(config-if-vlan)# vrf attach TABLE-11
Core-1(config-if-vlan)# exit
```

6. Display the Layer-3 interfaces attached to TABLE-11 VRF.

```
Core-1(config)# show ip interface brief vrf TABLE-11
Interface     IP Address       Interface Status
                               link/admin
vlan1111      No Address       up/up
vlan1112      No Address       up/up
```

What are the IP addresses of the SVIs? ______________________________

Note

When moving a Layer-3 interface (either routing port or SVI) from one VRF to another, it loses all its IP settings. Therefore, you must configure those parameters again.

7. Assign former IP addresses to interface **VLAN 1111 and 1112**.

```
Core-1(config)# interface vlan 1111
Core-1(config-if-vlan)# ip address 10.11.11.1/24
Core-1(config-if-vlan)# exit
```

```
Core-1(config)# interface vlan 1112
Core-1(config-if-vlan)# ip address 10.11.12.1/24
Core-1(config-if-vlan)# exit
```

8. Repeat step 6.

```
Core-1(config)# show ip interface brief vrf TABLE-11
Interface          IP Address          Interface Status
                                       link/admin
vlan1111           10.11.11.1/24         up/up
vlan1112           10.11.12.1/24         up/up
```

Note

IP connectivity is reestablished in VLANs X11 and X12; however all the typical Layer-3 diagnostic and configuration commands will now be VRF dependent. This means commands will require the VRF name in the command syntax.

9. Display your customer's routing table. You will need the VRF command extension at the end of the line.

```
Core-1(config)# show ip route vrf TABLE-11
Displaying ipv4 routes selected for forwarding
'[x/y]' denotes [distance/metric]
10.11.11.0/24, vrf TABLE-11
        via  vlan1111,  [0/0],  connected
10.11.11.1/32, vrf TABLE-11
        via  vlan1111,  [0/0],  local
10.11.12.0/24, vrf TABLE-11
        via  vlan1112,  [0/0],  connected
10.11.12.1/32, vrf TABLE-11
        via  vlan1112,  [0/0],  local
```

Are the former IP segments shown in the output? ________________

10. Ping PC-3 and PC-4. You will need the VRF command extension at the end of the line. Ping should be successful.

```
Core-1(config)# do ping 10.11.11.103 vrf TABLE-11
PING 10.11.11.103 (10.11.11.103) 100(128) bytes of data.
108 bytes from 10.11.11.103: icmp_seq=1 ttl=128 time=18.8 ms
108 bytes from 10.11.11.103: icmp_seq=2 ttl=128 time=0.807 ms
108 bytes from 10.11.11.103: icmp_seq=3 ttl=128 time=0.750 ms
108 bytes from 10.11.11.103: icmp_seq=4 ttl=128 time=0.794 ms
108 bytes from 10.11.11.103: icmp_seq=5 ttl=128 time=0.613 ms

--- 10.11.11.103 ping statistics ---
5 packets transmitted, 5 received, 0% packet loss, time 4108ms
rtt min/avg/max/mdev = 0.613/4.362/18.847/7.242 ms
```

```
Core-1(config)# do ping 10.11.12.104 vrf TABLE-11
PING 10.11.12.104 (10.11.12.104) 100(128) bytes of data.
108 bytes from 10.11.12.104: icmp_seq=1 ttl=128 time=19.7 ms
108 bytes from 10.11.12.104: icmp_seq=2 ttl=128 time=0.694 ms
108 bytes from 10.11.12.104: icmp_seq=3 ttl=128 time=0.809 ms
108 bytes from 10.11.12.104: icmp_seq=4 ttl=128 time=0.909 ms
108 bytes from 10.11.12.104: icmp_seq=5 ttl=128 time=0.856 ms

--- 10.11.12.104 ping statistics ---
5 packets transmitted, 5 received, 0% packet loss, time 4056ms
rtt min/avg/max/mdev = 0.694/4.613/19.797/7.592 ms
```

Tip

Some diagnostic commands like ping, traceroute, ssh session initiation, etc. are not natively supported in the global configuration context. However, you can import them from manager context by beginning the command with a "do" like in the examples above.

Task 2: Save Your Configurations

Objectives

You will now proceed to save your configuration.

Steps

Core-1 (via PC-1)

1. Save the current Core-1's configuration in the startup checkpoint.

```
Core-1# write memory
Configuration changes will take time to process, please be patient.
```

You have completed Lab 7!

Learning Check

Chapter 7 Questions

IP Network Mask

1. Given IP address 172.20.3.54, and a mask of 255.255.255.0, what can be accurately stated about this addressing?
   a. The host portion of the address is .3.54.
   b. This network portion of the address is 172.20.3.
   c. Host 172.20.3.89 would be on the same network.
   d. A switch might use this address to forward the packet.
   e. You could also indicate this mask as "/24."

IP Routing Table

2. A router's IP routing table has an entry with a Next-Hop IP Address of 10.30.233.1. What does this number represent?
   a. The packet destination
   b. The next Layer-2 switch that should receive the packet
   c. The cached ARP entry for the destination MAC address
   d. The next Layer-3 device that should receive the packet
   e. The router's own egress interface for routing

Packet Delivery

3. Which of the options below accurately describe a typical packet delivery process?
    a. Access switches used their MAC address table to forward frames.
    b. Multilayer switches use their MAC address table to forward frames.
    c. Multilayer switches add 802.1q tags before sending frames to other switches.
    d. Multilayer switches use an IP routing table to forward packets.
    e. Access switches add 802.1q tags before sending frames to endpoints.
    f. The source and destination IP addresses remain consistent throughout the packet delivery process, but the MAC addresses change.

8 VRRP

EXAM OBJECTIVES

- ✓ Explain the need for L3 redundancy and First Hop Redundancy protocols
- ✓ Describe VRRP and VRRP instances
- ✓ Describe master election
- ✓ Describe failover operation
- ✓ Explain VRRP preemption
- ✓ Describe VRRP and MSTP coordination

Overview

In this module, you will learn how to eliminate a potentially costly single point of failure: the endpoint's Default Gateway (DG). You will come to understand how a single DG can cause major outages, and why you cannot simply add a second DG.

You need to understand the Virtual Router Redundancy Protocol (VRRP), and how it automatically mitigates downtime upon DG failures. You will learn about VRRP operation, including how to load balance endpoint traffic by configuring multiple VRRP instances on a single set of routers.

You learn about the Master election process and how to control it by configuring priority values. You also learn about preemption options, to control what happens when a failed Master comes back online.

Finally, you learn about the importance of coordinating Layer-3 VRRP redundancy with Layer-2 MSTP redundancy, to avoid strange network outages and unpredictable behavior. Then you will apply this knowledge with a lab activity

Need for Layer-3 Redundancy

In the previous module you learned about the benefits of a Default Gateway (DG) for endpoints. Recall that an endpoint may only have one DG, and a single DG means a single point of failure. In the example shown in Figure 8-1, if Core-1 fails, PC-1 and all other hosts using it for the DG are now isolated. What can you do?

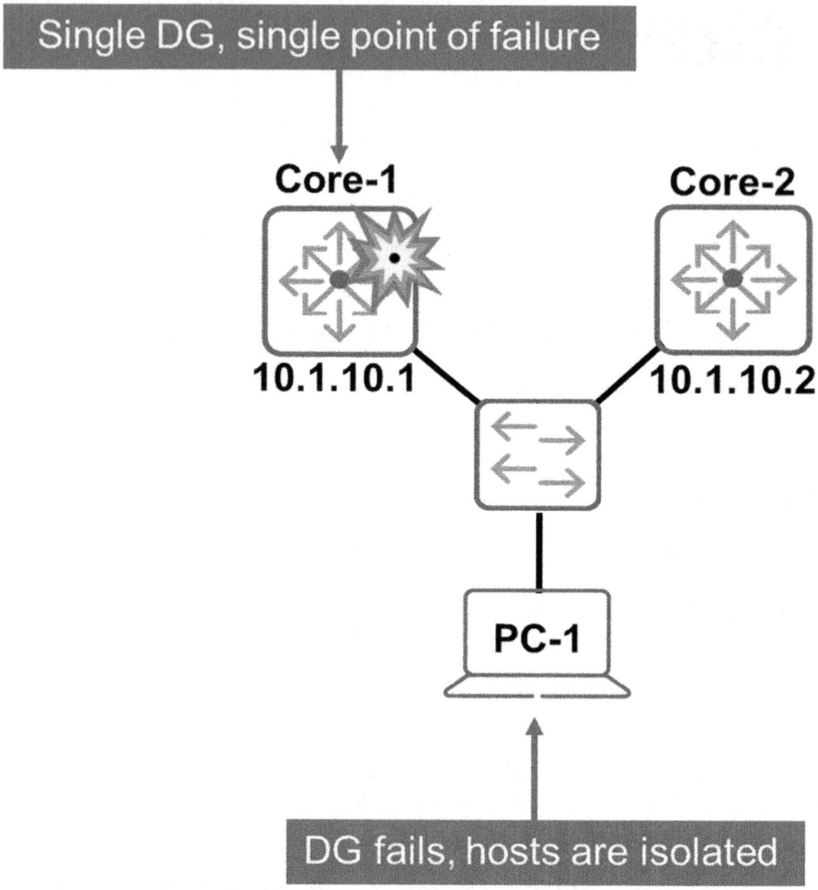

Figure 8-1 Need for Layer-3 Redundancy

You could add another DG for redundancy. This seems like an easy solution, but maybe not. Each endpoint's DG is either configured manually or obtained via DHCP. When Core-1 fails, you must either manually reconfigure each host with a new DG or reconfigure the DHCP scope. Then ask all end users to disconnect from the network and reconnect, power cycle their PC, or teach them how to trigger a DHCP release and renew action. (In a Windows command prompt for example, use **IPconfig /release**, then **IPconfig /renew**). However you do it, these methods are not very elegant or scalable, and may be disruptive for end users. (Figure 8-1).

There must be a better way, right?

First Hop Redundancy Protocol

The real solution for this challenge can be resolved from the network side instead from the endpoint side, using some kind of First Hop Routing Protocol (FHRP). This adds resiliency for endpoints by using a coordinated gateway solution, no change to endpoint IP configuration, no DHCP modifications, and no end user disruption. It is automatic!

Note
The term resiliency refers to the ability of the network to adapt to changes and failures.

An FHRP solution creates a single coordinated gateway from two or more physical routers. The two physical routers present themselves to endpoints as a single device, with a single Virtual IP (VIP) address. This VIP acts as the endpoint's DG (Figure 8-2).

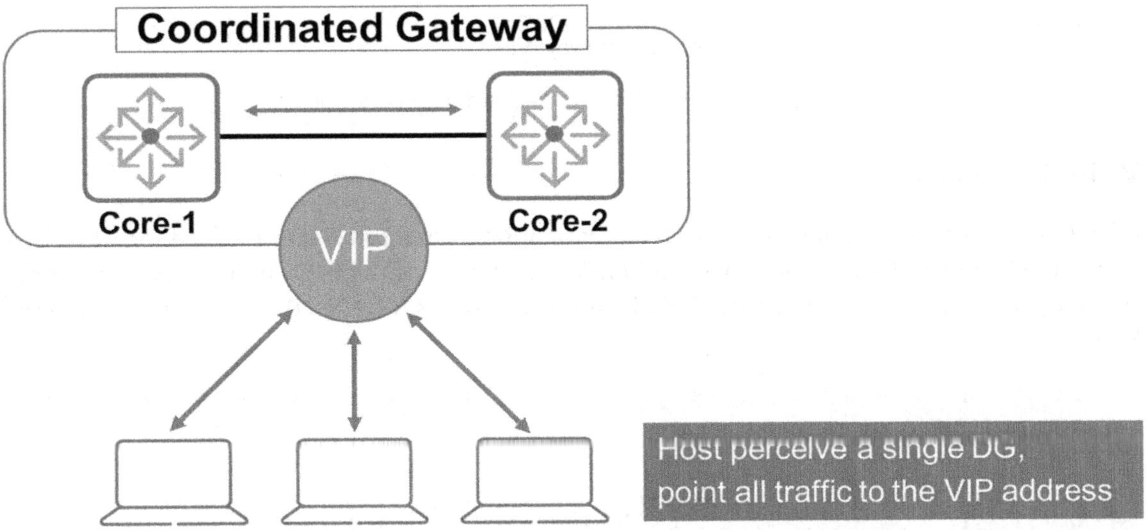

Figure 8-2 FHRP

Normally, the Primary routing device serves the DG role, forwarding traffic for endpoints. The Secondary unit monitors the Primary device state. If the Primary fails, the Secondary device takes over. It takes on the Primary role and VIP and forwards endpoint traffic. From the endpoint perspective the Virtual IP address is always available. There is no DG address change, and there is no disruption for end users.

Virtual Router Redundancy Protocol

RFC 5798 defines the Virtual Router Redundancy Protocol (VRRP), a standard FHRP that enables two or more routing devices to provide gateway redundancy for endpoints.

VRRP uses a Master-Standby architecture. Only one gateway actively forwards traffic sent to the VIP address. This primary forwarding device is called the **Master**, while the non-forwarding device is the **Backup** (Figure 8-3).

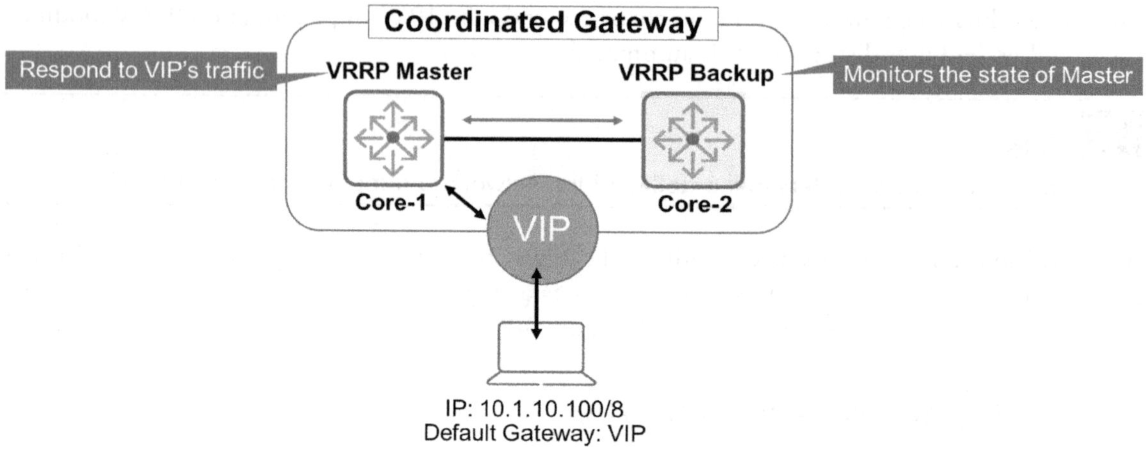

Figure 8-3 Virtual Router Redundancy Protocol

VRRP Instances

AOS-CX allows you to deploy multiple instances of VRRP, often to balance the load for VLANs, as shown in Figure 8-4. Each instance has a unique Virtual Router ID (VRID) number, AOS-CX refers as Group ID as shown in the figure. VRRP instance 1 serves VLAN 10, while instance 2 serves VLAN 20.

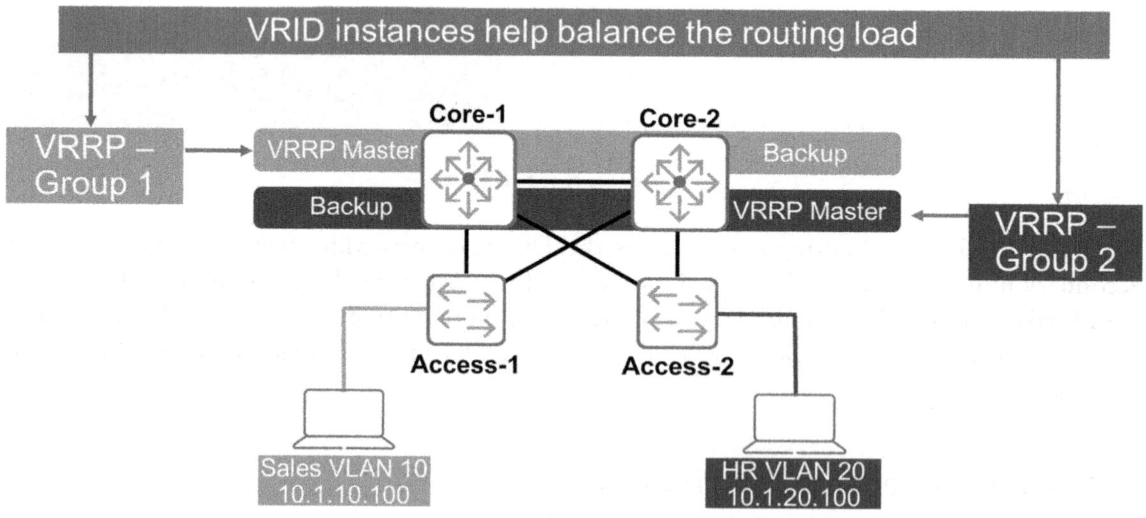

Figure 8-4 Virtual Router Redundancy Protocol Instances

Switch Core-1 is the Master or active forwarder for VLAN 10, with Core-2 as the Standby. Meanwhile, Core-2 is the Master for VLAN 20, with Core-1 as the Standby. This gives you a nice load balancing capability.

VRRP Instances Validate Capacity

Instances are also known in VRRP as Virtual Router IDs (VRIDs), the number of available VRIDs that a switch supports depends on the switch capacity. In AOS-CX you can verify the capacities of your switch using the **show capacities VRRP** command (Figure 8-5).

```
6300# show capacities vrrp

System Capacities: Filter VRRP
Capacities Name                                                                    Value
-----------------------------------------------------------------------------------------
Maximum number of unique IPv4 VRRP VRIDs configurable between 1 to 255                 8
Maximum number of VRRP IPv4 addresses supported                                     1024
Maximum number of VRRP IPv4 addresses supported per virtual router                    16
Maximum number of VRRP IPv4 virtual routers supported per port                         8
Maximum number of VRRP virtual routers supported                                     256
<<<<Omitted output>>>>
```

Figure 8-5 VRRP Show Capacity

Master Election

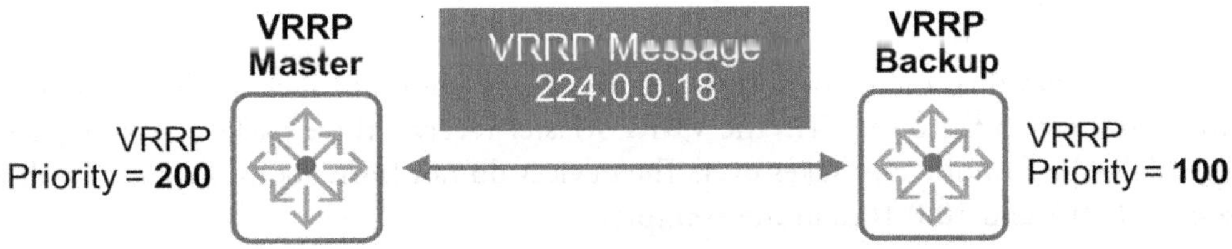

Figure 8-6 Master Election

VRRP members exchange multicast advertisement messages to elect the Master gateway, using address 224.0.0.18, IP protocol number 112. To control the Master election, you set a priority value from 1 to 255 where the highest priority wins. If both devices have the same priority, then the gateway with the highest IP address wins the election. In AOS-CX the default priority value is set to 100 (Figure 8-6).

Virtual IP Address

The Virtual IP (VIP) address is the result of the Gateway coordination. You assign a unique, "real" IP address to each individual physical gateway, as normal. The VIP address must also be unique. In Figure 8-7, you assigned 10.0.10.1 to the Master, 10.0.10.2 to the Backup, and 10.0.10.3 is used as the VIP.

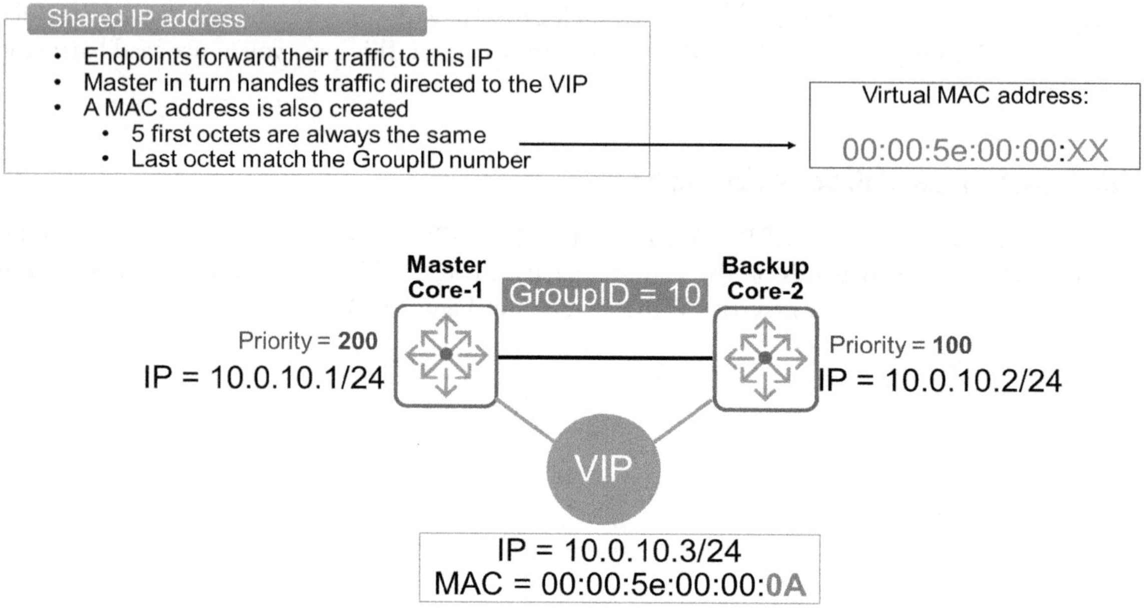

Figure 8-7 Virtual IP Address

Each VRRP instance has a unique VRRP address. 10.0.10.3 might be the VIP address for Instance 10, used for VLAN 10. Meanwhile, 10.0.20.3 might be the VIP address for Instance 20, used for VLAN 20.

You must ensure that this VIP address is configured as the endpoint Default Gateway. Thus, endpoints forward their traffic to the VIP. The VRRP Master receives these packets and routes them. If the Master fails, the Standby unit takes over. The devices do not learn about the router's physical IP addresses: 10.0.10.1 and 10.0.10.2 in the example.

A virtual MAC address (vMAC) is automatically assigned to the VIP. As defined in the standard, this address shall be 00:00:5e:00:00:XX, where XX = the VRID. In Figure 8-7, the VRID = 10, and so the vMAC is 00:00:5e:00:00:0A (Hex A = 10 in decimal). Thus, when endpoints ARP for their DG address of 10.0.10.3, they will learn the vMAC address, and add it to their ARP table.

VRRP Failover Operation

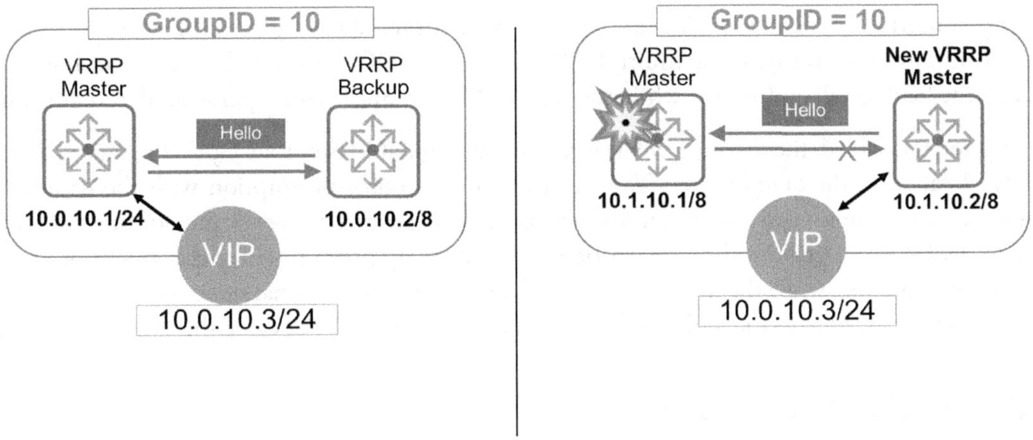

Figure 8-8 VRRP Failover Operation

Figure 8-8 shows a scenario where two Core switches run VRRP. Core-1 on the left has a higher priority, and so is the VRRP Master. Core-2 on the right is the VRRP Standby constantly monitoring Core-1 status via a keepalive mechanism. Endpoints forward their traffic to 10.0.10.3, which is services by the VRRP Master.

Then the Master fails. The standby stops receiving keepalive messages, and so knows that the Master is down. The former Standby takes over as the new VRRP master and begins to forward traffic for VIP 10.0.10.3.

VRRP Preemption

We are continuing our discussion from the previous Figure 8-8 about failover operation. You saw that Core-1 failed and so Core-2 took over as the new Master. What happens when Core-1 comes back online? This depends on how you configure VRRP preemption (Figure 8-9).

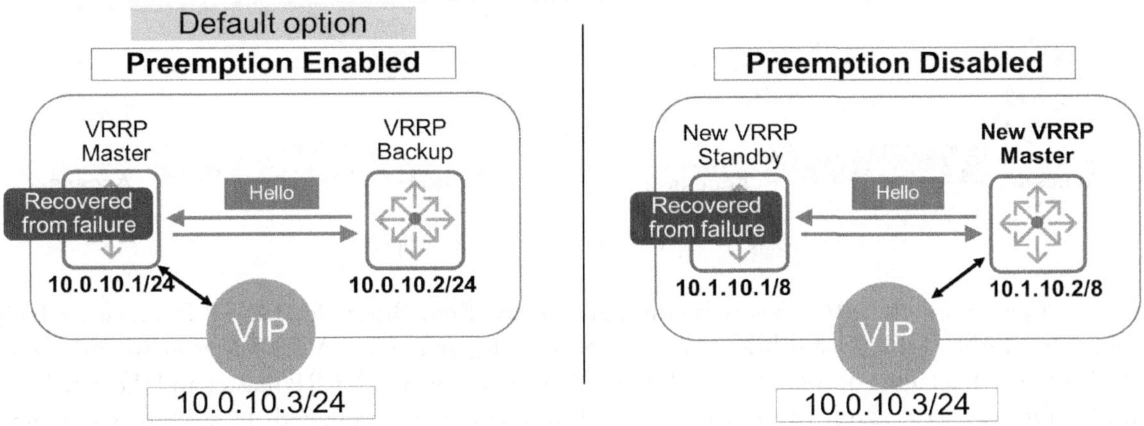

Figure 8-9 VRRP Preemption

If Preemption is enabled, then Core-1 will reassume its original Master role and Core-2 reverts to its Standby role. This is the AOS-CX default setting. It is nice because you know that under normal operating conditions, when all devices are up, the same router always acts as the Master. This can be especially important if you are using multiple VRRP instances. If a Master fails, the remaining device(s) will carry the load for all endpoints, while the former Master, once again operational, remains unused.

If Preemption is disabled, then Core-1 will not resume its original Master role. Core-2 remains the Master, and Core-1 takes on the Standby role. You must manually disable preemption with the command **no prempt**. With preemption disabled you lose the benefits described above. Some administrators might choose to disable preemption if they are worried about the (very brief) time lag that might occur during the preemption process; while the routers switch back over to new operational states, potentially during the middle of a busy day. Due to the high-performance nature of AOS-CX devices, this is rarely a concern.

VRRP and MSTP Coordination

You may have noticed in the previous scenario that a Layer-- 2 Loop can be created between Access-1 and the Core switches. You know how to avoid this, enable Spanning Tree.

In these scenarios there must be coordination between the MSTP Root Bridge and the VRRP Master. This ensures proper traffic forwarding, Layer-2 and Layer-3 protocols converge with the same devices.

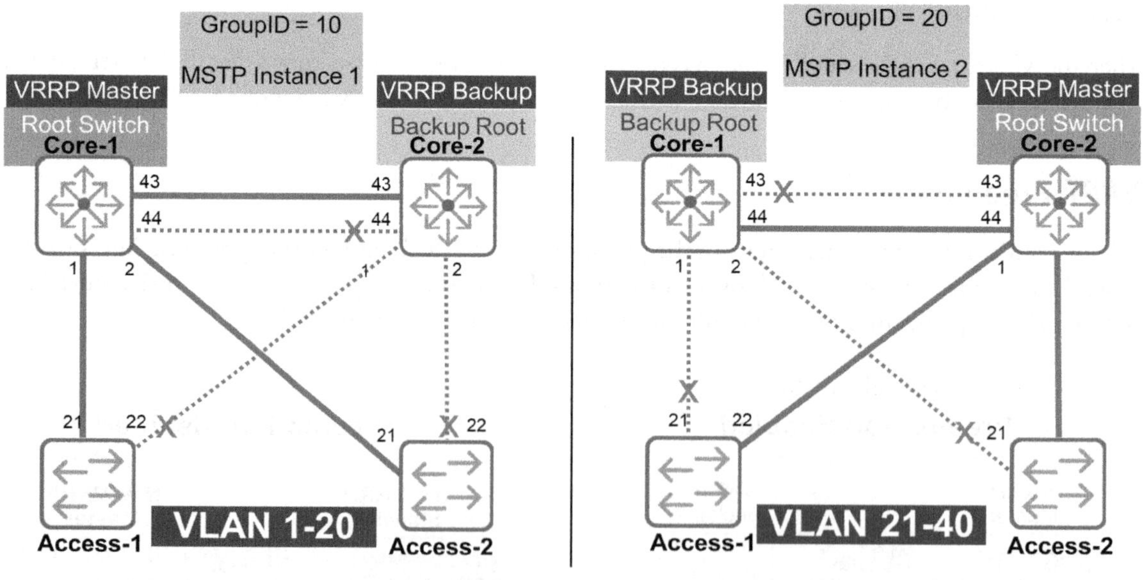

Figure 8-10 VRRP and MSTP Coordination

For example, in Figure 8-10, Core-1 is configured as the Root Bridge for MSTP Instance 1 which supports VLANs 1-20. Meanwhile, Core-1 is also configured as the VRRP Master for this same VLAN range. If a failure occurs on Core-1, Core-2 becomes the new VRRP master and the new Root Bridge for Instance 1. Both Layer-2 and Layer-3 protocols are coordinated, L2 STP uses the same forwarding path as L3 routing. This is vital to avoid unexpected behaviors.

Lab 8: Deploying VRRP

Overview

Once IP routing was deployed successfully, you approached management and made them aware of how much the network routing relies on Core-1 and how it became a single point of failure in the current infrastructure. You have explained that if Core-1 goes down, VLAN 1111 and VLAN 1112 will not be able to reach one another. One of them asked you, "how can we fix that?" Your proposal is to deploy a standard First Hop Redundancy Protocol (FHRP) called Virtual Router Redundancy Protocol (VRRP).

Note: References to equipment and commands are taken from Aruba's hosted remote lab. These are shown for demonstration purposes in case you wish to replicate the environment and tasks on your own equipment.

Objectives

After completing this lab, you will be able to:

- Enable routing functions on Core-2
- Deploy VRRP on both core switches
- Test failover and failback
- Enable VRRP and MST coordination (Figure 8-11).

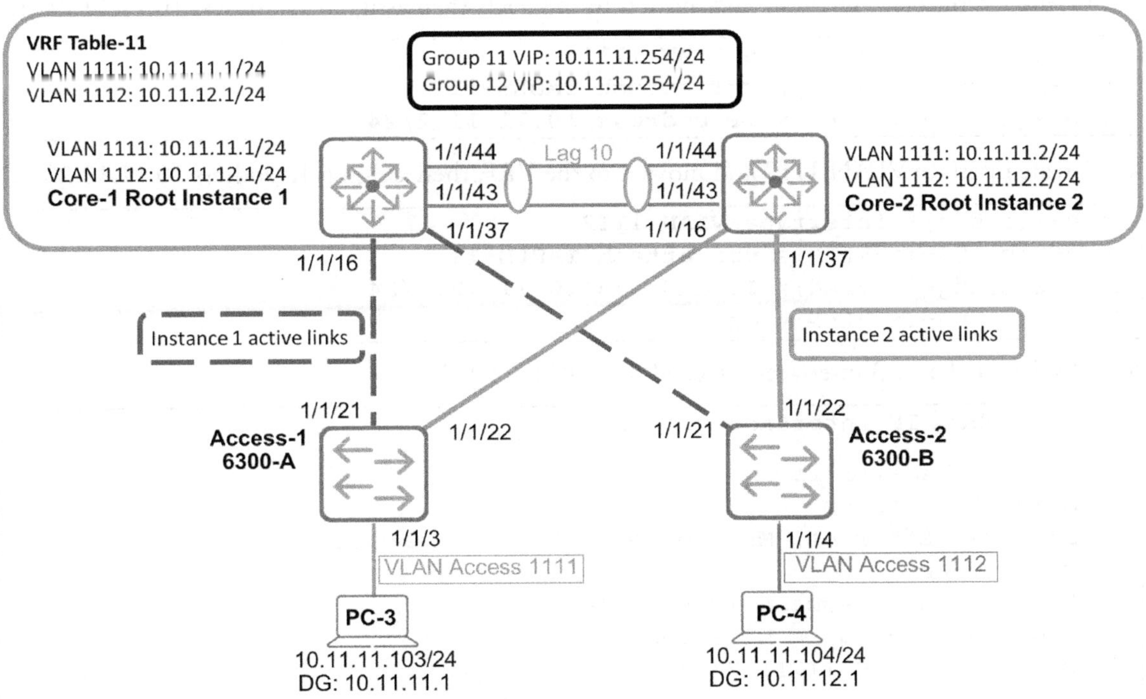

Figure 8-11 Lab Topology

Task 1: Enable IP Settings in Core-2

Objectives

In the following steps you will configure in Core-2 the same VRF and SVIs you already have in Core-1, assign them IP addresses and verify Layer-3 connectivity.

Steps

Core-2 (via PC-1)

1. Open the SSH session to Core-2. Login using **cxf11/aruba123**.
2. Create TABLE-11 VRF.

```
Core-2# configure terminal
Core-2(config)# vrf TABLE-11
Core-2(config-vrf)# exit
```

Notice

VRF names are case sensitive in both cases: when you create them and when you apply them to Layer-3 interfaces, make sure you are using the right capitalization.

---

3. Create interface VLAN 1111 and move it to the VRF, then assign it IP address 10.11.11.2/24.

```
Core-2(config)# interface VLAN 1111
Core-2(config-if-VLAN)# vrf attach TABLE-11
Core-2(config-if-VLAN)# IP address 10.11.11.2/24
```

4. Create interface VLAN 1112 and move it to the VRF, then assign it IP address 10.11.12.2/24.

```
Core-2(config)# interface VLAN 1112
Core-2(config-if-VLAN)# vrf attach TABLE-11
Core-2(config-if-VLAN)# IP address 10.11.12.2/24
Core-2(config-if-VLAN)# end
```

5. Display the Layer-3 interfaces attached to TABLE-11 VRF.

```
Core-2# show IP interface vrf TABLE-11

Interface VLAN1111 is up
  Admin state is up
  Hardware: Ethernet, MAC Address: 90:20:c2:bc:3f:00
  IP MTU 1500
  IP Directed Broadcast is Disabled
  IP Neighbor flood is Disabled
  IPv4 address 10.11.11.2/24
  L3 Counters: Rx Disabled, Tx Disabled
```

```
Interface VLAN1112 is up
  Admin state is up
  Hardware: Ethernet, MAC Address: 90:20:c2:bc:3f:00
  IP MTU 1500
  IP Directed Broadcast is Disabled
  IP Neighbor flood is Disabled
  IPv4 address 10.11.12.2/24
  L3 Counters: Rx Disabled, Tx Disabled
```

What are the IP addresses of the SVIs? ______________________________

6. As a sanity check, confirm you can ping **Core-1** using both SVIs.

```
Core-2# ping 10.11.11.1 repetitions 2 vrf TABLE-11
PING 10.11.11.1 (10.11.11.1) 100(128) bytes of data.
108 bytes from 10.11.11.1: icmp_seq=1 ttl=64 time=16.8 ms
108 bytes from 10.11.11.1: icmp_seq=2 ttl=64 time=0.258 ms

--- 10.11.11.1 ping statistics ---
2 packets transmitted, 2 received, 0% packet loss, time 1001ms
rtt min/avg/max/mdev = 0.258/8.538/16.818/8.280 ms
```

```
Core-2# ping 10.11.12.1 repetitions 2 vrf TABLE-11
PING 10.11.12.1 (10.11.12.1) 100(128) bytes of data.
108 bytes from 10.11.12.1: icmp_seq=1 ttl=64 time=17.9 ms
108 bytes from 10.11.12.1: icmp_seq=2 ttl=64 time=0.286 ms

--- 10.11.12.1 ping statistics ---
2 packets transmitted, 2 received, 0% packet loss, time 1000ms
rtt min/avg/max/mdev = 0.286/9.129/17.973/8.844 ms
```

Task 2: Deploying VRRP

Objectives

Next you will enable a VRRP instance, creating a virtual address and using it as the default gateway on PC-3. You will also track the processes' roles, discover the virtual MAC address used for the Virtual IP, and witness the effect of preemption.

Steps

Core-2 (via PC-1)

1. Open the SSH session to Core-2.
2. Move to interface VLAN 1111 and create the VRRP routing process using Group (Virtual Router ID) 11.

Note

VRRP Group number IS NOT table dependent.

```
Core-2(config)# interface VLAN 1111
Core-2(config-if-VLAN)# VRRP 11 address-family IPv4
```

3. Define **10.11.11.254** as the virtual IP address; then enable the group.

```
Core-2(config-if-VRRP)# address 10.11.11.254 primary
Core-2(config-if-VRRP)# no shutdown
Core-2(config-if-VRRP)# exit
Core-2(config-if-VLAN)# exit
```

4. Display the VRRP process information.

```
Core-2(config)# show VRRP interface VLAN1111

VRRP is enabled

Interface VLAN1111 - Group 11 - Address-Family IPv4
  State is MASTER
  State duration 01 mins 17.300 secs
  Virtual IP address is 10.11.11.254
  Virtual MAC address is 00:00:5E:00:01:0B
  Advertisement interval is 1000 msec
  Version is 2
  Preemption is enabled
    min delay is 0 sec
  Priority is 100
  Master Router is 10.11.11.2 (local)
  Master Advertisement interval is 1000 msec
  Master Down interval is 3609 msec
```

What is the Virtual Router state? ____________________

What is the VIP? ____________________

What version is the configuration using? ____________________

What is the default priority value? ____________________

What is the default advertisement interval? ____________________

What is the default master down interval? ____________________

VRRP needs to be enabled per group and globally in the switch. Since Core switches are a shared resource, the feature has been already enabled using the following command:

```
Core-2(config)# router VRRP enable
```

You will now procced configuring its counterpart Core-1.

Core-1 (via PC-1)

5. Open the SSH session to Core-1.
6. Repeat steps 2 to 3.

```
Core-1# configure terminal
Core-1(config)# interface VLAN 1111
Core-1(config-if-VLAN)# VRRP 11 address-family IPv4
Core-1(config-if-VRRP)# address 10.11.11.254 primary
Core-1(config-if-VRRP)# no shutdown
```

7. Define priority 254, then enable process globally.

```
Core-1(config-if-VRRP)# priority 254
Core-1(config-if-VRRP)# exit
Core-1(config-if-VLAN)# exit
```

8. Display the VRRP process information.

```
Core-1(config)# show VRRP interface VLAN1111

VRRP is enabled

Interface VLAN1111 - Group 11 - Address-Family IPv4
  State is MASTER
  State duration 12.501 secs
  Virtual IP address is 10.11.11.254
  Virtual MAC address is 00:00:5E:00:01:0B
  Advertisement interval is 1000 msec
  Version is 2
  Preemption is enabled
    min delay is 0 sec
  Priority is 254
  Master Router is 10.11.11.1 (local)
  Master Advertisement interval is 1000 msec
  Master Down interval is 3007 msec
```

What is the preemption setting and priority value? ________________

What is the VRRP router state? ________________

Answer

Because preemption is enabled, and Core-1's priority is higher than its peer, Core-2, Core-1 became MASTER and Core-2 BACKUP. This means that Core-1 is now the one in charge of advertising the hello packets.

What is the Virtual MAC address? ______________________________

Using your conversion skills acquired on Lab 1, take the last 2 hexadecimal digits of the Virtual MAC and convert them into decimal. What is the result? ______________

Is the result close to any previously defined variable? If so, which one? ______________

PC-3

9. Move to PC-3.
10. Open **Wireshark,** there should be a shortcut on the Desktop.
11. Open your connected NIC to the labs. In this example, we will use the "**Lab NIC**" entry (Figure 8-12). That will begin the packet capture on that interface. You will see VRRP packets right away.

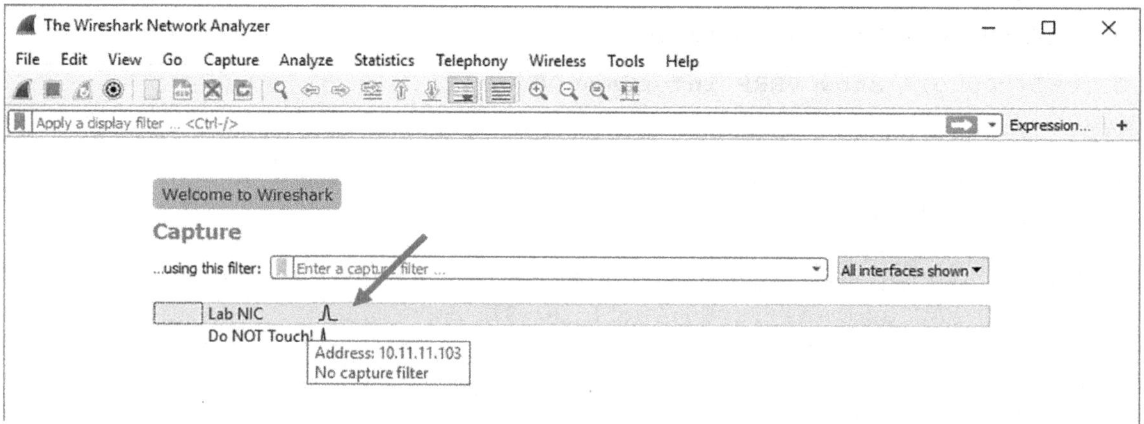

Figure 8-12 Wireshark

12. Stop the capture.
13. Select any of the VRRP packets (Figure 8-13).

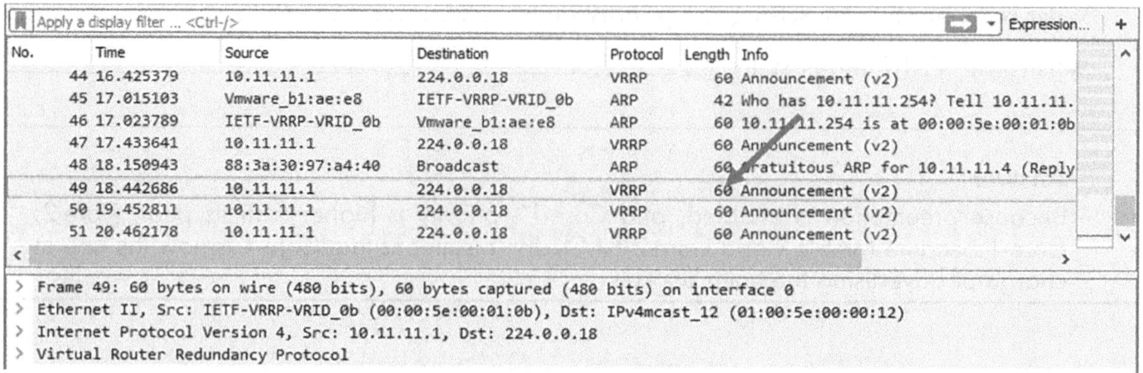

Figure 8-13 VRRP Packet Capture

What are source and destination MAC addresses in the Ethernet header? ______________

What kind of address is the destination address? ______________

What are the source address and destination address in the IP header? ______________

What kind of address is the destination address? ______________

14. Expand the IP header.

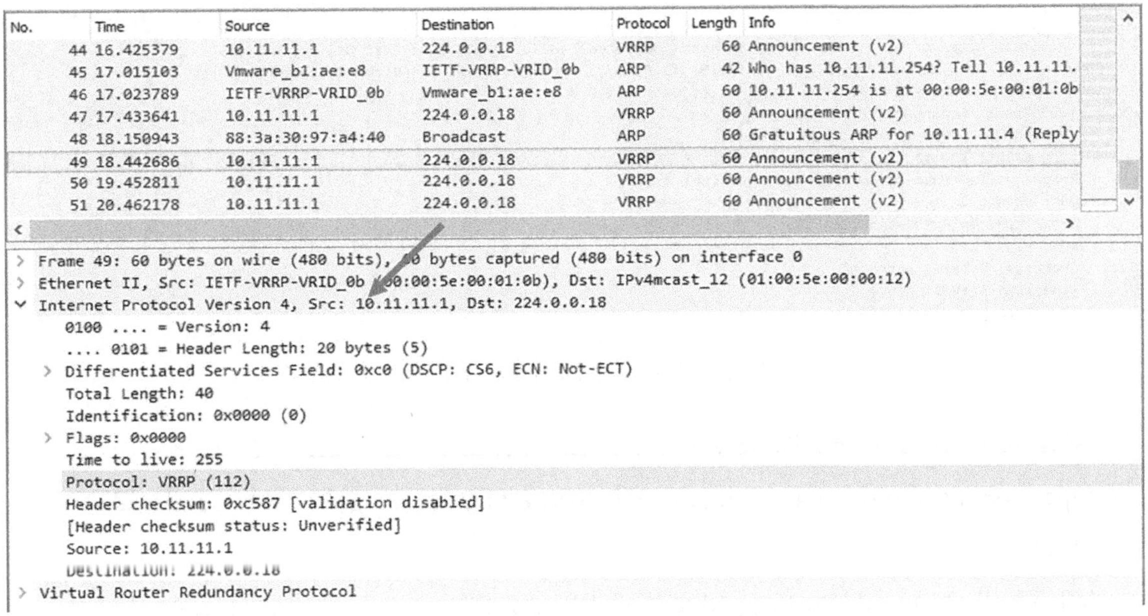

Figure 8-14 VRRP Packet Details

What is the IP protocol number? ______________

15. Expand the VRRP header (Figures 8-14 and 8-15).

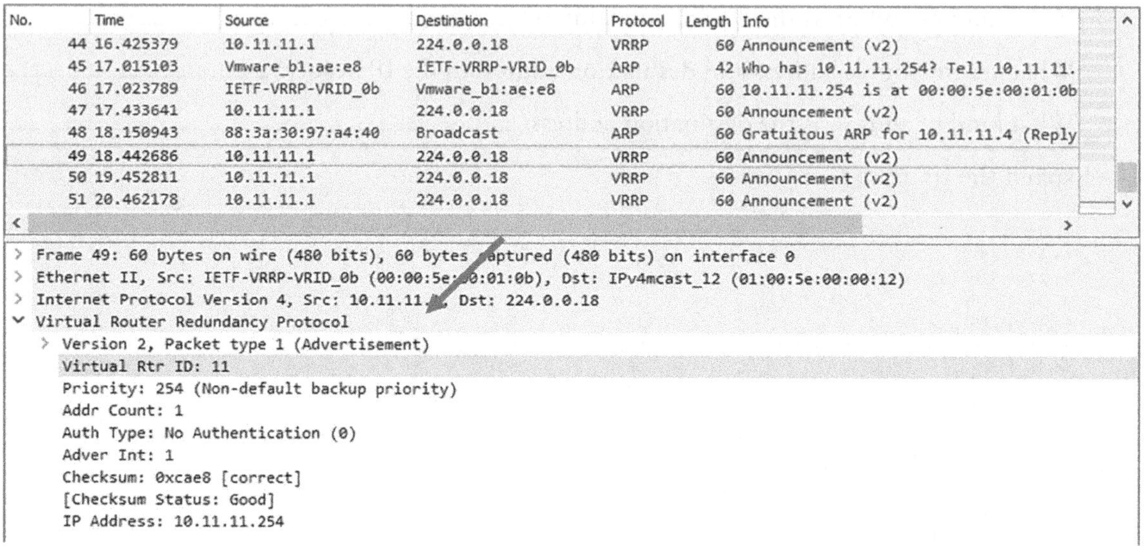

Figure 8-15 VRRP Packet Details 2

What parameters are familiar to you? ______________________________

16. Open command prompt and ping the VIP (**10.11.11.254**). Ping should be successful.

17. Display the ARP table (Figure 8-16).

What is the MAC address mapped to the VIP? ______________________________

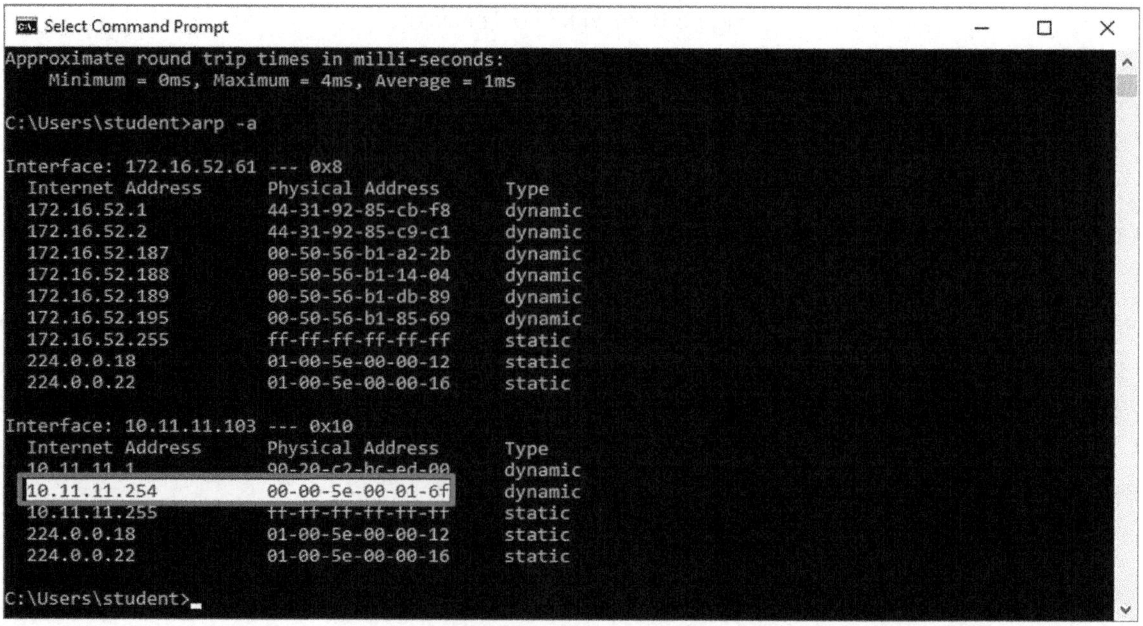

Figure 8-16 PC-3's ARP Table

Not that you know how VRRP works, you will proceed with configuring Virtual Router ID 12 for VLAN X12.

18. Core-1 (via PC-1)
19. Open the SSH session to Core-1.
20. Repeat steps 2 and 3 for VLAN 1112 using 12 and 10.11.12.254 as the VRRP group and VIP, respectively.

Note
VRRP Group number IS NOT table dependent.

```
Core-1# configure terminal
Core-1(config)# interface VLAN 1112
Core-1(config-if-VLAN)# VRRP 12 address-family IPv4
Core-1(config-if-VRRP)# address 10.11.12.254 primary
Core-1(config-if-VRRP)# no shutdown
Core-1(config-if-VRRP)# exit
```

Core-2 (via PC-1)

21. Open the SSH session to Core-2.
22. Repeat step 19.

```
Core-2(config)# interface VLAN 1112
Core-2(config-if-VLAN)# VRRP 12 address-family IPv4
Core-2(config-if-VRRP)# address 10.11.12.254 primary
Core-2(config-if-VRRP)# no shutdown
Core-2(config-if-VRRP)# end
```

23. Run "**show VRRP brief | include VLAN1**". Core-2 should be BACKUP of both groups.

```
Core-2# show VRRP brief | include VLAN11
 VLAN1111        11  IPv4 100  3647        N   Y  BACKUP    10.11.11.1
10.11.11.254
 VLAN1112        12  IPv4 100  34          N   Y  BACKUP    10.11.12.1
10.11.12.254
```

Task 3: Test VRRP Failover

Objectives

In this task you will finally test the resiliency that VRRP can offer to the hosts' default gateway.

Steps

PC-4

1. Access PC-4.
2. Change the default gateway in "**Lab NIC**" interface to **10.11.12.254** (Figure 8-17).

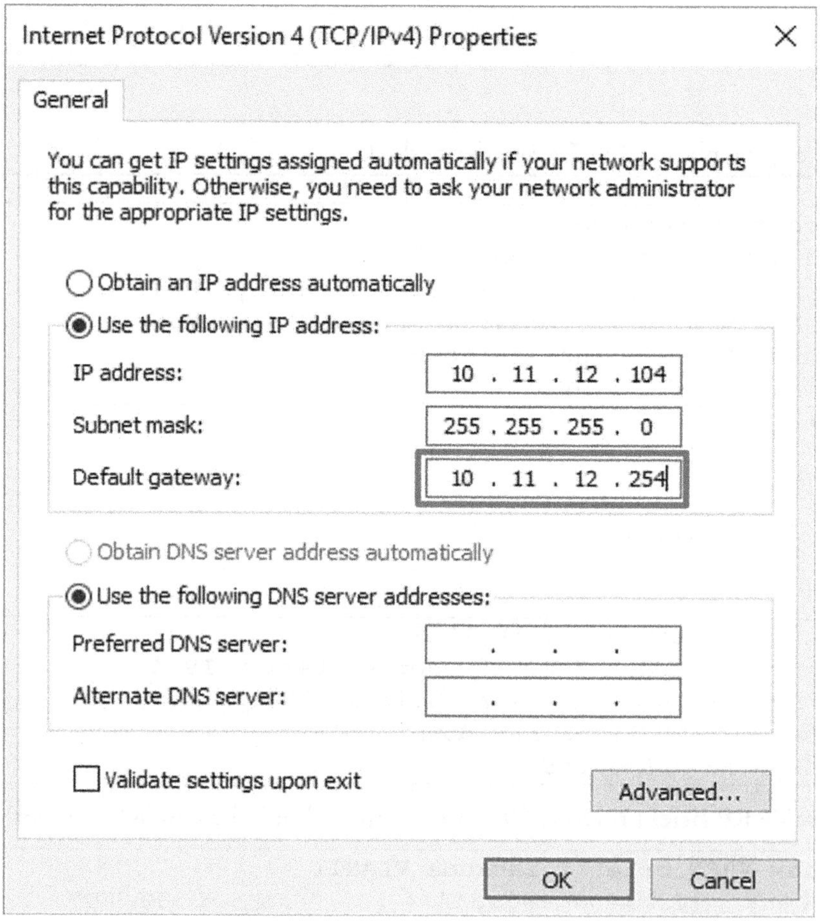

Figure 8-17 PC-4's Default Gateway

PC-3

3. Access PC-3.
4. Change the default gateway in "**Lab NIC**" interface to **10.11.11.254** (Figure 8-18).

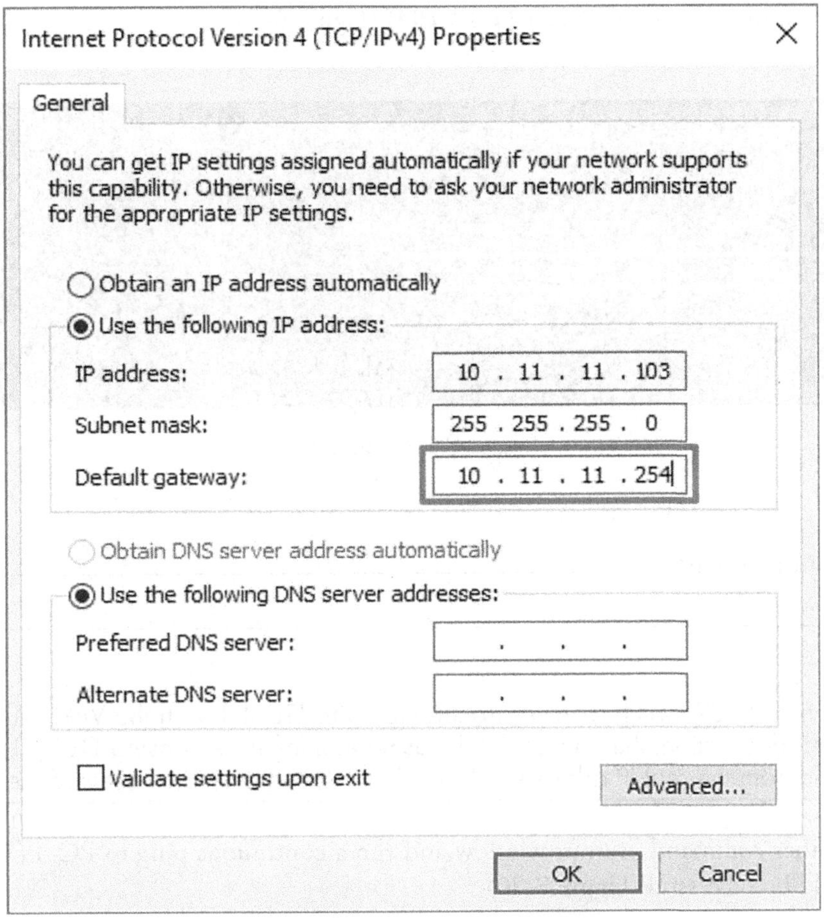

Figure 8-18 PC-3's Default Gateway

5. Run a traceroute towards PC-4 (**10.11.12.104**) (Figure 8-19).

```
Command Prompt
Microsoft Windows [Version 10.0.17134.441]
(c) 2018 Microsoft Corporation. All rights reserved.

C:\Users\student>tracert 10.11.12.104

Tracing route to 10.11.12.104 over a maximum of 30 hops

  1    <1 ms    <1 ms    <1 ms  10.11.11.1
  2    <1 ms    <1 ms    <1 ms  10.11.12.104

Trace complete.

C:\Users\student>
```

Figure 8-19 Traceroute

Who is your first hop? ____

Note

When an AOS-CX switch receives traceroutes with TTL of 1 with the VRRP MAC address as Layer-2 destination, the packet will die as normal (after decreasing TTL by 1), and reply will come from the real IP address of Layer-3 interface the switch received the packet on.

6. Open another command prompt window and run a continuous ping to PC-4 (**10.11.12.104**). Ping should be successful (Figure 8-20).

```
Command Prompt - ping -t 10.11.12.104
Microsoft Windows [Version 10.0.17134.441]
(c) 2018 Microsoft Corporation. All rights reserved.

C:\Users\student>ping -t 10.11.12.104

Pinging 10.11.12.104 with 32 bytes of data:
Reply from 10.11.12.104: bytes=32 time<1ms TTL=127
Reply from 10.11.12.104: bytes=32 time=1ms TTL=127
Reply from 10.11.12.104: bytes=32 time<1ms TTL=127
Reply from 10.11.12.104: bytes=32 time<1ms TTL=127
Reply from 10.11.12.104: bytes=32 time<1ms TTL=127
```

Figure 8-20 Ping to PC-4

Core-1 (via PC-1)

7. Open the SSH session to Core-1.
8. Disable interface VLANs 1111 and 1112. This will simulate a failure in Core-1 without affecting the other tenants.

```
Core-1(config)# interface VLAN 1111-1112
Core-1(config-if-VLAN-<1111-1112>)# shutdown
```

PC-3

9. Move back to PC-3 (Figure 8-21).

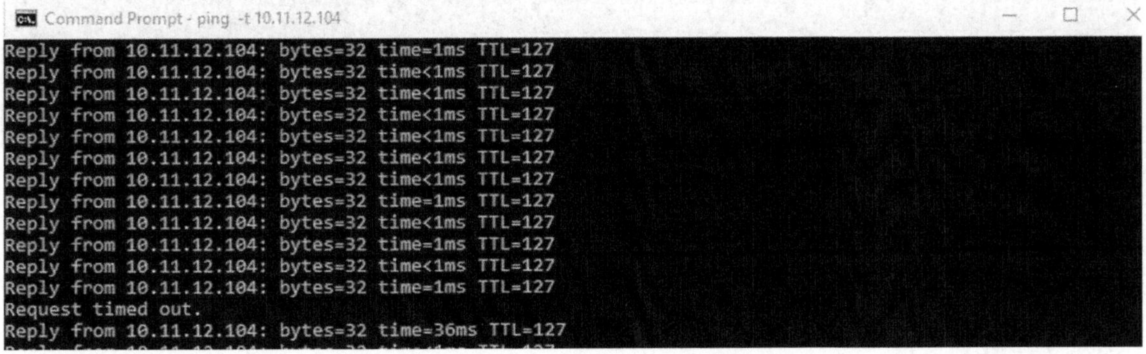

Figure 8-21 Second Ping to PC-4

How many pings did you miss? ______________________________

Is that what you expected? ______________________________

10. Repeat the traceroute (Figure 8-22).

```
Command Prompt
Microsoft Windows [Version 10.0.17134.441]
(c) 2018 Microsoft Corporation. All rights reserved.

C:\Users\student>tracert 10.11.12.104

Tracing route to 10.11.12.104 over a maximum of 30 hops

  1    <1 ms    <1 ms    <1 ms  10.11.11.1
  2    <1 ms    <1 ms    <1 ms  10.11.12.104

Trace complete.

C:\Users\student>tracert 10.11.12.104

Tracing route to 10.11.12.104 over a maximum of 30 hops

  1    14 ms    <1 ms    <1 ms  10.11.11.2
  2     1 ms    <1 ms    <1 ms  10.11.12.104

Trace complete.
```

Figure 8-22 Repeat Traceroute

Who is your first hop now? ______________________________

Core-2 (via PC-1)

11. Move back to Core-2.

12. Display the brief version of VRRP. Core-2 should be MASTER on both groups.

```
Core-2# show vrrp brief | include VLAN11
 VLAN1111       11   IPv4 100 1            N    Y   MASTER    10.11.11.2
10.11.11.254
 VLAN1112       12   IPv4 100 2            N    Y   MASTER    10.11.12.2
10.11.12.254
Core-2# show VRRP brief
```

Core-1 (via PC-1)

13. Move back to Core-1

14. Enable interface VLANs 1111 and 1112.

```
Core-1(config)# interface VLAN 1111-1112
Core-1(config-if-VLAN-<1111-1112>)# no shutdown
```

Task 4: VRRP and MST Coordination

Objectives

As seen in Task 2, in case of a priority tie the current MASTER remains MASTER. This makes Core-1 control both VIPs under some situations e.g. a power outage when both Core switches go down and Core1 beats Core2 during the boot process.

The problem with this is that Layer-3 load balancing is not guaranteed.

You currently have load sharing at Layer-2 by distributing the different MST instances' root bridges. A best practice is to coordinate both MST and VRRP as seen in Figure 8-23. This way, under normal conditions Core-1 is both the root bridge for instance 1 (where VLAN 1111 belongs) and the VRRP Master for VLAN 1111's VIP. Likewise, Core-2 is both the root bridge for instance 2 (where VLAN 1112 belongs) and the VRRP Master for VLAN 1112's VIP. The ultimate result is when traffic must go out the local segment. As soon as traffic hits either Core switch at Layer-2, that device is the gateway in charge of routing the traffic at Layer-3.

The next step raises the priority of Core-2 to achieve the desired behavior.

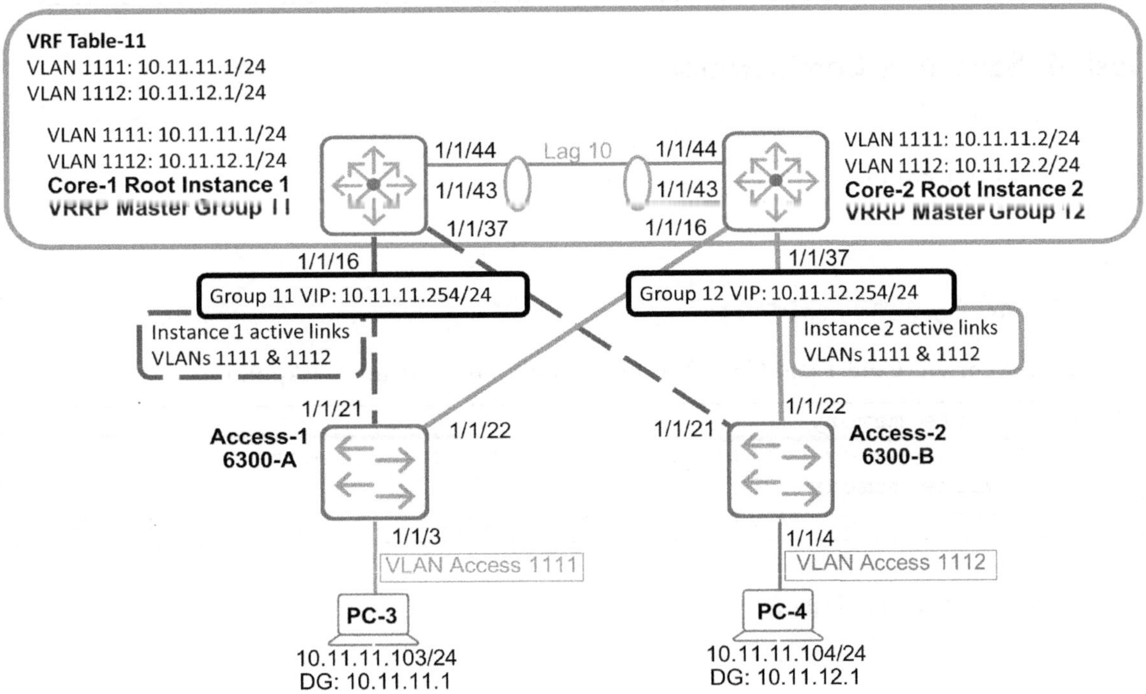

Figure 8-23 MST and VRRP Coordination

Steps

Core-2 (via PC-1)

1. Move back to Core-2.
2. Increase the VRRP group 12 priority 254.

```
Core-2(config)# interface VLAN 1112
Core-2(config-if-VLAN)# VRRP 12 address-family IPv4
Core-2(config-if-VRRP)# priority 254
Core-2(config-if-VRRP)# end
```

3. Display the VRRP process information. Core-2 should be BACKUP of group 11 and MASTER of 12.

```
Core-2# show VRRP brief | include VLAN11
 VLAN1111        11   IPv4 100  1659         N     Y    BACKUP     10.11.11.1
10.11.11.254
 VLAN1112        12   IPv4 254  1667         N     Y    MASTER     10.11.12.2
10.11.12.254
```

Task 4: Save Your Configurations

Objectives

You will now proceed to save your configuration.

Steps

Core-1 and Core-2 (via PC-1)

1. Save the current Core-1 and Core-2 configuration in the startup checkpoint.

```
Core-1# write memory
Configuration changes will take time to process, please be patient.
Core-2# write memory
Configuration changes will take time to process, please be patient.
```

You have completed Lab 8!

Learning Check

Chapter 8 Questions

VRRP Master Election

1. Which of the statements below accurately describe VRRP concepts and operation?
   a. A unique VRRP instance can run in an Aruba Switch.
   b. To control VRRP master election between two routers, you must configure a priority on both devices.
   c. If two VRRP routers have the same priority, the router with the highest IP address becomes the VRRP Master.

VRRP Preemption

2. You have configured a basic VRRP configuration, leaving all default options in place. What happens when the Master fails, and then comes back online four hours later?
   a. The Standby has become the new Master, and so remains the new Master
   b. The new Master coordinates with Layer-2 MSTP switches to adjust settings accordingly.
   c. The original Master resumes its Master role once it comes back online.
   d. A new election occurs, which the original Master, now back online, will lose.
   e. The original Master regains its Master role once you reconfigure it to be the Master again.

9 IP Routing - Part 2

EXAM OBJECTIVES

✓ Describe and perform subnetting

✓ Explain the advantages of VLSM and CIDR

Overview

This module should serve to significantly elevate your ability to design and deploy more complex, scalable IP networks. You will leverage your knowledge of binary and decimal number systems as you explore subnetting and how to use available IP address more efficiently. Related concepts include the various address classes and reserved address space, and why classful routing can seem quite rigid when compared to classless routing. Now you can apply your subnetting knowledge to network design and analysis scenarios.

Then you will explore Variable Length Subnet Masking (VLSM) and Classless Interdomain Routing (CIDR). VLSM helps you to assign address space more efficiently, while CIDR helps the routers to advertise and work with that address space more efficiently. Finally, a lab activity will give you more experience with these concepts.

Subnetting

IPv4 Address Classes

The available IPv4 address space is divided into five classes, Class A to E, which each class designed for a particular purpose. This is summarized in the table, which shows each class and its address range.

It also shows the first few most-significant bits of the address, if the range was converted to binary. For example, Class A address always have the most significant bit set to 0, Class B addresses always begin with the two most significant bits set to 10, and Class C addresses always begin with the three most significant bits set to 110.

Note

This training is focused on Classes A through C, which are used for Unicast addressing. These are by far the most common addresses that you will work with in your career.

Table 9-1 IPv4 Address Classes

Network Class	Address scope	Leading bits	Description
Class A	0.0.0.0. to 127.255.255.255	0000	Unicast address
Class B	128.0.0.0 to 191.255.255.255	1000	
Class C	192.0.0.0 to 223.255.255.255	1100	
Class D	224.0.0.0 to 239 255.255.255	1110	Multicast address
Class E	240.0.0.0 to 255.255.255.255	1111	Reserved for future or experimental purposes

Table 9-1 also shows that the first octet of any address reveals its Network class. This is important for you to know, as it will help you with upcoming concepts and activities, and prepare you for real-world design, administration, and troubleshooting tasks. The main difference between address classes A-C is first octet's range, and the distribution of Network ID and Host ID within the address. Here is how it works:

- Class A: The first octet is between 0 and 127. The first octet is reserved for the Network ID, which means that 3 octets (24 bits) are available to assign to hosts on that network.
- Class B: The first octet is between 128 and 191. The first two octets (16 bits) are reserved for the Network, which leaves 16 bits available for host assignment on that network.
- Class C: The first octet is between 192 and 223. The first 24 bits are reserved to specify the subnet, leaving only 8 bits available to specify hosts on that subnet.

IPv4 Address Classes and Default Masks

From the previous discussion, you might realize that there is a fixed Network Mask for each class. Think of a classful network as a network that uses these default Network Masks for their corresponding Network Class in Table 9-2.

Table 9-2 IPv4 Address Classes and Default Masks

		IPv4 address			
Network class	**Network mask**	**Octet 1**	**Octet2**	**Octet3**	**Octet4**
Class A	255.0.0.0	**Network**	Host	Host	Host
Class B	255.255.0.0	**Network**	**Network**	Host	Host
Class C	255.255.255.0	**Network**	**Network**	**Network**	Host

For example, a Class A network might be 10.0.0.0/8. With 24 bits to specify hosts, you can have a lot of hosts ranging from 10.0.0.1 to 10.255.255.254 usable.

Look at the Class B example, network 172.16.0.0/16. With 16 bits to specify hosts, you have 172.16.0.1 – 172.16.255.254.

The Class C example is network 192.168.1.0/24, leaving only 8 bits available to specify hosts on that network. You can have 192.168.1.1 – 192.168.1.254.

Notice the numbers in the example. Why didn't we assign 192.168.1.0 to a host? Why didn't we assign 192.168.1.255 to a host? Because these addresses are reserved. They have a special meaning.

Reserved Addresses

In any network there are two reserved addresses that cannot be assigned to the hosts. The first one is the Network ID or Network Number and the second one is the Local Broadcast Address looking at Figure 9-1.

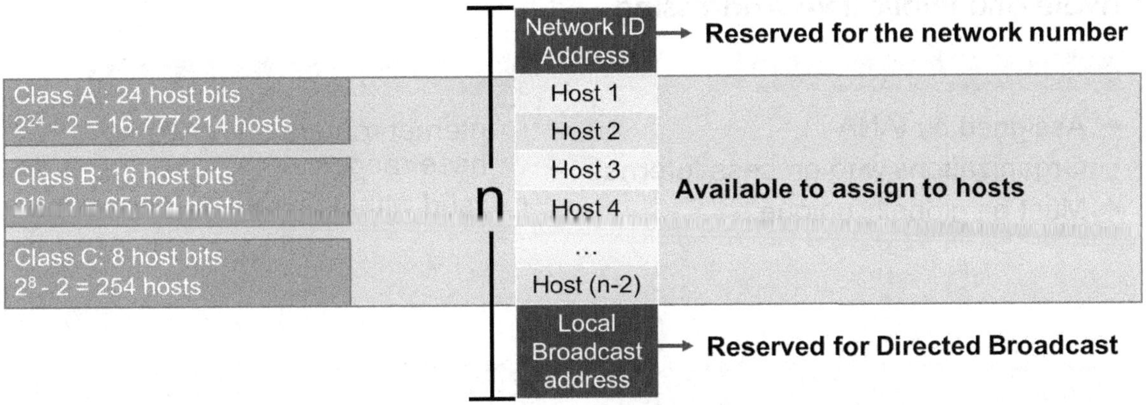

Figure 9-1 Reserved Addresses

As in the previous Class C example, IP address 192.168.1.0 cannot be assigned to a host, this number is reserved to mean "the network itself". Assigning this address to a host would be like telling your mail delivery person that your address is "Main Street". You cannot just live in the middle of the street, you must have a street address, "123 Main Street". Another way of saying this is that the network number is indicated when all host bits are binary 0s. This reserved network number is used by routers to find the best path to a subnet.

Similarly, you cannot assign the address 192.168.1.255 to a host. This is reserved for the broadcast address. It means, "Attention everyone on this subnet." Assigning this address to a host would be like having a child and naming her "Everyone".

So, the first available number is always the network ID (10.0.0.0, 172.16.0.0, 192.168.1.0), and the last available number is always reserved for a directed broadcast (10.255.255.255, 172.16.255.255, or 192.168.1.255).

The figure also indicates how many hosts you can have on a particular network, with the variable n. "n" represents how many unique numbers can be created, given the number of available hosts bits. To do this, use the formula 2^n (2 raised to the nth power).

Class A networks only use 8 bits for the network number, so 24 bits are available to specify hosts. 2^24 = 16,777,216 numbers, minus the 2 reserved addresses = 16,777,214 addresses, that is how many hosts you can have on a Class A subnet.

Class B networks use 16 bits for the network number, leaving 16 bits available to specify hosts. 2^16 = 65, 536 – 2 = 65,534 hosts on any Class B network.

Class C networks use up 24 bits to specify the network number, leaving only 8 bits available to specify hosts. 2^8 = 256 – 2 = 254 hosts on a Class C network.

Private and Public IPv4 Addressing

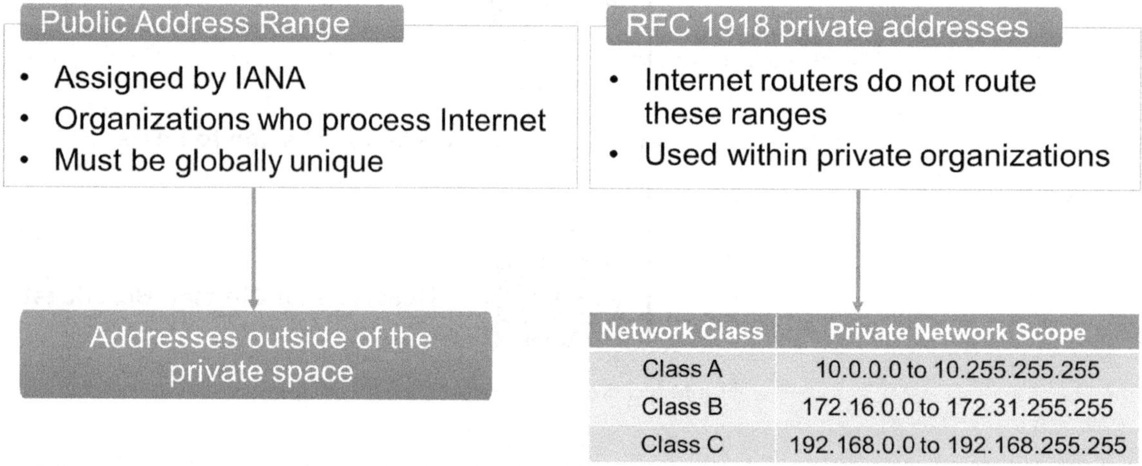

Figure 9-2 Private and Public IPv4 Addressing

In Figure 9-2, the IPv4 addressing scope is divided into private and public addresses. Typically, the public address space is assigned by the Internet Assigned Numbers Authority (IANA), for organizations that need to process packets from the Public Internet (typically Internet Service Providers). This is globally unique address space.

The private address space is defined in the RFC 1918 document published by the IETF organization (https://tools.ietf.org/html/rfc1918). This address space is reserved for private organizations to use within the confines of their organization. Traffic with these addresses should never be sent to the

Internet, nor ever be seen by the Internet. If an Internet router within your ISP sees these as destination IP addresses, they will not route that traffic. It will be discarded because it is not globally unique.

RFC 1918 defines three private address ranges, as shown in Figure 9-2.

Note

If this private traffic cannot be routed on the connected Internet, how do private organizations who use this space connect to the internet? Later you will learn about Network Address Translation (NAT), which solves this issue. NAT converts private addresses into public addresses before forwarding packets to the connected Internet.

Classful Network Disadvantage

Table 9-3 Available Classful Networks and Hosts

Network Class	Network Mask	Available Networks Using Private Scope	Available Hosts
Class A	255.0.0.0	1	16,777,214
Class B	255.255.0.0	16	65,524
Class C	255.255.255.0	256	254

When you deploy a Classful network, you can allocate a fixed number of hosts for each network type in this case, as previously calculated, and shown in Table 9-3. This approach has some disadvantages:

- The fixed host number for each class will unlikely accommodate organizational needs. Suppose that you need a network to allocate 2,000 endpoints. Of course, a Class B network will do the job, but what would you do with the remaining 63,000? They are wasted.
- Classful networks restrict the use of the number of networks and hosts that can be used. Imagine that you must set up 50 networks with 2000 on each network. This is simply not possible since none of the Network classes accomplish this task.

Thankfully, this is only an issue if we use the default network masks shown in Figure 9-3. We can resolve many of these issues by changing the default masks, using a process called subnetting.

Subnetting

Subnetting enables you to break up a single classful network into smaller pieces called subnetworks, or simply, subnets. Thus, you can create logical network numbers to accommodate the physical design of your network infrastructure. The advantages include:

- Smaller broadcast domains: Reduces broadcast overhead, potentially increasing performance.
- Ease of management: You create the number of networks and hosts that you need.

- Flexible network: Addressing can change and grow along with your business.
- Security features are applied easily: You can segment traffic and apply unique security to each subnet.

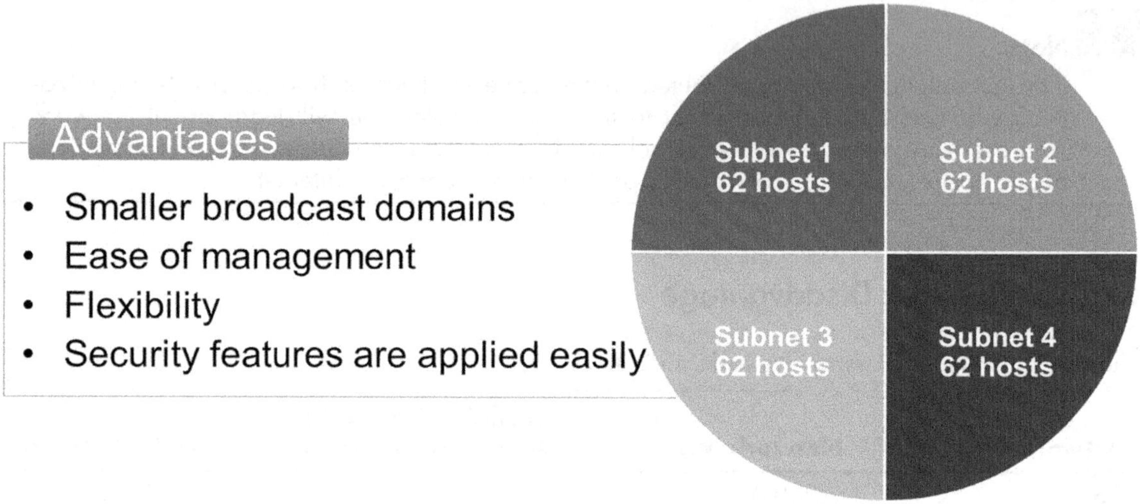

Figure 9-3 Subnetting

Figure 9-3 shows how a single Class C network with 254 hosts is broken up into four subnets, each with 62 hosts. You might notice that 62 times 4 is 248 and we have six missing addresses, those addresses are assigned to the Network and Local Broadcast addresses.

OK, let us explore how this works.

Subnet Masking Using Binary

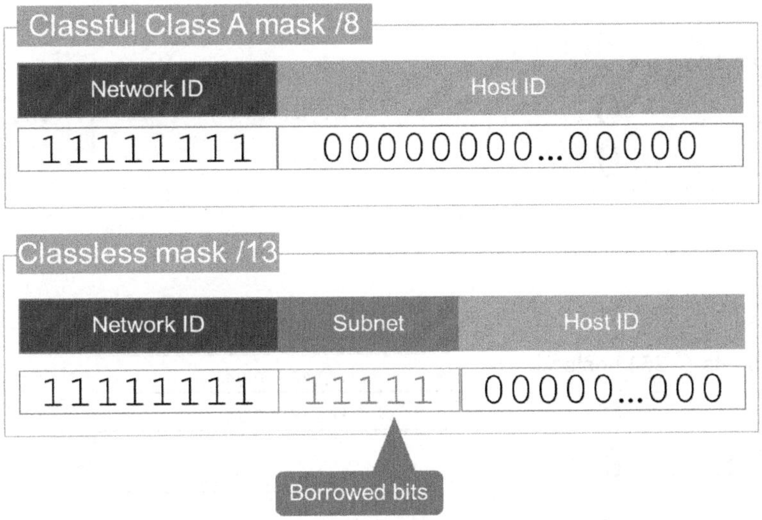

Octet (Decimal)	Octet (Binary)	Number of binary 1s
0	00000000	0
128	10000000	1
192	11000000	2
224	11100000	3
240	11110000	4
248	11111000	5
252	11111100	6
254	11111110	7
255	11111111	8

Figure 9-4 Subnet Masking Using Binary

To accomplish the task of dividing a network, you must use a custom network mask. Figure 9-4 shows borrows borrowing masked bits from the host portion of an IP address to create subnets. This mask is known as the subnet mask. This mask is known as a Classless mask.

Notice that each time that we refer to the term "borrow" it means that the bits must be set to one. Also, a subnet mask follows the same rule as the Network mask, its format is a sequence of ones followed by a block of zeros.

In Chapter 6, we introduced the two notations a Network Mask can have: Dot-decimal and prefix. Understanding subnetting will require for you to quickly convert a mask from one notation to the other.

Class B Subnet Mask Example

Classful

1 network		65,534 hosts	
172.	16.	0.	0
255.	255.	0.	0

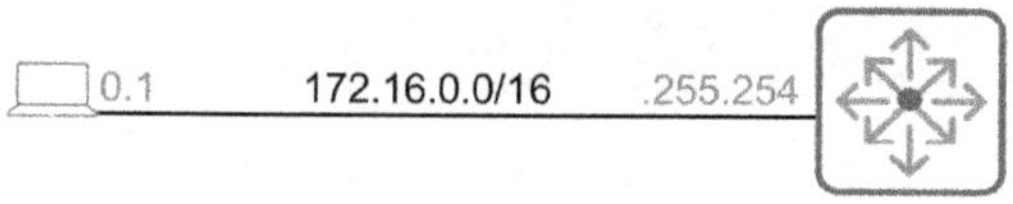

Classless: Borrow host bits for subnets

1 network		254 subnets	254 hosts
172.	16.	x.	0
255.	255.	255.	0

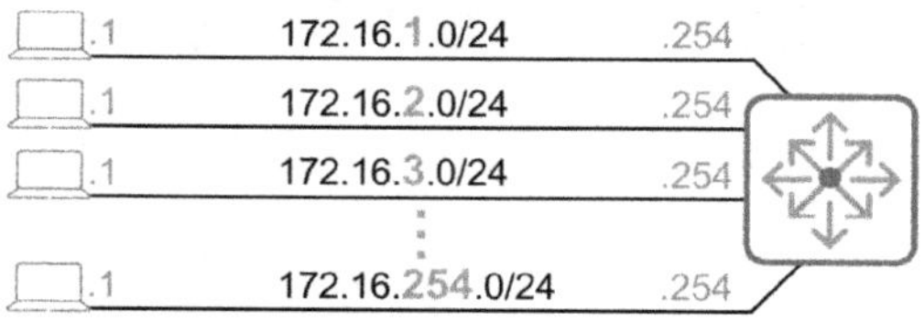

Figure 9-5 Class B Subnet Mask Example

Look at the top example in the figure, which uses the Class B default mask. This means that you can have 1 network, and on that network, you can have 65,534 hosts. The problem is that you have 150 networks, and you never have more than 200 hosts on each network. You might think that you can use 172.17.0.0, 172.18.0.0, up to 172.255.0.0.

You cannot do this because your department has been assigned the 172.16.0.0 address space, while your co-workers have been assigned 172.17.0.0 and 172.18.0.0.

You must therefore customize the network mask. You borrow host bits to create subnetworks, using a subnet mask, as shown in the bottom example.

Now you have Class B network 172.16.0.0, split into 254 subnetworks, 172.16.1.0/24, 172.16.2.0/24, and so on, up to 172.16.255.0/24. You still have 8 bits left over to specify hosts on each subnet. So, each subnet can have 254 hosts, as shown in Figure 9-5.

Note

In this document, the term "Network Mask" specifically refers to a Classful Network. The term "Subnet Mask" refers to a Classless Network (which is a Network using the non-default masks).

Class C Subnet Mask Example

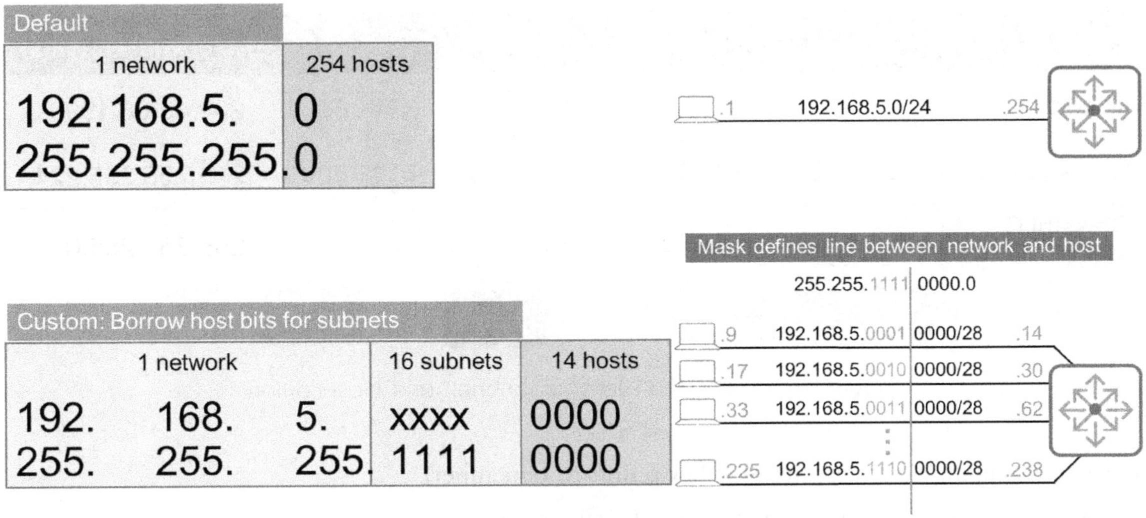

Figure 9-6 Class C Subnet Mask Example

Figure 9-6 shows an identical example to the Class B example, only using a Class C address. To subnet this you must think in binary, at least for the octet that is "split into two" by the subnet mask. The 3rd octet is split into two by the mask in this case, so only that octet is shown in binary, the others are shown in decimal.

The top example in Figure 9-6 uses the default /24 mask for a Class C address, 255.255 .255.0. This means that you can have a single subnet with 254 hosts. However, you have 10 subnets, and each subnet has 12 hosts. You can do the same exact thing you did in the previous example, take host bits to use for subnetting. Thus, we look at the last octet in its binary format.

We stake the first 4 bits of the host portion to use for subnetting, leaving the last 4 bits available for hosts. 2^4 = 16, and so 16 unique numbers can be created with 4 bits, minus the reserved 0000 for the network number, and the reserved 1111 for directed broadcast means you can have 14 hosts.

You also have 16 network numbers. Most modern implementations allow you to use all 16 of them. In some rare cases, some legacy or specialty equipment may have issues with the "all zeros' subnet" or the "all ones' subnet", but they are usually OK to use.

Look at top subnet in the example: 192.168.5.0001 0000/28. that forth octet, 0001000 = 16 in binary. So, the reserved subnetwork number is 192.168.5.0/28. The reserved broadcast is 192.168.5.15. Therefore, assignable host addresses on this subnet end in .1 through .14.

The remaining subnets are similarly addressed. Let us look at this in a bit more detail.

Finding the Network, Subnet, and Host Portion

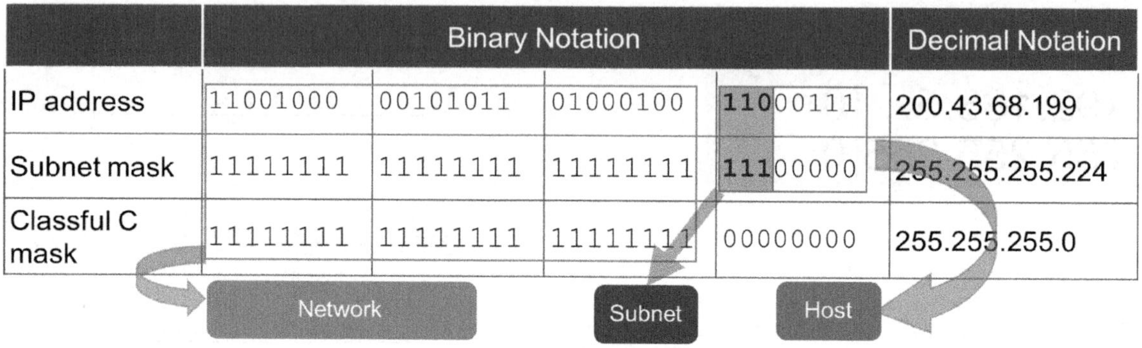

Figure 9-7 Finding the Network, Subnet, and Host Portion

Looking at Figure 9-7, there are some key points to remember:

- The Network part is always defined by the Classful Network mask (not the subnet mask).
- The Host part is always defined by the zeros in the subnet mask.

As an example, consider the following IP and Subnet mask broken down in Figure 9-7: 200.43.68.100/25. To understand the process this explanation will use the Binary notation.

- The first step is to convert the IP address and the subnet mask into its binary form.
- The network side is always obtained from the Classful Mask. In this case since the IP address is a Class C network, the first 24 bits will represent the Network side.
- To obtain the Host side this is simply the bits in the subnet mask that are set to zero. In this example those bits are the last seven.
- Finally, the Subnet side is what is not Network or Host, this is simply the bit 25.

Subnetting and Network Design

Designing with subnets

- Plan when and where routing will be placed.
- Determine the number of broadcast domains (subnets).
- Determine the number of host per subnet.

Formulas:

- **Number of subnets = 2^s**, where **s** represents the number of bits borrowed.
- **Number of hosts per subnet = 2^h-2**, where **h** is the number of binary bits used in the host portion.

Figure 9-8 Subnetting and Network Design

Subnetting has an important implication for network administrators because it helps to design broadcast domains. This dictates where and when routing must be done (Figure 9-8).

Subnetting is typically based on the number of Subnets needed and the number of Hosts per subnet that are required. To determine this information, two formulas can be used:

- Number of subnets = 2^s, where **s** represents the number of bits borrowed.
- Number of hosts per subnet = 2^h-2, where **h** is the number of binary bits used in the host portion.

Note

Remember that we need to subtract the 2 addresses because those are reserved to the Network ID and to the Local Broadcast address.

Subnetting Design Example

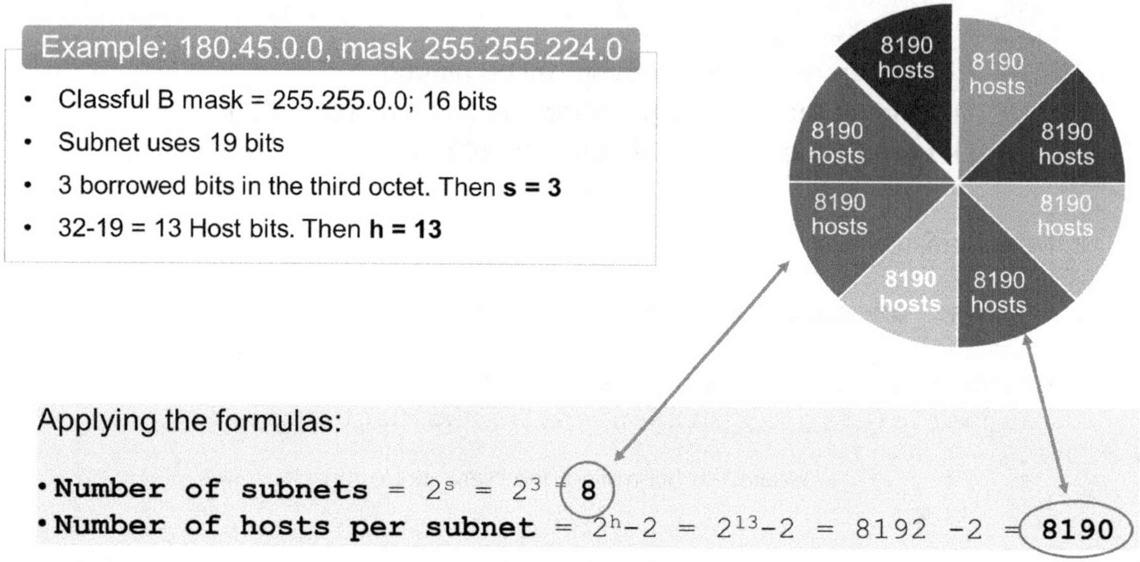

Figure 9-9 Subnetting Design Example

As an example (Figure 9-9) consider the Class B network, 180.45.0.0 with a subnet mask of 255.255.224.0. From this information you can determine the following:

- The classful mask for a class B is 16 bits.
- The subnet mask uses 19 bits.
- There are three borrow bits in the third octet. Then s = 3.
- Host part is determined by a simple subtraction. Host = 32 – bits set to 1. In this case 13. Therefore h = 13.

We can now apply the two formulas:

- Number of subnets = 2^3 = 8.

The number of hosts that these subnets can use depends on the reminder zeros in the subnet mask, in this case we have 21 zeros.

- Number of hosts per subnet = 2^{13}-2 = 8192 – 2 = 8190.

Subnetting Tasks

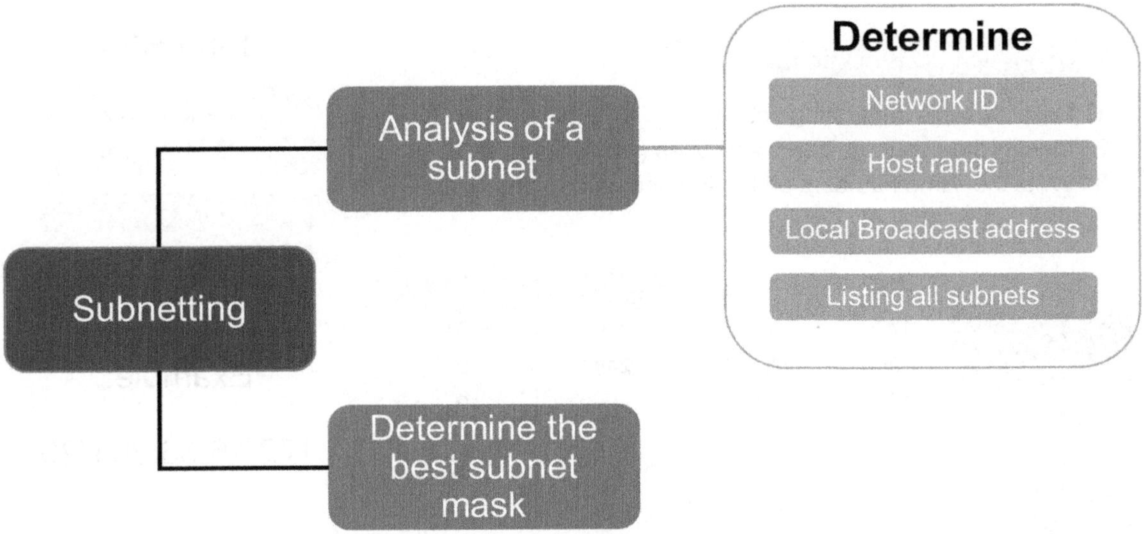

Figure 9-10 Subnetting Task

The analysis of the subnet requires that you determine the following:

- The Network address or Network ID (obtain to what network an IP belongs).
- The Local Broadcast address.
- Assignable range of addresses to hosts.
- Listing the subnets (optional) (Figure 9-10).

Note

Decimal and Binary approaches can be used to determine the previous parameter; however in real life the Binary approach is not common to be used since it takes more time. This training then considers the analysis using only the decimal notation.

Defining what would be the best subnet mask that suites an organization's need is based on the number of host and networks.

Subnet Analysis Introduction

Determine the subnet address

1. Create a table separating octets.
2. Identify the octet with zeros and ones (**working** octet)
3. Write the same numbers on the left and zero to the right.

	1	2	3	4
IP address	172	16	53	201
Subnet mask	255	255	**240**	0
Network ID	172	16		0
1st address				
Last address				
Broadcast address				

Determine

- Network ID
- First address
- Last address
- Broadcast address

Example:

172.16.53.201/20

Figure 9-11 Subnet Analysis Introduction

Determining the Subnet address

As an example, consider the following IP and mask: 172.16.53.201/20 (Figure 9-11).

Steps

1. First create a simple table where you can separate the different octets and write down the IP address and the network mask.
2. Identify the octet with zeros and ones. This octet will require all our attention. In this case a quick analysis of the subnet mask (the octet that is not 255 or 0) indicates that the third octet is the one that meets this criterion. This will be our working octet.
3. Write down the same numbers of the IP address on the left octets of the working octet. And write a zero on the right octets of the working octet.

Subnet Analysis

4. In the **working** octet determine the increment number.

```
Increment = 2z, where z is the number of 0s in
the working octet.
```

Example.

- 240 equals to 11110000
- Increment = 2^4 = 16

	1	2	3	4
IP address	172	16	53	201
Subnet mask	255	255	**240**	0
Network ID	172	16		0
1st address				
Last address				
Broadcast address				

Determine

- Network ID
- First address
- Last address
- Broadcast address

Example:

172.16.53.201/20

Figure 9-12 Subnet Analysis Step 4

4. In the working octet, determine the increment number. This number is determined with the formula:

Increment = 2z, where **z** equals the number of zeros in the working octet. In this case the third octet has four zeros on it, which implies that the increment is 16 (2^4) (Figure 9-12).

5. Find a multiple of the increment number (**closest but not greater**)

Multiple	Increment value
1	16
2	32
3	**48**

	1	2	3	4
IP address	172	16	53	201
Subnet mask	255	255	**240**	0
Network ID	172	16	48	0
1st address				
Last address				
Broadcast address				

Determine

- Network ID
- First address
- Last address
- Broadcast address

Example:

172.16.53.201/20

Figure 9-13 Subnet Analysis Step 5

5. Find a multiple of the increment number that is closest to but not greater than the IP address's working octet value. And write down the value in the working octet.

In this example the multiple that is closest to the IP is 48 (Figure 9-13).

Determining the First Address in the Subnet

Rule for the 1st available address

```
First address = Subnet address + 1
```

Example:
First address = 172.16.48.0 + 1 = 172.16.48.1

	1	2	3	4
IP address	172	16	53	201
Subnet mask	255	255	**240**	0
Network ID	172	16	48	0
1st address	172	16	48	1
Last address				
Broadcast address				

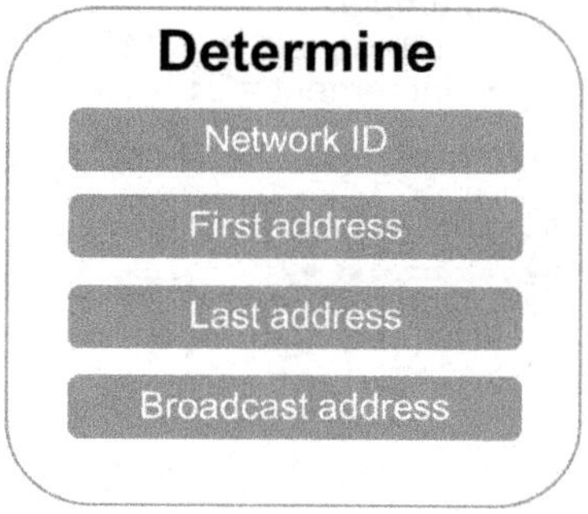

Example:

172.16.53.201/20

Figure 9-14 First Address in the Subnet

Use the following rule for the first address.

First address = Subnet address + 1.

In the example: First address = 172.16.48.0 + 1 = 172.16.48.1 (Figure 9-14).

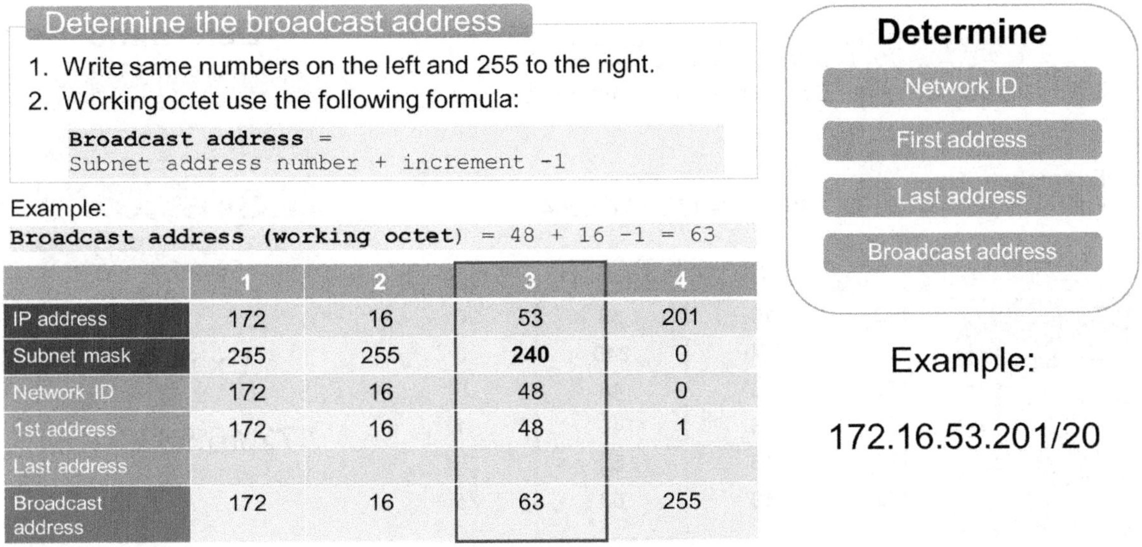

Figure 9-15 Determining the Broadcast Address

Determining the Broadcast Address

1. Write down the same numbers of the IP address on the left octets of the working octet and write a 255 on the right octets of the working octet.

2. For the working octet follow the next formula:

Broadcast address (working octet) = Number of the Subnet address in the working octet + increment – 1.

In the example using Figure 9-15:

Working octet in broadcast address = 48 + 16 -1 = 63.

Determining the Last Address in the Subnet

Rule for last available address

```
Last address = Broadcast address - 1
```

Example:
Last address = 172.16.63.255 - 1 = 172.16.63.254

	1	2	3	4
IP address	172	16	53	201
Subnet mask	255	255	**240**	0
Network ID	172	16	48	0
1st address	172	16	48	1
Last address	172	16	63	254
Broadcast address	172	16	63	255

Determine

- Network ID
- First address
- Last address
- Broadcast address

Example:

172.16.53.201/20

Figure 9-16 Determining the Last Address in the Subnet

1. Use the following formula:

Last address = Broadcast address – 1.

In the example shown in Figure 9-16: Last assignable address = 172.16.63.255 - 1 = 172.16.63.254.

Listing the Available Subnets

Process

- Based on the increment number.
- Use the following formula:

  Total number of subnets = $2^{\#\_of\_ones\_in\_working\_octet}$

Given 172.16.53.201/20, list all possible subnets

1. Analysis of the IP address and subnet:
   - IP address is a Class B address.
   - Working octet is third one.
   - Increment number is 16.
2. Total number of subnets:

   Total number of subnets = 2^4 = 16

Figure 9-17 Available Subnets

Listing all subnets that are available is based on the increment number. To know how many networks will be generated you can use the following formula:

Total number of subnets = $2^{\#\_of\_ones}$

The process is explained in the following example:

From the following IP address and mask list all possible subnets 172.16.53.201/20 (Figure 9-17).

Steps

1. From the previous section we know the following information:
    a. The IP address is a Class B address.
    b. The Increment number is 16.
    c. The Working octet is the third one.
2. Total number of subnets is $2^4 = 16$.

3. Write classful network as the first subnet.
4. Add the **increment** number to the working octet.
5. Repeat the previous step to list all networks.

	1	2	3	4
IP address	172	16	53	201
Subnet mask	255	255	240	0
Classful network	172	16	0	0
Next subnet	172	16	**16**	0

Subnet	Network address
1	172.16.0.0
2	172.16.16.0
3	172.16.32.0
...	

Subnet	Network address
...	
14	172.16.208.0
15	172.16.224.0
16	172.16.240.0

Figure 9-18 Available Subnets Continued

3. To define the first network simply write down the Classful network.
4. To obtain the next Network address, add the increment number to the working octet of the first subnet.
5. Repeat the previous step to obtain the rest of the addresses (Figure 9-18).

Determining the Best Mask

We now discuss how to determine the best mask that suites your organizational needs using Figure 9-19.

Example

XYZ Corp uses network 172.20.0.0 and requires:

- 50 subnets, with 40 hosts on each subnet

1. Determine subnet bits

Number of subnets <= 2^s, where **s** represents the number of bits borrowed.

Example: $50 <= 2^6$
$50 <= 64$

2. Determine host bits.

Number of hosts per subnet <= 2^h-2

Example: $40 <= 2^6-2$
$40 <= 62$

Figure 9-19 Determining the Best Mask

Suppose that an organization uses Class B network 172.20.0.0, which must be divided into 50 subnets. Each subnet must accommodate at least 40 hosts. This number considers the future growth for the next 5 years. Here is the process:

1. Determine how many subnet bits permit 50 subnets. You can use the following formula: Number of subnets <= 2^s

In this case we are using the formula in the inverse way: 50 <= 2^s. The best way to solve this equation is to replace **s** with different values and find which value is equal or greater than 50. In this case the result is 6, because 2^6 is 64.

In this case the number of bits borrowed from the host portion of the address is 6.

2. Determine how many host bits will be required to allocate the need. Use the formula: Number of hosts per subnet <= 2^h-2.

In this case we are using the formula in the inverse way: 40 <= 2^h-2. The best way to solve this equation is to replace **h** with different values. In this case the result is 6, because 2^6 is 64.

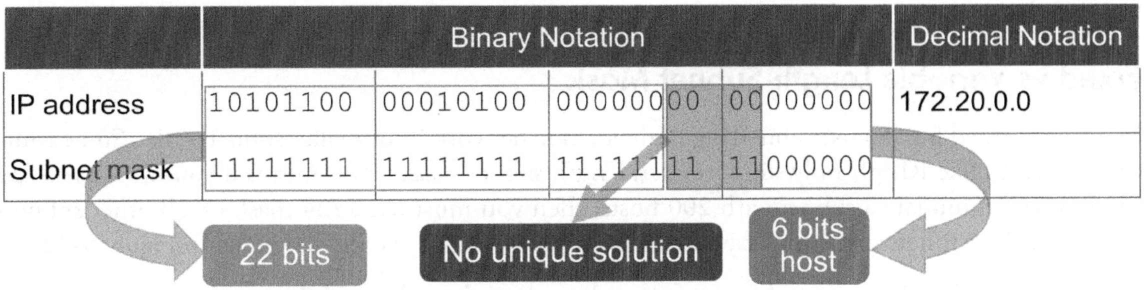

Figure 9-20 Determining the Mask Conclusion

From the previous results we can conclude the following:

- Since is a Class B address the network mask is 16 bits set to 1.
- We will need 6 borrow bits.
- We will need 6 host bits (Figure 9-20).

Now, you may wonder, what about the rest of the bits? How can we use them? This example simply does not have a unique answer that meets the original requirement. Let us continue to see how this plays out.

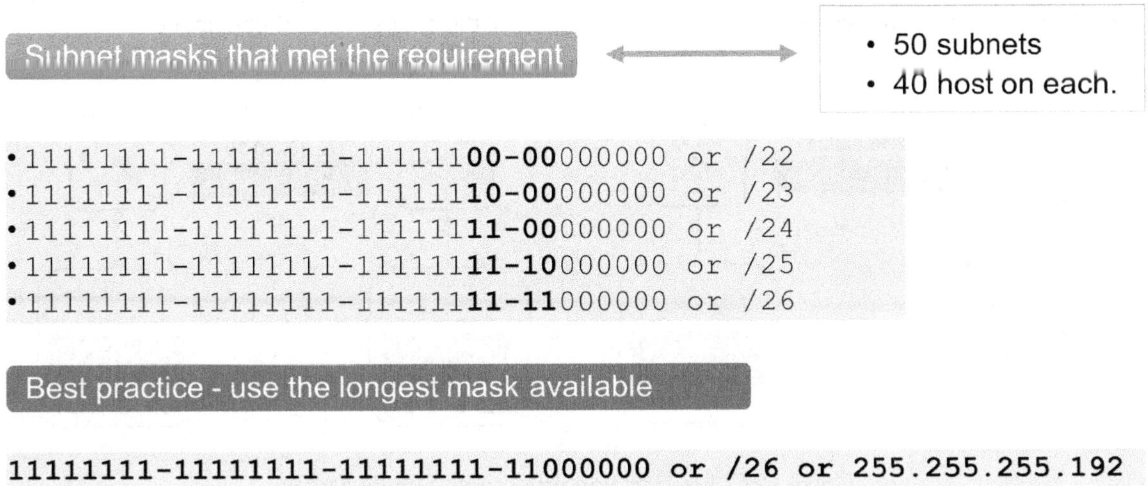

Figure 9-21 Subnet Mask that Meets Requirements

In case you run into this situation the best practice is to use the subnet mask that uses the longest number of bits set to one. In this case the subnet mask /26 would be the recommended answer (Figure 9-21).

VLSM and CIDR

Fixed vs Variable Length Subnet Mask

You have learned how to use subnetting to divide one network into smaller subnetworks. Some routing protocols, like RIPv1, only support fixed length subnet masks. This means if you must use a /24 mask to accommodate a subnet with 200 hosts, then you must use a /24 mask on all other subnets of the 172.16.0.0 network. This Fixed Length Subnet Masking (FLSM) is shown in Figure 9-22.

What a waste of address space. Many of the other networks only need 25 hosts, but the /24 mask means that those subnets can accommodate 254 hosts, over 200 IP addresses are wasted, never to be used. This is even worse on the point-to-point links between switches. These subnets will never need more than two IP addresses. One router has IP address 172.16.0.1, and the other has 172.16.0.2. The other 252 addresses are wasted. Because of RIPv1's FLSM requirement, you have used up subnets 172.16.1.0/24 – 172.16.5.0/24.

More sophisticated protocols like OSPF support Variable Length Subnet Masking (VLSM). Although one or more subnets may require a /24 mask to accommodate 200 hosts, you remain free to use different masks in the 172.16.0.0 address space.

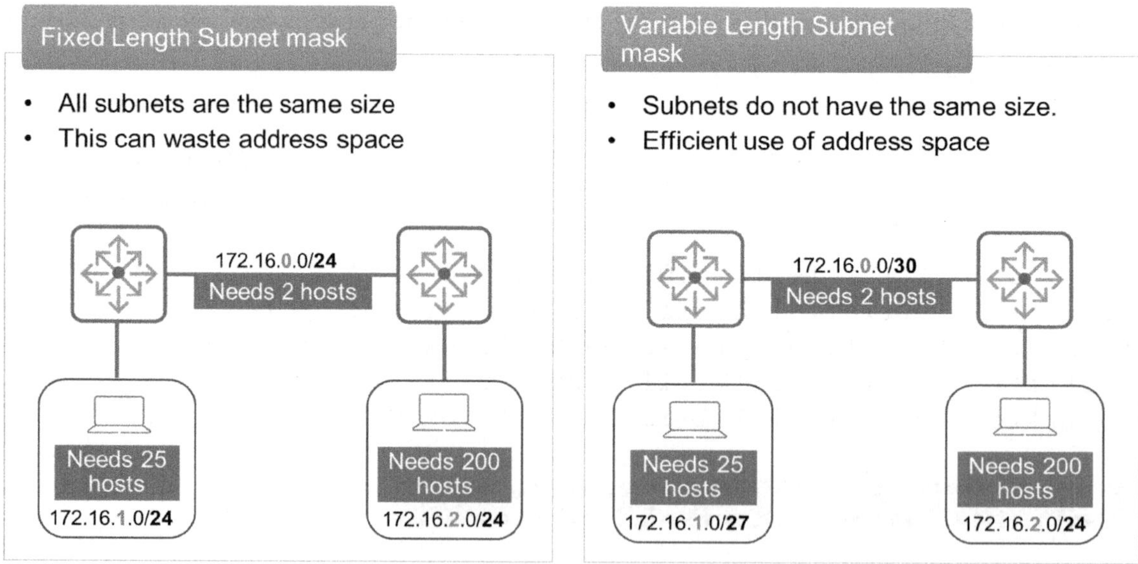

Figure 9-22 Fixed vs Variable Length Subnet Mask

In Figure 9-22, the bottom, right subnet must support 200 hosts, so you assign 172.16.2.0/24. Now, to accommodate the subnet with 25 hosts, you create subnets 172.16.1.0/27. Each can accommodate up to 30 hosts, and you still have subnets 172.16.1.32/27, 172.16.1.64, 172.16.1.96/27, 172.16.1.128/27, 172.16.1.160/27, 172.16.1.192/27 and 172.16.1.224/27 available for future growth.

To accommodate the point-to-point link, you create 172.16.0.0/30 again with plenty of subnets remaining for future growth. As you can see, this is far more efficient than FLSM. The only disadvantage of VLSM is that it requires you to think in binary, but you will soon master that anyway. Let us explore this concept further and show how you can derive network designs like this on your own.

VSLM Example

An example can help us to fully understand how VLSM can be used. In this case we have a network with the following requirements in Figure 9-23:

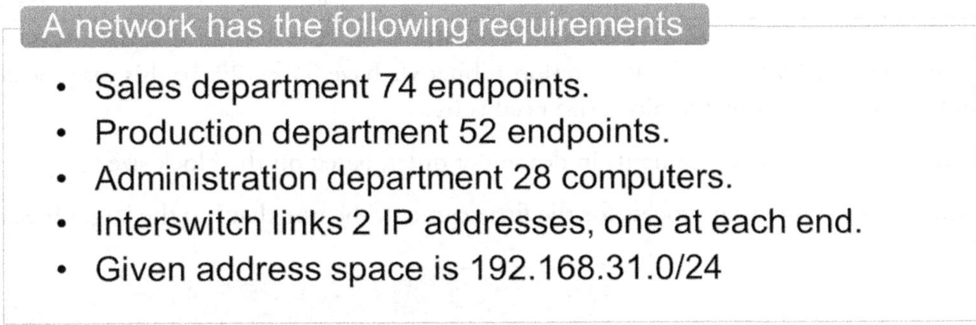

Figure 9-23 Network Requirements Example

Step by Step VLSM Subnetting

1. Consider the **real requirement**, including the reserved subnet and broadcast addresses. This number is obtained adding 2 to the Host requirement (Subnet address and the Local Broadcast address).
2. Select the appropriate block size. This number can be obtained from the formula.

Real requirement <= 2^h, where **h** is the number of hosts.

Note

You must select the highest value of **h** where the formula is true.

Table 9-4 VLSM Example

Segment	Host requirement	Real requirement (Subnet and Broadcast addresses	Block size
Sales	74	76	$2^7 = 128$
Production	52	54	$2^6 = 64$
Administration	28	30	$2^5 = 32$
Link1	2	4	$2^2 = 4$
Link2	2	4	$2^2 = 4$
Link3	2	4	$2^2 = 4$

In this case shown in Table 9-4, for Production subnet we have $54 <= 2^h$. In this case the answer is **h** = 6, and $2^6 = 64$. Therefore, the block size need is 64.

3. The next step is arranging segments in descender order, based on the block size.
4. Do the normal subnetting process for the first segment, the one that has the larger block size.

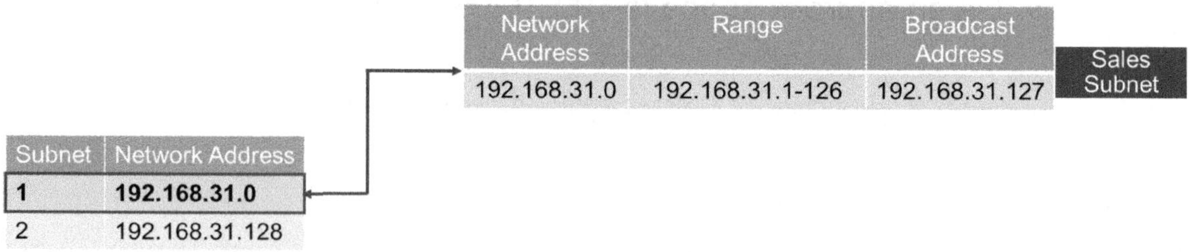

Figure 9-24 VLSM /25 Example

Analyzing the host needs in Figure 9-24, we can conclude that a /25 subnet mask is needed to allocate 126 endpoints. Notice that this subnet mask will divide the original network into 2 subnets. The first one can serve the Sales department needs and the second one becomes the subnet that will be divided to serve the next block size.

5. Apply the subnetting process for the next block size. The production department in this case.

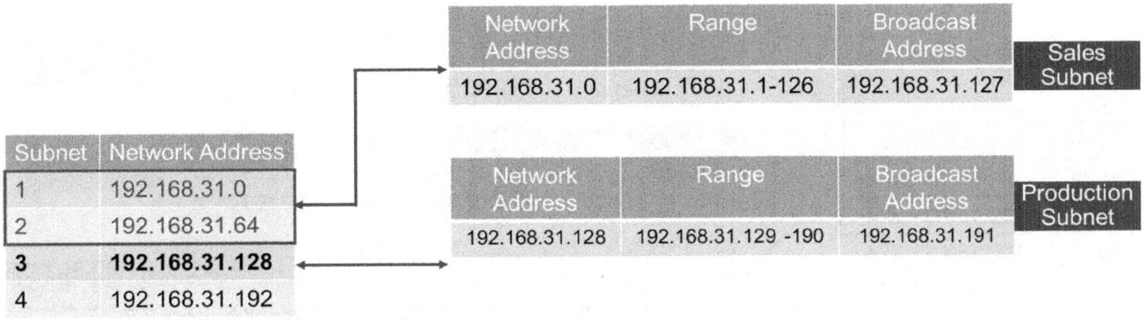

Figure 9-25 VLSM /26 Example

Analyzing the host count needed in Figure 9-25, we can conclude that a /26 network mask is required to accommodate 62 hosts. Using this subnet mask, it divides the original network into four different subnets. The first two subnets have been used by the previous department. So, we must start using the third one.

6. Apply the subnetting process for the next block size. The administrative department in this case.

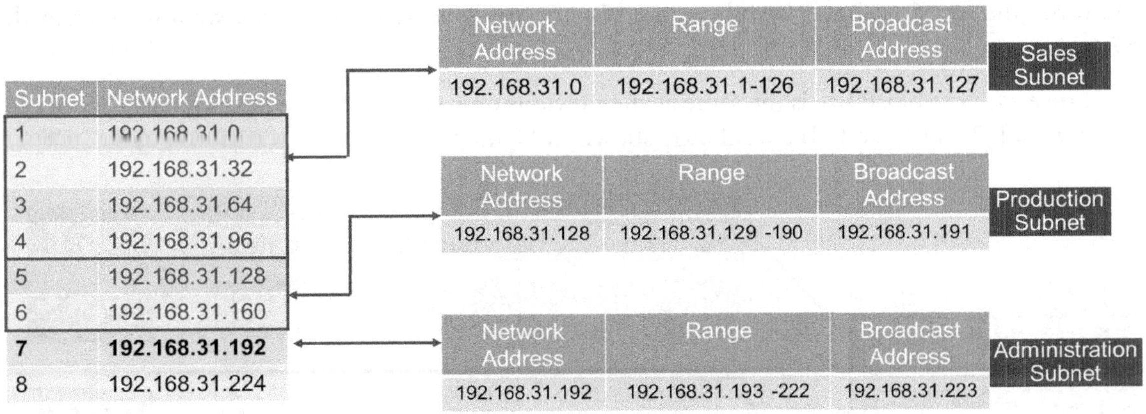

Figure 9-26 VLSM /27 Example

Analyzing the requirements in Figure 9-26, we conclude that a /27 network mask is needed to accommodate 30 hosts. Using this subnet mask, it divides the original network into eight subnets. However, the first two subnets have been used by the previous department. So, we must start at the seventh one for this use case.

7. Apply the subnetting process for the next block size, Link 1 in this case.

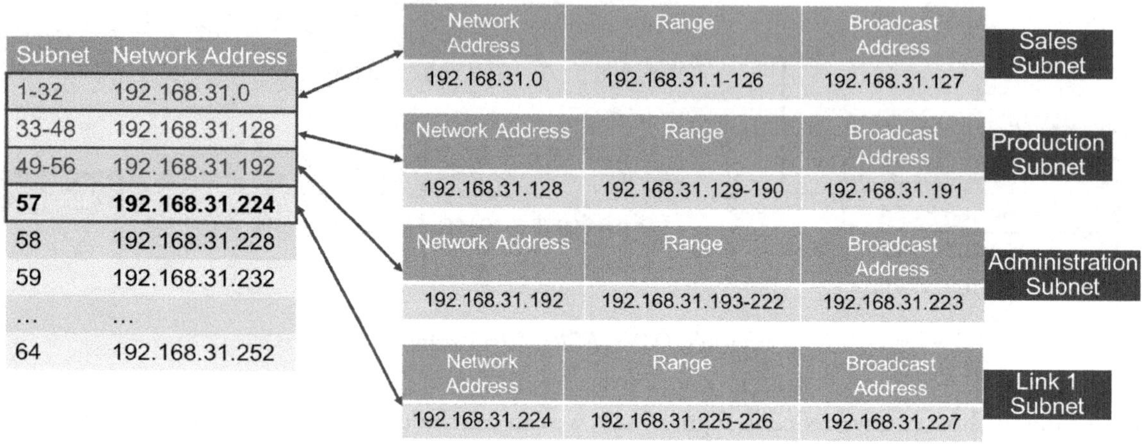

Figure 9-27 VLSM /30 Example

Analyzing the requirements in Figure 9-27, we conclude that a /30 network mask is needed to accommodate 2 hosts. Using this subnet mask, it divides the original Network into 64 different subnets. However, the first 56 subnets have been used by the previous department. So, we must start at the 57th one.

8. Since the next block size is the same as the previous one, simply use the next available subnet for the Link 2 and Link 3. The results are shown in Figure 9-28.

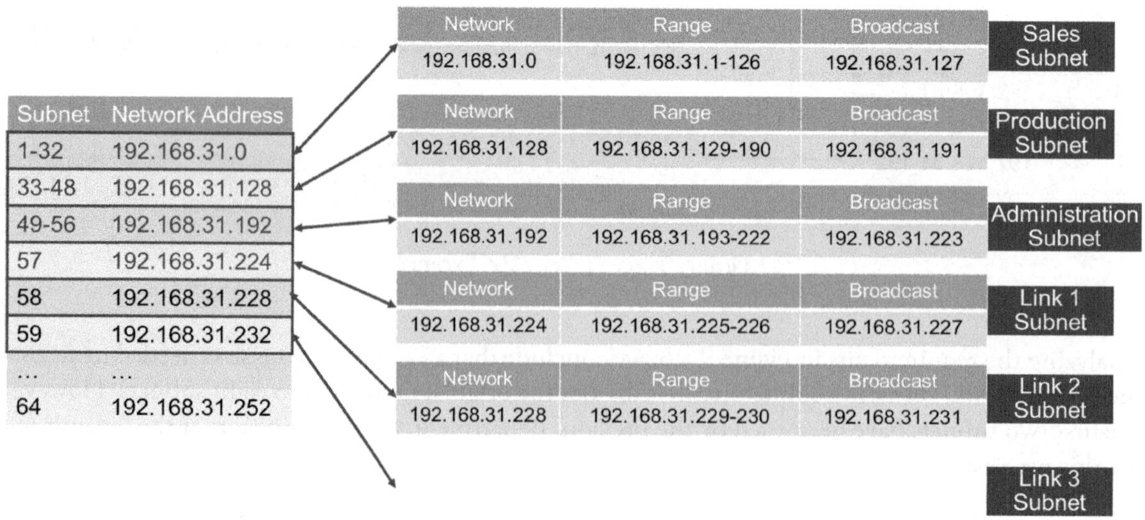

Figure 9-28 VLSM /30 Example Continued

Classless Inter-Domain Routing Introduction

CIDR is a method for allocating IP addresses and IP routing that replaces the previous architecture of Classful network design. CIDR standardizes the use of an IP address/subnet mask notation that we have already discussed in this module. CIDR also helps to aggregate routes to make a more efficient network.

You have learned how to divide a network address space into subnets to allocate organization's needs. The ability to break up one network into multiple subnets has great advantages for you as a design or administrative expert, and for the network. However, from the router's perspective, some new inefficiencies arise. Now they must store each individual subnet as a separate entity in their routing tables, and in their topology databases. This can use memory, processing, and bandwidth. It is not very efficient, especially when the next hop for all those subnets is the same device. The individual subnets are maintained, but several entries can be grouped into a single, unique entry that summarizes all individual entries.

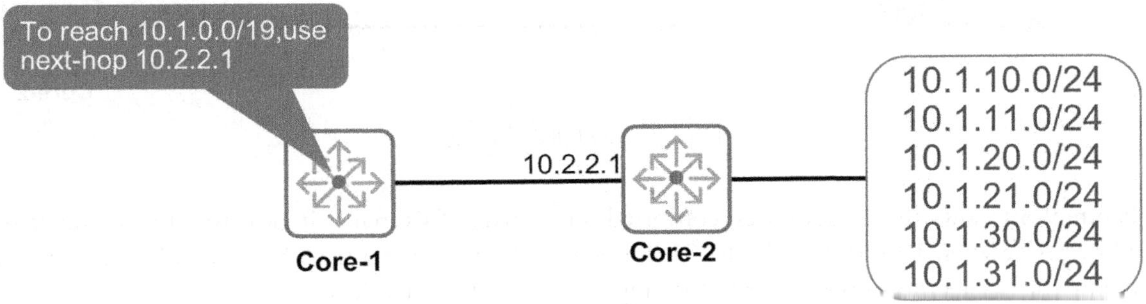

Figure 9-29 CIDR

Figure 9-29 shows a scenario where Core-2 has six subnets, which you have recently created. Without CIDR implemented in Core-1, each individual network will be listed as an entry in the Routing table. So, six entries in Core-2 means six entries in Core-1. Six hundred entries in Core-2 means 600 entries in Core-1.

Instead, your routers can evaluate the common bits among these addresses and perform a route summarization.

CIDR Example

Subnet	Binary Notation				Decimal Notation
Subnet 1	00001010	00000001	00001010	00000000	10.1.10.0
Subnet 2	00001010	00000001	00001011	00000000	10.1.11.0
Subnet 3	00001010	00000001	00010100	00000000	10.1.20.0
Subnet 4	00001010	00000001	00010101	00000000	10.1.21.0
Subnet 5	00001010	00000001	00011110	00000000	10.1.30.0
Subnet 6	00001010	00000001	00011111	00000000	10.1.31.0

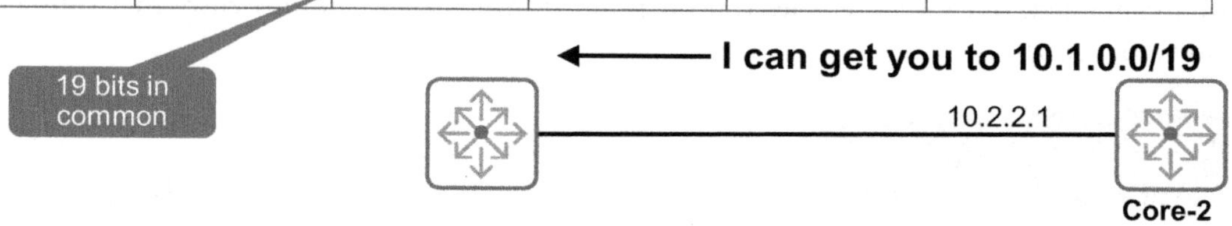

Figure 9-30 CIDR Example

Figure 9-30 shows the six addresses, converted into binary. This makes it clear that for the range of addresses between 10.1.10.0 and 10.1.31.0, the first 19 bits are identical. States another way, if you ignore the last 13 bits of the address, this range of addresses is identical.

This means that Core-2 can perform this calculation, and instead of advertising six addresses with a /24 mask, it advertises one address with a /19 mask as 10.1.0.0/19. Understand that routing has not changed. The individual subnets still exist on Core-2. Core-2 is simply summarizing what it says to Core-1. Core-2 is saying, "if you need to route a packet to any destination where the first 19 bits match the pattern 00001010.00000001.000, just send those packets to me."

Note

CIDR implicitly uses VLSM when summarization takes place in a router or multilayer switch. Not all the entries in routing tables on these devices will have the same subnet mask.

Lab 9: Subnetting and VLSM

Overview

BigStartup has plans to expand the network starting with the acquisition of Internet links from two different carriers, followed by adding a Server Switch, and investing in an Aruba Instant Solution.

You have been asked to interconnect the Core Switches with a Perimeter firewall pair that will connect to these ISP links, using non-/24 prefixes. They also want you to reserve two IP segments for connections to the Server Switch and another one for hosting up to 500 WiFi clients. Therefore, you have decided to review and practice subnetting before jumping into any configuration.

Note: References to equipment and commands are taken from Aruba's hosted remote lab. These are shown for demonstration purposes in case you wish to replicate the environment and tasks on your own equipment.

Objectives

After completing this lab, you will be able to:

- Subnet Class A, B and C networks into smaller IP segments.
- Calculate the total number of networks and hosts that a subnet process generates.
- Identify the Network ID and broadcast IP of a Subnet.
- Identify assignable IP address in a particular Subnet.

Task 1: Class A Subnetting

Objectives

Subnet the prefix using the information below:

Network Address: **43.0.0.0**

Number of needed Subnets: **9**

Steps

1. List all subnets in Table 9-5 down below.

   What is the address class? ____________________

   What is the default subnet mask? ____________________

   What is the required subnet mask? ____________________

   How many subnets will be generated with equal length subnet mask? ____________________

   What is the total number of assignable addresses per subnet? ____________________

   How many bits were borrowed from the host portion in the default mask for creating subnets? ____________________

Table 9-5 Subnetting Task 1

Subnet #	Network Identifier	First Assignable Address	Last Assignable Address	Broadcast Address
Subnet 0				
Subnet 1				
Subnet 2				
Subnet 3				
Subnet 4				
Subnet 5				
Subnet 6				
Subnet 7				
Subnet 8				

Task 2: Class B Subnetting

Objectives

Subnet the prefix using the information below:

IP Address: **132.89.5.10**.

Number of needed Subnets: **20**.

Steps

1. List all subnets in Table 9-6 down below.

   What network does the address belong to? ____________________

   What is the address class? ____________________

   What is the default subnet mask? ____________________

   What is the required subnet mask? ____________________

   How many subnets will be generated with equal length subnet mask? ____________________

   How many bits were borrowed from the host portion in the default mask for creating subnets?____________________

Table 9-6 Subnetting Task 1

Subnet #	Network Identifier	First Assignable Address	Last Assignable Address	Broadcast Address
Subnet 0				
Subnet 1				
Subnet 2				
Subnet 3				
Subnet 4				
Subnet 5				
Subnet 6				
Subnet 7				
Subnet 8				
Subnet 9				
Subnet 10				
Subnet 11				
Subnet 12				
Subnet 13				
Subnet 14				
Subnet 15				
Subnet 16				
Subnet 17				
Subnet 18				
Subnet 19				

Task 3a: Class C Subnetting Part 1

Objectives

Subnet the prefix using the information below:

Network Address: **192.168.1.0**.

Number of needed assignable host addresses: **2**.

Steps

2. List the first 4 subnets and the last one in Table 9-7

   What is the address class? ____________________

   What is the default subnet mask? ____________________

   What is the required subnet mask? ____________________

   How many subnets will be generated with equal length subnet mask? ____________________

   What is the total number of assignable addresses per subnet? ____________________

   How many bits were borrowed from the host portion in the default mask for creating subnets? ____________________

Table 9-7 Subnetting Task 3

Subnet #	Network Identifier	First Assignable Address	Last Assignable Address	Broadcast Address
Subnet 0				
Subnet 1				
Subnet 2				
Subnet 3				
Subnet 4				

Task 4a: VLSM Prefixes

Objectives

Subnet the prefix using the information below:

Network Address: **10.0.0.0**.

Number of needed assignable host addresses: **254**.

Steps

3. List 1st, 2nd, 3rd, 21st, 22nd, and the 101st subnets in Table 9-8 down below

   What is the address class? ____________________

   What is the default subnet mask? ____________________

   What is the required subnet mask? ____________________

   How many subnets will be generated with equal length subnet mask? ____________________

   What is the total number of assignable addresses per subnet? ____________________

   How many bits were borrowed from the host portion in the default mask for creating subnets? ____________________

Table 9-8 Subnetting Task 4a

Subnet #	Network Identifier	First Assignable Address	Last Assignable Address	Broadcast Address
Subnet 0				
Subnet 1				
Subnet 2				
Subnet 20				
Subnet 21				
Subnet 100				

Task 4b: VLSM — Point to Point Segments

Objectives

Subnet the prefix using the information below:

Take the first /24 subnet of exercise 4a and subnet it again with segments that support up to 2 assignable addresses.

Steps

1. List the first 5 subnets in Table 9-9.

   What is the required subnet mask? ____________________

   How many bits were borrowed from the host portion in the default mask for creating subnets?____________________

Table 9-9 Subnetting Task 4b

Subnet #	Network Identifier	First Assignable Address	Last Assignable Address	Broadcast Address
Subnet 0				
Subnet 1				
Subnet 2				
Subnet 3				
Subnet 4				

IMPORTANT

It is always a best practice to deploy a /30 prefix when the segment will be used on a link (physical or virtual) that only interconnects two Layer-3 devices; for example ethernet links between two routers or multilayer switches, GRE tunnels, and serial links.

You have completed Lab 9!

Learning Check

Chapter 9 Questions

IPv4 Address Classes, Reserved Addresses, Private, and Public IPv4 Addressing

1. Which statements are true about classful IP addressing?
   a. Class A addresses support more networks and more hosts than Class C addresses.
   b. If you must support 255 hosts on a single network, you can use a Class C address.
   c. Your ISP's routers will analyze the network portion of destination address 172.16.3.7, and route that packet toward its destination.
   d. Public address ranges are globally unique.

Class B Subnet Masking Example

2. You are using a /24 subnet mask with the Class B address 172.20.0.0. Which options describe a valid result of this scenario?
   a. You cannot do this. Class B addresses use a /16 mask.
   b. You can assign addresses to over 200 networks.
   c. Each subnet can support 65,534 hosts.
   d. If you must support more than 300 subnets, you must choose a different mask.

VLSM Example, CIDR Example

3. Which statements below are true?
   a. Given address 172.20.66.5/19, the subnet is 172.20.64.0.
   b. Subnetting a Class A address will increase the number of possible host addresses.
   c. Given address 10.1.187.5/16, this scheme allows for a total of 65,534 hosts on the subnet.
   d. When you use CIDR to aggregate a group of routes, assigned IP addresses are modified.

10 IP Routing - Part 3

EXAM OBJECTIVES

- ✓ Describe the operation and use of route types and Administrative Distance
- ✓ Explain Layer-3 scalability issues
- ✓ Routing Protocols
- ✓ Distance vector routing protocols
- ✓ Link-state routing protocols

Overview

In this module, you will learn about Route types, how a router can learn about the same path from different sources, and then use Administrative Distance to choose the most trustworthy source. Next you will learn to apply this knowledge with a technique known as floating static routes, before exploring some Layer-3 scalability issues

You will learn about the routing protocols that help to scale the routing solution. You will also know the difference between distance vector and link-state routing protocols.

Finally, a lab activity will give you more experience with these concepts.

Route Types and Administrative Distance

Route Types in AOS-CX

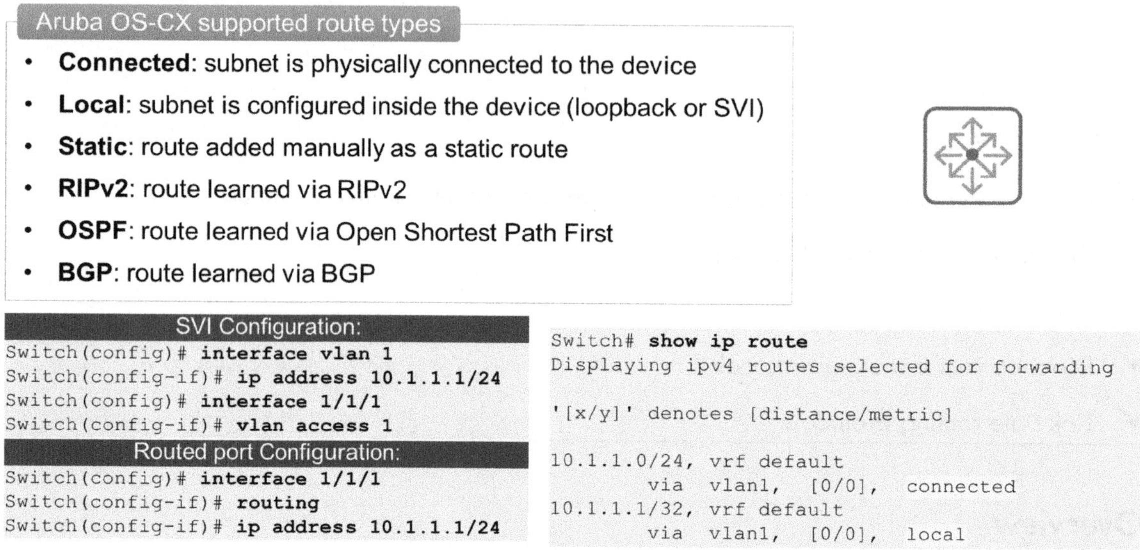

Figure 10-1 Route Types in AOS-CX

You learned about the IP routing table in module 6, and that a routing device makes Layer-3 forwarding decisions based on the best-path entries in this table. The entries in the routing table are populated manually or through a routing protocol. See Figure 10-1 for the different route types.

Connected and Local entries

Consider the following configuration, where the Switching Virtual Interface (SVI) for VLAN1 receives an IP address and port 1/1/1 is assigned to VLAN 1.

```
Switch(config)# interface vlan 1
Switch(config-if)# ip address 10.1.1.1/24
Switch(config)# interface 1/1/1
Switch(config-if)# no routing
Switch(config-if)# vlan access 1
```

This configuration generates some entries in the routing table. You can verify it using the **show IP route** command.

An example of the output is shown in Figure 10-1 where you can see that two entries are created in the routing table. The first entry is listed as 10.1.1.0/24 and is a connected type route. This entry means that the Subnet is available physically connected to the switch and there is no need for a next hop device.

The second entry is listed as 10.1.1.1/32 and is a local type route. This entry means that the IP address that was previously configured is available for the routing process inside the switch. This could be a loopback interface, or as shown here; a Switch Virtual Interface (SVI) for VLAN 1.

Note

You may notice that the local entry uses a /32 subnet mask. This is a special mask that indicates that subnetting cannot happen (no divisions are permitted) in the address space provided. This mask is useful to refer to individual hosts. In this case only one IP address is permitted to be configured in the SVI.

Static Routes

You need a static route when the destination network is not directly or physically connected to the switch or router, and no routing protocols like OSPF are advertising that route. In this case, you manually define the destination network and the next hop in the path. The next hop path must be directly connected to the device where you apply the static route.

In AOS-CX, use the **IP route** command to build a static route.

```
Switch(config)# ip route <remote-network/mask> <next-hop> vrf <vrf-id>
```

Suppose that you need endpoints in subnet 10.1.10.0 to communicate with others in 10.1.20.0. Core-1 switch has two physically connected networks: 10.1.10.0/24 and 10.1.12.0/30. However, the switch is not physically connected to 10.1.20.0/24 subnet. So, you add the route below as shown in Figure 10-2:

```
Core-1(config)# ip route 10.1.20.0/24 10.1.12.2 vrf table1
```

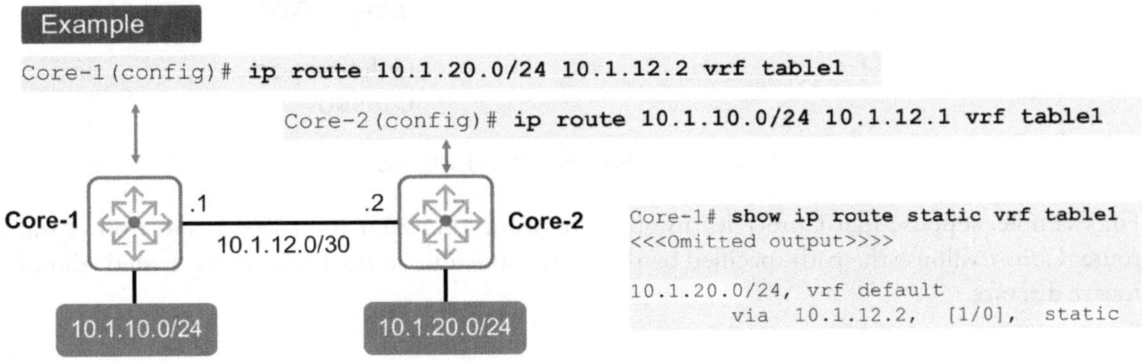

Figure 10-2 Static Route Example

Core-2 switch also needs a static route to complete the path, from its perspective it only has entries in its routing table for 10.1.20.0/24 and 10.1.12.0/30 networks. You must add a new route:

```
Core-2(config)# ip route 10.1.10.0/24 10.1.12.1 vrf table1
```

To verify this entry exists on the routing table issue the **show IP route VRF table1** command.

Administrative Distance

Sometimes a router will learn a route from two different sources. Maybe a router is running BGP, and OSPF, and you have entered some static routes. Perhaps all three methods have taught the router about network 10.1.20.0/24. Which source for routing information should the router trust? The source with the lowest Administrative Distance.

This is very much like humans learning information. You are hopefully very close to your mother, you trust her. You might say she has a very low administrative distance. If some stranger gives you conflicting advice, you may choose to listen to your mother. The stranger has a higher administrative distance.

Figure 10-3 shows the Administrative Distances for each routing protocol.

Overview

- A trust rating for route entries
- Used if one route is learned by two or more methods
- Lower distance is more preferred

```
Switch# show ip route

Displaying ipv4 routes selected for forwarding

'[x/y]' denotes [distance/metric]

10.1.20.0/24, vrf default
        via  10.1.12.2,   [1/0],   static
10.1.20.0/24, vrf default
        via  10.1.12.2,   [110/200],   ospf
```

Populating method	Administrative Distance
Directly connected	0
Static Route	1
External BGP	20
OSPF	110
Internal BGP	200
Unknown or unused	255

Figure 10-3 Administrative Distances

For example, suppose that Core-1 learns about network 10.1.20.0 from OSPF and from a static route. Core-1 will use the path specified by the static route, due to the lower, more trusted administrative distance.

Floating Static Routes

Manipulating the administrative distance can be used to create primary and backup routes, to improve network resiliency.

Example

- Prefer ISP1 Internet connection over ISP2
- In case ISP1 router fails, ISP2 should be used

```
Core-1(config)# ip route 0.0.0.0/0 10.1.251.2
Core-1(config)# ip route 0.0.0.0/0 10.1.252.2 distance 10
```

```
Core-1# show ip route

0.0.0.0/0, vrf default via  10.1.251.2,[1/0],static
0.0.0.0/0, vrf default via  10.1.252.2,[10/0],static
```

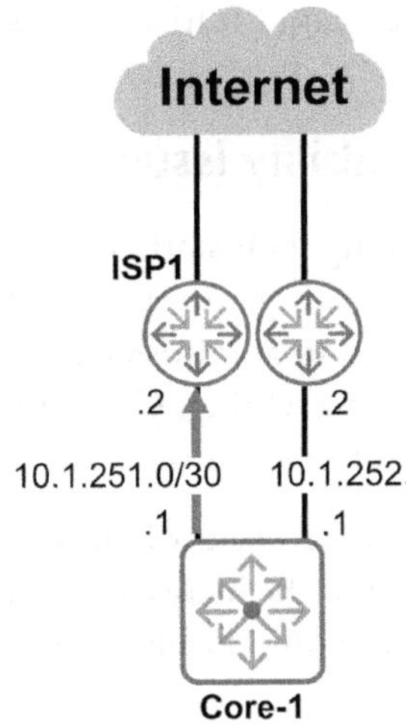

Figure 10-4 Floating Static Routes

Imagine that you have two Internet connections that use different ISPs as shown in Figure 10-4. The first connection has a higher bandwidth than the second one and therefore the administrator wants to use it as the primary connection. The secondary ISP connection will be a backup, waiting to be used in case the primary link fails.

To do this, configure two static routes. One to the "all routes" destination of 0.0.0.0 with ISP-1 as the next hop. You let its default administrative distance remain at 0.

Configure a second static route to the "all routes" destination of 0.0.0.0 with ISP-2 as the next hop, changing the administrative distance to 10.

```
Core-1(config)# ip route 0.0.0.0/0 10.1.251.2
Core-1(config)# ip route 0.0.0.0/0 10.1.252.2 distance 10
```

Since the ISP-1 route has a lower administrative distance it will be used exclusively. The ISP-2 path shall only be used if the primary link fails. You can verify this behavior using the **show IP route** command.

> **Note**
> The Network 0.0.0.0 with a subnet mask of 0.0.0.0 is a super network that summarizes all possible addresses in the IPv4 scope. It means any address.

Is important to differentiate between default gateway and default route. The first concept refers to a device that does not have the routing feature enabled, such as a host or a Layer-2 switch. In that situation we just provide the information about where to send packets that are not in the same subnet. Default route defined as 0.0.0.0/0 is used in devices where the routing process is enabled, such as routers and Multi-Layer Switches.

Scalability Issues

Working with static routes is simple and easy for small networks that have a few subnets. However, when an organization has hundreds or even thousands of subnets, static routing is not an efficient method to administer subnets. There is no automatic route advertisement, you must manually configure everything. Other than the simple Floating Static routes you just learned, there is no dynamic failover mechanism.

The human factor is also a big consideration. Administrators can cause serious problems if a route is placed in the incorrect device or if the route is not properly configured. This can create Layer-3 route loops, traffic "black-holing," and lost connectivity (Figure 10-5).

Static routes

- Suitable for simple networks.
- No automated failover.
- Human factor can cause outages.
- Maintenance could be challenge.

Dynamic routes

- Scale to any size.
- Offer automatic failover.
- Router exchanges improve availability.
- Maintenance is simple.

Figure 10-5 Scalability Issues

Recovering from a routing device failure could be slow if static routing is used. You must manually configure new alternative paths. This is inconvenient at best, especially when dynamic routing would automatically do this for you.

Dynamic routing protocols are far more scalable, handling thousands or even millions of routes across multiple routing devices. They automatically failover to alternate paths with little to no downtime. This is because routers constantly exchange messages that keep the network available and minimize your managerial workload.

Routing Protocols

Interior and Exterior Gateway Protocols

An Autonomous System (AS) is a collection of routers under a common administrative domain. Your Internet Service Provider (ISP) owns their own internal network, they have autonomy over this system, it is their AS. Each corporation has autonomy over their network, it is their AS.

To route packets inside an AS, each company chooses an Interior Gateway Protocol (IGP). An IGP is simply a routing protocol that runs inside an AS. Examples of IGPs include the Routing Information Protocol (RIP), Intermediate System–Intermediate System (IS-IS), and Open Shortest Path First (OSPF). Each company can use the IGP that works best for them.

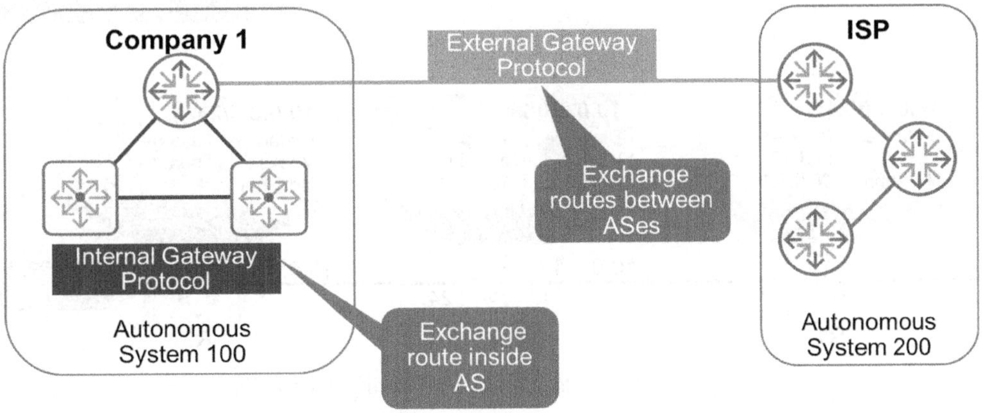

Figure 10-6 Interior and Exterior Gateway Protocols

In Figure 10-6 AS 100 has three routing devices. They may use RIP or OSPF (or both) to exchange network information in order to discover best paths within their own AS. This company could then connect to the internet, via an ISP that owns AS 200. Robust, enterprise-class routing between these Autonomous Systems requires an Exterior Gateway Protocol (EGP). The only EGP currently in use today is the Border Gateway Protocol (BGP).

Distance Vector Routing Protocols

The earliest methods devised to exchange IP information use Distance Vector algorithms. Each router advertises its distance from each network, and the vector or direction packets must travel to get to that network. The distance used with RIP for example is measured in "hop count". In Figure 10-7, how many routers must R3 "hop over" to get to network 10.0.3.0/24? The answer is 0 routers, it is directly connected to that network.

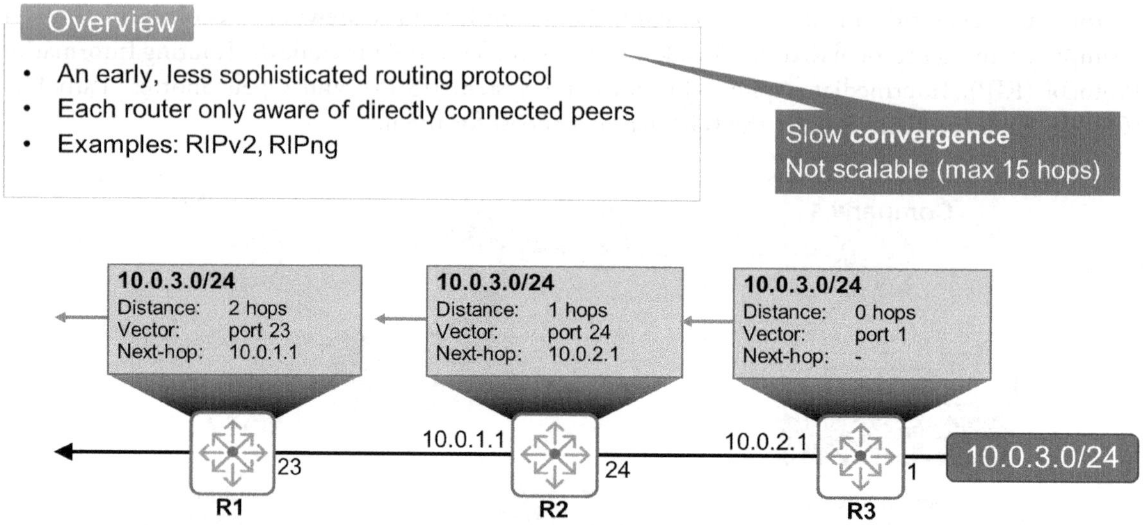

Figure 10-7 Distance Vector Routing Protocols

What vector or direction must R3 forward packets to reach 10.0.3.0/24? The answer is "out port 1". It is as if the router says, "to get to any host on destination network 10.0.3.0/24, which is 0 hops away, I must forward packets out my local Port 1. Using something like RIP or RIPv2, R3 advertises its distance and vector to R2.

R2 receives this and knows, "If R3 is 0 hops away, and I must hop over R3 to get to that network, then I am 1 hop away. To get to destination 10.0.3.0/24, which is 1 hop away, R2 must forward packets out local port 24, to next-hop router 10.0.2.1. R2 advertises its distance and vector to R1.

R1 receives this and knows, "If R2 is 1 hop away, and I must hop over R2 to get to the destination, then I am 2 hops away". To get to 10.0.3.0/24, which is 2 hops away, R3 forwards packets out local port 23, to next-hop router 10.0.1.1".

Distance Vector RIP routers are not aware of the entire network topology. They only perceive their directly connected routing peers. This simplifies operation, but also limits operation:

- Slow convergence: When a failure occurs, Distance Vector protocols can take minutes to converge, depending on network size, complexity, and architecture.
- Limited scalability: Each router can be no more than 15 hops away from any other router. Understand that you could still have dozens, or even hundreds of routers, as long as it is a relatively flat architecture.

Distance Vector protocols include the Routing Information Protocol (RIP), RIP version 2 (RIPv2), and RIP Next Generation (RIPng). RIP does not support security feature to protect the advertisement messages that are exchanged between routing devices. Due to their limited scalability, performance, and security, the AOS-CX does not support any Distance Vector protocols. Instead, Aruba supports the more robust Link State routing protocols OSPFv2 and OSPFv3.

Link-State Routing Protocol

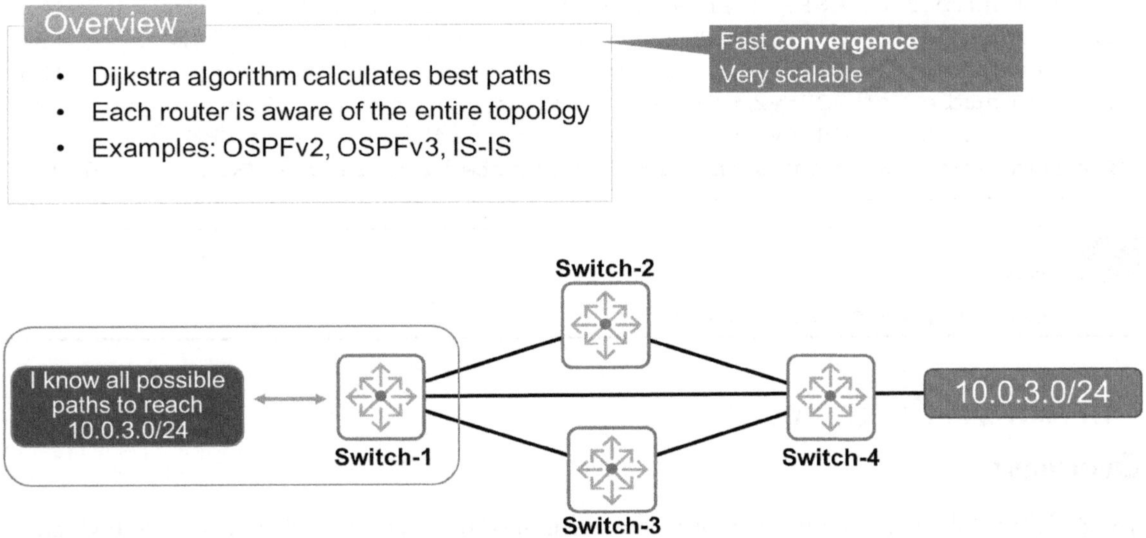

Figure 10-8 Link-State Routing Protocol

Link-State protocols resolve limitations and disadvantages of the Distance Vector protocols. Routers that run Link-State protocols possess information about the complete network topology. This approach enables them to independently calculate their routing table using the more sophisticated Dijkstra algorithm to select the best path for every network destination (Figure 10-8).

Actual implementations of Link-State protocols include Open Shortest Path First version 2 (OSPFv2), which is used for IPv4; OSPFv3, which is used for IPv6, and Intermediate System to Intermediate System (IS-IS). IS-IS is far less common than OSPFv2, and so this module is focused on OSPFv2. These protocols provide faster convergence times compared with Distance Vector protocols. Another advantage is that scalability for large networks is not a concern.

Many years ago, one disadvantage of protocols like OSPF is that they created more CPU, memory, and bandwidth utilization than protocols like RIP. However, routers have become more capable over the years, and our ability to design more efficient network architectures has greatly reduced this concern. Furthermore, the AOS-CX multilayer switches are designed to meet today's network requirements, supporting OSPFv2 and OSPFv3 but not IS-IS. You can verify this information by running the **show capacities OSPFv2** command.

```
Switch-6300# show capacities ospfv2
System Capacities: Filter OSPFv2
Capacities                                                          Name
Value
-------------------------------------------------------------------------
Maximum number of OSPFv2 areas configurable in the system            128
Maximum number of OSPFv2 interfaces configurable in the system       128
Maximum number of OSPFv2 interfaces per area in the system           128
Maximum number of OSPFv2 neighbors allowed across all VRFs           128
Maximum number of OSPFv2 processes supported across each VRF           1
Maximum number of routes in OSPFv2 supported across all VRFs       64000
```

Note

This training will focus on OSPFv2.

Lab 10: Static Routes

Overview

The goal of the following tasks is to complete the dual-homed Internet Service deployment for BigStartup. The customer wants load balancing across both carriers and redundancy in case of failure. They want assurance that if either link fails, traffic can still go out through the alternate ISP. This will require the configuration of static and floating routes, which you will apply on the Core switches.

Note: References to equipment and commands are taken from Aruba's hosted remote lab. These are shown for demonstration purposes in case you wish to replicate the environment and tasks on your own equipment.

Objectives

After completing this lab, you will be able to:

- Configure Core switches to Perimeter Firewall links using a /30 prefix
- Calculate and deploy Variable Length Subnet Mask (VLSM) prefixes
- Configure static routes
- Add a default route into the routing table for providing internet access
- Manipulate administrative distances in order to configure floating routes
- Validate proper load sharing and failover

Note

IP prefix is an aggregation of IP addresses and is usually used to refer to an IP network or subnet in general.

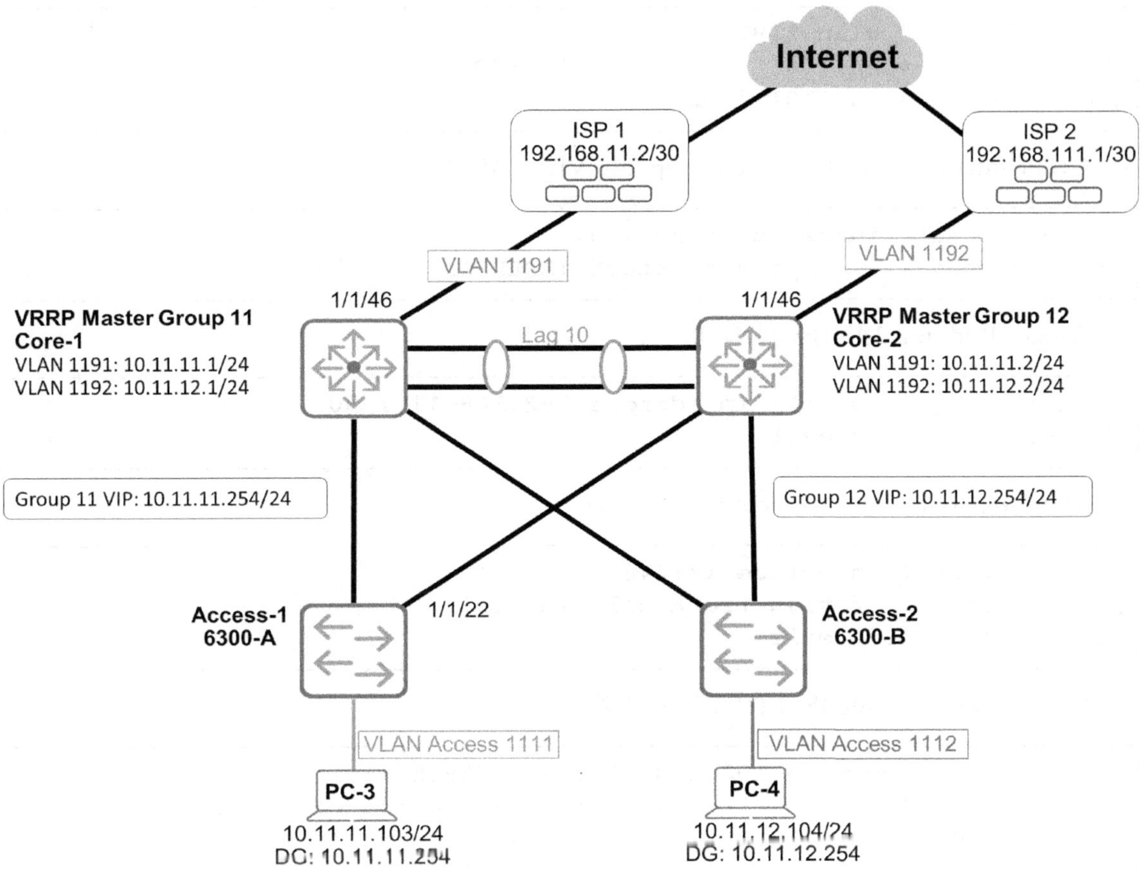

Figure 10-9 Lab Topology Task 1

Task 1: Add Links to ISPs

Objectives

In this task, you will prepare the network for future changes such as the addition of internet connections by assigning the /30 segments you calculated on Lab 9.1 Task 3b to VLANs 1191 and 1192 on Core-1 and Core-2 respectively (Figure 10-9).

Steps

Core-1 (via PC-1)

1. Open the SSH session to Core-1. Login using **cxf11/aruba123.**
2. Create VLAN 1191 and add the description TO_T11-ISP-1.

```
Core-1(config)# vlan 1191
Core-1(config-vlan-1191)# name TO_T11-ISP-1
Core-1(config-vlan-1191)# exit
```

3. Create interface VLAN 1191 and map it to VRF TABLE-11.

```
Core-1(config)# interface vlan 1191
Core-1(config-if-vlan)# vrf attach TABLE-11
```

4. Assign IP address 192.168.11.1/30.

```
Core-1(config-if-vlan)# ip address 192.168.11.1/30
Core-1(config-if)# exit
```

5. Move to port 1/1/46 and allow VLAN 1191.

```
Core-1(config)# interface 1/1/46
Core-1(config-if)# vlan trunk allowed 1191
Core-1(config-if)# exit
```

6. Confirm you can ping ISP1 (192.168.11.2).

```
Core-1(config)#do ping 192.168.11.2 vrf TABLE-11
PING 192.168.11.2 (192.168.11.2) 100(128) bytes of data.
108 bytes from 192.168.11.2: icmp_seq=1 ttl=64 time=13.4 ms
108 bytes from 192.168.11.2: icmp_seq=2 ttl=64 time=0.172 ms
108 bytes from 192.168.11.2: icmp_seq=3 ttl=64 time=0.162 ms
108 bytes from 192.168.11.2: icmp_seq=4 ttl=64 time=0.159 ms
108 bytes from 192.168.11.2: icmp_seq=5 ttl=64 time=0.154 ms

--- 192.168.11.2 ping statistics ---
5 packets transmitted, 5 received, 0% packet loss, time 4049ms
rtt min/avg/max/mdev = 0.154/2.810/13.405/5.297 ms
```

TIP

Some commands like copy, ping, or traceroute are not natively available at configuration context, however you can use the "do" command to import them from privileged context.

Core-2 (via PC-1)

7. Open the SSH session to Core-2
8. Repeat steps 2 to 6 using VLAN 1192, TO_T11_ISP-2 description and 192.168.111.2/30 IP address.

```
Core-2(config)# vlan 1192
Core-2(config-vlan-1192)# name TO_T11_ISP-2
Core-2(config-vlan-1192)# exit
Core-2(config)# interface vlan 1192
Core-2(config-if-vlan)# vrf attach TABLE-11
Core-2(config-if-vlan)# ip address 192.168.111.2/30
Core-2(config-if-vlan)# exit
Core-2(config)# interface 1/1/46
Core-2(config-if)# vlan trunk allowed 1192
Core-2(config-if)# exit
Core-2(config)# do ping 192.168.111.1 vrf TABLE-11
PING 192.168.111.1 (192.168.111.1) 100(128) bytes of data.
108 bytes from 192.168.111.1: icmp_seq=1 ttl=64 time=11.6 ms
108 bytes from 192.168.111.1: icmp_seq=2 ttl=64 time=0.216 ms
108 bytes from 192.168.111.1: icmp_seq=3 ttl=64 time=0.229 ms
108 bytes from 192.168.111.1: icmp_seq=4 ttl=64 time=0.180 ms
108 bytes from 192.168.111.1: icmp_seq=5 ttl=64 time=0.178 ms

--- 192.168.111.1 ping statistics ---
5 packets transmitted, 5 received, 0% packet loss, time 4108ms
rtt min/avg/max/mdev = 0.178/2.488/11.640/4.576 ms
```

Task 2: Adding Static Routes

Objectives

Right now, the links between the Core Switches and Perimeter Firewalls are up and running, however internet access is not available yet. In this task you will add static routes in order to send all non-local traffic to the carriers who will take care of the delivery process. Core-1 will be pointing to ISP1 and Core-2 will point to ISP2 in order to achieve a load balancing effect (Figure 10-10).

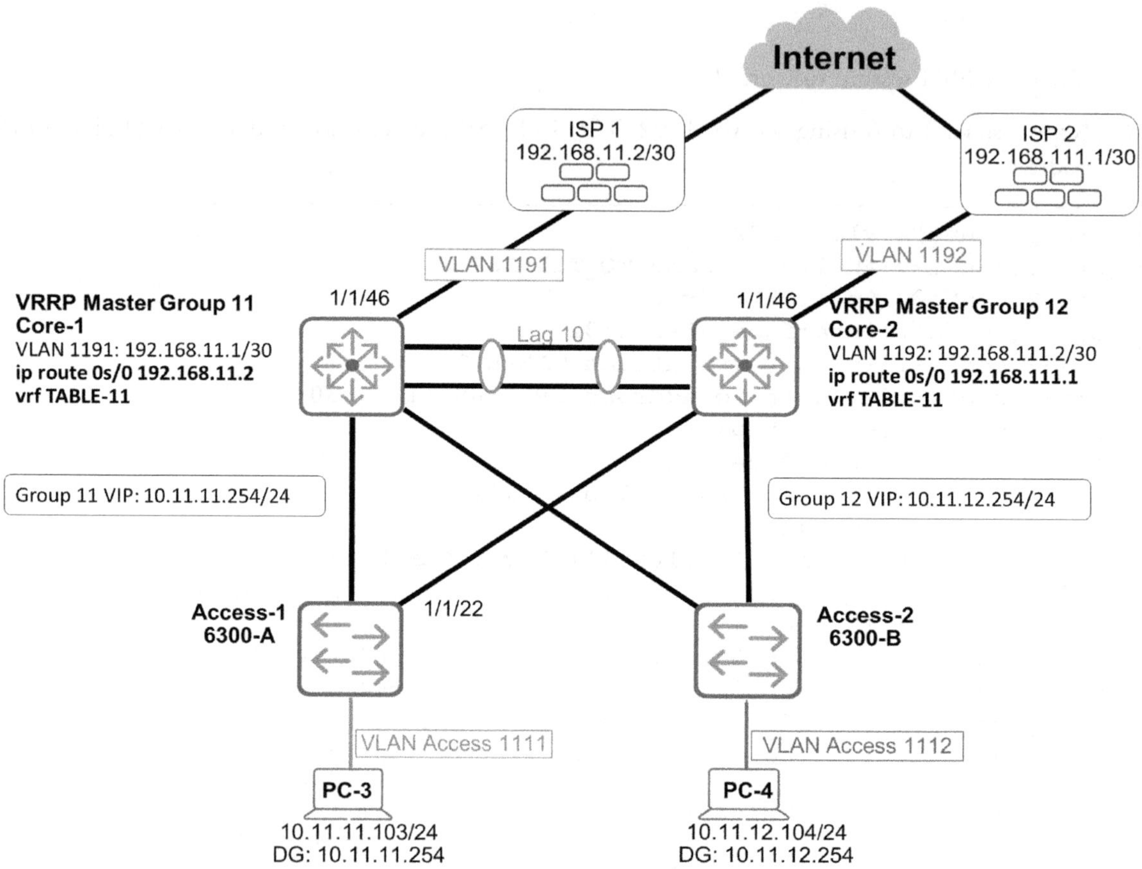

Figure 10-10 Lab Topology Task 2

Steps

Core-1 (via PC-1)

1. Open the SSH session to Core-1.
2. Create a static default route (also known as 0's prefix) pointing to ISP-1 (192.168.11.2) on TABLE-11.

```
Core-1(config)# ip route 0.0.0.0/0 192.168.11.2 vrf TABLE-11
```

3. Use "show ip route static vrf" and validate the route is listed.

```
Core-1(config)# show ip route static vrf TABLE-11

Displaying ipv4 routes selected for forwarding

'[x/y]' denotes [distance/metric]

0.0.0.0/0, vrf TABLE-11
        via  192.168.11.2,  [1/0],  static
```

What is the metric value and what is it for? ____________________

____

What is the distance value and what is it for? ____________________

____

4. Ping the 8.8.8.8 IP address. Ping should be successful.

```
Core-1(config)# do ping 8.8.8.8 datagram-size 32 vrf TABLE-11
PING 8.8.8.8 (8.8.8.8) 32(60) bytes of data.
40 bytes from 8.8.8.8: icmp_seq=1 ttl=51 time=8.09 ms
40 bytes from 8.8.8.8: icmp_seq=2 ttl=51 time=7.84 ms
40 bytes from 8.8.8.8: icmp_seq=3 ttl=51 time=7.82 ms
40 bytes from 8.8.8.8: icmp_seq=4 ttl=51 time=8.00 ms
40 bytes from 8.8.8.8: icmp_seq=5 ttl=51 time=8.07 ms

--- 8.8.8.8 ping statistics ---
5 packets transmitted, 5 received, 0% packet loss, time 4005ms
rtt min/avg/max/mdev = 7.822/7.968/8.097/0.160 ms
```

TIP

In addition to specifying the VRF, outbound ICMP echo packets can be manipulated by using the "**ping**" command followed by these options:

```
data-fill         Specify the ping packet data pattern in hexadecimal
digits
datagram-size     Specify the size of ping datagram
interval         Specify the interval between successive ping requests
ip-option          Specify an IP option to be used in ping packet
repetitions       Specify the number of ping packets to be sent
source              Specify the ping source IPv4 address or source
interface
timeout           Specify the ping timeout in seconds
tos               Specify IP TOS to be used in ping request
vrf               Specify the VRF to use
```

If there is no prefix in the routing table for the 8.8.8.8 IP address, what prefix is taking care of routing this traffic?____

PC-3

5. Access PC-3 and open a command prompt.
6. Ping the 8.8.8.8 IP address (Figure 10-11).

   Is ping successful?____

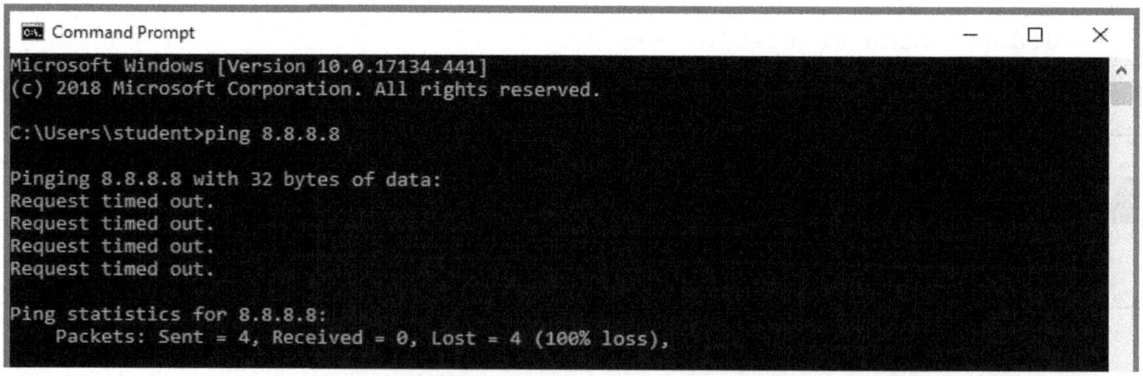

Figure 10-11 Failed Ping

7. Attempt a traceroute to the same address (Figure 10-12).

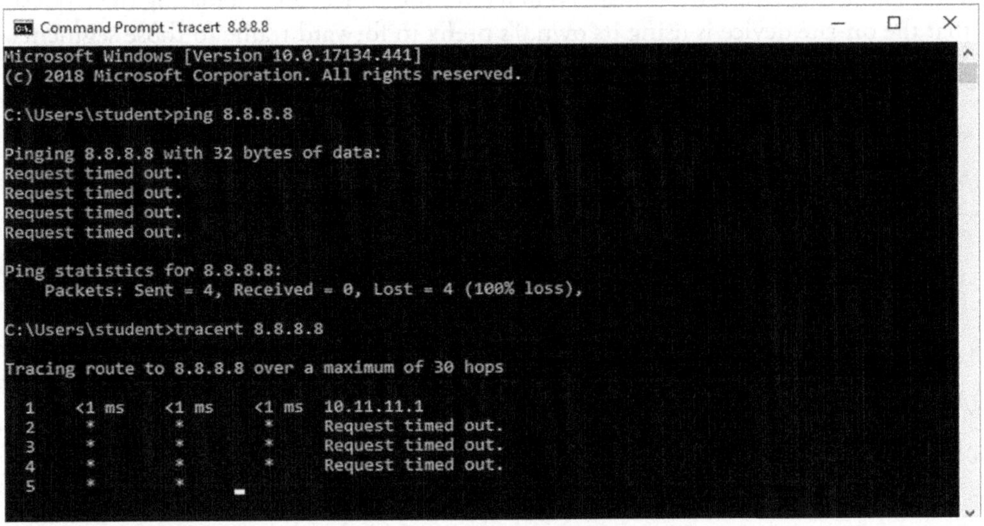

Figure 10-12 Traceroute

What is the last hop your trace is reaching?____

What is the last hop your trace is reaching?____

There could be many reasons why the ping is not working:

- An ACL in the firewall that filters the packets out.
- The lack of Network Address Translation (NAT) which sends the packets with the original source IP address making it impossible for the destination to properly respond back to you from the internet.
- A missing route for your local segment (10.1.0.0/16) in the service provider equipment causing it to drop the returning traffic or route it somewhere else.

At this point any of them is possible, however since Core-1 was able to reach the 8.8.8.8 address then it is most likely that the ISP device (Perimeter Firewall) does not contain your prefix in its routing table. After all, you must remember that when testing access from Core-1, packets had the 192.168.11.1 source IP address which is a segment ISP1 implicitly knows (connected network). On the other hand, packets sent by PC-3 had the 10.11.11.103 address, therefore, you must make sure the carrier has this route in their device pointing to Core-1's IP address as the next hop in VLAN 1191.

You have contacted ISP1 and asked if their device was setup properly, ensuring at a minimum the 10.11.11.0/24 and 10.11.12.0 were included in its routing table. After validating the request, the ISP realizes that the on-site device is using its own 0's prefix to forward traffic to those segments.

```
P52-6300-AB# show ip route 10.11.11.0 vrf CXF_ISP1

Displaying ipv4 routes selected for forwarding

'[x/y]' denotes [distance/metric]

0.0.0.0/0, vrf CXF_ISP1
        via  192.168.253.254,   [1/0],   static

P52 -6300-AB# show ip route 10.11.12.0 vrf CXF_ISP1

Displaying ipv4 routes selected for forwarding

'[x/y]' denotes [distance/metric]

0.0.0.0/0, vrf CXF_ISP1
        via  192.168.253.254,   [1/0],   static

P52-6300-AB#
```

To solve this, you request the ISP to add the network 10.X.0.0/16 pointing to 192.168.11.1 IP address (Core-1) as the next hop.

Note

In the next steps you will pretend to be the ISP1 technician.

ISP1 (via PC-1)

8. Using Putty, open an SSH session to ISP1 (Figure 10-13).

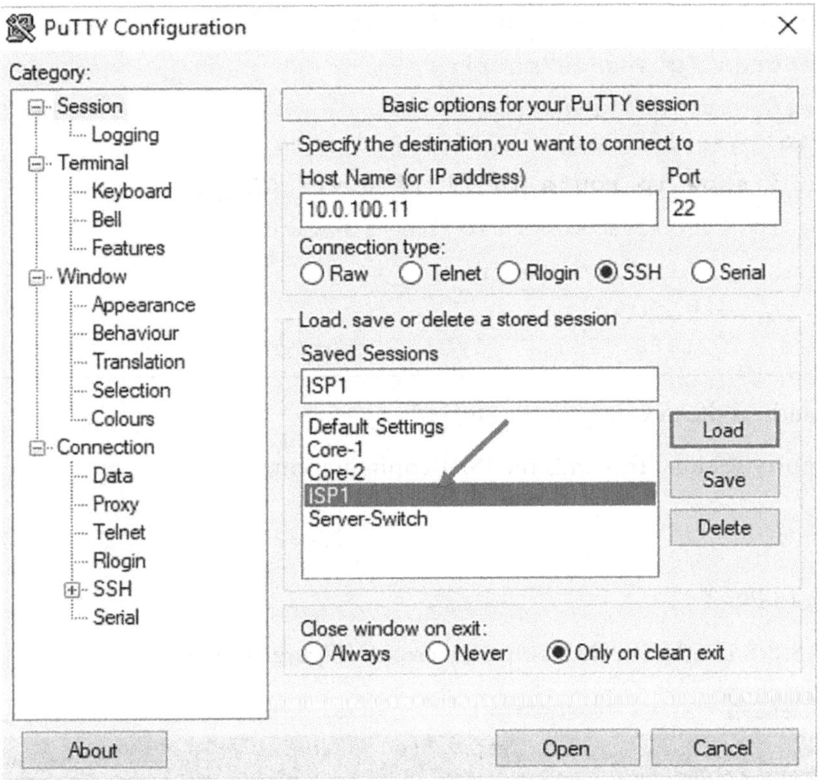

Figure 10-13 SSH to ISP1

9. Login using username: cxf11/aruba123.

10. Configure the missing static route: **10.11.0.0/16** via **192.168.11.1** on ISP1 VRF.

```
P52-6300-AB(config)# ip route 10.11.0.0/16 192.168.11.1 vrf CXF_ISP1
P52-6300-AB(config)# end
```

11. Use the "**show ip route**" command for validating there is an entry in the routing table for properly forwarding traffic to 10.11.11.0/24 and 10.11.12.0/24.

```
P52-6300-AB# show ip route 10.11.11.0 vrf CXF_ISP1
Displaying ipv4 routes selected for forwarding
'[x/y]' denotes [distance/metric]
10.11.0.0/16, vrf CXF_ISP1
        via  192.168.11.1,  [1/0],  static
P52-6300-AB# show ip route 10.11.12.0 vrf CXF_ISP1
Displaying ipv4 routes selected for forwarding
'[x/y]' denotes [distance/metric]
10.11.0.0/16, vrf CXF_ISP1
        via  192.168.11.1,  [1/0],  static
```

Is Core-1's IP address the next-hop in the entries?

12. Close the putty session. This ends the ISP1 configuration.

PC-3

13. Move back to PC-3.

14. Ping the 8.8.8.8 IP address, then run a traceroute (Figure 10-14).

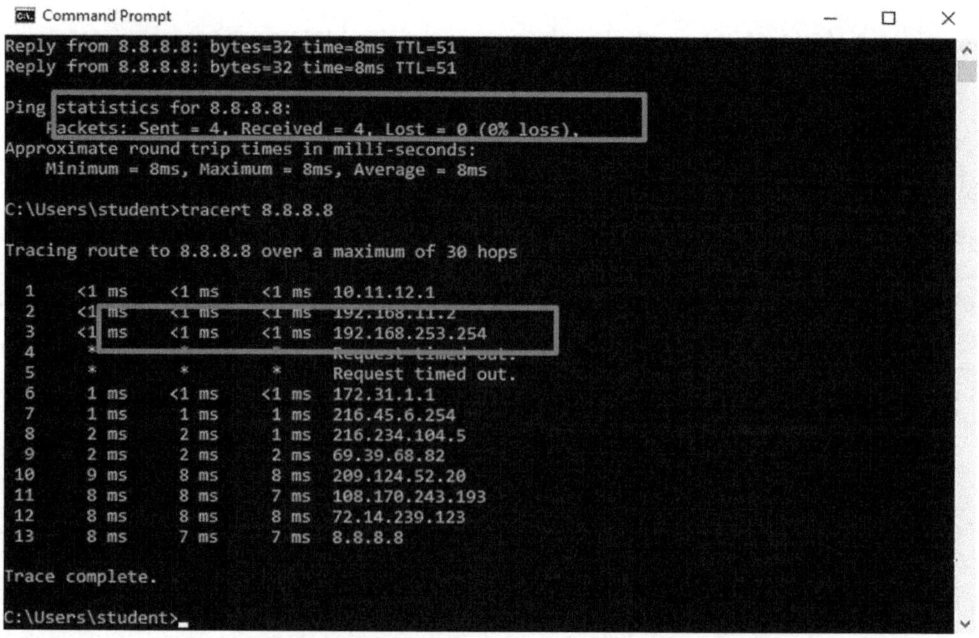

Figure 10-14 Ping Successful

Is ping successful? ______________________________

IMPORTANT

In IP networking, most communications are bidirectional, therefore adding a route with the destination prefix on the layer 3 device next to the source, is just as important as adding a route with the source prefix on the device next to the destination. If NAT isn't used, then all Layer-3 devices in between the source and the destination must have both prefixes in their routing tables as well.

What are the first and second hops? ______________________________

Core-2 (via PC-1)

15. Open the SSH session to Core-2.
16. Repeat steps 2 to 4 using 192.168.111.1 as your next hop.

```
Core-2(config)# ip route 0.0.0.0/0 192.168.111.1 vrf TABLE-1
```

```
Core-2(config)# show ip route static vrf TABLE-11
Displaying ipv4 routes selected for forwarding
'[x/y]' denotes [distance/metric]
0.0.0.0/0, vrf TABLE-11
        via  192.168.111.1,  [1/0],  static
```

What is the next hop? ______________________________

What will happen if that device goes down? ______________________________

```
Core-2(config)# do ping 8.8.8.8 datagram-size 32 vrf TABLE-11
PING 8.8.8.8 (8.8.8.8) 32(60) bytes of data.
40 bytes from 8.8.8.8: icmp_seq=1 ttl=52 time=8.45 ms
40 bytes from 8.8.8.8: icmp_seq=2 ttl=52 time=8.14 ms
40 bytes from 8.8.8.8: icmp_seq=3 ttl=52 time=7.88 ms
40 bytes from 8.8.8.8: icmp_seq=4 ttl=52 time=8.01 ms
40 bytes from 8.8.8.8: icmp_seq=5 ttl=52 time=7.91 ms

--- 8.8.8.8 ping statistics ---
5 packets transmitted, 5 received, 0% packet loss, time 4004ms
rtt min/avg/max/mdev = 7.889/8.082/8.459/0.216 ms
```

PC-4

17. Access PC-4 and open a command prompt.
18. Ping the 8.8.8.8 IP address. Ping should be successful
19. Run a traceroute to 8.8.8.8 (Figure 10-15).

```
Select Command Prompt
(c) 2018 Microsoft Corporation. All rights reserved.

C:\Users\student>tracert 8.8.8.8

Tracing route to 8.8.8.8 over a maximum of 30 hops

  1    <1 ms    <1 ms    <1 ms  10.11.12.2
  2    <1 ms    <1 ms    <1 ms  192.168.111.1
  3     1 ms    <1 ms    <1 ms  192.168.254.254
  4     *        *        *     Request timed out.
  5     *        *        *     Request timed out.
  6     2 ms     1 ms     1 ms  172.31.1.1
  7     2 ms     1 ms     1 ms  216.45.6.254
  8     2 ms     2 ms     1 ms  216.234.104.5
  9     3 ms     2 ms     2 ms  69.39.68.82
 10     8 ms     9 ms     8 ms  209.124.52.20
 11     8 ms     8 ms     8 ms  108.170.243.193
 12     9 ms     8 ms     9 ms  216.239.47.129
 13     8 ms     8 ms     7 ms  8.8.8.8

Trace complete.

C:\Users\student>_
```

Figure 10-15 Traceroute

What are the first and second hops? ______________________________

Are they the same as in step 14? ______________________________

IMPORTANT

Traffic from users in VLAN 1111 is using Core-1 as the gateway, who in turn uses ISP-1 as the next hop. Users in VLAN 1112 use Core-2 as the gateway and ISP-2 as the next hop (see Figure 10-15). This behavior provides a load balancing effect across both ISPs. It leverages the customer's two services.

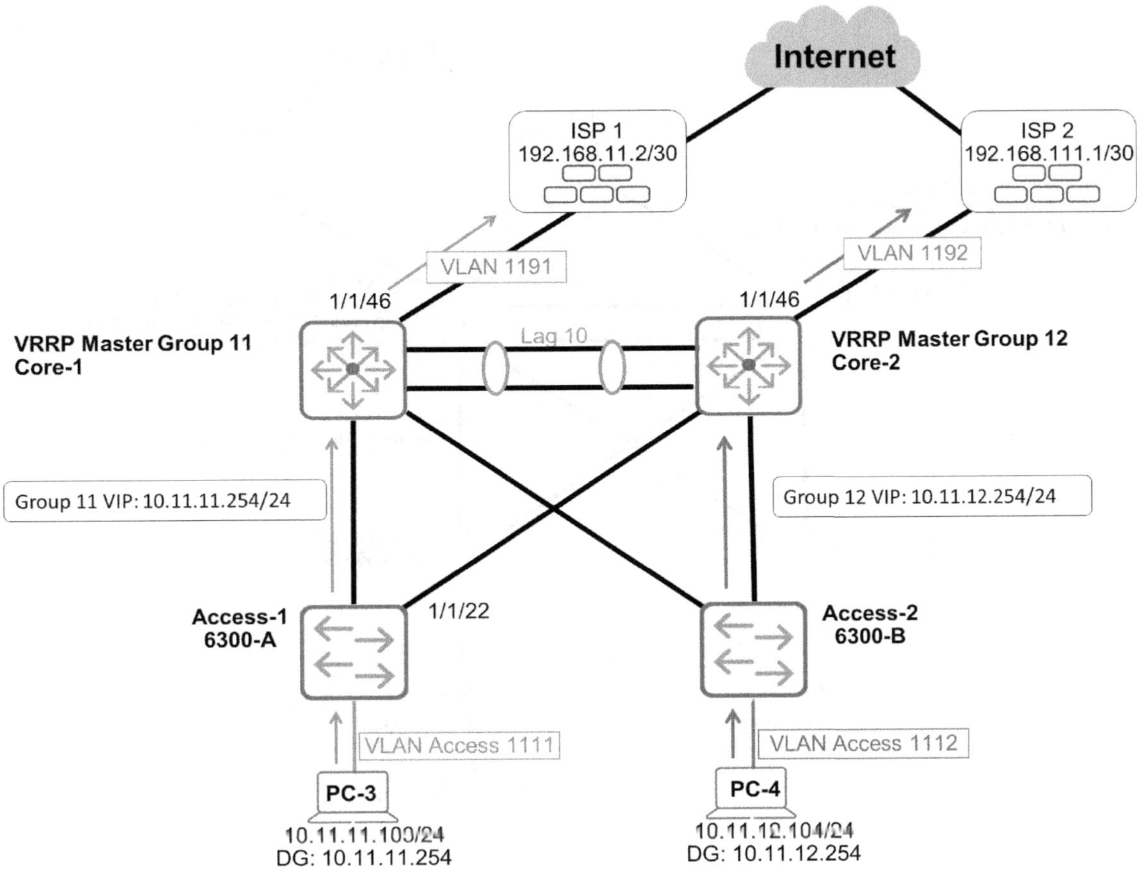

Figure 10-16 Traffic Path

Task 3: Redundancy with Floating Routes

Objectives

Your current deployment has proven more efficient, however, it still has a weak point - it contains single points of failure. If the link to ISP1 fails, then users in VLAN 1111 lose internet access. A similar result would occur to VLAN 1112 clients if ISP2 fails. The solution to this is the creation of static floating routes (Figures 10-16 and 10-17).

In this task, you will create a second prefix on each Core pointing to the other Core. However, these prefixes will have a lower preference because of an increased administrative distance. When the main internet link on either Core is active, then the floating routes are not present in the routing table and not used. However, if the connection to either carrier goes down, the main route vanishes, and the floating route is inserted and makes the switch route data traffic through its neighbor. Additionally, there will be a new IP segment used as a Layer 3 transport between the Cores. You already calculated this segment in Lab 9 Task 4b (Subnetting and VLSM).

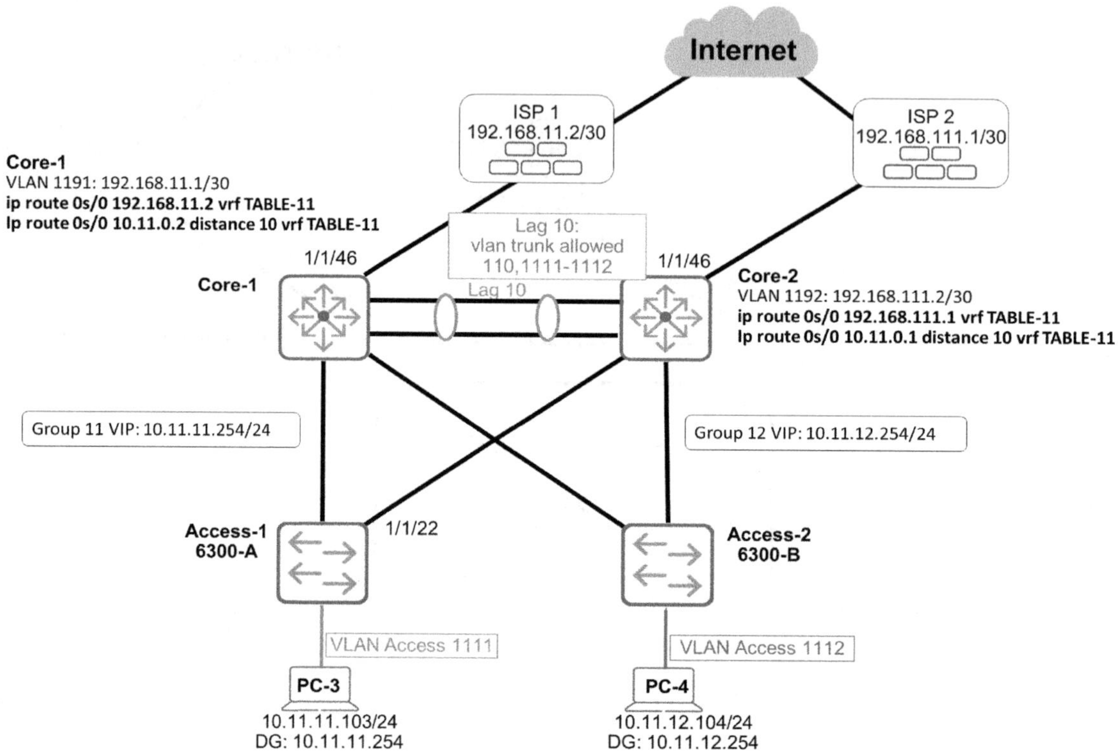

Figure 10-17 Lab Topology Task 3

Steps

Core-1 (via PC-1)

1. Open an SSH session to Core-1.
2. Create VLAN 110 and name it CORE-1&2_TABLE-11.

```
Core-1(config)# vlan 110
Core-1(config-vlan-110)# name CORE-1&2_TABLE-11
Core-1(config-vlan-110)# exit
```

3. Allow VLAN 110 to LAG 10.

```
Core-1(config)# interface lag 10
Core-1(config-lag-if)# vlan trunk allow 110
Core-1(config-lag-if)# exit
```

4. Create interface VLAN 110 and map it to VRF TABLE-11, then assign it the 10.11.0.1/30 IP address.

```
Core-1(config)# interface vlan 110
Core-1(config-if-vlan)# vrf attach TABLE-11
Core-1(config-if-vlan)# ip address 10.11.0.1/30
Core-1(config-if-vlan)# exit
```

5. Create a static default route in VRF TABLE-11 pointing to 10.11.0.2 and assign it a distance 10 (future Core-2 address in VLAN 110).

```
Core-1(config)# ip route 0.0.0.0/0 10.11.0.2 distance 10 vrf TABLE-11
```

6. Show the static routes of VRF TABLE-11.

```
Core-1(config)# show ip route static vrf TABLE-11

Displaying ipv4 routes selected for forwarding

'[x/y]' denotes [distance/metric]

0.0.0.0/0, vrf TABLE-11
        via  192.168.11.2,  [1/0],  static
```

How many entries do you have? ______________________________

What is the next hop? ______________________________

Core-2 (via PC-1)

7. Open an SSH session to Core-2.
8. Repeat steps 2 to 6 assigning 10.11.0.2/30 to Core-2 and use 10.11.0.1 as the route's next hop.

```
Core-2(config)# VLAN 110
Core-2(config-vlan-110)# name CORE-1&2_TABLE-11
Core-2(config-vlan-110)# exit
Core-2(config)# interface lag 10
Core-2(config-lag-if)# vlan trunk allow 110
Core-2(config-lag-if)# exit
Core-2(config)# interface vlan 110
Core-2(config-if-vlan)# vrf attach TABLE-11
Core-2(config-if-vlan)# ip address 10.11.0.2/30
Core-2(config-if-vlan)# exit
Core-2(config)# ip route 0.0.0.0/0 10.11.0.1 distance 10 vrf TABLE-11
Core-2(config)# show ip route static vrf TABLE-11

Displaying ipv4 routes selected for forwarding

'[x/y]' denotes [distance/metric]

0.0.0.0/0, vrf TABLE-11
        via  192.168.111.1,  [1/0],  static
```

Creating identical routes on two Layer-3 devices pointing to each other may lead to Layer-3 loops. In our scenario, that would occur if both ISP links go down. In this unlikely case, if Core-1 receives traffic to the internet it would use Core-2 as next hop, who, in absence of its main internet link, would then send traffic back to Core-1, who would repeat the same process over and over and over.

Although there is a built-in Layer-3 loop attenuation mechanism in the IP header called Time to Live (TTL), monitoring the validity of the floating route through Service Level Agreements (SLAs) based tracking is always recommended in order to prevent this issue from happening, otherwise loop packets would consume data plane resources before they die.

Note that SLAs are outside the scope of this training.

As alternative to floating routes you can combine static routes along with either BGP conditional advertisement or IGPs default route injection. This approach prevents Layer-3 loops entirely. You will examine the IGP default route injection approach in the next lab.

In this part of the process, routes and traffic paths remain as they were in the end of task 2. You will now simulate a failure and confirm the resulting path.

PC-3 and PC-4

9. Access both PCs.
10. Run a continuous ping toward 8.8.8.8. Pings should be successful.

Core-1 (via PC-1)

11. Move back to Core-1.
12. Disable interface VLAN 1191.

```
Core-1(config)# interface vlan 1191
Core-1(config-if-vlan)# shutdown
```

13. Display the VRF TABLE-11 routing table.

```
Core-1(config-if-vlan)# show ip route static vrf TABLE-11

Displaying ipv4 routes selected for forwarding

'[x/y]' denotes [distance/metric]

0.0.0.0/0, vrf TABLE-11
        via  10.11.0.2,  [10/0],  static
```

What is the next hop of the 0's prefix now? ______________________

PC-3

14. Move to PC-3 (Figure 10-18).

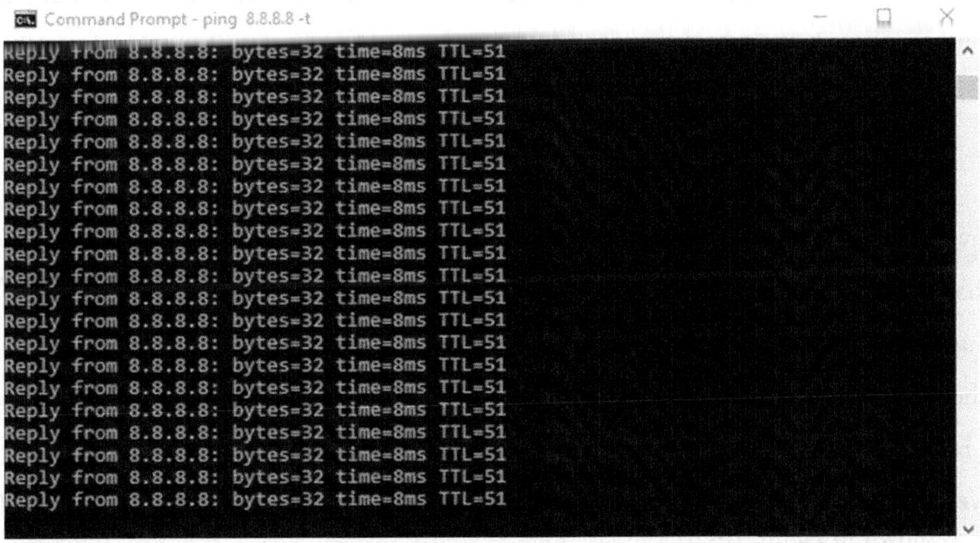

Figure 10-18 ping -t

What is the ping status? ______________________

15. Run a traceroute toward 8.8.8.8 (Figure 10-19).

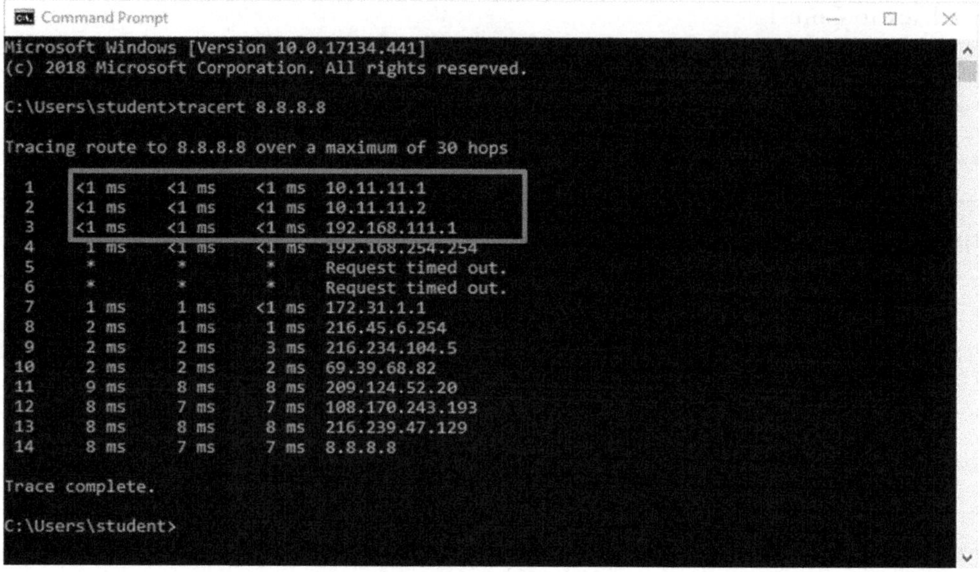

Figure 10-19 Traceroute

What are the first three hops?

1st hop: ______________________________

2nd hop: ______________________________

3rd hop: ______________________________

PC-4

16. Move to PC-4 then repeat step 15 (ping 8.8.8.8).

What is the ping status?

What are the first 2 hops?

1st hop: ______________________________

2nd hop: ______________________________

You have successfully deployed internet access redundancy and made BigStartup network resilient to failures, as shown in Figure 10-20.

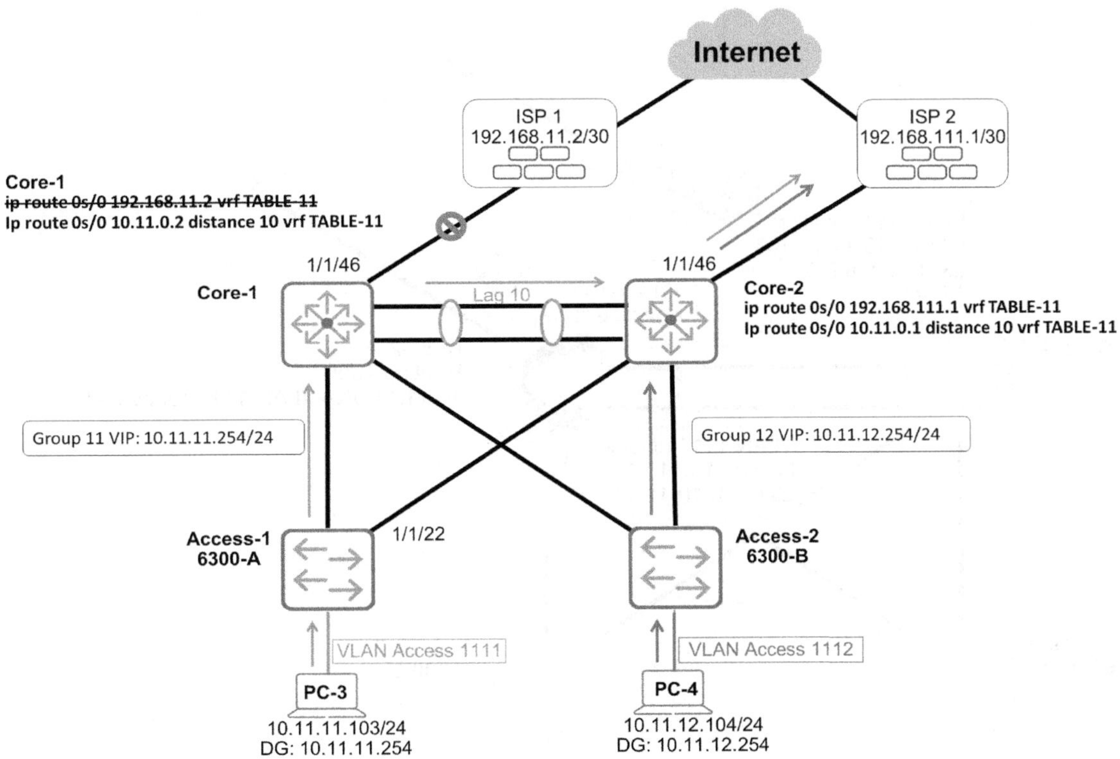

Figure 10-20 Floating Routes Failover

Pay attention to Step 15: PC-3's second hop. Since Core-1 is delivering the packet to Core-2 on VLAN 110, then you would normally expect that hop 2 should be 10.11.02, however it is not. The logic behind this behavior is that when Core-2 receives from Core-1 the ICMP echo with TTL=1 then it subtracts 1, TTL becomes 0 and the packet dies as normal.

Here Core-2 needs to respond back to the source (PC-3) with an "ICMP Time Exceeded" message (which is what you see on the tracert command's output), however according to Core-2's routing table, PC-3's IP address 10.11.11.103 isn't reachable via Core-1 on VLAN 110, but via VLAN 1111 as a connected network (see output below), therefore it delivers the packet using Layer-2. It uses the address it has from VLAN 1111. This is called asymmetric routing (Figure 10-21).

```
Core-2# show ip route 10.11.11.103 vrf TABLE-11
Displaying ipv4 routes selected for forwarding
'[x/y]' denotes [distance/metric]
10.11.11.0/24, vrf TABLE-11
        via  vlan1111,  [0/0],  connected
```

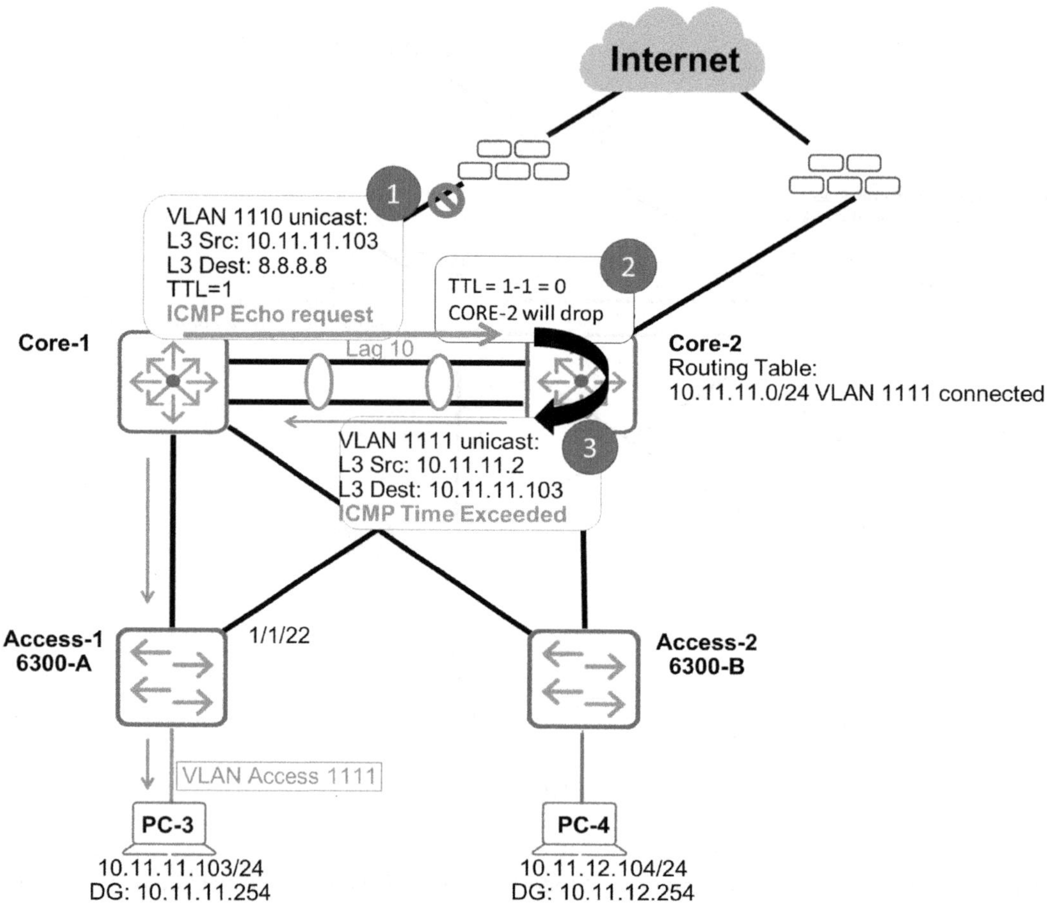

Figure 10-21 ICMP Time Exceeded

Core-1 (via PC-1)

17. Move back to Core-1.
18. Enable interface VLAN 1191.

```
Core-1(config-if-vlan)# no shutdown
Core-1(config-if-vlan)# end
```

Task 4: Save Your Configurations

Objectives

You will now proceed to save your configuration.

Steps

Core-1 and Core-2 (via PC-1)

1. Save the current Cores' configuration in the startup checkpoint.

```
Core-1# write memory
Configuration changes will take time to process, please be patient.
```

```
Core-2# write memory
Configuration changes will take time to process, please be patient.
```

You have completed Lab 10!

Learning Check

Chapter 10 Questions

Administrative Distance

1. Suppose that a router has learned about network 172.18.37.0/24 from three sources – OSPF, Internal BGP, and a static route. Which statements are true about this router's path selection?
    a. The router chooses the OSPF route because it is trusted more than BGP.
    b. The router chooses the best path based on the lowest cost.
    c. The router chooses the option with the highest Administrative Distance.
    d. The router chooses the static route.

Routing Protocols

2. Which of the statements below accurately describe link state routing protocols?
    a. They can be used to route packets between Autonomous Systems.
    b. They can be used to route packets inside an Autonomous System.
    c. They use a Distance Vector algorithm.
    d. They are more scalable than protocols like RIP.
    e. OSPFv2 is a very popular choice for Exterior Gateway Protocol-based routing.

11 OSPFv2 Single Area

EXAM OBJECTIVES

- ✓ Describe OSPF general operation.
- ✓ Explain areas and Router IDs.
- ✓ Describe hello messages.
- ✓ Describe OSPF network types.
- ✓ Describe DR election and neighbor states.
- ✓ Explain OSPF LSA types, path selection, and convergence.
- ✓ Configure OSPF.
- ✓ Use Path costs to manipulate routes.
- ✓ Describe and configure passive interfaces.

Overview

OSPF may be the most popular option for corporations to route traffic within their organization. OSPFv2 is used to route IPv4 packets within a corporate internetwork. You will explore OSPF operation, including OSPF areas, Router IDs, and various message types and neighbor states.

You will learn how subnet information is advertised by various types of Link State Advertisements (LSAs). Then you will learn how these LSAs build a database of all paths, and how that database is then used to build a routing table as a list of best paths over which to forward end user data traffic.

Finally, you will learn how to configure OSPF, and apply that knowledge with a hands-on lab activity.

OSPFv2 Router ID and Messaging

OSPF Introduction

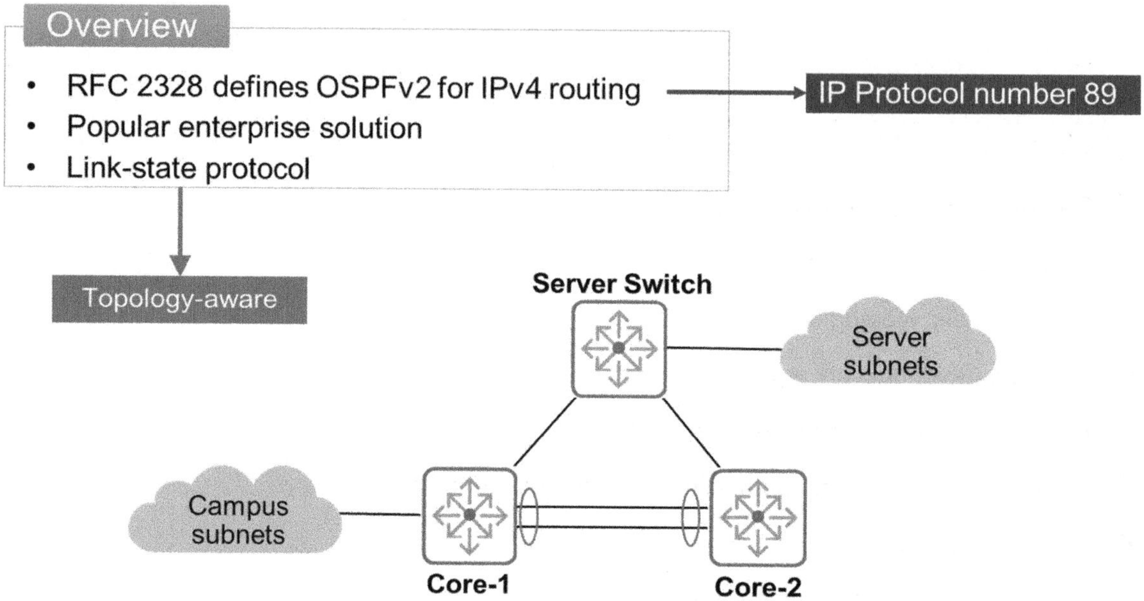

Figure 11-1 OSPF Introduction

RFC 2328 defines OSPFv2 to route IPv4 packets. OSPF does not use TCP or UDP – OSPF advertisements are placed directly inside an IP packet. Therefore, it does not have a TCP or UDP port number; it has IP protocol number 89 (Figure 11-1).

Note

The IP protocol number is a number associated to the protocol that is in use in Layer-4. The IP protocol number is included as a field in the Layer-3 header. This announcement in Layer-3 helps network devices to be aware of the Layer-4 protocol that is in use without decapsulating the packet. TCP uses the protocol number 6 and UDP uses the protocol number 17.

This is an extremely popular enterprise IGP routing solution, due to its hierarchical scalability and security mechanisms. For example, OSPF peers can authenticate packets exchanges. As a Link-State protocol, OSPF enabled routers advertise information about their connected Layer-3 interfaces and networks (links) and the cost associated with that interface. Let us see how it works.

Router ID Overview and Selection Criteria

All OSPF routers require a unique Router Identifier (RID), a 32-bit IP address in dotted-decimal notation. Routers include their ID in all OSPF packets that they send. Humans might look at the figure and see "Core-1, Core-2 and Sever Switch." The routers might identify themselves as 10.1.100.1, 10.1.100.2 and 10.0.100.0.

You can depend on each router to automatically identify itself, or you can take control of the situation and manually assign RIDs. Automatic assignment is tempting since it requires so little effort. However, many experienced engineers prefer to manually assign RIDs, due to certain documentation, troubleshooting, and management advantages.

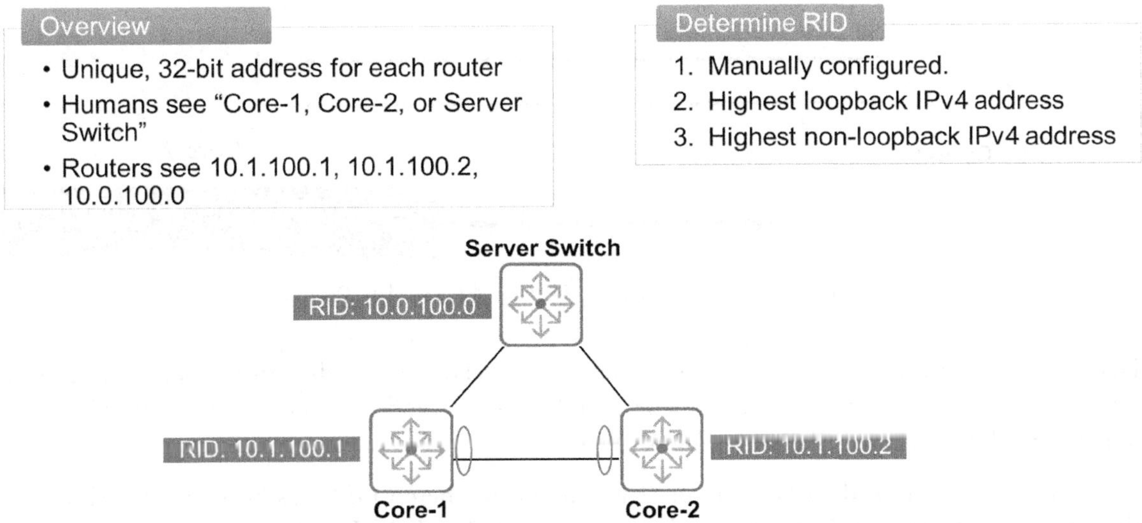

Figure 11-2 Router ID and Selection Criteria

AOS-CX uses the following sequence shown in Figure 11-2 to determine the Router ID:

1. If you manually specify the RID, then that is what the router uses.
2. If you do not specify the RID, the loopback interface with the highest IP address becomes the RID.
3. If no loopback interfaces exist, the regular non-loopback interface with the highest IP address becomes the RID. Non-functional Interfaces that are in a down state are not considered.

A Loopback interface is defined as a logical interface that is always in an up state (unless you manually disable it). This interface is useful for processes and protocols that depend on the interface status to work. The IP address associated to a loopback interface is routable, which means that external devices can initiate communication to it. As you gain more education and experience, you will continue to learn about the advantages of loopback interfaces: for scalability, troubleshooting, and network management.

OSPF General Operation Overview

Phase 1: Build a Neighbor Table

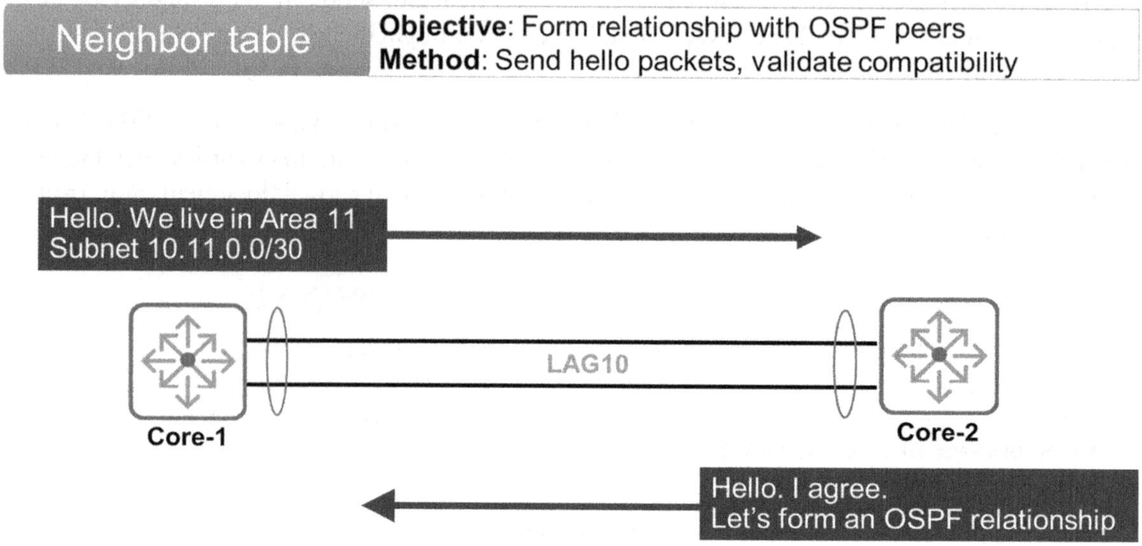

Figure 11-3 Building an OSPF Neighbor Table Phase 1

First, directly connected OSPF neighbors introduce themselves to their directly connected neighbors. The objective is to validate that they are compatible. The method is to send OSPF "Hello" packets out each OSPF interface as shown in Figure 11-3.

For example, Core-1 sends hellos out all of its interfaces where OSPF has been enabled shown in Figure 11-3, including out LAG10, on subnet 10.11.0.0/30, "Hello. I am Core-1 and I think that we live in Area 11, a normal area, and that we do not need to use secure authentication. We are connected on subnet 10.110.0/30." Core-2 sends similar information in its hello packet out LAG10. As long as the criteria match, the OSPF routers agree to be neighbors and they form an OSPF neighbor relationship. If any of these parameters do not match (typically due to misconfiguration), the routers refuse to form a neighbor relationship, and your network is broken. Let us assume that all routers in the figure successfully formed an adjacency with each directly connected peer. This will be reflected in each router's neighbor table.

Note

Only a small part of Hello packet contents is shown and discussed here, to convey the main idea. There is much more information exchanged in hello packets, about which you will soon learn.

Note

The term adjacency refers to a couple of routers that are physically connected to each other. This term is different from OSPF neighboring since an OSPF neighbor relationship can be established between a couple of routers that are not physically connected.

Phase 2: Build a Topology Database

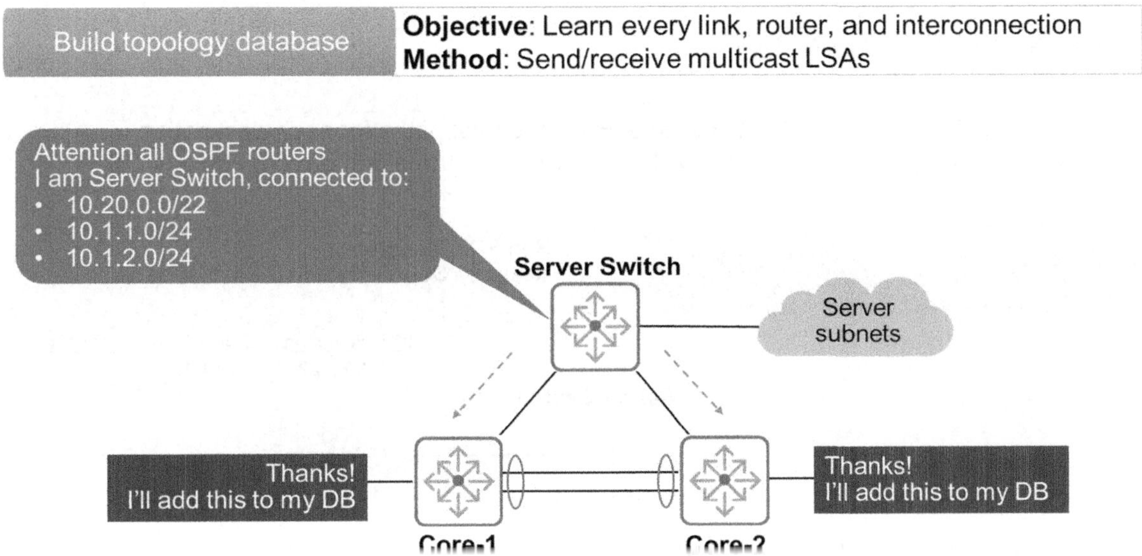

Figure 11-4 Build a Topology Database in Phase 2

The topology database is also called a Link State Database (LSDB). This is where a router shares known subnets with other routers If and only if an adjacency is fully formed. The objective is to build a topology database as a list of every single link (subnet), every single router, and exactly how those routers and subnets are interconnected. The method is to send multicast Link State Advertisements (LSAs).

Server Switch sends LSAs out all of its interfaces, "Attention all OSPF routers. I am Server Switch, and I am directly connected to 10.1.1.0/24, 10.1.2.0/24, 10.20.0.0/22. Every other OSPF router receives these LSAs and adds the information to its Topological database. Soon, every router has received LSAs from every other router. Thus, each router has a full topology database. This database is essentially the diagram you see in Figure 11-4, in a numerical format. As a result, each OSPF router has an identical topological database.

Note

The figure only shows Server Switch advertising its directly connected subnets, because that is all that it currently knows. However, once Server Switch receives LSAs from the other routers (as they have just received from Server Switch) it will advertise those routes as well. Routers advertise the entire contents of their topology database to all other routers. The topology database is also known as the link-state database.

Phase 3: Build the OSPF Table

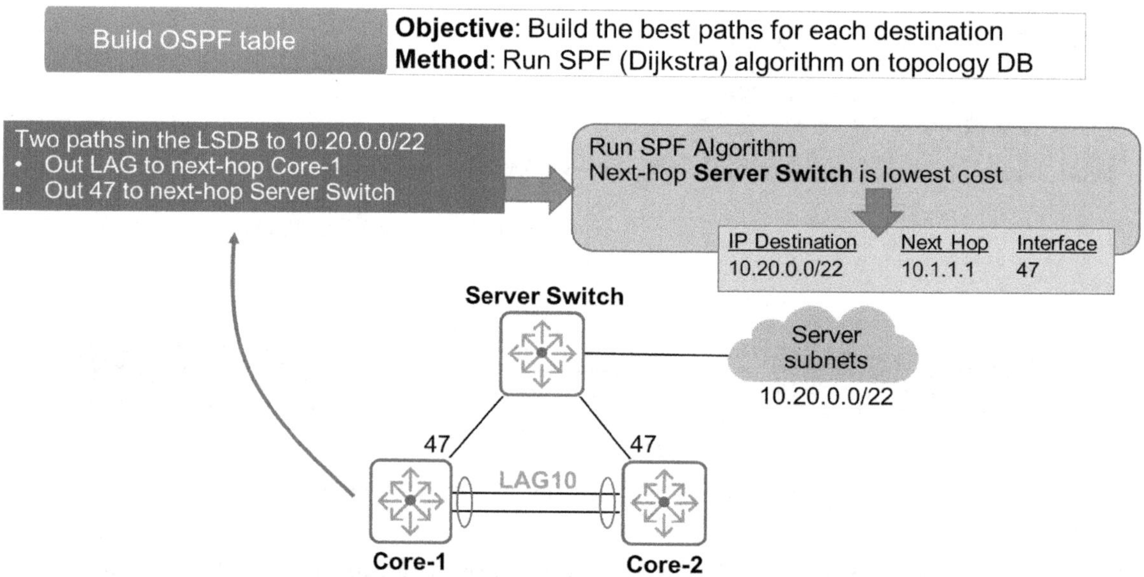

Figure 11-5 Building the OSPF Table for Phase 3

Although there is only one topology, each router's position and connectivity within that topology is unique. Thus, each router's objective is to determine the best path to each link from where they sit within the topology. The method is to run the SPF (Dijkstra) algorithm on the topology Database or LSDB.

Looking at Figure 11-5, Core-1's SPF algorithm analyzes the topology database and sees that Core-2 could reach destination 10.20.0.0/22 by routing packets out port LAG10. And Server Switch can reach the same destination out of port 47. The algorithm considers the cost associated with each path (based on bandwidth) and chooses the lowest cost (fastest) path. The best path shown in Figure 11-5 is to send the traffic directly to Server Switch.

Phase 4: Build a Routing Table

Build FIB table	**Objective**: Publish the best path on the FIB

```
Core-1# show ip route

10.20.0.0/22, vrf default
        via  10.1.1.1,   [110/200],   ospf
```

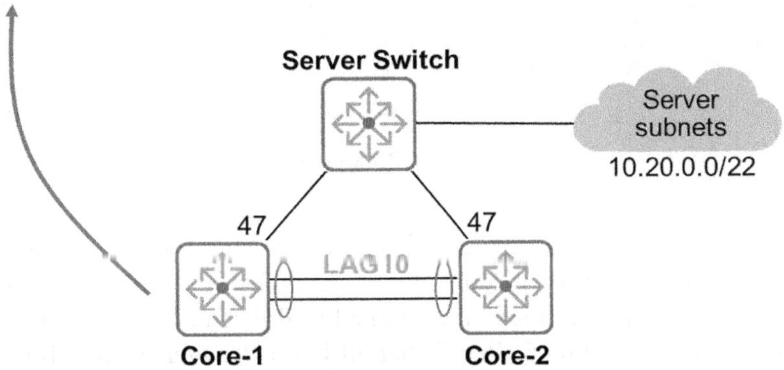

Figure 11-6 Building a Routing Table in Phase 4

In Figure 11-6, the best path previously calculated by OSPF is published on the Routing table (FIB). In this case the best path from Core-1 to Server Subnets uses the path through Server Switch.

OSPFv2 Neighbors

Hello Messages

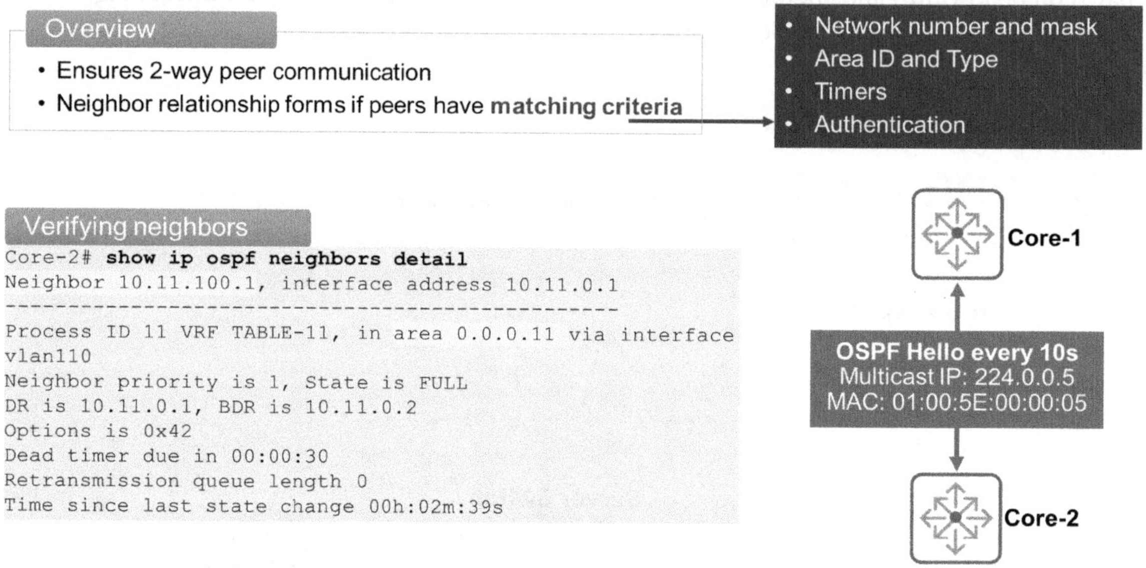

Figure 11-7 Hello Messages

Directly connected OSPF routers send hello packets to ensure 2-way communication, and to act as a failure detection mechanism. By default, these packets are sent every 10 seconds to Multicast IP address 224.0.0.5. This is the reserved "attention all OSPF routers" multicast address. Its associated MAC address is 01:00:5E:00:00:05. Recall that all Layer-2 switches flood broadcast and multicast frames out all ports in the broadcast domain, so all directly connected routers exchange Hellos; the first packet to be sent in the OSPF exchange process (Figure 11-7).

Remember that another main purpose of a Hello packet is to build and maintain a neighbor table. Peers only form a neighbor relationship if they are compatibly configured. They must agree that they are on the same subnet and have the same subnet mask. They must be in the same area and agree on the area type. Their timers must match (10-second OSPF hello timer, etc.), and they must be configured to use the same authentication type.

To verify the hello interval, you can use the **show IP OSPF neighbor detail** command.

In AOS-CX the hello interval is 10 seconds; however you can customize the interval from 1 to 65553 seconds.

```
Switch(config)# interface <interface-id>
Switch(config-if)# IP OSPF hello-interval <seconds>
```

Dead interval is the interval of time after which a neighbor is declared dead. Typically, this value is four times the Hello interval. This value also must match to create a neighbor relationship.

OSPF Neighbor States

OSPF uses a Finite State Machine (FSM) to process the neighbor state transitions between routers when certain conditions are satisfied. This process can be divided into two main phases:

- Establish Neighbor Adjacencies.
- Synchronize OSPF databases.

It is important to clarify that in a Broadcast Network, database synchronization only happens between the Designated Router (DR) and DROTHER routers and between the Backup Designated Router (BDR) and DROTHER routers. In other words, DROTHER routers only establish neighbor adjacencies and stay in the 2-WAY state (which is considered a stable state) but never synchronize databases.

As an example, consider Figure 11-8 where two core switches attempt to become OSPF neighbors over a Broadcast Network.

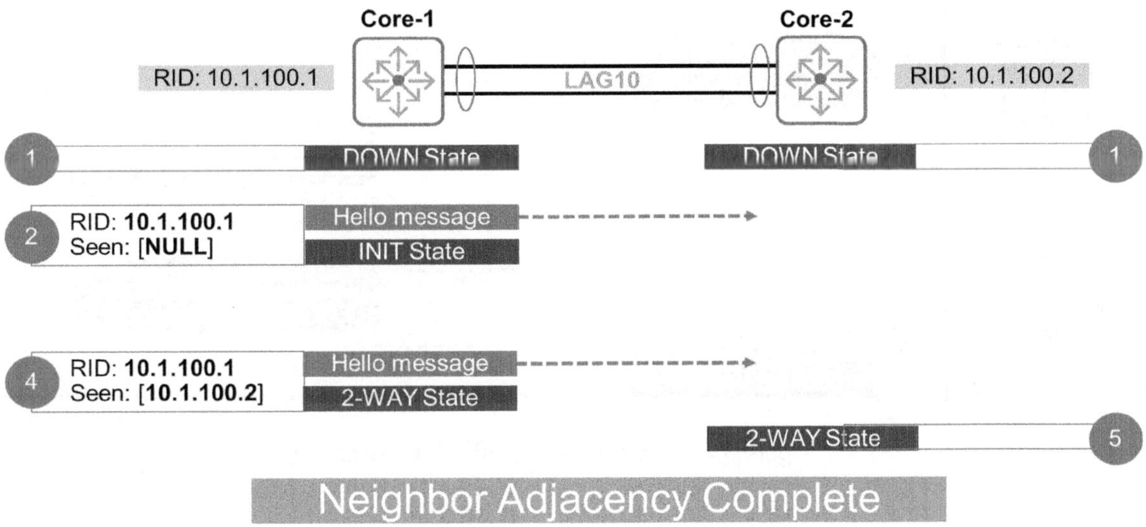

Figure 11-8 Establish Neighbor Adjacencies

Establish Neighbor Adjacencies:

1. Figure 11-8 starts with Core-1 and Core-2 starts with the DOWN neighbor state.
2. Core-1 transits to the INIT state when it sends the first Hello message. This message includes Router ID = 10.1.100.1; the Hello message includes a field from which routers have Core-1 received hellos. Since this is the first Hello message the field has a NULL value.
3. Core-2 receives Core-1's Hello message and responds, indicating that the message has been seen and values are compatible. Core-2 transits to INIT state.
4. Core-1 receives the Hello message and transits to the 2-WAY state. This device sends again the Hello message to Core-2 but this time it includes both Router IDs in the seen field.
5. Core-2 receives this message and moves to the 2-WAY state.

Synchronize OSPF Databases

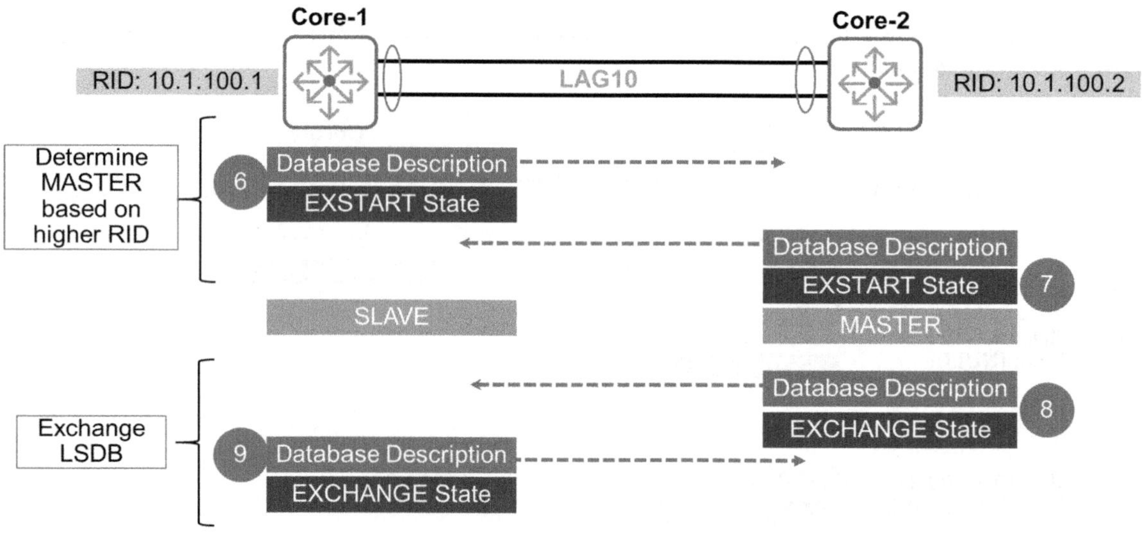

Figure 11-9 Synchronize OSPF Databases

In the example, Core-1 and Core-2 are the only two devices in the network, and so they continue to the database synchronization process (Figure 11-9).

6. Core-1 initiates the synchronization process by sending a Database Description packet. The switch transits to the EXSTART neighbor state.
7. Core-2 does a similar process when it moves to the EXSTART state by sending a Database Description packet.

The goal of the EXSTART state is to determine which switch will become the MASTER on the link, based on the highest Router ID. Understand that the MASTER role defines only which switch will initiate the Database exchange process. This role has nothing to do with DR/BDR – it is only for Link State Database (LSDB) exchange. In this example, Core-2 has a higher Router-ID and becomes the MASTER.

8. Core-2 sends another Database Description packet as it transitions to the EXCHANGE state. Core-2 is now sharing a summary of the contents of its LSDB with Core-1.
9. Core-1 also sends a Database Description packet and moves to the EXCHANGE state, sharing its LSDB with Core-2.

After several packets sent and received in the EXCHANGE state, each router will have a summary of the others entire LSDB. They compare the information received and, in the next step, request the missing information.

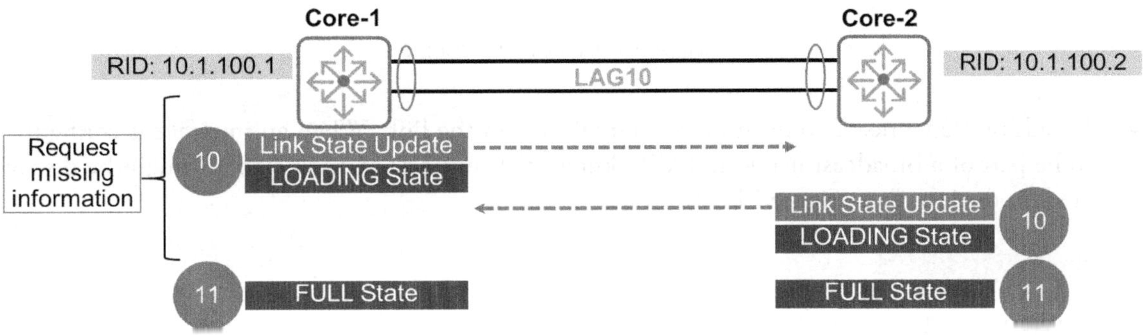

Figure 11-10 Synchronize OSPF Databases Continued

10. Figure 11-10 shows Core-1 and Core-2 request the missing information using Link State Update (LSU) packets. The other peer answers by sending the requested database information. Both switches transition to the LOADING neighbor state.

This state is the actual routing information exchange.

11. Core-1 and Core-2 move to the FULL state when there is no more information to be exchanged, and both devices have the same Link-State Database (LSDB).

You can verify the OSPF neighbor state using the **show IP OSPF neighbors** command.

```
Core-1# show IP OSPF neighbors
Neighbor ID        Priority       State        Nbr Address     Interface
---------------------------------------------------------------------------
10.1.100.2         1              FULL/DR      10.11.0.2       LAG10
```

OSPFv2 Operations

OSPF Network Types

From the protocol perspective two options exist for network types:

- Point-to-Point Network: Only two peers are on the link in Figure 11-11. When an interface is configured to be part of a Point-to-point link, OSPF knows that a single neighbor device is expected on the interface. PPP Serial links (deprecated in networks nowadays) are an example of this network types.

Figure 11-11 Point to Point

- Broadcast Networks: Two or more peers might be on the link. When an interface is configured to be part of a broadcast network, OSPF knows that more than one neighbor might be discovered on the interface (Figure 11-12).

Figure 11-12 Broadcast

In AOS-CX, interfaces default to the broadcast network type, but you can modify this with the **IP OSPF network** command.

```
Switch(config)# interface <interface-id>
Switch(config-if)# IP OSPF network {broadcast | point-to-point}
```

To verify the type of network that is in use you can use the **show IP OSPF interface** command. Unless you truly have multiple routers in the same broadcast domain, it is a recommended to configure switch-to-switch links with the point-to-point network type.

The network type is a concept that was used many years ago when Ethernet was not fully accepted as the unique Layer-2 protocol. Back in those days, serial communication was used more often, where it is only possible to have one device at each end of the link. This led to the concept of point-to-point network type. Meanwhile, you know that Ethernet is designed to have multiple devices connected to the same broadcast domain. This led to the concept of a Broadcast Network type.

OSPF can also use the Non-Broadcast Multiaccess (NBMA) Network type. This network can support multiple devices (multi-access) but does not support the broadcast capability. Frame Relay is an example of this network type. The use of this type of network is deprecated for modern networks, and so will not be covered in this course.

Broadcast Network Scalable Problem

The amount of information that can be exchanged between OSPF peers could be high in a medium-sized enterprise network. In a Broadcast network type this could easily increase since each router can have multiple peers. This could impact router performance when hundreds or thousands of routes must be computed for each OSPF peer. We need a solution.

OSPF solves this scalability challenge by electing a Designated Router (DR) in the broadcast domain. This device maintains a complete full neighbor state with the rest of the devices (which implies that databases are exchanged with the peers). However, the non-designated routers do not exchange database information with each other. This helps to reduce the amount of information that each router in the domain must process.

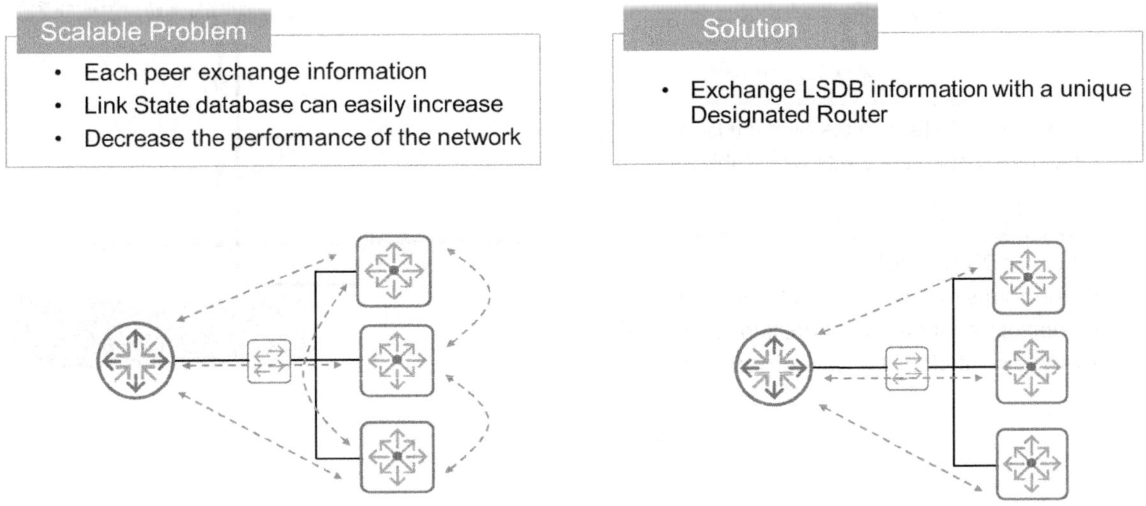

Figure 11-13 Scalability and Solution

To maintain high availability, you can elect a Backup Designated Router (BDR) to avoid a single point of failure. This device also maintains a full state with all devices in the Broadcast network. However, it only advertises information when the primary DR is no longer available.

Designated Router and Backup Designated Router

In a Broadcast network OSPF routers expect to have formed neighbor relationships with more than one peer. This situation could potentially be inefficient when there is a topology change, LSAs can be flooded and re-flooded in the broadcast domain. The solution is to elect a single point of contact as a Designated Router (DR). This helps to coordinate peer interactions in the broadcast domain. It forms full adjacencies with all other OSPF peers in the broadcast domain, so that it can receive and flood LSAs.

A Backup Designated Router (BDR) is elected to take over if the DR fails. The BDR also forms a full adjacency with the DR, and all other peers in the broadcast domain.

Any router not elected to be the DR or BDR is labeled as DROTHER, "Some router other than me is the DR." These routers only form a full adjacency with the DR and the BDR. This is where the efficiency is realized. Whether there are 3 routers or 30 routers in the broadcast domain, DROTHERs need only form Full adjacencies with 2 peers as the DR and BDR.

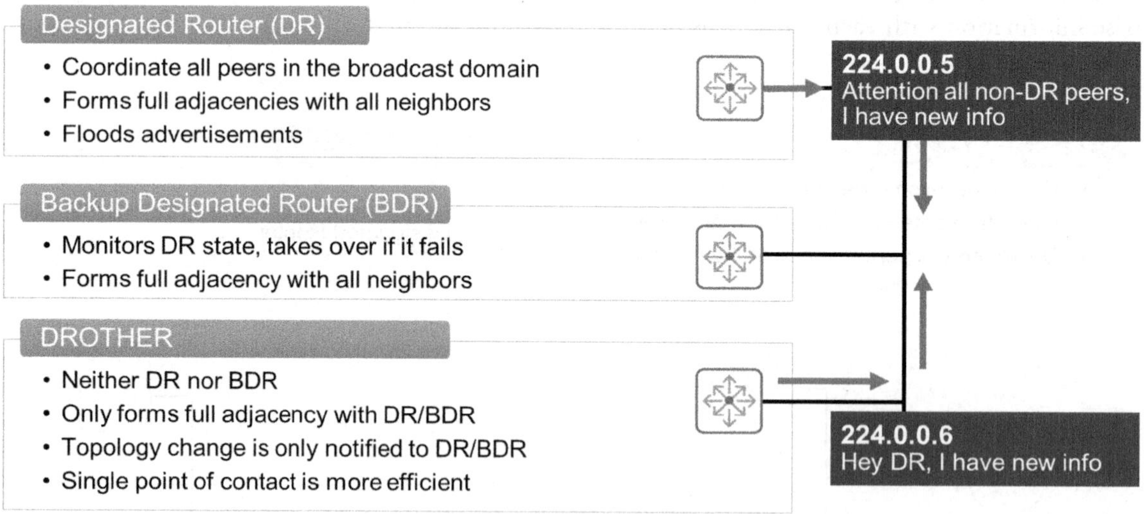

Figure 11-14 DR and BDR

In Figure 11-14, one of the DROTHERs detects a topology change on one of its other interfaces. It need not communicate to every other router in the broadcast domain, only the DR and BDR. So, it sends a multicast LSA using destination IP address 224.0.0.6 as the reserved address that says, "attention DR and BDR."

The DR is functional, so it receives this packet. It updates its topology database and informs all other DRs in the link with a multicast LSA to 224.0.0.5, "Attention all DROTHERs, I have new information."

Designated Router Election

DR and BDR election is based on a priority value assigned to an interface – the highest priority value wins the election. In case of a tie, the router with the higher Router-ID becomes the DR.

AOS-CX follows certain rules related to the priority value:

- The default priority value is 1.
- Valid priority values are 0-255.
- A priority value of 0 means that the router does not participate in DR election.

You can perform this configuration at the interface level as shown:

```
Switch(config)# interface <interface-id>
Switch(config-if)# IP OSPF priority <priority-value>
```

To verify the priority value and the elected DR, use the command **show IP OSPF interface**, or **show IP OSPF neighbors**.

```
Switch# show IP OSPF interface
Transit delay 1 sec, Router priority 1
    Designated Router IP: 10.0.13.2
    Backup Designated Router IP: 10.0.13.1
```

OSPF Area

An Area is a group of OSPF routers that share the same Link State database. All router must be part of an area.

OSPF Area

- Group of OSPF routers with same LSDB
- Hierarchy improves scalability

Backbone area

- Always Area 0
- All other areas must connect to Area 0

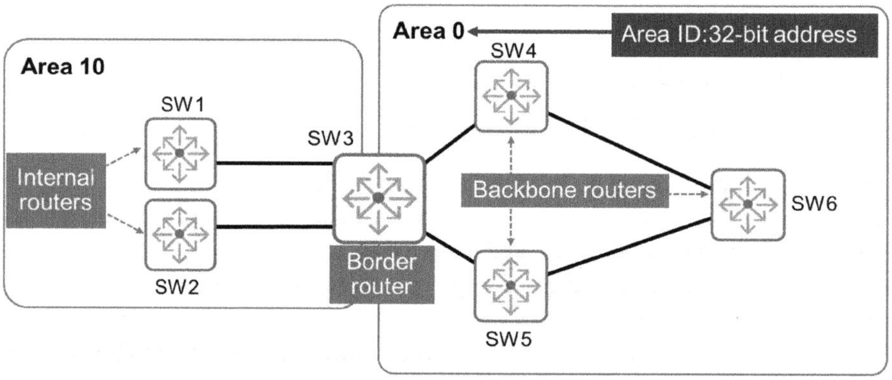

Figure 11-15 Backbone and Normal Areas

When you split a large network into separate areas, you reduce the size of the LSDB in each router, lower CPU utilization, and increase overall network stability. This is because each router in an area must only maintain the topology for that area.

For example, in Figure 11-15; SW1, SW2, and SW3 need not learn about the entire topology. They only need to know about the Area 10 topology.

Routers SW1 and SW2 are called "Internal routers." All their interfaces are in a single area. If an internal router must route outside of its area, it simply forwards packets to its Area Border Router (ABR). An ABR is a router connected to two or more areas. SW3 is the ABR for Area 10, with two interfaces in Area 10 and two interfaces in Area 0.

ALL areas must connect directly to the special backbone Area 0. This is the most important area in the hierarch, and so should have a redundant design. So, Area 10 cannot connect directly to any other area that is not 0. Communication between 2 non-backbone areas MUST communicate via the backbone area 0. Routers with interfaces in Area 0 are called backbone routers. Routes SW4, 5, and 6 have all interfaces in a single area, so they are also Internal routers. You can call them Internal Backbone routers.

You assign interfaces to an area by assigning them to an area ID - a 32-bit long address that can be written in dot-decimal notation (Area 0.0.0.0), or in decimal notation Area 0, as shown in Figure 11-15. AOS-CX supports both notations. This course is only focused on single-area designs, in which all router interfaces are in Area 0. You can learn more about hierarchical OSPF solutions in the advanced courses.

OSPF LSA Type 1

OSPF routers generate different types of Link State Advertisements (LSAs), each with a different purpose and scope in the OSPF routing domain. Each LSA includes the Link-State identifier which describes the portion of the network that a router announces. You will learn about these LSA types, starting with LSA Type 1 shown in Figure 11-16.

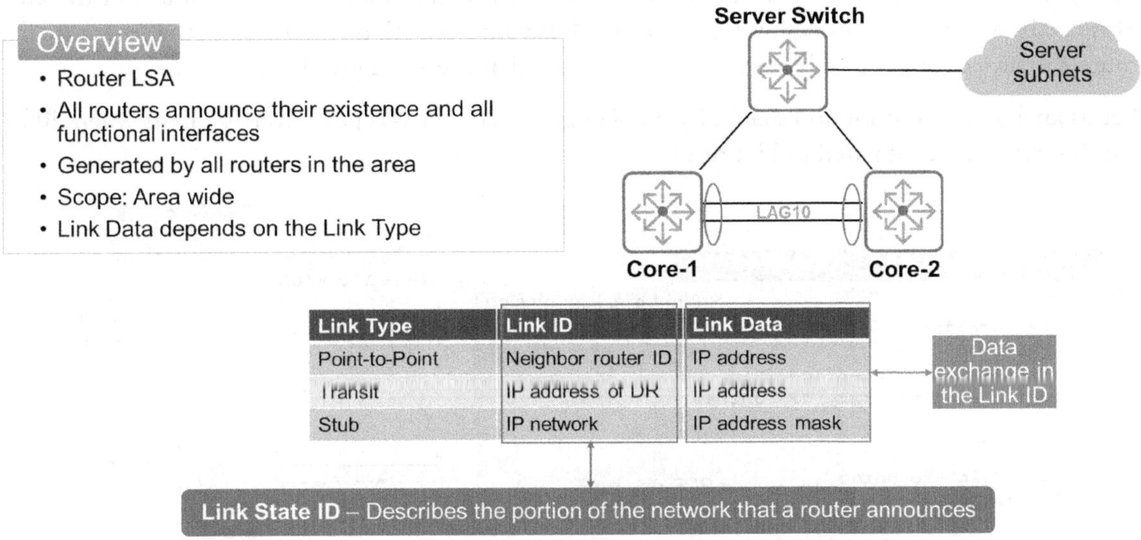

Figure 11-16 LSA Type 1

The purpose of LSA Type 1 is for a router to announce itself. That is why they are called "Router LSAs." You might walk into a room and say, "Hello everyone, my name is James Bond." Similarly, routers use a Type 1 LSA to say, "Hello everyone, I am RID 10.1.100.1, and I have 3 interfaces that are functional, and are participating in this OSPF area."

It is important to remember that the information shared on LSA Type1 depends on the Link Type. Consider what information will be shared by the Server Switch when different link types are configured. In addition to defining the network type, OSPF also defines the link types, which are two different concepts. Link types are primarily used to describe the interfaces or neighbors of an OSPF router.

- Stub Link: Used when OSPF is enabled on an interface and no OSPF neighbor exists on the interface. For example, a Loopback interface is considered stub Network.

- Transit Link: Used in a Broadcast network with two or more OSPF neighbors.
- Point-to-point Link: Used in Point-to-point networks, only one OSPF neighbor is expected in the link.

> **Note**
>
> The Link Type is a consequence of setting up the network-id and the number of neighbors that are in the link. When the network type is set to point-to-point then the router expects a single device on the link. When the network type is set to Broadcast then the stub or transit link type is used. Stub for no neighbor and Transit for one or more neighbors.

In AOS-CX you can verify this information by using the **show IP OSPF LSDB** command. In the example shown in Figure 11-16, router Core-1 has learned that there are three routers in the area. This can be a powerful troubleshooting command. If your network diagram shows that there are five routers in area 0, but you only see 3 listed, you know that there is a problem.

Let us analyze the information shared by the Server Switch's LSA-Type1 advertisements when different link types are configured in Figure 11-17.

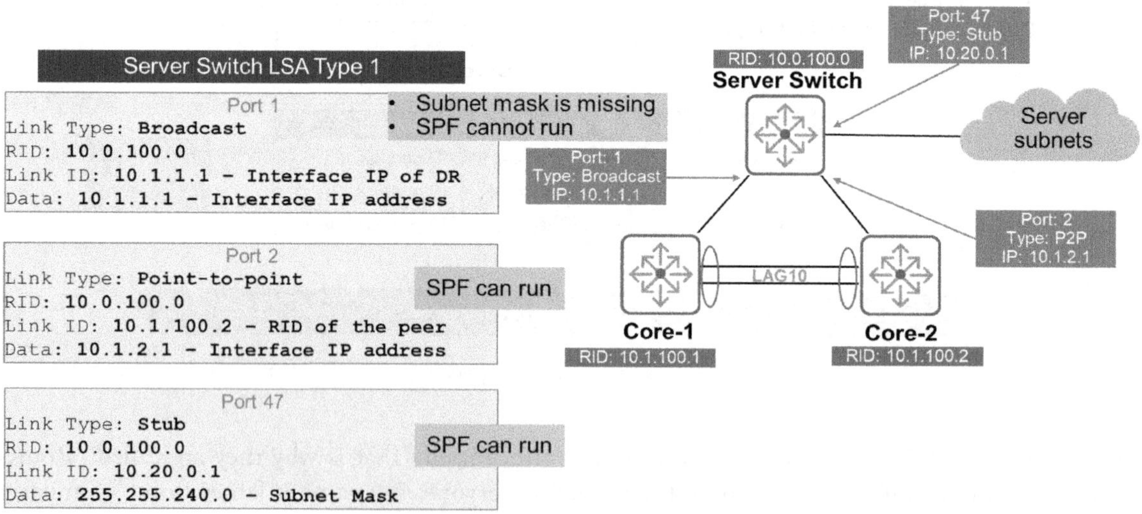

Figure 11-17 LSA Type 1 Continued

Now analyze the information received from Core-1 and Core-2 perspective.

First, the Stub Link type includes the Subnet and the Mask, this information is enough to run the SPF algorithm locally to reach the destination.

Second, the Point-to-point interface includes the Router ID of the peer and the local interface used. From Core-1 perspective the link details are not complete, Core-1 needs the data of the other peer on the link. This information will be known when Core-1 receives the LSA Type 1 from Core-2. When we receive the information from both parties then Core-1 can run the SPF algorithm.

Finally, the broadcast interface will include only the IP address of the Router ID, but in this case no subnet information will be included using LSA Type1. How can we solve this problem?

The answer is to use the LSA Type 2

In AOS-CX you can verify this information by using the **show IP OSPF LSDB** command.

OSPF LSA Type 2

The LSA Type 2 is used when there is a Broadcast network type link, which has an elected DR and BDR. Routers on point-to-point network types do not generate a Type 2 LSA. In this case the Link-state ID is the IP address of the Designated Router. These LSAs are known as Network LSAs, because routers advertise the networks for which it is the DR.

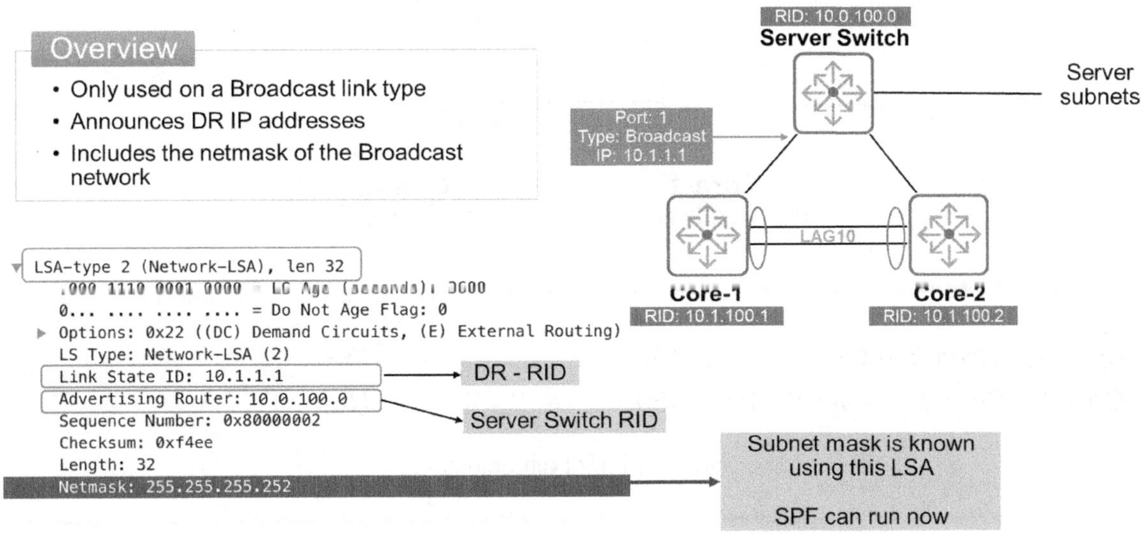

Figure 11-18 OSPF LSA Type 2

The image shows a packet capture using Wireshark where the netmask is included in the LSA (Figure 11-18). This information helps to run the SPF algorithm. The missing information that was missing in Type 1 is now known.

In the show IP OSPF LSDB output, the Network Link State Advertisement section shows you a list of DRs.

Path Selection

After all routers have successfully exchanged LSAs and LSUs, they all have an identical LSDB, a topology database. Remember, the LSDB is a list of very links, every router, and how those routers and links are interconnected. It is a list of every path.

Now routers must run the Shortest Path First (SPF) (Dijkstra's algorithm) to find the best paths to each destination subnet. The best path is the one with the lowest cost, and cost is based on bandwidth. Therefore, if there are multiple paths to a single subnet, OSPF chooses the path with the lowest cumulative cost, the fastest path.

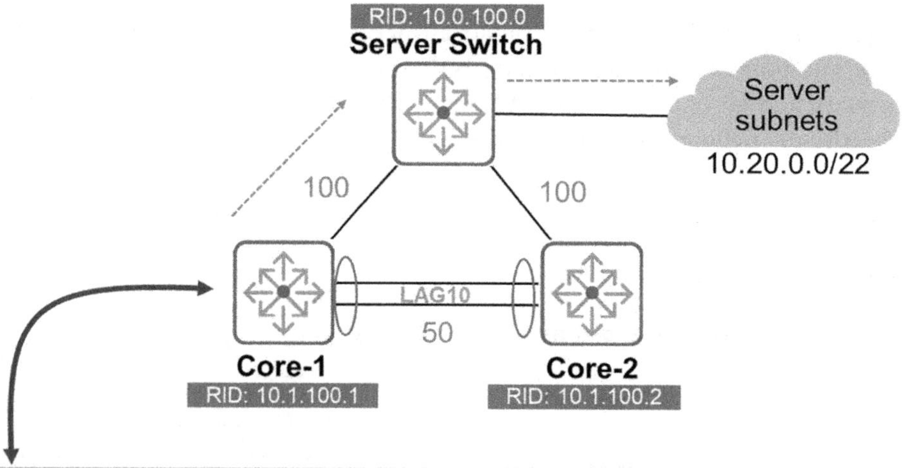

Route	Cumulative Cost	Best path
Core-1 – Sever Switch	100	Yes
Core-1 – Core-2 – Sever Switch	150	No

Figure 11-19 Path Selection

Consider the topology shown in Figure 11-19. Core-1 has two paths to reach destination subnet 10.20.0.0/22. To determine each path's cost, simply add the values indicated for each link. Here is what you get:

- Using Core-2 as the next hop, the cost is 100 = 100.
- Using Server-Switch as the next hop, the cost is 100+50 = 150.

Obviously, using Server-Switch results in the lowest cost, and so that path is added to the route table.

OSPF Convergence

There are two components to OSPF routing convergence:

- Detect topology changes.
- Recalculate routes.

Topology change detection is supported in two ways by OSPF. The first, and quickest, is a failure or change of status on the physical interface. The second is a timeout of the OSPF hello timer. An OSPF neighbor is deemed to have failed if the time to wait for a hello packet exceeds the dead timer, which defaults to four times the value of the hello timer. The default hello timer is 10 seconds, so the default dead timer is 40 seconds.

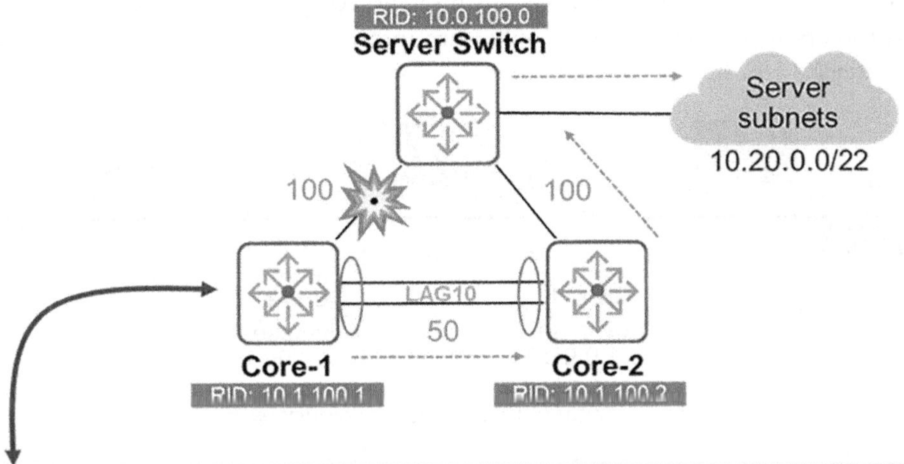

Route	Cumulative Cost	Best path
~~Core-1 – Sever Switch~~	~~100~~	NA
Core-1 – Core-2 – Sever Switch	150	Yes

Figure 11-20 Convergence

When a change is detected, an LSA is sent to all routers in the OSPF area to signal the topology change. In Figure 11-20, the link between Core-1 and Sever Switch has failed. Server Switch and Core-1 detect this outage and their links go from an UP state to a DOWN state. Thus, Server Switch and Core-1 originate the topology change LSA. Then they run the SPF algorithm to calculate their best new paths to any affected network, such as 10.20.0.0/22. The Server switch will not make any changes as the best path is directly connected. Core-1 on the other hand will recalculate its best path. In this case it will use the path using Core-2.

Ultimately, Core-2 receives LSAs about the change, but no recalculation is needed from its point of view. Each router performs route recalculation after a failure has been detected. This causes all routers to recalculate all their routes using the Dijkstra (SPF) algorithm.

Passive Interfaces

OSPF configuration involves enabling the protocol on logical and physical interfaces. Thus, the router can generate LSAs to advertise subnets to other routers. This implies that the router sends periodic Hello messages on all OSPF-enabled interfaces.

In some cases, this is not desired. The most common example is when only hosts exist on that subnet. Router constantly sends OSPF packets on a network where nobody cares. Hosts do not respond to OSPF multicast 224.0.0.5 and 224.0.0.6. It simply wasted processing cycles and bandwidth on the link. If bad actors are on the link, they could learn information about your network, and potentially mount an attack.

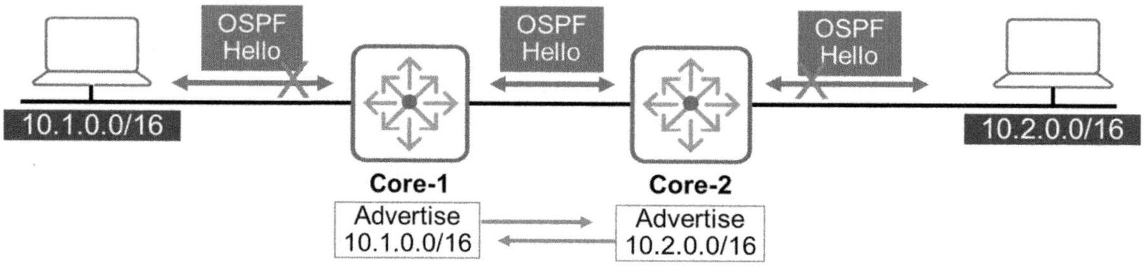

Figure 11-21 Passive Interfaces

The solution is to configure these host-facing router interfaces as passive. When an interface is passive, it stops sending and accepting OSPF packets out that interface. However, it continues to advertise that network to other routers. In Figure 11-21, Switch-1 does not send hello packets out its 10.1.0.0/16 network, but it will tell Switch-2 about that network. Switch-2 has a similar arrangement, as relates to the 10.2.0.0/16 link.

In AOS-CX you can use the **IP OSPF passive** command in the interface context to enable a passive interface.

```
Switch(config)# interface <interface-id>
Switch(config-if)# IP OSPF passive
```

OSPF Scalability

During the previous discussion, did you notice a potential scalability challenge with OSPF? You learned that every single router sends LSAs that advertise nearly the entire contents of their LSDB to every other router. With hundreds of thousands of routers, these LSA packets can begin to consume significant bandwidth. The LSDB (topology database) can grow quite large, consuming memory resources on each router. The SPF algorithm must then run on this exceptionally large database, consuming CPU cycles. This is not scalable. The solution shown in Figure 11-22 is OSPF hierarchy implemented by splitting the network up into Areas.

Challenge	• Every router process information about every other router • LSAs use bandwidth, LSDP uses memory, SPF algorithm uses CPU
Solution	• Split the network up into hierarchical OSPF **areas**.

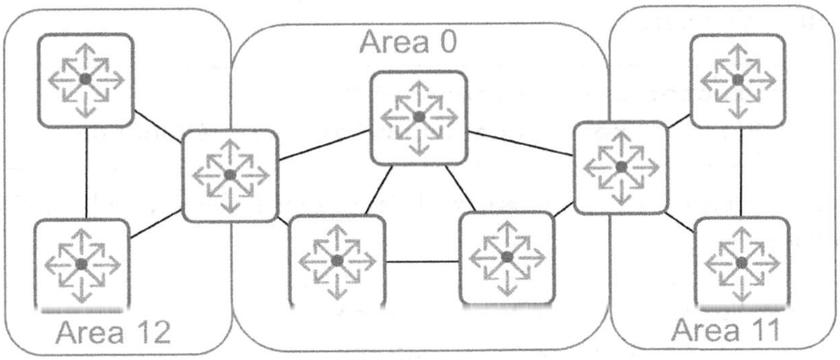

Figure 11-22 OSPF Scalability

Using Cost to Manipulate Routes

The cost associated for each interface is calculated using this formula:

$$\text{OSPF Cost value} = \frac{\text{Reference Bandwidth}}{\text{Interface Bandwidth}}$$

AOS-CX uses a default reference value of 100000 Mbps. You can verify this value using the **show IP OSPF** command.The result of the OSPF cost formula can be displayed using the **show IP OSPF interface** command. Notice in Figure 11-23 that a 10Gbps port has assigned the Cost of 10.

Verify

```
Switch # show ip ospf | include Bandwidth
Reference Bandwidth: 100000 Mbps
```

```
Switch# show ip ospf interface

IP address 10.0.13.1/24, Process ID 1 VRF default, area 0.0.0.0
    State Backup-dr, Status up, Network type Broadcast
    Link Speed: 10000 Mbps
    Cost Configured NA, Calculated 10
    Transit delay 1 sec, Router priority 1
```

Figure 11-23 Route Manipulation

Configuring Cost Value

AOS-CX allows to modify the cost of an interface in two different ways:

Modifying the reference bandwidth value. This method is applied to the entire OSPF process, which means that will affect all interfaces.

```
Switch(config)# router OSPF <process-id>
Switch(config-OSPF-1)# reference-bandwidth <1- 4000000>
```

Modifying the cost associated with an interface. This approach allows to only modify the cost value to a specific interface.

```
Switch(config)# interface <interface-id>
Switch(config-if)# IP OSPF cost <cost-value>
```

When this command is applied the router is no longer considered the cost formula but instead simply uses the manual value that was entered. Validate using the **show IP OSPF interface** command.

```
Switch# show IP OSPF interface
Interface 1/1/27 is up, line protocol is up
--------------------------------------------

IP address 10.0.34.3/24, Process ID 1 VRF default, area 0.0.0.0
    State Backup-dr, Status up, Network type Broadcast
    Link Speed: 10000 Mbps
    Cost Configured 40, Calculated 40
    Transit delay 1 sec, Router priority 1
```

Configuring OSPF in AOS-CX

1. Enable OSPF process. AOS-CX is capable to run a single OSPF process per VRF. The **router OSPF <process-id>** command is used to enable the OSPF process and assigns a process value to it, this value is a number between 1 and 63.

```
Switch(config)# router OSPF <process-id>
```

2. Configure the Router-ID.

```
Switch(config-OSPF-1)# router-id <a.b.c.d>
```

3. Create the OSPF area. AOS-CX allows to configure the Area ID in dot-decimal value or digital format. For example, 0.0.0.0 is equivalent to 0.

```
Switch(config-OSPF-1)# area <area-id>
```

4. Enable OSPF in the interface.

```
Switch(config)# interface <interface-id>
Switch(config-if)# IP OSPF <process-id> area <area-id>
```

5. Set the network type.

```
Switch(config)# interface <interface-id>
Switch(config-if)# IP OSPF network {broadcast | point-to-point}
```

6. Optional, set the OSPF cost associated to the interface.

```
Switch(config)# interface <interface-id>
Switch(config-if)# IP OSPF cost <cost-value>
```

Lab 11: Static Routes

Overview

The goal of the following tasks is to complete the dual-homed Internet Service deployment for BigStartup. The customer wants load balancing across both carriers and redundancy in case of failure. They want assurance that if either link fails, traffic can still go out through the alternate ISP. This will require the configuration of static and floating routes, which you will apply on the Core switches.

Note that references to equipment and commands are taken from Aruba's hosted remote lab. These are shown for demonstration purposes in case you wish to replicate the environment and tasks on your own equipment.

Objectives

After completing this lab, you will be able to:

- Configure Core switches to Perimeter Firewall links using a /30 prefix.
- Calculate and deploy Variable Length Subnet Mask (VLSM) prefixes.
- Configure static routes.
- Add a default route into the routing table for providing internet access.
- Manipulate administrative distances in order to configure floating routes.
- Validate proper load sharing and failover.

Note

IP prefix is an aggregation of IP addresses and is usually used to refer to an IP network or subnet in general.

Lab 11.1: Open Shortest Path First Single Area

Overview

This morning, while drinking your coffee and browsing your email, you notice a message from BigStartup titled: "PO: Professional Services, Server Switch Integration." A few hours later, you meet your customer and find out that the servers they ordered months ago have finally arrived, along with a Data Center grade 8325 AOS-CX switch intended for connecting them. Although another supplier, called NetAmateur, will oversee that switch's implementation, they want you to take care of the Core part.

They also have plans for expanding and extending the network to remote locations in the following years, and they will want these locations to be able to access the servers. You have advised them this is a good time to design and deploy a dynamic routing protocol called OSPF.

Objectives

After completing this lab, you will be able to:

- Define an OSPF router ID.
- Create VRF-specific OSPF process.
- Create an Area and assign it to interfaces.
- Build neighbor relationships.

- Validate OSPF-learned prefixes.
- Deploy DHCP Helper role (Figure 11-24).

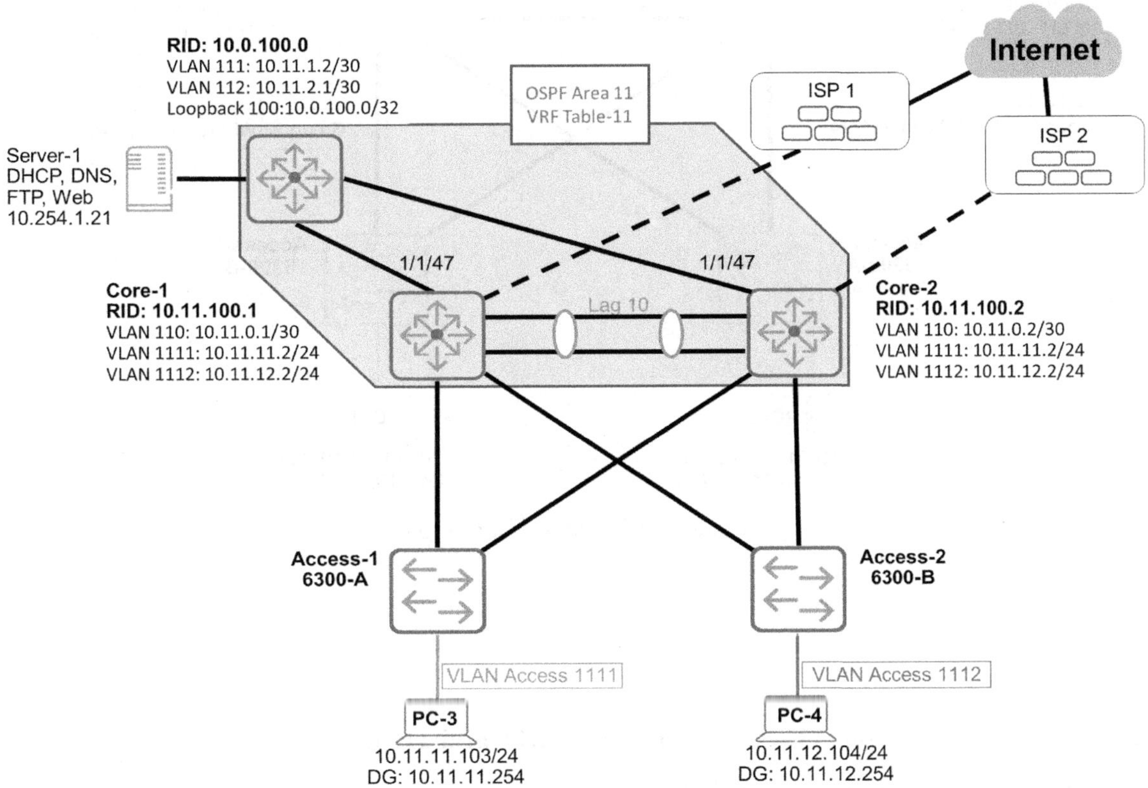

Figure 11-24 Lab Topology

Task 1: OSPF Single Area Between Cores

Objectives

You are about to run an OSPF single Area deployment on your core switches. This includes defining a unique Router ID, enabling the process and mapping it to a VRF, creating an OSPF area and assigning it to interfaces. You will begin with the link between Cores. Once the tasks are completed you will proceed with neighbor discovery validation (Figure 11-25).

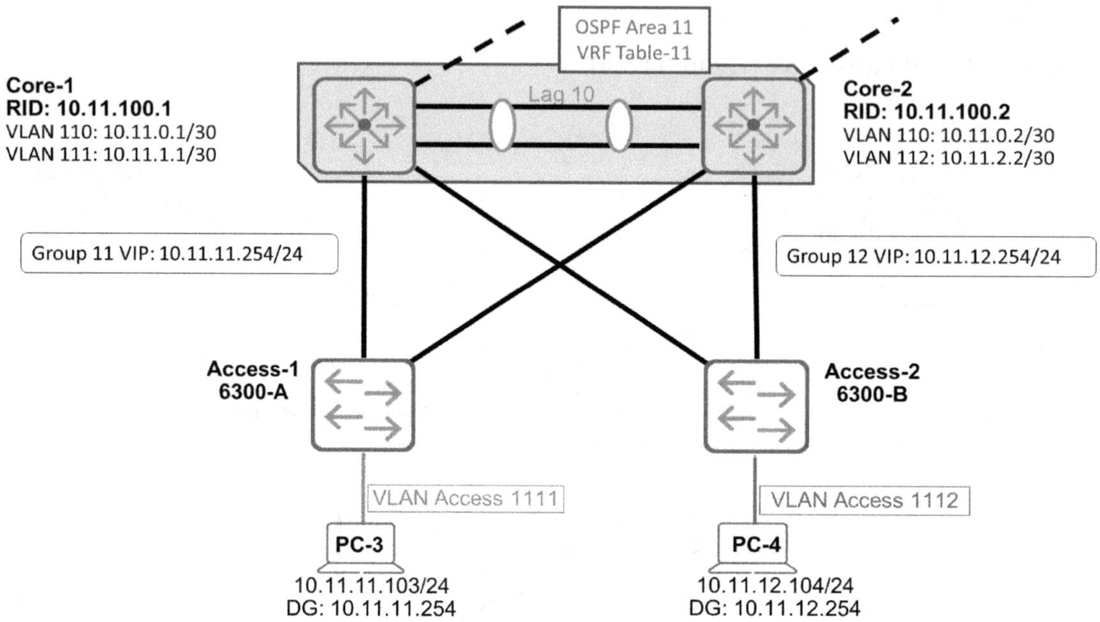

Figure 11-25 Task 1 Topology

Steps

Core-1 (via PC-1)

1. Open the SSH session to Core-1. Login using **cxf11/aruba123**.
2. Define the height of the page to 40 lines.

```
Core-1# page 40
```

3. Create the OSPF process number 11 and map it to VRF TABLE-11.

```
Core-1(config)# router OSPF 11 VRF TABLE-11
```

4. Assign Router ID 10.11.100.1 and create area 11.

```
Core-1(config-OSPF-11)# router-id 10.11.100.1
Core-1(config-OSPF-11)# area 11
```

5. Enable the process.

```
Core-1(config-OSPF-11)# enable
Core-1(config-OSPF-11)# exit
```

Note

At this point OSPF is up and running in Core-1, however it is not sending Hello messages yet because you have not enabled it on any interfaces. You will now enable it on the link to Core-2.

6. Assign OSPF process 11 area 11 on interface VLAN 110.

```
Core-1(config)# interface VLAN 110
Core-1(config-if-VLAN)# IP OSPF 11 area 11
Core-1(config-if-VLAN)# end
```

7. Review the OSPF process state on VRF TABLE-11.

```
Core-1# show IP OSPF VRF TABLE-11
Routing Process 11 with ID : 10.11.100.1 VRF TABLE-11
-----------------------------------------------------

OSPFv2 Protocol is enabled
Graceful-restart is configured
Restart Interval: 120, State: inactive
Last Graceful Restart Exit Status: none
SPF: Start Time: 200ms, Hold Time: 1000ms, Max Wait Time: 5000ms
Maximum Paths to Destination: 4
Number of external LSAs 0, checksum sum 0
Number of areas is 1, 1 normal, 0 stub, 0 NSSA
Number of active areas is 1, 1 normal, 0 stub, 0 NSSA
BFD is disabled
Reference Bandwidth: 100000 Mbps
Area (0.0.0.11) (Active)
  Interfaces in this Area: 1 Active Interfaces: 1
  Passive Interfaces: 0 Loopback Interfaces: 0
  SPF calculation has run 4 times
  Area ranges:
  Number of LSAs: 1, checksum sum 30066
```

What routing ID is this OSPF router using? ____________________

What is the state of the protocol? ____________________

How many areas are created and what is the Area ID? ____________________

How many LSAs have been created? ____________________

What LSA type do you think it is? ____________________

8. Display the status of OSPF interfaces on VRF TABLE-11.

```
Core-1# show IP ospf interface VRF TABLE-11
Interface VLAN110 is up, line protocol is up
---------------------------------------------

IP address 10.11.0.1/30, Process ID 11 VRF TABLE-11, area 0.0.0.11
    State Dr, Status up, Network type Broadcast
    Link Speed: 1000 Mbps
    Cost Configured NA, Calculated 100
    Transit delay 1 sec, Router priority 1
    Designated Router IP: 10.11.0.1
    No backup designated router on this network
    Timer Intervals: Hello 10, Dead 40, Retransmit 5
    No authentication
    Number of Link LSAs: 0, checksum sum 0
    BFD is disabled
```

What interface is running the protocol? ______________________________

What area is the interface on? ______________________________

What are the default Hello and Dead timers? ______________________________

Note

Right now, Core-1 is sending hello messages out of Interface VLAN 110, however, there is no other OSPF router on that segment yet. You will proceed to deploy the counterpart on Core-2.

Core-2 (via PC-1)

9. Open the SSH session to Core-2.

10. Repeat steps 2 to 6 using Router ID 10.11.100.2.

```
Core-2# page 40
Core-2# configure terminal
Core-2(config)# router OSPF 11 VRF TABLE-11
Core-2(config-OSPF-11)# router-id 10.11.100.2
Core-2(config-OSPF-11)# area 11
Core-2(config-OSPF-11)# enable
Core-2(config-OSPF-11)# exit
Core-2(config)# interface VLAN 110
Core-2(config-if-VLAN)# IP OSPF 11 area 11
Core-2(config-if-VLAN)# end
```

11. List all OSPF neighbors that Core-2 has discovered. Include the details.

```
Core-2# show IP OSPF neighbors detail VRF TABLE-11
Neighbor 10.11.100.1, interface address 10.11.0.1
-------------------------------------------------

Process ID 11 VRF TABLE-11, in area 0.0.0.11 via interface VLAN110
Neighbor priority is 1, State is FULL
DR is 10.11.0.1, BDR is 10.11.0.2
Options is 0x42
Dead timer due in 00:00:30
Retransmission queue length 0
Time since last state change 00h:02m:39s
```

What neighbor has Core-2 discovered? List the Router ID? ______________________

What is the adjacency state? ______________________

What is the Designated Router and what is the Backup? ______________________

Since both nodes have a default priority of 1, how was Designated Router (DR) elected? ______________________

12. Write down the roles for the links between the cores in Figure 11-26.

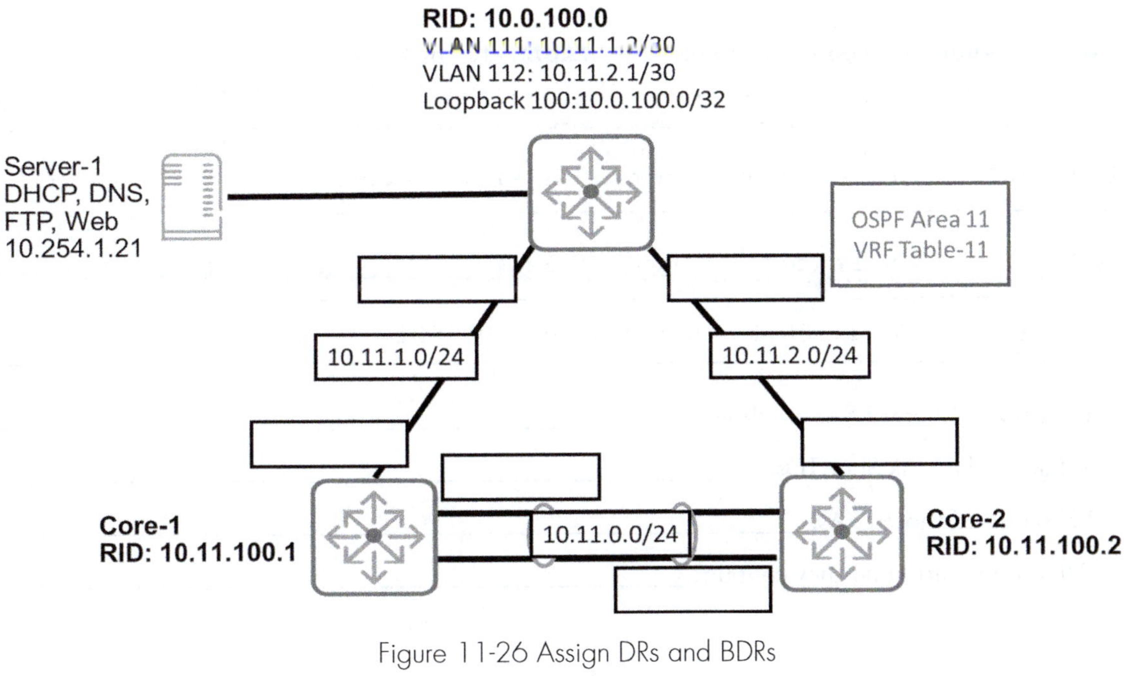

Figure 11-26 Assign DRs and BDRs

13. Display the Router LSAs that Core-2 knows.

```
Core-2# show IP OSPF 11 LSDB VRF TABLE-11 router
OSPF Router with ID (10.11.100.2) (Process ID 11 VRF TABLE-11)
================================================================

Router Link State Advertisements (Area 0.0.0.11)
-------------------------------------------------

LSID          ADV Router     Age     Seq#          Checksum    Link
Count
-----------------------------------------------------------------------
10.11.100.1   10.11.100.1    1318    0x80000006    0x00009138  1
10.11.100.2   10.11.100.2    1324    0x80000006    0x00008f37  1

Core-2#
```

How many Router LSAs are shown? ______________________________

What are the Link State IDs? ______________________________

Who created those LSAs? ______________________________

What information do they contain? ______________________________

14. Display the Network LSAs that Core-2 knows.

```
Core-2# show IP OSPF 11 LSDB VRF TABLE-11 network
OSPF Router with ID (10.11.100.2) (Process ID 11 VRF TABLE-11)
================================================================

Network Link State Advertisements (Area 0.0.0.11)
--------------------------------------------------

LSID          ADV Router     Age     Seq#          Checksum
---------------------------------------------------------------
10.11.0.1     10.11.100.1    1479    0x80000001    0x00003b9b
```

How many Router LSAs are shown? ______________________________

What are the Link State IDs? ______________________________

Who created those LSAs? ______________________________

What information do they contain? ______________________________

Core-1 (via PC-1)

15. Move to Core-1.
16. Display the Router LSAs.

```
Core-1# show IP OSPF 11 LSDB VRF TABLE-11 router
OSPF Router with ID (10.11.100.1) (Process ID 11 VRF TABLE-11)
===============================================================

Router Link State Advertisements (Area 0.0.0.11)
-------------------------------------------------

LSID          ADV Router         Age     Seq#          Checksum      Link
Count
----------------------------------------------------------------------------
10.11.100.1   10.11.100.1        1318    0x80000006    0x00009934    1
10.11.100.2   10.11.100.2        1324    0x80000006    0x00009733    1
```

Are these LSAs like the ones that Core-2 has? ______________________________

____

> **Tip**
> To confirm if they are the same version, you have to compare the LSID and Sequence number.

How many links do each of them announce? ______________________________

____

> **Note**
> Right now, only one link is contained within the Router LSA (10.11.0.0/30).

Task 2: Add the Server Switch

Objectives

The next phase in this integration will be to build the interconnection with the Server Switch using the two links that have already been plugged in. You will use VLANs 111 and 112 for that as shown in figure 11-27. Remember that you will only take care of Core switches configuration, while the Server Switch is being configured by another partner.

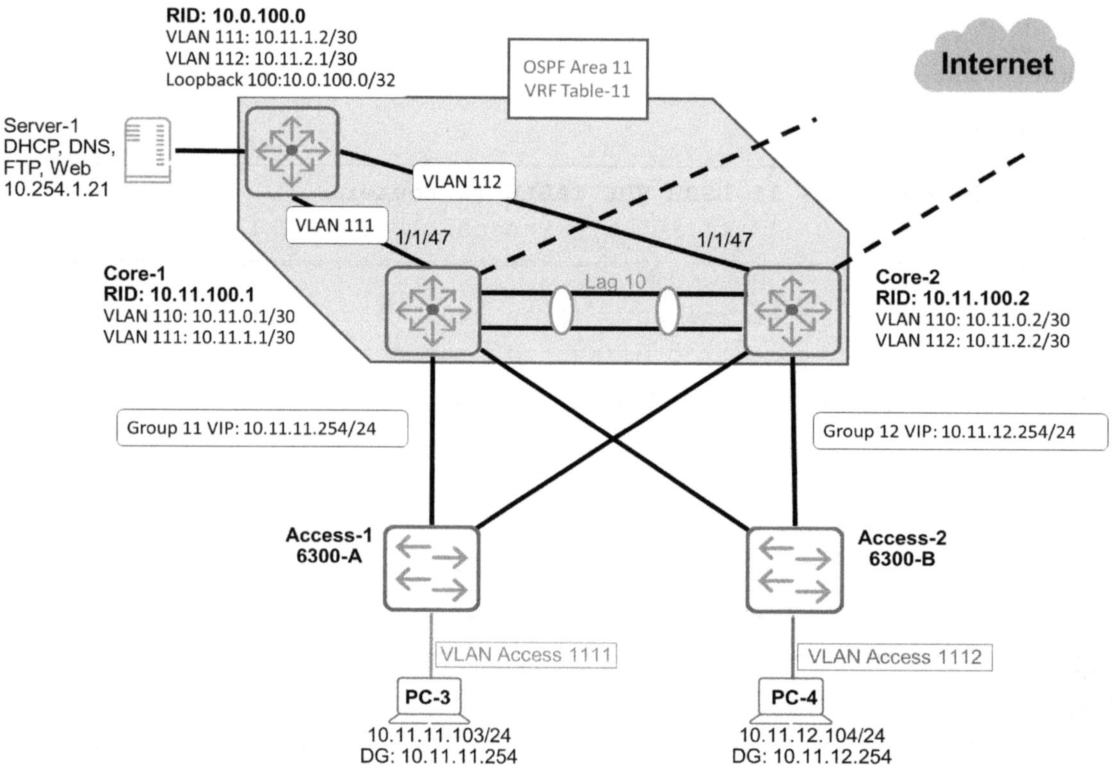

Figure 11-27 Task 2 Topology

Steps

Core-1 (via PC-1)

1. Open the SSH session to Core-1.
2. Create VLAN 111 and put a description. This will be the transport for the uplink to the Server Switch.

```
Core-1(config)# VLAN 111
Core-1(config-VLAN-111)# name TO_SERVER-SWITCH_TABLE-11
Core-1(config-VLAN-111)# exit
```

3. Tag it on port 1/1/47.

```
Core-1(config)# interface 1/1/47
Core-1(config-if)# VLAN trunk allowed 111
Core-1(config-if)# exit
```

4. Create interface VLAN 111 and map it to TABLE-11 VRF, put the 10.11.1.1/30 IP address and enable the OSPF process on it.

```
Core-1(config)# interface VLAN 111
Core-1(config-if-VLAN)# VRF attach TABLE-11
Core-1(config-if-VLAN)# IP address 10.11.1.1/30
Core-1(config-if-VLAN)# IP OSPF 11 area 11
Core-1(config-if-VLAN)# end
```

5. Display the list of neighbors Core-1 has now.

```
Core-1# show IP OSPF neighbors detail VRF TABLE-11
Neighbor 10.11.100.2, interface address 10.11.0.2
-------------------------------------------------

Process ID 11 VRF TABLE-11, in area 0.0.0.11 via interface VLAN110
Neighbor priority is 1, State is FULL
DR is 10.11.0.1, BDR is 10.11.0.2
Options is 0x42
Dead timer due in 00:00:36
Retransmission queue length 0
Time since last state change 00h:03m:11s
Neighbor 10.0.100.0, interface address 10.11.1.2
------------------------------------------------

Process ID 11 VRF TABLE-11, in area 0.0.0.11 via interface VLAN111
Neighbor priority is 1, State is FULL
DR is 10.11.1.2, BDR is 10.11.1.1
Options is 0x42
Dead timer due in 00:00:31
Retransmission queue length 0
Time since last state change 00h:00m:08s
```

Did you discover any new neighbors? ____

Who are the neighbors? ____

6. Write down the role for the links between Core-1 and the Server Switch in Figure 11-27.

Core-2 (via PC-1)

7. Move to Core-2.
8. Repeat steps 2 to 4 using VLAN 112 and 10.11.11.2/30 for the IP address.

```
Core-2(config)# VLAN 112
Core-2(config-VLAN-112)# name TO_SERVER-SWITCH_TABLE-11
Core-2(config-VLAN-112)# exit
Core-2(config)# interface 1/1/47
Core-2(config-if)# VLAN trunk allowed 112
Core-2(config-if)# exit
Core-2(config)# interface VLAN 112
Core-2(config-if-VLAN)# VRF attach TABLE-11
Core-2(config-if-VLAN)# IP address 10.11.2.2/30
Core-2(config-if-VLAN)# IP OSPF 11 area 11
Core-2(config-if-VLAN)# end
```

9. Display the list of neighbors Core-2 has now.

```
Core-2# show IP OSPF neighbors VRF TABLE-11
OSPF Process ID 11 VRF TABLE-11
================================

Total Number of Neighbors: 1

Neighbor ID     Priority    State        Nbr Address   Interface
-----------------------------------------------------------------
10.11.100.1     1           FULL/DR      10.11.0.1     VLAN110
```

How many entries are listed? ______________________________

Is there any device missing? ______________________________

10. Confirm OSPF is properly enabled on interface VLAN 112.

```
Core-2# show IP OSPF interface VLAN112 VRF TABLE-11
Interface VLAN112 is up, line protocol is up
---------------------------------------------

IP address 10.11.2.2/30, Process ID 11 VRF TABLE-11, area 0.0.0.11
    State Dr, Status up, Network type Broadcast
    Link Speed: 1000 Mbps
    Cost Configured NA, Calculated 100
    Transit delay 1 sec, Router priority 1
    Designated Router IP: 10.11.2.2
```

```
No backup designated router on this network
Timer Intervals: Hello 10, Dead 40, Retransmit 5
No authentication
Number of Link LSAs: 0, checksum sum 0
BFD is disabled
```

What is the status of the interface and protocol? ________________________________

Tip

By looking at the configuration, it seems everything is in order. You will most likely have to look at packet statistics in order to see what packets are being exchanged between Core-2 and the Server switch.

---

11. Display the OSPF packet statistics for interface VLAN 112.

```
Core-2# show IP OSPF statistics interface VLANX2 VRF TABLE-11
OSPF Process ID 11 VRF TABLE-11, interface VLAN112 statistics  (cleared
0h1m57s ago)
=====================================================================
=================

Tx Hello Packets      : 11           Rx Hello Packets      : 0
Tx Hello Bytes        : 704          Rx Hello Bytes        : 0
Tx DD Packets         : 0            Rx DD Packets         : 0
Tx DD Bytes           : 0            Rx DD Bytes           : 0
Tx LS Request Packets : 0            Rx LS Request Packets : 0
Tx LS Request Bytes   : 0            Rx LS Request Bytes   : 0
Tx LS Update Packets  : 0            Rx LS Update Packets  : 0
Tx LS Update Bytes    : 0            Rx LS Update Bytes    : 0
Tx LS Ack Packets     : 0            Rx LS Ack Packets     : 0
Tx LS Ack Bytes       : 0            Rx LS Ack Bytes       : 0

Total Number of State Changes : 6
Number of LSAs                : 0
LSA Checksum Sum              : 0
Total Transmit Failures       : 0
Total OSPF Packets Discarded  : 10

Reason                        Packets Dropped
-----------------------------------------------
Invalid type                  0
Invalid length                0
Invalid checksum              0
```

```
Invalid version                  0
Bad or unknown source            0
Area mismatch                    0
Self-originated                  0
Duplicate router ID              0
Interface standby                0
Total Hello packets dropped      5
  Network Mask mismatch          0
  Hello interval mismatch        5
  Dead interval mismatch         0
  Options mismatch               0
  MTU mismatch                   0
  Neighbor ignored               0
Authentication errors            0
  Type mismatch                  0
  Authentication failures        0
Wrong protocol                   0
Resource failures                0
Bad LSA length                   0
Bad DD packets                   0
Others                           5

Total LSAs Ignored : 0
Bad Type           : 0
Bad Length         : 0
Invalid Data       : 0
Invalid Checksum   : 0
```

Has Core-2 received any hello packet? ________________________________

Has Core-2 dropped any hello packet? ________________________________

Why? ________________________________

Answer

Core-2 has dropped hello packets because of a hello interval mismatch. Although you know Core-2 is running the default value of 10 seconds, you are not certain of what interval value the Server Switch is using. You will have to run debugs in order to find out.

12. Clear the debug buffers.

```
Core-2# clear debug buffer
```

13. Display the OSPFv2 debugs stored in buffers. This debug is on by default.

```
Core-2# show debug buff module OSPFv2 | begin 2 10.0.100.0
2020-01-29:08:31:33.460518|hpe-routing|LOG_ERR|AMM|-|OSPFV2|OSPFV2|OSPF
268708866 Hello packet with mismatched hello interval received from router
10.0.100.0.
2020-01-29:08:31:33.460536|hpe-routing|LOG_ERR|AMM|-|OSPFV2|OSPFV2|My
Hello Interval = 10
2020-01-29:08:31:33.460550|hpe-routing|LOG_ERR|AMM|-|OSPFV2|OSPFV2|Neighb
oring Hello Interval = 20
```

What information is the show debug displaying? ______________________________

Is there any complaint about contents in hello messages?______________________________

Note

The output is clear, incoming hello packets interval is two times higher than usual. Since this is a parameter that must match between two OSPF routers, the mismatch prevents the neighbor relationship from forming. When you share this information with the partner deploying the server switch (NetAmateur), you realize he is not an expert in the matter and does not understand what you are asking. However, he allows you to fix what you need to make this integration work.

Server Switch (via PC-1)

14. Using Putty, open an SSH session to the Server Switch.

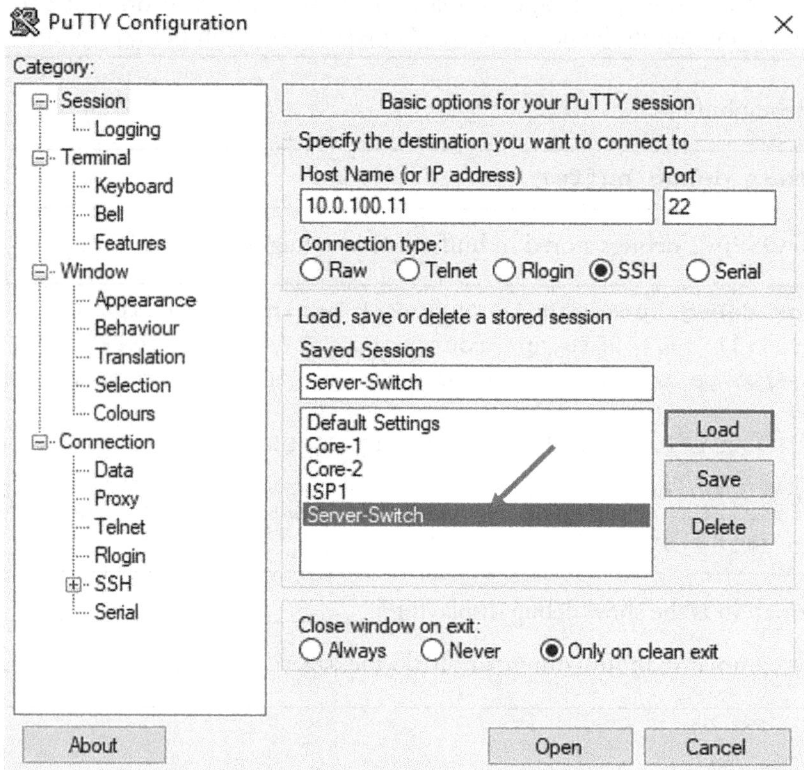

Figure 11-28 SSH to Server Switch

15. Login using Username: **cxf11/aruba123**.

16. Decrease hello interval from 20 to 10 seconds on interface VLAN 112.

```
P52-6300-AB (config)# interface VLAN 112
P52-6300-AB (config-if-VLAN)# IP OSPF hello-interval 10
P52-6300-AB (config-if-VLAN)# end
```

17. Close the putty session.

Core-2 (via PC-1)

18. Move back to Core-2.

19. Display the neighbors again. Server switch should be there.

```
Core-2# show IP OSPF neighbors detail VRF TABLE-11
Neighbor 10.11.100.1, interface address 10.11.0.1
-------------------------------------------------

Process ID 11 VRF TABLE-11, in area 0.0.0.11 via interface VLAN110
Neighbor priority is 1, State is FULL
DR is 10.11.0.1, BDR is 10.11.0.2
Options is 0x42
Dead timer due in 00:00:37
Retransmission queue length 0
Time since last state change 00h:15m:12s
Neighbor 10.0.100.0, interface address 10.11.2.1
------------------------------------------------

Process ID 11 VRF TABLE-11, in area 0.0.0.11 via interface VLAN112
Neighbor priority is 1, State is FULL
DR is 10.11.2.2, BDR is 10.11.2.1
Options is 0x42
Dead timer due in 00:00:35
Retransmission queue length 0
Time since last state change 00h:02m:04s
```

Did you discover any new neighbors? ______________________________

What are their IP addresses? ______________________________

20. Write down the role for the links between Core-1 and the Server Switch.

____

Note

Right now, Core switches have each other and have the Server Switch as a neighbor. Therefore, they should be receiving Link State Updates that include the server's segment.

21. Display the routing table, including only the newly learned OSPF prefixes.

```
Core-2# show IP route OSPF VRF TABLE-11

Displaying ipv4 routes selected for forwarding

'[x/y]' denotes [distance/metric]
```

```
10.0.100.0/32, VRF TABLE-11
        via  10.11.2.1,  [110/125],  OSPF
10.11.1.0/30, VRF TABLE-11
        via  10.11.0.1,  [110/200],  OSPF
        via  10.11.2.1,  [110/200],  OSPF
10.254.1.0/24, VRF TABLE-11
        via  10.11.2.1,  [110/125],  OSPF
```

What networks have Core-2 discovered? ____________________

What networks is the Server Switch a next hop for? ____________________

____

Answer

Server Switch (10.11.2.1) is the next hop for 10.0.100.0/32 and 10.254.1.0/24, its loopback and the servers' segment, respectively.

What Is the Administrative Distance and metric for those segments? ____________________

Core-1 (via PC-1)

22. Move back to Core-1.
23. Display the routing table, including only the newly learned OSPF prefixes.

```
Core-1# show IP route OSPF VRF TABLE-11

Displaying IPv4 routes selected for forwarding

'[x/y]' denotes [distance/metric]

10.0.100.0/32, VRF TABLE-11
        via  10.11.1.2,  [110/125],  OSPF
10.11.2.0/30, VRF TABLE-11
        via  10.11.1.2,  [110/200],  OSPF
        via  10.11.0.2,  [110/200],  OSPF
10.254.1.0/24, VRF TABLE-11
        via  10.11.1.2,  [110/125],  OSPF
```

What is the next-hop IP address for those networks learned from the server switch? ____________

____

Note

Based on the outputs, both Cores are using their direct link to the server switch to reach segments that are beyond it (Figure 11-29). This also means that traffic from VLANs whose default gateway is Core-1 will be forwarded across VLAN 111, and traffic of VLANs whose default gateway is Core-2 will use the VLAN 112 uplink.

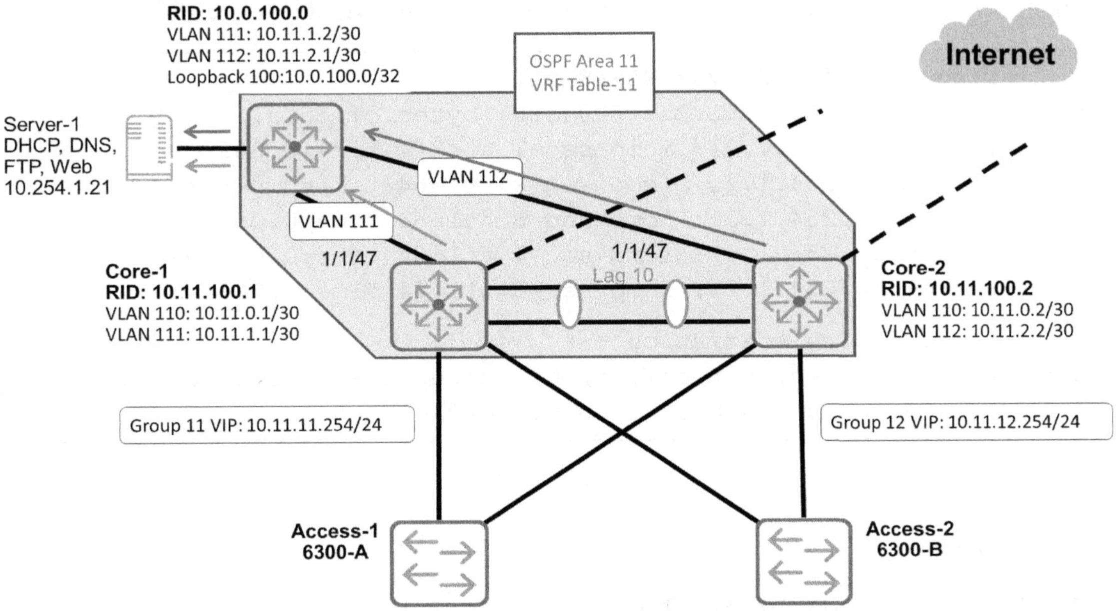

Figure 11-29 Upstream Traffic

Now you will run some connectivity tests.

24. From Core-1, ping the Server Switch's loopback IP address (10.0.100.0). The ping should be successful.

```
Core-1# ping 10.0.100.0 VRF TABLE-11
PING 10.0.100.0 (10.0.100.0) 100(128) bytes of data.
108 bytes from 10.0.100.0: icmp_seq=1 ttl=64 time=0.168 ms
108 bytes from 10.0.100.0: icmp_seq=2 ttl=64 time=0.164 ms
108 bytes from 10.0.100.0: icmp_seq=3 ttl=64 time=0.188 ms
108 bytes from 10.0.100.0: icmp_seq=4 ttl=64 time=0.166 ms
108 bytes from 10.0.100.0: icmp_seq=5 ttl=64 time=0.164 ms

--- 10.0.100.0 ping statistics ---
5 packets transmitted, 5 received, 0% packet loss, time 4100ms
rtt min/avg/max/mdev = 0.164/0.170/0.188/0.009 ms
```

25. Ping the Windows Server IP address (10.254.1.21). The ping should be successful.

```
Core-1# ping 10.254.1.21 VRF TABLE-11
PING 10.254.1.21 (10.254.1.21) 100(128) bytes of data.
108 bytes from 10.254.1.21: icmp_seq=1 ttl=64 time=0.063 ms
108 bytes from 10.254.1.21: icmp_seq=2 ttl=64 time=0.066 ms
108 bytes from 10.254.1.21: icmp_seq=3 ttl=64 time=0.068 ms
108 bytes from 10.254.1.21: icmp_seq=4 ttl=64 time=0.068 ms
108 bytes from 10.254.1.21: icmp_seq=5 ttl=64 time=0.067 ms

--- 10.254.1.21 ping statistics ---
5 packets transmitted, 5 received, 0% packet loss, time 4072ms
rtt min/avg/max/mdev = 0.063/0.066/0.068/0.007 ms
```

PC-3

26. Move to PC-3.

27. Ping the Windows Server (10.254.1.21).

    Was ping successful? ______________________

    Run a traceroute towards Windows Server. Was it successful? ______________________

```
Select Command Prompt - tracert 10.254.1.21
C:\Users\student>ping 10.254.1.21

Pinging 10.254.1.21 with 32 bytes of data:
Request timed out.
Request timed out.
Request timed out.
Request timed out.

Ping statistics for 10.254.1.21:
    Packets: Sent = 4, Received = 0, Lost = 4 (100% loss),

C:\Users\student>tracert 10.254.1.21

Tracing route to 10.254.1.21 over a maximum of 30 hops

  1    <1 ms    <1 ms    <1 ms  10.11.11.1
  2     *        *        *     Request timed out.
  3     *        *        *     Request timed out.
  4     *        *        *     Request timed out.
  5     *        *        *     Request timed out.
  6     *        *        *     Request timed out.
  7     *        *        *     Request timed out.
```

Figure 11-30 Failed Traceroute

Why? ____

Answer

Traffic is failing for the same reason the first test to the Internet failed in lab 10 (Figure 11-30). (Static Routes Task 2 Step 7). Communications are bidirectional, it is not enough to know how to reach the remote destination but is also necessary that the other end knows how to send the replies.

Task 3: Advertise LAN Segments

Objectives

In this activity you will advertise your LAN prefixes, so the Server Switch knows how to reach the client PCs.

Steps

Core-1 (via PC-1)

28. Open the SSH session to Core-1.
29. Enable OSPF process 11 area 11 on interface VLANs 1111 and 1112.

```
Core-1(config)# interface VLAN 1111-1112
Core-1(config-if-VLAN-<1111-1112>)# IP OSPF 11 area 11
Core-1(config-if-VLAN-<1111-1112>)# end
```

30. Display the Router LSAs.

```
Core-1# show IP OSPF 11 LSDB VRF TABLE-11 router
OSPF Router with ID (10.11.100.1) (Process ID 11 VRF TABLE-11)
===============================================================

Router Link State Advertisements (Area 0.0.0.11)
-----------------------------------------------

LSID            ADV Router    Age     Seq#          Checksum          Link
Count
--------------------------------------------------------------------------------
10.0.100.0     10.0.100.0    73     0x80000013     0x0000d456       2
10.11.100.1    10.11.100.1   14     0x80000046     0x0000bc01       4
10.11.100.2    10.11.100.2   1737   0x8000004b     0x00006576       2
```

How many Router LSAs do you have now? ______________________________

Who do they belong to? ______________________________

How many links are counted for Core-1? ______________________________

What links do they correspond to? ______________________________

31. Confirm segments 10.11.11.0/24 and 10.11.12.0/24 are now part of the OSPF routing process.

```
Core-1# show IP OSPF 11 routes VRF TABLE-11
Codes: i - Intra-area route, I - Inter-area route
       E1 - External type-1, E2 - External type-2

OSPF Process ID 11 VRF TABLE-11, Routing Table
---------------------------------------------

Total Number of Routes : 8

10.0.100.0/32       (E1)
     via 10.11.1.2 interface VLAN111, cost 125 distance 110
10.11.0.0/30        (i) area: 0.0.0.11
     directly attached to interface VLAN110, cost 100 distance 110
10.11.1.0/30        (i) area: 0.0.0.11
     directly attached to interface VLAN111, cost 100 distance 110
10.11.2.0/30        (i) area: 0.0.0.11
     via 10.11.0.2 interface VLAN110, cost 200 distance 110
10.11.2.0/30        (i) area: 0.0.0.11
     via 10.11.1.2 interface VLAN111, cost 200 distance 110
10.11.11.0/24       (i) area: 0.0.0.11
     directly attached to interface VLAN1111, cost 100 distance 110
10.11.12.0/24       (i) area: 0.0.0.11
     directly attached to interface VLAN1112, cost 100 distance 110
10.254.1.0/24       (E1)
     via 10.11.1.2 interface VLAN111, cost 125 distance 110
```

Core-2 (via PC-1)

32. Move to Core-2.

33. Repeat step 2.

```
Core-2(config)# interface VLAN 1111-1112
Core-2(config-if-VLAN-<1111-1112>)# IP OSPF 11 area 11
Core-2(config-if-VLAN-<1111-1112>)# end
```

Task 4: Testing Services

Objectives

In this activity you will start using one of the services that users in VLANs 1111 and 1112 have been waiting for: DHCP. Since Layer-3 connectivity has been enabled all the way from the LAN segments up to the server's VLAN, then you can easily receive DHCP Discover messages at the Core switch and relay them up to the server. For redundancy, you will do it on both Cores.

Steps

Core-1 (via PC-1)

34. Open the SSH session to Core-1.
35. Move to interfaces VLAN 1111 and 1112, then enable the DHCP relay function.

```
Core-1(config)# interface VLAN 1111-1112
Core-1(config-if-VLAN-<1111-1112>)# IP helper-address 10.254.1.21
Core-1(config-if-VLAN-<1111-1112>)# end
```

Core-2 (via PC-1)

36. Open the SSH session to Core-2.
37. Repeat step 2.

```
Core-2(config)# interface VLAN 1111-1112
Core-2(config-if-VLAN-<1111-1112>)# IP helper-address 10.254.1.21
Core-2(config-if-VLAN-<1111-1112>)# end
```

PC-3

38. Access PC-3.
39. Under the search field in the task bar, type “control panel.” Windows will automatically display all items matching the string.
40. Click the top result (Control Panel). A new window will pop up.
41. In Control Panel, click “View network status and tasks” under Network and Internet.
42. Click “Lab NIC” under Access type Connections. A new window will pop up.
43. In Lab NIC status window, click “Properties” button.

44. In Lab NIC Properties section, select "Internet Protocol Version 4 (TCP/IPv4), then click "Properties" button.
45. In Internet Protocol Version 4 (TCP/IPv4) Properties, choose "Obtain an IP address automatically" under General tab.
46. Then choose "Obtain DNS server address automatically" (Figure11-31).

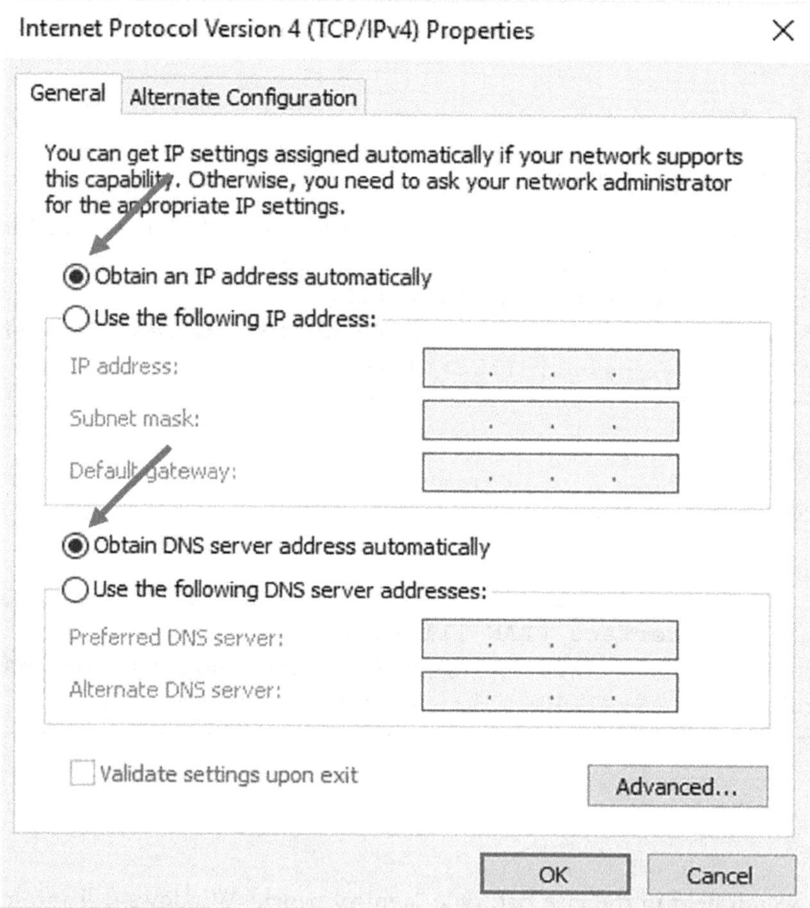

Figure 11-31 Obtain an IP Address Automatically

47. Click "OK" button; then "Close" once.
48. Still in Lab NIC window, click the "Details..." button (Figure 11-32).

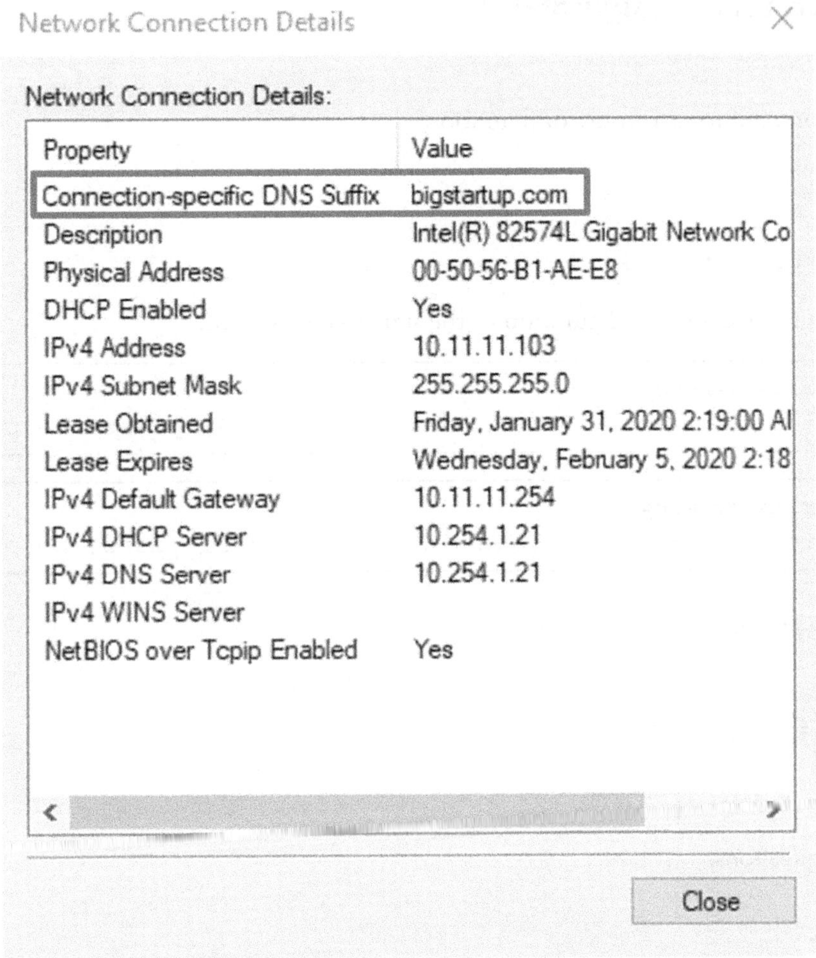

Figure 11-32 Network Connection Details

What connection-specific DNS Subfix did you get? ______________________________

What IP address and subnet mask did you get? ______________________________

What IPv4 Server was assigned to PC-3? ______________________________

PC-4

49. Access PC-4.

50. Repeat steps 5 to 15.

Task 5: Save Your Configurations

Objectives

You will now proceed to save your configuration.

Steps

Core-1 and Core-2 (via PC-1)

51. Save the current Cores' configuration in the startup checkpoint.

```
Core-1# write memory
Configuration changes will take time to process, please be patient.
```

```
Core-2# write memory
Configuration changes will take time to process, please be patient.
```

You have completed Lab 11.1!

Learning Check

Chapter 11 Questions

There are no questions.

12 Stacking

EXAM OBJECTIVES

- ✓ Describe device operational planes.
- ✓ Describe stacking technologies and benefits.
- ✓ Explain and configure VSF.
- ✓ Trace Layer-2 traffic.
- ✓ Describe VSF failover mechanisms.
- ✓ Describe VSX.

Overview

The knowledge you gain from this module about stacking technologies will help you to design, implement, and configure more resilient, reliable, high-performing networks. You first explore device operational planes using the control, management, and data plane, and the relationship between them. You will learn how this relates to stacking technologies and features that let you group multiple physical switches into a single virtual switch.

Then you learn about Aruba's stacking technology called Virtual Switching Framework (VSF). You will explore VSF operation, requirements, roles, members, and ports; then you will learn how to configure VSF, along with VSF use cases and about tracing Layer-2 traffic in a VSF scenario. You will look at VSF failover scenarios, and how to improve upon them with Split Detection. Then you will get a brief introduction to Aruba's Virtual Switching eXtension (VSX) technology.

Stacking Technologies

Operational Planes: Control, Management, and Data

A network device is logically composed of three operational planes, and each plane performs specific tasks (Figure 12-1).

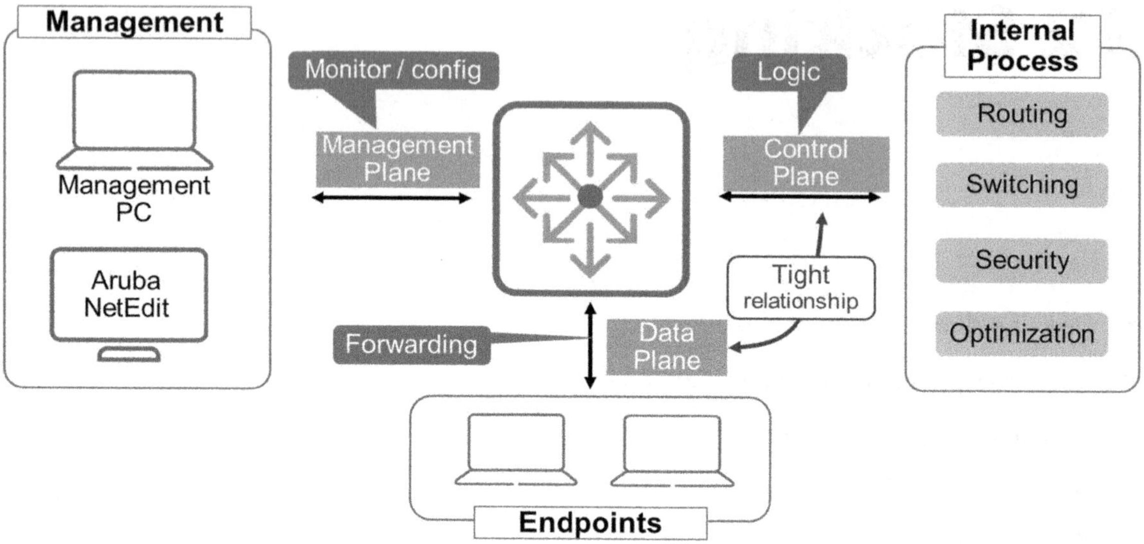

Figure 12-1 Control, Management, and Data Planes

Data Plane

The data plane receives and sends frames using specialized hardware called Application-Specific Integrated Circuits (ASIC), which is much faster than using software. ASICs modulate and demodulate data, and handle other functions related to frame transmission and receipt.

Control Plane

The control plane logic determines what to do with the data that has been received. These decisions are made with internal processes, routing, switching, security, and flow optimization. Data plane and Control planes have a tight relationship, to process any data as fast as possible.

Management Plane

You use the management plane to monitor and configure the device. This plane must be separate from the data plane, for security and accessibility reasons. You do not want your access to the device to be completely reliant on things like VLANs or VRF. You must be able to access the device even if the control and data planes fail. Also, you do not want end users to gain access to the management plane; this could be an egregious security issue.

Note
AOS-CX devices have a specific Interface and VRF that is used for Out-of-Band Management which maintains a total separation from the data plane.

Introduction to Stacking Technologies

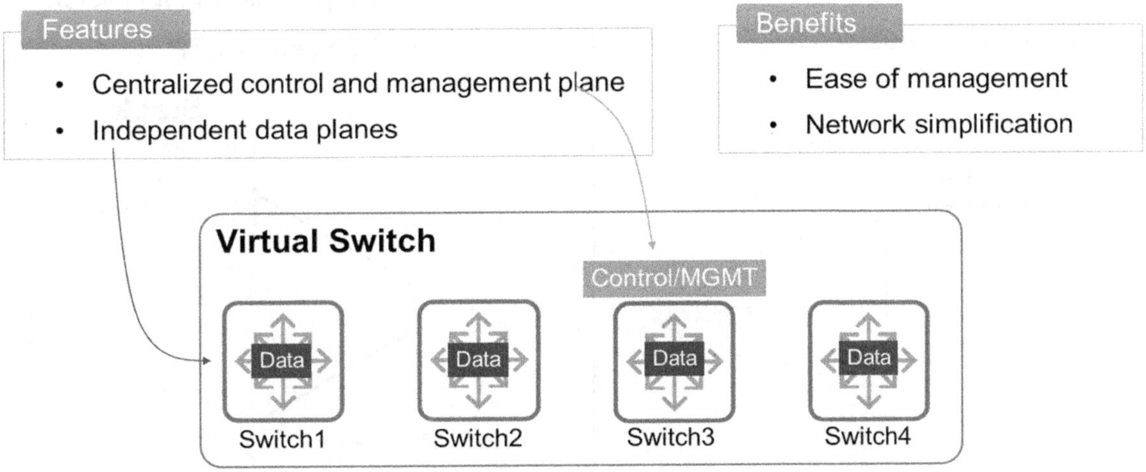

Figure 12-2 Stacking Technologies

Stacking technology allows you to manage a group of switches as a single device, a Virtual Switch. Control and Management Plane functions are centralized in one group member, but each member runs its own independent data plane. The tight relationship between the control and data planes is maintained; it just happens on an inter-switch basis (Figure 12-2).

Stacking benefits include:

- Ease of management: You no longer need to connect to, configure, and manage each individual switch. You simply configure the primary switch. That configuration is then automatically distributed to other virtual switch members. This simplifies network setup, operation, and maintenance.
- Network simplification: Since multiple devices share a common control plane, routing protocols and Spanning-Tree are no longer needed inside the stacking group. Connected devices perceive the group as a single device.

Aruba switching families support two primary stacking technologies: Virtual Switching Framework (VSF) and Virtual Switching Extension (VSX). You will be introduced to VSX, but this training is focused on VSF.

Distributed Data Plane and Distributed Link Aggregation

Stacking technologies maintain the data plane distributed across all the members; this implies each physical device individually creates and populates forwarding tables like ARP and MAC. These tables are then shared across all members using the control plane (Figure 12-3).

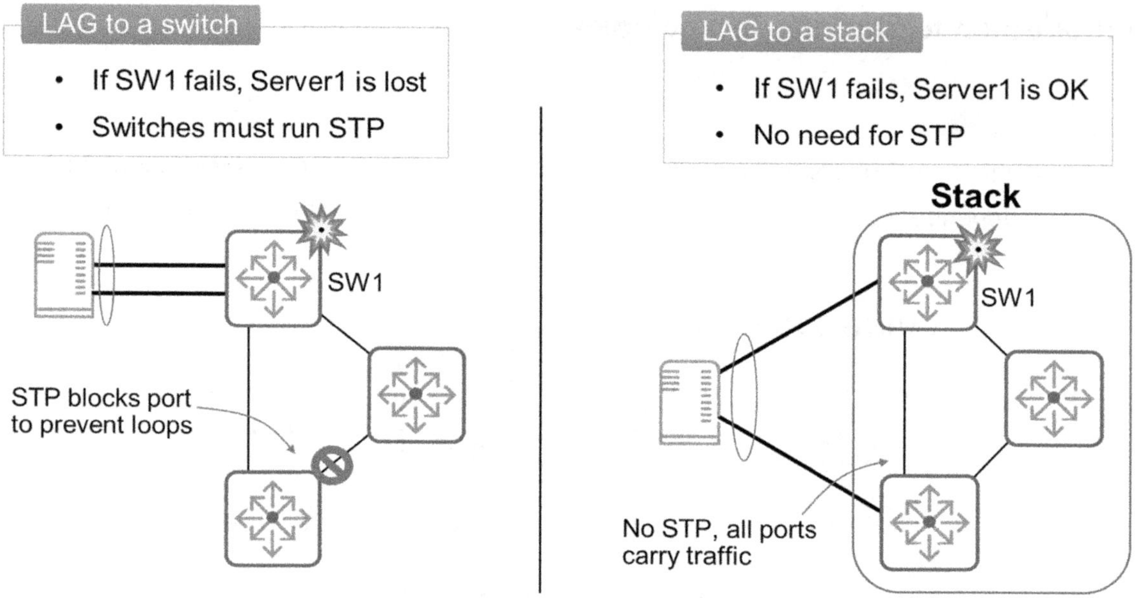

Figure 12-3 Distributed Data Plane and Distributed Link Aggregation

Mobility Controllers, Firewalls, and servers can benefit from the stacking with LAG enable switches, since they perceive a LAG connection to a single device. However physical links terminate in different Stack members. If SW1 fails in the example shown, the traffic can still use other LAG links. LAG and Stacking features enable the network to fully use all available links at the same time. Notice that Spanning-Tree is not needed because the stack operates from a single control plane. Aruba highly recommends this implementation.

Aruba VSF Stacking Solution and Platforms

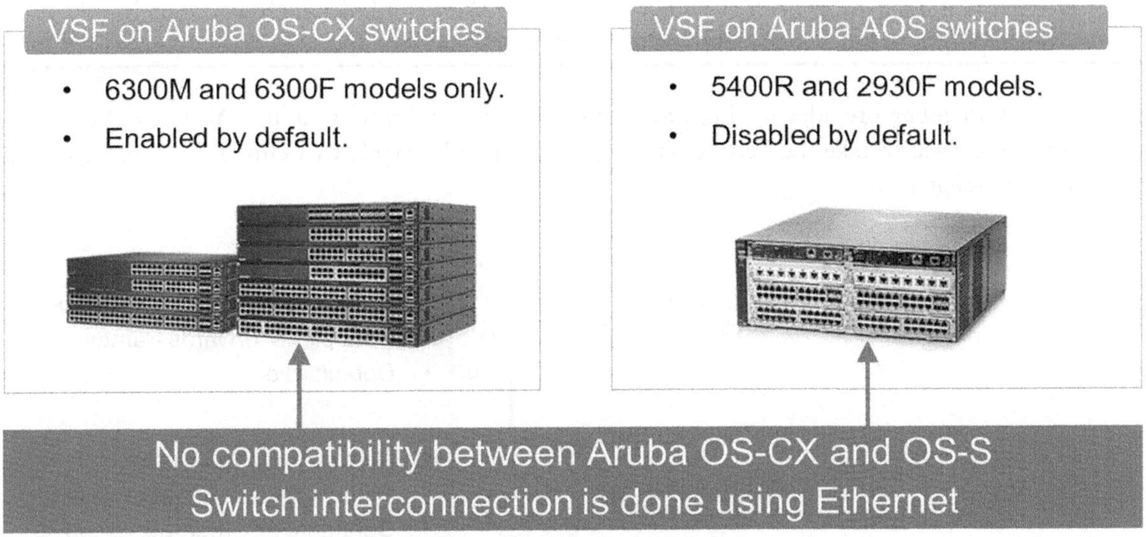

Figure 12-4 Aruba VSF Stacking Solution and Platforms

Aruba Virtual Switching Framework (VSF) defines a virtual switch, which is composed by individual physical switches interconnected using Ethernet links. All member switches share a single control plane. Devices connected to the VSF perceive a single device. As you recently learned, this virtual switch behavior has significant benefits related to simplified management and improved connectivity

In AOS-CX, VSF is supported on the 6300M and 6300F models only; other models use a different technology, called VSX. You can configure a maximum of 10 members in the stack. This feature is enabled by default (Figure 12-4).

The VSF feature is also available in the Aruba AOS switching family, including the 5400 and 2930 series, but the feature is disabled by default. Understand that the VSF feature is not compatible between OS-CX and AOS platforms. You cannot form a VSF stack with switches from different OS families. This means that VSF can only be formed using any combination of 6300 AOS-CX switching series.

VSF Member Roles and Links

Aruba VSF creates a single control plane that runs on a single VSF member. This is the Primary member and always uses member ID 1. This device assumes the Master role in the stack (Figure 12-5).

Note
A factory-default Aruba 6300 switch boots up as VSF-enabled switch with member ID 1. This implies that the switch behaves as the Primary member.

A Secondary member provides for high availability in case of Primary failure. You can choose any member in the stack to take the Secondary role, but it must be explicitly defined. Just configure any member ID except 1.

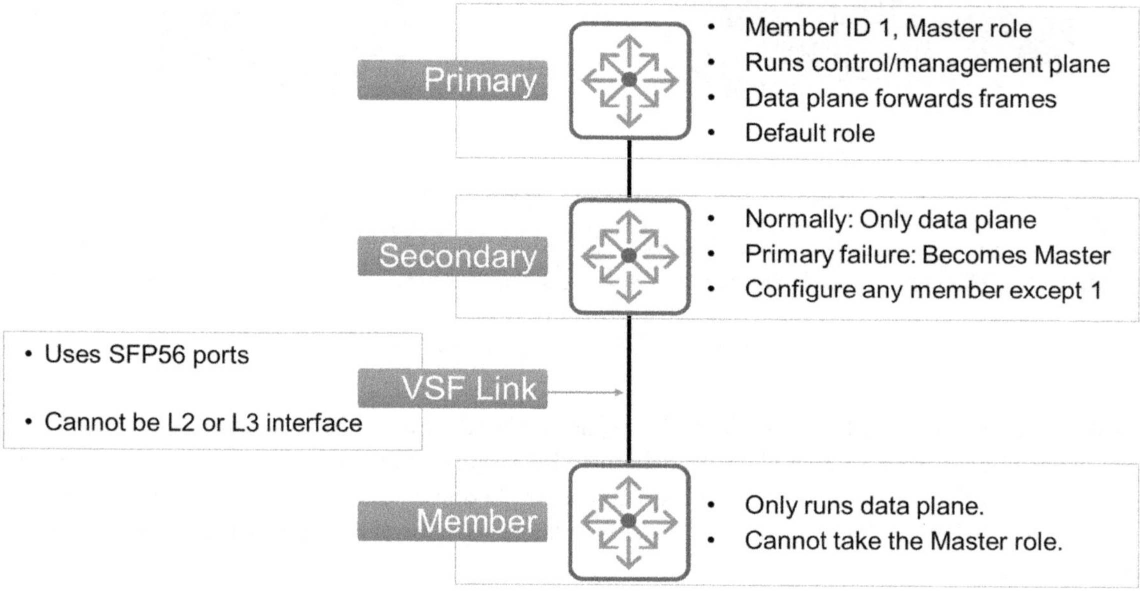

Figure 12-5 VSF Member Roles and Links

The other devices in the VSF are Members, which only run the data plane, and cannot assume the Master role.

VSF switches are interconnected using SFP56 ports. When you configure a port for VSF it can no longer be used as a Layer-2 or Layer-3 interface. In other words, the port does not belong to the switch's Data plane.

VSF Open Virtual Switch Database

In Chapter 2 you learned about the Current State Database. As the most important element of the AOS-CX architecture, it is contacted by all control and management protocols. In a VSF stack this database runs on the Master switch.

When VSF runs on a group of switches the Open Virtual Switch Database (OVSDB) is also created. This new database runs in the Master switch and contains state and configuration data for the VSF Stack itself (Figure 12-6).

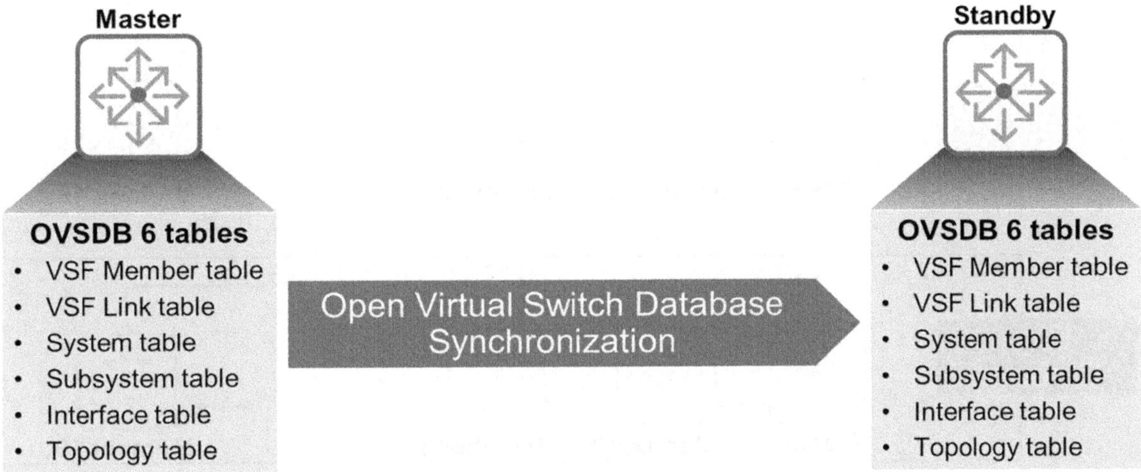

Figure 12-6 VSF Open Virtual Switch Database

The Master switch synchronizes OVSDB content with the standby, to ensure that it can quickly take over the master role without interruption.

The OVSDB database includes six tables:

- VSF member table
- VSF link table
- System table: Includes the number of members, MAD status, fragment status, and topology type
- Subsystem table: Boot time for each member
- Interface table
- Topology table

VSF Topologies

Of course, VSF members must be physically connected to form the switching stack, in one of two topologies: Daisy chain or Ring (Figure 12-7).

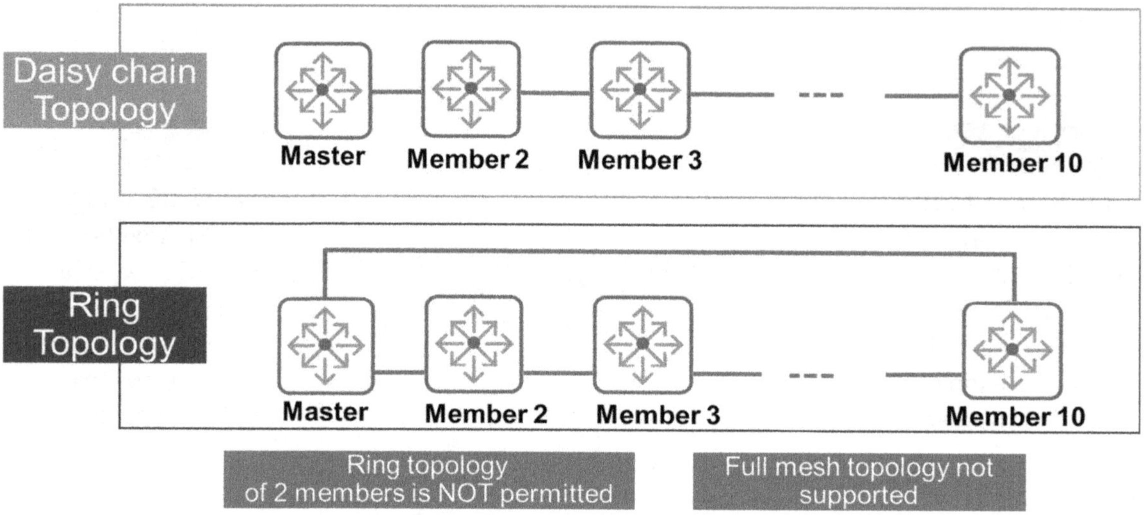

Figure 12-7 VSF Topologies

- Daisy Chain: As the name implies, this topology interconnects VSF members with a single chain of Ethernet connections. From the figure you can easily see that a switch or link failure causes the stack to be split. This means that part of the stack is unable to provide endpoint connectivity.
- Ring Topology: This topology is recommended since it offers a backup path in case of a switch or link failure.

Note

A ring topology created with a couple of switches is not permitted, since a unique link between two members most exist, this last rule takes precedence. Full mesh topology is not supported.

VSF Requirements

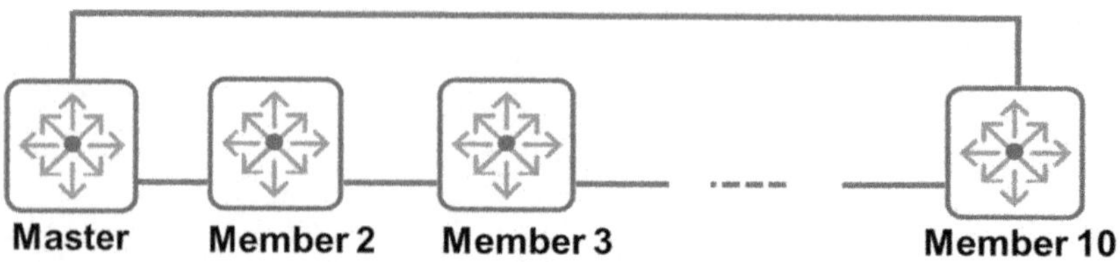

Figure 12-8 VSF Requirements

VSF has some requirements that you must meet:

- Use AOS-CX version 10.4 or higher.
- All members must run the same OS-CX version.
- Only 6300 switch models can form the stack, but model combination is allowed.
- A single link is only allowed for VSF Link.
- VSF Link uses regular Ethernet port.
- Recommended to use the uplink ports which support 10, 25, or 50 Gbps.
- Maximum 10 members are supported (Figure 12-8).

VSF Member ID and Port Numbers

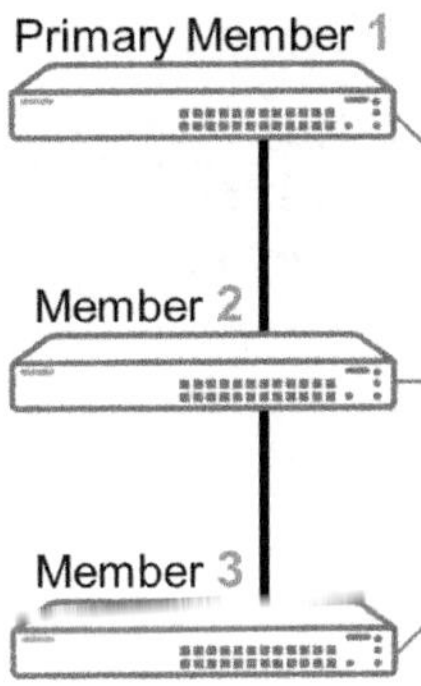


```
Access-6300# show interface brief
-----------------------------------------------------------------
Port     Native  Mode    Type          Enabled Status     Speed
         VLAN                                             (Mb/s)
-----------------------------------------------------------------
1/1/1    1       access  SFP+DAC1      yes     up         10000
1/1/2    1       access  SFP+DAC1      yes     up         10000
...
2/1/1    1       access  SFP+DAC1      yes     up         10000
2/1/2    1       access  SFP+DAC1      yes     up         10000
...
3/1/1    1       access  SFP+DAC1      yes     up         10000
3/1/2    1       access  SFP+DAC1      yes     up         10000
```

Figure 12-9 VSF Member ID and Port Numbers

When the VSF stack forms, all physical devices use a single Control Plane. This means that all switch interfaces are be available for configuration, using the standard AOS-CX Member/Slot/Port notation, as shown in Figure 12-9. Use the command show interface brief to see all available ports for all switches in the stack.

Note

Since all 6300 switch series models are fix switches, the slot number is always 1.

VSF Configuration Example

Consider the scenario where a couple of 6300 switches are assigned to the same VSF stack (Figure 12-10).

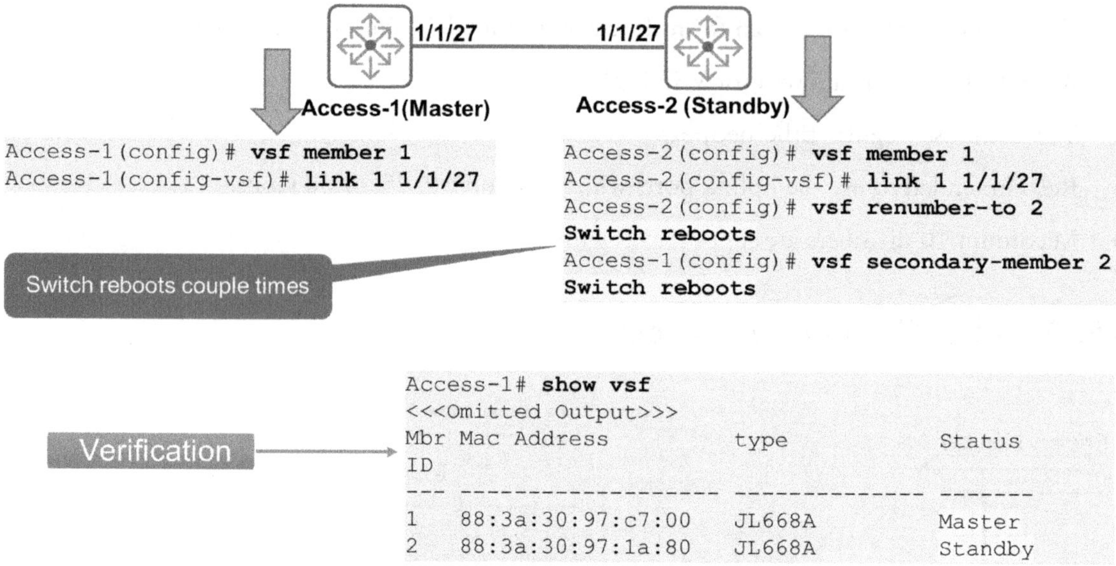

Figure 12-10 VSF Configuration Example

```
Access-1(config)# vsf member 1
Access-1(config-VSF)# link 1 1/1/27
Access-2(config)# VSF member 1
Access-2(config-VSF)# link 1 1/1/27
Access-2(config)# VSF renumber-to 2
Access-2(config)#! Switch reboots
```

Adding a secondary member.

```
Access-1(config)# VSF secondary-member 2
Access-1(config)#! Switch reboots
```

Use the **show VSF** command to determine member status and role.

VSF Pre-Provisioning

AOS-CX supports member pre-provisioning. This enables you to prepare the VSF Link and member configuration for a specific 6300 switch model before the switch is connected to the stack. When the switch joins the stack, it boots up with the proper configuration.

```
Switch-6300(config-VSF)# VSF member 4
Switch-6300(config-VSF)# type jl658a
Switch-6300(config-VSF)# link 1 1/1/25
Switch-6300(config-VSF)# link 2 1/1/26
```

The following table indicates the available options (Figure 12-11).

P/N	Model
JL658A	6300M 24SFP+/4SFP56
JL659A	6300M 48SR PoE CLS 6/4SFP56
JL660A	6300M 24SR PoE CLS 6/4SFP56
JL661A	6300M 48G PoE CLS 4/4SFP56
JL662A	6300M 24G PoE CLS 4/4SFP56
JL663A	6300M 48G/4SFP56
JL664A	6300M 24G/4SFP56
JL665A	6300F 48G PoE CLS 4/4SFP56
JL666A	6300F 24G PoE CLS 4/4SFP56
JL667A	6300F 48G/4SFP56
JL668A	6300F 24G/4SFP56

Figure 12-11 VSF by Model

Tracing Layer-2 Unicast Traffic

When a VSF member receives a frame for Layer-2 forwarding, it consults the L2 forwarding table to determine the egress interface. As shown in Figure 12-12, it forwards the frame out this interface, which might be local or on another member. If the egress interface is on another member, the source member forwards the packet on the VSF link.

```
Switch# show mac-address
MAC Address          VLAN      Type          Port
-------------------------------------------------
90:20:c2:bc:ee:00    10        dynamic       2/1/1
00:0b:86:b4:eb:37    10        dynamic       3/1/1
```

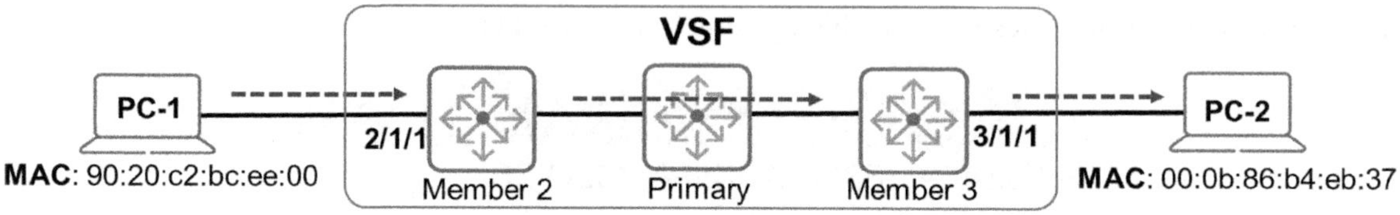

Figure 12-12 Tracing Layer-2 Unicast Traffic

A VSF fabric is like any switch configured with link aggregation. It learns MAC addresses on a logical LAG entity, as opposed to the physical interfaces. It selects one LAG member link for forwarding each conversation.

However, VSF overrides the typical LAG hash function used for physical interface selection. A VSF member prefers to use their own local links (shown in Figure 12-13), and to avoid using VSF links. If the member has multiple local links in the aggregation, then it uses the typical hashing mechanism to choose between those.

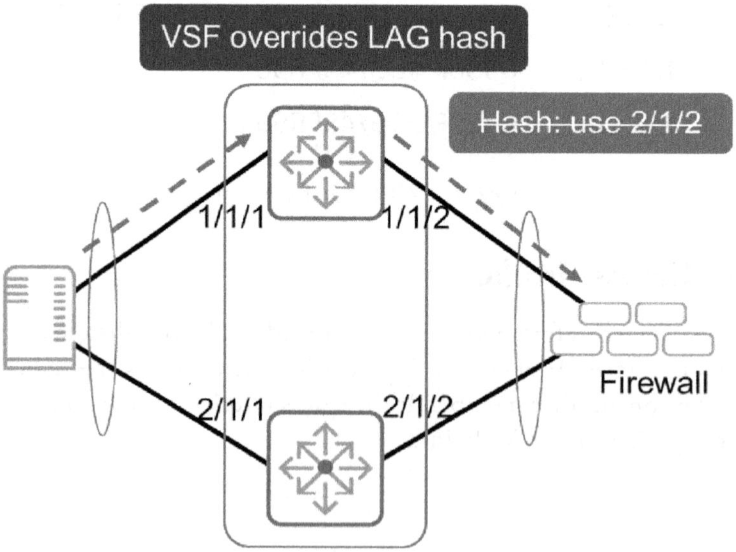

Figure 12-13 VSF Hash

VSF Failover and OSPF Graceful-Restart

The Primary member is the most important device in the stack; it runs the control and management plane. External devices exchange routing and switching protocols directly to this member. If this device fails like in Figure 12-14, the entire stack is down. You should configure a VSF Secondary member for redundancy.

The Secondary assumes the Master role upon Primary failure. The new master runs all Control plane protocols, uses the configuration databases, and responds to management sessions.

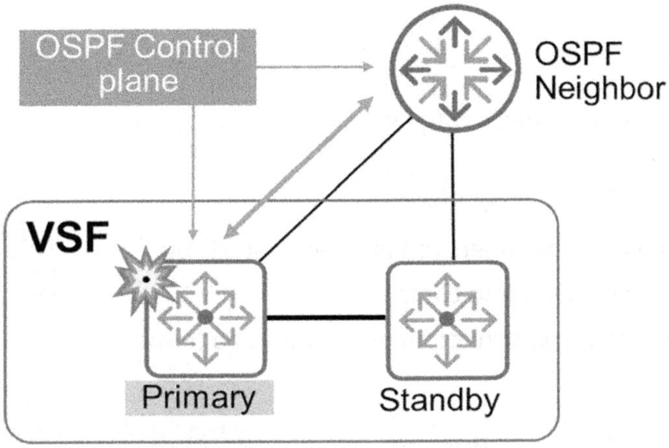

Figure 12-14 OSPF Graceful-Restart

In Figure 12-15, when the Primary member fails, Layer-2 traffic continues to be forwarded without disruption. Layer-3 protocols such as OSPF perform graceful restart by notifying peers of the failover event. This triggers a rebuild of OSPF adjacencies. During convergence, the switch continues to route traffic based on the last-known routing information, prior to the failure. This typically only lasts a few seconds. After OSPF is fully operational, routing uses the new information.

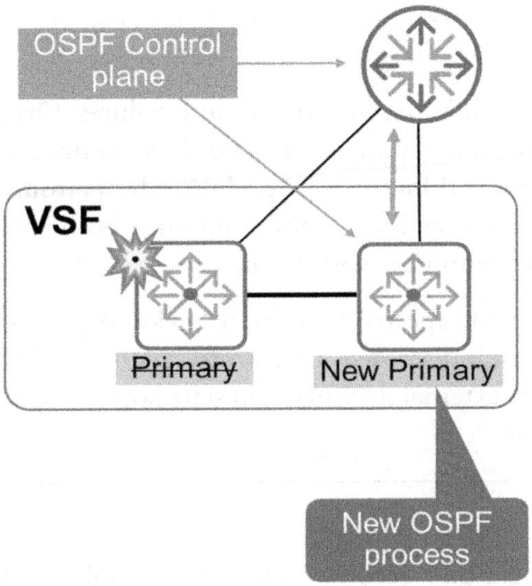

Figure 12-15 Graceful-Restart New Primary

Note

With VSF there is **no preemption;** this means that when the failed member re-joins the stack it will not replace the current Master of the stack, instead it takes the Standby role.

VSF Link Failure

VSF Link failures could cause a fragmented stack.

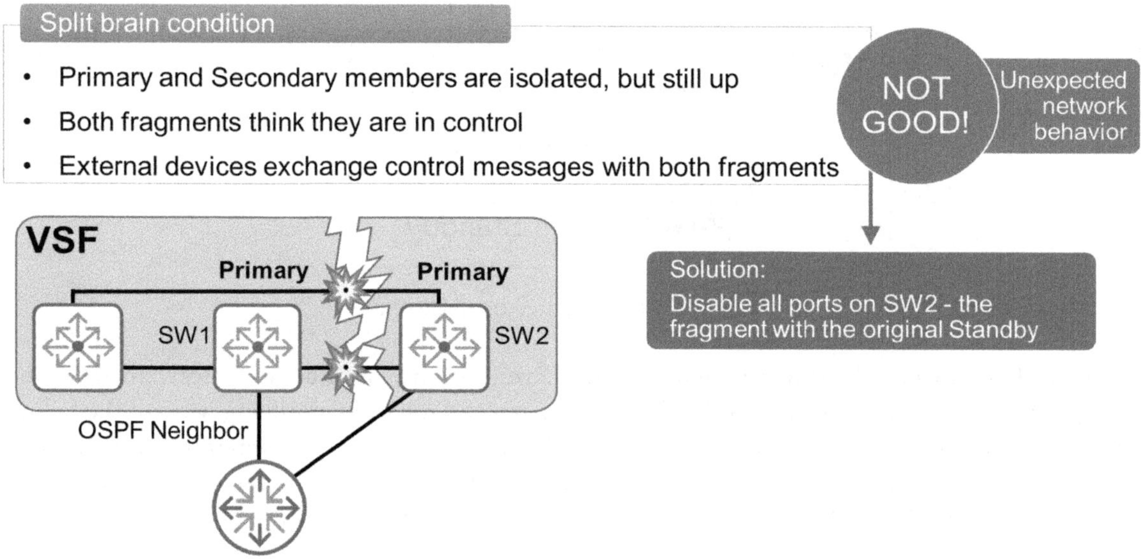

Figure 12-16 VSF Link Failure

Figure 12-16 shows a fragmented VSF stack, due to link failures. Originally, SW1 was Primary and SW2 was Secondary. After fragmentation, there is no direct connection between the two switches. SW1 continues to think that it is Primary. SW2 no longer hears from SW1, and so now thinks that it is the Primary. This is known as Split-brain condition; both fragments continue to function although there is no communication between them.

Split-brain can cause unstable, unexpected network behavior. A packet received in one fragment and destined for the other fragment is discarded. Even worse, both segments use the same IP address and the same routing information; external devices could start populating duplicated data. This can cause very strange network behavior.

Note

Split-brain situation could also occur if a VSF member fails in a Daisy chain topology. The best way to solve a split-brain situation is to disable the ports one of the segments.

Split Detection Using Multi-Active Detection

You can use Multi-Active Detection (MAD) to avoid split-brain situations. Thus, if a VSF link failure occurs, the segment that includes the Standby member verifies Primary member status. If the original Primary is up, then all members in the fragment that does not include the Primary member will disable all their ports (Figure 12-17).

VSF uses two mechanisms to detect and verify the status of the Primary member.

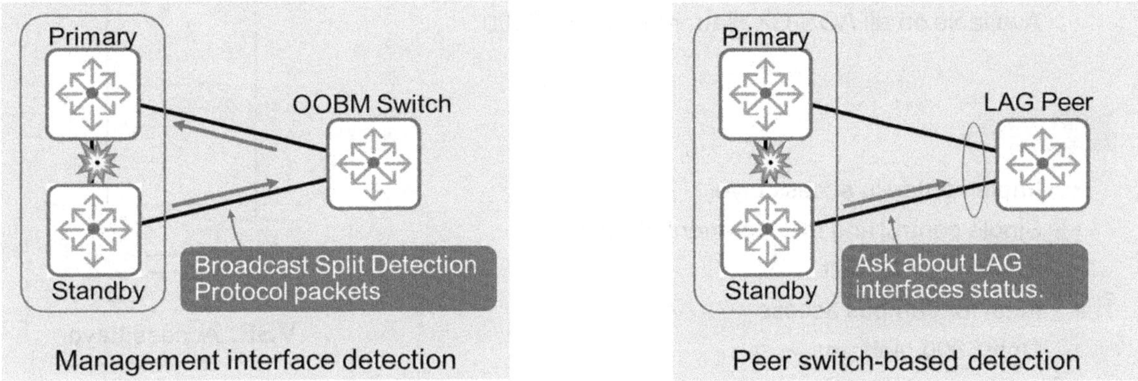

Figure 12-17 Multi-Active Detection

Management Interface Split Detection

This method requires you to connect Out-Of-Band Management (OOBM) interfaces to primary and secondary stack members. These interfaces must be in the same Layer-2 broadcast domain (VLAN). This network is used to identify active stack fragments. Each member broadcast Split Detection Protocol Packets to identify stack fragments that are currently operational.

Peer Switch-Based Detection

This method does not require additional connections and relies on the Link Aggregation Group (LAG) implementation. Switches ask the LAG Peer about its interface states using those interfaces connected to primary and secondary stack fragments. If the LAG peer indicates that its interfaces toward the Primary member are up, then the Standby member has detected a Split-brain situation, and shuts down its interfaces.

VSX Introduction

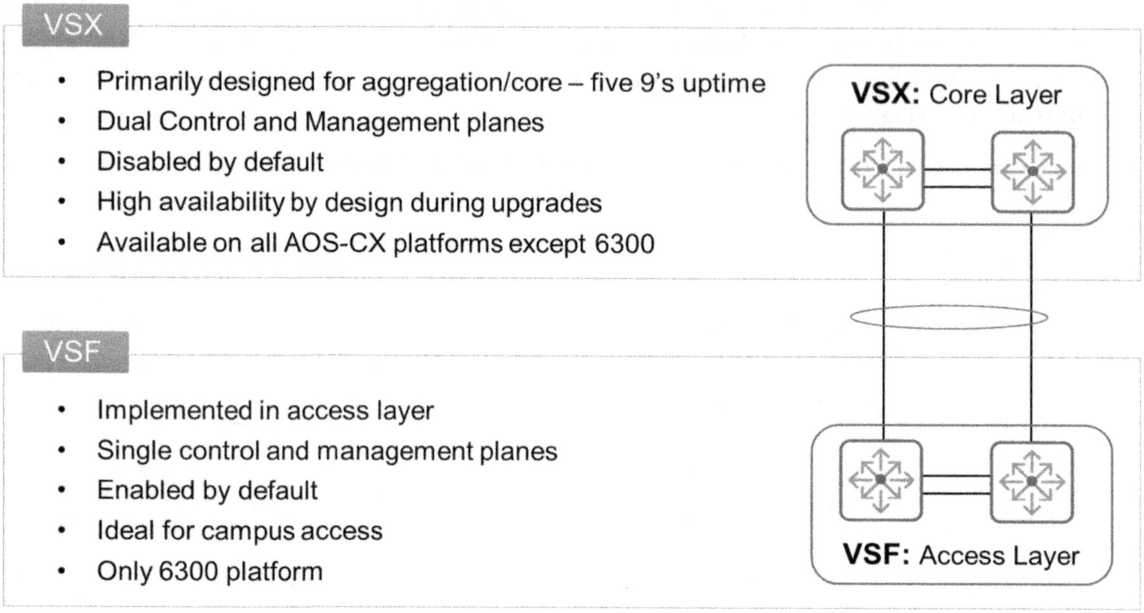

Figure 12-18 Comparing VSF to VSX

Aruba Virtual Switching Extension (VSX) is a virtualization technology for AOS-CX switches. This technology can be run in all the AOS-CX portfolio models except the 6300 series, which only runs VSF. VSX is commonly implemented in core devices and at data centers. VSF is suitable for the Access Layer.

VSX improves data plain performance. With VSF the control plane only can be run in the Primary member. Thus, some time is wasted when non-primary members ask the Control plane how to handle packets. With VSX, each member runs its own Control plane, allowing for faster decisions, reduced latency, and better performance.

Although VSX switches run separate control planes, they still maintain database synchronization for the configuration. Unlike VSF, each switch can modify and populate the Control plane, while presenting themselves as one virtualized switch to other devices. VSX allows you to upgrade members with near zero downtime and with continuous packet forwarding (Figure 12-18).

Lab 12: Static Routes

Overview

The goal of the following tasks is to complete the dual-homed Internet Service deployment for BigStartup. The customer wants load balancing across both carriers and redundancy in case of failure. They want assurance that if either link fails, traffic can still go out through the alternate ISP. This will require the configuration of static and floating routes, which you will apply on the Core switches.

Objectives

After completing this lab, you will be able to:

- Configure Core switches to Perimeter Firewall links using a /30 prefix.
- Calculate and deploy Variable Length Subnet Mask (VLSM) prefixes.
- Configure static routes.
- Add a default route into the routing table for providing internet access.
- Manipulate administrative distances in order to configure floating routes.
- Validate proper load sharing and failover.

Note

IP prefix is an aggregation of IP addresses and is usually used to refer to an IP network or subnet in general.

Lab 12.1: Create a Virtual Switching Framework Stack

Overview

It has been one year since BigStartup started business and increased profits are making it possible to open additional offices. This new project for additional offices begins next month and they want you to take care of the entire network deployment. This project will take several months, and you might not be able to assist with Level 1 support. You suggest handing over control of the access switches to an internal staff member. He is not very experienced in networking and does not feel confident managing multiple independent switches.

To simplify the deployment, you plan to create a single stack of switches using a technology called Virtual Switching Framework (VSF), so he only will need to deal with one logical unit.

Note that references to equipment and commands are taken from Aruba's hosted remote lab. These are shown for demonstration purposes in case you wish to replicate the environment and tasks on your own equipment.

Objectives

After completing this lab (Figure 12-19), you will be able to:

- Create a VSF stack.
- Define stack roles.
- Verify VSF topology.
- Configure distributed Link Aggregation.

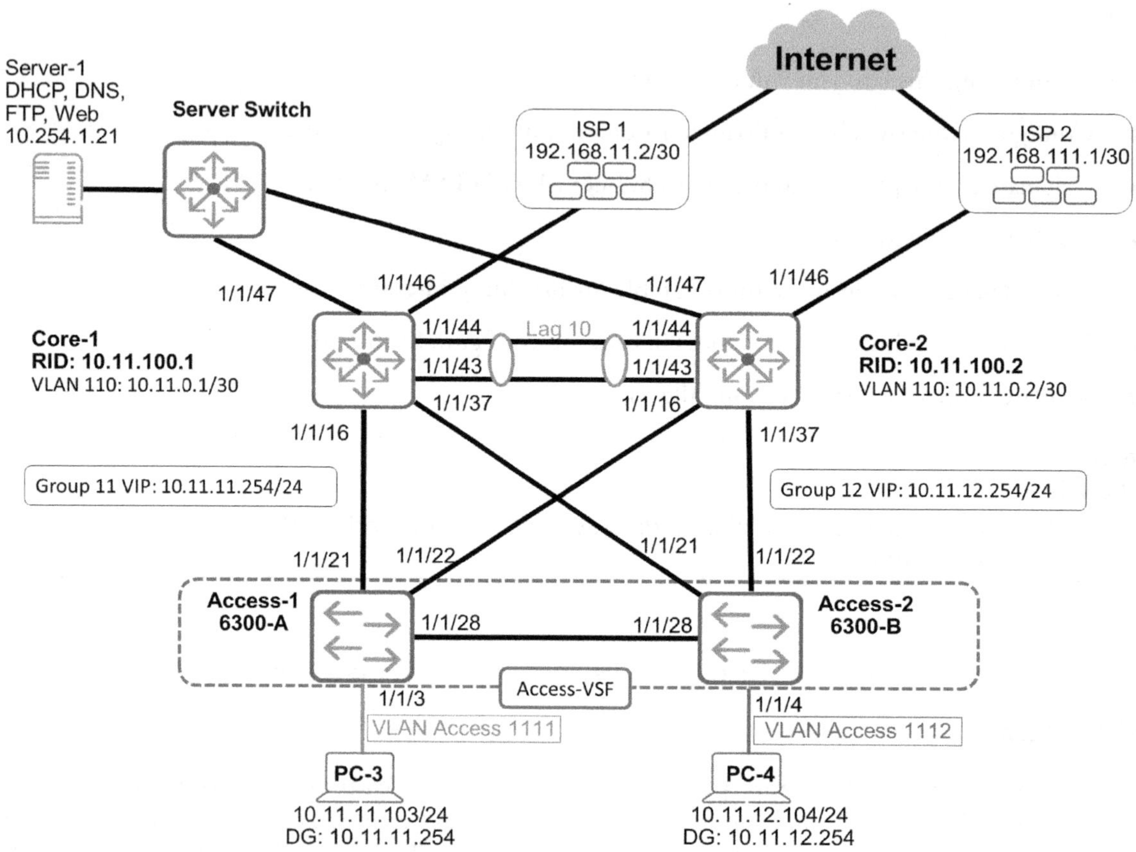

Figure 12-19 Lab Topology

Task 1: Deploy a VSF Stack

Objectives

You are about to create a VSF stack. This involves rebooting one of the units which might affect users connected to it. Although you know the process will take no more than 5 minutes, you have requested a 30-minute maintenance window. To further minimize the inconvenience, you have scheduled the maintenance window during lunch.

In this task, you will create a VSF stack with both Access switches using port 1/1/28. Then you will explore the stack properties and normalize the port configuration on member 2.

Steps

PC-4

1. Open a console session to PC-4.
2. Run a continuous ping to 8.8.8.8. Ping should be successful.

Access-1

3. Open a console session to Access-1.
4. Create VSF link 1 using port 1/1/28.

```
T11-Access-1(config)# vsf member 1
T11-Access-1(VSF-member-1)# link 1 1/1/28
T11-Access-1(VSF-member-1)# exit
```

Access-2

5. Open a console session to Access-2.
6. Create VSF link 1 using ports 1/1/28.

```
T11-Access-2(config)# VSF member 1
T11-Access-2(VSF-member-1)# link 1 1/1/28
T11-Access-2(VSF-member-1)# exit
```

7. Renumber the switch to VSF member 2. You will be prompted to save configuration and reboot the unit. Answer "**y**".

```
T11-Access-2(config)# VSF renumber-to 2
This will save the VSF configuration and reboot the switch.
Do you want to continue (y/n)? y
```

The system will reboot and be back online after a few minutes.

8. Log in with admin and no password.

```
T11-Access-2 login: admin
Password:

member#
```

What is the new prompt shown in the switch's CLI? ________________________________

Access-1

9. Move back to Access-1.

10. Run the "**show VSF**" command.

```
T11-Access-1(config)# show VSF

MAC Address                 : 88:3a:30:98:30:00
Secondary                   :
Topology                    : Chain
Status                      : No Split
Split Detection Method      : None


Mbr Mac Address          type           Status
ID
--- ------------------- -------------- ---------------
1   88:3a:30:98:30:00   JL668A         Master
2   88:3a:30:97:a4:40   JL668A         Member
```

What is the Stack's MAC address? ____________________

What is the topology used in the stack? ____________________

How many members are part of the stack? ____________________

Does the stack MAC address match any of the member's? ____________________

Whose? ____________________

What is status (role) of Member 1? ____________________

What is status (role) of Member 2? ____________________

11. Run the detailed version of the output.

```
T11-Access-1(config)# show VSF detail
VSF Stack
        MAC Address                 : 88:3a:30:98:30:00
        Secondary                   :
        Topology                    : chain
        Status                      : No Split
        Split Detection Method      : None
        Software Version            : FL.10.04.0003

        Name                        : Aruba-VSF-6300
        Contact                     :
        Location                    :
```

```
Member ID                          : 1
        MAC Address                : 88:3a:30:98:30:00
        Type                       : JL668A
        Model                      : 6300F 24-port 1GbE and 4-port SFP56
                                     Switch
        Status                     : Master
        ROM Version                : FL.01.05.0003
        Serial Number              : SG90KN70HX
        Uptime                     : 4 days, 10 hours, 4 minutes
CPU Utilization            : 1%
        Memory Utilization         : 17%
VSF Link 1                 : Up, connected to peer member 2, link 1
VSF Link 2                 :

Member ID                          : 2
        MAC Address                : 88:3a:30:97:a4:40
        Type                       : JL668A
        Model                      : 6300F 24-port 1GbE and 4-port SFP56
                                     Switch
        Status                     : Member
        ROM Version                : FL.01.05.0003
        Serial Number              : SG90KN70HB
        Uptime                     : 2 minutes
CPU Utilization            : 1%
        Memory Utilization         : 8%
VSF Link 1                 : Up, connected to peer member 1, link 1
VSF Link 2                 :
```

What is the switch type (part number) of both members? ______________________

What is the switch type (Model) of both members? ______________________

What is the CPU and memory utilization of Member 1? ______________________

What is the CPU and memory utilization of Member 2? ______________________

12. Use the "**show VSF topology**" for looking at logical connections between members.

```
T11-Access-1(config)# show VSF topology
Mstr
+---+     +---+
| 2 |1==1| 1 |
+---+     +---+
```

What is the logical link that connects both units? ______________________

13. Run the "**show VSF link**" for displaying the physical port members of logical link 1.

```
T11-Access-1(config)# show VSF link

VSF Member 1
     Link       Peer    Peer
Link State      Member  Link   Interfaces
---- ---------- ------- ------ ---------------------------
1    up         2       1      1/1/28


VSF Member 2

     Link       Peer    Peer
Link State      Member  Link   Interfaces
---- ---------- ------- ------ ---------------------------
1    up         1       1      2/1/28
```

What ports are used in Member 1 for creating VSF link 1? ______________

What ports are used in Member 2 for creating VSF link 1? ______________

Both members are now part of the same logical stack. They share the same control plane and management plane, although data plane is distributed among them. It means that the physical interfaces of both units can be managed by the Master.

14. Run the "**show interface brief**" and confirm you can see ports of both members.

```
T11-Access-1(config)# show interface brief
--------------------------------------------------------------------------------
Port         Native   Mode    Type                 Enabled  Status   Reason
Speed
VLAN                                                                      (Mb/s)
--------------------------------------------------------------------------------
1/1/1     1112    access 1GbT           yes     up                         1000
1/1/2      1       access 1GbT            yes      down    Administratively
down   --
1/1/3     1111    access 1GbT           yes     up                         1000
1/1/4      1       access 1GbT            no       down    Administratively
down   --
                        <----- output omitted --->
1/1/21     1      trunk  1GbT           yes     up                         1000
1/1/22     1      trunk  1GbT           yes     up                         1000
1/1/23     1       access 1GbT            no       down    Administratively
down   --
1/1/24     1       access 1GbT            no       down    Administratively
down   --
```

```
1/1/25    1      access SFP+DAC1       no      down    Administratively
down   --
1/1/26    1      access SFP+DAC1       no      down    Administratively
down   --
1/1/27    1      access SFP+DAC1       no      down    Administratively
down   --
1/1/28    --     routed SFP+DAC1      yes    up                  10000
2/1/1      1        access 1GbT             yes      down    Waiting for
link         --
2/1/2      1        access 1GbT             yes      down    Waiting for
link         --
2/1/3      1        access 1GbT             yes      down    Waiting for
link         --
2/1/4     1      access 1GbT          yes    up                   1000
                  ←---- output omitted ---→
2/1/21    1      access 1GbT          yes    up                   1000
2/1/22    1      access 1GbT          yes    up                   1000
2/1/23     1        access 1GbT             yes      down    Waiting for
link         --
2/1/24     1        access 1GbT             yes      down    Waiting for
link         --
2/1/25    1      access SFP+DAC1      yes    up                  10000
2/1/26     1        access SFP+DAC1         yes      down    Waiting for
link         --
2/1/27     1        access SFP+DAC1         yes      down    Waiting for
link         --
2/1/28    --     routed SFP+DAC1      yes    up                  10000
VLAN1       --            --             yes      up
```

Can you see ports of member 1 and member 2?____

What is the mode of interfaces used for the VSF link?____________________________________

Answer

These interfaces lost their previous configuration, moved to routed ports, and are now exclusively used for VSF. Due to their routed mode properties Layer-2 loops cannot be created through them.

What VLANs are assigned to ports 1/1/1 and 1/1/3 (PC-1 and PC-3)?____________________

What VLAN is assigned to port 2/1/4 (PC-4)?____

What is the port mode of interfaces 1/1/21 and 1/1/22 (uplinks of Member1)?______________

What is the port mode of interfaces 2/1/21 and 2/1/22 (uplinks of Member2)?______________

PC-4

15. Move back to PC-4.

    Is the ping still going? ______________________________

NOTICE

When Member 2 came back from rebooting and joined the stack, it lost its previous configuration, wiping the ports' settings out and putting them in default values. This process is obviously affecting PC-4 who can no longer access internet.

You realize you only have 10 minutes left before the maintenance window is over. So, you better hurry up and restore the configuration on those ports!

Do not panic! You do not have to create the VLANs or Spanning-Tree configuration all over again; they are already part of the global VSF stack configuration that Member 1 manages. The only thing you must do is to provision the ports properly.

Access-1

16. Move back to Access-1.

17. Disable all Member 2's ports but the VSF connections?

```
T11-Access-1(config)# interface 2/1/1-2/1/27
T11-Access-1(config-if-<2/1/1-2/1/27>)# shutdown
T11-Access-1(config-if-<2/1/1-2/1/27>)# exit
```

18. Enable Member 2's uplinks to Core-1 and Core-2 and allow VLANs 1111 and 1112 (2/1/21 and 2/1/22).

```
T11-Access-1(config)# interface 2/1/21-2/1/22
T11-Access-1(config-if-<2/1/21-2/1/22>)# no shutdown
T11-Access-1(config-if-<2/1/21-2/1/22>)# VLAN trunk allowed 1111-1112
T11-Access-1(config-if-<2/1/21-2/1/22>)# exit
```

19. Enable the port that connects to PC-4 (2/1/4); then make it member of VLAN 1112.

```
T11-Access-1(config)# interface 2/1/4
T11-Access-1(config-if)# no shutdown
T11-Access-1(config-if)# VLAN access 1112
T11-Access-1(config-if)# exit
```

Well done! You have restored connectivity in record time! Now that the urgency is over, you can change the hostname of the system to something more appropriate.

20. Change the hostname to T11-Access-VSF.

```
T11-Access-1(config)# hostname T11-Access-VSF
```

PC-4

21. Move back to PC-4.

    Is the ping working now? ____________________

22. Stop the ping.

Task 2: Configure Distributed Link Aggregation.

Objectives

Right now, the stack is up and running. However, because of your Spanning-Tree knowledge, you know that only two out of the four uplinks are actively in use: 1/1/21 is root port for Instance 1 and alternate for Instance 2 while 1/1/22 is root port for Instance 2 and alternate for Instance 1. The other two uplinks 2/1/21 and 2/1/22 are alternate of both instances.

Therefor you must complete the deployment by configuring Link aggregation between the Stack and both Cores.

You will first create LAG X1 in both the VSF stack and Core-1. Then you will create LAG X2 in Core-2 and the VSF stack (Figure 12-20).

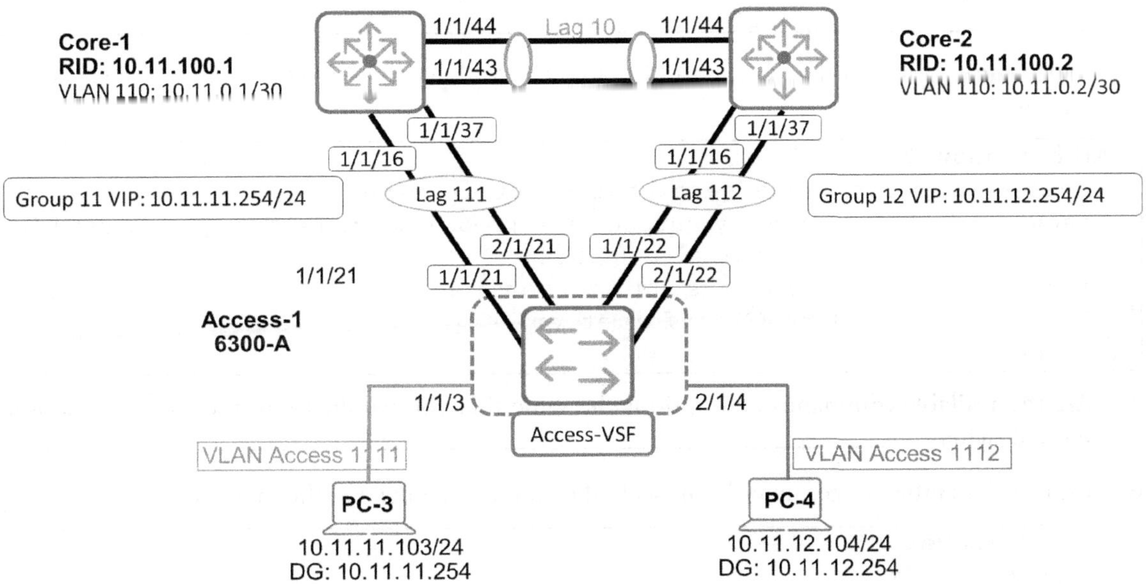

Figure 12-20 LACP Topology

Steps

PC-3

1. Access PC-3.
2. Run a continuous ping to PC-4 (10.X.12.104). Ping should be successful.

Access-VSF: Member 2

3. Open a console session to Access-VSF: Member 2 (formerly known as Access-2).
4. Hit the "**?**" question mark. You will get the help as the output.

```
member# ?
  diagnostics         Change diagnostic commands availability
  exit                Exit current mode and change to previous mode
  list                Print command list
  member              VSF member selection
  no                  Negate a command or set its defaults
  page                Enable page break
  show                Show running system information
  start-shell         Start Bash shell
VSF-factory-reset  Clear all VSF configurations and boot as the primary
                      switch
```

5. Type "**show**" followed by "**?**" question mark. You will get the "show" command's help as the output.

```
member# show ?
   session-timeout  Idle session timeout in minutes
   tech             Display output of a predefined command sequence used by
                    technical support
   version          Displays switch version
VSF               Show VSF information
member#
```

   Are the available commands and options the same that you would see in the Master or a non-stacked switch? ______________________________

6. Run the "**member 1**" command; this will take you to Member 1's (the master) CLI.

```
member# member 1
T11-Access-VSF#
```

7. Create LAG111 with the following settings:
   a) Description: **TO_CORE-1**
   b) Allowed VLANs: **1111 and 1112**
   c) LACP rate: **fast**
   d) LACP mode: **active**
   e) Enabled: **yes**

```
T11-Access-VSF# configure terminal
T11-Access-VSF(config)# interface LAG 111
T11-Access-VSF(config-LAG-if)# description TO_CORE-1
T11-Access-VSF(config-LAG-if)# VLAN trunk allowed 1111-1112
T11-Access-VSF(config-LAG-if)# LACP mode active
T11-Access-VSF(config-LAG-if)# LACP rate fast
T11-Access-VSF(config-LAG-if)# no shutdown
T11-Access-VSF(config-LAG-if)# exit
```

8. Associate ports 1/1/21 and 2/1/21 to LAG 111.

```
T11-Access-VSF(config)# interface 1/1/21
T11-Access-VSF(config-if)# LAG 111
T11-Access-VSF(config-if)# exit
T11-Access-VSF(config)# int 2/1/21
T11-Access-VSF(config-if)# LAG 111
T11-Access-VSF(config-if)# exit
```

PC-3

9. Move back to PC-3 (Figure 12-21).

   Is the ping still running? ______________________________

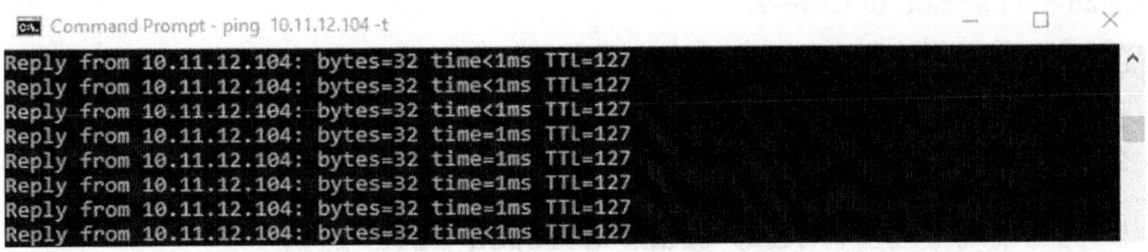

Figure 12-21 Ping to Pc4

Core-1 (via PC-1)

10. Open an SSH session to Core-1. Log in using cxf11/aruba123.
11. Create LAG111 with the following settings:
    a) Description: **TO_T11-ACCESS-VSF**
    b) Routing: **no**
    c) Allowed VLANs: **1111 and 1112**
    d) LACP rate: **fast**
    e) LACP mode: **active**
    f) Enabled: **yes**

```
Core-1(config)# interface LAG 111
Core-1(config-LAG-if)# description TO_T11-ACCESS-VSF
Core-1(config-LAG-if)# no routing
Core-1(config-LAG-if)# VLAN trunk allowed 1111-1112
Core-1(config-LAG-if)# LACP mode active
Core-1(config-LAG-if)# LACP rate fast
Core-1(config-LAG-if)# no shutdown
```

12. Associate ports 1/1/16 and 1/1/37 to LAG111.

```
Core-1(config)# interface 1/1/16
Core-1(config-if)# LAG 111
Core-1(config-if)# exit
Core-1(config)# interface 1/1/37
Core-1(config-if)# LAG 111
Core-1(config-if)# exit
```

Core-2 (via PC-1)

13. Open an SSH session to **Core-2**.
14. Repeat steps 11 and 12, creating LAG112 instead.

```
Core-2(config)# interface LAG 112
Core-2(config-LAG-if)# description TO_T11-ACCESS-VSF
Core-2(config-LAG-if)# no routing
Core-2(config-LAG-if)# VLAN trunk allowed 1111-1112
Core-2(config-LAG-if)# LACP mode active
Core-2(config-LAG-if)# LACP rate fast
Core-2(config-LAG-if)# no shutdown
Core-2(config-LAG-if)# exit
```

```
Core-2(config)# interface 1/1/16
Core-2(config-if)# LAG 112
Core-2(config-if)# exit
Core-2(config)# interface 1/1/37
Core-2(config-if)# LAG 112
Core-2(config-if)# exit
```

PC-3

15. Move back to PC-3 (Figure 12-22).

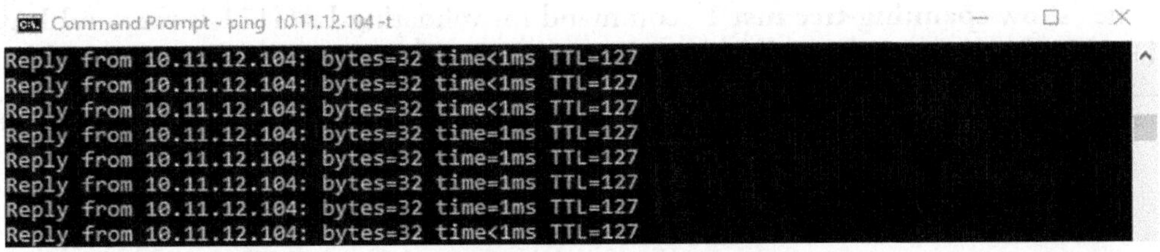

Figure 12-22 Ping PC4

Is the ping still running? ______________________________

Access-VSF: Member 1

16. Move to Member 1.

17. Repeat step 14 using TO_CORE-2 as description and mapping the LAG to ports 1/1/22 and 2/1/22 instead.

```
T11-Access-VSF(config)# interface LAG 112
T11-Access-VSF(config-LAG-if)# description TO_CORE-2
T11-Access-VSF(config-LAG-if)# VLAN trunk allowed 1111-1112
T11-Access-VSF(config-LAG-if)# LACP mode active
T11-Access-VSF(config-LAG-if)# LACP rate fast
T11-Access-VSF(config-LAG-if)# no shutdown
T11-Access-VSF(config-LAG-if)# exit
T11-Access-VSF(config)# interface 1/1/22
T11-Access-VSF(config-if)# LAG 112
T11-Access-VSF(config-if)# exit
T11-Access-VSF(config)# interface 2/1/22
T11-Access-VSF(config-if)# LAG 112
T11-Access-VSF(config-if)# end
```

18. Run the "**show LACP interfaces**" command; then confirm all four uplinks are UP.

```
T11-Access-VSF# show LACP interfaces | begin 8 Actor
Actor details of all interfaces:
-----------------------------------------------------------------------------
IntfAggr       Port  Port  State   System-ID        System Aggr Forwarding
Name        Id    PriPri     Key  State
-----------------------------------------------------------------------------
1/1/21  LAG111     22    1     ALFNCD  88:3a:30:98:30:00 65534  111  up
2/1/21  LAG111     86    1     ALFNCD  88:3a:30:98:30:00 65534  111  up
1/1/22  LAG112     23    1     ASFNCD  88:3a:30:98:30:00 65534  112  up
2/1/22  LAG112     87    1     ASFNCD  88:3a:30:98:30:00 65534  112  up
```

19. Use the "**show spanning-tree mst 1**" command for validating LAG111 is root and LAG112 is Alternate.

```
T11-Access-VSF# show spanning-tree mst 1 | begin 60 Port | exclude Disabled
                Port:LAG111, Cost:20000, Rem Hops:19

Port          Role           State        Cost     Priority   Type
-------------- -------------- ------------ ------- ---------- ----------
1/1/1         Designated     Forwarding   20000    128        point_to_point
1/1/3         Designated     Forwarding   20000    128        point_to_point
2/1/4         Designated     Forwarding   20000    128        point_to_point
LAG111        Root           Forwarding   20000    64         point_to_point
LAG112        Alternate      Blocking     20000    64         point_to_point

Topology change fLAG            : True
Number of topology changes      : 11
Last topology change occurred : 239 seconds ago
```

20. Use the "**show spanning-tree mst 2**" command for validating LAG112 is root and LAG111 is Alternate (Figure 12-23).

```
T11-Access-VSF# show spanning-tree mst 2 | begin 60 Port | exclude Disabled
               Port:LAG112, Cost:20000, Rem Hops:19

Port          Role           State        Cost     Priority   Type
-------------- -------------- ------------ ------- ---------- ----------
1/1/1         Designated     Forwarding   20000    128        point_to_point
1/1/3         Designated     Forwarding   20000    128        point_to_point
2/1/4         Designated     Forwarding   20000    128        point_to_point
LAG111        Alternate      Blocking     20000    64         point_to_point
LAG112        Root           Forwarding   20000    64         point_to_point
Topology change fLAG            : True
Number of topology changes      : 16
Last topology change occurred : 256 seconds ago
```

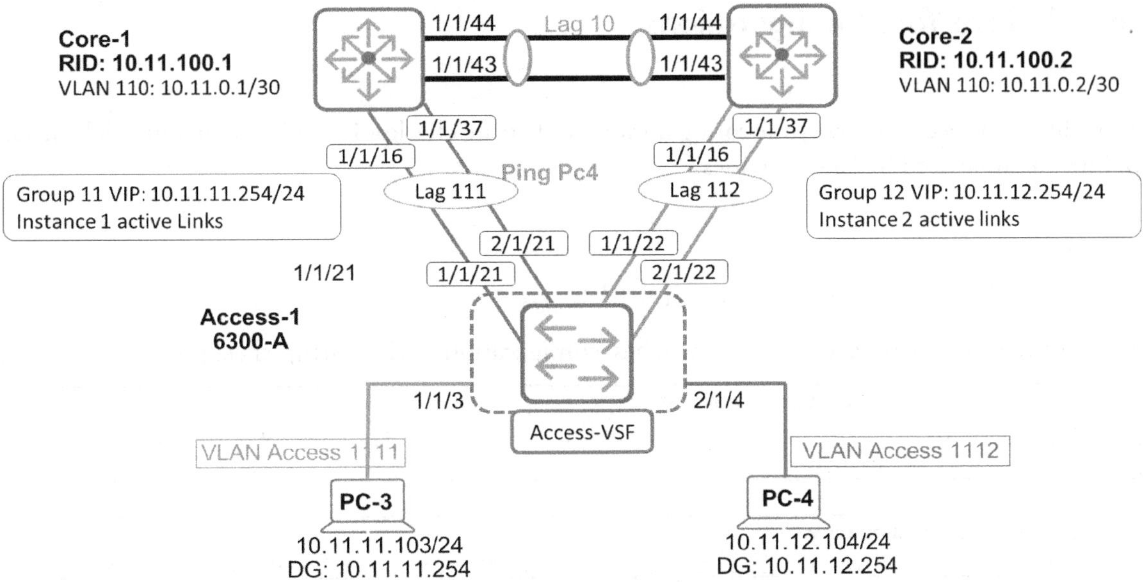

Figure 12-23 Spanning-Tree MST

PC-3

21. Move back to PC-3 (Figure 12-24).

    Is the ping still running? ______________________________

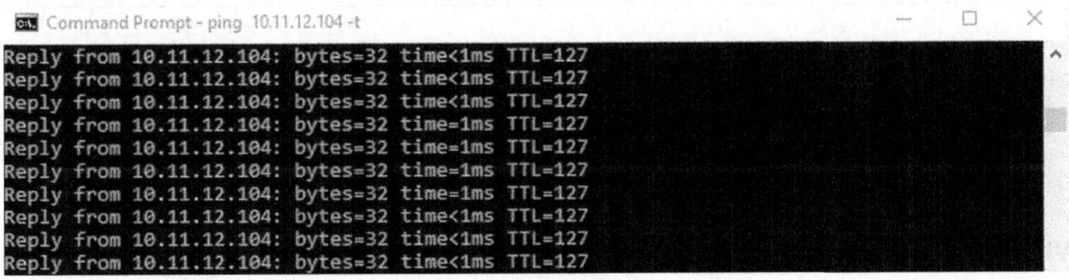

Figure 12-24 Ping to PC-4

Task 3: Save Your Configurations

Objectives

You will now proceed to save your configurations and create checkpoints. Notice that final lab checkpoints might be used by later activities.

Steps

Access-VSF, Core-1, and Core-2 (via PC-1).

1. Save the current Access and Core switches' configuration in the startup checkpoint.

```
T11-Access-VSF # write memory
Configuration changes will take time to process, please be patient.
T11-Access-VSF #
```

```
Core-1# write memory
Configuration changes will take time to process, please be patient.
```

```
Core-2# write memory
Configuration changes will take time to process, please be patient.
```

Access-VSF

2. Backup the current Access-VSF's configuration as a custom checkpoint called **Lab12-1_final**.

```
T11-Access-VSF # copy running-config checkpoint Lab12-1_final
Configuration changes will take time to process, please be patient.
```

You have completed Lab 12.1!

Lab 12.2: Maintaining the VSF Stack

Overview

After deploying VSF and centralizing both the control and management plane, the next phase is to assure there is no single point of failure that could prevent the stack from working. This is done by enabling two main features: standby member and split detection. To test these features BigStartup has authorized another maintenance window.

Objectives

After completing this lab (Figure 12-25), you will be able to:

- Increase the stack resiliency by adding a standby member.
- Provide stack stability using splitdetection.
- Validate the proper performance of the features.

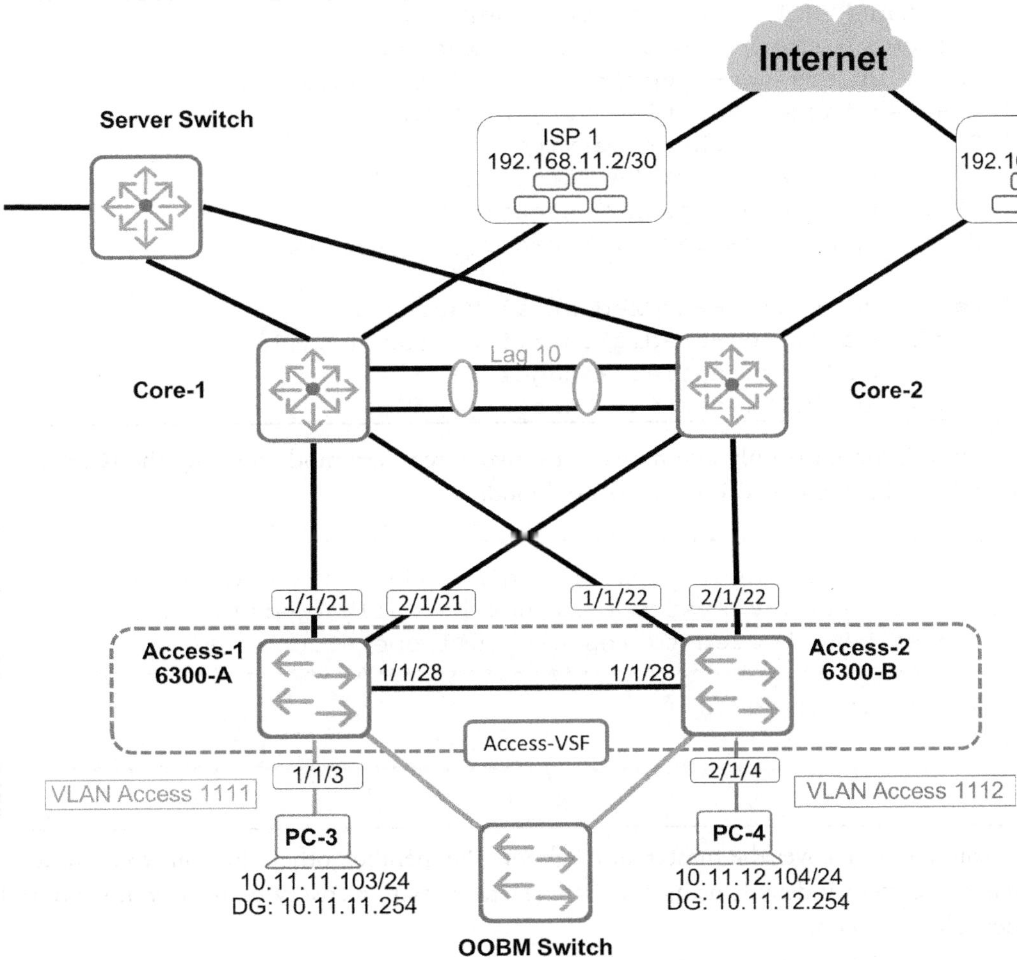

Figure 12-25 Lab Topology

Task 1: Secondary Member

Objectives

Once the stack is created and traffic is flowing, the next step is to maintain the stack and make sure it is as stable as possible. Currently there is a single Master taking care of the management and control plane duties. If that switch happens to fail, then the stack will lose its main point of control and the whole stack goes down, getting stuck in the boot process as seen in console output below.

```
[  OK  ] Started PVNET namespace move script.
[FAILED] Failed to start HPE Credential Manager.
See 'systemctl status hpe-credmgr.service' for details.
[  OK  ] Reached target VSF Discovery System.
[  OK  ] Started HA Type Check Service.
[  OK  ] Reached target Check HA Target to Boot.
[  OK  ] Stopped HPE Credential Manager.
         Starting HPE Credential Manager...

[FAILED] Failed to start HPE Credential Manager.
See 'systemctl status hpe-credmgr.service' for details.
[  OK  ] Stopped HPE Credential Manager.
         Starting HPE Credential Manager...
```

In order to break this loop, the only alternative is to invoke recovery mode pressing the [**Ctrl**]+[**C**] key sequence, taking the member(s) into "**recovery**" mode.

```
*********************************************************************
WARNING! Entering emergency support login mode. This mode is for
support use only and the system will not be fully operational.
The system must be rebooted to restore full operation.
*********************************************************************
T11-Access-VSF login: admin
Password:

recovery#
```

In such case, you have to recover the master and "reboot" the member, otherwise you would have to set the switches into factory default using the "VSF-factory-reset" recovery context command and configure them all over again.

```
recovery# ?
boot                 Reboot all or part of the system; configure default boot
                       parameters
  copy                 Copy data or files to/from the switch
  erase                Erase device information or files
  exit                 Exit current mode and change to previous mode
  list                 Print command list
```

```
  show                   Show running system information
  start-shell            Start Bash shell
VSF-factory-reset  Clear all VSF configurations and boot as the primary
                     switch
recovery#
```

In order to prevent this situation from happening, you can assign (in advance) the "standby" role (secondary member) to any other member of the stack. Once assigned, upon failure of the master, the standby member will take over the master role.

In this lab you will assign the standby role to Member 2 and simulate a failure on Member 1 (see Figure 12-26).

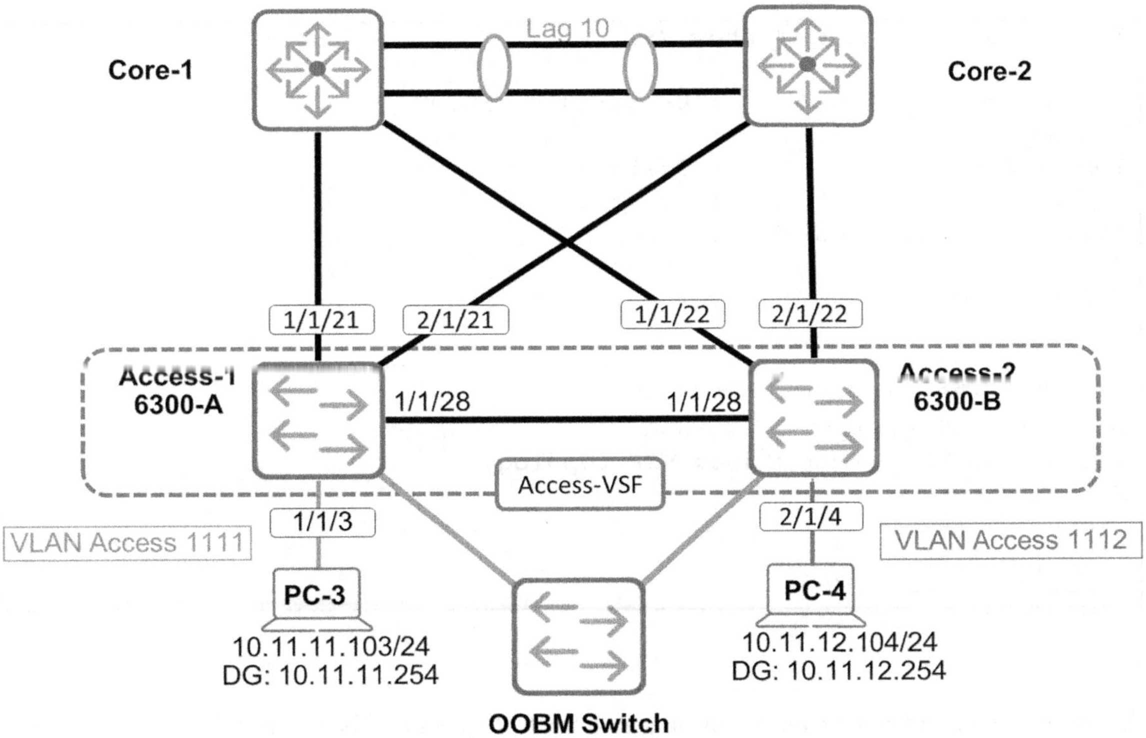

Figure 12-26 Master Standby

Steps

Access-VSF: Member 1

1. Access Member 1's console session.
2. Assign the standby member role. Member 2 will reboot.

```
T11-Access-VSF# configure terminal
T11-Access-VSF(config)# VSF secondary-member 2
This will save the configuration and reboot the specified switch.
Do you want to continue (y/n)? y
```

3. After a few minutes issue the "**show VSF**" and "**show VSF topology**" command to see the new role assigned to Member 2.

```
T11-Access-VSF(config)# show VSF

MAC Address                 : 88:3a:30:98:30:00
Secondary                   : 2
Topology                    : Chain
Status                      : No Split
Split Detection Method      : None

Mbr Mac Address          type            Status
ID
--- ------------------- -------------- ---------------
1   88:3a:30:98:30:00   JL668A          Master
2   88:3a:30:97:a4:40   JL668A          Standby
T11-Access-VSF(config)# show VSF topology
StdbyMstr
 +---+     +---+
 | 2 |1==1| 1 |
 +---+     +---+
```

PC-4

4. Access PC-4 and run a continuous ping to 8.8.8.8. Ping should be successful.

Next you will simulate a failure by rebooting the Master unit.

Access-VSF: Member 1

5. Move to Member 1.
6. Reboot it.

```
T11-Access-VSF# VSF member 1 reboot
The master switch will reboot and the standby will become the master.
Do you want to continue (y/n)? y
```

PC-4

7. Move back to PC-4 (Figure 12-27).

```
Command Prompt
Reply from 8.8.8.8: bytes=32 time=8ms TTL=51
Reply from 8.8.8.8: bytes=32 time=8ms TTL=51
Reply from 8.8.8.8: bytes=32 time=8ms TTL=51
Reply from 8.8.8.8: bytes=32 time=8ms TTL=51
Reply from 8.8.8.8: bytes=32 time=8ms TTL=51
Reply from 8.8.8.8: bytes=32 time=8ms TTL=51
Reply from 8.8.8.8: bytes=32 time=8ms TTL=51
Reply from 8.8.8.8: bytes=32 time=8ms TTL=51
Reply from 8.8.8.8: bytes=32 time=8ms TTL=51
Reply from 8.8.8.8: bytes=32 time=8ms TTL=51
Reply from 8.8.8.8: bytes=32 time=8ms TTL=51
Reply from 8.8.8.8: bytes=32 time=8ms TTL=51
Reply from 8.8.8.8: bytes=32 time=8ms TTL=51
Reply from 8.8.8.8: bytes=32 time=8ms TTL=51
Reply from 8.8.8.8: bytes=32 time=8ms TTL=51
Reply from 8.8.8.8: bytes=32 time=8ms TTL=51
Reply from 8.8.8.8: bytes=32 time=8ms TTL=51
Reply from 8.8.8.8: bytes=32 time=8ms TTL=51
Request timed out.
Reply from 8.8.8.8: bytes=32 time=8ms TTL=51
Request timed out.
Request timed out.
Reply from 8.8.8.8: bytes=32 time=8ms TTL=51
Reply from 8.8.8.8: bytes=32 time=8ms TTL=51
Reply from 8.8.8.8: bytes=32 time=8ms TTL=51
Reply from 8.8.8.8: bytes=32 time=8ms TTL=51
Reply from 8.8.8.8: bytes=32 time=8ms TTL=51
Reply from 8.8.8.8: bytes=32 time=8ms TTL=51
Reply from 8.8.8.8: bytes=32 time=8ms TTL=51
```

Figure 12-27 Ping to Internet

Is the ping still running? ______________________________

How many packets did you lose? ______________________________

Access-VSF: Member 2

8. Move to Member 2. As you can see the unit is still alive.

9. Issue the "show VSF" command.

```
T11-Access-VSF# show VSF

MAC Address                : 88:3a:30:98:30:00
Secondary                  : 2
Topology                   : Standalone
Status                     : Active Fragment
Split Detection Method     : None
```

```
Mbr Mac Address          type           Status
ID
--- ------------------- -------------- ---------------
1                        JL668A         Not Present
2   88:3a:30:97:a4:40    JL668A         Master
```

What is the topology? ____________________

What is the status of the fragment? ____________________

What role does the member have? ____________________

10. Wait until Member1 recovers; then repeat step 9.

```
T11-Access-VSF# show VSF

MAC Address                : 88:3a:30:98:30:00
Secondary                  : 2
Topology                   : Chain
Status                     : No Split
Split Detection Method     : None

Mbr Mac Address          type           Status
ID
--- ------------------- -------------- ---------------
1   88:3a:30:98:30:00    JL668A         Standby
2   88:3a:30:97:a4:40    JL668A         Master
```

What role did Member 1 get when it came back?

____

Note

The Master role in VSFis not preemptable: current Master remains the master.

11. Issue the "**VSF switchover**" for restoring the Master role to Member 1.

```
T11-Access-VSF# VSF switchover
This will cause an immediate switchover to the standby
and the master will reboot.
Do you want to continue (y/n)? y
T11-Access-VSF#
Feb  4 20:25:49 hpe-mgmtmd[2986]: RebootLibPh1: Reboot triggered due to
Reboot requested through database
```

Access-VSF: Member 1

12. Move to Member 1. You will see that due to the "switchover" event, any previous console session that Member 1 had was closed and you will have to log in again.

```
The current session terminated due to a failover event. Login again to
access the router.

  (C) Copyright 2017-2019 Hewlett Packard Enterprise Development LP

                         RESTRICTED RIGHTS LEGEND
  Confidential computer software. Valid license from Hewlett Packard
Enterprise
  Development LP required for possession, use or copying. Consistent
  with FAR 12.211 and 12.212, Commercial Computer Software, Computer
  Software Documentation, and Technical Data for Commercial Items are
  licensed to the U.S. Government under vendor's standard commercial
  license.

We'd like to keep you up to date about:
   * Software feature updates
   * New product announcements
   * Special events
Please register your products now at: https://asp.arubanetworks.com


T11-Access-VSF login:
```

Task 2: Split-Brain Detection

Objectives

After a Master failure, the standby member switch or fragment remains alive. This is because the fragment senses when the links to the Master go down and assumes the Master went down as well. However, what would happen if connections between the two devices fail rather than the master switch? You will discover what happens in the next task.

Steps

PC-3 and PC-4

13. Move to PC-3.
14. Run 3 continuous pings to: PC-3's gateway (10.11.11.254), PC-4 (10.11.12.254), and 8.8.8.8. Pings should be successful.
15. Move to PC-4.
16. Run 3 continuous pings to: PC-4's gateway (10.11.12.254), PC-3 (10.11.11.254), and 8.8.8.8.

Access-VSF: Member 1

17. Move to Member 1.
18. Disable the physical port of the VSF link. This will trigger a split-brain event.

```
T11-Access-VSF(config)# interface 1/1/28
T11-Access-VSF(config-if-VSF)# shutdown
This may cause the stack to split.
Do you want to continue (y/n)? y
T11-Access-VSF(config-if-vsf)#
```

PC-3 and PC-4

19. Move to PC-3 (Figure 12-28).

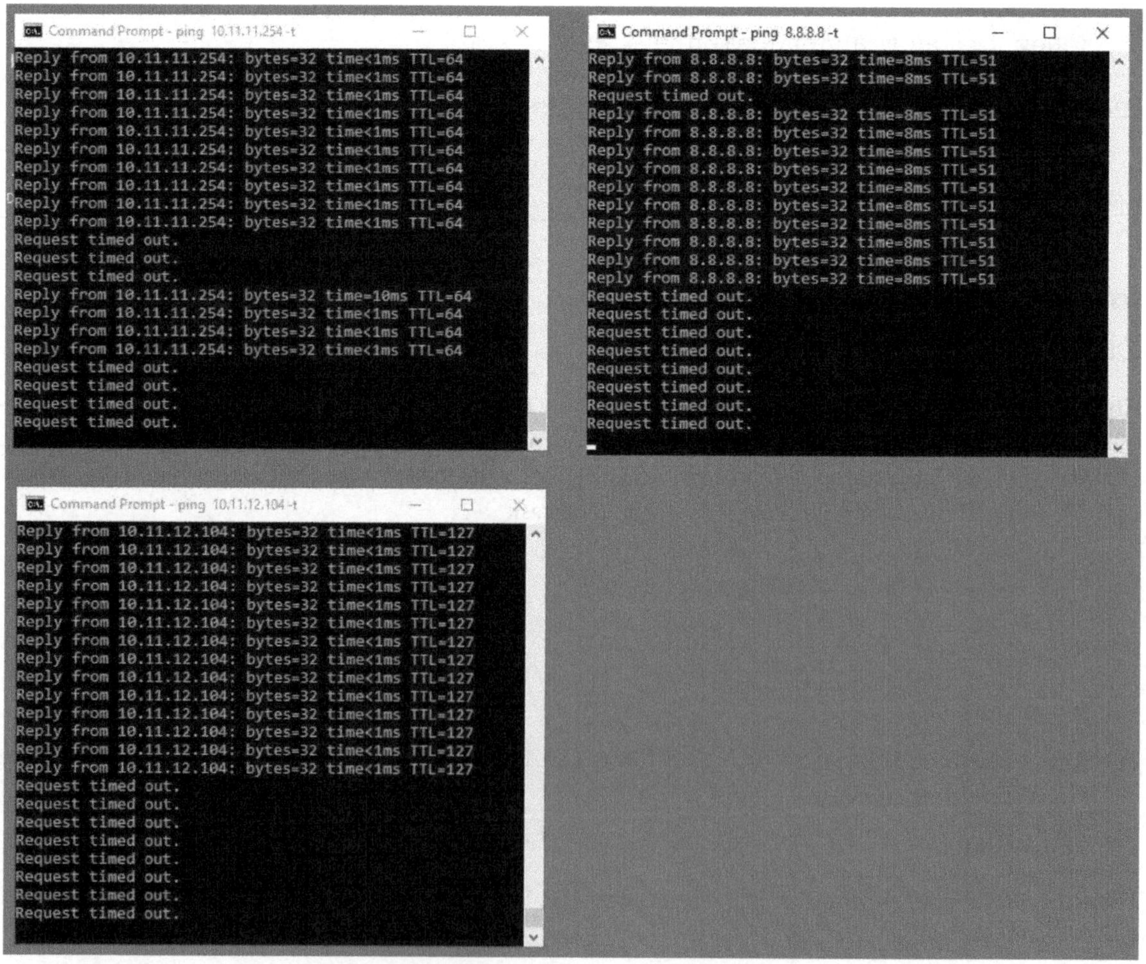

Figure 12-28 Multiple Pings from PC-3

How are the pings behaving? ______________________________

20. Move to PC-4 (Figure 12-29).

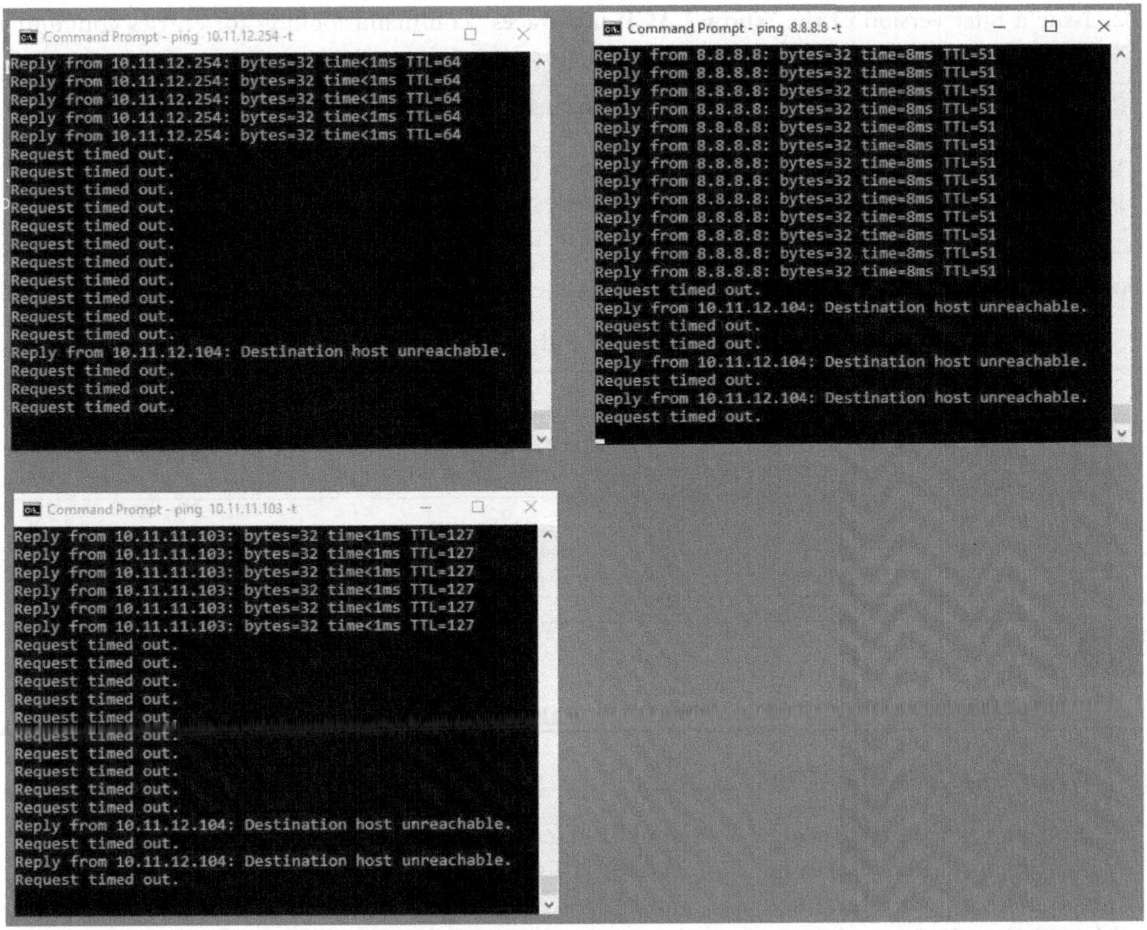

Figure 12-29 Multiple Pings from PC-4

How are the pings behaving? ______________________________

What is the status of your stack members? ______________________________

Core-1

21. Move to Core-1.
22. Issue a filter version of the "**show LACP interfaces**" command looking for entries containing LAG111 (this is the LAG that connects to your stack).

```
Core-1# show LACP interfaces | include 111
1/1/16  LAG111      17    1      ASFNCD  90:20:c2:bc:ed:00 65534 111 up
1/1/37  LAG111      38    1      ASFNCD  90:20:c2:bc:ed:00 65534 111 up
1/1/16  LAG111      22    1      ASFNCD  88:3a:30:98:30:00 65534 111
1/1/37  LAG111      86    1      ASFNCD  88:3a:30:98:30:00 65534 111
```

Focus at the first two entries; what is the status of the interfaces? ____________

23. Issue the "**show interface LAG brief**" command. The output may be longer than the one below.

```
Core-1# show interface LAG brief
--------------------------------------------------------------------------------
Port     Native  Mode   Type          Enabled Status  Reason              Speed
VLAN                                                                     (Mb/s)
--------------------------------------------------------------------------------
LAG10      1     trunk  --              yes     up      --                2000
LAG101     1     trunk  --              yes     up      --                2000
LAG111     1     trunk  --              yes     up      --                2000
```

Note

Since Core-1 is a shared resource you may get more entries in the command's output.

What is the status of LAG111? ____________

The problem you are experiencing is a result of having two stack fragments (Member 1 and Member 2), both acting as masters shown in Figure 12-30. This causes the members using not only the same configuration, but also the same Layer-3 and Layer-2 addressing. Therefore, they are sending identical LACP Data Units on the interfaces that are configured to be part of the same LAG (1/1/21 and 2/1/21 to Core-1 and 1/1/22 and 2/1/22 to Core-2).

Since the Core switches receive these incoming LACP Data Units as normal, they are not aware of any failure and maintain their LAGs and forward traffic across them as usual, based on the source and destination IP addresses.

Note

If your connectivity test from PC-3 to 8.8.8.8 is still working successfully, then it is likely that the behavior explained in the lines above is taking place on another of your pings.

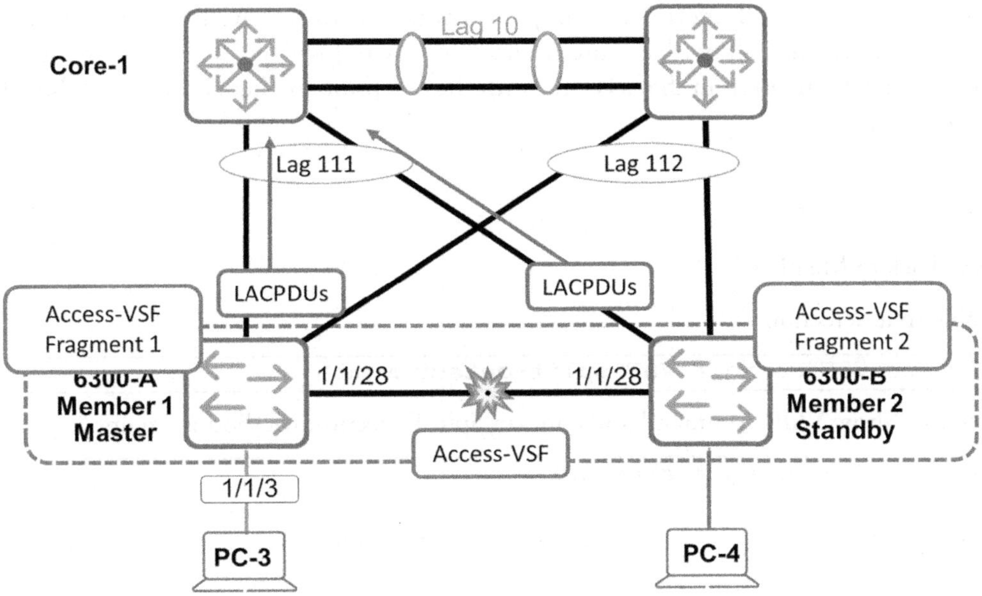

Figure 12-30 Split Brain

Access-VSF: Member 1

24. Move back to Member1.
25. Enable the port of the VSF link. Member2 will merge and reboot.

```
T11-Access-VSF(config-if-VSF)# no shutdown
```

Access-VSF: Member 2

26. Move to Member 2. You shall notice the member switch will reboot as part of the re-merge process.

```
T11-Access-VSF#
Feb  4 20:48:14 VSFd[719]: RebootLibPh1: Reboot triggered due to Reboot of
Member ID 2, Lost merge
```

Now you will enable management port-based, split-brain detection. When this feature is enabled, the Master and Standby Member will exchange broadcast-based heartbeats when they sense a failure in the VSF links. If the Standby member does not receive any of these messages, then it concludes that the Master itself has failed, not just the VSF links. Therefore, it keeps working as normal. However, if the Master is alive and continues to advertise split-detect messages, then the Standby Member's fragment changes its status to inactive and disables all its ports except the management and VSF interfaces. This isolates it from the rest of the network and prevents the Cores from sending traffic to it.

Although this behavior will affect every endpoint connected to the inactive fragment, those connected to the Active one will not have any connection loss and will always be able to establish connections with any destination in the network, with the exception of clients connected directly to the inactive fragment.

Access-VSF: Member 1

27. Move back to Member 1.
28. Enable split detection.

```
T11-Access-VSF(config)# VSF split-detect mgmt
```

29. Issue the "**show VSF**" command and confirm Split Detection Method is "mgmt.".

```
T11-Access-VSF(config)# show VSF

MAC Address                 : 88:3a:30:98:30:00
Secondary                   : 2
Topology                    : Chain
Status                      : No Split
Split Detection Method      : mgmt

Mbr Mac Address          type            Status
ID
--- ------------------- -------------- ---------------
1   88:3a:30:98:30:00   JL668A         Master
2   88:3a:30:97:a4:40   JL668A         Standby
```

30. Disable the physical port of the VSF link. This will trigger split-detect messages from the Standby Member, see Figure 12-31.

```
T11-Access-VSF(config)# interface 1/1/28
T11-Access-VSF(config-if-VSF)# shutdown
This may cause the stack to split.
Do you want to continue (y/n)? y
T11-Access-VSF(config-if-VSF)#
```

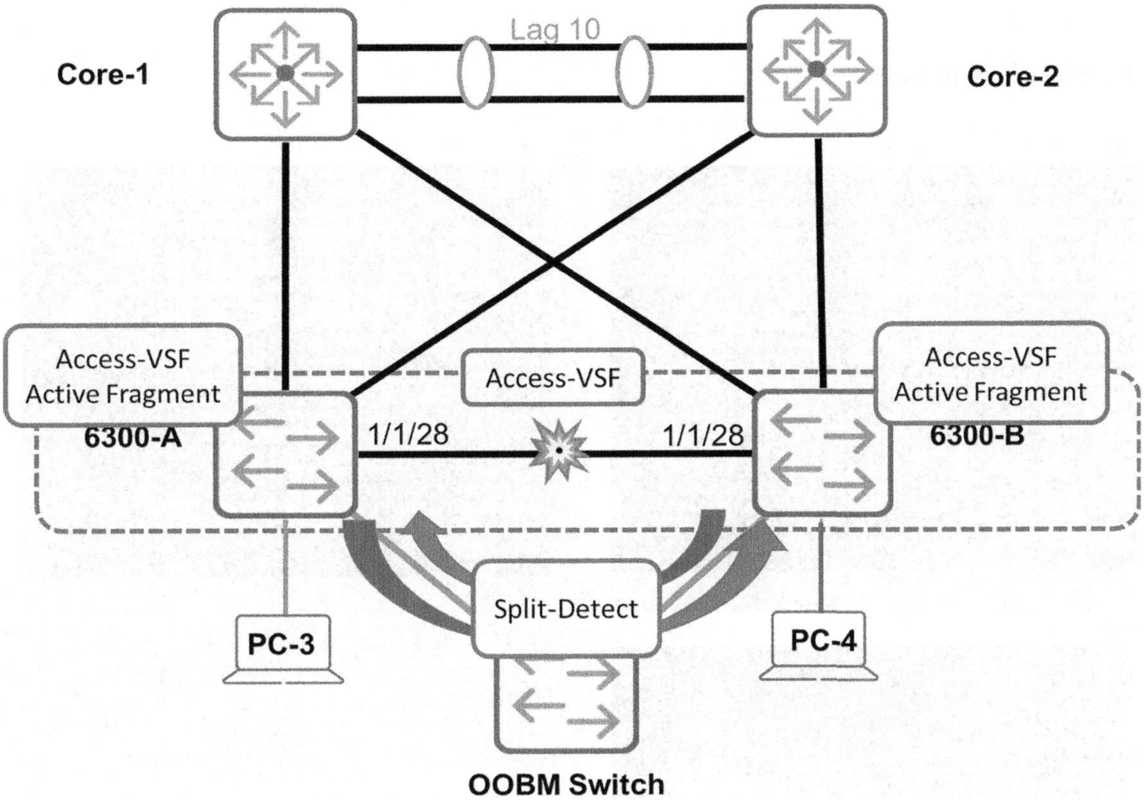

Figure 12-31 Split Detection

Notice

Split detect uses Ethertype 0xf8f8. If you happen to deploy any Layer-2 filtering tool in the Out-of-Band Management switch, then make sure these packets are explicitly permitted.

PC-3 and PC-4

31. Move back to PC-3.

Figure 12-32 Multiple Pings from PC-3

In Figure 12-32, are pings still running? ______________________________

Which one is falling? ______________________________

Is this result what you expected? ______________________________

32. Move back to PC-4.

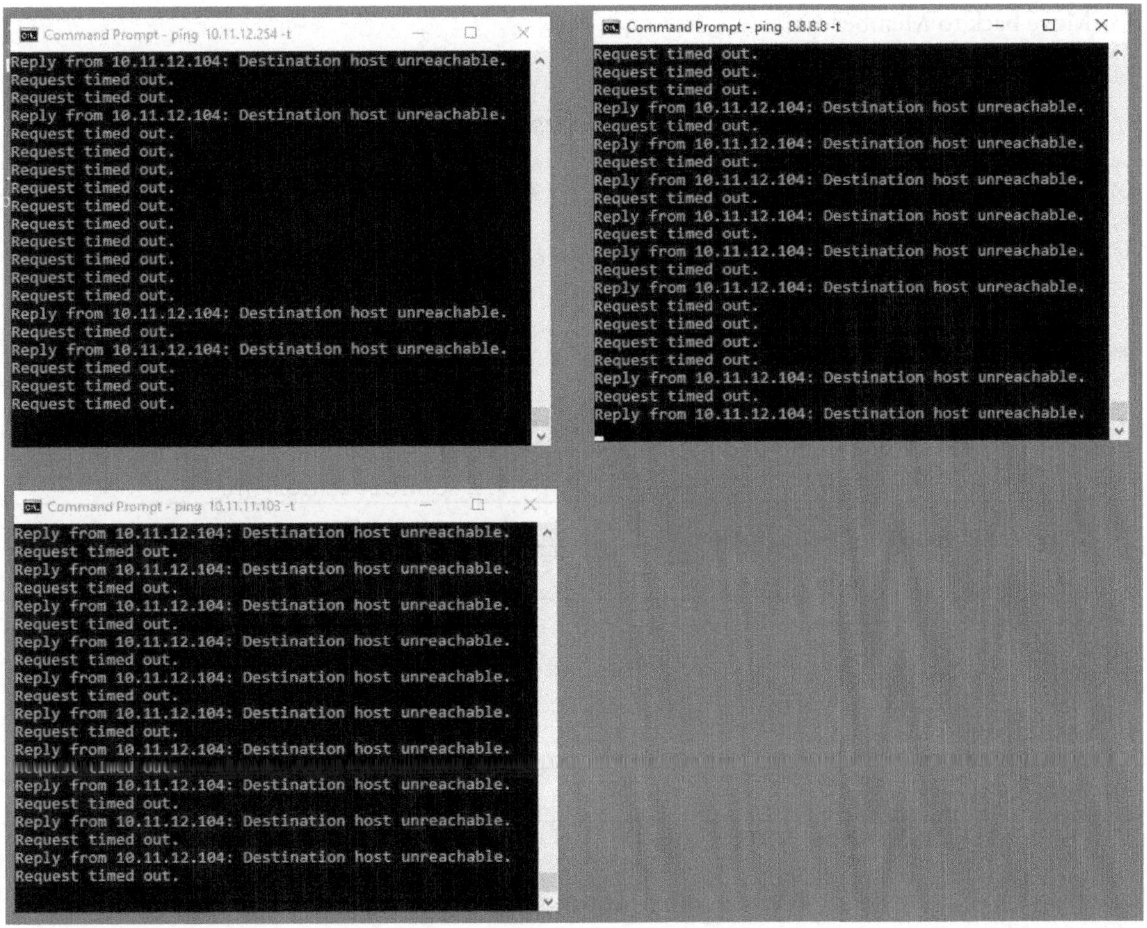

Figure 12-33 Multiple Pings from PC-4

In Figure 12-33, are pings still running? ______________________________

Which one is falling? ____

Is this result what you expected? ________________________________

Access-VSF: Member 1

33. Move back to Member 1.

34. Issue the "**show VSF**" command.

```
T11-Access-VSF(config-if-VSF)# show VSF

MAC Address                  : 88:3a:30:98:30:00
Secondary                    : 2
Topology                     : Standalone
Status                       : Active Fragment
Split Detection Method       : mgmt
Mbr Mac Address            type           Status
ID
--- ------------------ -------------- ---------------
1   88:3a:30:98:30:00  JL668A         Master
2                      JL668A         In Other Fragment
```

What is the status of the fragment? ______________________________

What is the status of Member 2? ______________________________

Access-VSF: Member 2

35. Move back to Member 2.

36. Repeat step 21.

```
T11-Access-VSF# show VSF

MAC Address                  : 88:3a:30:98:30:00
Secondary                    : 2
Topology                     : Standalone
Status                       : Inactive Fragment
Split Detection Method       : mgmt

Mbr Mac Address            type           Status
ID
--- ------------------ -------------- ---------------
1                      JL668A         In Other Fragment
2   88:3a:30:97:a4:40  JL668A         Master
T11-Access-VSF#
```

What is the status of the fragment? ______________________________

What is the status of Member 2? ______________________________

37. Use the "**show interface brief**" command and look for the status of both uplinks and connection to PC-4.

```
T11-Access-VSF# show interface brief | exclude no
--------------------------------------------------------------------------------
Port     Native   Mode    Type       Enabled   Status   Reason            Speed
VLAN                                                                     (Mb/s)
--------------------------------------------------------------------------------
2/1/4    1112     access  1GbT       yes       down     Disabled by VSF   --
2/1/21   1        trunk   1GbT       yes       down     Disabled by VSF   --
2/1/22   1        trunk   1GbT       yes       down     Disabled by VSF   --
2/1/28   --       routed  SFP+DAC1   yes       down     Waiting for link  --
VLAN1    --       --                 yes       down                       --
LAG111   1        trunk   --         yes       down     --               auto
LAG112   1        trunk   --         yes       down     --               auto
T11-Access-VSF#
```

What is the status of these ports? ____________________

What is the reason? ____________________

Your result should be similar to the one shown in Figure 12-31 above. ____________

Access-VSF: Member 1

38. Move back one last time to Member 1.

39. Enable the ports.

```
T11-Access-VSF(config-if-VSF)# no shutdown
T11-Access-VSF(config-if-VSF)# end
```

Task 3: Save Your Configurations

Objectives

You will now proceed to save your configurations and create checkpoints. Notice that final lab checkpoints might be used by later activities.

Steps

Access-VSF, Core-1, and Core-2 (via PC-1)

1. Save the current Access-VSF's configuration in the startup checkpoint.

```
T11-Access-VSF # write memory
Configuration changes will take time to process, please be patient.
```

Access-VSF

40. Backup the current Access-VSF's configuration as a custom checkpoint called **Lab12-2_final**.

```
T11-Access-VSF # copy running-config checkpoint Lab12-2_final
Configuration changes will take time to process, please be patient.
```

You have completed Lab 12.2!

Learning Check

Chapter 12 Questions

Operational Planes – Control, Management, and Data

1. Which of the statements below accurately describe network devices operational planes?
   a. The control plane is used to control the switch configuration.
   b. The management plane manages internal Layer 2 and Layer 3 switch processes.
   c. The data plane moves data from ingress to egress port.
   d. The control and management planes are tightly integrated.

Aruba VSF Stacking Solution and Platforms, VSF Member Roles and Links

2. Which of the options below describe a valid VSF scenario?
   a. An Aruba OS-CX switch acts as the primary and an Aruba AOS switch has a backup role.
   b. Configure two switches: one as Primary and one as member using a single VSF Link.
   c. Configure VSF on 5 8325 Aruba OS-CX switches.

VSF Topologies, VSF Requirements, VSF Configuration

3. Which of the statements describe valid VSF requirements and specifications?
   a. You can daisy-chain up to 10 VSF members.
   b. You can connect 10 VSF members in a ring topology.
   c. You can mesh multiple members together for redundancy.
   d. If you use an Aruba 6300 series as the master, you can connect Aruba 5300's as members.
   e. The configuration of VSF may cause members to reboot.

13 Secure Management and Maintenance

EXAM OBJECTIVES

- ✓ Describe the OOBM port and management VRF.
- ✓ Explain secure management protocols.
- ✓ Describe RADIUS-based management authentication.
- ✓ Explain SNMP.
- ✓ Describe configuration file management.
- ✓ Describe OS image management.
- ✓ Restore and AOS-CX device to factory default and perform password recovery.

Overview

Network management is a vital skill for prospective network administrators and engineers. This module will give you the foundational knowledge to understand and perform the most important network management skills.

First you will learn about how AOS-CX devices have isolated the management and data planes using Virtual Routing and Forwarding (VRF). You see how a separate management VRF supports the OOBM interface which is purely for management operations. These devices also have a default VRF for typical data plane operations, to support connectivity for end users and other network devices.

You will explore secure management protocols, including SSH for CLI access, HTTPS for GUI access, AAA, and RADIUS for centralized security, RBAC for efficient, role-based security. You will also learn about the SNMP operation, architecture, and configuration.

The journey continues as you dive into configuration file management and Operating System image management. Then you learn how to restore an AOS-CX device to a factory default state and perform password recovery.

Management and Maintenance

Out-Of-Band Management Port

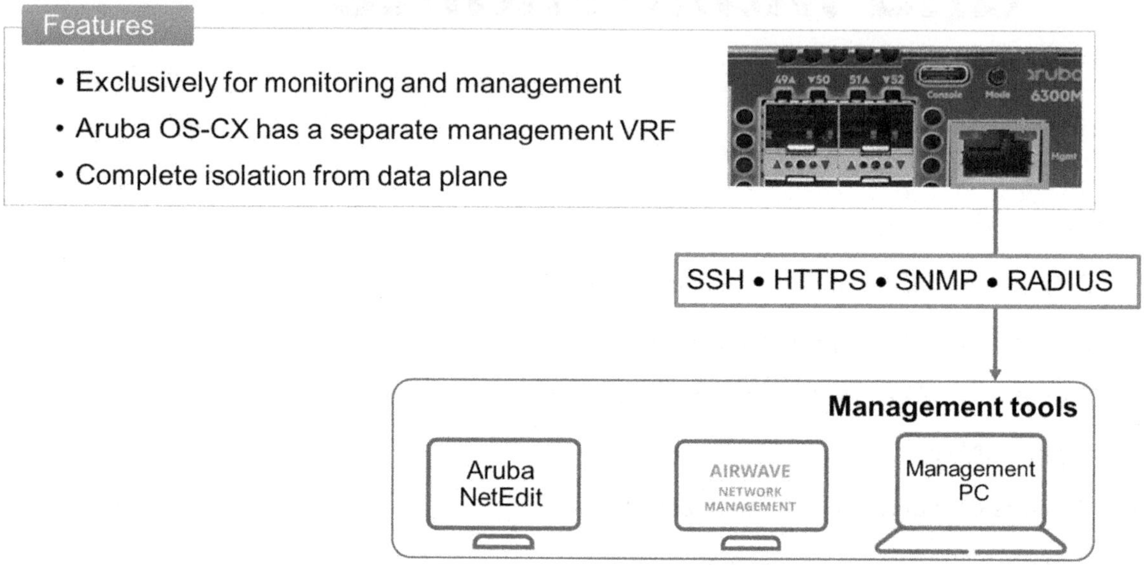

Figure 13-1 Out-Of-Band Management Port

The AOS-CX switch families include an Out-Of-Band Management (OOBM) port in Figure 13-1, used exclusively to monitor and manage the switch. Because AOS-CX has a separate management VRF, there is complete isolation between the management and data planes. Data traffic can never see or use this port. Due to this complete isolation, management traffic does not use any *bandwidth* in the data plane. This is commonly referred as Out-of-Band Management or OOBM.

You do have the option of remotely connecting to and managing the switch via a normal Ethernet port in the data plane. This is referred to as In-Band Management. This can seem convenient but is not recommended. A misconfiguration of switch routing (or switching protocol) could cause you to lose administrative access to the device. There is also a security concern. Without manually configured security controls, it is possible for hackers to access your switch configuration and take control of the device.

Management VRF

You learned about Virtual Routing and Forwarding (VRF) in Module 6 of this course. VRF creates separate virtual routers inside a physical router, with separate routing tables. AOS-CX devices have a default VRF for the data plane, and a separate mgmt VRF for the Management port to handle OOBM traffic.

The AOS-CX mgmt interface is enabled by default. It is configured to receive its IP parameters using DHCP. Use the **show interface mgmt** command in Figure 13-2 to verify the state of this interface. If preferred, you can manually configure IP parameters on the management interface, as shown in Figure 13-2.

```
Switch(config)#interface mgmt
Switch(config-if-mgmt)# ip static <IP-address/Mask>
Switch(config-if-mgmt)# default-gateway <Default-gateway-IP>
Switch(config-if-mgmt)# nameserver <DNS-Primary-server>
```

Verification

```
Switch# show interface mgmt
  Address Mode                       : static
  Admin State                        : up
  Mac Address                        : 88:3a:30:97:c7:01
  IPv4 address/subnet-mask           : 10.251.1.4/24
  Default gateway IPv4               : 10.251.1.254
  Primary Nameserver                 : 10.253.1.21
<<<Omitted output>>>>
```

Figure 13-2 Show Interface Mgmt Command

Ping and Traceroute in the Management VRF

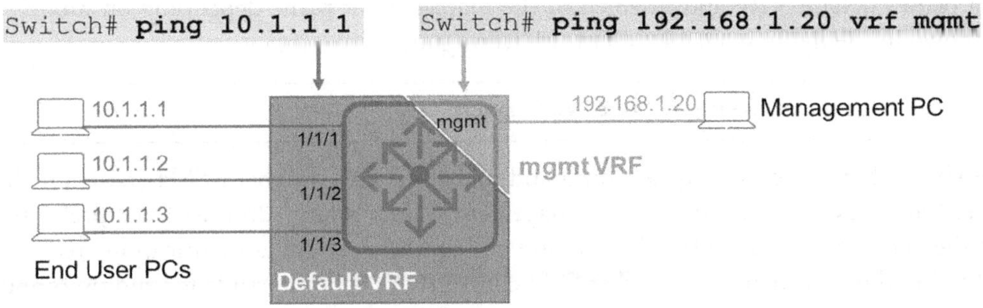

Figure 13-3 Ping and Traceroute

By default, AOS-CX switch ping and traceroute commands are generated for the data plane's default VRF. To verify connectivity on the mgmt VRF, you must use special ping and traceroute syntax to specify the mgmt VRF, as shown in Figure 13-3.

SSH for AOS-CX

Objective Secure protocol for switch CLI access

Aruba OS-CX 6300 series
- Enabled by default on and **mgmt** and **default** VRF

Aruba OS-CX non 6300 series
- Enabled by default on **mgmt** VRF

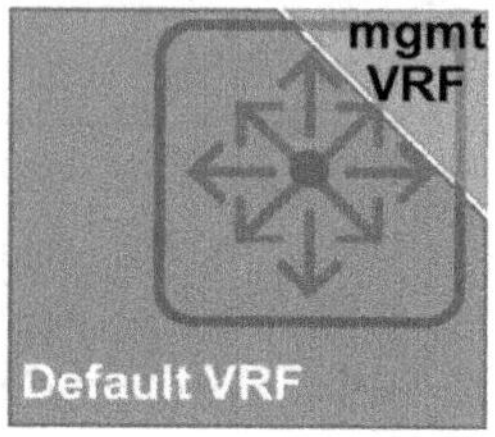


```
8325(config)# ssh server vrf default
8325# show ssh server vrf default

SSH server configuration on VRF default :

    IP Version          : IPv4 and IPv6     SSH Version           : 2.0
    TCP Port            : 22                Grace Timeout (sec)   : 60
    Max Auth Attempts : 6
    Host-keys           : ECDSA, ED25519, RSA
```

Figure 13-4 SSH for AOS-CX

You must use the Secure Shell (SSH) protocol to connect to the AOS-CX switch CLI. SSH provides secure communications between the switch and your management PC. SSH is enabled by default in the data plane's default VRF and disabled in the management plane depending on model. Use the syntax shown in the figure to enable SSH for VRF mgmt.

```
Switch(config)# ssh server vrf mgmt
```

Use the **show SSH server vrf mgmt** command in Figure 13-4 to check SSH status on the mgmt interface. Once SSH is enabled in the management plane, many administrators prefer to disable SSH in the data plane. Although SSH is secure and requires proper authentication credentials, disabling SSH in the data plane ensures that SSH connectivity is not possible for end users and potential bad actors.

HTTPS for AOS-CX

Objective Secure protocol for switch GUI access

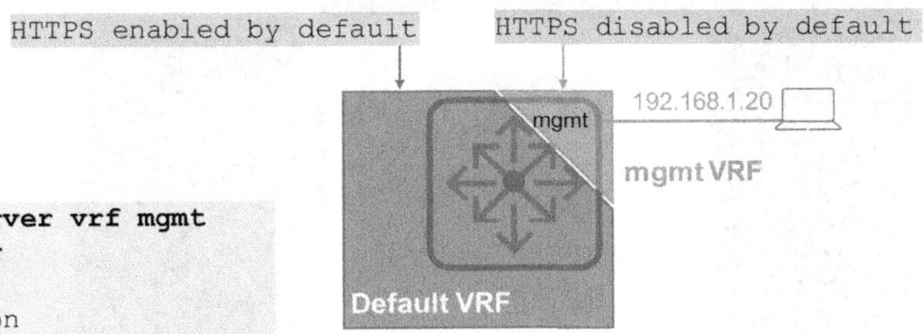


```
Switch(config)# https-server vrf mgmt
Switch# show https-server

HTTPS Server Configuration
----------------------------
 VRF                   : mgmt, default

 REST Access Mode      : read-write
```

Figure 13-5 HTTPS for AOS-CX

HTTPS provides secure GUI access to the switch. Like SSH, HTTPS is enabled by default in the default VRF, and disabled in the management plane depending on model. Treat HTTPS like SSH; enable it in the management plane using the syntax shown in Figure 13-5. Then disable it in the data plane's default VRF to maximize security.

```
Switch(config)# https-server vrf mgmt
```

Use the **show HTTPS-server** command to verify HTTPS status.

To disable the HTTPS service in the VRF default:

```
Switch(config)# no https-server vrf default
```

Web Interface

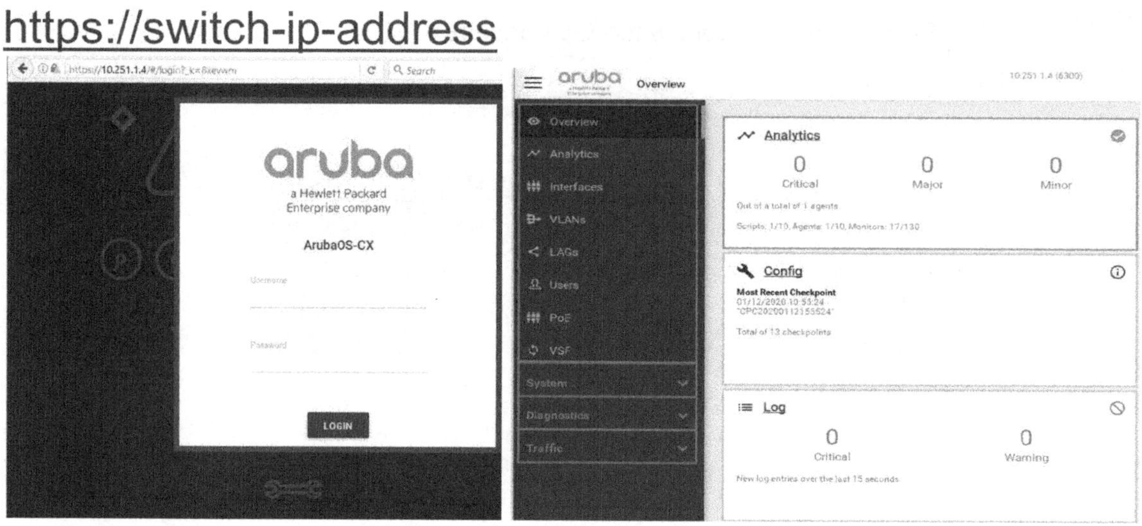

Figure 13-6 Web Interface

AOS-CX switches integrate a GUI web interface for device monitoring and management. To use this interface, open a web browser and enter the switch IP address: https://switch-ip-address

The menu on the left is divided into four different sections:

- Overview: Displays basic protocols and feature information. Those include Analytics, Interfaces, VLANs, LAGs, Users, Power over Ethernet, and VSF.
- System: Displays Environmental information, Log, DNS servers, SNMP configuration, and Configuration management.
- Diagnostics: Include features like Ping and Traceroute.
- Traffic: This menu includes information about Spanning-Tree.

Remember that it is a best practice to permit HTTPS/GUI use only in the mgmt VRF (Figure 13-6).

Authentication, Authorization, and Accounting

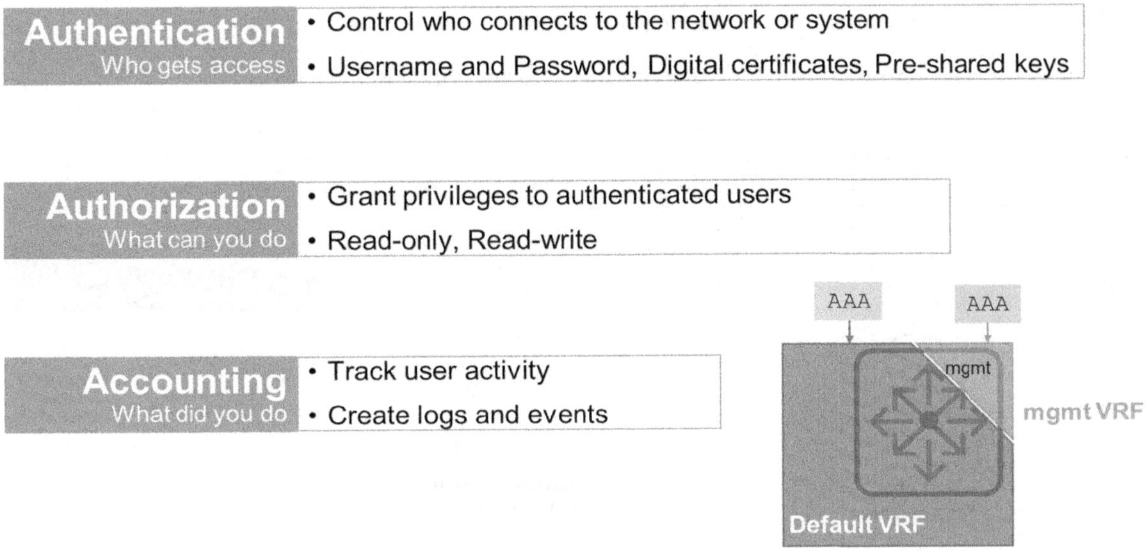

Figure 13-7 Authentication, Authorization, and Accounting

AAA is a security concept that involves three individual processes (Figure 13-7):

- Authentication controls who gets access. The system validates credentials as users attempt data plane connectivity to the default VRF, or management connectivity to the mgmt. VRF. The credentials can be in the form of usernames and password, digital certificate, or Pre-Shared Keys (PSK).
- Authorization controls what you can do upon authentication. This process grants privileges to authenticated users. Can you connect to the network and use resources? Can you have read-only access to the switch CLI or GUI? Can you have full read/write access to the switch CLI? This depends on your level of authorization.
- Accounting tracks what you did by creating event logs, for example, Jose Rodrequez accessed his sales files at 3:30pm, John Smith deleted accounting files at 2:00am, and Mary Owens modified the switch CLI last Thursday at 12:45.

AAA is often implemented with a Remote Authentication Dial-In User Service (RADIUS) server, about which you will soon learn.

Role-Based Access Control (RBAC)

Administrators can access and configure the switch. They have full visibility of all switch processes. This is perfect for well-trained, trustworthy employees, but others should be restricted based on their expertise and job function. This concept is known as Role-Based Access Control or RBAC.

AOS-CX applies RBAC defining user-groups, where each group is manually configured with specifically allowed switch commands. AOS-CX defines three default user-groups: administrators, auditors, and operators, which can neither be deleted nor edited.

Use the **show user-group** command to verify this information (Figure 13-8).

```
Switch# show user-group
GROUP NAME     GROUP TYPE  INCLUDED GROUP  NUMBER OF RULES
-------------- ----------- --------------- --------------
Administrators built-in       n/a             n/a
auditors       built-in       n/a             n/a
operators      built-in       n/a             n/a
```

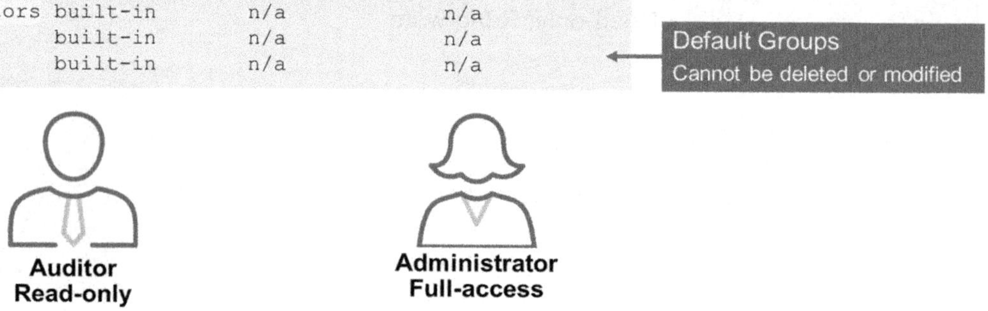

Figure 13-8 Show User-Group Command

RBAC Configuration

Define new user-groups as shown:

```
Switch(config)# user-group <group-name>
```

Map a user account to a defined group as shown:

```
Switch(config)# user <username> group <user-group> password
plaintext <password>
```

Use rules to define the commands that will be available, as shown:

```
Switch(config)# user-group monitoring
Switch(config-usr-grp-monitoring)# permit cli command "<command>"
```

In Figure 13-9 below, a group named monitoring can only use the commands **show version** and **show interface 1/1/1**.

Example

```
Switch(config)# user-group monitoring
Switch(config-ur-grp-monitoring)# 10 permit cli command "show version"
Switch(config-ur-grp-monitoring)# 20 permit cli command "show interface 1/1/1"
```

Pattern matching language:
Regular Expressions (Regex)

Figure 13-9 User-Group Monitoring Example

AOS-CX accepts complete command syntax and accepts Regular Expression (Regex) syntax. This is a set of variables and logic symbols that let you specify a group of commands with less typing.

RADIUS-Based Management Authentication

For authentication, some administrators define local credentials on each switch. This is good for smaller environments but becomes a burden as the network grows. If you have 100 network devices, you must maintain 100 separate credential databases, and try to keep them consistent.

Many people prefer to centralize AAA services on a Remote Authentication Dial-In User Service (RADIUS) server. Hundreds and thousands of devices can use the RADIUS protocol (UDP port 1812) to access a centralized RADIUS server—a centralized repository for credentials.

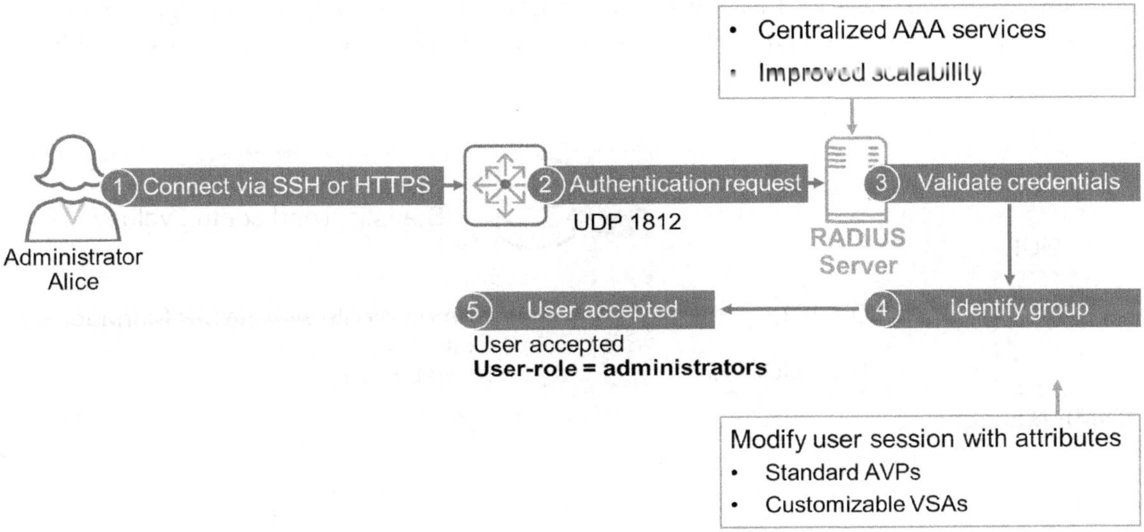

Figure 13-10 RADIUS-Based Management Authentication

A user or administrator asks the switch if it can connect, and the switch in turn asks the RADIUS server, “Hey, I have user Alice, with password Secret123. Should I grant them access?”

The RADIUS server receives this request, validates credentials against its database, and responds to the switch with an ACCEPT message or a REJECT message. RADIUS messages can also include attributes. These are like “notes” that can modify how a connection session shall proceed.

For example, in Figure 13-10 user Alice attempts to login into a switch, which sends Alice’s credentials to the RADIUS server. The server validates these credentials and sends an ACCEPT message, which can include an attribute that helps the AOS-CX switch to place Alice in the Administrator user-group.

One reason for the RADIUS standard’s popularity is that it was designed to be customizable by equipment manufacturers and vendors, using Vendor-Specific Attributes (VSA). Aruba has created VSAs that are specific for its products, to enhance usability and features. By default, RADIUS servers use standard attributes called Attribute Value Pairs (AVP). Custom VSAs must be manually added to the RADIUS server. Aruba ClearPass is a powerful RADIUS server that uses Aruba VSAs by default, without need for manual addition.

Simple Network Management Protocol (SNMP)

SNMP is an application-layer protocol defined in RFC 1157 for exchanging management information between network devices. This protocol is a popular method to configure, manage, and monitor network elements from any vendor. Figure 13-11 shows the SNMP architecture, as described below:

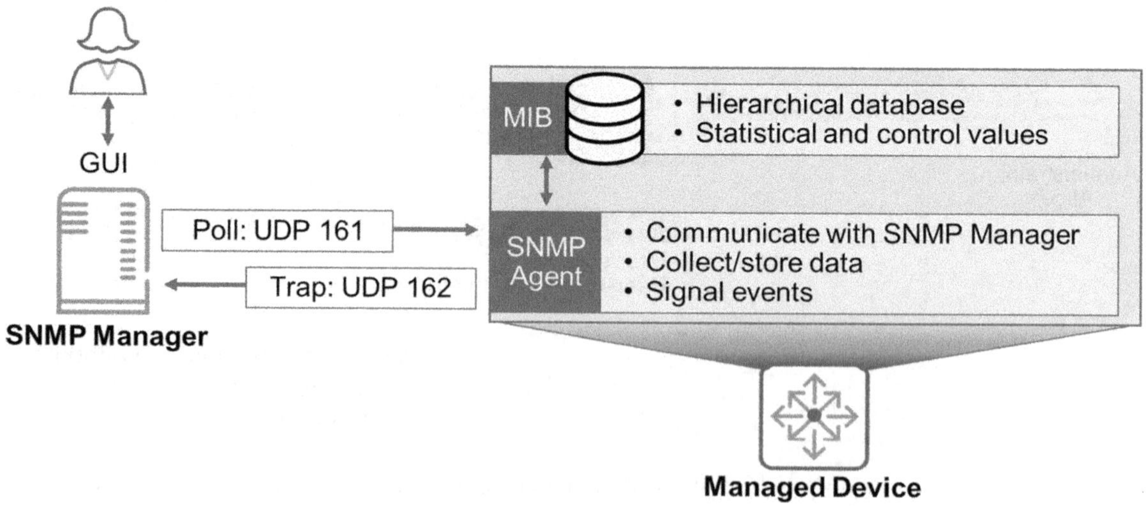

Figure 13-11 SNMP

SNMP Manager

It is typically a dedicated server that communicates with SNMP agent. It often has a GUI, so administrators can view and change parameters for many network devices from a single interface. The manager uses several message types to gather and modify network device parameters. Some of its key functions include:

- Queries agents.
- Gets responses from agents.
- Sets variables in agents.
- Acknowledges asynchronous events from agents.

Managed Devices

The routers, switches, firewalls, wireless controllers, access points, and any other network devices should be centrally monitored, managed, and configured. Internally, these managed devices have two main SNMP components.

1. The SNMP Agent collects information and communicates with the SNMP Manager about device configuration and status. It stores and retrieves this information in a Management Information Base (MIB).
2. The MIB is a hierarchical database that stores device status, statistics, and configuration information. This is the information that is exchanged between the SNMP Manager and the managed device.

Communication and Ports

Usually, SNMP Manager to Agent communications is a "pull" mechanism. When this device requires to get information from the managed device it requests the information using simple commands such as GET, GET NEXT, GET BULK. Changes in the device are done using the SET command. This communication uses UDP 161.

The exception to the "pull" mechanism is when the managed device has important information that cannot wait for the manager's period polling. "Newsflash!! My CPU utilization is dangerously high". In cases like this, the managed device "pushes" information to the manager without being asked, using an SNMP Trap. SNMP Traps use UDP 162.

SNMP Versions

The different SNMP versions are described below:

SNMP Version 1

This is the first version of the SNMP protocol and uses a community-based security mechanism. The "community string" is like a simple pre-shared passcode. If the Managed device has a community string of **public**, then any SNMP manager that can reach the device can access the agent's MIB, as long as **community string = public** is used.

SNMP Version 2c

This is the revised protocol, which includes enhancements of SNMPv1 in the areas of protocol packet types, transport mapping, MIB structure elements. This version also uses a community-based security mechanism.

SNMP Version 3

This provides a higher level of security, including message integrity, authentication, and encryption. A simple configuration using SNMP version 2 in AOS-CX is presented in Figure 13-12:

SNMP version 2 configuration in ArubaOS-CX:

Aruba OS-CX by default:
- Community "public" read-only

```
Switch(config)# snmp-server community <community-string>
Switch(config)# snmp-server vrf <vrf-name>
```

> **Note**
> By default, SNMP read-only community is set to **public** in AOS-CX. Read-write community is not set, therefore not accessible. AOS-CX switches are read-only by default.

Configuration File Management

An AOS-CX switch uses RAM and Flash memory to save configuration files. You should be aware of RAM and Flash memory characteristics, as they relate to the storage of device configuration files.

RAM memory is used to save the configuration that is currently running on the device; the running-config. Remember that RAM is not permanent storage. The contents of RAM are lost when a device reboots or powers down. If you modify the running-config and the switch reboots, your changes are lost. Use the command **show running-config** to view this file.

Flash memory is used to permanently save a configuration file. The contents of flash memory survive during reboot or power off. Use the **show startup-config** command to verify the contents on this file.

Of course, any time you make changes to the running-config, you should copy those changes to the startup-config using the **copy** command. To permanently save the configuration that is running in the device, use the command **copy running-config startup-config**.

Note

Alternatively, you can use the command **write memory** which does the exact same task.

If you need to restore a configuration from the startup-config use the command **copy startup-config running-config**.

As a best practice, you should export the running and the startup configuration files to an external file server. This will help you to recover from catastrophic device failures. To accomplish this task, you can use the **copy** command, as shown in Figure 13-12.

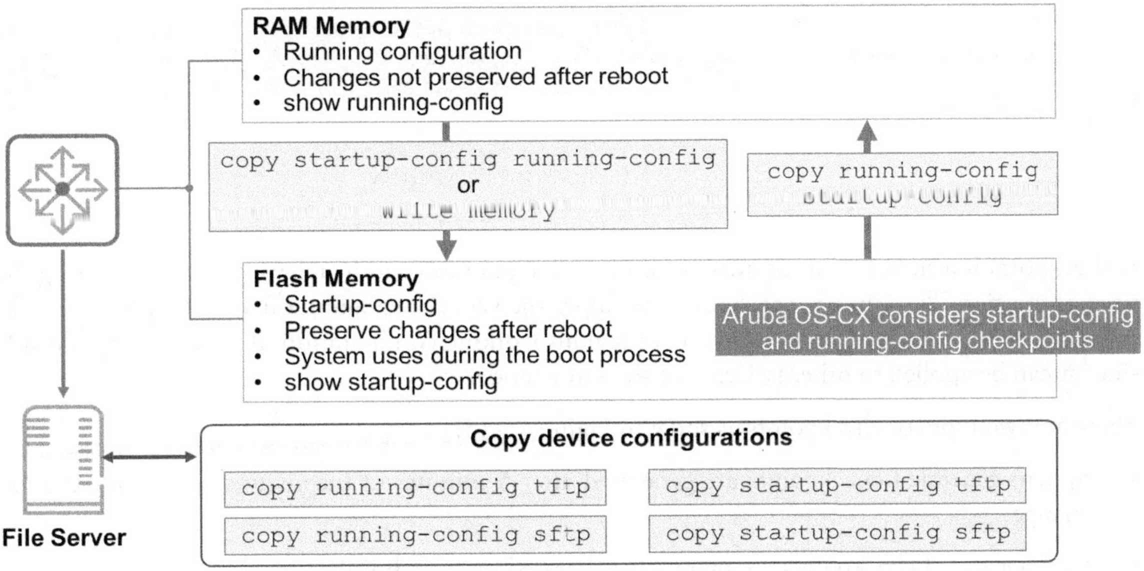

Figure 13-12 Configuration File Management

For example, to copy the running-config to a TFTP server with IP address 10.253.1.21, use the command **copy running-config tftp://10.253.1.21/switch_config.cfg**

AOS-CX switches also allow you to copy files to a USB flash drive, which can be directly connected to the switch. To copy your running or startup-config to a USB device, use the following syntax:

```
Switch# copy {running-config | startup-config} usb:/file
```

AOS-CX considers startup and running-config checkpoints; you will learn about checkpoints in the next slide.

Checkpoint Overview

Using the copy commands, you just learned how to save your configurations to an external file server. This allows you to store configuration files and recover lost configurations in case of a power outage or administrative mistake. This is a good thing, but these files do not include any additional data about the state of networking processes. For a true recovery, a new approach is needed.

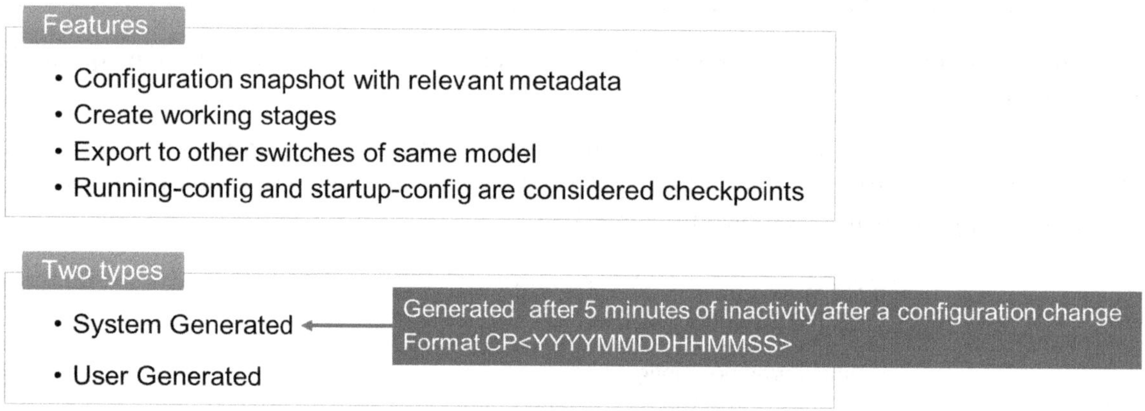

Figure 13-13 Checkpoint Overview

A checkpoint is a snapshot of the switch running configuration and its relevant metadata during the time of creation. You can use checkpoints to apply the switch configuration stored within a checkpoint whenever needed, such as revert to a previous working configuration. A checkpoint is flexible since it can be applied to other switches of the same model.

There are two types of checkpoints as show in Figure 13-13:

- System generated checkpoints are generated after 5 minutes of inactivity after a configuration change.
- User generated checkpoints are manually generated by the administrator.

Note
AOS-CX considers startup and running-config checkpoints.

Checkpoint Configuration

To create a checkpoint, use the **copy** command.

```
Switch# copy {running-config | startup-config} checkpoint
<checkpoint-name>
```

To verify the checkpoint list, use the command **show checkpoint list all**.

To revert the switch from a checkpoint, use the following command:

```
Switch# copy checkpoint <checkpoint-name> {running-config |
startup-config}
```

Note
You can export a checkpoint file to an external server.

Alternatively, you can use the **checkpoint rollback** command. This command only restores the configuration to the running-config file. The **checkpoint rollback** command does the same thing as **copy checkpoint running-config** command.

```
Switch# checkpoint rollback <checkpoint-name>
```

Checkpoint Auto Mode

There are situations when applying a configuration could lock out your access to the switch. This leaves no other option but to locally connect to the device using the console port and remove the offending configuration lines. The checkpoint auto mode feature addresses this problem in an elegant way. The solution includes a timer that you set. The system then creates a checkpoint with the current state. You then make your desired configuration changes, which the system applies after a confirmation. If the configuration lines did not affect your access, you will be able to confirm the change. If your changes locked you out of the device, confirmation does not occur. The switch thus automatically reverts to the latest snapshot after the time expires.

To use this mode, issue the following command in Figure 13-14:

1. Administrator enables checkpoint auto mode.

```
Switch# checkpoint auto <minutes>
```

2. The system generates a checkpoint and starts a timer.

If no confirmation received, system rolls back to checkpoint.

3. Administrator configures the device.

4. Administrator must confirm the changes to be permanent.

```
Switch# checkpoint auto confirm
```

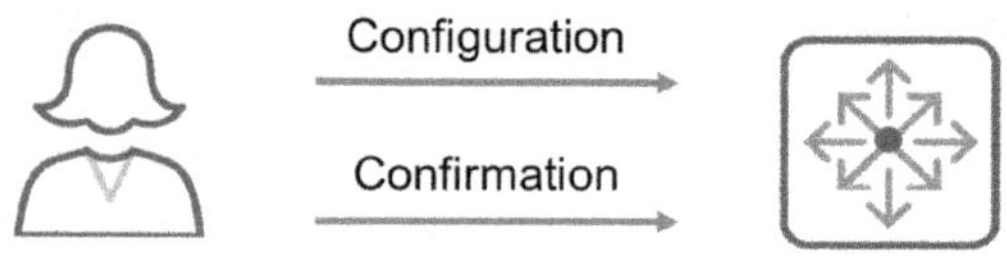

Figure 13-14 Checkpoint Auto Mode

Operating System Image Management Introduction

AOS-CX switches have two flash memory modules or partitions for storing switch software image files. AOS-CX refers to those modules as primary and secondary images.

Having two flash memory locations helps to manage the switch more easily, and to plan firmware upgrades. For example, you can download a new firmware code in the flash memory that is not currently in use and then instruct the switch to boot from it during a maintenance window.

The **show images** command used below in Figure 13-15 shows information about the software in the primary and secondary images.

2 partitions:
- **Primary**
- **Secondary**

```
Switch# show images
---------------------------------------------------------------------------
ArubaOS-CX Primary Image
---------------------------------------------------------------------------
Version : GL.10.04.0003
Size    : 415 MB
Date    : 2019-10-31 12:33:52 PDT
SHA-256 : 794336ee0b1f941aac421bec5333f16b4ebbcd1f4035a388d3b79aa
---------------------------------------------------------------------------
ArubaOS-CX Secondary Image
---------------------------------------------------------------------------
<<<<<Omitted output>>>>>>

Default Image : primary
------------------------------------------------------
Management Module 1/1 (Active)
------------------------------------------------------
Active Image       : primary
Service OS Version : GL.01.05.0002
BIOS Version       : GL-01-0013
```

Figure 13-15 Show Images Command

Operating System Image Management Access

You can update the switch using the GUI (shown in Figure 13-16) or the CLI. Using the GUI for this task is simple. Just navigate to **System → Firmware Update** submenu. Then browse for the file in your local machine, select the flash partition, and click Upload.

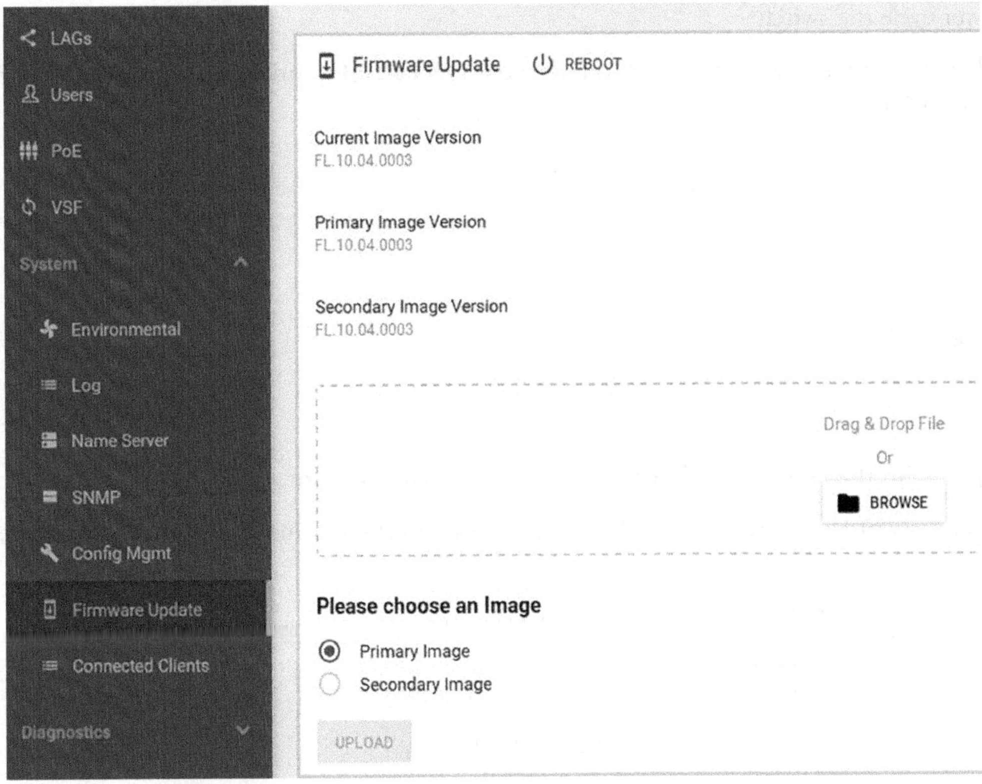

Figure 13-16 Update Using the GUI

Using the CLI issue the **copy** command.

```
Switch# copy {tftp://|sftp://USER@}{IP|HOST}[:PORT][;blocksize=VAL]/
FILE {primary | secondary}
```

Suppose that you want to copy the image file GL.10.04.0003.swi from the TFTP server with IP address 10.253.1.21 to the Primary partition. Use the following command:

```
Switch# copy tftp://10.253.1.23/GL.10.04.0003.swi primary
```

To use Secure FTP with the username admin, use the following command:

```
Switch# copy sftp://admin@10.253.1.21/GL.10.04.0003.swi primary
```

Password Recovery Process

In case that the credentials do not work to login into the switch a password recovery process has to be performed.

1. Connect to the switch using the console port.
2. Power cycle the switch.
3. When the system prompts, select the **Service OS console** option by typing **0** highlighted in Figure 13-17.

```
Boot Profiles:

0. Service OS Console
1. Primary Software Image [FL.10.04.0003]
2. Secondary Software Image [FL.10.04.0003]

Select profile(primary): 0
```

Figure 13-17 Boot Profiles

4. Log in with the user admin. No password is set for this account.
5. Enter password keyword and type the new password for the admin account shown in Figure 13-18.

```
ServiceOS login: admin
SVOS> password
Enter password: ********
Confirm password: ********
```

Figure 13-18 Login

6. Enter **boot**.
7. Log in using the admin username and the password that was set on step 5.

Reset to Factory Default

The command **erase all zeroize** restores the switch to its factory default configuration shown in Figure 13-19. You will be prompted before the procedure starts. Once complete, the switch will restart from the primary image with factory default settings.

The command **erase-startup** erases the startup checkpoint. Using the zeroize command shown here erases ALL checkpoints.

Zeroize

- Deletes all checkpoints in the system
- Returns the system to factory default

Erase-startup

- Deletes only the startup checkpoints in the system
- No factory default

```
switch(config)# erase all zeroize
This will securely erase all customer data and reset the switch to factory
defaults. This will initiate a reboot and render the switch unavailable until
the zeroization is complete.
This should take several minutes to one hour to complete. Continue (y/n)? y
The system is going down for zeroization.
```

Figure 13-19 Reset to Factory Default

Lab 13: Secure Management Access

Overview

After deploying VSF and instructing the staff member how to gain console access to the system, you get a few queries from him and his manager. They commented that going to the IDF every time a change is needed, consumes a considerable amount of time. They ask if remote access is possible since they have it with the Core switches. Additionally, they are also interested in any graphical interface alternatives for monitoring system parameters like, CPU, memory, ports, and the stack status.

After the meeting, the manager comments behind closed doors that he is aware of the technician's limited training. He wants to restrict the technician's configuration tasks to provisioning the first nine ports of each stack member into the proper VLAN.

Note: References to equipment and commands are taken from Aruba's hosted remote lab. These are shown for demonstration purposes in case you wish to replicate the environment and tasks on your own equipment.

Objectives

After completing this lab (Figure 13-20), you will be able to:

- Enable remote access in through the mgmt. port only.
- Enable local command authorization.
- Deploy RADIUS-based AAA Role-Based Access Control.
- Explore AOS-CX web-based UI.

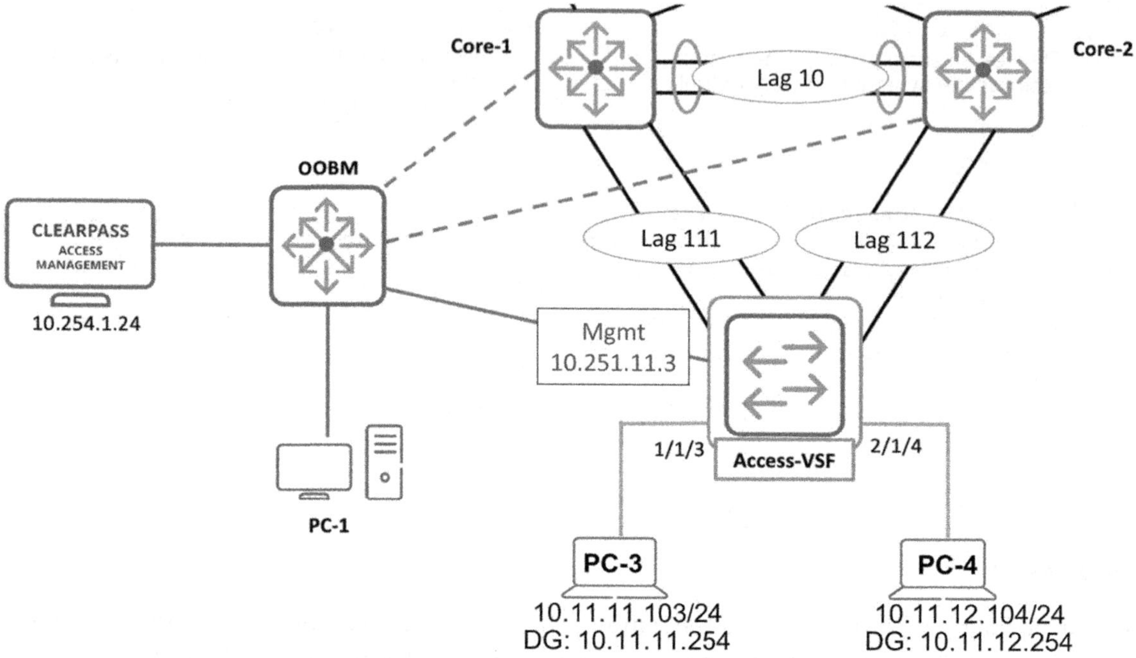

Figure 13-20 Lab Topology

Task 1: Management Port

Objectives

To comply with your customer's requirements, you must first assign an IP address to the management port. Remember, this port belongs to an exclusive management-specific VRF. Unlike regular data VRFs, where either static or dynamic routing is supported, the management one uses a default gateway, as if it was a host.

Steps

Access-VSF: Member 1

1. Access Member 1's console session.
2. Move to "mgmt" interface and assign the 10.251.11.3/24 IP address.

```
T11-Access-VSF(config)# interface mgmt
T11-Access-VSF(config-if-mgmt)# ip static 10.251.11.3/24
```

3. Assign the 10.251.11.254 and 10.254.1.22 as gateway and DNS servers, respectively.

```
T11-Access-VSF(config-if-mgmt)# default-gateway 10.251.11.254
T11-Access-VSF(config-if-mgmt)# nameserver 10.254.1.22
T11-Access-VSF(config-if-mgmt)# exit
```

4. Display the "mgmt" VRF.

```
T11-Access-VSF(config)# show vrf mgmt
VRF Configuration:
------------------
VRF Name    : mgmt
use "show interface mgmt" for mgmt interfaces
```

What interfaces are associated to this VRF? ______________________________

5. Display the "mgmt" interface settings. Confirm the parameters are correct.

```
T11-Access-VSF(config)# show interface mgmt
Address Mode                     : static
  Admin State                    : up
  Mac Address                    : 88:3a:30:98:30:01
  IPv4 address/subnet-mask       : 10.251.11.3/24
  Default gateway IPv4           : 10.251.11.254
  IPv6 address/prefix            :
  IPv6 link local address/prefix :
  Default gateway IPv6           :
Primary Nameserver               : 10.254.1.22
  Secondary Nameserver           :
```

6. Ping the default gateway (10.251.11.254). Ping should be successful.

```
T11-Access-VSF(config)# do ping 10.251.11.254 vrf mgmt
PING 10.251.11.254 (10.251.11.254) 100(128) bytes of data.
108 bytes from 10.251.11.254: icmp_seq=1 ttl=64 time=4.20 ms
108 bytes from 10.251.11.254: icmp_seq=2 ttl=64 time=0.224 ms
108 bytes from 10.251.11.254: icmp_seq=3 ttl=64 time=0.231 ms
108 bytes from 10.251.11.254: icmp_seq=4 ttl=64 time=0.230 ms
108 bytes from 10.251.11.254: icmp_seq=5 ttl=64 time=0.224 ms

--- 10.251.11.254 ping statistics ---
5 packets transmitted, 5 received, 0% packet loss, time 4076ms
rtt min/avg/max/mdev = 0.224/1.022/4.201/1.589 ms
```

7. Display the SSH servers on all VRFs.

```
T11-Access-VSF(config)# show ssh server all-vrfs | include SSH
SSH server configuration on VRF default :
  IP Version          : IPv4 and IPv6        SSH Version        : 2.0
SSH server configuration on VRF mgmt :
  IP Version          : IPv4 and IPv6        SSH Version        : 2.0
```

What VRFs have an SSH server? ______________________________

8. Display the SSH servers on all VRFs.

```
T11-Access-VSF(config)# show https-server

HTTPS Server Configuration
----------------------------

VRF                    : mgmt, default

REST Access Mode       : read-write
```

What VRFs have an HTTPS server? ______________________________

Note

In 6300 and 6400 series switches, SSH and HTTPS services are running by default in both the "mgmt" and "default" VRFs; however in the case of 8300 and 8400s these services are only running in the "mgmt" VRF.

Also REST Access mode comes as read-write in the 6000 platforms, while in the 8000s it begins as "read-only".

9. Disable SSH and HTTPS services from default VRF. This will prevent this traffic from being processed in the regular data VRF.

```
T11-Access-VSF(config)# no ssh server vrf default
Active SSH sessions will be terminated.
Do you want to continue (y/n)? y
T11-Access-VSF(config)# no https-server vrf default
```

Task 2: RBAC

Objectives

The next step to comply with your customer's desires is to enable local command authorization. That is achieved by creating user-groups and local user accounts in AOS-CX. In this task, you are going to define a list of allowed commands. To reduce the number of lines needed for the task you will leverage the power of Regular Expressions (REGEX).

Notice

Regular expressions are text strings used for describing a search pattern; they are considered the next step in the evolution of wildcards. Several features and tools in networking, IT, engineering, science, etc. use REGEX for matching strings. You might find it useful to start learning about them.

Steps

Access-VSF: Member 1

1. Access Member 1's console session.
2. Create a user-group called "port-prov"; then allow the following:
    1. Access to global configuration context.
    2. Access to first 9 ports on both VSF members.
    3. Change VLAN membership on those ports.
    4. Enable ports.
    5. Display a list of interfaces, VLANs, and user information.

```
T11-Access-VSF(config)# user-group port-prov
T11-Access-VSF(config-usr-grp-port-prov)# permit cli command
"configure terminal"
T11-Access-VSF(config-usr-grp-port-prov)# permit cli command
"interface [1-2]/1/[1-9]$"
T11-Access-VSF(config-usr-grp-port-prov)# permit cli command
"vlan access"
T11-Access-VSF(config-usr-grp-port-prov)# permit cli command
"no shutdown"
T11-Access-VSF(config-usr-grp-port-prov)# permit cli command
"show interface brief"
T11-Access-VSF(config-usr-grp-port-prov)# permit cli command
"show vlan"
T11-Access-VSF(config-usr-grp-port-prov)# permit cli command
"show user information"
T11-Access-VSF(config-usr-grp-port-prov)# exit
```

TIP

Defining commands of different user-groups supports REGEX. For example, in the second rule [1-2] means that the character could take either value "1" or "2", likewise [1-9] represents any number in the range from 1 to 9, and "$" means this is the end of the line and nothing else can follow.

3. Display the user-groups.

```
T11-Access-VSF(config)# show user-group
GROUP NAME     GROUP TYPE     INCLUDED GROUP     NUMBER OF RULES
-------------- -------------- ------------------ ----------------
administrators built-in       n/a                n/a
auditors       built-in       n/a                n/a
operators      built-in       n/a                n/a
port-prov      configuration  --                 7
```

In addition to "port-prov" what groups are listed? ________________________________

The "operator" context enables you to execute commands to view, but not change, the configuration. This group has privilege level 1. Users with "auditor" rights have access to show accounting, events, and logging commands and the ability to use copy show commands to direct output onto a USB or remote storage. The prompt for this kind of session is "auditor>". This group has privilege level 19. Administrator group grants "manager" access (full access) to every aspect of the system. This group has privilege level 15.

4. Display the details of your group. You will notice all the rules you have defined with sequence numbers in steps of 10.

```
T11-Access-VSF(config)# show user-group port-prov
User-Group Summary
==================
Name              : port-prov
Type              : configuration
Included Group    : --
Number of Rules   : 7
```

```
User-Group Rules
================
SEQUENCE NUM  ACTION     COMMAND                              COMMENT
------------------------------------------------------------------------
10            permit     configure terminal
20            permit     interface [1-2]/1/[1-9]$
30            permit     vlan access
40            permit     no shutdown
50            permit     show interface brief
60            permit     show vlan
70            permit     show user information
```

5. Create the "cxf11-local" user account password "aruba123". Map the account to the "port-prov" group you just created.

```
T11-Access-VSF(config)# user cxf11-local group port-prov password
plaintext aruba123
```

6. Display the local user list. You will see only two accounts.

```
T11-Access-VSF(config)#  show user-list
USER                              GROUP
----------------------------------------
admin                             administrators
cxf11-local                       port-prov
```

Note
Although the scenario is asking for secure RBAC, the "admin" account should remain untouched with no password. This eases the assistance and reset procedures that the lab help desk might need to run.

PC-1

7. Access PC-1's console session.
8. Open putty.
9. Run an SSH session to the management IP address of the Access-VSF (10.251.11.3) (Figure 13-21).

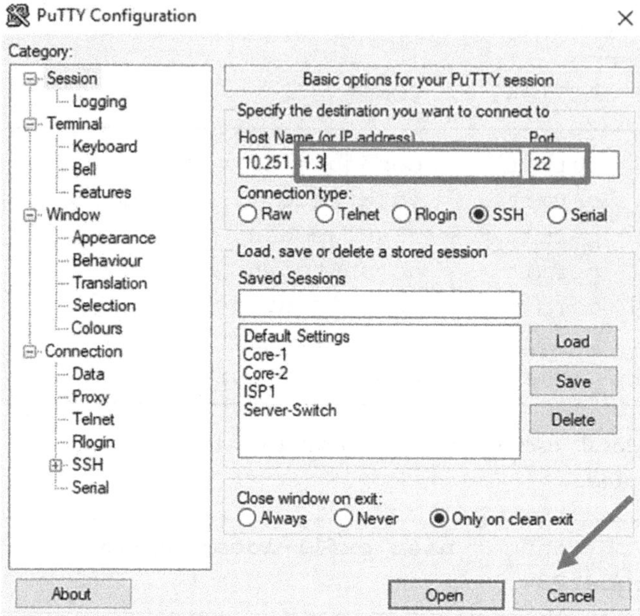

Figure 13-21 Putty

Access-VSF (via PC-1)

10. Log in with cxf11-local/aruba123.

```
Login as: cxf11-local
(C) Copyright 2017-2019 Hewlett Packard Enterprise Development LP
                    ←---- output omitted ---→
cxf11@10.251.11.3's password:aruba123
```

11. Try the "**show user information**" command. You shall see the user you are using for this session and the user-group it belongs.

```
T11-Access-VSF# show user information
Username              : cxf11-local
Authentication type   : local
User-group            : port-prov
User privilege level  : N/A
```

12. Move port 2/1/4 to VLAN 1111.

```
T11-Access-VSF(config)# interface 2/1/4
T11-Access-VSF(config-if)# vlan access 1111
T11-Access-VSF(config-if)# end
```

13. Display VLAN 1111 and confirm port 2/1/4 is there.

```
T11-Access-VSF# show vlan 1111
-----------------------------------------------------------------------
VLAN  Name       Status  Reason  Type    Interfaces
-----------------------------------------------------------------------
1111  EMPLOYEES  up      ok      static  1/1/3,2/1/4,lag111-lag112
```

14. Display the running configuration.

```
T11-Access-VSF# show running-config
Cannot execute command. Command not allowed.
```

15. Access lag 111 interface, then port 1/1/10.

```
T11-Access-VSF(config)# interface lag 111
Cannot execute command. Command not allowed.
T11-Access-VSF(config)# interface 1/1/10
Cannot execute command. Command not allowed.
```

Did you experience any issues trying out any of those 3 commands? ______________

What is most likely the cause? ______________

PC-4

16. Move to PC-4.
17. Run Command Prompt as administrator (Figure 13-22).

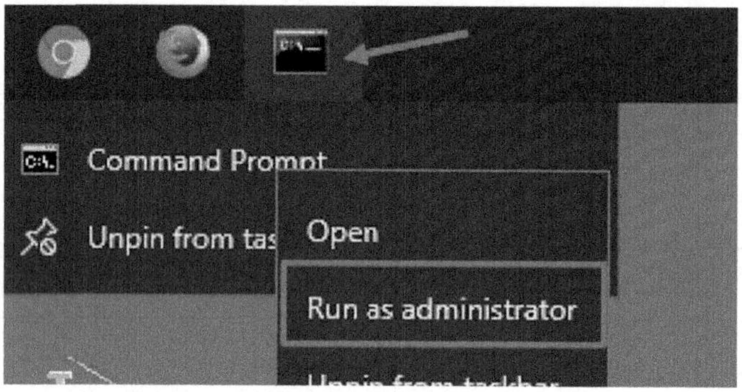

Figure 13-22 Run as Administrator

18. Run "**ipconfig-renew**" to request an IP address from VLAN 1111.

TIP

If you are not allowed to run the command, then make sure your NIC is setup as DHCP client.

Task 3: RADIUS-Based Management

Objectives

After testing the command-based authorization with your customer and demonstrating the power of this management control, you explain that local accounts are not always the best option, especially with fast growing networks like BigStartup. Having operator accounts that need to be created at every single switch and system does not scale well. This is especially true when a password change or account revocation is required. Therefore, you offer to deploy a ClearPass demo to give them a taste of account centralization and also demonstrate the power of the ClearPass product.

In this task you will enable RADIUS-based authentication for SSH and HTTPS sessions.

Steps

Access-VSF: Member 1

1. Access Member 1's console session.

2. Define a RADIUS server with the 10.254.1.24 IP address. Use "aruba123" as the shared secret and map it to VRF mgmt.

```
T11-Access-VSF(config)#radius-server host 10.254.1.24 key plaintext
aruba123 vrf mgmt
```

3. Display the newly created RADIUS server. Confirm all settings are in order.

```
T11-Access-VSF(config)# show radius-server | begin 3 SERVER
SERVER NAME                                        | PORT  | VRF
------------------------------------------------------------------
10.254.1.24                                        | 1812  | mgmt
------------------------------------------------------------------
```

4. Set the RADIUS group, then the local username database as authentication groups for HTTPS and SSH services.

```
T11-Access-VSF(config)# aaa authentication login https-server group
radius local
T11-Access-VSF(config)# aaa authentication login ssh group radius
local
```

It is a best practice to have a local database backup a remote authentication group when configuring AAA management access. This prevents locking out the administrator's account if the AAA server fails or becomes unreachable.

PC-1

5. Access PC-1's console session.
6. Run an SSH session to the management IP address of the Access-VSF.

```
Login as: cxf11
(C) Copyright 2017-2019 Hewlett Packard Enterprise Development LP
                    ←---- output omitted ---→
cxf11@10.251.11.3's password:aruba123
```

7. Log in with cxf11/aruba123. This account is stored in ClearPass.

8. Try the "show user information" command.

```
T11-Access-VSF# show user information
Username               : cxf11
Authentication type    : RADIUS
User-group             : administrators
User privilege level : 15
```

What is the Authentication type?________________

To what user-group does the user belong?________________

What is the privilege level?________________

You will now proceed to remove local command authorization.

9. Delete the local account.

```
T11-Access-VSF(config)# no user cxf11-local
User cxf11-local's home directory and active sessions will be
deleted.
Do you want to continue (y/n)? y
```

10. Delete the port-prov authorization group.

```
T11-Access-VSF(config)# no user-group port-prov
```

Task 4: Explore AOS-CX Web UI

Objectives

Your customer's final request is to use a graphical interface for monitoring the system. You invite the executives from BigStartup to explore AOS-CX Web User Interface.

Steps

PC-1

1. Access the console session of PC-1.
2. Open a browser and point it to your Access-VSF management IP address (10.251.11.3).
3. Log in using **cxf11/aruba123** (Figure 13-23).

Figure 13-23 Web Login Page AOS-CX

4. Accept the pre-login banner. You will be taken to the Overview page (Figure 13-24 and 13-25).

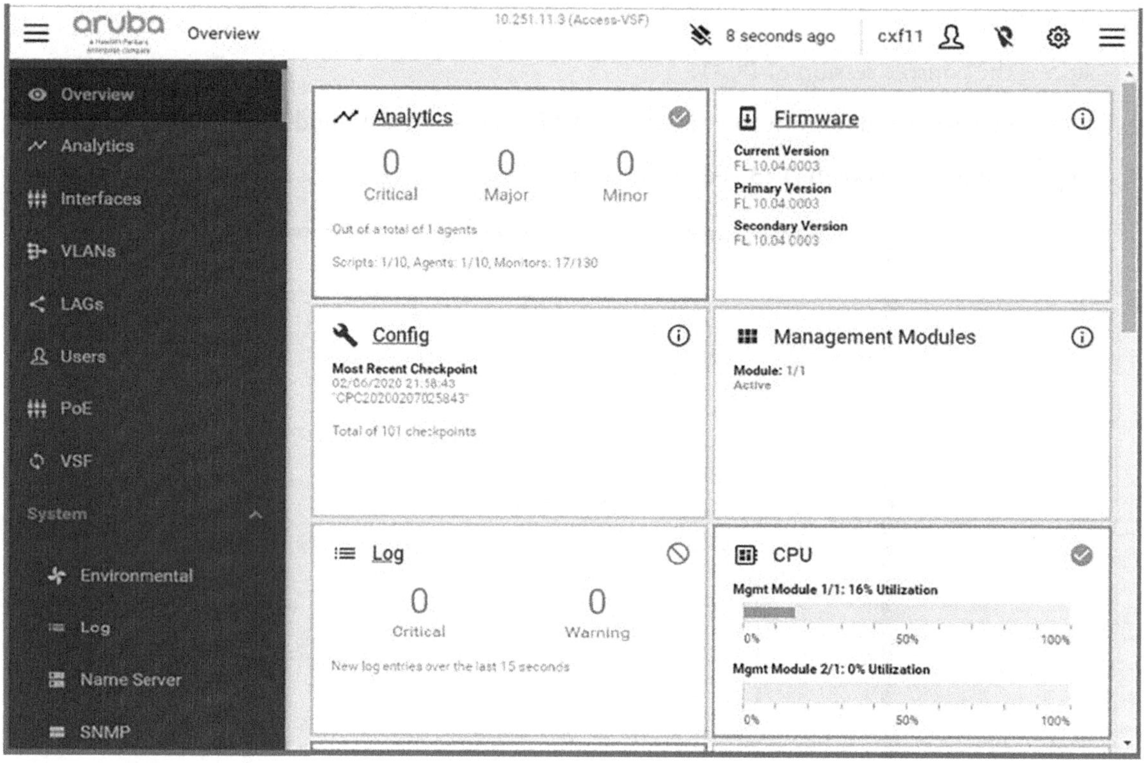

Figure 13-24 Overview

What is the Firmware version running in the stack? ______________________________

Are there any new logs? ______________________________

What is the CPU utilization on each stack member? ______________________________

5. Scroll down.

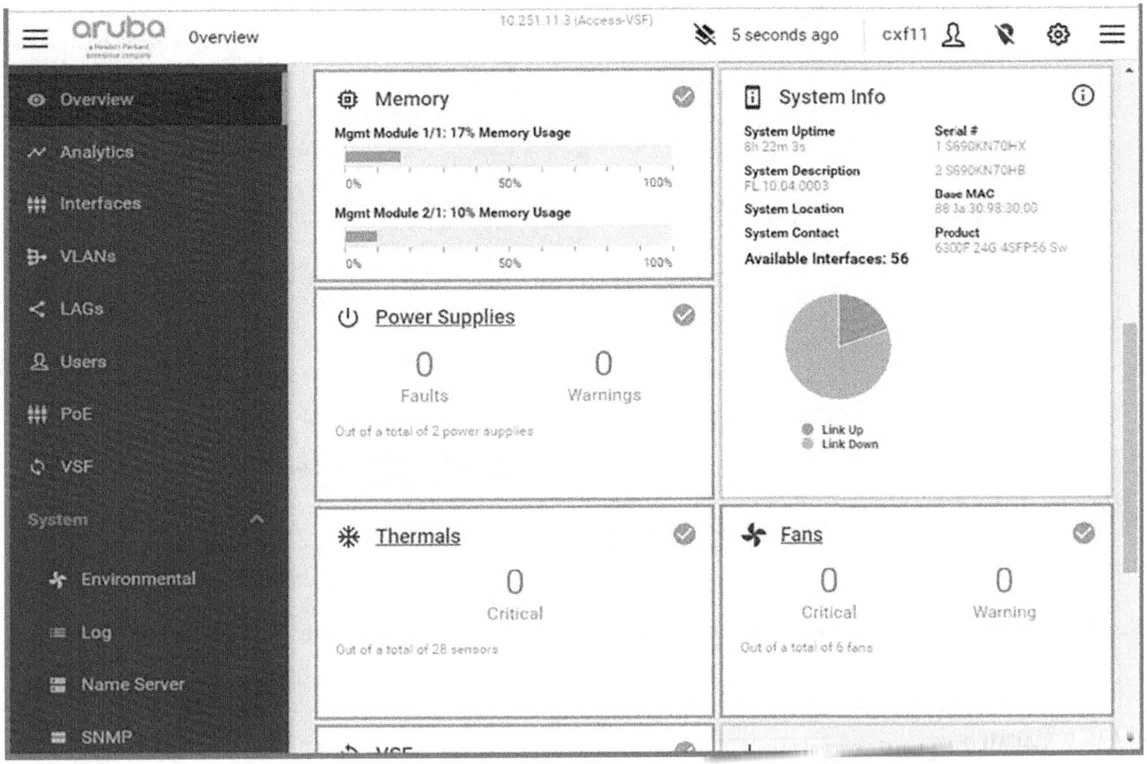

Figure 13-25 Overview Continued

What is the Memory utilization on each stack member?

What are the serial numbers of both units? ____________________

What percentage of interfaces are down? ____________________

Is there any thermal or fan alarm? ____________________

6. Scroll down; then click the "+" sign in an open widget slot. It will ask for an interface number.

7. Select port 1/1/3 to start monitoring the interface (Figure 13-26).

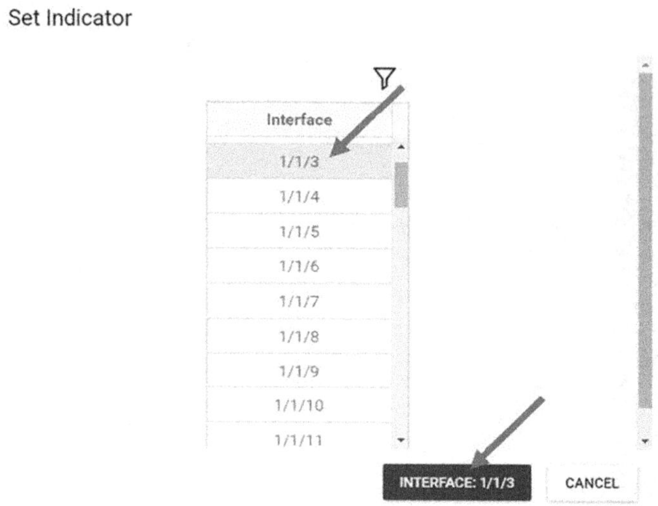

Figure 13-26 Physical Interfaces

8. Repeat step 7 with ports 1/1/21 and 2/1/21; these are uplinks to Core-1 (Figure 13-27).

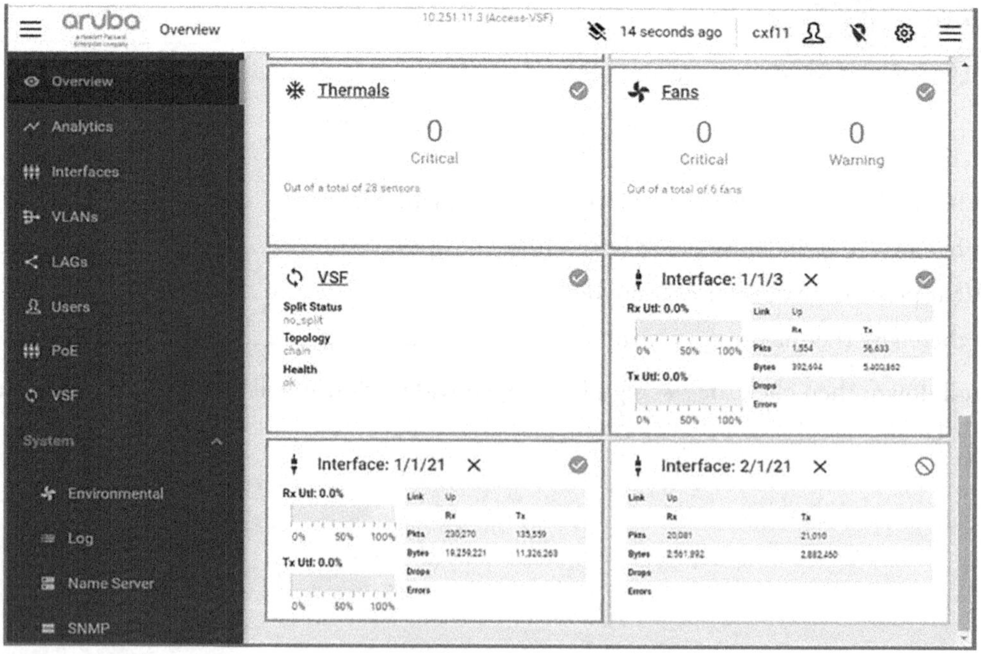

Figure 13-27 Overview Continued

What is the status of port 1/1/3? ____________________

Access-VSF: Member 1

9. Access Member 1's console session.
10. Disable port 1/1/3.

```
T11-Access-VSF(config)# interface 1/1/3
T11-Access-VSF(config-if)# shutdown
```

PC-1

11. Move back to the web session (Figure 13-28).

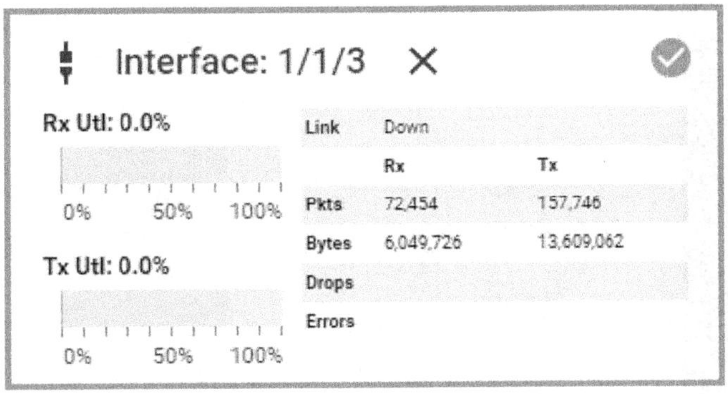

Figure 13-28 Interface 1/1/3

Was there any change the link status (Figure 13-28) from the previous Figure 13-27? ______________________

Access-VSF: Member 1

12. Move back to Member 1.
13. Enable the port.

```
T11-Access-VSF(config-if)# no shutdown
```

PC-1

14. Move back to the web session.

Was it the VSF Split status? ______________________

Was it the VSF topology? ______________________

Was it the VSF Health? ______________________

15. Click at the VSF hyperlink. That will take you to the VSF page (Figures 13-29 and 13-30).

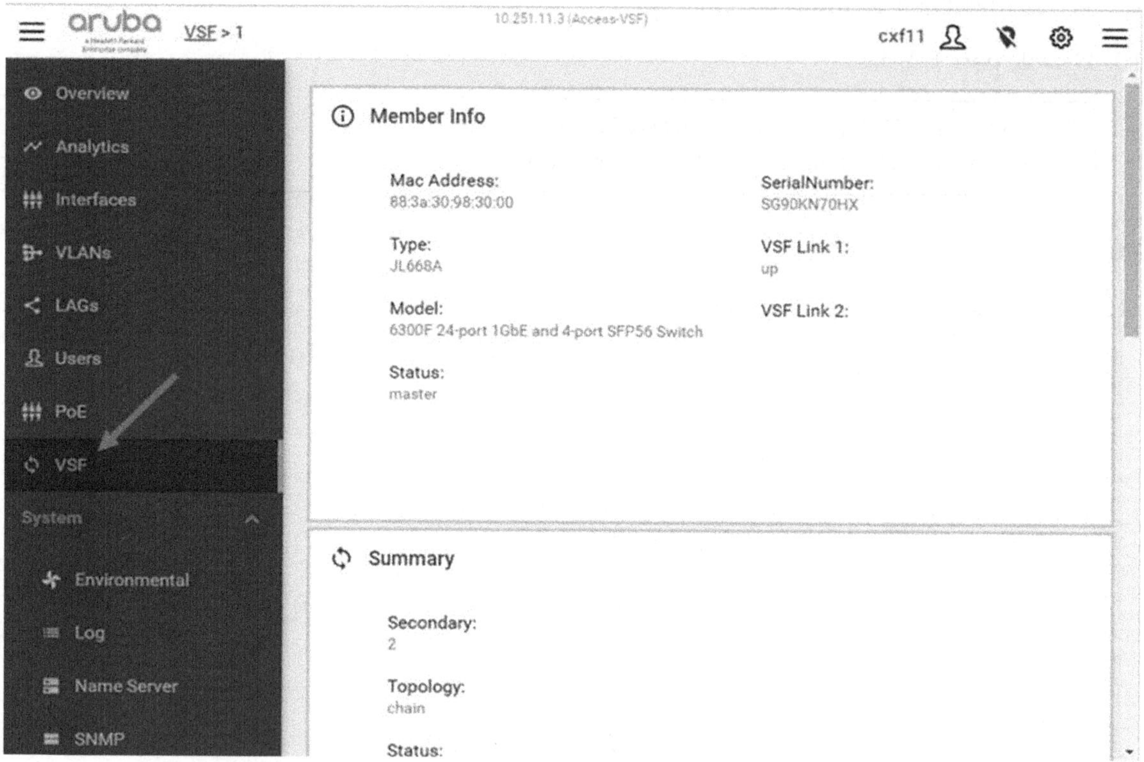

Figure 13-29 VSF

Whose information is shown? Member 1 or member 2? ______________________

16. Scroll down.

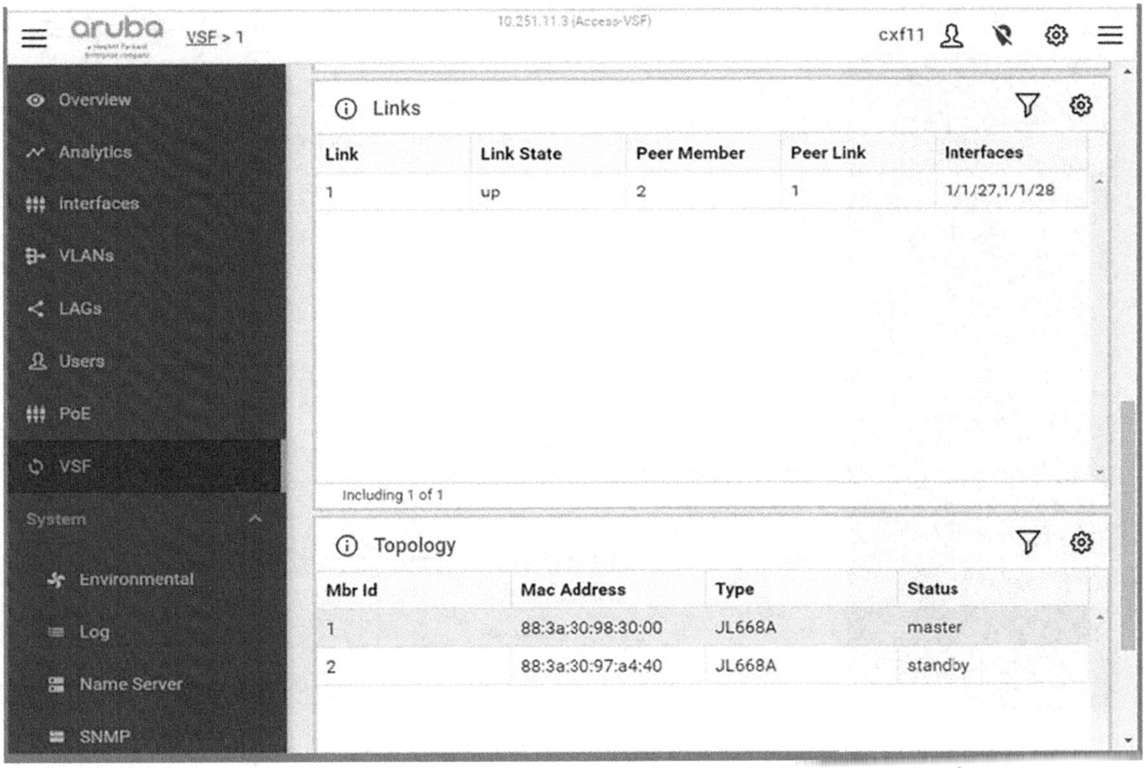

Figure 13-30 VSF Continued

What physical ports are being used for the logical VSF link? ____________________

17. Select member 2 in the topology table (Figure 13-31).

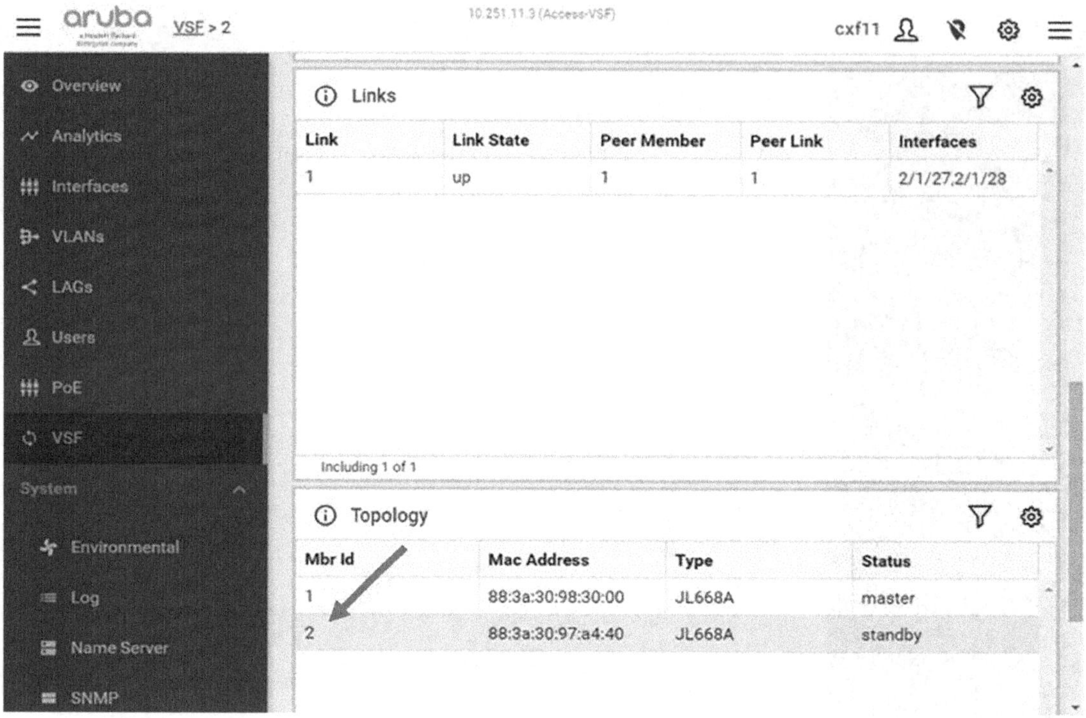

Figure 13-31 VSF Member 2

What physical ports are being used for the logical VSF link? ______________________________

18. Click on "Interfaces" in the left navigation pane (Figure 13-32).

Figure 13-32 Front Pane

How many ports do the switches have? ______________________________

What interfaces are up on member 1? ______________________________

What interfaces are up on member 2? ______________________________

19. Click on "VLANs" in the left navigation pane (Figure 13-33).

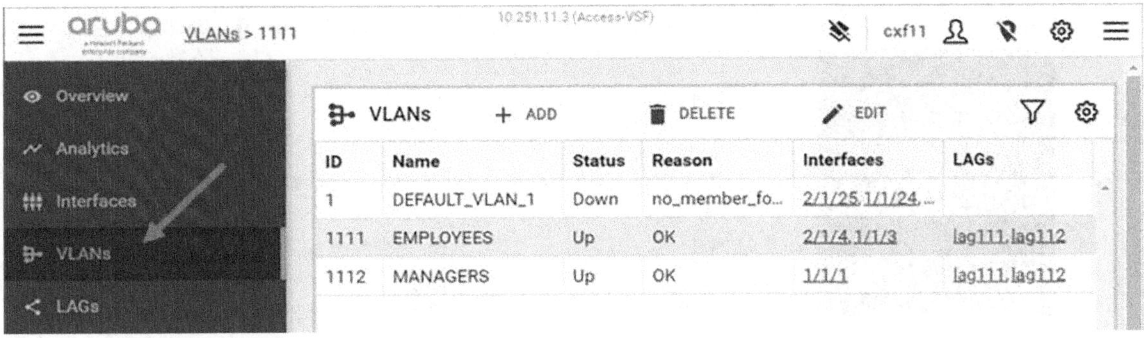

Figure 13-33 VLANs

How many VLANs are listed and what are their names? ______________________

What ports are members of VLAN 1112? ______________________

20. Click on "LAGs" in the left navigation pane (Figure 13-34).

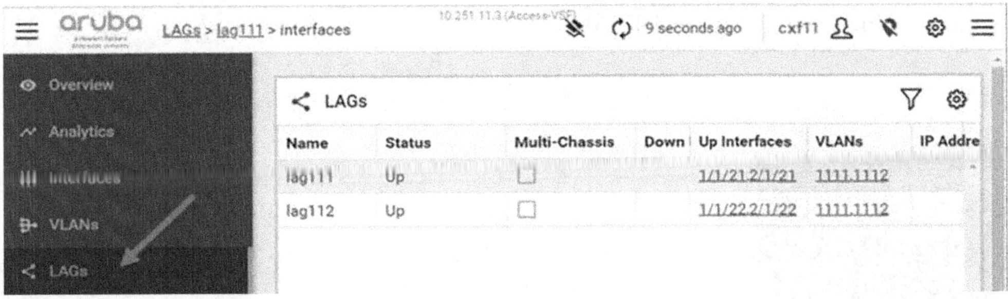

Figure 13-34 LAGs

How many LAGs are created? ______________________

Ports are used in these LAGs? ______________________

21. Expand “System” on the left navigation pane. Then click on “Environmental” (Figure 13-35).

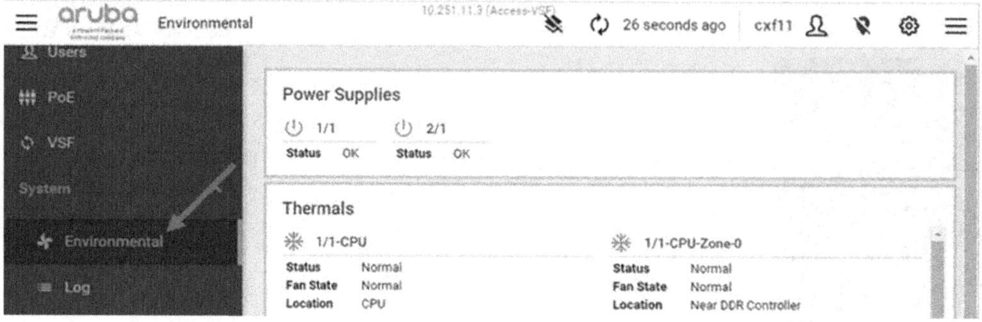

Figure 13-35 Environmental

How many power supplies does the stack have?____________________________

What is the current temperature of CPU 1/1?____________________________

What is the current temperature of CPU 1/1 Zones 0 to 4?____________________________

22. Click **System -> Log**.

23. Select any of the entries (Figure 13-36).

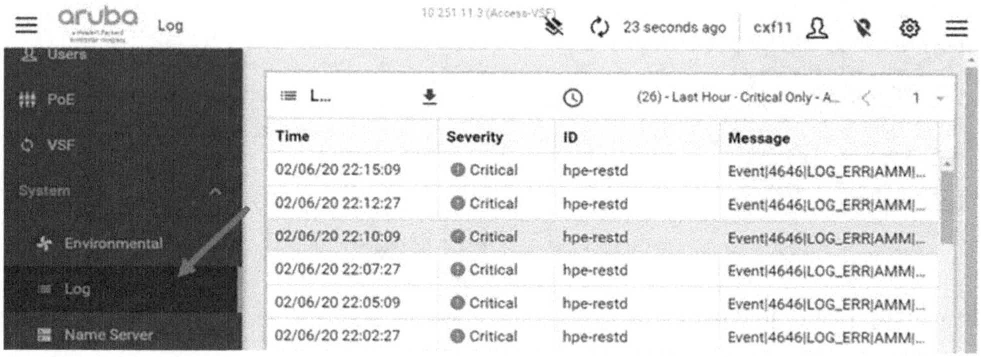

Figure 13-36 Log

What is the severity of the log record?____________________________

What is the message of the log record?____________________________

Note

It is likely the log refers to the lack of connectivity to Aruba Activate. The switches do not currently have internet access.

Note

Aruba Activate provides Zero Touch Provisioning and can facilitate centralized management platforms.

24. Click on **System -> Connected Clients;** then scroll down. This shows the LLDP table with all discovered neighbors (Figure 13-37).

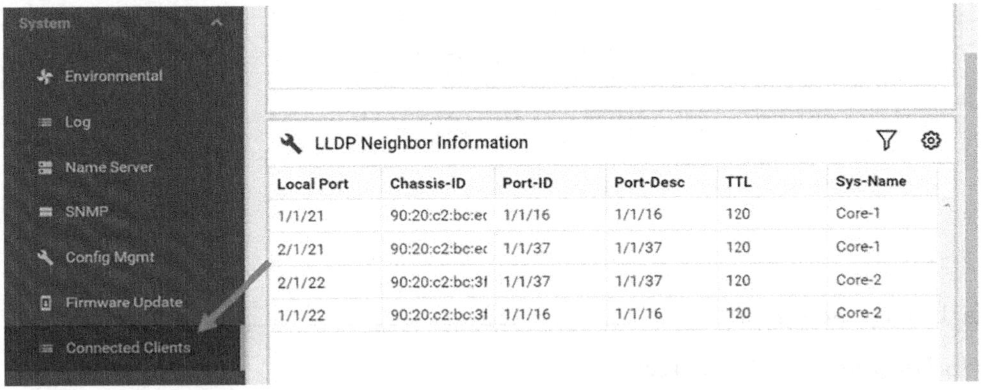

Figure 13-37 Connected Clients

25. Expand Diagnostics; then click on Ping.

26. Type 10.251.11.200 as IPv4 Target, then check "Use Management Interface" checkbox. This IP address is owned by the NETEDIT system you will use in the next lab (Figure 13-38).

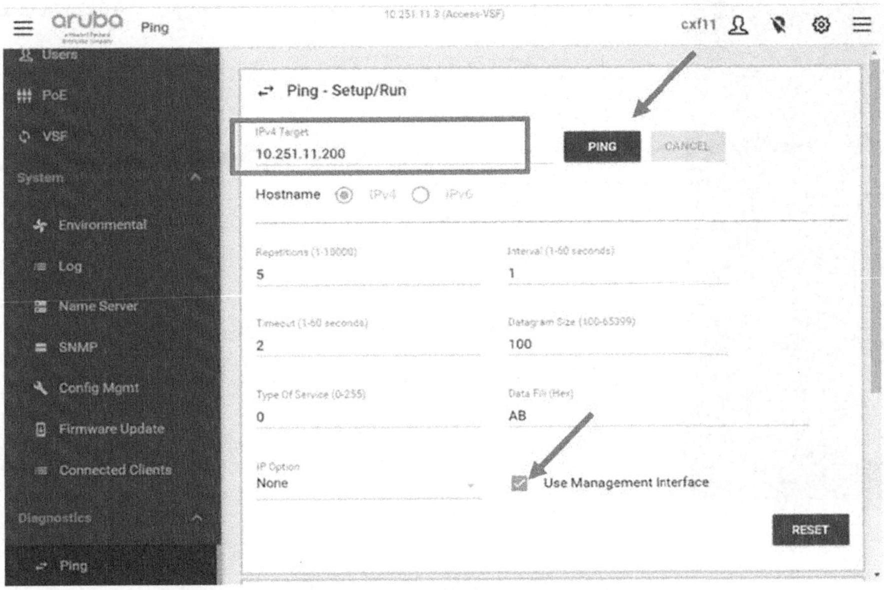

Figure 13-38 Diagnostics Using Ping

27. Press the "PING" button and wait (Figure 13-39). Be patient…

```
Ping - Output (5/5)

1/5: PING 10.251.11.200 (10.251.11.200) 100(128) bytes of data.
108 bytes from 10.251.11.200: icmp_seq=1 ttl=64 time=0.938 ms

2/5: PING 10.251.11.200 (10.251.11.200) 100(128) bytes of data.
108 bytes from 10.251.11.200: icmp_seq=1 ttl=64 time=0.544 ms

3/5: PING 10.251.11.200 (10.251.11.200) 100(128) bytes of data.
108 bytes from 10.251.11.200: icmp_seq=1 ttl=64 time=0.599 ms

4/5: PING 10.251.11.200 (10.251.11.200) 100(128) bytes of data.
108 bytes from 10.251.11.200: icmp_seq=1 ttl=64 time=0.675 ms

5/5: PING 10.251.11.200 (10.251.11.200) 100(128) bytes of data.
108 bytes from 10.251.11.200: icmp_seq=1 ttl=64 time=0.578 ms
```

Figure 13-39 Ping Result

Was the ping successful?____

28. Go to **Diagnostics -> Show Tech**.

29. Click on "GENERATE". This will create the "Show Tech" support file.

30. Click on "EXPORT". This will download the file through the browser. The file will show up at the bottom of the browser (Figure 13-40).

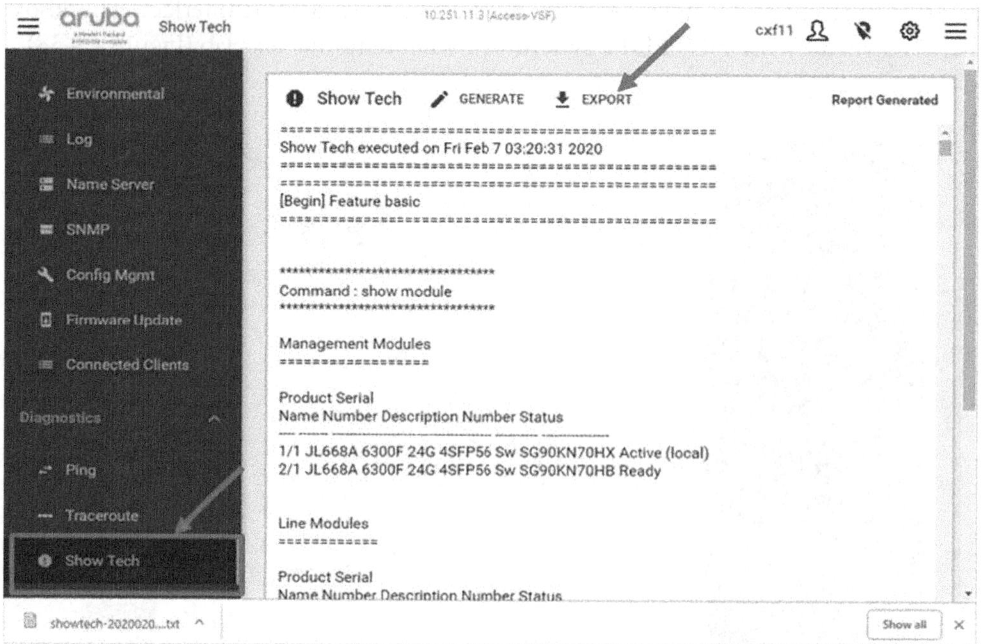

Figure 13-40 Show Tech

Note

When opening a Technical Assistance Center (TAC) support case, one of the pieces of information they will first ask for is this output. It is always a good practice to generate it and download it in advance.

31. Click on the gear icon in the top right corner; then select "V10.04 API". This will open another browser tab and display the AOS-CX REST API documentation (Figures 13-41 and 13-42).

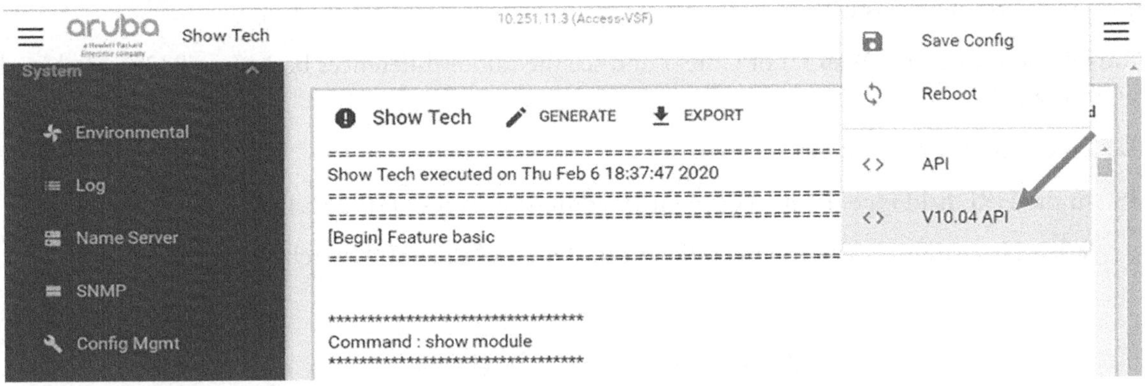

Figure 13-41 API

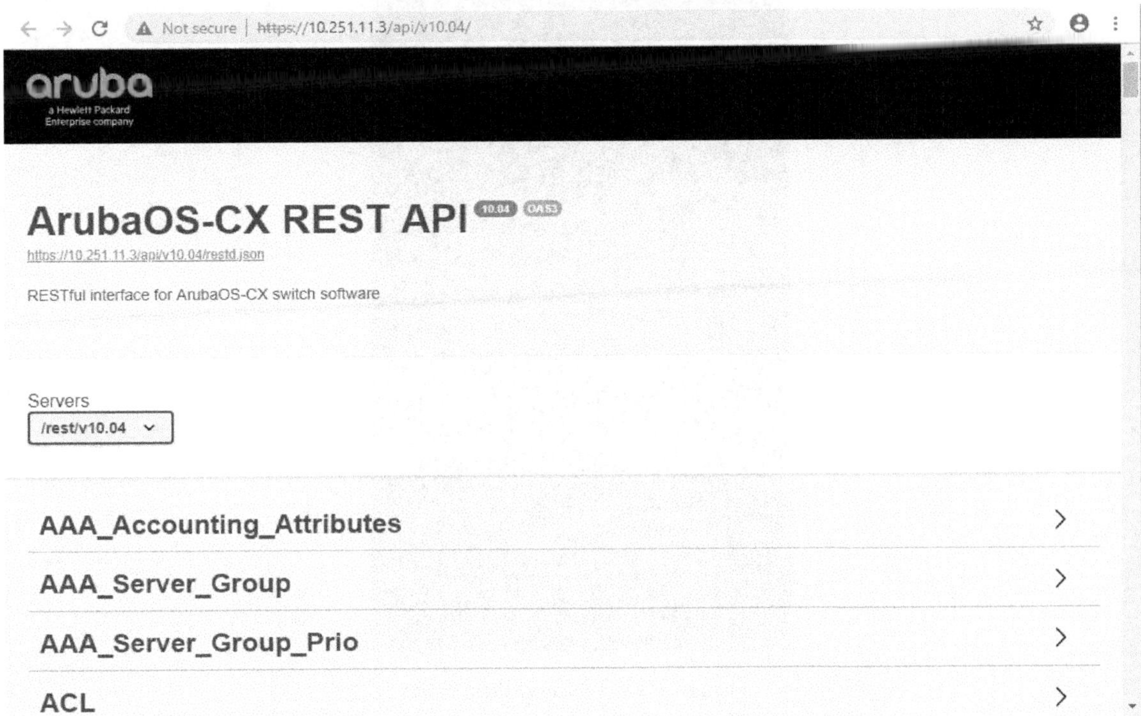

Figure 13-42 AOS-CX REST API

Switches running the AOS-CX software are fully programmable with a REST (Representational State Transfer) API, allowing easy integration with other devices both on premises and in the cloud. This programmability, combined with the Aruba Network Analytics Engine, accelerates a network administrator's understanding and response to network issues.

The AOS-CX REST API enables programmatic access to the AOS-CX configuration and state database at the heart of the switch. By using a structured model, changes to the content and formatting of the CLI output do not affect the programs you write. And, because the configuration is stored in a structured database instead of a text file, rolling back changes is easy. This reduces the risk of downtime and performance issues.

You will now access the Web UI of Core-1 and see the minor differences between a 8325 switch and a 6300 switch.

32. Open another browser tab.
33. In the URL field type the management IP address of Core-1 (10.251.11.201).

    What Navigation Pane option is different to the UI of the 6300 switches?

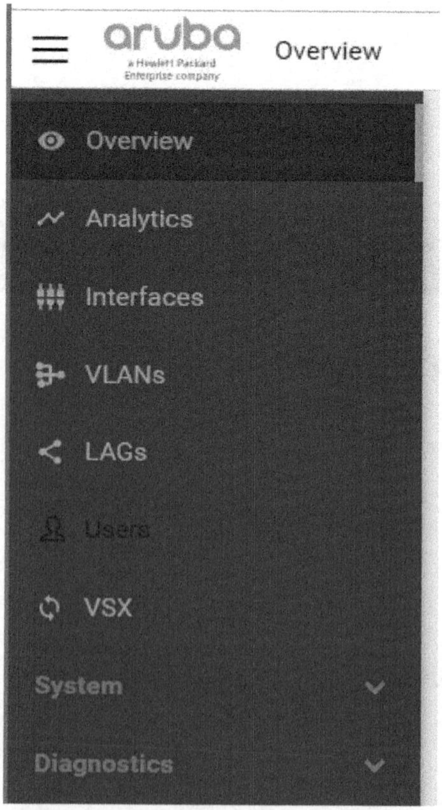

Figure 13-43 Navigation Pane

34. Click on **Interfaces** (Figures 13-43 and 13-44).

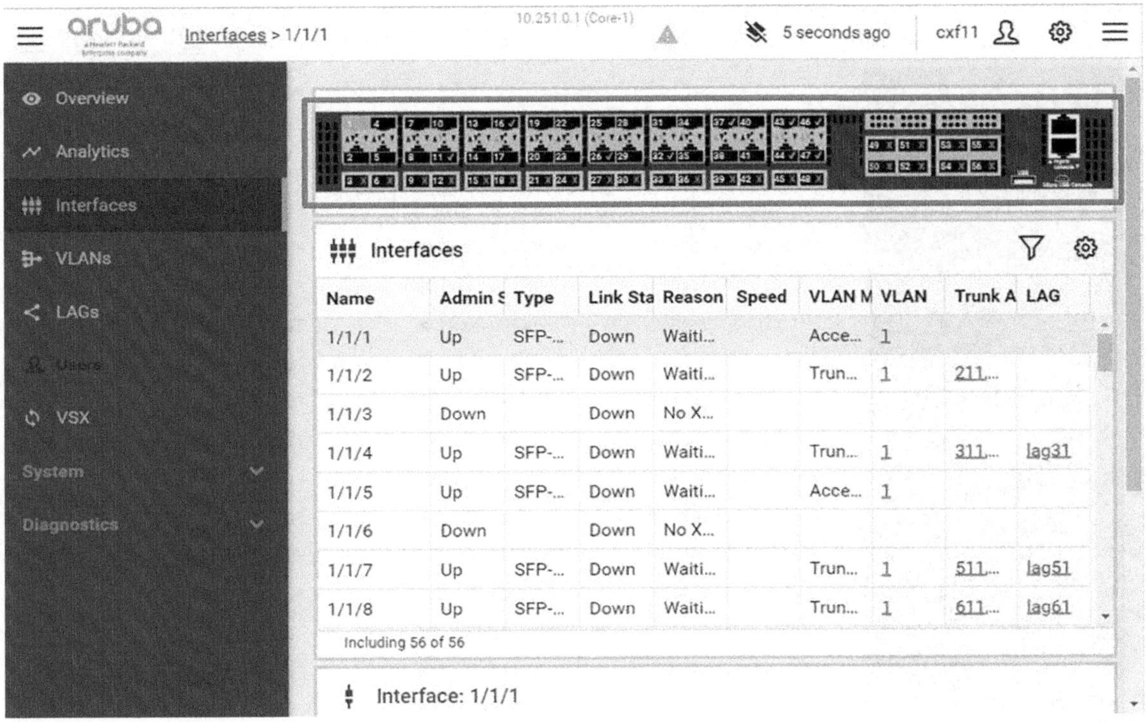

Figure 13-44 8325 Interfaces

What differences can you see to the panel shown in the 6300's UI (step 18)? ________________

Task 5: Save Your Configurations

Objectives

You will now proceed to create a checkpoint; save your configuration and download it as a file in order to keep a backup of the current configuration.

Steps

PC-1

1. Move back to the browser tab of the 6300's UI; you might need to log in using "cxf11/aruba123".

2. Click on **Config Mgmt** (Figure 13-45).

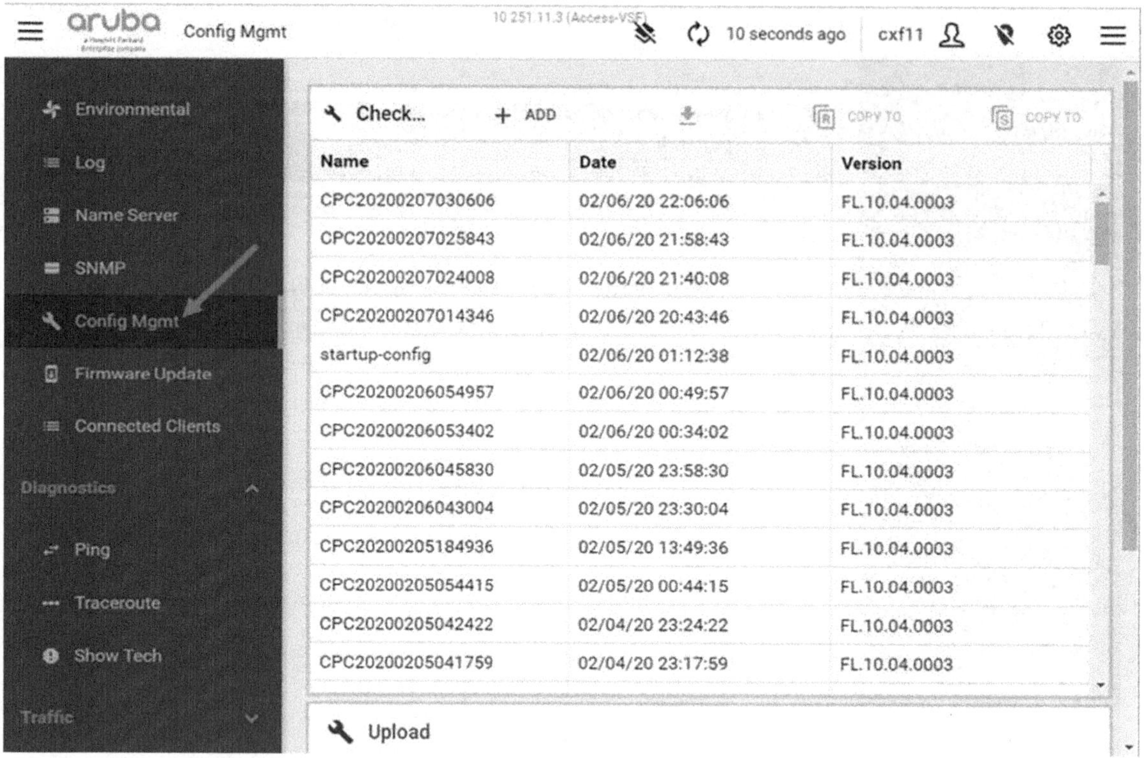

Figure 13-45 Configuration Management

3. Click on "**ADD**".

4. Type "**Lab13_final**" as the checkpoint name; then click on **Create Checkpoint**, and **close** when done (Figure 13-46).

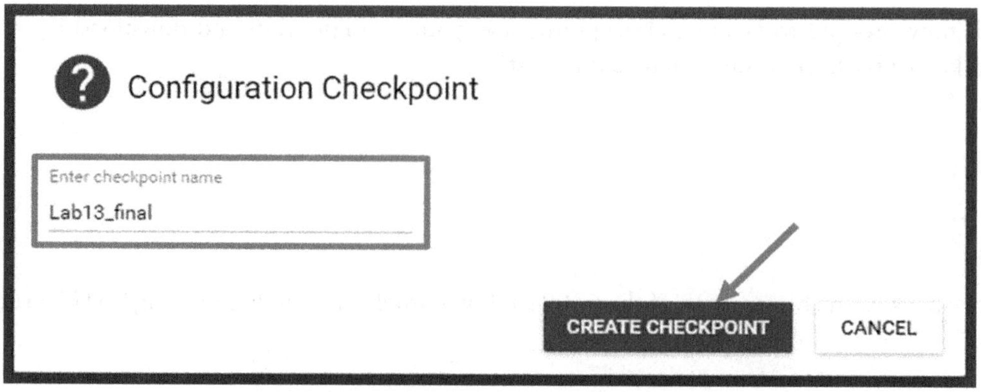

Figure 13-46 Configuration Checkpoint

5. Select Lab13_final checkpoint; then click on "Copy to Startup" button (Figure 13-47).

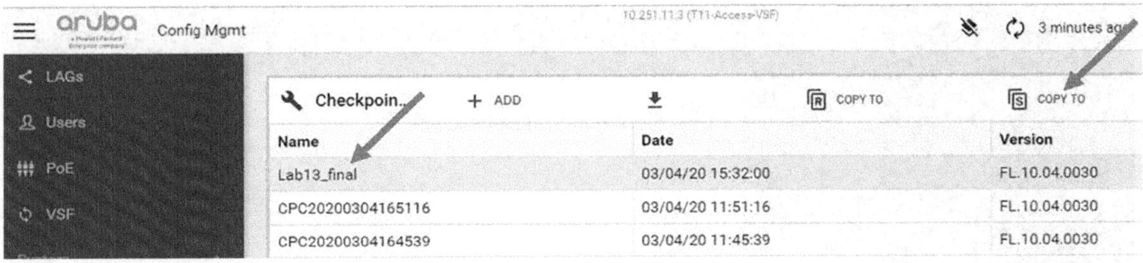

Figure 13-47 Configuration Checkpoint Continued

6. Click on "Copy" button; then close (Figure 13-48).

Figure 13-48 Configuration Copy

7. Select **Lab13_final** checkpoint; then click on the "download" button; the backup will show up at the bottom of the browser (Figure 13-49).

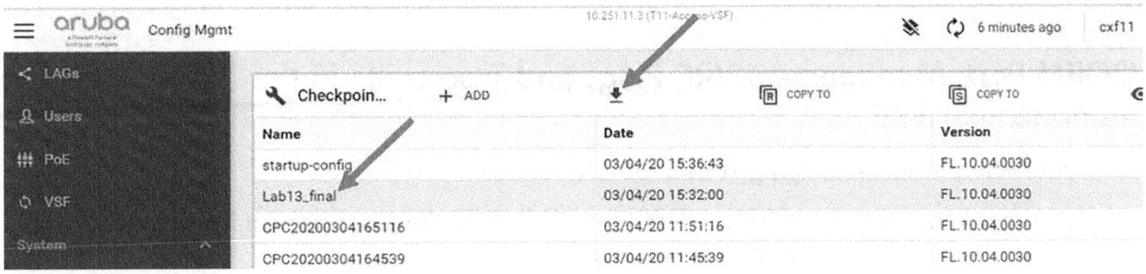

Figure 13-49 Checkpoint Download

8. Click on "Close" button (Figure 13-50).

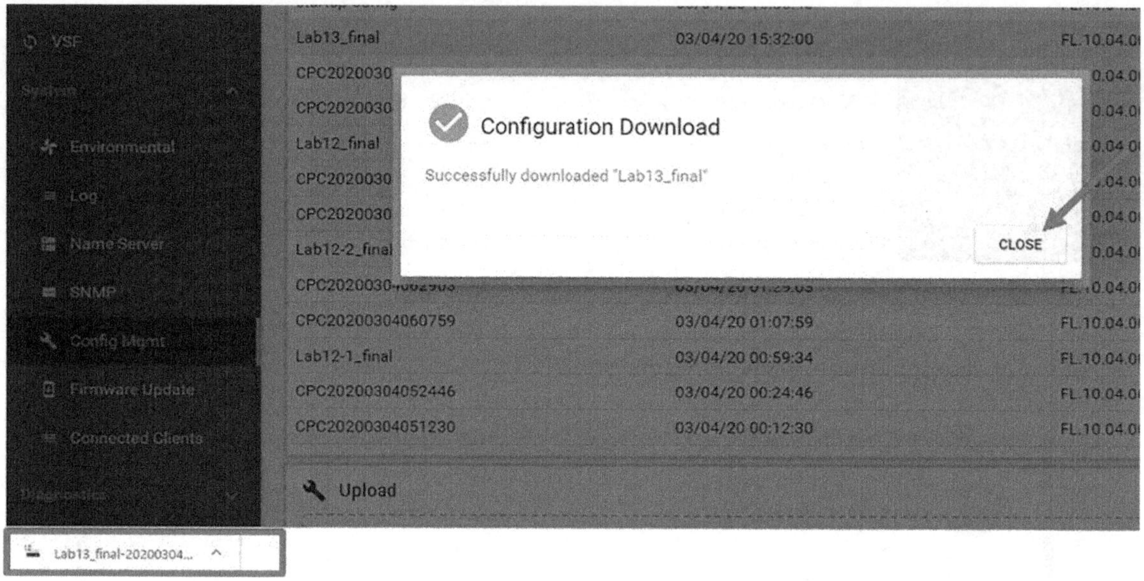

Figure 13-50 Confirm Configuration Download

9. Click on the "Close" button.

You have completed Lab 13!

Learning Check

Chapter 13 Questions

OOBM Port, Management VRF, Ping, and Traceroute in the Management VRF

1. What is true about managing Aruba OS-CX devices?
    a. You can connect using SSH, HTTPS, and SNMP on the management interface and on any typical access interface on the switch.
    b. The control plane uses a special management VRF.
    c. The management interface can acquire an IP address via DHCP or by manual configuration.
    d. You can use the command "ping 10.1.1.1" to ping a PC at that address which has been connected to a switch OOBM port.

SSH for Aruba OS-CX, HTTPS for Aruba OS-CX, Web Interface

2. Which of the options below accurately describe accessing a 6300 ArubaOS-CX device for CLI or GUI access?
   a. By default, SSH is enabled in the management and default VRF.
   b. By default, HTTPS is enabled in the default VRF.
   c. SSH is the preferred method for GUI access.
   d. It is a best practice to only enable GUI access on the management VRF.

AAA, RBAC, RADIUS-based Management Authentication

3. Which of the statements describe valid Aruba OS-CX secure management access concepts?
   a. AAA Accounting controls what you can do once you login to the device.
   b. AAA services can be used in both the management VRF and the default VRF.
   c. Role-Based Access Control (RBAC) is based on a user's group assignment.
   d. Advantages of using a RADIUS server include simplicity and faster authentication operations.
   e. An easy way to modify several users' access is to modify the "operators" group.

Configuration File Management, Checkpoint Overview, Password Recovery

4. What is true about Aruba OS-CX configuration file management?
   a. It is a good idea to copy the running configuration to the startup configuration after you have made changes to the configuration file that is currently in use.
   b. The configuration file that is used while the switch is in operation is typically stored in a flash file system.
   c. The advantage of a "Checkpoint" is that it stores operational metadata, in addition to the device configuration.
   d. Checkpoints are files – a snapshot of the configuration at a given time.

14 AOS-CX Management Tools

EXAM OBJECTIVES

✓ Describe NetEdit features, configuration, and access.

✓ Configure switches to support NetEdit.

✓ Describe the Aruba CX Mobile app.

Overview

This module covers useful AOS-CX management tools in order to improve your network administration efficiency, and the ease with which you perform many configuration and monitoring tasks. You will begin by exploring NetEdit features, installation, configuration, and access, before learning how to configure AOS-CX switches to support NetEdit. Finally, you will explore the Aruba CX Mobile App.

Management Tools

Introduction to Aruba NetEdit

As networks grow, they become more challenging to maintain, especially when introducing a new protocol or feature. Changes to large networks must be prepared, designed, configured, and validated on every single network device. CLI is a powerful configuration tool, but it is not scalable.

Aruba NetEdit provides for coordinated switch configuration, monitoring, and troubleshooting. It provides for intelligent, error-free configuration with validation for consistency and compliant, and the automation of multi-device change workflows without the overhead of programming. IT teams can coordinate end-to-end service roll outs, automate rapid network-wide changes, and ensure policy conformance after network updates.

Aruba NetEdit works closely with the embedded analytics in each AOS-CX switch, provided by the Aruba Network Analytic Engine (NAE). You get intelligent assistance and continuous validation, with compliance and design validation, analytics, and troubleshooting.

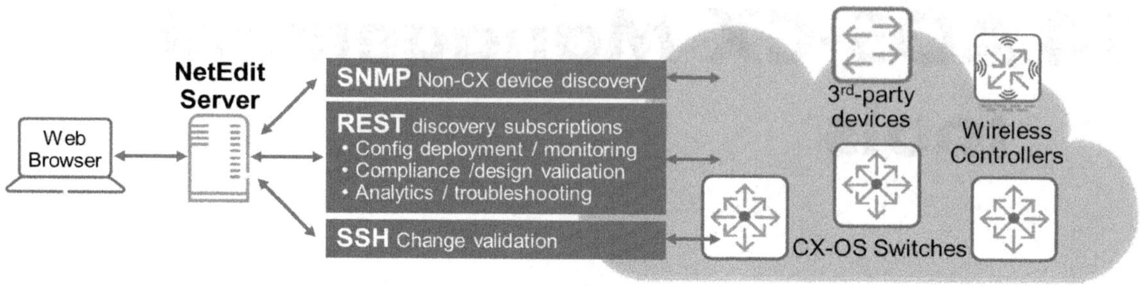

Figure 14-1 NetEdit

As shown in Figure 14-1, NetEdit works with AOS-CX switches via a Representational State Transfer Application Programming Interface (REST API). NetEdit uses SSH for change validation and supports SNMPv2c and SNMPv3 for non-CX device discovery.

NetEdit Installation

Aruba NetEdit is a web-based application and runs as an Open Virtualization Application (OVA) Virtual Machine (VM) (Figure 14-2).

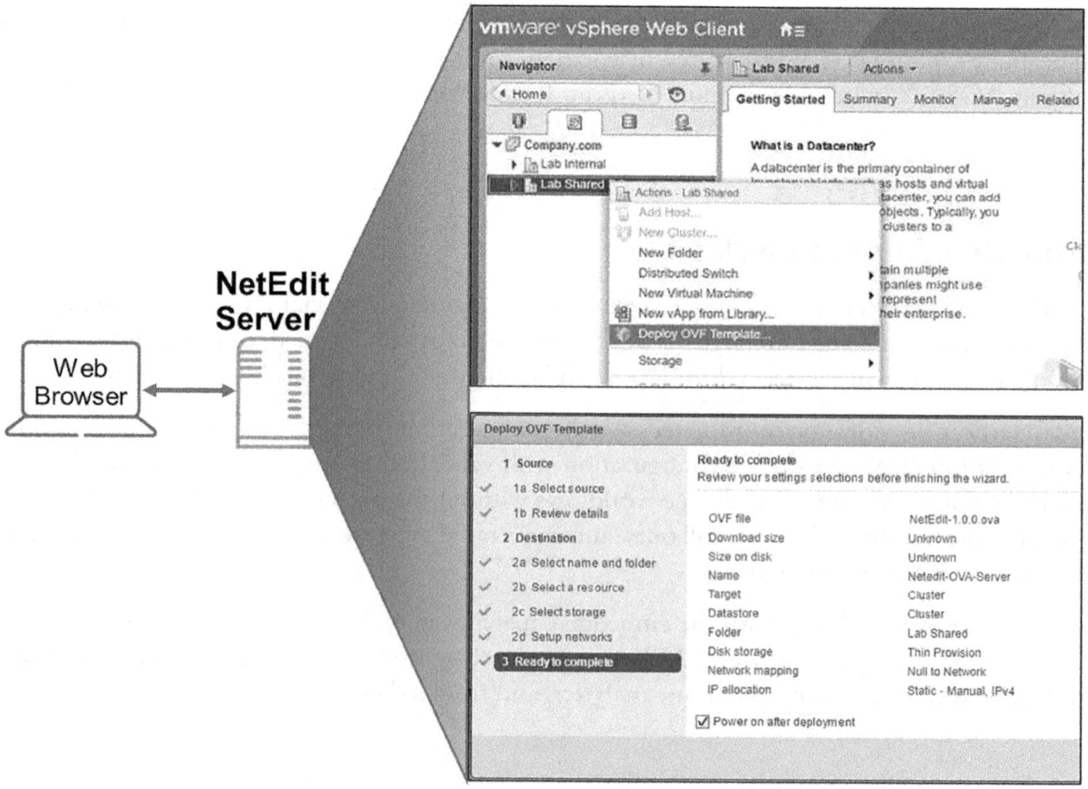

Figure 14-2 NetEdit Installation

A NetEdit deployment in VMWare vSphere version 6.0 or higher has the following requirements:

- 6 CPUs
- 32 GB RAM
- 115 GB disk space
- Network connectivity to the target switches to be managed

Install Procedure

1. Select the Host and Cluster and deploy the OVF Template.
2. Complete the wizard to deploy the OVF. After it the VM will be installed in the vSphere system.

NetEdit Initial Configuration

Set Password

1 In vSphere interface, select the NetEdit VM, open a console, and log in as neadmin

```
netedit-server login: neadmin
```

2 NetEdit will prompt to reset the password

```
Debian GNU/Linux 9 netedit-server ttyl

netedit-server login: neadmin
You are required to change your password immediately (root enforced)
New password:
Retype new password:
```

3 After password reset, prompted again for new password, configuration starts automatically

Figure 14-3 NetEdit Initial Configuration—Setting the Password

Licensing

NetEdit is currently available on a trial basis for up to 25 network switches. There are also licensing options for one- and three-year subscriptions for Aruba Support Services (Figures 14-4 to 14-5).

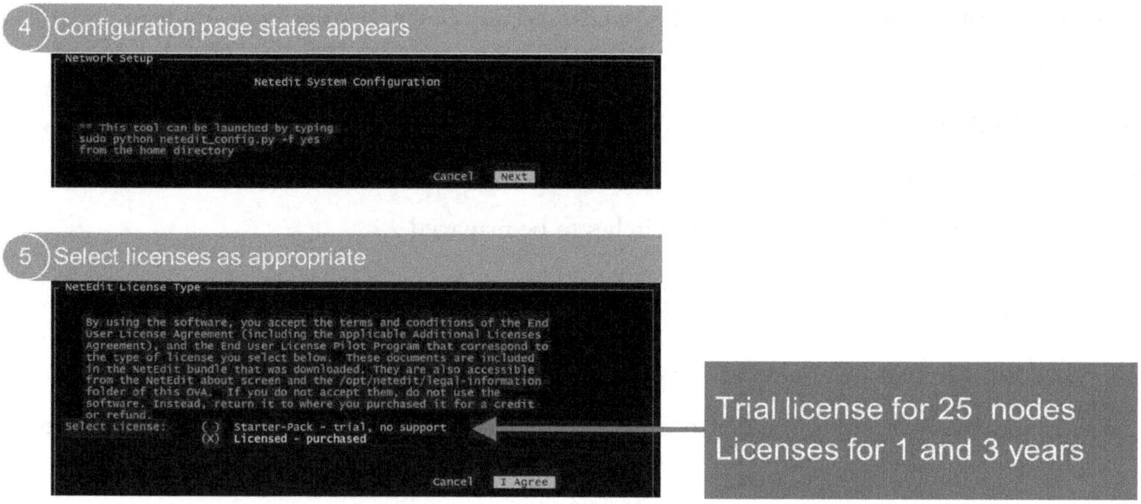

Figure 14-4 NetEdit Initial Configuration—Licensing

Network Configuration

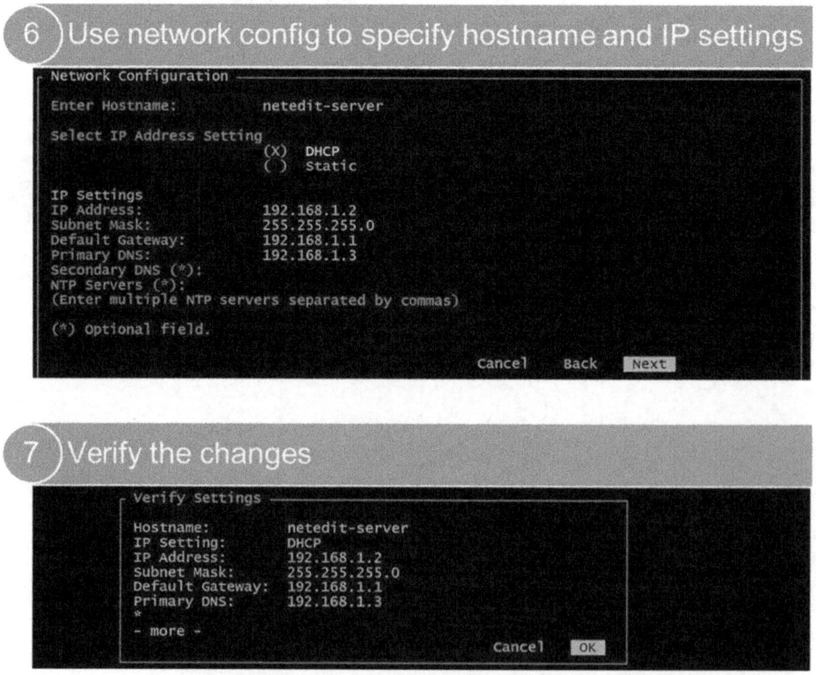

Figure 14-5 NetEdit Initial Configuration—Network Configuration

NetEdit GUI Login

Log in to NetEdit using the GUI per Figure 14-6.

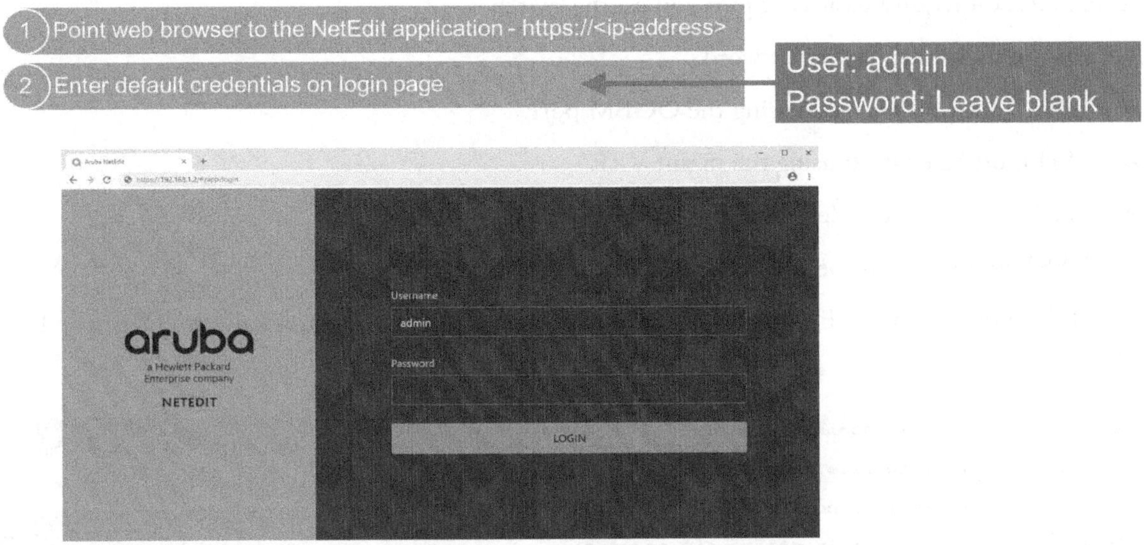

Figure 14-6 NetEdit GUI Login

Change Password

At the first login, a prompt to change the password displays. This will take you to overview page displays. Successfully logging in means that NetEdit is ready to use (Figure 14-7).

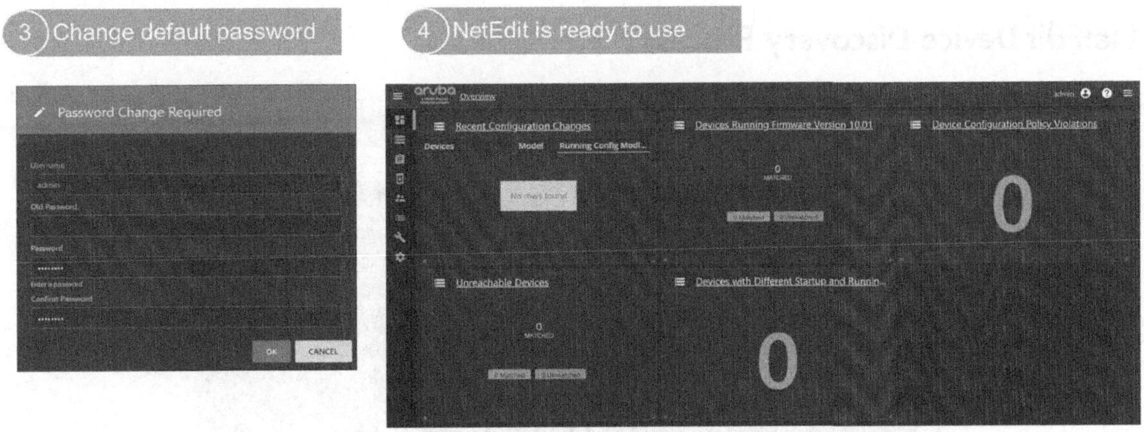

Figure 14-7 Change Password

NetEdit Device Discovery

Configure Switches to Support NetEdit

Aruba NetEdit requiresbasic configuration on the switches.

- Admin user must have a password.
- Device must be reachable using the OOBM port.
- SSH must be enabled using the mgmt VRF.
- HTTPS must be enabled using the mgmt VRF.
- REST interface must be enabled in read-write mode.

The following script in Figure 14-8 can be used to meet these requirements (Figures 14-9 to 14-12).

```
Switch(config)# user admin password                      <-- Set Admin password

Switch(config)# interface mgmt
Switch(config-if-mgmt)# no shutdown
Switch(config-if-mgmt)# ip static <ip-address>           <-- OOBM port reachability
Switch(config-if-mgmt)# default-gateway <default-gateway-IP>

Switch(config)# ssh server vrf mgmt
Switch(config)# https-server vrf mgmt                    <-- Enable SSH, HTTPS, REST
Switch(config)# https-server rest access-mode read-write
```

Figure 14-8 Device Setup for NetEdit

NetEdit Device Discovery Process

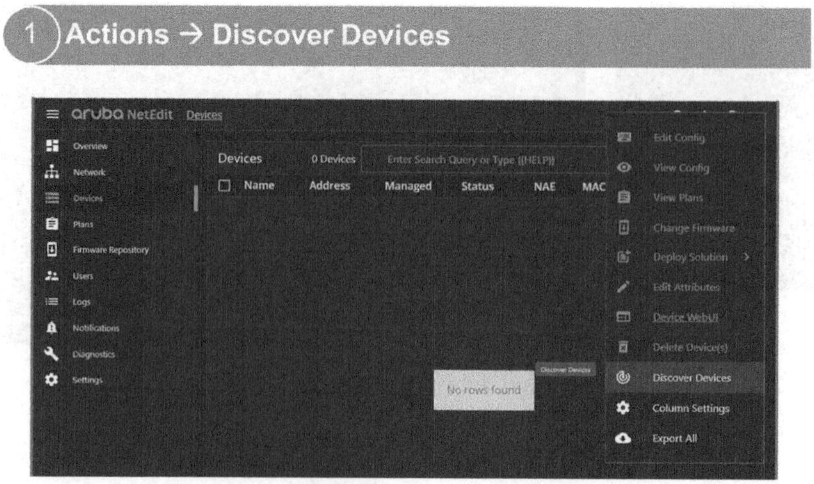

Figure 14-9 Discover Devices

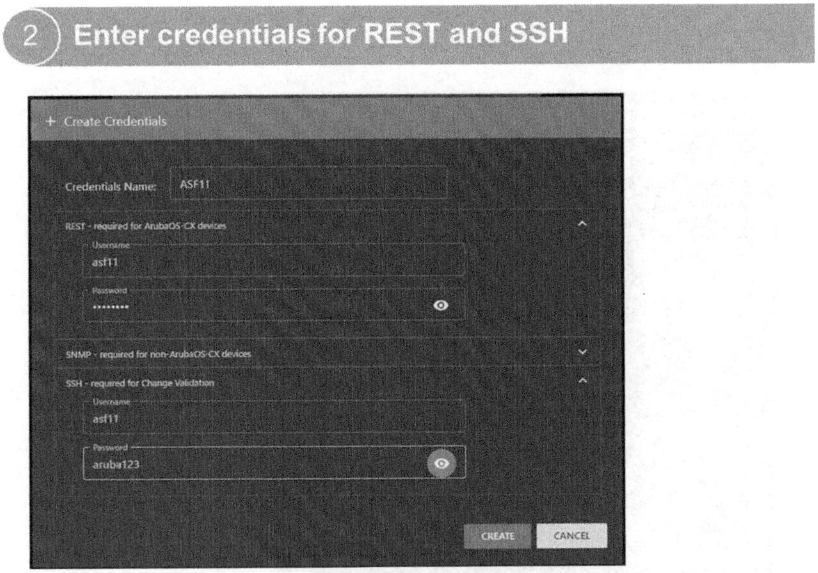

Figure 14-10 REST and SSH Credentials

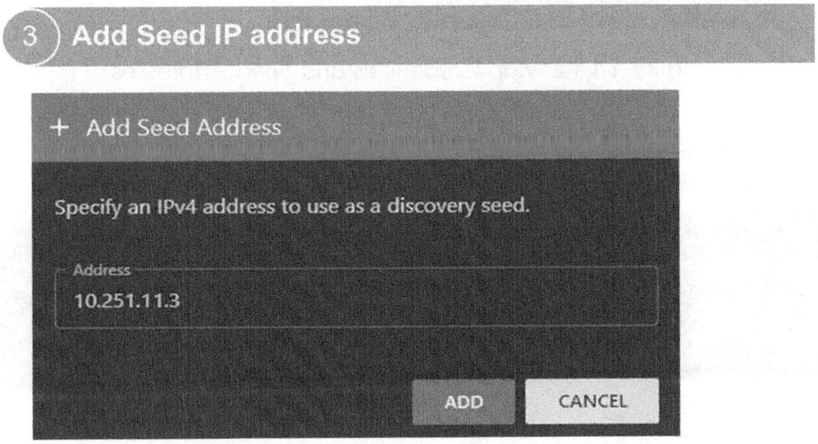

Figure 14-11 Adding a Seed IP Address

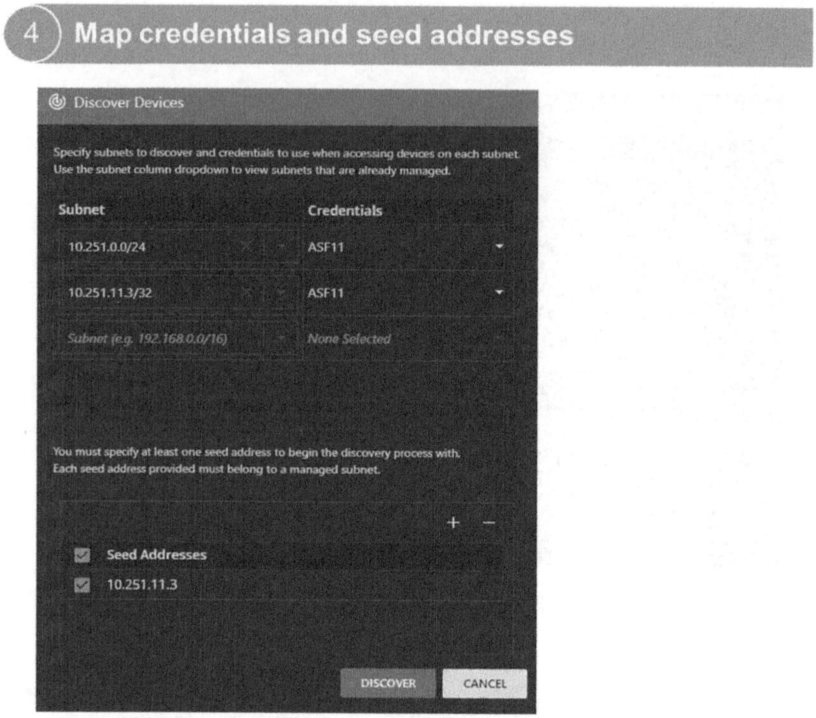

Figure 14-12 Map Credentials and Seed Addresses

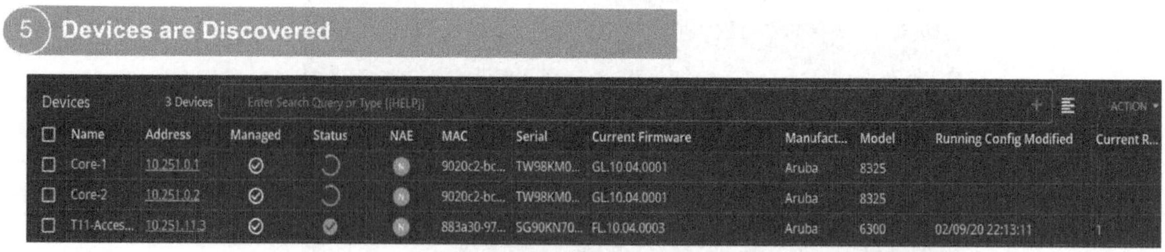

NetEdit Device Monitoring

NetEdit—Device Details

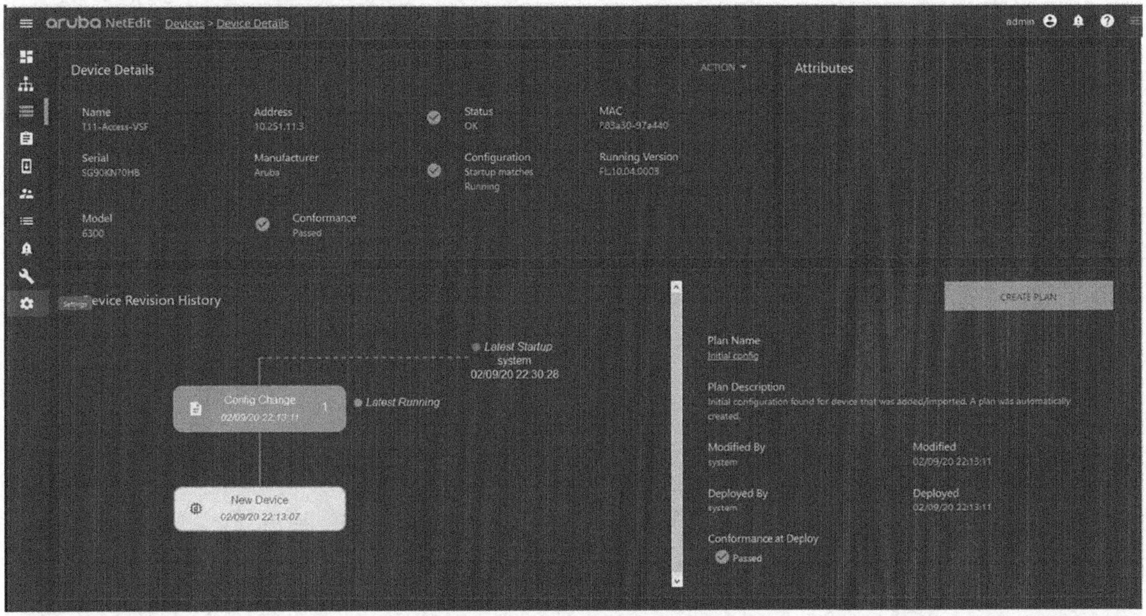

Device Details

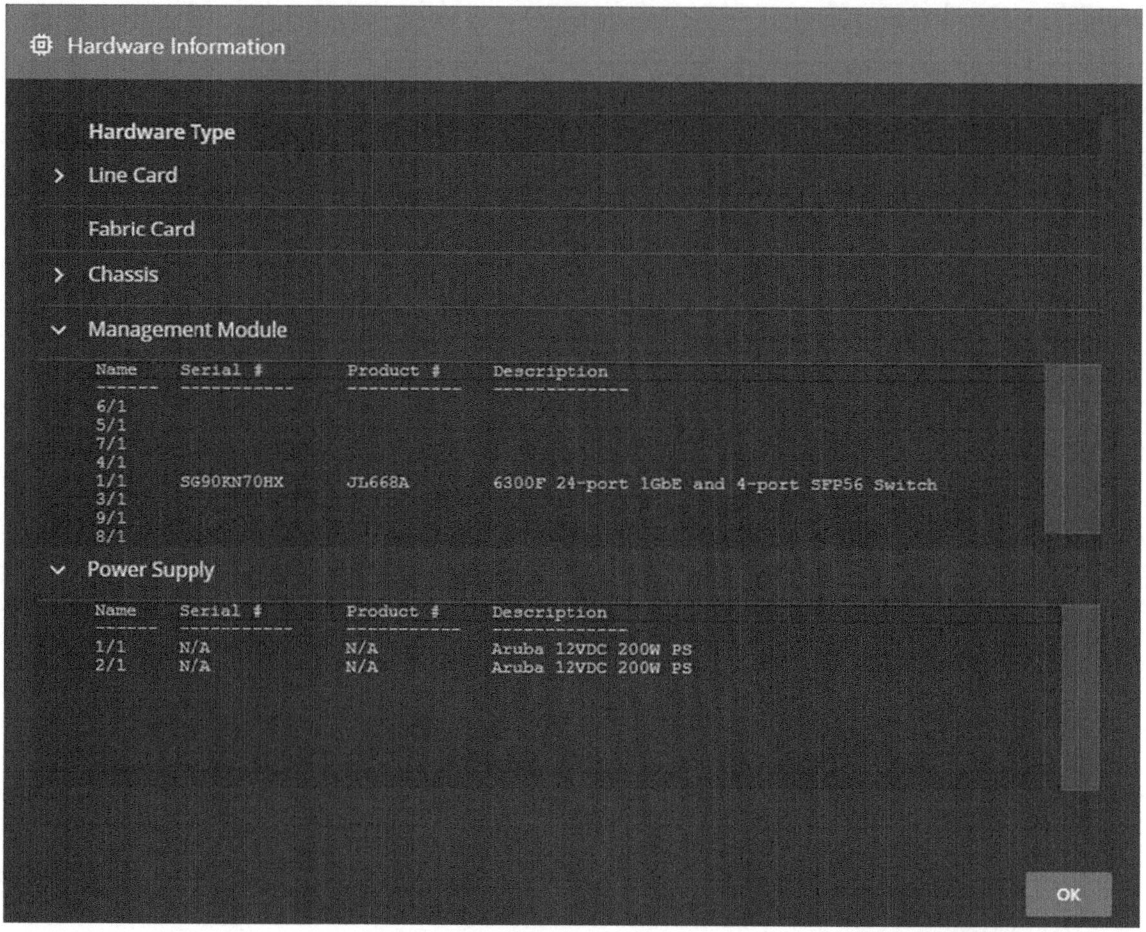

Hardware and Firmware Information

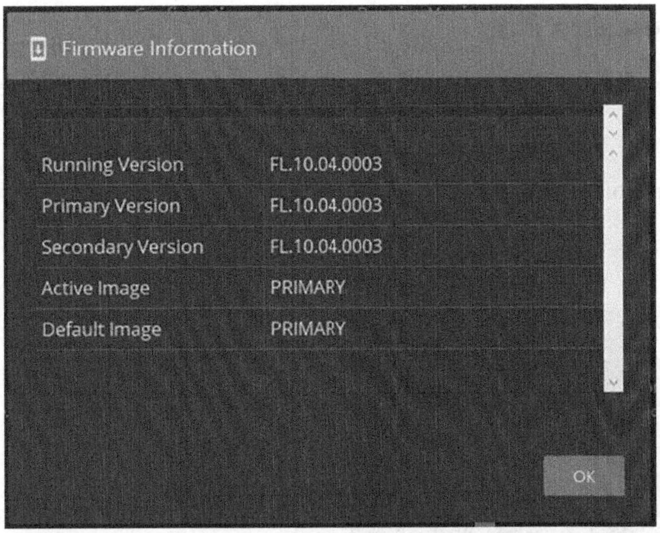

Current Configuration

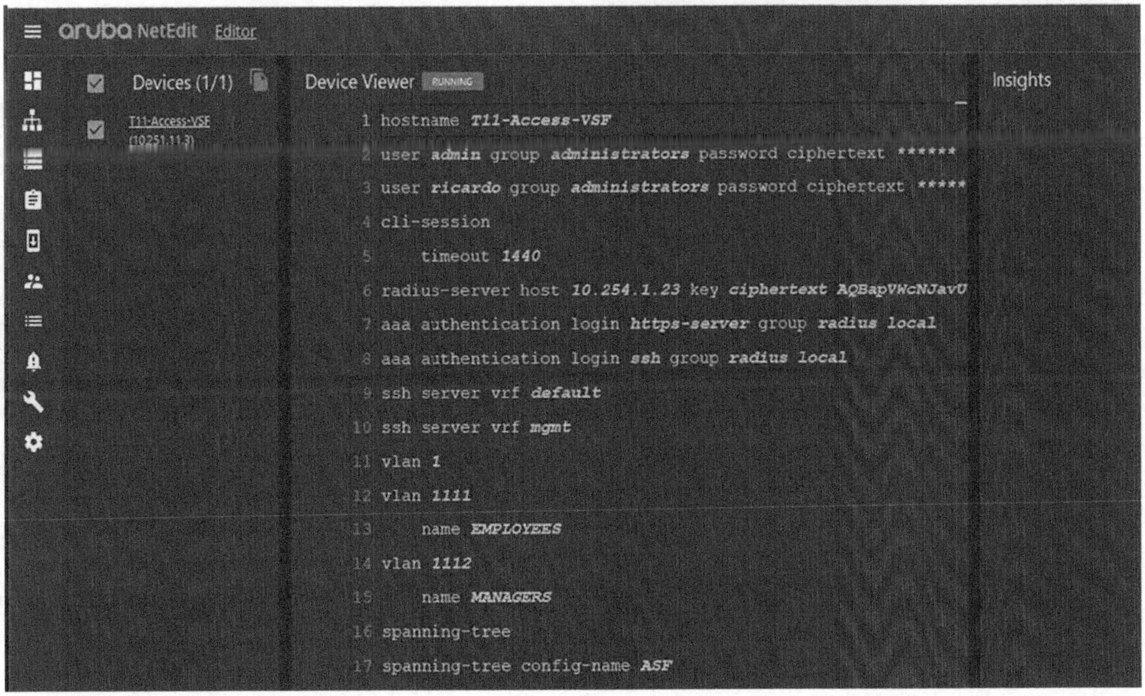

NetEdit Device Management

Create a Configuration Plan

Start by creating a new VLAN and assign to a port. Figure 14-13 shows the steps in NetEdit.

1. Create a Plan.
2. Edit the configuration.
3. Validate the changes.

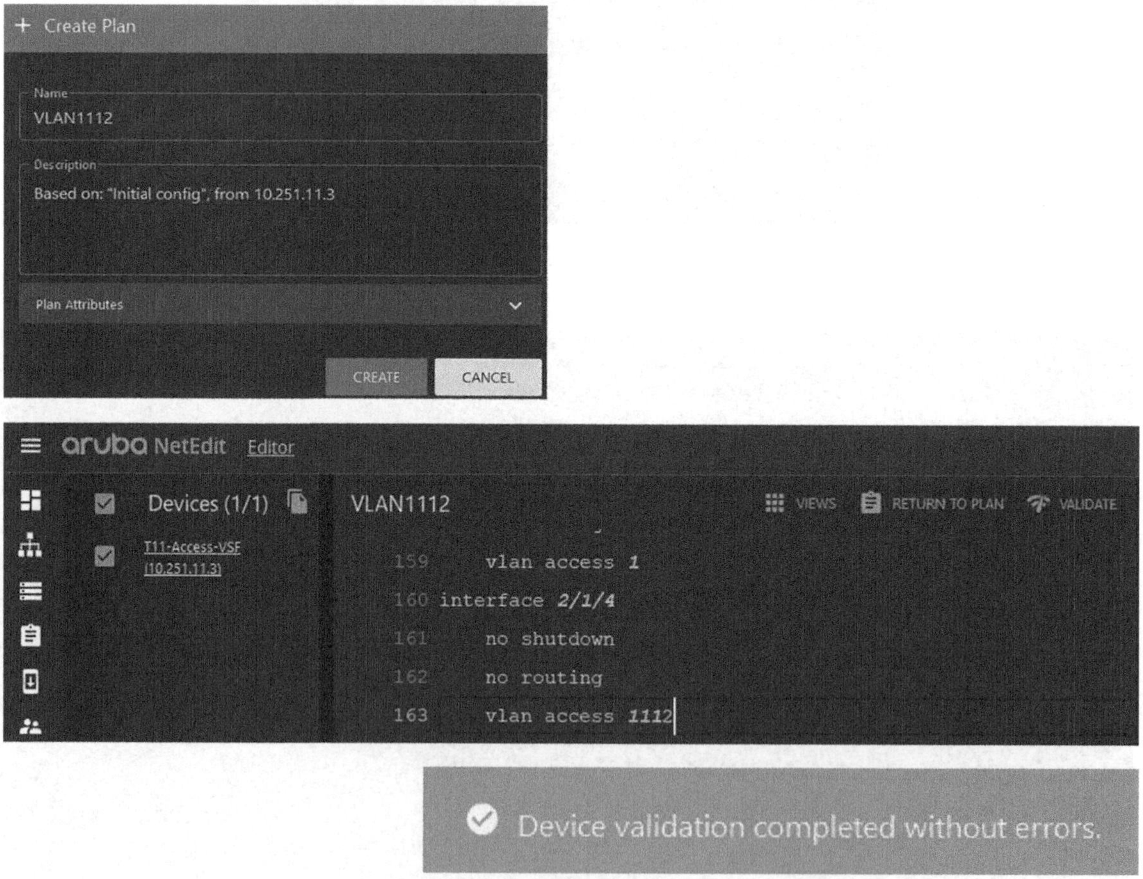

Figure 14-13 Create a Configuration Plan

Deploy the New Vlan

4. Deploy the change per Figure 14-14 below by selecting **Deploy**.

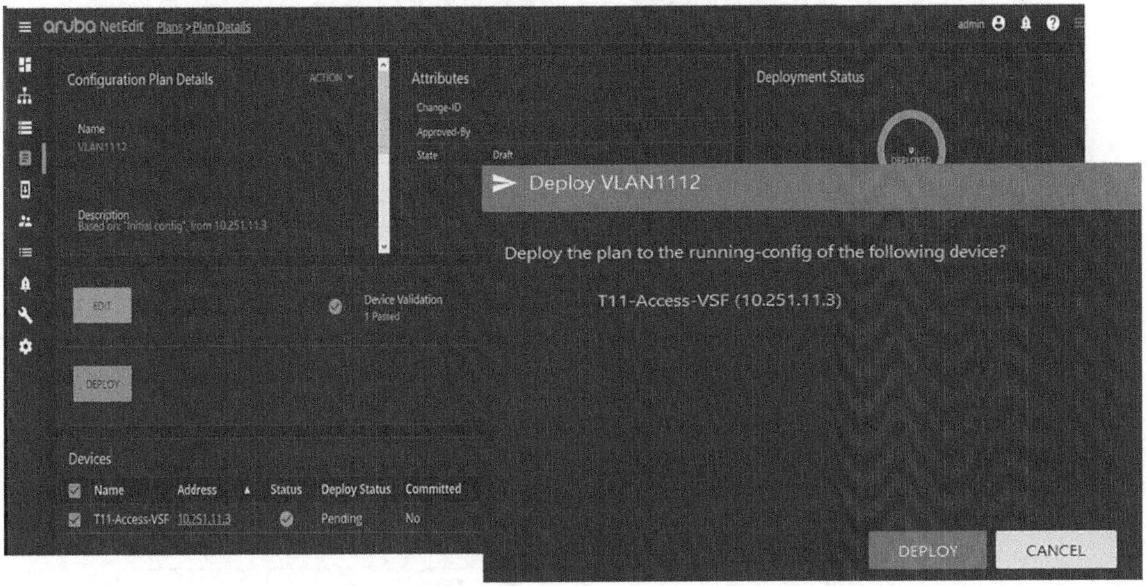

Figure 14-14 Deploy the Plan

5. Verify the change from switch console in Figure 14-15.

```
T11-Access-VSF# show int 2/1/4 brief
-----------------------------------------------------------------------------------------
Port      Native  Mode    Type          Enabled Status  Reason                  Speed
          VLAN                                                                  (Mb/s)
-----------------------------------------------------------------------------------------
2/1/4     1112    access 1GbT           yes     up                              1000
```

Figure 14-15 Confirm VLAN

Aruba CX Mobile App Overview

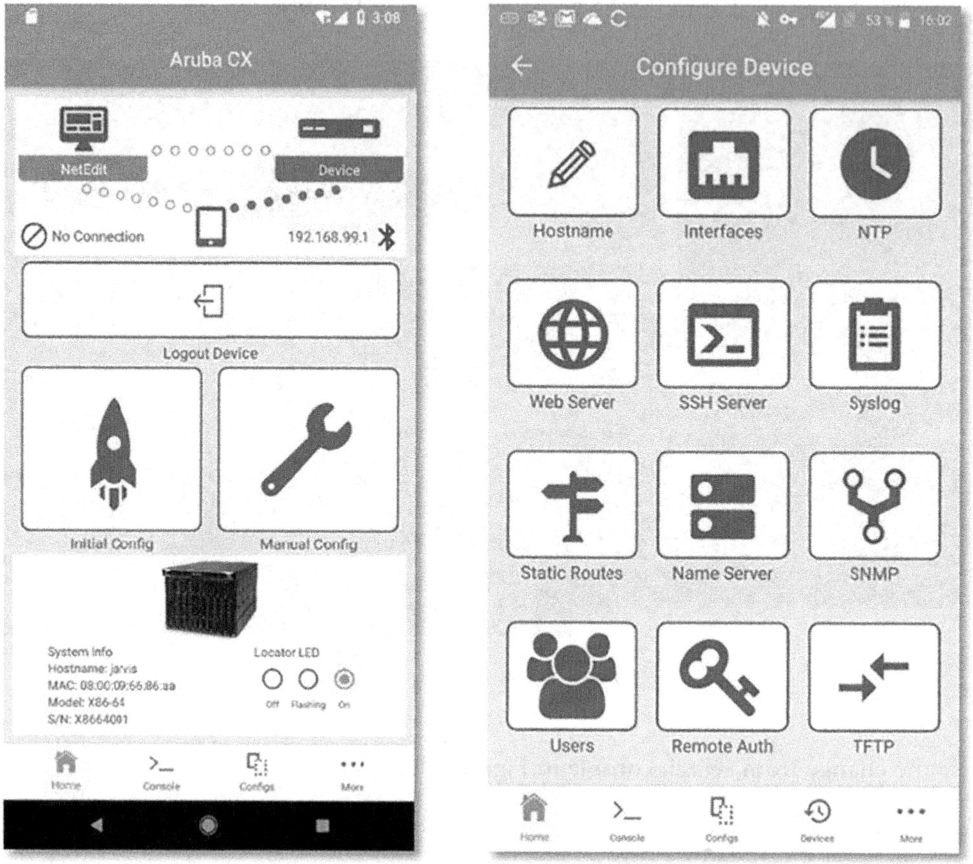

Figure 14-16 Aruba CX Mobile App Overview

The Aruba CX Mobile App accelerates day zero configuration and deployment of AOS-CX switches. No need for physical switch connections, connect your Apple or Android device via Bluetooth or Wi-Fi, for easy monitoring and configuration workflows and templates. Configure and monitor virtual switch stacks and PoE usage.

This application was created to address the complexity of switch configuration and installation for large deployments. You can validate that switches were configured and installed correctly, without relying on a network administration team for confirmation. The Aruba CX application integrates with Aruba NetEdit for intelligent configuration management, continuous validation, and overall network health (Figure 14-16).

Note

AOS-CX switches must run at least version 10.02.0001 for 8400, 8320, and 8325 models. The minimum code version for 6300 and 6400 switch series is 10.4. Your mobile device must be an Apple device running iOS version 12 or higher, or an Android device running version 5.0 or higher.

Aruba CX Mobile App Features

Here are the key features of the Aruba CX Mobile App:

- The application uses Bluetooth and Wi-Fi to communicate with AOS-CX switches.
- Is available for Apple iOS 12 or higher and Android 5.0 or higher platforms.
- Configuration of basic operational settings eliminates having to connect a console cable.
- Built-in configuration templates and ability to customize your own.
- Easily manage the running and startup configuration (see Figure 14-15).
- Access the Switch CLI.
- Check PoE budget utilization.
- Transfer files between the switch and your mobile device.
- Role-based Access Control (RBAC)
- Firmware updates via HTTPS.
- Stacking automation (see Figure 14-15).
- Monitoring of PoE utilization (Figure 14-17).

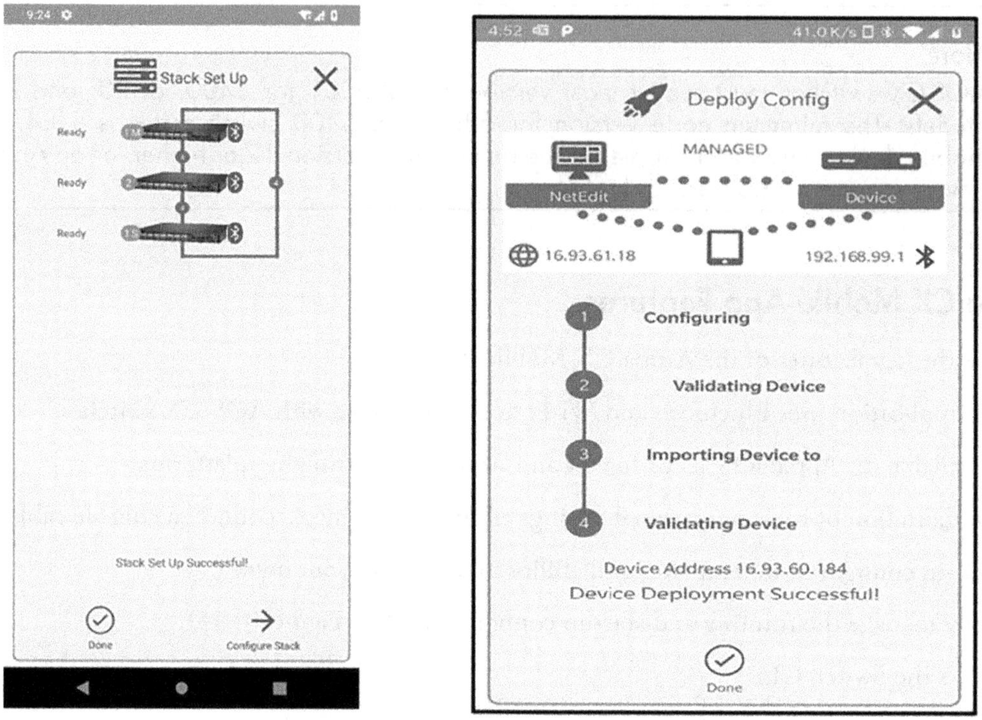

Figure 14-17 Stacking and NetEdit

Lab 14: Monitoring Devices with Aruba NetEdit

Overview

After enabling remote management, BigStartup's IT staff wants to know if there is a way to monitor and manage both the main office and the remote locations from a single pane of glass. Currently they are opening individual web sessions to each switch. To provide a consolidated monitoring and management service, you will demonstrate Aruba NetEdit.

Note: References to equipment and commands are taken from Aruba's hosted remote lab. These are shown for demonstration purposes in case you wish to replicate the environment and tasks on your own equipment.

Objectives

After completing this lab, you will be able to:

- Access NetEdit and update admin credentials.
- Discover switching devices.
- Monitor switching devices.
- Run a Deployment Plan.
- Commit a deployment.
- Inspect the logs (Figure 14-18).

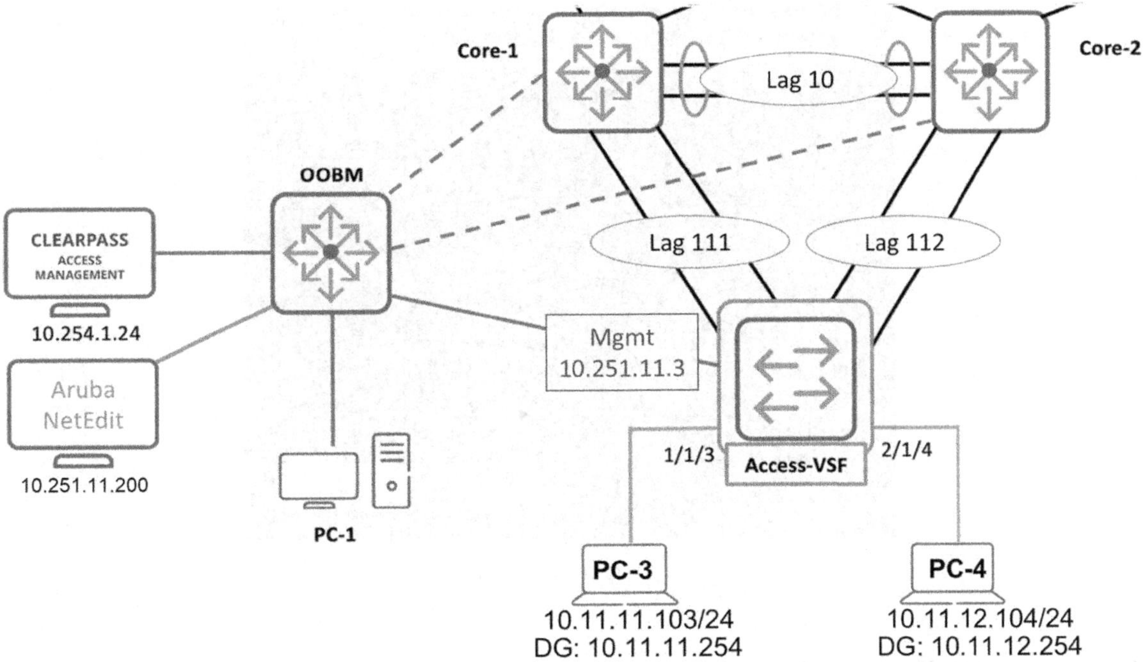

Figure 14-18 Lab Topology

Task 1: Discovering Devices in NetEdit

Objectives

In this lab you will access NetEdit for the first time; therefore you will be asked to update the "admin" credentials. Once inside you are going to add devices into its management database and proceed with regular monitoring and exploration tasks.

Steps

PC-1

1. Access PC-1.
2. Open a browser and type the NetEdit IP address in the URL field (10.251.11.200).
3. Log in with **admin** and **aruba123**.
4. In the Password Change Required dialog box type "aruba123" with no quotes under the Password and Confirm Password fields (Figure 14-19).

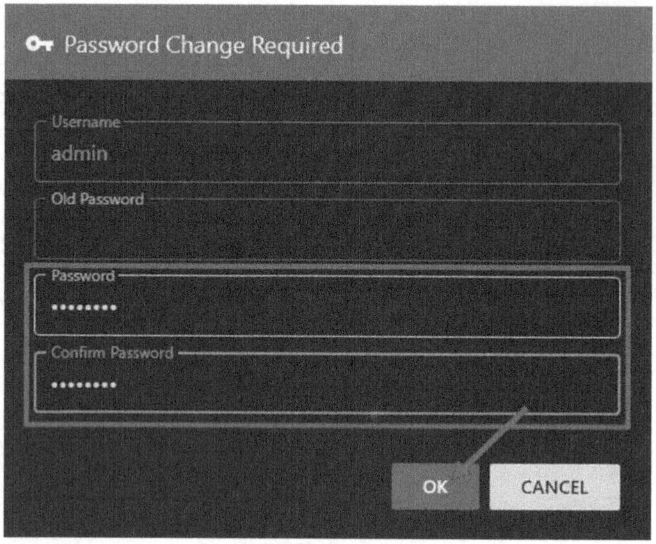

Figure 14-19 Password Change

5. Click the "OK" button. That will take you to NetEdit "Overview" (Figure 14-20).

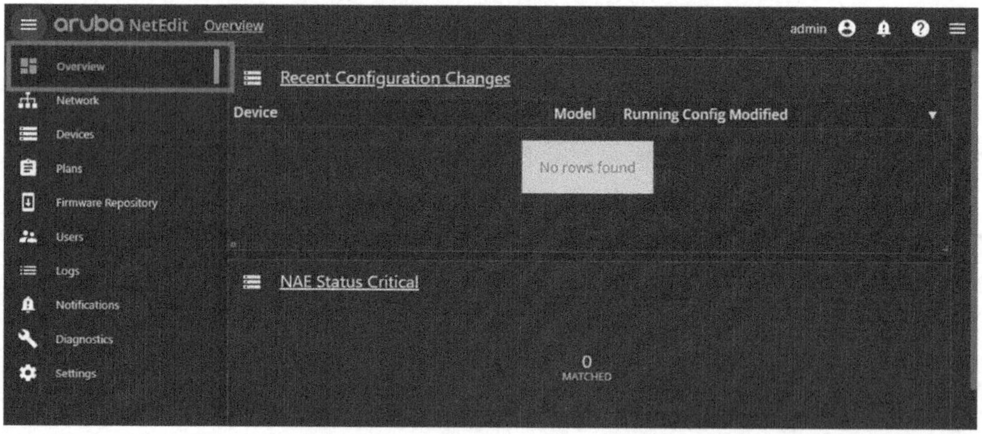

Figure 14-20 NetEdit Overview

6. In the left navigation panel click on "Devices".
7. At the far right click on the "Action" button; then select "DiscoverDevices" from the menu that appears. A dialog box will show up (Figure 14-21).

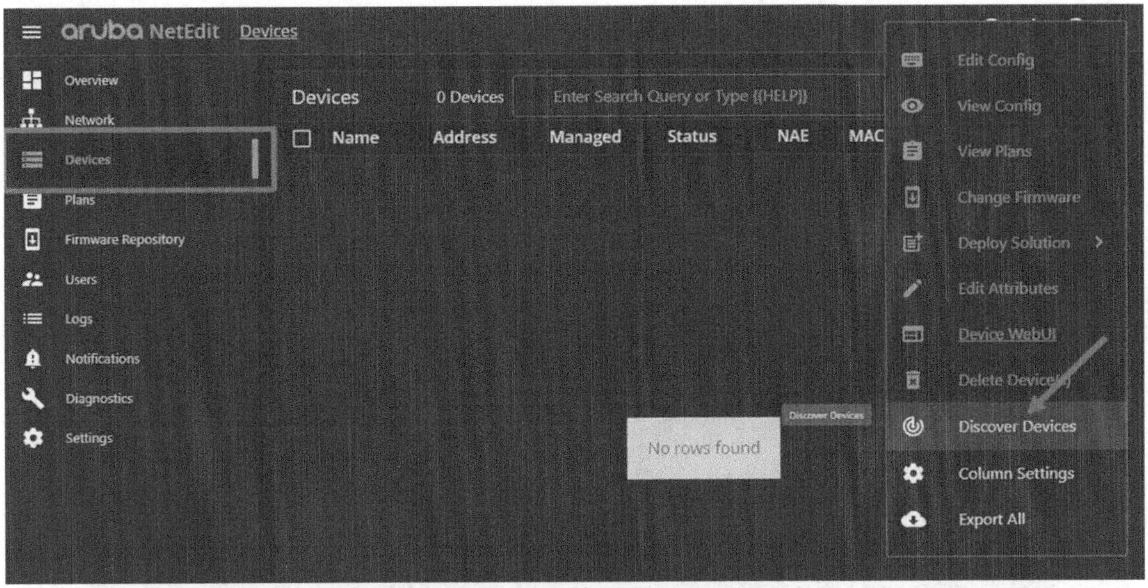

Figure 14-21 NetEdit Devices

8. Under Subnet type "10.251.11.3/32".
9. Click on "Add Credentials". A new dialog box appears (Figure 14-22).

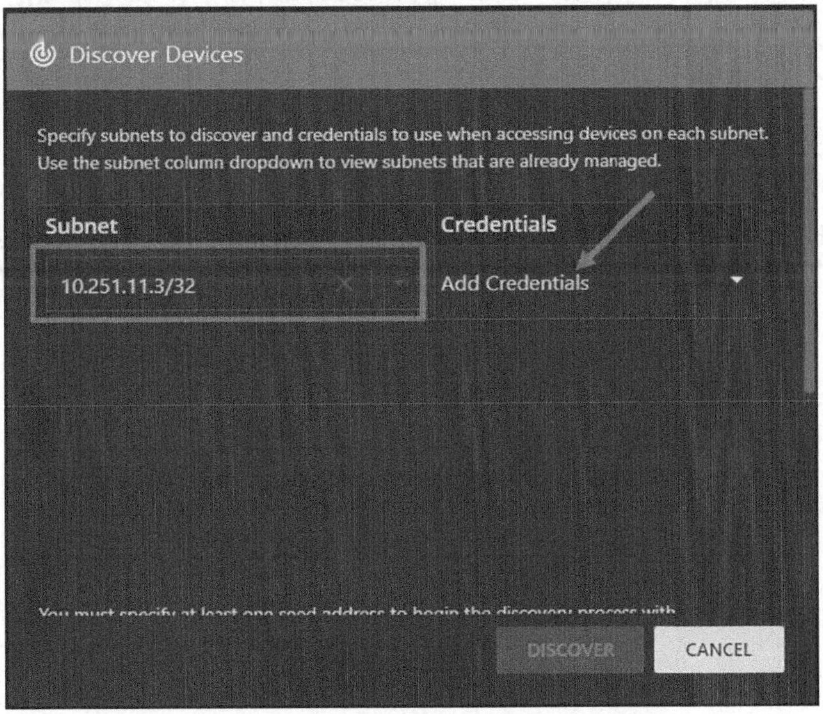

Figure 14-22 Discover Devices

10. On credentials Name type **cxf11**.
11. Expand "REST, required for AOS-CX devices"; then type **cxf11** as username and **aruba123** as password.
12. Repeat step 11 under "SSH, required for Change Validation".
13. Click on the "eye" icon to confirm the password (Figure 14-23).

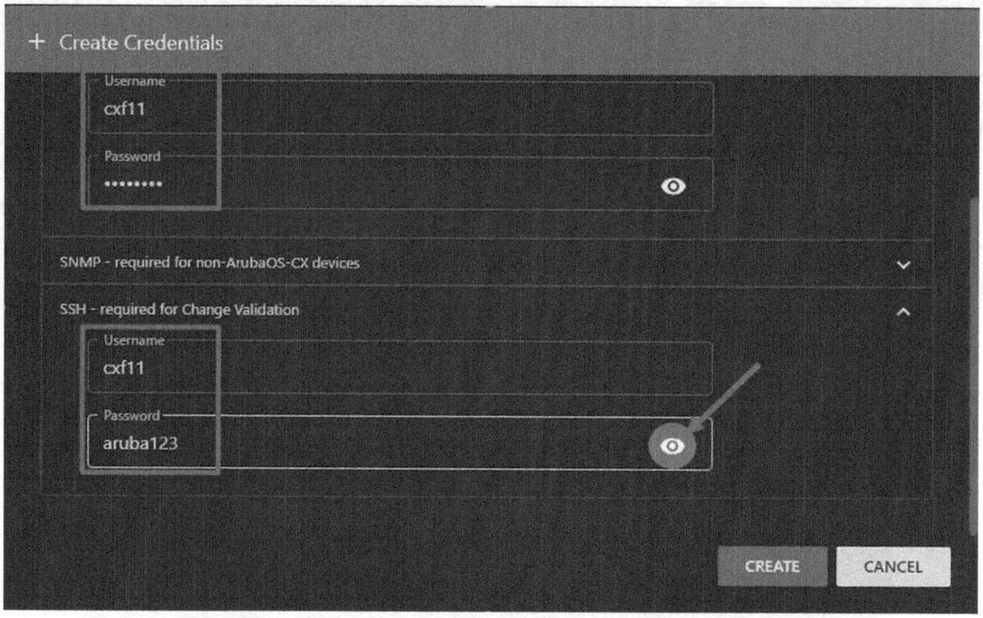

Figure 14-23 Create Credentials

14. Click "CREATE" button.
15. Back in the Discover Devices dialog box, scroll down; then in the Seed Addresses area click the "+" sign. A new dialog box will show up.

16. Type **10.251.11.3**; then click "ADD" button (Figure 14-24).

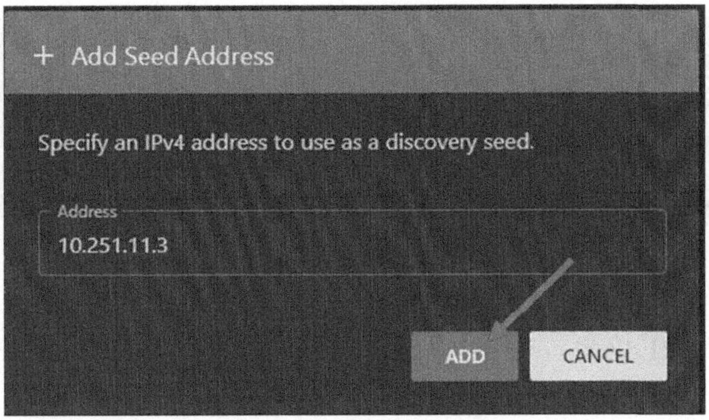

Figure 14-24 Add Seed Address

17. Check the newly added Seed Address; then click the **Discover** button (Figure 14-25).

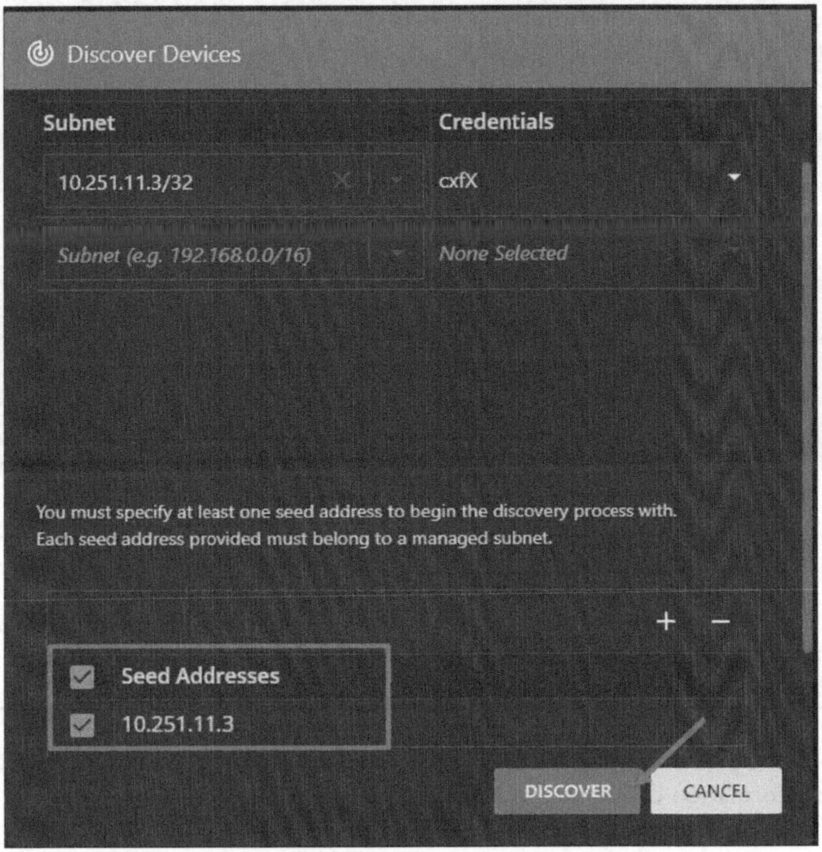

Figure 14-25 Discover Devices

18. Wait a minute; then refresh the browser. You will have a device entry (Figure 14-26).

Figure 14-26 NetEdit Devices Continued

What device has NetEdit discovered? ____________________

What version is listed under Current Firmware column? ____________________

What model is it? ____________________

19. Click on the IP address of Access-VSF. That will take you to the Device Details page (Figure 14-27).

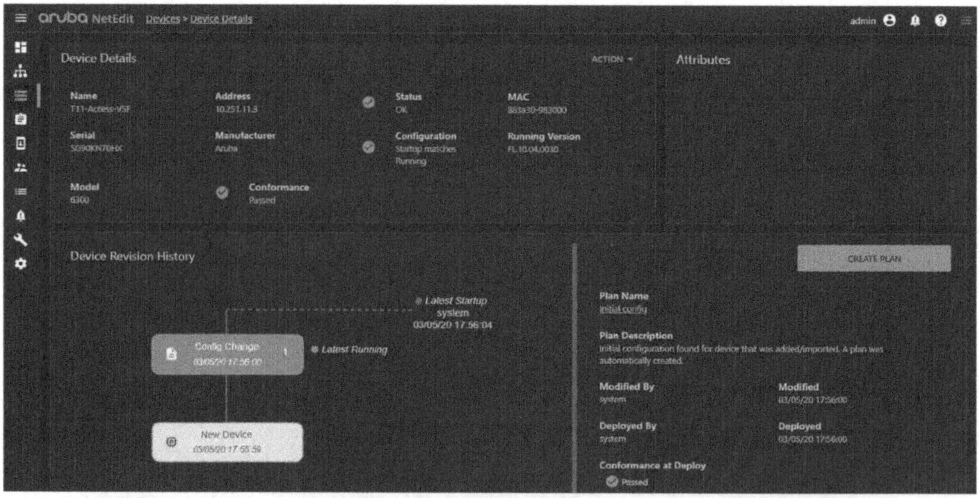

Figure 14-27 Device Details

Note

In addition to the regular details (Name, model, serial number, address, and Code version) you can also see whether or not the Startup and Running configurations match, as well as their current Conformance and Status states.

20. Click the "Action" button; then select "Hardware Information" from the menu that appears. The Hardware Information dialog box will show up.

21. Expand the "Management Module" and "Power Supply" sections (Figure 14-28).

    What Member of the VSF stack is considered the Management module? ____________

    How many power supplies are listed? ____________

    What physical device do they relate to? ____________

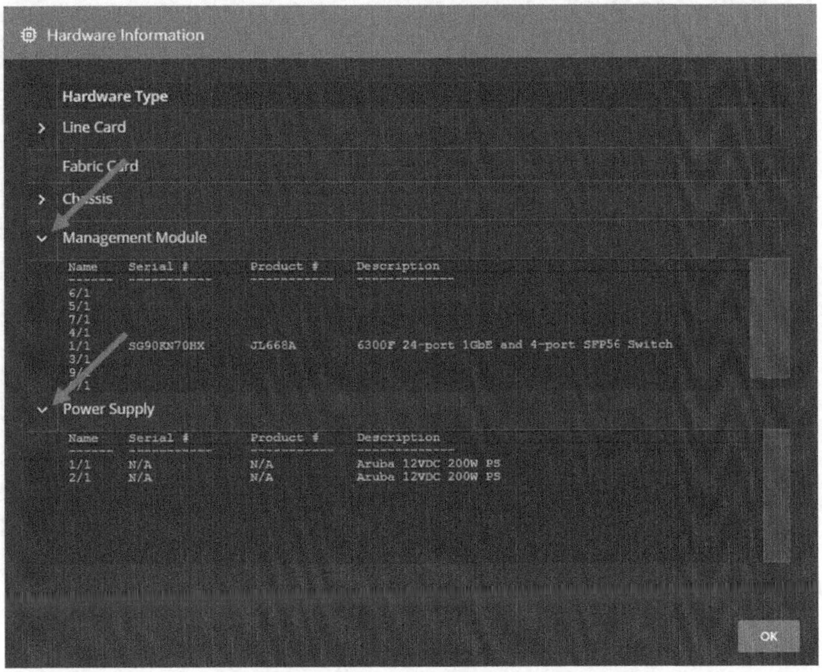

Figure 14-28 Hardware Information

22. Click the **OK** button.

23. Click the "Action" button; then select "View Firmware Information" from the menu that appears. The Firmware Information dialog box will show up (Figure 14-29).

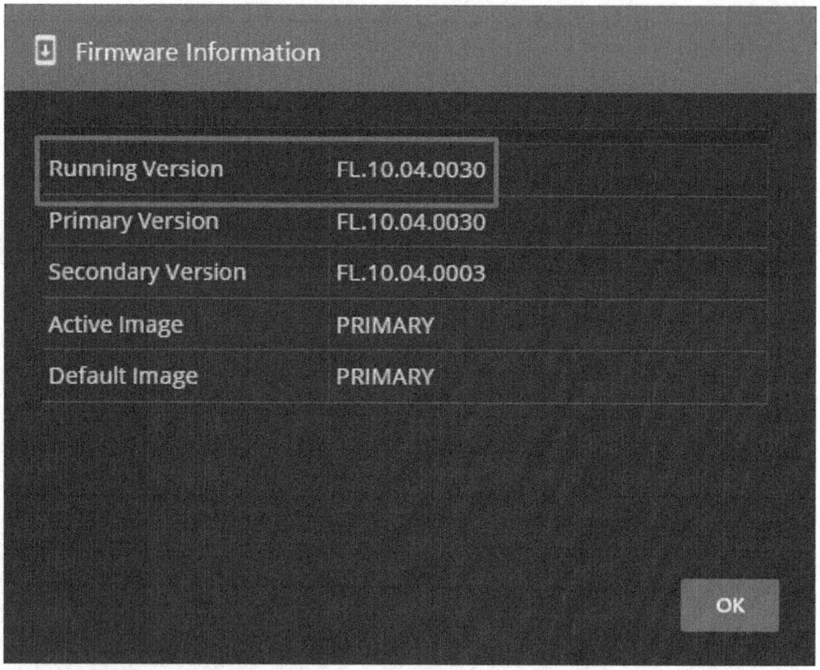

Figure 14-29 Firmware Information

What version of code is running in the system? ____________________

What AOS-CX code versions are stored on Primary and Secondary partitions? ____________

24. Click **OK** button.

25. Click the "Action" button; then select "View Running Config" from the menu that appears. The "Device Viewer RUNNING" section for Access-VSF shows up and will display the running configuration (Figure 14-30).

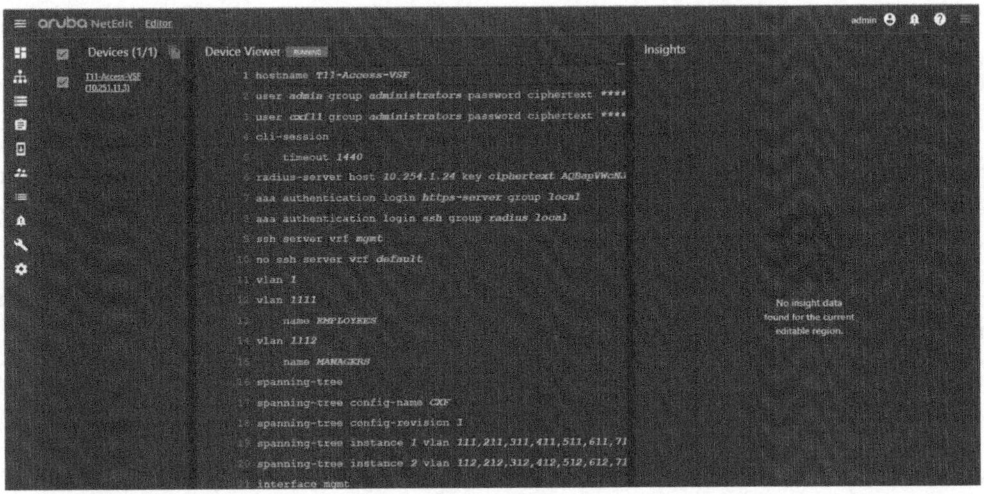

Figure 14-30 Device View

26. Click the "Overview" button () in the navigation panel (Figure 14-31).

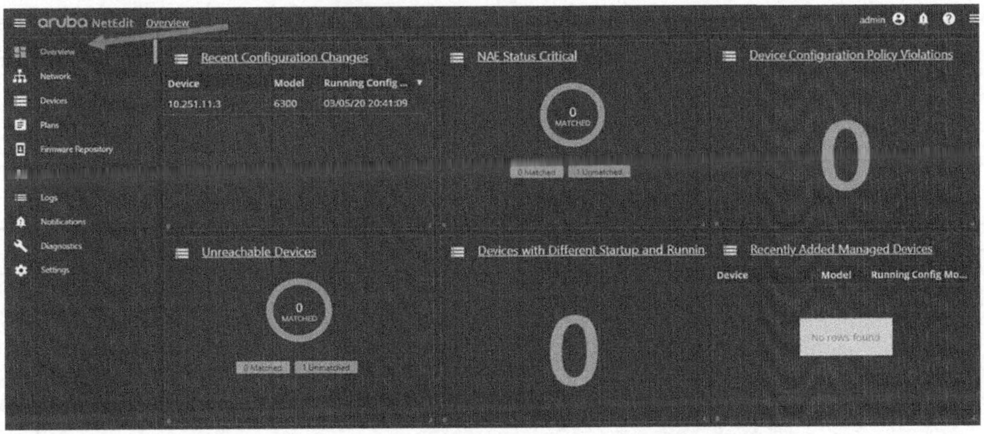

Figure 14-31 NetEdit Overview Continued

Are there any unreachable devices? ______________________________

Do any devices have different Startup and Running Configurations? If so, what are they? ______________________________

Task 2: Deployment Plan

Objectives

The IT Staff at BigStartup seem quite impressed by NetEdit and its monitoring capabilities. However, they are wondering if configuration changes can be made from the tool. Next you will demonstrate NetEdit's script deployments capabilities as well as roll back options in case of configuration mistakes.

In this task you will run a deployment plan and commit it, so the configuration changes remain even if the devices reboot. Then you will inspect the NetEdit logs.

Steps

Access-VSF

1. Move to Access-VSF's console.
2. Display the brief information of port 2/1/4.

```
T11-Access-VSF# show interface 2/1/4 brief
--------------------------------------------------------------------------------
Port      Native  Mode   Type      Enabled Status  Reason         Speed
          VLAN
(Mb/s)
--------------------------------------------------------------------------------
2/1/4     1111    access 1GbT         yes     up                   1000
```

What VLAN is the port mapped to? ________________________________

PC-1

3. Access PC-1.
4. Open a browser and type the NetEdit IP address in the URL field **10.251.11.200**; then hit [Enter].
5. Log in with **admin** as username and **aruba123** as password.
6. Click on "Devices" in the navigation pane ( ) (Figure 14-32).
7. Check the checkbox next to Access-VSF's IP address (10.251.11.3).

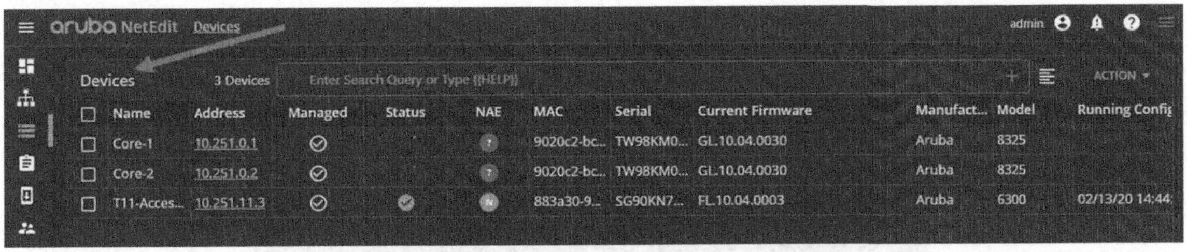

Figure 14-32 NetEdit Devices Continued

8. Click "ACTION" at far right; then select "Edit Config" from the menu that appears. This takes you to PLAN section and shows a Create Plan dialog box (Figure 14-33).
9. Under name type **VLAN1112**.

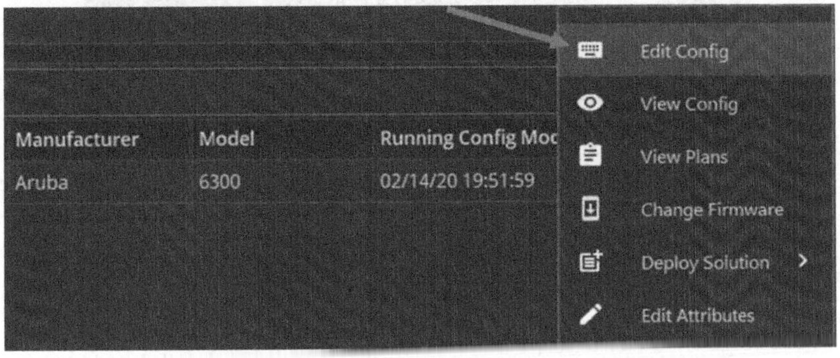

Figure 14-33 Actions Edit Config

10. Under Description type "Assign VLAN1112 to port 2/1/4" (Figure 14-34).
11. Click on the "CREATE" button.

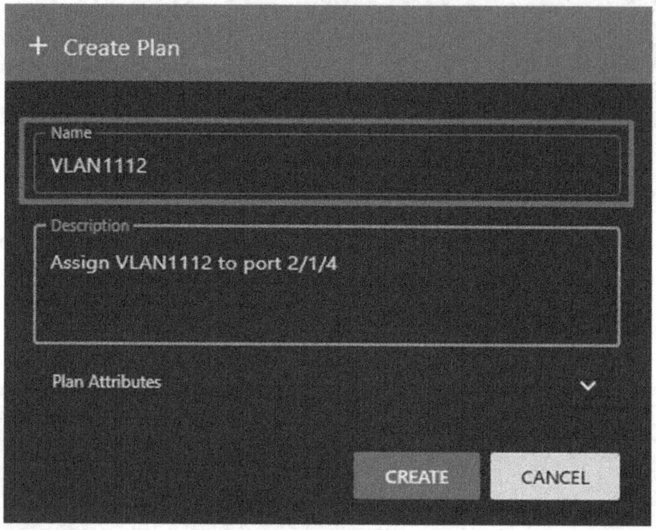

Figure 14-34 Create Plan

12. In the configuration section, scroll down to interface 2/1/4.
13. Click on "vlan access 1111" and change it to **vlan access 1112** (Figure 14-35).
14. Click on "VALIDATE". The plan will be validated and should be successful (Figure 14-36).

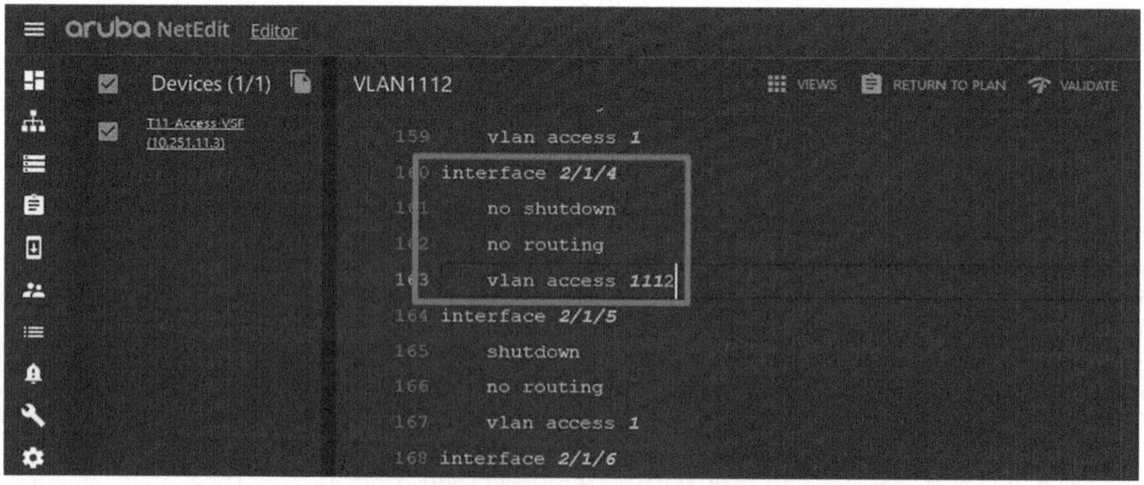

Figure 14-35 VLAN 1112 Configuration Plan

15. Click on "RETURN TO PLAN". This takes you to "*Plans > Plans Details*" (Figure 14-37).

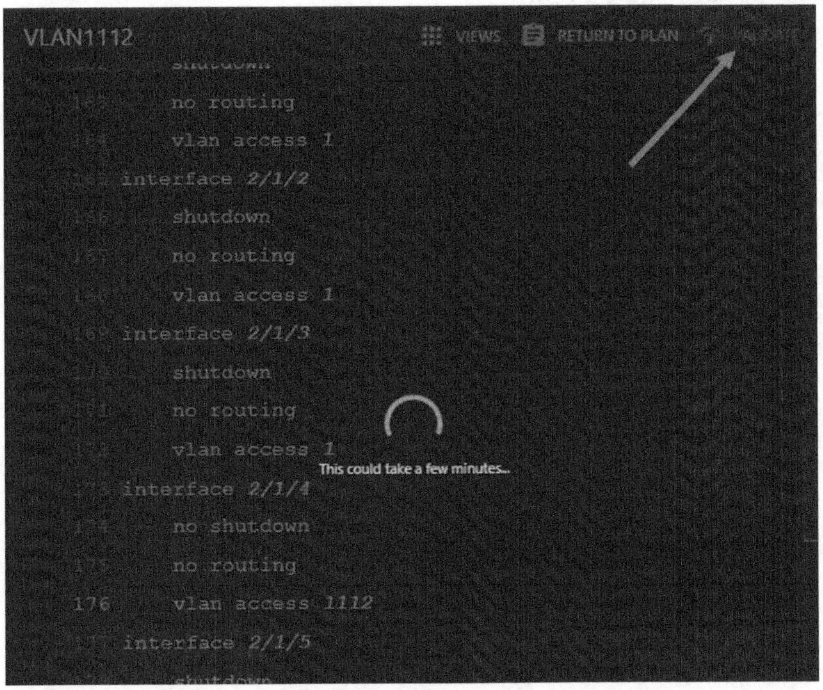

Figure 14-36 Plan Validation

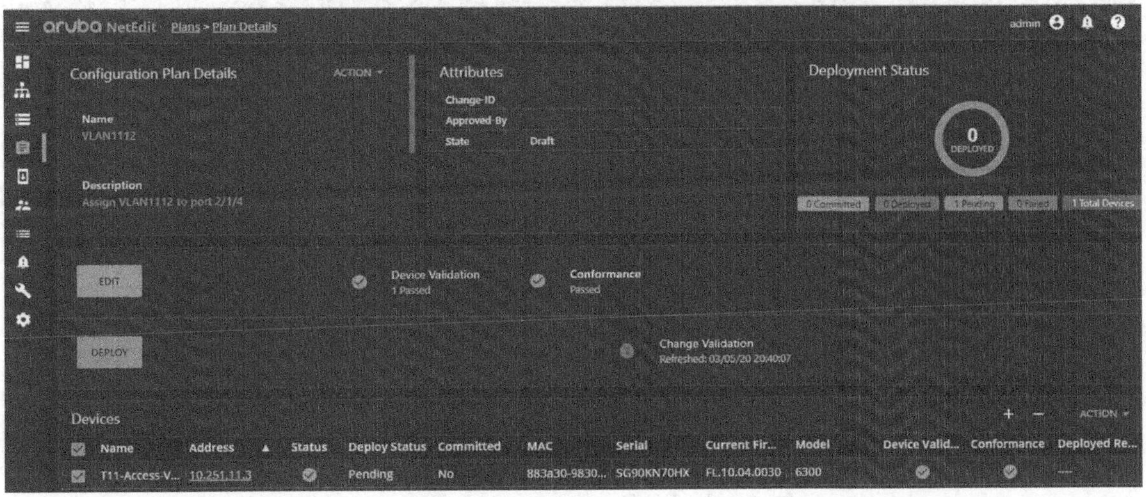

Figure 14-37 Plan Details

16. Confirm that your newly created plan is listed. Then click the purple "DEPLOY" button. A dialog box appears (Figure 14-38).

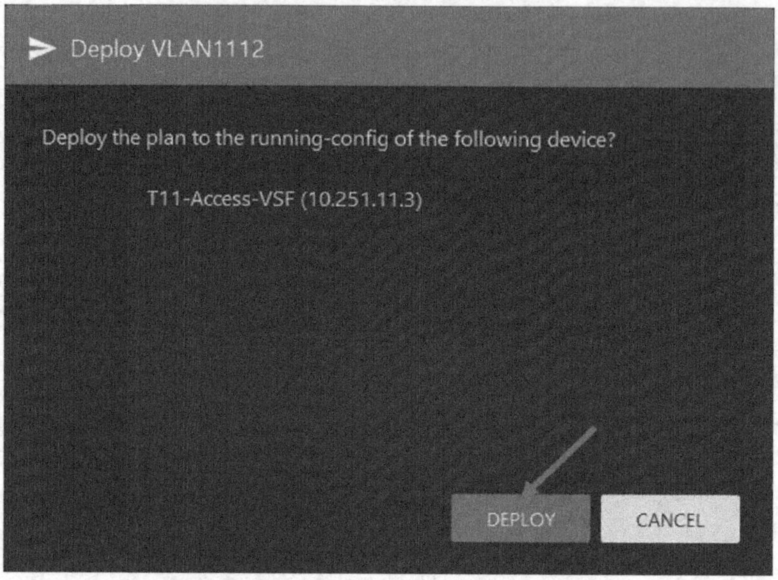

Figure 14-38 Deploy VLAN1112

17. Click the blue "DEPLOY" button; you should receive a "*Deployment is in progress…*"message at the bottom right (Figure 14-39).

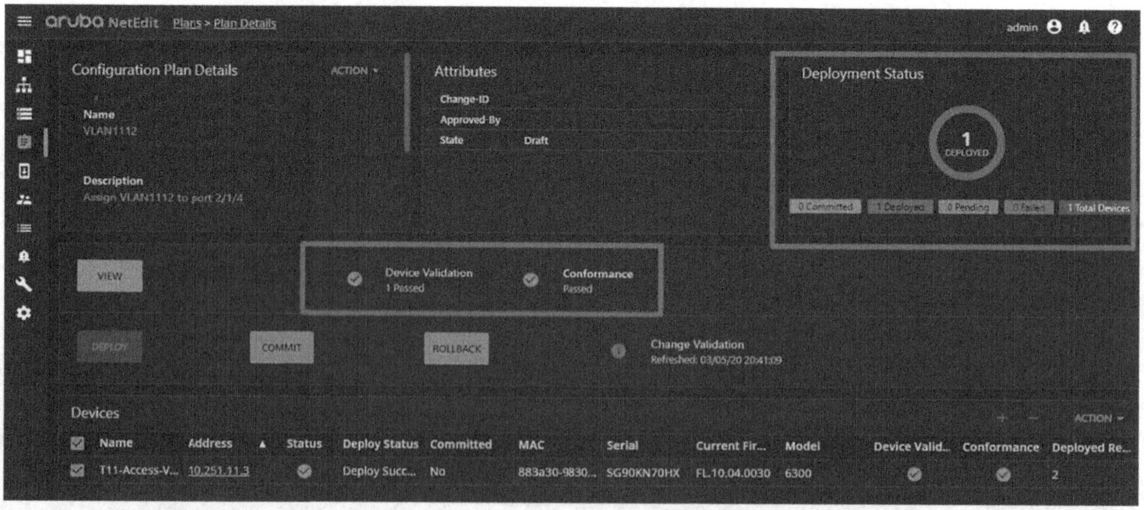

Figure 14-39 Deployment is in Progress

What was the Device Validation Result? ______________________________

What was the Conformance Result? ______________________________

What is the Deployment Status?______________________________

18. Click on “COMMIT”. A dialog box appears (Figure 14-40).

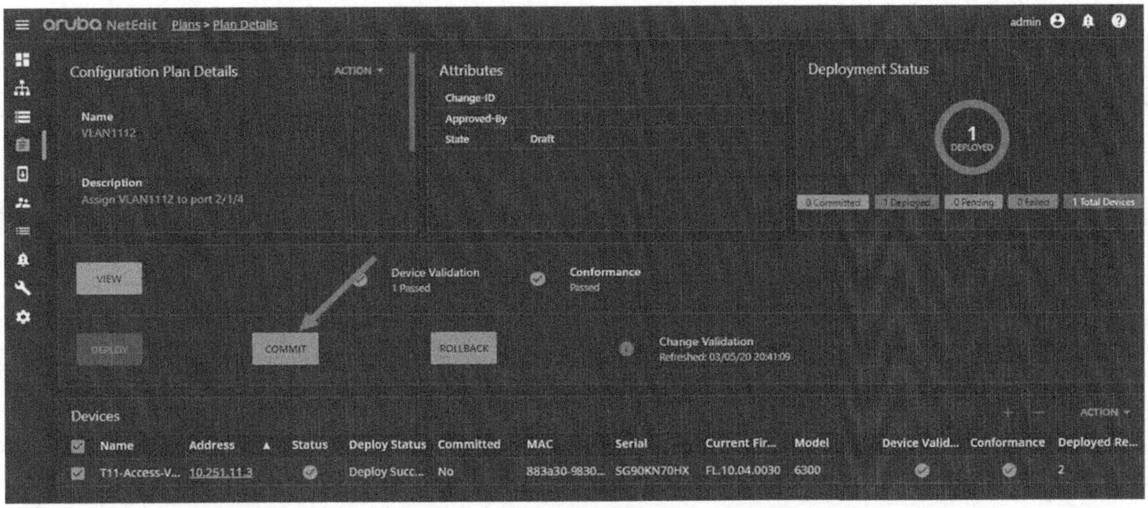

Figure 14-40 Deployed Plan

19. Click on “COMMIT” again. This will save the current configuration in the “startup-config” checkpoint (Figure 14-41).

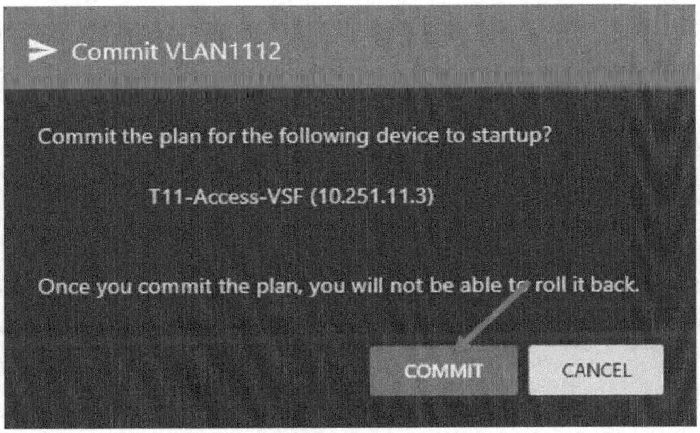

Figure 14-41 Committing a Plan

What is the Deployment Status now?____

Access-VSF

20. Move back to Access-VSF's console.
21. Display the brief information of port2/1/4.

```
T11-Access-VSF# show interface 2/1/4 brief
---------------------------------------------------------------------------------
Port     Native   Mode      Type     Enabled Status  Reason              Speed
         VLAN                                                           (Mb/s)
---------------------------------------------------------------------------------
2/1/4   1112     access   1GbT       yes     up                          1000
```

What VLAN is the port mapped to now? ______________________________

PC-1

22. Move back to PC-1.
23. Click on "Logs" in the left navigation pane (☰). You will see evidence of the previous deployment (Figure 14-42).

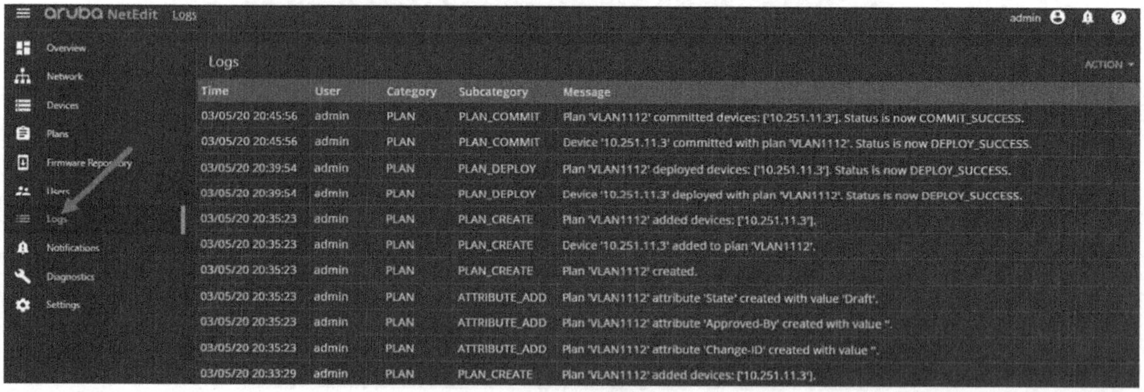

Figure 14-42 NetEdit Logs

You have completed Lab 14!

Learning Check

Chapter 14 Questions

Introduction to Aruba NetEdit

1. What is true about Aruba NetEdit connectivity options?
   a. It uses SNMPv3 to discover and manage Aruba OS-CX switches.
   b. It can use SNMPv2c to discover 3rd-party devices.
   c. Many useful functions are available via a REST API.
   d. You can simultaneously view and edit multiple devices.

NetEdit Installation, NetEdit Initial Configuration – Licensing, NetEdit GUI Login, Configure Switches to Support NetEdit

2. Which of the options below describe valid NetEdit installation and configuration options?
   a. NetEdit is a web-based application that runs on VMware.
   b. The NetEdit trial license is limited to 25 weeks.
   c. Initial NetEdit Web login requires username = admin, password = admin.
   d. NetEdit connects to switches via any available switchport.
   e. You can enable either SSH, HTTSP, or REST.

Aruba CX Mobile App Overview, Aruba CX Mobile App Features

3. What is true about the Aruba CX Mobile App?
   a. Android devices connect to OS-CX switches via Bluetooth or Wi-Fi.
   b. Apple iOS devices connect to OS-CX switches via Bluetooth or Wi-Fi.
   c. The app integrates with NetEdit.
   d. The app can use SNMPv2c for integration with 3rd-party devices.
   e. You can transfer files between the switch and your mobile device.

Practice Test

Authorized Practice Test for the ACSA Certification Exam

INTRODUCTION

The Aruba Certification Switching Associate (ACSA) certification validates your knowledge of the features, benefits, and functions of Aruba switching network components and technologies. This certification validates your skills on the networking fundamentals of Aruba CX and AOS switches and file structures including VLANs, secure access, redundancy technologies, and Aruba's Virtual Switching Framework (VSF). It verifies your knowledge of configuring and maintaining routed networks utilizing static, default, and dynamic routes along with the dynamic routing protocol OSPF. The certification tests your understanding of choosing, installing, and configuring the appropriate Aruba technology at the correct OSI layer. Finally, you should be able to validate management software and configurations on Aruba CX and AOS switches.

The intent of this guide is to set expectations about the context of the exam and to help candidates prepare for it. Recommended training to prepare for this exam can be found at the HPE Certification and Learning website (Https://certification-learning.hpe.com). It is important to note that, although training is recommended for exam preparation, successful completion of the training alone does not guarantee that you will pass the exam. In addition to training, exam items are based on knowledge gained from on-the-job experience and from other supplemental reference material such as the ACSA Study Guide.

Minimum Qualifications

To achieve the Aruba Certified Switching Associate certification, you must pass the HPE6-A72 exam. Candidates should have a thorough understanding of Aruba switching implementations in small-to-medium businesses (SMBs). To pass the exam, you should have at least six months experience deploying small-to-medium enterprise-level networks. You should have an understanding of wired technologies used in edge and simple core environments.

HPE6-A72 Exam Details

The following are details about the HPE6-A72 exam:

- Exam type: Proctored
- Number of items: 60

- Exam time: 90 minutes
- Passing score: 75%
- Item types: Multiple choice (single and multiple response), drag and drop, and diagram selection
- Reference material during testing: No online or hard copy reference material is allowed during testing.

HPE6-A72 Testing Objectives

23% Identify, Describe, and Apply Foundational Networking Architectures and Technologies.

- Describe and explain the OSI Model.
- Describe and explain the most common layer media (Layer-1).
- Describe the basics of Layer-2 Ethernet, including broadcast domains and ARP messages.
- Interpret an IP routing table and explain default routes, static routing, and dynamic routing, including OSPF.
- Define and recognize the purpose and interaction of Layer-4 (Transport) protocols in an IP network.
- Identify and describe multicast traffic and its purpose on a network.
- Identify the role of TFTP, SFTP, FTP, Telnet, and SNMPv2 in managing Aruba network devices and how to apply the appropriate security for these features.
- Identify and describe the concept of QoS and explain its significance in converged networks.
- Describe and explain basic network security setup on Aruba switches.
- Describe Layer-2 redundancy technologies such as STP/RSTP/MSTP and VSF, including their benefits.
- Describe and apply link aggregation.
- Identify, describe, and explain VLANs.
- Describe network management.
- Describe the concepts of server-related networking (NIC and CNA).

17% Identify, Describe, and Differentiate the Functions and Features of Aruba Products and Solutions.

- Identify basic features and management options for Aruba wired products.
- Compare and contrast Aruba Networking solutions and features and identify the appropriate product for an environment.
- Identify which Aruba Networking products should be positioned given various customer environments and infrastructure needs (include the criteria needed to make such a recommendation).
- Identify and describe available toolsets for managing Aruba Networking products (CLI-based, web, scripted, SNMP, NetEdit, mobile app, and API).

27% Install, Configure, Set Up, and Validate Aruba Solutions.

- Perform an environmental survey for site readiness.
- Configure basic features on Aruba switches, including initial settings and management access.
- Configure Aruba switches with Layer-2 technologies such as RSTP/MSPT, link aggregation, VLANs, LLDP, and device profiles.
- Configure basic IP routing with static routes or OSPF on Aruba switches.
- Configure the management software and manage configuration files on Aruba switches. Manage the software and configuration files on Aruba switches; NetEdit
- Validate the installed solution via debug technology, logging, and show commands.

13% Tune, Optimize, and Upgrade Aruba Solutions.

- Optimize Layer-2 and Layer-3 infrastructures via broadcast domain reduction, VLANs, and VSF.
- Manage network assets using Aruba tools.
- Verify L3 routing tables convergence and scalability (OSPF, RIP, static routes, ECMP, directly connected).
- Assess how to optimize network availability (VRRP, VSF, Trunks, MSTP, additional hardware redundancy).

12% Tune, Optimize, and upgrade Aruba Solutions.

- Optimize Layer-2 and Layer-3 infrastructures via broadcast domain reduction, VLANs, and VSF.
- Manage network assets using Aruba tools.
- Verify L3 routing tables convergence and scalability (OSPF, RIP, static routes, ECMP, directly connected).
- Assess how to optimize network availability (VRRP, VSF, Trunks, xSTP, additional hardware redundancy).

8% Manage, Monitor, Administer, and Operate Aruba Solutions.

- Perform network management according to best practices.
- Perform Administrative tasks (Moves / Adds / Changes / Deletions) (Add new devices, VLAN assignment.)

Test Preparation Questions and Answers

The following question will help you to measure your understanding of topics that may be covered in exam. Read all the choices carefully since there may be more than one correct answer. Choose all correct answers for each question.

Questions

1. Which layer of the OSI model is responsible for setup, maintenance, and tear down of sessions between two computing devices?
    a. Presentation Layer
    b. Session Layer
    c. Physical Layer
    d. Network Layer

2. With what other technology does Full-Duplex communication closely match?
    a. CB radio using push-to-talk
    b. a mobile phone call
    c. a point-to-point connection between a switchport and a hub port
    d. a single fiber-optic strand allowing transmit or receive

3. Review the exhibit.

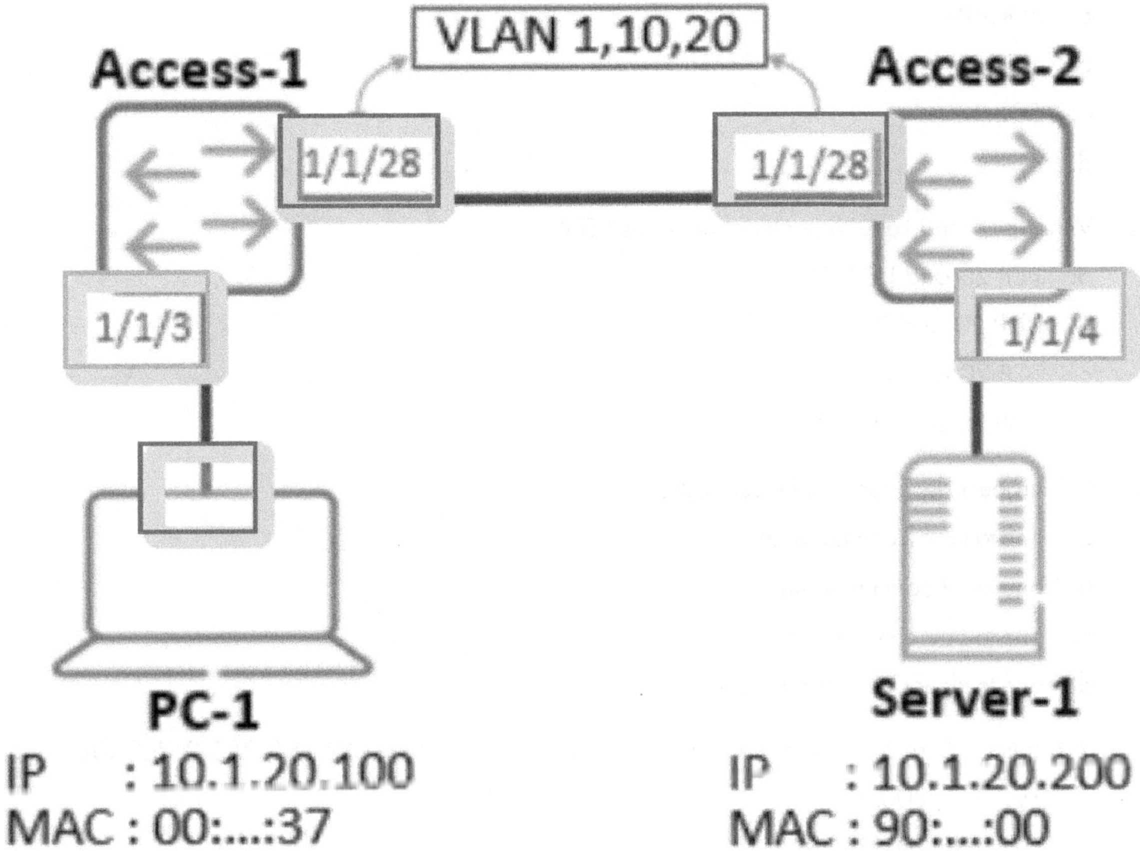

Server-1 is not running a hypervisor or virtual switch. Which ports should be configured as **Trunk** ports? (Select two.)

a. PC-1 NIC (Network Interface Card)

b. Access-1 port 1/1/3

c. Access-1 port 1/1/28

d. Access-2 port 1/1/28

e. Access-2 port 1/1/4

4. Which of the following is a MAC (Media Access Control) address?

a. 8c:85:90:76:6c:95

b. 8c:85:90:76:6g:95

c. 8c:85:90:76:6c:95:75

d. 2001::1

5. Which of the following is a Layer-3 Routing protocol?
   a. PVRSTP+
   b. MST
   c. 802.1x
   d. BGP
6. What port and Layer-4 protocol matches FTP?
   a. TCP 20 and UDP 21
   b. UDP 20 and TCP 21
   c. TCP 20 and TCP 21
   d. UDP 20 and UDP 21
7. Which best describes Multicast traffic?
   a. one-to-many communication
   b. one-to-all communication
   c. one-to-one communication
   d. one-to-closest communication
8. What is the broadcast address of the network 192.168.201.112 255.255.255.240?
   a. 192.168.200.127
   b. 192.168.201.127
   c. 192.168.201.255
   d. 192.168.201.119
9. What command reboots an AOS-CX switch?
   a. Switch# reload
   b. Switch# reboot
   c. Switch# boot system in-place checkpoint <checkpoint-name>
   d. Switch# boot system
10. Which Ethernet port combination does the Aruba 2930M switch series support?
    a. 10/100 Megabit Ethernet, Gigabit Ethernet, and 40 Gigabit Ethernet
    b. 10/100 Megabit Ethernet, Gigabit Ethernet, and 100 Gigabit Ethernet
    c. Gigabit Ethernet, 25 Gigabit Ethernet, and 40 Gigabit Ethernet
    d. 10/100 Megabit Ethernet, Gigabit Ethernet, 25 Gigabit Ethernet, and 100 Gigabit Ethernet

11. What is a benefit of a 2-Tier design over a 3-Tier?
    a. Offloading processing from the Core without routing at the Access layer.
    b. Lowering the cost of a deployment due to needing less switches overall.
    c. Can use lower speed links between Core to Aggregation and Aggregation to Access given the use of an Aggregation layer.
    d. Gaining the flexibility to connect the Data-Center to any Access layer switch.

12. What is the maximum number of switches supported in an Aruba Virtual Switching Framework (VSF) stack?
    a. Two
    b. Four
    c. Ten
    d. Eight

13. Which option correctly describes a LAN network?
    a. A group of compute resources that communicates between geographically separate location
    b. Compute resources that are networked locally over different Layer-2 switches
    c. A network of devices over long distances but between different ISPs
    d. The connection between several devices using Bluetooth

14. Currently, the prompt on the AOS-CX switch displays:

```
Core-1(config)# interface 1/1/5
Core-1(config-if)#
```

In Aruba AOS-CX, what command will immediately return the prompt to Privileged mode?

a. The command **exit**
b. Pressing **ctrl+w**
c. The command **quit**
d. Pressing **ctrl+z**

15. Which transport legacy protocol allows unsecure remote access to manage a network device? (Select two.)
    a. HTTP
    b. SSH
    c. FTP
    d. Telnet
    e. RadSec

16. What statement is true when it comes to managing Aruba AOS-CX switches?
    a. The management VRF is considered part of the switch control plane.
    b. You can assign an IP address to the management interface using DHCP.
    c. SSH can only be enabled on the management VRF (Virtual Route Forwarder).
    d. The VRF assigned to the management interface can be used on other ports.

17. An administrator has advised you use the **checkpoint auto 15** command prior to making remote management port changes. What does this command do on Aruba AOS-CX switches?
    a. Allow the creation of a checkpoint that will automatically roll back in 15 minutes unless changes have been committed.
    b. This will place a bookmark in the running-configuration of the switch to more easily return to configuring commands, should you lose your place.
    c. A checkpoint called "auto 15" will be created that you can use to manually restore if an error occurs.
    d. This creates a backup of the configuration that requires the administrator to have privilege level 15 to restore.

18. What is an available command on an Aruba AOS-CX switch that would back up the secondary image to a remote repository?
    a. Copy secondary tftp://admin@10.1.1.21/GL.10.04.0003.swi
    b. Backup secondary sftp://admin@10.1.1.21/GL.10.04.0003.swi
    c. Copy sftp://admin@10.1.1.21/GL.10.04.0003.swi secondary
    d. Secondary copy sftp://admin@10.1.1.21/GL.10.04.0003.swi

19. What switch function(s) occur at the Control plane?
    a. Receives and sends frames by using Application-Specific Integrated Circuits (ASICs).
    b. Handles switch monitoring.
    c. Switches packets faster than using software.
    d. Determines packet forwarding using routing, switching, security, and flow optimization.

20. Refer to the exhibit.

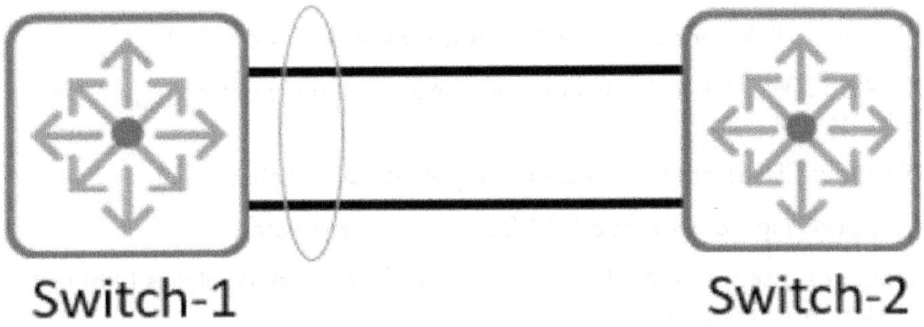


```
Switch-1# configure terminal
Switch-1(config)# interface lag 1
Switch-1(config-lag-if)# lacp mode active
Switch-1(config-lag-if)# lacp rate fast
Switch-1(config-lag-if)# vlan trunk allowed 1,11,12
Switch-1(config-lag-if)# no shutdown
Switch-1(config-lag-if)# exit
Switch-1(config)# interface 1/1/27-1/1/28
Switch-1(config-if-<1/1/27-1/1/28>)# lag 1
Switch-1(config-if-<1/1/27-1/1/28>)# exit
Switch-1(config)# show lacp interfaces
```

The above configuration shows Switch-1 is configured for Link Aggregation Control Protocol (LACP). Switch-2 has configured matching ports for manual link aggregation (LAG) and has not enabled LACP. What will be the LACP Forwarding State of ports 1/1/27 and 1/1/28 on Switch-2?

a. LACP-block

b. Down

c. Up

d. LACP-enabled

21. Which two statements are true about the state of a new AOS-CX 6300M switch at factory defaults? (Select two.)
    a. LLDP is enabled on up-link ports and switchports for the AOS-CX 6300M.
    b. For the AOS-CX 6300M switch, all up-link ports and switchports are configured as routed mode by default.
    c. LLDP is enabled, but CDP is not supported on any AOS-CX switches.
    d. The 6300M supports high power IEEE 802.3bt power-over-ethernet.
    e. The 6300M requires a separate NAE license to enable Network Analytics Engine support. It handles switch monitoring.
22. What command will automatically timeout the terminal session in 20 minutes of no use?
    a. Core-1(config)# terminal-session
       Core-1(config-cli-session)# logout 2 0
    b. Core-1(config)# session-logout 120
    c. Core-1(config)# session-timeout 20
    d. Core-1(config)# session-timeout 2 0
23. What command could be used to test reachability from an AOS-CX switch?
    a. Ping6
    b. Tracert
    c. Pathping
    d. Netstatus
24. Refer to the exhibit.

```
Temperature information
------------------------------------------------------------------------------
                                                          Current
Mbr/Slot-Sensor                        Module Type      temperature  Status
------------------------------------------------------------------------------
ACCESS-1# 
```

What command could be used to verify the temperature of an AOS-CX switch?

a. Show temperature
b. Show system temperature
c. Show chassis temperature
d. Show environment temperature

25. What is true about VSX?
    a. VSX keeps the control planes separate for stack members.
    b. VSX is available on all Aruba OS-CX switches except the 6300F model.
    c. VSX is ideal for small branch access layer deployments.
    d. VSX is implemented on static port switches with VSX-plus needed to stack chassis together.

26. Which AOS-CX supported version of Spanning-Tree allows the use of different instances mapped one or more VLANs?
    a. IEEE 802.1d Spanning Tree Protocol (STP)
    b. IEEE 802.1s Multiple Spanning Tree (MST)
    c. IEEE 802.1w Rapid Spanning Tree Protocol (RSTP)
    d. Cisco Rapid Per VLAN Spanning Tree (RPVST)

27. What are two switch requirements to be discovered by NetEdit?
    a. Enabling SSH access
    b. A REST API license installed on the switch
    c. HTTP server being enabled
    d. Enabling REST with read-write capabilities
    e. Enabling Telnet access

28. Which routing protocol is considered a link-state protocol and is supported on Aruba AOS-CX switches?
    a. IS-IS
    b. BGP
    c. OSPFv2
    d. RIPv2

29. What is true regarding Spanning-Tree on AOS-CX switches at factory default?
    a. Spanning-Tree is disabled on all AOS-CX switches.
    b. 6200, 6300, and 6400 switches have Spanning-Tree enabled by default. 8320, 8325, and 8400 switches disable Spanning-Tree at defaults.
    c. Spanning-Tree is enabled on all AOS-CX switches.
    d. 6200, 6300, and 6400 switches have Spanning-Tree disabled by default. 8320, 8325, and 8400 switches enable Spanning-Tree at defaults.

30. Refer to the exhibit showing the topology and configuration on Switch-A.

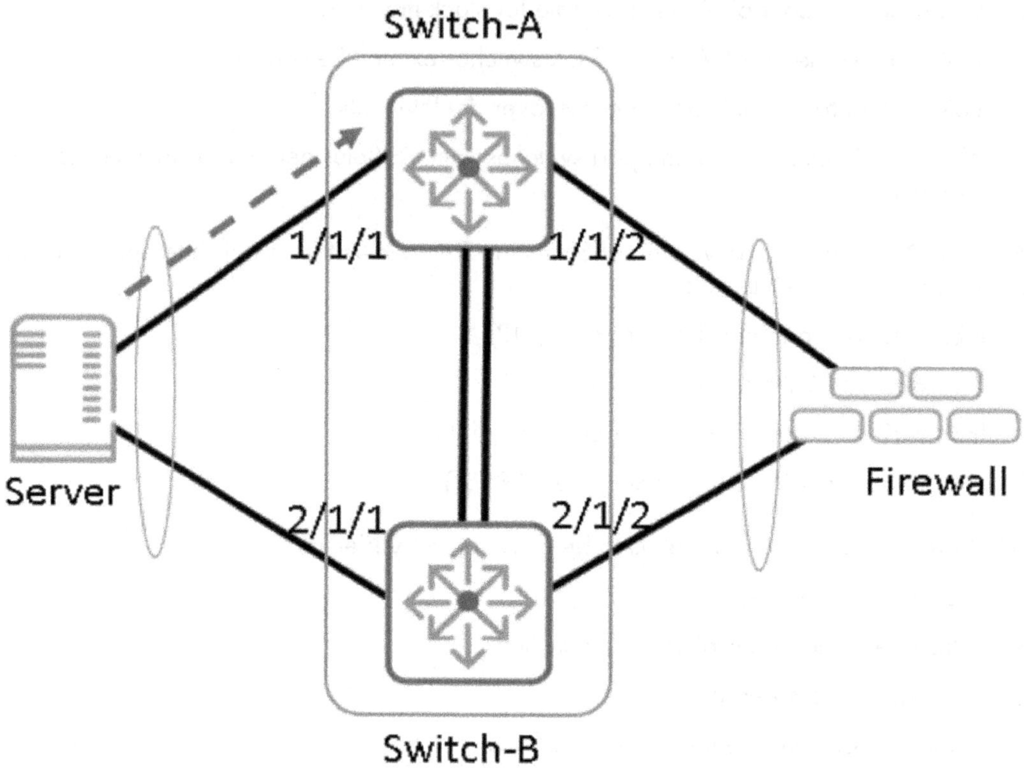


```
Switch-A# configure terminal
Switch-A (config)# vsf member 1
Switch-A (vsf-member-1)# link 1 1/1/27
Switch-A (vsf-member-1)# link 1 1/1/28
Switch-A (vsf-member-1)# exit
Switch-A (config)# show vsf

MAC Address                : 88:3a:30:98:30:00
Secondary                  :
Topology                   : Chain
Status                     : No Split
Split Detection Method     : None

Mbr Mac Address            type       Status
ID
--- ------------------     ------     ------
1   88:3a:30:98:30:00      JL668A     Master
2   88:3a:30:97:a4:40      JL668A     Member
```

Switch-A and Switch-B are stacked together using VSF. They are connected on ports 1/1/27 and 1/1/28 from Switch-A to Switch-B. What happens if Switch-A is shut down?

a. Switch-B remains a Member. Traffic between the Server and the Firewall will automatically be routed across the LAG.

b. Switch-B continues to reboot until Switch-A resumes its role as Master. No traffic will pass from the Server to Firewall.

c. Switch-B will be elected as the new Master. Traffic will continue between the Server and the Firewall uninterrupted.

d. Switch-B remains up as a Member but will disable all multi-chassis LAG ports. This will disrupt traffic between the Server and the Firewall.

Answers

1. Which layer of the OSI model is responsible for setup, maintenance, and tear down of sessions between two computing devices?

   ☑ **B** is correct. Layer-5, the Session Layer is responsible for setup, maintenance, and tear down of sessions between two computing devices.

   ☒ **A**, **C**, and **D** are incorrect. **A** is incorrect because the Presentation Layer transforms data into the formats that the application accepts and includes processes such as compression/decompression, encryption/decryption, and code translation (EDCDIC to ASCII). **C**; the Physical Layer dictates the physical aspects of how signals are transmitted and received across some media. **D**; the Network Layer is used to establish device communications across multiple LANs or WANs, using the best available path.

2. With what other technology does Full-Duplex communication closely match?

   ☑ **B** is correct.

   ☒ **A**, **C**, and **D** are incorrect. **A** is incorrect because describes a send *or* receive option with a CB radio that is indicative of half-duplex communication. **C** shows a scenario where even full-duplex cable devices such as a PC network interface card or (in this example) a switchport will normally switch to half-duplex when connected to a shared medium like a hub. **D** is wrong given that communication over fiber requires at least two-strands to permit communication in both directions simultaneously.

3. Review the exhibit.

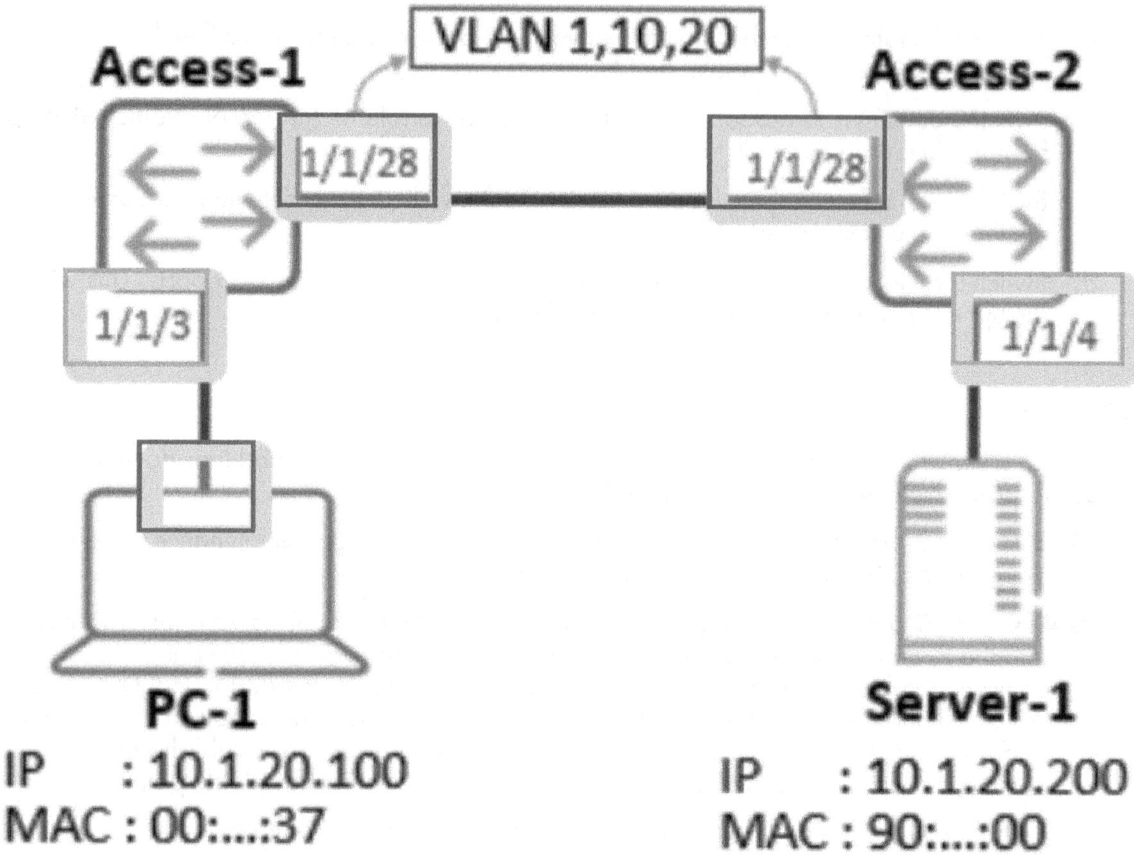

Server-1 is not running a hypervisor or virtual switch. Which ports should be configured as **Trunk** ports? (Select two.)

☑ **C** and **D** are correct.

☒ **A**, **B**, and **E** are incorrect. **A** is incorrect because a client device (as is Server-1) so long as there is no switch running on the client or server. If there was a hypervisor or virtual switch on PC-1 or Server-1, then you would typically Trunk multiple vlans to those appliances. **B** and **E** would be set as an Access port to service the clients in a single vlan.

4. Which of the following is a MAC (Media Access Control) address?

☑ **A** is correct. **A** is a MAC address represented correctly as twelve hexadecimal characters with the 48-bits required.

☒ **B**, **C**, and **D** are incorrect. **B** is incorrect because of the use of the letter "g" being outside the hexadecimal range (0-9 and A-F). **C** has too many characters at fourteen. **D** is in hexadecimal; however, it is an IPv6 address.

5. Which of the following is a Layer-3 Routing protocol?

☑ **D** is correct as the Border Gateway Protocol.

☒ **A**, **B**, and **C** are incorrect. **A** and **B** are incorrect because Spanning Tree protocols used for loop-prevention at Layer-2. **C** is an authentication protocol used for enterprise AAA deployments. Other options for routing protocols include OSPF, IS-IS, RIP, and EIGRP as popular options. Only BGP and OSPF are supported currently on HPE AOS and OS-CX switches.

6. What port and Layer-4 protocol matches FTP?

☑ **C** is the correct option given that FTP uses sequencing, windowing, and TCP-handshake for allowing a recoverable connection between endpoints. Compare this with TFTP which uses only UDP 69 (option **B**).

☒ **A**, **B**, and **D** are incorrect. **A** and **D** also use correct port numbers but include UDP.

7. Which best describes Multicast traffic?

☑ **A** is correctly describing multicast as one transmitter to multiple receivers.

☒ **B**, **C**, and **D** are incorrect. **B** describes flooding or broadcast traffic. Unicast with a single sender to a single receiver is option **C**. **D** is an IPv6 behavior called Anycast which replaces Broadcasts found in IPv4.

8. What is the broadcast address of the network 192.168.201.112 255.255.255.240?

☑ **B** is correct. A subnet mask of 225.255.255.240 or /28, increments subnets by 0.0.0.16. Given that the given address is 192.168.201.112, you can find the scope as an increment of 16 in the fourth octet. This means that the address is the subnet of the scope beginning with 192.168.201.112 and ending with the broadcast of 192.168.201.127. The next subnet would be between with 192.168.201.128 (also a multiple of 0.0.0.16). The correct answer then is **B**.

☒ **A**, **C**, and **D** are incorrect. **A** is wrong given the third octet is 200 instead of 201. **C** is incorrect as it is outside the scope even though it is a broadcast in 192.168.201.240. **D** is wrong as it is a normal host address; however, it is within the correct scope.

9. What command reboots an AOS-CX switch?

☑ **D** is correct. **D** will reboot the AOS-CX switch with options to choose the Primary or Secondary operating system on boot.

☒ **A**, **B**, and **C** are incorrect. **A** is incorrect as there is no "reload" command on AOS-CX. **B** will reboot the switch if you break the boot and enter the SVOS but not during normal operation. **C** shows the correct "boot system"; however, there are no options for "in-place checkpoint <checkpoint-name>.

10. Which Ethernet port combination does the Aruba 6300M switch series support?

☑ **A** is correct given that the 2930M series has options for 10/100/1000 MbE ports or 8 smart-rate 1/2.5/5/10 GbE ports along with modular support for 10GbE or 40GbE uplinks.

☒ **B**, **C**, and **D** are incorrect. **B** and **D** are incorrect given the 100 GbE port requirements that are available only on the AOS-CX series 6400, 8325, and 8400. Option **C** is incorrect because of the inclusion of the 25 GbE. 25GbE is currently supported on the 6300, 6400, 8325, and 8400. The AOS switches support only up to 10 GbE and 40 GbE.

11. What is a benefit of a 2-Tier design over a 3-Tier?

☑ **B** is the correct answer given that a 2-Tier design does not use an Aggregation layer and therefore requires less switches.

☒ **A**, **C**, and **D** are incorrect. **A** describes a 3-Tier benefit. In a 2-Tier the Core has additional processing when not routing at the Access Layer; all routing must be handled by the Core. **C**; there is no use of an Aggregation layer so this answer is incorrect. **D** describes a Spine-Leaf design found in mid to large datacenter deployments and is therefore unique from 2-Tier and 3-Tier designs.

12. What is the maximum number of switches supported in an Aruba Virtual Switching Framework (VSF) stack?

☑ **C** is correct as the VSF protocol supports a maximum of 10 member-ids uniquely attached to each switch member in the stack.

☒ **A**, **B**, and **D** are incorrect. **A** describes a Virtual Switching Extension (VSX) stack which is limited to two members. **B** and **D** are incorrect.

13. Which option correctly describes a LAN network?

☑ **B** is correct given that the endpoints are within the same subnet even if different Layer-2 devices are used.

☒ **A**, **C**, and **D** are incorrect. **A** and **C** both fall under a WAN or VPN connection given the geographically separate locations. **D** refers to a PAN or Personal Area Network rather than a LAN.

14. Currently, the prompt on the AOS-CX switch displays:

```
Core-1(config)# interface 1/1/5
Core-1(config-if)#
```

In Aruba AOS-CX, what command will immediately return the prompt to Privileged mode?

☑ **D** is correct; however, you could also enter "end".

☒ **A**, **B**, and **C** are incorrect. **A** would take you back to Global Configuration mode and then Privileged mode but not immediately. **B** would erase the last word entered. **C** was taken from Comware and does not apply to AOS-CX.

15. Which transport legacy protocol allows unsecure remote access to manage a network device? (Select two.)

    ☑ The correct answers are **A** and **D** as both carry configuration traffic without any encryption.

    ☒ **B**, **C**, and **E** are incorrect. **B** (SSH) is similar to Telnet in that it carries CLI commands; however, SSH uses a cryptographical strong authentication and encryption. **C** (FTP) is not designed for any time of management other than exchanging files. **E** (RadSec) carries RADIUS authentication and accounting data over a secure TLS tunnel. While you could argue that RADIUS has aspects of management, the use of RadSec is secure, not unsecure.

16. What statement is true when it comes to managing Aruba OS-CX switches?

    ☑ The correct answer is **B** where the management interface supports both DHCP and Static IP address assignment.

    ☒ **A**, **C**, and **D** are incorrect. **A** is incorrect as the management VRF is still part of the data plane. **C** is wrong given that the SSH server can be enabled on the management and any other VRF at the same time. The management interface can only belong to the "mgmt" VRF making **D** incorrect.

17. An administrator has advised you use the **checkpoint auto 15** command prior to making remote management port changes. What does this command do on AOS-CX switches?

    ☑ The correct answer is **A**. Checkpoint auto command is useful in scenarios where management access may drop and the administrator is cut off from the switch. With **checkpoint auto 15**, the admin has fifteen minutes to complete their task and commit changes. If they have lost connectivity, the switch will restore itself given that no commit command was issued.

    ☒ Options **B, C,** and **D** are incorrect.

18. What is an available command on an Aruba OS-CX switch that would back up the secondary image to a remote repository?

    ☑ The correct answer is **A**. The syntax for a **copy** command is "copy <from> <to>".

    ☒ **B**, **C**, and **D** are incorrect. This means that option **C** tries to copy from an sftp server to the secondary which is not what we want. **D** fails to place the copy command first. **B** uses the wrong command instead of copy.

19. What switch function(s) occur at the Control plane?

    ☑ The correct answer is **D** and includes functions for route discovery and ARP table maintenance.

    ☒ **A**, **B**, and **C** are incorrect. Option **A** describes the Data plane, **B** is Management plane, and **C** is Application-Specific Integrated Circuits (ASICs).

20. Refer to the exhibit.

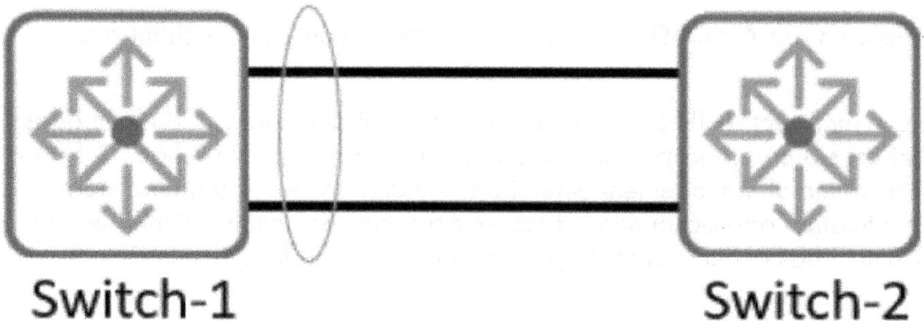


```
Switch-1# configure terminal
Switch-1(config)# interface lag 1
Switch-1(config-lag-if)# lacp mode active
Switch-1(config-lag-if)# lacp rate fast
Switch-1(config-lag-if)# vlan trunk allowed 1,11,12
Switch-1(config-lag-if)# no shutdown
Switch-1(config-lag-if)# exit
Switch-1(config)# interface 1/1/27-1/1/28
Switch-1(config-if-<1/1/27-1/1/28>)# lag 1
Switch-1(config-if-<1/1/27-1/1/28>)# exit
Switch-1(config)# show lacp interfaces
```

The above configuration shows Switch-1 is configured for Link Aggregation Control Protocol (LACP). Switch-2 has configured matching ports for manual link aggregation (LAG) and has not enabled LACP. What will be the LACP Forwarding State of ports 1/1/27 and 1/1/28 on Switch-2?

☑ The correct answer is **C**. Even though the switches cannot agree on using LACP, Switch-2 will always show "up" for the LAG forwarding state given that it does not rely on LACP.

☒ **A**, **B**, and **D** are incorrect. Switch-1 will show option **A** given that LACP has failed. If Switch-2 were to shut down the matching ports then Switch-1 would show the Forwarding State as "down" in option **B**. Option **D**; this command is not used.

21. Which two statements are true about the state of a new AOS-CX 6300M switch at factory defaults? (Select two.)

☑ The correct answers are **A** and **D**. LLDP and CDP are enabled at defaults along with 802.3bt 60 watt uPoe with 90 watt to be supported in a future release.

☒ **B**, **C**, and **E** are incorrect. **B** is incorrect as all ports on the 6200, 6300M/F, and 6400 series are switchports at default. The 8320, 8325, and 8400 are routed ports at default in contrast. **C** is incorrect as stated. **E** is incorrect as NAE requires no licensing.

22. What command will automatically timeout the terminal session in 20 minutes of no use?

☑ **C** is correct.

☒ **A**, **B**, and **D** are incorrect. **A** and **B** are not viable commands in AOS-CX. **D** is the correct command, but the value is only measured in minutes using the first number. Zero would not be accepted.

23. What command could be used to test reachability from an AOS-CX switch?

☑ **A** is correct. **A** is the only accepted command in AOS-CX commands shown. You could also use ping, traceroute, and traceroute6.

☒ **B**, **C**, and **D** are incorrect. **B, C,** and **D** are all Microsoft commands not used in AOS-CX.

24. Refer to the exhibit.

```
Temperature information
--------------------------------------------------------------------------------
                                                         Current
Mbr/Slot-Sensor                  Module Type             temperature  Status
--------------------------------------------------------------------------------
ACCESS-1#
```

What command could be used to verify the temperature of an AOS-CX switch?

☑ **D** is correct. The command **show environment** has options for seeing the status of fans and power supplies as well.

☒ **A**, **B**, and **C** are incorrect. **A, B,** and **C** do not exist. There is an option for **show system** but not with temperature.

25. What is true about VSX?

☑ **A** is correct. VSX uses separate control planes compared to VSF where only the Master switch acts as a single control plane.

☒ **B**, **C**, and **D** are incorrect. **B** is incorrect in that the 6400, 8320, 8325, and 8400 are the only switches that support VSX. VSF using 6300M/F and 6200s would apply in small deployments such as an Access closet (IDF) or branch deployment. VSX offers more control and reliability needed for Aggregation, Core, and Data-Center deployments making **C** incorrect. **D** is wrong given that there is no such thing as "VSX-plus".

26. Which AOS-CX supported version of Spanning-Tree allows the use of different instances mapped one or more VLANs?

    ☑ **B** is correct.

    ☒ **A**, **C**, and **D** are incorrect. **A** and **C** both utilize a single instance for calculating Spanning-Tree root and port assignments. Option **D** could have applied except that RPVST can only match an instance to a single vlan and not multiple vlans.

27. What are two switch requirements to be discovered by NetEdit?

    ☑ **A** and **D** are correct.

    ☒ **B**, **C**, and **E** are incorrect. **B**; Aruba switch features require no licensing on the switches themselves. Enabling the HTTPS server is a requirement to carry the REST protocol. However, AOS-CX switches do not support enabling HTTP or Telnet making **C** and **E** incorrect.

28. Which routing protocol is considered a link-state protocol and is supported on AOS-CX switches?

    ☑ **C** is correct.

    ☒ **A**, **B**, and **D** are incorrect. Option **A** is a link-state protocol as well but not supported by AOS-CX switches at this time. **B** is supported on AOS-CX and used to route between Autonomous Systems but is not considered link-state. **D** is not support by AOS-CX and is also not link-state.

29. What is true regarding Spanning-Tree on AOS-CX switches at factory default?

    ☑ **B** is correct. For any of the 6XXX series AOS-CX Spanning-Tree is enabled and all ports are designated as switchports. This is for using these switches at the access layer where running Layer-2 may introduce more loops in the network. The 8XXX series AOS-CX switches have all their ports disabled and routed so the need for Spanning-Tree to be enabled is diminished. Options **A, C,** and **D** are incorrect.

30. Refer to the exhibit showing the topology and configuration on Switch-A.

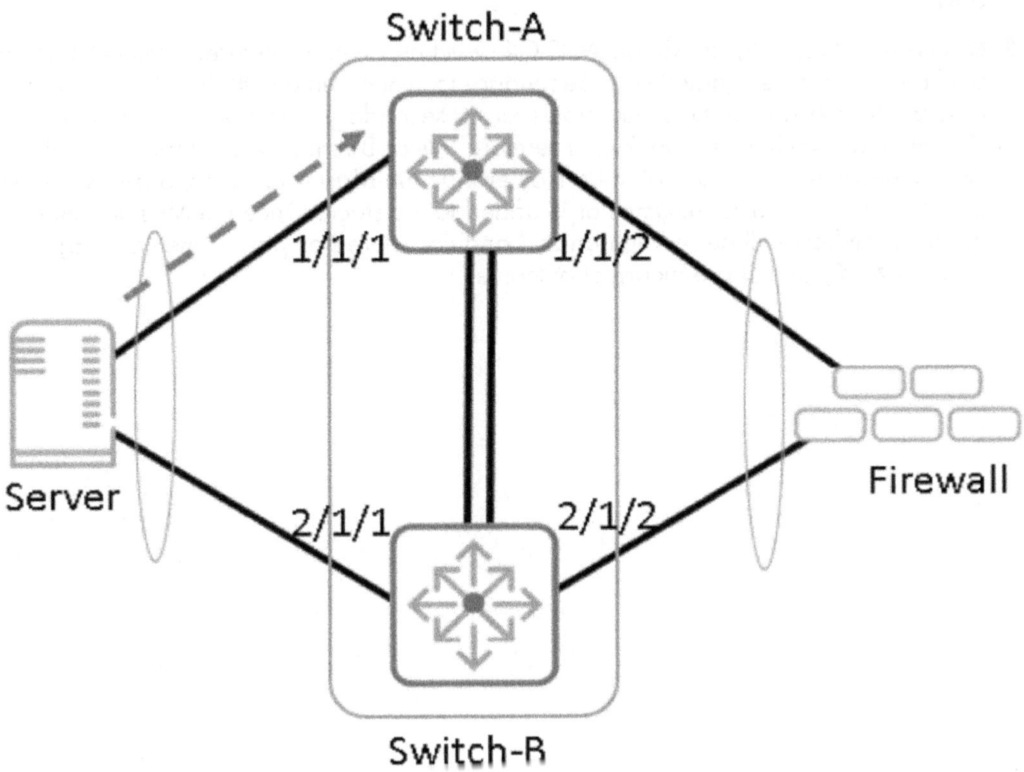


```
Switch-A# configure terminal
Switch-A (config)# vsf member 1
Switch-A (vsf-member-1)# link 1 1/1/27
Switch-A (vsf-member-1)# link 1 1/1/28
Switch-A (vsf-member-1)# exit
Switch-A (config)# show vsf

MAC Address                 : 88:3a:30:98:30:00
Secondary                   :
Topology                    : Chain
Status                      : No Split
Split Detection Method      : None

Mbr Mac Address             type      Status
ID
--- -----------------       ------    ------
1   88:3a:30:98:30:00       JL668A    Master
2   88:3a:30:97:a4:40       JL668A    Member
```

Switch-A and Switch-B are stacked together using VSF. They are connected on ports 1/1/27 and 1/1/28 from Switch-A to Switch-B. What happens if Switch-A is shut down?

☑ **B** is correct. Normally in VSF on AOS-CX switches when the Master Switch-A has failed a backup switch is designated as a Secondary to synchronize with the Master and take over the Master role in the stack. However no secondary command was issued designating Switch-B as a backup. Therefore Switch-B remains just another member and cannot become the Master. Members other than the Master (or Secondary) will enter a boot-loop until a Master resumes or is added to the stack. Once the Master comes back up, the Members will be resynchronized and configured as part of the stack again. Options **A, C,** and **D** are incorrect outcomes.

Appendix
Learning Checks

Chapter 1 Answers

Computer Networks

1. Which of the following are concepts or technologies that are **specific** to a LAN? Pick two.

    a. **Ethernet**

    b. **Wi-Fi**

The OSI Model

2. Which of the following are aspects of Layer-4 of the OSI model? Pick three.

    a. **TCP**

    c. **UDP**

    d. **Segmentation**

Physical Media

3. Under which circumstances is it most appropriate to use Single Mode fiber optic mode? Pick two.

    b. **When you must connect two buildings that are 10km apart**

    c. **When you are concerned about electromagnetic interference**

Binary to Decimal Conversion

4. What does 11010110 equal to in decimal?

    c. **214**

5. What does 10101110 equal to in decimal?

    c. **174**

6. What does 01000101 equal to in decimal?
   d. **69**
7. What does 11111110 equal to in decimal?
   a. **254**
8. What does 10000001 equal to in decimal?
   d. **129**

Chapter 2 Answers

The OSI Model

1. Which of the options below accurately describe MAC addresses?
   a. **They are used at Layer 2 of the OSI model.**
   d. **They are 48-bits long.**
   e. **They are used for Ethernet and Wi-Fi technologies, among others.**

Networking Devices

2. Which components and concepts are directly focused on Layer-2 communications?
   a. **Switch**
   c. **Multi-Layer Switch**
   d. **MAC addresses**
   f. **Access Points**
3. Which components and concepts are directly focused on Layer-3 communications?
   b. **Router**
   c. **Multi-Layer Switch**
   e. **IP addresses**
4. Which of the following statements accurately describe common networking services?
   d. **The advantage of HTTPS over HTTP is that it is more secure.**

Chapter 3 Answers

Network Design

1. Which options below describe differences between 3-tier and 2-tier network designs?

   d. **A 3-tier design might be more scalable than a 2-tier design.**

Switch Platforms

2. What are some advantages of a modular, chassis-based switch?

   a. **They are more scalable.**

   e. **They are more flexible.**

Console Port

3. What kind of cables might you use to connect to an Aruba OS-CX Switch console port?

   c. **USB cable**

   d. **Serial cable**

Getting Switch Information

4. Which command could you use to validate network connectivity for an AOS-CX switch?

   a. **show interfaces brief**

Network Discovery

5. Which of the options below accurately describe network discovery commands or techniques?

   a. **LLDP is a Layer-2 discovery protocol.**

   d. **The ping command leverages ICMP echo requests and echo replies.**

Chapter 4 Answers

Domains

1. Which of the options below accurately describe collision domains and broadcast domains?

   a. Collision domains relate to Layer-2 processes, while broadcast domains are a Layer-3 concept.

   d. A routing device defines the edge of a broadcast domain.

VLANs

2. What are the benefits of creating VLANs?

   c. **Smaller broadcast domains can improve performance.**

   d. **MAC address tables are smaller.**

802.1Q

3. What is true from the following lines of configuration?

```
SW1(config)# interface 1/1/24
SW1(config-if)# vlan trunk allow 1,20
```

   d. **Native VLAN is VLAN-1.**

MAC Address and ARP Tables

4. Which options below accurately describe MAC address and ARP tables?

   d. **The ARP table maps IP addresses to MAC addresses.**

   e. **Switches use the MAC address table to properly forward frames.**

Frame Delivery

5. When does a switch add a VLAN tag to a frame?

   c. **When it forwards the frame to another switch.**

Chapter 5 Answers

Redundancy

1. Which of the following are issues created from redundant Layer-Two loops?

   a. Routing loops

   b. **Broadcast storms**

   c. **Multiple frame copies**

   d. Voltage drops to Power-Over-Ethernet ports

   e. **Instability of the MAC address sable**

Spanning-Tree Protocol

2. Which Spanning-Tree protocols are considered open standards?
    a. PVRSTP+
    b. GLBP
    c. 802.1D
    d. 802.1W
    e. 802.11AX
    f. 802.1S

RSTP Operation

3. What is the command to enable an **edge** port in Aruba OS-CX?
    a. **Spanning-tree port-type admin-edge**
    b. Spanning-tree port-type edge
    c. Port-type admin-edge
    d. Spanning-tree port-type access.

Chapter 6 Answers

Static and Dynamic LAG

1. What is correct when referring to Static versus Dynamic LAG?
    a. Static Link Aggregation mode devices do not exchange any control information.
    b. Switches can establish a LAG between each other as long as one side is Dynamic.
    c. Dynamic LAG uses the Aruba proprietary LACP protocol.
    d. LACP is not available on Layer-Three routed ports.
    e. Dynamic LAG can detect link failures and ensure that LAG port members terminate on the same device.

Load Sharing

2. What can be used to determine the hashing algorithm used for load balancing traffic across a LAG in Aruba OS-CX switches?
   - **a. Layer-4 TCP/UDP ports**
   - **b. Layer-3 Source and Destination IP addresses**
   - **c. Layer-2 Source and Destination MAC addresses**
   - d. Layer-1 Port numbers
   - e. Layer-7 application type if Deep-Packet inspection is enabled.

Deploying LACP

3. What is the command to enable a Link Aggregation interface 99 in Aruba OS-CX?
   - a. SW1(config)# interface LAG 99
   - b. SW1(config)# Dynamic LAG 99
   - c. SW1(config)# Static LAG 99
   - d. **SW1(config)# LAG 99**

Chapter 7 Answers

IP Network Mask

1. Given IP address 172.20.3.54, and a mask of 255.255.255.0, what can be accurately stated about this addressing?
   - **b. This network portion of the address is 172.20.3**
   - **c. Host 172.20.3.89 would be on the same network.**
   - **e. You could also indicate this mask as "/24."**

IP Routing Table

2. A router's IP routing table has an entry with a Next-Hop IP Address of 10.30.233.1. What does this number represent?
   - **d. The next Layer-3 device that should receive the packet.**

Packet Delivery

3. Which of the options below accurately describe a typical packet delivery process?

   a. Access switches used their MAC address table to forward frames.

   b. Multilayer switches use their MAC address table to forward frames.

   c. Multilayer switches add 802.1q tags before sending frames to other switches.

   d. Multilayer switches use an IP routing table to forward packets.

   f. The source and destination IP addresses remain consistent throughout the packet delivery process, but the MAC addresses change.

Chapter 8 Answers

VRRP Master Election

1. Which of the statements below accurately describe VRRP concepts and operation?

   c. **If two VRRP routers have the same priority, the router with the highest IP address becomes the VRRP Master.**

VRRP Preemption

2. You have configured a basic VRRP configuration, leaving all default options in place. What happens when the Master fails, and then comes back online four hours later?

   c. **The original Master resumes its Master role once it comes back online.**

Chapter 9 Answers

IPv4 Address Classes, Reserved Addresses, Private, and Public IPv4 Addressing

1. Which statements are true about classful IP addressing?

   d. Public address ranges are globally unique.

Class B Subnet Masking Example

2. You are using a /24 subnet mask with the Class B address 172.20.0.0. Which options describe a valid result of this scenario?

   b. You can assign addresses to over 200 networks.

   d. If you must support more than 300 subnets, you must choose a different mask.

VLSM Example, CIDR Example

3. Which statements below are true?

   a. Given address 172.20.66.5/19, the subnet is 172.20.64.0.

   c. Given address 10.1.187.5/16, this scheme allows for a total of 65,534 hosts on the subnet.

Chapter 10 Answers

Administrative Distance

1. Suppose that a router has learned about network 172.18.37.0/24 from three sources – OSPF, Internal BGP, and a static route. Which statements are true about this router's path selection?

   d. The router chooses the static route.

Routing Protocols

2. Which of the statements below accurately describe link state routing protocols?

   b. They can be used to route packets inside an Autonomous System.

   d. They are more scalable than protocols like RIP.

Chapter 12 Answers

Operational Planes – Control, Management, and Data

1. Which of the statements below accurately describe network devices operational planes?

   c. The data plane moves data from ingress to egress port.

   d. The control and management planes are tightly integrated.

Aruba VSF Stacking Solution and Platforms, VSF Member Roles and Links

2. Which of the options below describe a valid VSF scenario?

   b. Configure two switches: one as Primary and one as member using a single VSF Link.

VSF Topologies, VSF Requirements, VSF Configuration

3. Which of the statements describe valid VSF requirements and specifications?

    a. You can daisy-chain up to 10 VSF members.

    b. You can connect 10 VSF members in a ring topology.

    e. The configuration of VSF may cause members to reboot.

Chapter 13 Answers

OOBM Port, Management VRF, Ping, and Traceroute in the Management VRF

1. What is true about managing Aruba OS-CX devices?

    a. You can connect using SSH, HTTPS, and SNMP on the management interface and on any typical access interface on the switch.

    b. The management interface can acquire an IP address via DHCP or by manual configuration.

SSH for Aruba OS-CX, HTTPS for Aruba OS-CX, Web Interface

2. Which of the options below accurately describe accessing a 6300 Aruba OS-CX device for CLI or GUI access?

    d. It is a best practice to only enable GUI access on the management VRF.

AAA, RBAC, RADIUS-based Management Authentication

3. Which of the statements describe valid Aruba OS-CX secure management access concepts?

    b. AAA services can be used in both the management VRF and the default VRF.

    c. Role-Based Access Control (RBAC) is based on a user's group assignment.

Configuration File Management, Checkpoint Overview, Password Recovery

4. What is true about Aruba OS-CX configuration file management?

    a. It is a good idea to copy the running configuration to the startup configuration after you have made changes to the configuration file that is currently in use.

    b. The advantage of a "Checkpoint" is that it stores operational metadata, in addition to the device configuration.

    c. Checkpoints are files – a snapshot of the configuration at a given time.

Chapter 14 Answers

Introduction to Aruba NetEdit

1. What is true about Aruba NetEdit connectivity options?
   - **b. It can use SNMPv2c to discover 3rd-party devices.**
   - **c. Many useful functions are available via a REST API.**
   - **d. You can simultaneously view and edit multiple devices.**

NetEdit Installation, NetEdit Initial Configuration – Licensing, NetEdit GUI Login, Configure Switches to Support NetEdit

2. Which of the options below describe valid NetEdit installation and configuration options?
   - **a. NetEdit is a web-based application that runs on VMware.**

Aruba CX Mobile App Overview, Aruba CX Mobile App Features

3. What is true about the Aruba CX Mobile App?
   - **a. Android devices connect to OS-CX switches via Bluetooth or Wi-Fi.**
   - **b. Apple iOS devices connect to OS-CX switches via Bluetooth or Wi-Fi.**
   - **c. The app integrates with NetEdit.**
   - **e. You can transfer files between the switch and your mobile device.**

Index

A

D

E

F

H

I

T